"Belonging to the World"

BICENTENNIAL ESSAYS ON THE BILL OF RIGHTS

Cosponsored by Oxford University Press
and the Organization of American Historians

Kermit L. Hall, General Editor

EDITORIAL BOARD
Michal Belknap, Harold M. Hyman, R. Kent Newmyer,
William M. Wiecek

Fair Trial
Rights of the Accused in American History
David J. Bodenhamer

The Guardian of Every Other Right
A Constitutional History of Property Rights, Second Edition
James W. Ely, Jr.

Promises to Keep
*African Americans and the Constitutional Order,
1776 to the Present*
Donald G. Nieman

"Belonging to the World"
Women's Rights and American Constitutional Culture
Sandra F. VanBurkleo

"Retained by the People"
A History of American Indians and the Bill of Rights
John R. Wunder

"Belonging to the World"

Women's Rights and American Constitutional Culture

SANDRA F. VANBURKLEO

New York   Oxford
OXFORD UNIVERSITY PRESS
2001

Oxford University Press

Oxford   New York
Athens   Auckland   Bangkok   Bogotá   Bue nos Aires   Calcutta
Cape Town   Chennai   Dar es Salaam   Delhi   Florence   Hong Kong   Istanbul
Karachi   Kuala Lumpur   Madrid   Melbourne   Mexico City   Mumbai
Nairobi   Paris   São Paulo   Shanghai   Singapore   Taipei   Tokyo   Toronto   Warsaw

and associated companies in
Berlin   Ibadan

Published by Oxford University Press, Inc.
198 Madison Avenue, New York, New York, 10016
http://www.oup-usa.org

Oxford is a registered trademark of Oxford University Press

Library of Congress Cataloging-in-Publication Data

VanBurkleo, Sandra F.
    "Belonging to the world" : women's rights and American constitutional culture / by
Sandra F. VanBurkleo.
        p. cm. — (Bicentennial essays on the Bill of Rights)
    Includes bibliographical references and index.
    ISBN 0-19-506971-4 (cloth : alk. paper) — ISBN 0-19-506972-2 (pbk. : alk paper)
    1. Women—United States—Civil rights—History. 2. Women's rights—United
States—History. I. Title. II. Series.

KF4758.V36 2000
323.3'4'0973—dc21   00-029349

Printing number: 9 8 7 6 5 4 3 2 1

Printed in the United States of America
on acid-free paper

For Edward Martin Wise
and to the memory of Mary K. Bonsteel Tachau,
kindred spirits
and citizens of the world

"I went there to assert a principle—a principle relevant to the circumstances of that convention, and one which would promote *all* good causes and retard *all* bad ones. I went there, as an item of the world, to contend that the sons and daughters of the race, without distinction of sex, sect, class or color, should be recognized as belonging to the world, and I planted my feet upon the simple *rights of the delegate*. I asked no favor as woman, or in behalf of woman; no favor as a woman advocating temperance; no recognition of the cause of woman above the cause of humanity; the indorsement of no 'ism' and of no measure; but I claimed, in the name of the world, the rights of a delegate in a world's convention."

—Reverend Antoinette Brown, 1853

Contents

Editor's Preface   viii

Preface   ix

Acknowledgments   xviii

PART ONE: "THE WAY OF OBEDIENCE": FOUNDATIONS   1

1 Governing Women in British North America   5
2 Toward the Revolutionary Settlement   36

PART TWO: "TALK IS THE FOUNTAIN-HEAD OF ALL THINGS":
REPUBLICAN SPEECH COMMUNITIES AND COEQUALITY   59

3 Law, Gender, and Domestic Culture   63
4 Republican Speech Communities   81
5 Toward Coequality and Self-Possession   103
6 Capitalism and the New American Empire   125
7 The Civil War Settlement   139

PART THREE: "GOVERNMENTS TRY THEMSELVES":
DEMOCRATIC SUFFRAGE COMMUNITIES AND EQUALITY   175

8 Democratic Suffrage Communities   181
9 Economic Protection versus Equal Rights   210
10 Physical Protection versus Self-Sovereignty   239
11 The Civil Rights Settlement   256
12 Afterword   307

Notes   316

Bibliographic Essay   362

Index of Cases   391

Index   395

Editor's Preface

"Belonging to the World": Women's Rights and American Constitutional Culture is another volume in the Bicentennial Essays on the Bill of Rights, a series that has resulted from the fruitful collaboration of the Organization of American Historians' Committee on the Bicentennial of the Constitution and Oxford University Press. The committee in 1986 concluded that one of the most appropriate ways in which historians could commemorate the then forthcoming bicentennial of the Bill of Rights was to foster better teaching about the history of liberty. Too often, the committee concluded, undergraduate students could have learned more about that subject if only they would have had basic texts analyzing the evolution of central concepts associated with the Bill of Rights. Previous volumes, for example, have treated the rights of the accused to fair trial and the rights of individuals to use and hold their property freely. The committee, however, also wanted volumes that would deal with groups, such as African Americans, Native Americans, and women, for whom gaining and maintaining rights has proven difficult. The committee also knew that it did not want books that would be strictly guides to legal issues, although readers of this and the other volumes in the series will discover that each gives attention to case law and doctrinal developments. That is as it should be, of course; the histories of law and liberty, at least in the American experience, are inextricably joined. Yet the history of liberty has necessarily been a human drama, one in which lawyers, judges, plaintiffs, defendants, and organized social groups have shaped the development and adaptation of the first ten amendments and, more generally, the entire constitutional order, to social change. The law has had an important role in organizing this human drama, but these books are at their core about people making choices, sometimes through the law, often times outside of it, to challenge the established order in the hope of broadening the bounds of liberty.

Nowhere has this human drama been more vivid and the consequences for understanding the course of liberty more arresting than in the history of women's rights. Sandra F. VanBurkleo has met the challenge of not only filling the many gaps in this story but also in relating those developments to the shifting social status of women in America. Like the other books in this series, *"Belonging to the World"* offers a synthetic examination of its subject rooted in the best and most recent literature in history, political science, law, and in this instance, women's history and studies. Like the other authors in this series, Sandra VanBurkleo has taken as her goal charting the history of liberty across a constantly changing sea of social, cultural, and political development.

Mary K. B. Tachau had originally agreed to prepare this volume, but her untimely death robbed this series and the historical profession of one its most gifted interpreters. We are grateful to Sandra VanBurkleo for filling the resulting void with lucidity and imagination.

Kermit L. Hall
General Editor

Preface

For many decades, Americans have been announcing, as did Radcliffe president Mary Bunting in 1961, that "the bitter battles for women's rights are history" and the "cause . . . won."[1] At the dawn of a new millennium, college students regularly tell their professors that extended talk about women's struggle for equality (to quote one of my students) is "old news" and "paranoid." Writers proclaim the death and intellectual dearth of feminism. They also celebrate the arrival of the Postfeminist Woman—a motorcycle-riding femme fatale with a Ph.D. in computer science—in the place of "women's libbers," still characterized in some circles as humorless fanatics who are determined to smash the family and dress women in army boots.

This book could be read as a meditation on the merits of these claims. *Has* women's rights agitation run its course, or run the wrong course? Clearly, modern women are better situated within the constitutional order than they were, say, in the 1840s, when organized women's rights agitation first appeared in the new republic. Women participate in public life differently and more fully than did Abigail Adams, who in 1776 reminded her husband, John Adams, to "remember the ladies" in the framing of new constitutions and statutes.[2] Female citizens regularly vote, sit on juries, make contracts and wills, earn Ph.D.s, and sue for equal wages. And, though burdened with racism and often with poverty, women of color nevertheless have both legal standing and electoral power. In 1848, when restive New Yorkers issued the Seneca Falls Declaration of Sentiments—a document commonly viewed as *the* manifesto for modern feminism—none of these rights, privileges, and possibilities attached ordinarily to women.

Nevertheless, women have not yet achieved full equality; nor have Americans rectified the sex's second-class citizenship and related absence, beyond the Nineteenth Amendment and assorted Supreme Court rulings, from basic constitutional texts. Personal security continues to elude the female majority: Despite public education programs and vastly improved law enforcement, wife beating, rape, and other forms of gender-specific violence steadily increase. Fortune 500 companies typically do not have female executives. And cultural forces continue to disable young women, so that "equal opportunity" in adult life is something of an empty promise. Young girls still learn that trucks are for boys and dolls are for girls; as women, they claim (in the words of other students) that they are not "very mechanical" and are not "into" math or statistics.

To some extent, these problems reflect the relative scarcity of sound information about how generations of American women have experienced government, freedom, and citizenship. Only a few years ago, a magazine editor asked me to confirm that women had not been citizens until the 1960s—as if female citizenship commenced with the Warren Court. At another extreme, in 1996, a commentator at a scholarly conference asserted that white women's complaints "paled" when compared to the "more legitimate" demands of blacks, as if racism and sexism compete for attention and the category "black" contains no women. Half-truths, in turn, fuel backlash, making it difficult indeed for Americans to credit feminists with widely popular achievements—among them, expanded reproductive freedom, day care centers, hot lines for battered wives, and higher wages.

The much-touted "glass ceiling" extends far beyond corporate boardrooms: Talented women of all races and classes, but especially women of color, seem to be stuck several rungs below men on economic and political ladders. Nor do judges seem eager, years after the defeat of the Equal Rights Amendment, to "find" an uncompromising equality for women in the Fourteenth Amendment's equal protection clause. Despite advances and notwithstanding white women's ameliorating proximity to powerful men, access to legal remedies for discriminatory practices still can depend on the goodwill of employers or judges.

Particularly troubling is women's steady loss of ground in the battle for subsistence. Conventional economic indicators make clear that despite an impressive array of civil rights statutes and amendments, female worker-citizens as a class are not clearly better off than they were several decades ago. To be sure, the gap between male and female wages has not grown dramatically wider and in some occupations has closed slightly, yet when analysts compare the wages of men and women who are similarly situated but not identically employed (such as male janitors and female housekeepers), the gap becomes a chasm. Remarkably, wage differences between men and women who are engaged in identical work have proved to be resistant even to the threat of lawsuits. Female workers congregate mainly in poorly paid "pink-collar" jobs, with dire consequences for female-headed households, women's aspirations, and the nation's economic prospects. Horror stories proliferate about women who protest harassment or sue for promotion, only to confront pornography in desk drawers and shredded work boots. Everywhere, modern spins on traditional limitations severely impinge on women's achievement and well-being—as when employers impose slow-track penalties for pregnancy or cling to work rules established decades ago, when both capitalists and unionists excluded women and organized the workplace accordingly.

We know, too, that the ballyhooed flood of female careerists was temporary, heaviest in fields traditionally associated with "women's work" (like teaching, caregiving, and home- or consumer-related industries), and bottom heavy. When women entered male-dominated fields in junior slots, they often stayed there, with commensurately lower salaries. They also had to adapt to standards set by and for men—as when a female police officer cross-dresses. As Carolen Bailey, a pioneering police commander from Minnesota, said, "When women were two or three percent of the force, a lot of women we saw coming in were trying to fit into the male mold. In fact, the uniforms do that. You put a male uniform on a woman and it looks like little boys trying to be big men."[3] And the plight of poor women is nothing short of desperate. Decades ago, poverty came to be feminized as well as racialized, and recent changes in welfare policy have made things much worse.

Women's declining presence in computer science—an icon of the postmodern age—makes part of the point. Contrary to "postfeminist" mythology and despite modest increases in the number of female physicists and engineers, computer science degrees go mostly to men. Scientific American reported a decline of 23.5 percent in the number of computer science bachelor's degrees awarded to women between 1983–84, when they earned 32,172 BAs or BSs in the field, and 1993–94. The magazine also noted a "shrinking-pipeline" effect between high school and college: Girls make up half the students in high school computer classes, yet in 1993–94 held only 5.7 percent of computer science full professorships in Ph.D.-granting universities.[4]

This book, then, is a beginning attempt to understand how women have been governed, how some of them have experienced freedom and public authority, and how reformers have tried to improve the female majority's access to the rights and obligations of citizenship. It also seeks to explain how and why American women seem to have entered the new millennium without firm constitutional standing and without affecting remedies for persistent forms of discrimination based on sex, notably in situations involving reproduction and physical security.

Two concepts essential to the book's organization require some clarification. The first is the notion of a settlement—an adaptation of a term first used by John Murrin to describe the periodic reordering of Anglo-American governments and the terms of citizenship during constitutional crises.[5] In this book, *settlement* describes both the dynamic process of renegotiating basic terms of legal-political discourse and the concrete results of renegotiation (constitutions, judicial affirmations of constitutions, popular identification with a new polity, and the like). The second is the idea of a speech community (or, as a variant, a suffrage community). Anthropologists and sociolinguists have developed the concept of *speech community* to help us understand certain aspects of citizenship and participation in a shared political culture that extends beyond the state in a formal sense. Nineteenth-century Americans regularly constructed small civil societies to articulate and resolve public questions. The concept of the speech community allows us to grasp how they addressed a host of issues related to the condition of women. In these communities, participants shared goals; a sense of fellowship; and, most important, a belief that through the act of speech, they could transform individuals as well as the republic. By coupling speech to a "generalized social bond" among individuals, as the anthropologist Victor Turner has explained, speech communities can become agents of change—agents that are often more influential than formal governmental institutions.[6] Suffrage communities likewise have been organized around the common act of voting; participating citizens believe that they can resolve social conflicts and advance civil society through voting—an act sometimes described as a "voice" or public "statement."

The book's three main parts coincide roughly with British North American, postrevolutionary, and post–Civil War developments. Part One lays the foundations for all that follows. It examines Anglo-American constructions of the female subject and citizen, as well as the evolution on New World soil of an American version of the sovereign head within family government—the kinglike husband whose sovereignty theoretically could not be divided without destroying the entire constitutional order. It also explores women's experiences with what we now would call freedom of speech, liberty of conscience, the right of locomotion, economic and political freedom, and equal protection or due process of law. In addition, it describes white middle-class women's loss of ground in the eighteenth century, roughly between the 1680s and the onset of resistance to British imperial policies in the 1760s, with particular attention to economic and social change. The concluding section describes the revolutionary settlement struck between the sexes during four decades of constitutional reinvention, from about 1764–65 until about 1805–07.

Part Two reconstructs the century surrounding the emergence of the first women's movement—the so-called first wave—roughly from the 1790s, when sustained criticism of the subjection of American women first emerged, into and slightly beyond the Civil War. During the age of revolution, the social compacts struck between male citizens for their mutual benefit confirmed the ongoing vitality of what women would come to call an "aristocracy of sex." Thus, Lockean contractualism, which helped republicans justify the drawing of a bright line between political and conjugal societies, in the short run probably hindered women's movement into public life. But the revolution also produced the "republican mother," a vision of the maternal female patriot linked, however precariously, to a bygone world of upper-class female influence. This new construction kept women out of political life in the formal sense, yet encouraged political labor in the domestic sphere—as when women sewed flags, wrote patriotic essays for publication, and waged economic boycotts. By vesting matrons with responsibility for maintaining civic virtue and transmitting revolutionary ideas into the next century, the Sons of Liberty feminized the soul of their revolution and situated Daughters of Liberty at its epicenter.

This is to say two separate things: On one hand, as Linda Kerber argues, an extended conversation in revolutionary America about the implications of republican political theory for women resulted by 1810 in a quasi-"Thermidorian" flight from a mixed-sex popular sovereign.[7] As in revolutionary France, the language of liberation embodied what Dorinda Outram calls a "Catch-22," in which women's reliance on republican imagery and arguments to secure freedom beyond the household invited ridicule and moral censure. Although the French and American Revolutions differed appreciably, women in both republics got to choose between "true womanhood" and full citizenship. Moreover, judges in the waning years of the American Revolution decided to perpetuate lordship in family governments. On the other hand, republican constitutionalism served as a limited but powerful tool for self-liberation and group mobilization, in part because it lent authority to the "otherwise compromised position of the female speaker" in public settings.[8] Armed with revolutionary texts, women formulated rights claims in terms that made sense to lawyers and began to construct a feminized, although not yet "feminist,"[9] variant of republican constitutionalism.

In turn, these formulations—wedded to ideas spawned by the Second Great Awakening and associated reform movements—provided scaffolding for the articulation of new women's rights platforms by 1850. Activists aimed first to reconstitute individual women through speech and to secure speech freedom for women. They also constructed republican speech communities from a shared belief in the women's rights creed. These communities were especially visible at women's rights conventions and in women's newspapers, but extended beyond such gatherings to encompass all who subscribed to the creed. Within these liminal spaces, women labored to refashion marriage, social custom, and the male monopoly of public life through rational conversation. The main goal of the majority in these decades was republican coequality, not gender-neutral democratic equality. But at every turn, other visions of freedom competed with the dominant strain for reformers' attention. While women often came to feminism as a result of antislavery work, I should add, their new communities were not identical with abolitionist communities. To the extent that abolitionist historians (the architects of modern history writing) encouraged scholars to think of the woman's movement as a subset of abolitionism, differences and nuances have been lost.

First-wave leaders abruptly shifted gears in the 1860s, when the trauma of the Civil War and a host of cultural changes redirected both the nation and its reformers. Part Two concludes with these troubling developments. Together, they constituted yet another renegotiation of relations between the sexes, which I call the Civil War settlement. As during the Revolution, constitutional change was a double-edged sword. Although rights-bearing language in statutes and constitutional amendments seemed to place all citizens on an equal footing, wartime developments compounded women's difficulties. In the end, Republican Party priorities and judicial interpretations of new constitutional texts affirmed the status quo for women and led many activists to fear that their sex had lost standing in relation to all men. Hence, women's rights leaders narrowed and legalized the agenda;

increasingly, they emphasized elements of republican citizenship, especially women's right to *act* in public as voters, jurors, lawyers, and officeholders.

To some extent, the decision to invade the polls reflected two interconnected sociopolitical processes. The first was the emergence, in the United States as elsewhere, of a mass electoral democracy. As political scientist Judith Shklar once explained, political modernization brought in its wake the notion of "citizenship as standing," the main elements of which were "voting" and "earning." Standing, in turn, came to be less a matter of self-respect than a question of "public respect" and the constitutional right *not* to be deprived of status as a citizen.[10] The second was the victory of common-law discourse in its century-long contest with political discourses. Increasingly, Americans spoke "law" as a primary language and understood political obligation to mean voting, jury duty, and military service—all of which were "gendered" male. By at least 1875, suffragists perceived that speech communities had failed; for their efforts, they had been denied access to emergent democratic suffrage communities, within which citizens "spoke" to one another vicariously, through ballots, political parties, and the press. Activists noted the end of an era, in some cases collapsing the demand for speech freedom into demands for ballots, and leaped headlong into organized suffragism.

Part Three begins with women's invasions of spaces previously taken to be profane. The federal government's involvement in black emancipation, combined with "new" social sciences and mounting interest in "social mothering," sent women's rights activists back to the drawing board. Into the twentieth century, thousands of Gilded Age and Progressive reformers (joined occasionally by radicals) hoped to extend domestic culture *into* the world, on the ground that industrial capitalism and filth threatened American families as never before. This drive to secure direct participation in government and cosovereignty within families also led reformers to support legislative protection for working women and children. Much as Populists sought to subject private railroad corporations to public scrutiny, so urban reformers tried to raze walls between "the state" and "the family"— not just to do public work *at* home, but to re-create the world *as* home. For them, the state was a megahousehold to be "ruled" by a male–female electorate. Casting ballots as individuals, suffragists would be able to defend themselves at the polls alongside men; at the same time, the presumably homogeneous "class" of female voters would protect families, sweep out city hall, and eliminate industrial abuse. Suffragists knew, too, that without judicial reconsideration of that remarkably durable vestige of medieval constitutional theory, the sovereign family "head," suffragism could not succeed. As lawyers began to pose hard questions about whether the right to vote implied cosovereignty and the division of the supposedly indivisible heads of households, the constitutional heart of the matter emerged unequivocally. Nothing impeded women more decisively than the fiction of the unitary domestic sovereign—the main enemy of many antebellum reformers and a monkey on every woman's back well into the modern era.

This paradigm more or less held firm until World War I and adoption of the Nineteenth Amendment. Thereafter, disagreements over the sufficiency of ballots and the merits of sex-specific economic protection led to renewed agitation, in the National Woman's Party (NWP) and elsewhere, for equal rights in economic as well as political life. At the same time, as Nancy Cott demonstrates, the "characteristic doubleness" of suffragism and feminism—their "simultaneous affirmation of women's human rights and women's unique needs and differences"—re-formed into recognizably modern political camps (such as "sameness" and "difference" feminism).[11] After 1923, liberals abandoned the NWP and lobbied hard for a long list of freedoms—among them, access to political conventions as delegates, professional education, improved reproductive control, officeholding, jury service, and fair wages—in some cases, on the ground of the sex's special attributes and needs. Radical feminists pressed for cultural transformation. The NWP, allied with free-market Republicans, emphasized passage of the Equal Rights Amendment (ERA), the equivalent for women of the Fourteenth Amendment's equal protection clause.

Perhaps ironically, feminists looked to the government for protection *against* the government. Modern American lawmakers had come to be capable of both protection of citizens' rights and unprecedented invasions of rights and liberties. Moreover, citizens came to think of rights not so much as zones of autonomy that remained free precisely because government was absent, but, rather, as positive entitlements or public grants, created and protected by the state. Hence, reformers and many public officials sought ways to wield parts of the government against other, repressive elements. Courts, for example, moved to protect citizens from invidious class-based legislation. Whereas many reformers in the 1850s had struggled unsuccessfully to keep various governments *out* of the business of policing women's bodies, law-minded feminists in the 1950s asked the courts to protect the female majority from such regulation—for instance, by extending the right to privacy to include reproductive decisions. Even as judges defended private spaces against legislative inroads, their posture was still protective: The government would be *present*, not absent, and could change the terms of its presence or withdraw, leaving women undefended.

Hence, by the early 1960s—initially from within its established liberal branches—a resurgent women's movement began to demand changes in the prevailing constructions of "man" and "woman" in American law. As groups like the National Organization for Women took up the NWP's ERA banner, liberal feminists hammered away at sex-specific legal classifications, pursued legislative and constitutional remedies for inequality, and began to mobilize against sex-based violence. Then, drawing on half-submerged memories of the first wave and on experiences in the civil rights movement, radical feminists began to press hard for cultural revolution. In their view, liberal legalism formed part of the problem, and ERA—the embodiment of laissez-faire constitutionalism—perpetuated racism and sexism by failing to criticize capitalism and the legal system itself. It is not surprising that Americans (including judges and legislators) rejected many of these ideas and, by the 1990s, forged a series of compromises, the terms of which I call the civil rights settlement. Recently, in response to the limits of that settlement (especially its reliance on equal rights jurisprudence), feminist scholars have begun to elaborate on the antebellum critique of law's operation within American culture. Some of them have concluded that throwing law at government is a lot like throwing red meat at hungry tigers, and that Americans will not achieve sex equality until capitalism and the governments supporting it have been reconfigured.

When possible, I let women speak for themselves and try *not* to put words in their mouths (or to substitute current terms for theirs), although from time to time, analysis requires a certain amount of translation and imposition. I have tried not to equate American constitutional experience with white male or federal judicial experience, and I give space alongside the public policy narrative to the manner in which politicized women have lived and resisted circumscription. These engagements have varied according to the norms and necessities of particular historical moments. Reformers have attempted, for example, to mold public opinion and so lessen customary restraints on women. Sometimes, they have tried to extend the home and its moral economy into the public sphere; on other occasions, women have created "free spaces" (to use Sara Evans's term) situated between family and government or have leaped into the political fray alongside men. These activities dramatically enrich what historians might say about authority and liberty in America by complicating our conception (again in Evans's words) of *who* participates in governance, *which* topics are taken to be "proper subjects for public discussion and decision," and *how* we define key terms like *public life* or *constitutional act*.[12] Few scholars doubt that judicial decisions and congressional debates of civil rights acts are fit subjects for constitutional history. What about suffrage vigils at the White House, the eviction of women from speakers' platforms, and mass arrests of women for dispensing or seeking birth control information?

And how exactly have women positioned *themselves* within constitutional culture? If culture can be defined, after Mary Beth Norton and David Sabean, as a "structure of shared values" articulated in a "series of arguments among people about the common things of their everyday lives,"[13] what has been shared and what has not when men and women talk about sovereignty and self-government? Little is known about women's shifting legal consciousness—how both rank-and-file and upper-class women conceived of rights, government, terms like *public* and *private,* and constitutional texts. Did freedom of speech or the right of locomotion mean the same thing to men and women? Despite increased interest in such questions, we know relatively little about how nonwhite, working-class, or lesbian women dealt with oppression or carved out zones of autonomy within restrictive communities. We don't even know if communities *were* uniformly restrictive across time and space. Little has been written about how men and women experienced criminal trials before the twentieth century; we know even less about women's ability to exercise freedoms beyond the right to deal in property or cast ballots. What *about* the "right to be let alone" (or privacy); the right of locomotion; procedural rights; and First Amendment liberties, notably freedom of speech? The last omission is especially startling. Speaking and listening are central democratic practices capable of altering what Susan Bickford calls "the field of meaning" in public life,[14] and gender ascriptions have clearly marked experiences of speech freedom. As a result, this book often can speak only of middle-class heterosexual white people and of rights—for example, the right to vote or economic equality—for which modernists have contended most successfully.

Equally troubling is the scarcity of writing about women's perceptions of their own situation (as contrasted to the government's official view) in the centuries before the Civil War. I devote much space to premodern developments, not to give short shrift to modernity, but to suggest that key elements of the story have been ignored. In the second third of the nineteenth century, political economy and law began to interact in recognizably modern ways, absorbing and expressing distinctly modern views of gender difference. Before modern times, women *had* constitutional experiences, thought about rights, and made use of constitutional discourse to resist circumscription and to demand a place in public life. Often, these experiences differed from men's; yet scholars have reconstructed only bits and pieces of developments that, once organized and explored more fully, may dramatically alter how we tell the story. Such elaborations may suggest, to give one example, that Americans into the twentieth century practiced indirect or virtual representation, contrary to revolutionary principles, and that the inspiring slogan, "No taxation without representation," was not manifest in public life until at least the 1920s.

I also hope to show how various extra-political governments, which are usually taken to be beyond the scope of constitutional history, powerfully shaped women's experiences of freedom. Constitutional historians typically emphasize the acts of political governments, especially at the federal level, and, within that zone, particularly of the Supreme Court. This preoccupation, however, squeezes out the better part of human experience with constitutionalism and imposes post–Civil War (and, in some respects, post–New Deal) conceptions of nation-state relations and citizenship on early America, when states, municipalities, and heads of families controlled access to many basic freedoms. For at least half of American history, after all, citizens looked to state rather than federal constitutions and statutes for affirmations of citizenship rights. In addition, challenges to women's autonomy have often occurred in settings remote from courts and legislatures, where customary constitutions—conditioned, to be sure, by formal constitutions but not identical with them—hold sway. Before recent times, husbands governed wives and children; pastors, magistrates, or presiding officers in meetings curtailed women's ability to speak or assemble in public. For such would-be orators, state and federal guarantees of speech freedom were little more than inspiring slogans. Temperance workers, abolitionists, and women's rights conventioneers hammered out the details of alternative constitutional regimes, elements of which made their way into formal constitutions; and, to make matters more complex, both formal and customary constitutions of restraint sometimes collided with "constitutions of aspiration," to borrow Hendrik Hartog's term.[15] At such times, constitutional culture changed, often in advance of or in opposition to formal developments.

Skeptics might say that informal rulers have not made "law" and so should remain offstage; others would argue, to the contrary, that the state has often relied on husbands and community gatekeepers to enforce law and custom and that courts have been only one site of constitutional evolution. Informal interventions can be riveting. In past centuries, uppity women were silenced by catcalls, arson, and muggings. They were committed to asylums; locked in closets; beaten for obstinacy; denied access to clubs and law firms; divested of personal property after their husbands' deaths; and, in a fascinating breach of the old principle by which the government cannot "take" property without compensation, relieved of property rights at marriage. When women resist circumscription on the ground, say, of inequality, constitutional culture mutates. In the 1980s, a female pipefitter noted that, "for a long time," she was not "allowed to do certain types of jobs. . . . Some of the men would take the tools out of my hands." She persisted. Now, she holds and uses tools without impediment. In such transactions, formalized in sexual harassment suits, men and women confront the belief that if "a woman can do it, it ain't that masculine, not that tough,"[16] and move toward equality.

Given the mandate of the Bill of Rights Essay Series, I can only sketch the borders of regions that beg to be charted in detail. Perhaps historians of women and of constitutionalism will begin to talk over scholarly fences more regularly so that, before more decades pass, someone will be able to write a new, woman-friendly textbook in American constitutional history. In that account, female citizens will occupy center stage with men as comakers of constitutional culture. Perhaps historians will come to see, too, that in the past, citizens inhabited different, adjacent stages, organized much like the circular arenas at a circus, in which the limelight shifts restlessly from ring to ring. Supreme Court justices will appear not as *the* makers of arenas, but as powerful boundary setters and actors in a larger cast of characters. Since the New Deal especially, the Supreme Court frequently has established the boundaries within which citizens experience freedom or its absence; at other moments, however—and sometimes even in the modern era—federal judicial policy has been secondarily important or irrelevant. This is particularly true in the case of women because they have been governed differently from men. But it is also true, say, in Appalachia, where (as Calvin Trillin's *Killings* so brilliantly suggests) customary constitutions shape judgments about the "rightness" of a man's decision to shoot a stranger for walking over his tobacco field.

Whatever else we may decide to do, historians need to tell the whole story about how American men and women have lived their constitutional heritage. Citizens deserve to know that the republicans' proud insistence on untrammeled access to liberty and to personally dignifying self-government still applies most fully to white men. We can use this knowledge to revitalize public life, or not, as we choose. *Do* Americans mean to create what Joan Wallach Scott calls an "equality that rests on differenc*es*"?[17] With luck, this book will make it easier to converse in classrooms, in public meetings, and at dinner tables. As antebellum feminists saw clearly, conversation can remake the world. In Susan Bickford's words, "If we are ever to move from our inegalitarian social order to a diverse, egalitarian, and democratic one, we must speak and listen in a way that sustains and extends the possibility of *actively making sense together*."[18]

Acknowledgments

These pages might never have emerged from the depths of my computer without the support of colleagues and friends. The Bill of Rights Essay Series' rule against bibliographic notes conceals the extent of my debt to scholars working in many disciplines. Without these scholars' efforts, there would have been little to say. A flood of recent writing—much of it emanating from fields beyond the history of public law—makes clear that the constitutional history of women will not long remain an unexplored country. Myriad path-breaking studies press beyond the frontier, exhibiting the kind of restless curiosity and tenacity that I associate with Old Mother Featherlegs (so-called because of the fringe on her chaps) and certain seafaring Scandinavians. Although the bibliographic essay conveys a slightly better sense of the universe, I wish to extend special thanks to the many scholars whose books, articles, and letters altered my angle of vision or provoked disagreement—among them, the oddly *present* Mary Beard, who still inspires us to look beyond legal formalities to culture and to women's achievements in the face of oppression.

I have been blessed as well with splendid research assistants. Joan Arnstein, Robert Buchta, Dominic DeBrincat, and Ann Marie Lehman cheerfully performed dull clerical tasks; tolerated abrupt shifts in gears; waded through piles of governmental documents; and, despite Paleolithic film readers in a key repository, unearthed piles of buried treasure. Leeann Ford, my undergraduate assistant in 1997–98, read women's newspapers with me for a summer and helped me to understand speech freedom. While working on another project, research assistants Yvonne Pitts, Jim Schwartz, and Bonnie Speck stumbled upon invaluable material. More than once, these scholars saved the day; together, they provide ample ground for optimism about the future of the academy.

Other generous people provided conversation in cafés, conference sessions, and e-mail exchanges. H-Law and H-Women subscribers provided citations and useful information. At a crucial moment, Sally Gordon and the late, much-lamented Betsy Clark affirmed the project's value. Through her work and in conversation, Betsy helped me to see the importance of religion in women's rights consciousness; Sally offered encouragement, tough questions, and help with Mormonism. The late and irreplaceable Paul Murphy made it possible for me to see speech freedom in odd places. I also thank Effie Ambler, Norma Basch, Susan Porter Benson, Eileen Boris, Christine Compston, Tiffany Dziurman, Sara Evans (who said, "Yes, it's important," at the right time), Zanita Fenton, Mike Grossberg, Alice Hearst, Dirk Hartog, Tim Huebner, Colette Hyman, Chris Johnson, Morton Keller (for helpful remarks at a 1991 conference), Nick Kyser, Lynn Laufenberg, Julie Longo, Mary Beth Norton (for a useful letter), Kitty Preyer (for bibliographic help and firm nudges), Marie Provine, Alan Raucher, Beth Onusko Savalox, Jane Schaberg, Stanley Shapiro, Debra Viles (for lessons in courage and for sharing research), the Vlasopolos-Ambrogio collective, Joseph Ward, and Bill Wiecek. Mary Farmer, Sally Gordon, Sue Grayzel, Cynthia Harrison, Peter Hoffer, David Konig, Kent Newmyer, Don Nieman, and Vicky Woeste bravely slogged through portions of the manuscript at various stages in its development; I am forever in their debt. My friend and colleague Marc Kruman read and reread chapters, tolerated my fits and starts, and gave meaning to old adages about how disagreement advances knowledge; he even gave up sightseeing in Rome to undertake a final read. Les Benedict challenged me to clarify elements of Part II; although I could not agree with him entirely, I adopted many suggestions and benefited from having to formulate responses, some of which appear in this book.

Many ideas arose first in classrooms. I recall the contributions of students enrolled in my once-in-a-lifetime 1993 legal history seminar, the Madison Foundation fellows gathered a few months later at American University, discussants at three women's studies brown bag lectures at Wayne State, participants in a 1994 National Endowment for the Humanities Institute at the University of Tulsa, discussion after a 1996 lecture sponsored by the Wayne State University (WSU) Center for Legal Studies, exchanges at the Ohio Legal History Colloquium in 1997, and a series of happenings in my constitutional history class during the otherwise dreary winter of 1997.

I am grateful, too, for WSU grants emanating from the Department of History, the Office of the Vice President for Research, and the Undergraduate Research Council, which together subsidized research assistants, travel expenses, and photocopying. Walter Edwards of the WSU Humanities Center provided a quiet place to write. Librarians expertly facilitated my work; I thank particularly the staff at WSU's Purdy and Neef Libraries, Detroit Public Library, the State Archives of Washington, University of Michigan Libraries, and the Library of Congress. Series editor Kermit Hall, as well as Nancy Lane, Gioia Stevens, Linda Jarkesy, Lisa Grzan, and Stacie Caminos of Oxford University Press, exhibited great patience as I crawled toward the finish line. Finally, near trail's end, two OUP readers provoked second thoughts with pages of detailed commentary.

Two sui generis human beings deserve special notice. Edward Martin Wise, my best friend and brilliant live-in lawyer, fetched books during sabbatical leaves; provided matchless editing, as well as laundry and cooking services; and ferreted out idiotic readings of legal texts. Mary K. Bonsteel Tachau made me promise to write this book (originally contracted to her) shortly before her death. She would have disagreed with many of my decisions. But, in the end, I think she might have forgiven me for them on the ground that they were not, after all, mistakes of fact, which she rarely forgave. Mary K. condemned Phyllis Schlafly as a "pink herring" during debates on the ERA in Kentucky, not because they disagreed with one another, but because she thought that Schlafly was spreading terrible lies.* Critics, one hopes, will follow suit, absolving from blame the many generous people who helped a rather traditionally educated constitutional historian find her way toward the history of women and then into and through this book—which, in the making, remade me. That, perhaps, has been the finest gift of all.

Detroit, Michigan
S. V. B.
August 2000

*Story told by Eric Tachau, Louisville, KY, 1992.

"Belonging to the World"

Part One

"The Way of Obedience"
Foundations

> The soul has naturally two elements, a ruling and a ruled; and each has its different goodness, one belonging to the rational and ruling element, and the other to the irrational and ruled. . . . The rule of the freeman over the slave is one kind of rule; that of the male over the female another.
>
> —ARISTOTLE, *The Politics* (c. 335–322 B.C.)[1]

I n the 1630s, as English settlement of North America began in earnest, all Europe grappled with widespread social unrest, the collapse of commodity markets, and the ravages of the Thirty Years' War. In Britain, Anglican persecutions of Puritans and other religious dissenters, combined with economic dislocations, spurred the Great Migration— by colonial Puritan lights, a divinely ordained exodus of Saints from a corrupted Old World. In the 1630s alone, more than 20,000 souls "flew out of England as out of Babylon."[2] A string of new English colonies, reaching from Plymouth and Massachusetts Bay in the North to the swamps of Virginia and to steamy Caribbean islands, readily absorbed this outpouring. In the upper South, white settlers multiplied from a handful in the 1610s to about 1,000 in 1620 and 10,000 by 1650; after 1619, the population included a small number of bonded Africans. In the colonies now called New England, settlements grew more rapidly, from a few hundred people in 1620 to 13,500 twenty years later.

Although North America held great promise for unhappy or restless Europeans, it was also a hazardous place, and as one moved from north to south, dangers proliferated. Francis Bacon and other boosters of empire encouraged enterprising young Englishmen to migrate alone: "When the plantation grows to strength," wrote Bacon in 1625, "then it is time to plant with women as well as with men."[3] Indeed, because of persistent sex imbalances (in the 1630s, about 6 men for each woman and by 1700, about 2.5 to 1) and lethal diseases, white populations in southern climes did not begin to reproduce themselves until the 1680s. The life expectancy for male émigrés in the South was about 43 years and slightly less for their female companions; in most cases, these figures were lower than in Great Britain. Children who were fortunate enough to survive infancy usually lost at least one parent well before adulthood; two-thirds of all marriages ended in fewer than ten years with the death of one partner. If female migrants lasted until age 45, they usually outlived their husbands; the Chesapeake evolved, as one historian puts it, into a "land of newcomers" as well as a "land of widows."[4] Labor shortages and influxes of shady characters plagued the colonial leadership; so did the loosely knit social fabric, restive servant populations, and rapid turnover among officeholders. Those who contracted for female servants probably hoped to obtain domestic labor, rather than to buy wives.

But if women sought husbands, sex imbalances ensured their success. In four Maryland counties before 1700, only *two* women died unmarried.

New England Congregationalists, in contrast, lived long enough to boast in doddering tones about their "city on a hill."[5] After the first winter, villagers in the Massachusetts Bay area enjoyed an abundant food supply and relative freedom from epidemic disease. Women and men survived to age 70 and sometimes to 90, thereby outliving their English counterparts and, indeed, living longer than their landless children who were waiting to marry found convenient. Because Puritans tended to migrate in families, first-generation communities had a relatively balanced sex ratio, although next-generation women in some towns outnumbered men 2 to 1; half the original female settlers of Andover, Massachusetts, for instance, bore eight to eleven children each. Ministers and magistrates closely supervised members of the community, and in attempts to revive what David Konig has called "old communal methods of achieving social harmony,"[6] Congregationalists labored to contain the related "infections" of antinomianism and economic individualism.

This is not to say that all New Englanders were Puritans. Numerous adventurers and ne'er-do-wells crowded the docks in Boston and Salem, drawn less by God's voice than by the promise of relatively high wages, upward mobility, or simply a chance to begin life anew. Mercantile houses flourished in virtually every big town with a decent harbor, and Massachusetts legislators painstakingly regulated economic development to prevent spiritual decline. It is to say instead that the mostly Anglican South, if only by default, more consistently tolerated social and economic independence. Stockholders in the Virginia Company wished heartily not only for more women, but for more clergymen and for settlers who were willing to grow food.

Colonial women initially benefited from the scarcity of labor and, in the South especially, skewed sex ratios. English women in America never entirely escaped the strictures of English law and custom. Nor did seventeenth-century men and women value independence of body and mind in a modern sense. But for a relatively brief time in the seventeenth century and in some locations into the eighteenth, the instability of new social and spiritual systems encouraged a certain regard for the female sex. In the North, the radical Protestant belief in the spiritual equality of men and women sometimes mitigated the formal harshness of the law of marriage and undermined parts of the Puritans' church-state machine. Women in New England seaports rarely became economic leaders, but their labor and capital permeated local markets. In New England port cities, Elaine Crane found seventeenth- and eighteenth-century women engaged in home work, as well as in salaried labor, in virtually every facet of the economy. Although working women lost ground during the eighteenth century and typically earned less than men who were engaged in similar work, they "taught school, ran inns and taverns, and sold rum. . . . They leased out land, houses, warehouses, horses, and slaves, and they lent money at interest." They also served as shopkeepers (in 1737, 57 of Boston's 133 licensed retailers were women), clerks, and bookkeepers.

> Women whitewashed houses, drove milk carts, ran lotteries, ground chocolate, sowed the ground, wintered the town bull, taught dance, and sold dung. They worked as shipwrights, apothecaries, and . . . brass founders. Women carted wood or hay, repaired the town highways, and kept the post office . . . made buttons and mourning rings in partnership with jewelers and prepared the dead for burial. Women made candles for export, nets for fishing voyages, and ships' bread for slaving ventures. They embroidered chair seats for up-

holsterers and painted Windsor chairs for cabinet-makers. They retailed the goods imported by merchant grandees and made wigs to cover up their scalps.[7]

As the colonists approached revolution, however, women's prospects deteriorated, especially in the commercializing North. As settlements grew dense, mortality increased and fertility rates decreased; in demographic terms, the New World was becoming more like the Old World. In planting colonies, where white women retained a certain amount of power and social influence into the late eighteenth century, the introduction of bonded African labor triggered a reorientation of both law and culture; new racialized stereotypes (such as the white "lady" and the black "wench") accompanied a refashioning of patriarchy wherever slavery took root. By the 1750s, and certainly by 1790, little remained of old ways of living and thinking. In the end, a number of factors—among them, the appearance of bourgeois leisure, liberal-republican political theory, the gradual division of white society into gendered "spheres," the related masculinization of public power, and the emergence of Republican Motherhood as a distinctively feminine way to express patriotism—promoted the constitutional and economic marginalization of women during the Age of the Democratic Revolution.

Chapter 1

Governing Women in British North America

Historians cannot say with certainty whether Mistresses Ann Hutchinson and Ann Hibbens knew one another, but the odds are good that they did. Both women came to New England from Lincolnshire, a Puritan hotbed. Both had married prominent merchants named William, and both had decided to migrate with their families, in 1630 and 1634 respectively, to be near John Cotton, a brilliant Puritan lecturer and newly appointed assistant pastor of the First Church of Boston in Massachusetts Bay. Mary Beth Norton and Jane Kamensky suspect that Hibbens witnessed and learned from Hutchinson's tribulations. At any rate, the two women participated in slightly different ways in the social and spiritual experimentation characteristic of newly established British colonial societies. Their stories tell us a great deal about their society's fear of unbounded women; they also reveal much about the colonists' vision of the "good" woman and about law's power in shaping the conditions of freedom for women in British North America. Especially in northern colonies, but also in the emerging plantation South, women (and, in different ways, men) found themselves surrounded by webs of government that both ensured and proscribed freedom.

"UNSAFE SPEECH"

In 1635, the learned and charismatic Hutchinson gained admission to the First Church of Boston, over the objections of several pastors who suspected her of antinomianism (the belief in the primacy of divine revelation and related skepticism about the absolute authority of the clergy and Mosaic law). With the encouragement of Cotton, Governor Harry Vane, and her fiery brother-in-law, the minister John Wheelwright, Hutchinson began to hold women's meetings at home—a common enough activity among English women—where she explicated biblical texts and criticized sermons, notably those of John Wilson, pastor of the First Church.[1]

The success of Hutchinson's meetings coincided with a colonywide revival and rapid expansion of church rolls; when religious zeal waned in 1636, Cotton began chiding other pastors for abandoning, solely to attract members, the "covenant of grace" in favor of a Popish "covenant of works." Hutchinson, who agreed with Cotton and had Vane's ear, emerged as the mainspring of a faction pitted against Wilson's ministry and John Winthrop's gubernatorial ambitions. Throughout the colony and against canon law and custom, her followers began to walk out of services and to heckle ministers about theological points.

Then, the tide began to turn against Vane's supporters. Feigning friendship, Wilson and other clerics visited Hutchinson's home in December 1636, ostensibly to discuss religion; Wilson secretly took notes, from which the group later compiled a list of doctrinal "errors." A month later, at Cotton's invitation, Wheelwright preached an incendiary fast-day sermon in which—to Cotton's horror—he condemned every local minister except his host for practicing a covenant of works and called for warfare against Satan's allies in local churches. The language of his jeremiad revealed ongoing associations between woman and the Antichrist. Said Wheelwright, good Christians relished battles between "Gods people and those that are not"; everyone knew "that the whore [or false church] must be burnt. . . . [I]t is not shaving of her head and paring her nayles and changing her rayment, that will serve . . . but this whore must be burnt." Fearing rebellion, the Massachusetts General Court (or provincial assembly) confiscated firearms from suspected Wheelwright supporters, who, in turn, circulated a remonstrance threatening an appeal to royal courts. Four months later, Winthrop won the governorship and Vane fled to London. In March 1637, magistrates started proceedings against Wheelwright, Hutchinson, and minor players in what came to be called the Antinomian Controversy. Convicted of sedition for his public condemnation of the clergy, Wheelwright was exiled, although he later returned to a prestigious lectureship at Harvard.

His sister-in-law fared less well. In September 1637, at an open meeting in Newtown (now Cambridge), a church-state synod examined Hutchinson, in keeping with English procedure, for evidence of sedition, heresy, blasphemy, and other crimes. Pregnant and faint, she faced three rows of hostile magistrates, deputies, and clergymen. Hutchinson, said Winthrop, had "troubled the peace of the commonwealth" and "spoken divers things . . . prejudicial to the honour of the churches and ministers." She had "maintained a meeting and an assembly" at home, even though the practice had been censured as "a thing not tolerable nor comely in the sight of God." The court hoped to "reduce" her; failing that, she would be condemned for pride and arrogance.

For a time, Hutchinson prevailed, ably challenging the court's questionable use of evidence obtained privately, its related refusal to let her examine Wilson's notebooks, and its failure to administer oaths. She was a keen student of biblical law and legal procedure and saw how weak the court's case really was. Winthrop had no hard evidence of sedition—by definition a public crime—and weak evidence of heresy. She had not signed the Wheelwright petition, had criticized ministers only at home, and had spoken with Wilson's allies as one speaks with "friends." As she reminded the court, Puritans respected private conversations and "matter[s] of conscience"; because she was correct, Winthrop acceded to her procedural demands.

Gradually, however, the focus shifted from theology to "natural" relations between the sexes, especially to Hutchinson's alleged usurpations of male prerogatives. More than once, the magistrates reminded her that men need not "discourse" with women, that a woman never could "call a company together" to preach, and that women could not offer testimony without judicial permission. Why had Hutchinson not taught women to "love their husbands and not to make them clash?" Surely her meetings, so "prejudicial to the state," led women to neglect their families and to believe, with their teacher, that "the fear of man is a snare." Domestic sabotage weakened the polity; as a minister later explained, God chose *not* to create church and state "at one stroke," but to lay "foundations both of State and Church, in a family"—the "Mother Hive" from which authority "issued forth." Thus, the court declared Wilson's notebooks a lawful source of evidence: When women attacked the polity at its taproot, confidences "counted for nothing."

In the end, Hutchinson decided to hold nothing back. She described her doctrinal positions in detail. She also claimed a God-given ability to distinguish between true and false voices. Hoping for evidence of heresy, the magistrates asked her to say more precisely how God communicated with her. "By an immediate voice," she replied. She reminded her accusers that because Jesus alone controlled her "body and soul," the court could only bring a "curse upon . . . posterity, and the mouth of the Lord hath spoken it." The magistrates breathed a sigh of relief: The "American Jezebel" (as she came to be called) had admitted antinomianism in public and could be exiled, should she arrogantly refuse to recant theological errors.

Jailed in a private home for the winter, Hutchinson awaited a church trial for violating the parish covenant by which Saints agreed to "walke in all sincere Conformity" with God's law as interpreted by the clergy; if guilty, she would be excommunicated. Wilson officiated at the church proceeding in March 1638. Hutchinson was too weak to attend the opening session, at which elders presented yet more evidence "taken from her owne Mouth" over the winter. Because she claimed to be ruled exclusively by God, not by men, the magistrates accused her of Familism—that is, sympathy with the "family of love" sect in which members collectively married Jesus and dispensed with ordinary matrimony.[2] As one critic put it, she plainly supported "that foule, groce, filthye, and abominable opinion held by Familists, of the Communitie of Weomen."

Hutchinson stoutly denied all ties to Familism and recanted several "errors," which should have saved her from condemnation: Puritans typically forgave and tried to rehabilitate Saints willing to humiliate themselves in public. But the woman in the dock had been demonized. Cotton reminded parishioners that although Hutchinson had done "much good," she was "but a Woman and many unsound and dayngerous principles are held by her." Did she not threaten the "very foundation of Religion" with the "filthie Sinne of the Communitie of Woemen and all promisc[uou]s and filthie cominge togeather of men and Woemen without Distinction or Relation of marriage?" He even accused her of marital infidelity on the ground that Familism always led to it.

At closing sessions in March 1638, Wilson read an even longer list of "errors," some compiled by Thomas Shepard and other embittered ex-disciples over the winter. Weakened by pregnancy and detention, Hutchinson said little. In any case, heretical doctrines had ceased to be the issue; she had been cast as the whore of Babylon and charged with sabotaging godly relations. An elder summarized charges: "[Y]ou have stept out of your place, you have rather bine a Husband than a Wife and a preacher than a Hearer, and a Magistrate than a Subject." Wilson called her a "dayngerous Instrument of the Divell." Others feared that the "Misgovernment of this Woman's tongue" portended grave "Disorder." Although some members objected to invasions of conscience, Cotton found biblical authority to exile her for perjury, blasphemy, and spiritual "seduction." The writ of excommunication ordered her to leave the parish "as a Leper."

Hutchinson walked out of church, followed by family members and her friend Mary Dyer (executed in 1660 for Quakerism). She then joined her husband William, who had fled to Rhode Island. There, she experienced what Winthrop soberly termed a "monstrous birth"—in his view, providential evidence of grotesque religious beliefs. Winthrop noted, too, that Dyer's "familiarity with the devill" earlier had produced a stillborn "monstrous" child, which Hutchinson and Dyer had concealed; both women were unnatural and perhaps diabolical. In 1639, elders (including William Hibbens) visited Rhode Island to check on the progress of censured members. Hutchinson slammed the door in their faces. She wanted no part of them; she was an ecstatic "spouse of Christ." Disconcerted visitors pronounced her a "Harlot" and begged the church to "cut her off" completely; Wilson gladly obliged.

The tale's end fit neatly into the narrative Winthrop later constructed to explain Hutchinson's exile. In the early 1640s, she had moved to New Netherland to find "peace";

there, Indians had killed the entire Hutchinson family except one child. Surely, the disaster had been providential: "I never heard that the Indians . . . did ever before this, commit the like outrage," Winthrop wrote. God had made of "this wofull woman" a "heavie
example of their cruelty," thereby confirming her diabolical nature. Meanwhile, and partly
in response to upheaval in England, Puritans everywhere began to close ranks, ruling out
female ministries and religious experimentation. As John Brinsley explained in a typical
1645 sermon in Yarmouth, England, "Sure we are, that . . . Women may not teach in
publick."

> And were there no other Reason for it, this alone might be sufficient to silent them. The
> woman by her taking upon her to teach . . . became the Instrument of Seduction, and Au-
> thor of Transgression to her husband, and consequently of ruine to him. . . . Henceforth
> then no more Women-Preachers. . . . [F]or women to take upon them the office of Teach-
> ing . . . [is] . . . a mingling of Heaven and earth together, an inversion of the course and
> order of nature.[3]

Ann Hibbens, in contrast, did not claim to be a prophet. No sooner had the well-to-
do Hibbens family sailed into Boston harbor in 1630 than Ann developed a reputation for
a sharp tongue and "crabbedness of . . . temper."[4] In Jane Kamensky's words, she "occupied a liminal position in the community's speech-status hierarchy, expected to articulate both the social elevation of her wealth and the 'natural' submission of her gender,' "
and failed to achieve the latter.[5] But serious trouble awaited in 1640, when she locked
horns with a carpenter who had raised his price after building a fancy bedstead. Hibbens
not only disputed the workman's claim and investigated prices charged by artisans in
neighboring towns, but also rejected the mediating efforts of another workman. As
Kamensky notes, Hibbens "spoke as a woman trying to participate in a rational society
with a developing economy; prices, value, and collusion, not inspiration and revelation,
were her province." But in the wake of Hutchinson's exile, women exhibited a "restless
tongue" at some peril. Puritans disliked female saboteurs even more than they hated
garden-variety shrews.[6]

In the autumn of 1640, the First Church began an examination of Hibbens to ferret
out evidence of "lying." This was a serious crime: The 1648 Massachusetts *Laws and Liberties* threatened a severe whipping for telling lies "pernicious to the publick weal," particularly those causing "damage or injurie of any particular person" or designed to "abuse
the people with false news."[7] The church court also sought evidence of scolding and un-
governed speech; the last straw apparently had been Hibbens's rejection of male mediation and her related decision to undertake a market survey. Hibbens, the court announced,
had been "proud & Contemptius and unreverent"; she had "used such speeches to . . .
Brother Davis and other workmen, *when they would not speak as you do.*" Against nature, she sought to convince men of her point of view; in Puritan towns, women imitated
men, not the other way around.[8]

As in Hutchinson's civil trial, charges quickly multiplied to include the contraven-
tion of natural relations between women and men. Judges charged Hibbens with laying
"infamy, disgrace, and reproach" on the carpenter; they also noted her refusal to answer
questions, her "carriage . . . so proud and contemptuous and irreverent . . . when the church
is dealing with her." She refused to answer questions; through a "Brother," she sardonically told judges that she dared not speak because God required silence of women. In the
end, examiners condemned her violations of "the rule of the Apostle in usurping author-

ity over him whom God hath made her head and husband, and in taking the power and authority which God hath given to him out of his hands." William had accepted the price; Ann's belief that she could "manage it better than her husband" was a "plain breach of the rule of Christ."

Had Hibbens used "indirect means" to rile up her neighbors? Such means could only be Satanic, but in 1640, churchmen settled for admonition and, when she refused to disavow "covetous distempers," excommunication. Hibbens supposedly merited damnation for "slandering and raising up an evil report of . . . Brethren," for the "sowing of discord," and for moving "with a restless and discontented spirit . . . from person to person, from house to house, and from place to place." She questioned her husband's "wise . . . head." She "usurped authority over him, grieved his spirit," behaved "as if he was a nobody," and rejected "the way of obedience," encouraging "unquietness of the family." Like Hutchinson, Hibbens flouted relational teachings and so threatened public peace; unlike Hutchinson, she had embraced the commercial spirit—an impulse entrusted primarily to strong-willed men.

Hibbens vanished from public view until 1654, when her well-regarded husband died; one historian thinks that without his protection, she no longer could fend off the "full weight of her neighbors' hatred." In 1655, the General Court convicted her of witchcraft. The magistrates refused the verdict and ordered a new trial; the jurors again condemned her. On June 19, 1656, she was executed as a witch—for being "turbulent in her passion, and discontented," and possessed of a "strange carriage." John Norton, a First Church minister, thought that she had been hanged "for having more wit than her neighbors"; she had "guessed that two of her persecutors, whom she saw talking in the street, were talking of her; which, proving true, cost her life."[9]

GOD'S LAW, THE KING'S LAW

To some extent, the punishment of Hibbens and Hutchinson for "unsafe" conduct partly reflected the Puritan magistracy's deep-seated fear of what Carole Pateman has called "the disorder of women."[10] Many believers saw women as instruments of "anarchie" and spiritual seduction. Expression had to be strictly policed; otherwise, as Winthrop explained in a 1637 attempt to justify new limits on religious dissent, "a wife, a childe, a servant may doe any thinge . . . though the husband, father, or master deny their consent."[11] Puritan sages believed, too, that females achieved Sainthood, not by being exemplary women, but by emulating men: As London's Reverend Robert Bolton put it in 1635, "Souls have no sexes. In the better part they are both men."[12] Hutchinson's ex-follower Shepard testified at her church trial that he had been bewitched by a "swarm of strange opinions," which "like flies" went to the "sores of men's heads and hearts." In the presence of a gifted seductress, "every man hath some drunken conceit that rocks him asleep," leading him away from God, much as Eve had led Adam astray.[13] Puritans' harsh treatment of Eve-like saboteurs vividly illustrated their capacity for "holy violence in the performance of all duties,"[14] including marital duties.

Beneath social theory and religious doctrine, however, lay a framework of biblical and civil law swathed in the legitimating cloak of antiquity. Nothing lent greater authority to a rule, whether in a meetinghouse or courtroom, than the claim that it had existed for time out of mind. In early modern England, husbands and magistrates jointly governed women; as J. H. Baker explains, marital subjection "profoundly affect[ed] property rights and contractual capacity, not to mention access to the common-law system itself." Wives were not the only group burdened with status disabilities; aliens, monks, serfs, servants, apprentices, and children occupied similarly low rungs on the legal ladder. But the law of marriage was the "most pervasive aspect of the English law of persons"—not only because of its consequences for married people, but also because it shaped the law of inheritance.[15]

With a few important exceptions, private law treated a never-married woman (a *feme sole*) more or less like a man of the same class: If men who were similarly situated in society could sell a wagon or be sued for nuisance, so could single women. In contrast, a married woman (or *feme covert*) labored under crushing legal disabilities. At marriage, a woman's legal personality was merged with and overshadowed by her husband's. While subject to the marital bond, a status variously called *coverture* or the *marital indenture*, a wife essentially became her husband's perpetual servant—or, as some scholars would say, his permanent debtor or tenant. She lost direct access to myriad rights that her husband, now her lord or *baron*, exercised in her stead; the couple acted as one person, usually through the husband. A wife's body was not precisely the husband's property. But he had exclusive property rights in her *company* as well as in her domestic and sexual *services*—that is, in what she might do with her body. As a result, he could decide (to give a few examples) whether she would bear children, have sexual intercourse, or write a letter in solitude.

Thus, English women did not undergo "social death"[16] so much as protective muzzling and curtailment. A wife experienced freedom of action vicariously, as when a man voted for his family, transacted business for his wife, or testified as to *their* intentions when a constable arrested *her* for a crime. Lawyers called this fusion of "two souls" into "one flesh" the "unity of person" or "marital unity" doctrine; the requirement that the wife adopt her husband's surname in place of her father's symbolized this merger as well as the transfer of interest in her labor from father to husband.[17]

The list of disabilities was daunting. By custom and at law, Anglo-Americans proscribed all women's freedom—by restricting university education to men, withholding political rights, or ruling out occupations that might "unsex" or scandalize women (such as lawyering, doctoring, lifting, and building). But a married woman's designated path was particularly narrow. During coverture, a husband and wife mutually served and exploited one another, in keeping with the feudal character of the marital relation. On the one side, men owed their wives bed and board, "pin money" (a common law term), physical protection, evenhanded governance, and sexual fidelity. On the other side, as the widely read Anglican clergymen Richard Allestree explained, wives owed their husbands "Fidelity . . . of the Bed" and "fidelity in the managing of those worldly Affairs he commits to her."[18]

Heading the list of disabilities were married women's loss of rights to property and locomotion (the common law right to move about freely). Bare title to all real estate owned by a woman before marriage remained with her unless she conveyed the land to her husband. Title to clothing, jewelry, and other personal possessions ("paraphernalia"), as well as effective managerial control over real estate, passed to her husband at the moment of union, unless a woman had acted against the presumption of unification in advance of marriage. The main instruments by which wives-to-be might reserve title to enumerated real and personal property were trusts and premarital agreements (sometimes called marriage settlements or antenuptial contracts). Usually, these set-asides occurred for the benefit of children. With rare exceptions, wives could not make contracts, become autonomous parties to lawsuits, retain earnings (although husbands could return wages to their wives as gifts), create separate wills, travel without permission, refuse sexual relations, claim separate residences, or retain custody of children after divorce or separation. A husband could sell or mortgage his wife's personal property without consulting her, even if it had belonged to her before marriage, because it now belonged to him. Yet he could not *bequeath* her paraphernalia or sell property inherited by her—and, in some colonies, land owned by the two of them—without judicial approval. And when women sought to convert property to joint ownership or convey land to husbands or their creditors, judges often suspected coercion and examined wives privately, usually in a chamber away from husbands, about their "true feelings."

Premarital agreements did *not* secure a married woman's managerial rights—the ability to use and enjoy property, to contract, to sell, or to will. Instead, a court-appointed trustee (who could be her husband) conducted business for her, limited only by his duty to consult with her and conserve assets for heirs. A woman's separate property could be abused; it was common, for instance, for a husband to transfer assets to a wife's estate, thus keeping his wealth from creditors, since her estate could not be tapped for his debts. Obsessive detail in premarital settlements betrayed much anxiety: Women aimed to secure children's inheritances against half-known men heavily favored at law. In one 1653 pact between Ann Allen and Joseph Jewett of Massachusetts, Ann promised to give 100 pounds "during her life to her children; that the eldest son by the former marriage would be brought up as a scholar, kept in school, kept well fed and clothed, and sent to University, fully paid for; other children the same." Ann secured horses for a son, a daughter's legacy, and the right to give "any of her children" such goods as "a feather bed, bolster and pillow, with a bedstead, . . . curtains and wrought vallance," and a "livery cupboard."[19]

In English colonies, settlements fell within the purview of chancery courts or, when they were unavailable, the equity side of common-law courts. Thus, women's security depended on the continuance of equity jurisdiction, which Americans gradually abolished or curtailed, and on the cooperation of husbands and judges, who could circumvent compacts without great trouble. In colonies with separate equity courts—among them, South Carolina, New York, Maryland, Virginia, and New Jersey—as well as those, such as Pennsylvania, where law courts enforced equitable agreements and otherwise protected wives from profligate husbands, women exercised limited control over property brought into marriage. Elsewhere, judges could subject women to the self-eradicating letter of the law. Few colonial women, moreover, enjoyed equitable protection; over time, no more than 8 percent benefited from premarital compacts. Poor or non-European wives and wives without lawyers had no such luxury. And as Marylynn Salmon points out, cultural and legal restraints may well have seemed so weighty that women "did not consider the possibility of employing separate estates," even when they had misgivings about marital erasure; at least in South Carolina, the "fear and distrust women exhibited by creating settlements" antagonized men.[20]

For many of the same reasons, married women's control over their own bodies was sorely limited. No man could lawfully force a wife to act against nature or the will of God, nor were men free to kill or severely maim women. But English judges recognized the *baron's* right to administer moderate corporal punishment, particularly when a wife scolded or brawled (for which crimes, a New Englander could choose to turn his wife over to the magistracy), withdrew domestic labor, or abandoned the marital bed. If a man disputed his wife's desire to go for a walk or attend a meeting, he could lock her in the house; if he wished to keep an estranged wife away from their children, he could lock her *out* of the house. Even if she feared or wished to avoid pregnancy, she could not lawfully refuse his sexual advances—not even when the sex act might jeopardize her life or health.

Few principles were better established than the husband's right of correction. The medieval writer Bracton explained, after Roman Catholic practice, that a wife was "under the rod" of her husband,[21] and though progressive Britons downplayed the old idea that men could beat wives as long as they used a rod no thicker than a thumb, the right to discipline wives and children physically persisted well into the nineteenth century and even found its way into Anglo-American culture by way of the stage and printing press. In 1639, a wag named John Taylor wrote these lines:

> He that marries a scold,
> He hath most cause to be merry,
> For when she's in her fits,
> He may cherish his wits,
> With singing, *Hey downe dery*, with a cup of sherry.
> . . . Dub a club, kill her with a club,
> Be thy wife's master:
> Each one can tame a shrew.[22]

Husbands' power to affect wives' physical security was formidable. When a "shrew" ran away, her *baron* could claim that the loss of her labor reduced his estate. Men could disclaim responsibility for debts incurred by runaway or estranged wives, offer rewards for women's return, and dispatch the sheriff to reclaim children, in whose labor fathers also had a property right. And because of men's exclusive conjugal rights, spousal rape was literally inconceivable; the Bay Colony excluded wives (and prepubescent girls, whose violation fell within a different rubric) from a 1646 law punishing with death or other "grievous punishments" men who "RAVISH[ED] any maid or single woman" older than ten years.[23] In early Anglo-America, the rape of a married woman by a man other than her husband was a capital crime, and because they had a property right in their wives' chastity, husbands could seek monetary damages when other men had "criminal conversation" with their wives, with or without the women's permission.

When her husband died, a woman's prospects changed dramatically, in some ways for the better. In the absence of a special provision in his will, a woman could hope only for the widow's portion of his estate, or "dower." In Massachusetts, for example, the widow (or *relict*) received as dower a life estate in one-third of all "houses, lands, tenements, rents and hereditaments as her said Husband was seized of," as well as ownership of one-third of his "monie, goods and chattels, real and person[al]," provided that she did not "committ or suffer any strip or waste." She could manage her third of the land and use income generated by it during her lifetime, but, in other respects, the *relict* functioned as a trustee for her husband's heirs, admonished not to alter property destined for others. This aversion to "waste" (a legal term encompassing both constructive improvement and ruination) persisted well into the eighteenth century; as late as 1818, a New England judge held that a widow could not "waste" her dower by cutting down timber.[24] Theoretically, neither husbands nor their creditors could touch dower rights before or after widowhood, but the rule could be surmounted easily. Legislators contributed to the erosion of dower;

in Connecticut, for example, lawmakers in 1673 passed a law for intestate cases (later reversed) stripping widows of dower in personal property and reducing their already precarious access to land.

For widows, much depended on the value of their dower, the charity of neighbors, and prospects for remarriage. To be sure, *relicts* had greater freedom than they enjoyed when married: As long as they lived, they managed their own property; retained earnings; and sometimes received charitable help with food, harvesting, and other necessities. In Charles County, Maryland, multiple marriages could empower women; mid-seventeenth-century widows took new husbands three times more often than widowers took new wives, which left some women in command of considerable property in several families. Generous husbands in the South and elsewhere sometimes left women more than their third or made them joint or full executors of estates; among ninety-three wills made by men in mid-to-late-seventeenth-century New Hampshire, for example, 75 percent to 80 percent named widows as executors. In such cases, women functioned after their spouses' deaths as "deputy husbands"[25] or agents, much as they had done when their husbands had temporarily left town.

But when a widow lacked money, lost a husband late in life, had unhelpful (or no) children, or lived amid a surplus of women, misery was the rule—even in New England, where male and female populations were relatively well balanced. Partly because New Englanders lived to be grandparents, but also because of a slight surplus of women in many eighteenth-century northern towns, widowhood occurred well after middle age and could last for as long as a decade. Acute labor shortages on farmsteads, poor health, and poverty haunted widows. In the coastal village of Gloucester in 1665, a widow named Bridgett Window received through her husband's will "al her wearing cloathes," a bed, a rug, and bolster "which she brought with her," and "one Iorn pot," a "bras pot," and "al other things that are left . . . of her houssal Stuff "; in 1666, aging and ill, she protested the behavior of "overseers" who had paid her only 30 shillings for a year's maintenance and withheld "bread and beer." Judges ordered the delivery of a cow; when she died in 1673, she left an estate of only 26 pounds. In 1742, a Boston census reported 1,200 widows, "1000 of them poor," in a growing city of 16,382 souls. Widowhood also meant isolation and loss of status: "Goodwife Jones" became "Widow Jones," a term that recast a productive, sexual being as a sexless social burden. As Cotton Mather explained in 1728, "A State of Widowhood is a state of Affliction; and very singularly so, if the widow is bereaved of the Main Support that after the Death of her Husband was left unto her. . . . And how much are her Sorrows Embittered, by New Anxieties and Encumbrances . . . ; Debts to be paid, and Mouths to be fed."[26]

Both politicians and clergymen were keenly interested in regulating marital beginnings and endings; unmarried people largely escaped the discipline of law, and the well-being of political society seemed to depend on the ongoing stability of "little commonwealths." Nonconforming Protestant views of family government reflected a seventeenth-century movement, apparent throughout much of Europe, toward the further secularization of marriage—a condition rooted at least as firmly in custom as in church law. In early modern Christian societies in general, marriage happened when a man and woman willed themselves wed; in Roman Catholic countries, the church blessed, regulated, and publicized their union for the benefit of children and to ensure social peace. Alone among Protestant nations, England into the eighteenth century was what historian Roderick Phillips terms a "special case";[27] church courts retained considerable (although incomplete and ever-diminishing) control over the law of marriage. In Protestant Switzerland, Germany, Scotland, and Scandinavia, lawmakers viewed marriage as a worldly, non-sacramental agreement or contract, to be blessed if newlyweds wished at the church steps. Because Puritans embraced contractualism and abolished church courts, they departed from English practice, but these changes were Protestant, rather than merely Puritan. By insisting on sacramental marriage and administering canon law in civil courts, Anglicans rowed against the Protestant current. But even radical Puritans thought that marriage, unlike simple civil agreements, had social and cultural implications and so could be regulated by secular authorities.

Christians strongly disputed the merits of divorce. The legalization of the practice in Europe correlated with state sponsorship of Protestantism—although England retained the Catholic ban at home and in Anglican colonies like Virginia, Carolina, and New York (after the Duke of York's laws were implemented). Before the Marriage Act of 1753, Anglicans allowed only permanent separation if the partners agreed to celibacy; annulment for impotence, affinity, and consanguinity; and a few Parliamentary divorces—forty-four in all between 1670 and 1769. Indeed, legislative divorce allowed Anglicans to circumvent the ban until a divorce bill was adopted in 1857. Colonists often responded more positively to pleas for marital dissolution, although practices varied wildly, with access to divorce increasing as one moved north. Only Massachusetts offered absolute legislative divorce to any woman for cause. But Connecticut lawmakers also granted divorces, and as of 1711, Rhode Island wives could sue for absolute divorce after a seven-year desertion.[28] Anglican South Carolina and Virginia extended no relief beyond annulment or permanent separation. In Catholic Maryland, spouses could obtain a separation (not absolute divorce) in chancery if they could prove extreme abuse or abandonment.

Yet, for all their liberality, Massachusetts and Connecticut recorded few divorces—in the 1690s, four and seven, respectively, in colonies boasting 70,000 and 30,000 residents. Puritans both allowed and discouraged marital failure; given the instability of colonial society, it perhaps would have been foolhardy to do otherwise. Disparate rules in adjoining colonies and the impossibility of verifying marital status abroad sorely tempted philanderers and bigamists, but, as Hendrik Hartog demonstrates, modernizing people had a fluid conception of marriage, particularly in unsettled territories. It was possible for a person to be half-married, almost married, or married differently to more than one person.[29] Non-Anglican lawmakers tended to allow divorce to facilitate sound remarriage, simultaneously strengthening political control over marriage and discouraging physical flight. Fearful that men with wives in England (and runaway wives working as indentured servants) might seduce unsuspecting locals or take multiple spouses, Bay Colony magistrates went so far as to deport individuals with wives and husbands "in England, or elsewhere" who might succumb to temptation. Lawmakers singled out men who committed "lewdnes and filthines heer among us," "make love to woemen, and attempt Marriage," or "live under suspicion of uncleannes," ordering them to return to their spouses or pay a steep fine.[30] Men and women who were unable to obtain divorces could move to other colonies and establish households. The risk of bigamy charges was small, and the social and economic costs of bad marriages were steep. Alternatively, couples might undertake customary divorce (for instance, by returning rings in the presence of witnesses) and notify officials of the deed, but the practice weakened state control over families and so was discouraged.

Scholars know little of divorce beyond New England. In colonies that were influenced by the Duke of York's Laws (Pennsylvania, Delaware, New York, New Jersey, and Maryland), the Anglican ban supposedly prevailed. But as elsewhere, colonists probably winked at the letter of the law, and customary practices probably undermined legal norms. New York recorded eight divorce decrees (several of them Dutch) in the seventeenth century; Pennsylvanians allowed divorce for adultery after 1682. In southern Anglican colonies, county courts heard marital disputes—a departure from English practice. But because justices of the peace followed canon law, divorce was banned until well after the American Revolution.[31] In the six New England colonies between 1620 and 1699, men submitted 31 petitions for separation and divorce to legislators, 9 of them in the Bay Colony; women submitted 67, 30 of them in Massachusetts. Men and women, moreover, sought divorce on different grounds. Half the women listed desertion, 12 listed adultery and desertion together, and 8 listed adultery alone. Men cited adultery (with occasional, secondary mention of desertion) in 23 of the 31 cases. No woman listed "refusal of intercourse" or "refusal to accompany," as did two men; no man pointed to cruelty, absence, heretical opinions, threats to life, and "oppression of spirit," as did 6 women. Wives complained of poverty or physical and emotional abuse; men cited rebellion and inconstancy.[32]

At least in Connecticut, legislators apparently did not heed women's complaints about imminent or actual harm; instead, they allowed divorce mainly when poorly kept wives or children might become expensive wards of the state or particular households seemed to be undermining the political "family." The Connecticut law of 1667, under which judges granted hundreds of divorces in the next century, allowed dissolution for "adultery, fraudulent contract, or willfull desertion for three years, with total neglect of duty, or seven years' providentiall absence." Adultery loomed largest in male petitions. Middle- and lower-class women did not usually escape dangerous or philandering husbands, and the marital prospects of women could be affected by rape, suggestions of promiscuity, or a man's public accusation of unwanted sexual overtures. Men accused of sex crimes suffered shaming, but, to a great extent, the sin lay in damaging another man's property. Because men were expected to "sow wild oats," elders tended to blink at "natural" expressions of sexuality; only women spoiled their marital prospects by being kissed in public.[33]

In the main, judges aimed less to ensure individual happiness than to bolster the family's ability to maintain social order, educate dependents, and produce wealth. Toward that end, officials sometimes took steps to protect society from women's supposedly inevitable lapses into carnality, duplicity, and anarchism. In the Bay Colony, for example, the General Court outlawed married women's entertainment of men in the absence of husbands. No such rule prevented husbands' entertainment of female friends. Winthrop's denunciation of Hutchinson's "misgovernment" of his wife's tongue epitomized European (that is, not peculiarly Puritan) conceptions of households as the basic *political* units of society. Marriage, wrote Samuel Pufendorf in 1672, created a "nuptial society" that was the "fountain-head and seed-plot" of the state; Winthrop cast the family as a "little common wealth, and a common wealth . . . a greate family."[34]

Within lawful marriages, couples sometimes ignored legal rules: William Hibbens probably viewed Ann as a partner. Even Cotton thought that women were "creatures without which there is no comfortable Living for man: it is of them what is wont to be said of Governments, *That bad ones are better than none*"; while some men called women "a *necessary Evil*," he knew them to be "a *necessary Good*." Time and again, legal theory diverged from social reality. Sometimes, spouses failed to meet obligations or administer punishment. Poverty might trump law, or a man might decide that a woman fit to be a wife was "too good to be thy servant, and worthy to be thy fellow."[35] But because the law *could* be invoked to control women, it coexisted uneasily with many men's good estimation of their wives and with contrary elements of Protestant religious belief. It was these opposing strands, in fact, that led women again and again to defy tradition and demand recognition as spiritual equals—and, by extension, as cosovereigns in families.

SPIRITUAL EQUALITY VERSUS DEPENDENCE

Law and custom were powerful. In witchcraft and sedition trials, judges portrayed married women exactly as the common law prescribed: as submissive domestic laborers to be governed by a pantheon of sovereign male "heads"; as the author of a respected discussion of the "Lawes Provision for Women" put it in 1632, "All [women] are understood either married or to be married." Among even the most enlightened Englishmen, a wife's divinely ordained task was to give "helpe and assistance in governme[n]t to the Master of the familie" as a respected "associate," not quite a cohead and never a "Prince." Political and legal theorists excluded wives (and, to some extent, potential wives) from the compact struck between king and subjects and so prevented women—along with servants, copyholders, and children—from becoming what Carol Pateman calls "civil individuals." As dependents, women had neither law-giving authority nor access to historic constitutional rights.[36]

Yet "holy violence" against eccentric women often stemmed from tensions between the traditional distrust of Eve's daughters and the reality of post-Reformation *advancement*. The wonder is not that magistrates harshly punished women like Hibbens and Hutchinson but, rather, that these women progressed so far with their projects before they collided with authority. Their peers, after all, granted both of them the capacity to influence public life. In the case of Hutchinson, magistrates asserted in open court that she could destroy Puritanism; Hibbens assumed, without much spousal opposition, that she *could* undertake market research, dash from town to town, and charge workers with fraud. Other groups spawned by the Radical Reformation embraced women's spiritual equality more comfortably, establishing foundations for Christian women's self-emancipation in later centuries. For Quakers, Anabaptists, and other radicals, baptism was an "equalizing covenant" analogous to betrothal. Women were "peers and companions in the faith, and mates in missionary enterprise"; marriage was a conjugal relationship between equal souls. Both sexes communed directly with God and made independent religious choices. In one historian's judgment, this insistence on "freedom of conscience for all adult believers," combined with the acceptance of women's lay ministries and (sometimes) ordination, represented a "major breach in patriarchalism and a momentous step in the western emancipation of women."[37]

Even the Counter Reformation offered Catholic women fresh opportunities for a significant public presence. In New France and New Spain, women worked alongside men or struck out on their own in missions, convents, hospitals, and schools. To be sure, Catholic women subordinated themselves to God and to his clergy without benefit of the Protestants' belief in immediate, direct "conversation" with God and between Saints. But woman-centered sanctuaries in both the Old and New Worlds functioned as spaces for Catholic women's education and politicization. These cracks in the dike of tradition greatly facilitated religious women's movement *into* the world as fully constituted teachers and agents. In the 1650s, Marguerite Bourgeoys, founder of Canada's Notre Dame Congregation, explained that her sisters left the cloister to be "wanderers." Although the old way had been a "protection for persons of our sex," they preferred to move about freely as "women of the parish," carrying God's message to the unconverted or needy.[38]

Thus, when Puritans tightened traditional connections between families and political governments, they typically granted "male heads of household a broader religious and supervisory role" than men had enjoyed in England.[39] The Puritan idea of spiritual self-examination could be dangerous. Sooner or later, introspective Saints might decide to communicate directly with God or challenge the clerical monopoly on biblical interpretation. Moreover, women who had been led to believe that sex did not control salvation might question the naturalness of "right relations," as William Gouge described them, between "[m]agistrate and subject, minister and people, husband and wife, parent and childe, master and servant, neighbors and fellowes."[40] Pastoral insistence on a woman's "subjection in all lawful things to her husband"[41] could not alter the fact of a large female foot in the door. As Michael Walzer explains, "Puritan writers insisted upon the inferiority of the female, but nevertheless recognized in her the potential saint"; the marriage contract, conceptualized as a "spiritual union" analogous to the "near bond of marriage" that the Saints collectively contracted with God, cast further doubt on men's authority (as distinguished from raw power, which they did possess) to silence or confine women.[42]

Consider the shift of ground between Church of England sermons about matrimony in 1563 and the lectures composed some decades later by Samuel Willard, pastor of Boston's Old South Church for thirty years. Among sixteenth-century Anglicans, the husband was the "Leader and Author of Love" and the wife a "weak Creature," without "strength and constancy of Mind"; because wives were "more prone to all weak . . . dispositions of Mind more than Men Be" and "vain in their Fantasies and Opinions," they were enjoined to "obey husbands" and "cease from commanding."[43] Willard disagreed. While not denying male supremacy, he held that spouses had a "joint Interest in governing the . . . Family. If God . . . hath bestowed on them Children or Servants, they have each of them a share in the government of them." Despite "an inequality in the degree of this Authority, and the Husband is to be acknowledged to hold a *Superiority*, which the Wife is practically to allow," the wife still was "invested with an Authority over them by God; and her Husband is to allow it to her . . . for tho' the Husband be the Head of the Wife, yet she is an Head of the Family." Among "all the Orders which are unequals," spouses came "nearest to an Equality." They made "a Pair," which implied "a Parity"; in God's eyes, they were "Yoke-Fellows." Nor could husbands pummel their mates. "Though the husband be the wives head," wrote the reform-minded English minister William Perkins, "yet it seemeth he hath no power nor liberties granted him" to warrant physical abuse. Here, the "unity doctrine" helped women. A man could "reprove & admonish her in word only," but never "chastise her either with stripes, or stroke." Why not? Because "wives are their husbands mates; and they two be one flesh. And no man will hate, much less beat his owne flesh."[44]

Thus, although the common law of England theoretically debased married women, other factors could and did ameliorate black-letter law. Without them, marriage would have been intolerable for women of all classes; in 1740, the English novelist Samuel Richardson accurately noted that matrimony could be a "state of humiliation for a lady."[45] As Hutchinson and Hibbens learned the hard way, many colonists subscribed to the view that women harbored great evil and promoted social mischief, and the law of marriage mirrored those beliefs. William Perkins purveyed common knowledge when he listed the "sins of wives"—a tendency to "be proud, to be unwilling to beare the authority of their husbands; to chide and braule with bitterness; to forsake their houses."[46] Only a few Protestants (among them, Quakers; the Dunkers, who renounced human sexuality; and

Moravians, organized in sex-segregated "choirs") managed to divide the sovereign authority of the family's petit king. Others decided that women approached the male standard and so merited elements of citizenship. Of "all inferiours," said William Gouge, wives were "farre the most excellent and therefore to be placed in the first ranke." Protestant reformer John Wesley granted spiritual independence and lay ministries to women but excluded them from governance.[47]

Having so decided, the colonists transplanted the monarchical household ruler onto New World soil, albeit with certain modifications. Mary Beth Norton thinks that monarchical (in her word, "Filmerian") family government survived the trans-Atlantic voyage *especially* among the Puritans.[48] Much as monarchical sovereignty could not be divided between a king and subject without destroying kingship and the English constitution, so British Americans painstakingly preserved an undivided baronial sovereignty within families. In the eyes of the law, women could hope at best to function not as coheads, possessed of their own sovereignty and lawmaking authority, but as junior partners to whom men might grant limited rights and privileges. Married women's primary obligations in the polity lay not with political governors, but with domestic governors, who made law for households. Only a few critics of monarchical constitutionalism assailed these feudal practices. As Montesquieu said in his 1748 discussion of women in Russia, "Everything is closely related: the despotism of the prince is naturally conjoined with the servitude of women, and the liberty of women with the spirit of the monarchy."[49]

FREEDOM, UNFREEDOM, AND THE POWER OF WORDS

Seventeenth-century Englishmen usually conceived of rights as grants of privilege by the Crown to subjects, to be used and enjoyed like property. The natural law-inspired notion that individuals carried innate, sacrosanct rights *into* the polity did not yet animate legislation or adjudication. But fully constituted subjects of kings and petty kings did claim certain ancient rights that the monarchs swore to uphold, among them the "right to law," or the right not to be governed arbitrarily. To be without law's guarantees of procedural regularity was to be profoundly unfree. The idea that the rule of law embodied liberty thus was English, not Puritan. When Winthrop explained in 1645 that Saints experienced liberty through "subjection to authority," he spoke first as an English constitutionalist; as a *Puritan*, Winthrop affirmed the primacy of God's law, in effect Christianizing legal discourse. In Winthrop's words, subjection to the king's law resembled Christian subjection; it produced the "same kind of liberty wherewith Christ hath made us free."[50]

For Puritan legalists, woman's subjectship within marriage provided *the* microcosmic example of how self-erasure expanded freedom. "The woman's own choice," said Winthrop, "makes . . . a man her husband; yet being so chosen, he is her lord, and she is to be subject to him, yet in a way of liberty, not of bondage." A wife thought of marriage as "her honor and freedom, and would not think her condition safe and free, but in her subjection to her king and husband; his yoke is so easy and sweet to her as a bride's ornaments; and if through forwardness or wantonness . . . she shake it off . . . she is at no rest . . . until she take it up again; and whether her lord smiles upon her . . . [or] frowns, or rebukes, or smites her, she apprehends the sweetness of his love . . . and is refreshed, supported, and instructed by every such dispensation of his authority over her."[51] Puritans thus created a well-governed female Saint—one whose "special proclivity for evil"[52] might *not* jeopardize society—by enjoining her to embrace "voluntary subjection" within a tight web of government.

Among religious dissenters especially, few attributes of a public personality mattered more than the related liberties of speech, conscience, and what modernists might call liberty of association. The English, with other Europeans, recognized that governmental control of printing, the spoken word, and message-bearing deportment prevented public violence. British intolerance for unsettling political speech was marked; neither men nor women could criticize the government or one another with abandon. But by circumscribing women's ability to learn and express opinions in public, officials nipped a supposedly malignant source of social derangement in the bud. Women who sought an active religious or scholarly vocation risked public humiliation. On one occasion, Puritan historian Edward Johnson castigated women who were interested in reading and writing about theology as "silly women laden with diverse lusts and phantastical madness." Winthrop opined that scholarship and the desire to teach would "drive a woman mad" and attributed the breakdown suffered by Connecticut Governor Edward Hopkins's wife to "excessive reading"—a condition later called "brain fever." If she had "attended her household affairs" and "such things as belong to women, and not gone out of her way and calling to meddle in such things as are proper for men, whose minds are stronger," said Winthrop, she might have "kept her wits."[53]

Because Puritans exalted and feared "the Word," they diligently ferreted out what Winthrop termed "unsafe speech" as well as unsafe conduct. Congregations came to know their spiritual condition through conversations undertaken within fixed boundaries of logic, legality, and propriety; "unsafe" speech, or speech "without faith," was both sinful and seditious. On the question of women's nonsubmissive speech or carriage, Puritan ministers enjoyed unanimity, particularly after 1640. The influential English scholar, Thomas Hooker, permitted female utterances in public only when oratory supported "*subjection, and so suit with their sexes.*" After the Antinomian Controversy, Cotton similarly relied on St. Paul and others to reassert the necessity of women's silence in public spaces, except to praise God or confess crimes. Because the singing of psalms was viewed as a variety of "prophesying," it could be forbidden alongside speech "by way of teaching" or "by way of propounding questions" with the goal of learning. A woman was supposed to direct such queries to "her husband at home." In Cotton's view, God forbade "all place of speech and power in the church" for women "unless it be to join with the rest of the church" in praising God; women lacked "some power, which Christ has given to the brotherhood. . . . I suffer not a woman to teach, nor to usurp authority over the man, but to be in silence."[54]

Women sometimes chafed under customary and formal proscriptions. Literary critics regularly tarred successful writers like London's Eliza Fowler—a widely read novelist and playwright who had abandoned her minister husband in 1721 to write fiction—for "shameless scribbling." Women, Fowler wrote, sensed the "injustice which has long been done them, and find a vacuum in their minds"; men saw that education put "the sexes too much on an equality" and would "destroy" women's "implicit obedience . . . to our commands: if once they have the capacity of arguing with us, where would be our authority!"[55] Massachusetts legislators reinforced the customary silencing of women with black-letter law, put scolds in the stocks or ducked them in ponds, and clamped down on ungodly symbolic speech. A judge offered Goody Hunter a choice between a soaking and a gagging for "speaking out of turn." Men were neither charged with scolding nor hauled before judges for interjecting thoughts at odd moments. Symbolic speech—often punished as general misconduct—also ran afoul of the constabulary. In 1662, Salemites carted Goody Wilson, as well as her mother and sister, through the town for the "barbarous and inhuman" offense of staging a protest by walking naked in public. When jurors convicted

Dorothy Hoyt of general misconduct for wearing men's clothing, she was given a choice between "whips and fines."[56]

The furor with which Bostonians greeted Hutchinson's influential ministry highlights the importance of what Amy Schrager Lang calls "female authorship" in women's struggle for public responsibility and self-definition."[57] Any acknowledgment of women's right to speak commandingly shook patriarchal government to its foundations; thus, officials zealously defended their monopoly of public power, which perpetuated unequal experiences of the rule of law. For example, attempts to control or discount women's speech during trials (as with the silencing of Hutchinson)—or judicial attempts to force women to speak against their will or conscience (as in Hibbens's trial)—resulted in procedural differences based on sex. When magistrates refused to "discourse" with women on their own terms or as equals, they effectively disallowed self-defense through speech; Bay Colony magistrates engaged publicly with the heretical Roger Williams in a pamphlet war, but invited no such exchange with Hutchinson or her followers. Nor did Puritan judges' deep-seated respect for the privilege against self-incrimination prevent incursions on a woman's conscience. To be sure, presiding officers often encouraged confession so that sinners might be readmitted into the community. But as Hutchinson's case and Wheelwright's countercase suggest, women's testimony was taken to be relatively "soft"; judges tended to think that women who were accused of wrongdoing did not know "truth." When judges tried to wrest incriminating evidence from Wheelwright, bystanders successfully intervened; Hutchinson's recantations were coerced, used against her, and discredited at the pleasure of the court.[58]

Perhaps more than any other group, the Quakers celebrated the free exchange of words without regard to sex. They aimed, says historian Barry Levy, to create an "ideal speech community" in which Friends would share "holy conversation"—a mixture of speech acts and deportment that organized holy lives, purified society, and carried the community toward spiritual perfection. Puritans also believed that law constructed and perfected reality; one believer said that a Saint was "taught by the law to know himself, so that he may learn to sing."[59] Quakers and, in a different way, Puritans carried this understanding of law's social operation into social practice. Margaret Fell, the English Quaker mistress of a sanctuary at Swarthmore Hall, insisted that all Saints were "children of God by faith . . . neither male nor female," but "all one" in Jesus. In *Womens Speaking Justified* (1666), written during her imprisonment under the English Quaker Act, Fell made women's speech a theological centerpiece: Was not the "church of Christ" the "spiritual Mother" of all Christians? Surely those who spoke "against the Womans speaking, speak against the Church of Christ, and the Seed of the Woman, which Seed is Christ." Although they were sex segregated, Quaker meetings granted credence to male *and* female testimony; women directly shaped public life when they scrutinized betrothed couples for "clearness" and "holy conversation."[60]

POLITICAL AND ECONOMIC DISABILITIES

Access to the lectern, witness table, and printing press did not exhaust the list of civic privileges from which women were excluded. Typically, only freeholders cast ballots and held office. In Pennsylvania, Delaware, and South Carolina, statutes barred women from voting. Elsewhere, mixtures of custom and formal property or freehold requirements disallowed female suffrage, although a few women (perhaps Quaker and Dutch) did vote in

Massachusetts, New Hampshire, Rhode Island, New York, Maryland, New Jersey, and Pennsylvania. In New England, Puritan women could not confer church membership, although they could *be* members and offered advice during screenings of new members; the right to confer membership implied sovereignty. Female candidates for membership confessed faith in private, rather than in the usual public way, after Cotton complained that his wife Sarah's open confession would violate "the apostle's rule" and "woman's modesty." Given woman's "feebleness" and "melanchollick fearfulness," Puritans decided to transcribe and read women's private confessions *for* them in public.[61]

Although the colonists reserved grand and petit jury service for enfranchised men, judges entrusted a slice of the public to women when trials involved women's bodies or the mysteries of reproduction. Responsibilities on matrons' juries, which were empaneled to gather sex-specific information from women's bodies in cases of infanticide, bastardy, or abortion-related homicide, as well as women's service as expert witnesses about domestic lore and childbirth, permitted midwives and other women to play what Mary Beth Norton calls a limited but "powerful role in . . . public life." Marylanders summoned matrons' juries only four times between 1656 and 1668. But lives hung in the balance: Women's testimony about the fact of recent childbirth or the identity of a bastard's father was often taken to be unimpeachable.[62]

Matrons' participation in criminal proceedings seemed overall to help women who were accused of crimes. But it could be a double-edged sword, both assisting women (as when midwives and other birth attendants identified men responsible for rape or bastardy) and condemning them (as when the charge was infanticide, and the accused denied having given birth). Ann Johnson, a Maryland midwife, forced a married woman to confess adultery so that the court might "lay the saddle upon the right horse" and relieve her husband of financial responsibility. Another Marylander cleared a woman of charges of infanticide by confirming that the child had been stillborn; yet another determined that, contrary to testimony, a woman recently had given birth, which was effectively a death sentence, even though the body had not been found. After 1624, English law required a woman to prove that her child had been born dead or to produce witnesses of natural death; otherwise, the courts presumed infanticide, particularly when the corpse had been concealed or lost. Colonists did not adopt the rule immediately; Mary Dyer's concealment of a "monstrous" child during the antinomian crisis was presumptive evidence perhaps of Satanism, but not of infanticide. Only in the 1690s did New Englanders make concealment of a corpse presumptive evidence of guilt.[63] Attempts to evade the gallows could be pathetic: Jane Crisp of Talbot County, Maryland, confessed that she had been "delivered of a Child" out of doors and "the Hoggs had Eaten it." Marylanders hanged Elizabeth Greene in 1664 for tossing a newborn boy "into the fire"; a midwife's testimony as to the presence of milk convicted her. Matrons also examined the bodies of accused female witches for "witch's teats"; men accused of witchcraft were not so examined.[64]

Other opportunities for community service existed, but are poorly understood. If women in ever-more-crowded colonial cities followed English patterns, for instance, they probably undertook social welfare projects, voluntary and otherwise. One scholar finds that among the working poor in seventeenth-century English cities, civic authorities asked homemakers—many of whom also produced goods for the market—to provide surrogate families for the poor, teach children to knit and weave, or nurse strangers to health in their homes. Although women were formally excluded from the polity in a modern sense, in early societies such work linked them to public life in ways that contemporaries took to be important and even indispensable.[65]

Indeed, the prospect of paid work and a good marriage market inspired thousands of women to board ships bound for North America, where settlements came to require women with domestic and artisanal skills and wages or marriage promised security and social advancement. As populations became more sex balanced and native born, home industry proliferated, mostly as a result of female labor. In New England, women pursued a boggling array of industries; by 1650, the demand for female servants temporarily increased in the heavily male Chesapeake, to supplement male labor and facilitate household production. Once possessed of the necessary equipment, Chesapeake wives, female servants, and children knitted for the market, brewed cider and beer, made cheese, salted meat, and wove textiles.[66] Men's and women's work were never entirely interchangeable, but, especially in the labor- and capital-scarce South, women undertook whatever job came to hand, including fieldwork. At the turn of the eighteenth century, a traveler named John Lawson called Carolina's sparse female population "the most industrious Sex." By their "good Housewifery," women and girls made a "great deal of Cloath of their own Cotton, Wool and Flax." Girls married "very young," he judged, "some at Thirteen or Fourteen; and She that stays till Twenty is reckoned a stale maid. . . . Many of the women are very handy. . . . They are ready to help their Husbands in any servile Work, as Planting." In the upcountry, girls were "not bred up to the Wheel and Sewing only, but [to] the Dairy, and affairs of the House . . . ; so that you shall see them, whilst very young, manage their Business with . . . Alacrity."[67]

Only with the arrival of African laborers did planters systematically keep white women out of the fields, in effect dividing the category of woman into black agricultural workers and white domestic or industrial workers. Put differently, the transition from indentured servitude to slavery, completed in the Chesapeake between 1680 and 1720, added race to an already complex social stew of gender and class difference. Whites assigned "sexually threatening, venal qualities" to a separate class of black laboring women and both piety and chastity to white women.[68] In 1705, the Virginian Robert Beverley noted a fresh distinction between "the Female-Servants, and Slaves: for a White Woman is rarely or never put to work in the Ground, if she be good for any thing else." Virginians hoped with new laws to "Discourage all Planters from using any Women so," imposed "the heaviest Taxes upon Female-Servants working in the Ground," and exempted "all other white Women" and black women employed "out of Doors." By 1750, with the introduction of crop diversification and plows, racialized gender distinctions proliferated. According to one historian, enslaved men "operated the plows" and became blacksmiths, coopers, and slave drivers; black women performed "the most basic and monotonous" field and domestic chores."[69]

Wives in South Carolina and Maryland enjoyed relatively extensive economic freedom. Fathers often willed land to sons and slaves to daughters; the resulting control over the workforce vastly strengthened female authority in households and enhanced marriage prospects. In three out of five wills granting slaves to daughters, Maryland fathers also *entailed* the slaves (that is, gave them "solely and only" to daughters and their progeny), which protected that portion of the estate from spousal interference. On other occasions, fathers gave daughters money or property, including slaves, for use during their lifetime. Historian Jean Lee concludes that these practices helped women, since husbands could not meddle with "lesser estates" during women's lives, but could easily make off with land, slaves, or other property received outright by will or inheritance.[70] Many daughters also ended up in charge of the labor force, which increased their power. Chesapeake planters rewarded wives handsomely for affection and labor; as noted earlier, widows frequently received more than their customary third. And though fewer daughters than sons got land, *some* daughters did. Among the landed testators with daughters in mid-eighteenth-century Maryland, one-third of the fathers and one-half the mothers left land to their daughters. Only 6.5 percent of those testators from 1740 to 1784 were women, yet one-fifth of all daughters received the use or ownership of land, sometimes to the exclusion of sons. Thus, while inheritances at midcentury did not ensure female autonomy, they did protect some white women from powerlessness and abject misery.[71]

When a husband absconded, went to sea, required extensive help from his wife in business, or was jailed, Parliament or a colonial assembly might license a wife as a female trader, to conduct business on her own and, if abandoned, to secure food and other necessities. The wife then became a *feme sole* (unmarried woman) in certain respects. Assemblymen in Pennsylvania (1718), South Carolina (1712 and 1744), and elsewhere formalized female traders' rights by statute, making women responsible for business debts; extending trader status to women whose husbands failed to support them; and, in the 1744 law, empowering women to sue in their own names, provided they also "nam[e] the husband for conformity." Assemblymen probably intended to avert fraud, not to expand women's rights. Both the 1712 and 1744 Carolina laws narrowly aimed to prevent the evasion of debt by "several" female traders; the 1712 measure pointed to women with a "design to defraud the persons to whom they are indebted by sheltering and defending themselves from any suit brought against them by reason of their coverture." In every instance, license was temporary, limited to specific activities, and at the pleasure of lawmakers. In Rhode Island, a 1711 statute allowed a wife without a husband for three years to "demand, sue for, recover, possess, and improve all lands and houses or other real estate and personal property" as if the husband had made her his attorney. But she could not sell property and was made to report periodically to "two freeholders" who served as trustees. For the initial three years, moreover, she and her family could not easily engage in economic self-defense.[72]

Then, as now, women's wages fell short of men's, although New England employers may have paid women proportionately more in the colonial years and in postwar periods than they did by 1815. Generally, the gap between men and women diminished where the division of labor was least well defined or tasks had not been subdivided into specialties. In New England, farm productivity rose by almost two-thirds between 1666 and 1777; as in England, a significant number of women labored for wages, yet they received less than male farmers for the same work. Among Massachusetts weavers, men and women earned similar pay for producing similar cloth, but few women undertook to produce the most complex weaves. In the 1750s, the number of women workers recorded in account books jumped sharply, from 3.8 percent of all workers to about 15 percent; within this group, boys earned about two-thirds of men's wages and women about one-half. In midcentury Chester County, women earned about 24 percent of men's farm-labor pay for domestic work and 33 percent of men's wages for spinning.

The law of inheritance, a sensitive barometer of attitudes toward women, reflected extraordinary English as well as colonial efforts to preserve male control over wealth. Eileen Spring shows that between the thirteenth and eighteenth centuries, the British manipulated the letter of statutes, dower rights, and strict settlements to eliminate the threat that the heiress-at-law had posed in the Middle Ages to family estates. When an Englishman accumulated property sufficient to yield a dower significantly more than subsistence level for his wife, he sometimes found ways to evade dower requirements. The idea was less to cheat wives than to ensure the transmission of property from fathers to sons;

women were said to require only enough to subsist and care for children. Much as the dower had become "conditional upon the husband's allowing it," so first-born English heiresses increasingly were at the mercy of fathers, brothers, and judges.[73]

Periodic displays of generosity did not disturb a pattern of loss and disinheritance. Seventeenth-century Pennsylvanians tended to allocate equal shares to all sons, disfavoring daughters. In the Chesapeake, male testators treated sons equally and, in terms of monetary value, left nearly equal portions to daughters, at the same time tying them up in life estates or irrevocable trusts so that daughters and sons-in-law might not dissipate the families' wealth. Sons often were instructed not to allow sisters to fall into poverty. But in a society that viewed a person's historic relationship to land as the fount of rights, largesse was a poor substitute for an estate. In Peter Hoffer's words, fathers protected women's property not to "inaugurate an era of feminism," but to keep property in their families.[74]

When women demanded formal rewards in exchange for economic contributions as taxpayers and entrepreneurs, the plea typically fell on deaf ears. In 1647–48, for example, the aristocratic Margarett Brent of Maryland, who served as the governor's executor in 1647 and managed a vast estate with her sister, requested an assembly vote for herself. She had been "received as his Lordship's Attorney," she said, yet had no voice; lawmakers denied that Brent "should have any vote in the house."[75] Decades later, a group of widows demanded public recognition of the wealth they contributed to the community, probably to no avail. "We the widdows of this city," they declared in a 1733 letter to the New York *Journal*, "have had a Meeting, and as our case is something Deplorable, we beg . . . that we may be Relieved. . . . We are House keepers, Pay our Taxes, carry on Trade, and most of us are she Merchants, and as we in some measure contribute to the Support of Government, we ought to be Intituled to some of the Sweets of it; but we find ourselves entirely neglected, while the Husbands that live in our Neighborhood are daily invited to Dine at Court; we have the Vanity to think we can be full as Entertaining."[76]

POLICING WOMEN'S BODIES

Husbands and magistrates also limited women's ability to control pregnancy and sexual activity. Bondswomen experienced the virtual eradication of personal liberty; indeed, the endemic rape of African "property" by whites vividly illustrated and caricatured the familial head's control over women's bodies. Because masters *owned* both the bodies and the labor of enslaved women, rape or assault victims lacked standing as persons in courts of law. They also risked life and limb when they resisted mastership. In 1743, North Carolinian Matthew Hardy beat his slave Lucy, tied her to a ladder, and burned her to death; because the assembly had declared it inconceivable that a master might destroy his own estate without cause, he was discharged.

In the Chesapeake and elsewhere, strict policing of interracial sexual liaisons impinged with particular cruelty on women and children. In 1662, for example, Virginia burgesses declared that the mulatto children of African bondswomen would be enslaved, following the status of their mother, and their children after them, as had been the case in ancient Rome. Two years later, Marylanders began deeding the children of English women and enslaved African men to the men's masters for thirty years, indenturing the white women to the same masters. Maryland thus departed from the old Roman rule by which the status of mixed-blood children followed the maternal line. By pronouncing white women's mixed-race progeny to be slaves "as their fathers were," the colony punished white women for carrying "black men's seed."[77]

Personal security increased dramatically in the leap from slavery to freedom. But even within the free classes, the boundaries around women's bodies were taken to be permeable, and most women experienced considerable insecurity. White women at least could prosecute men for assault or rape, if only through their husbands or fathers. And within limits, New England women who were violated by men may have been helped by the fact that Puritan judges expected everyone to sin, did not pathologize sex more than the English did generally, and could believe tales of male lust run amok. But the expectation of male misbehavior also subjected women to ongoing, low-level sexual "play," and judges, rather than women, drew the line between revelry and crime. Puritans encouraged moderate enjoyment of "the flesh," insisting that use of the marriage bed was "founded in man's Nature." Although they discouraged sexual relations outside betrothal and marriage, they forgave fleshly appetites and sometimes associated the veneration of "pure" women with the "Popish conceit of the Excellency of Virginity." Examples abound of assault that failed to impress judges because the behavior was so common. It was necessary only to avoid extremes (impotence and frigidity, on the one hand, and rape and enticement, on the other) and to ensure that sex not divert attention from God.[78]

At least in the early decades, women were not punished unremittingly for the loss of virginity or for fornication. In female-scarce Somerset County, Maryland, about one-third of all women in the seventeenth century were pregnant when they married—twice the English rate. Nor did communities seem to object, as long as marriage (and the regularization of inheritance) occurred; Maryland grand jurors presented no women for bridal pregnancy. To the north, Puritans apparently treated sexual transgressors with relative patience, emphasizing spiritual rehabilitation, rather than stern punishment or ostracization.[79] In Connecticut, where premarital pregnancy was commonplace, ministers and judges simply enjoined couples to marry; in Hingham, Massachusetts, between 1721 and 1800, 41 out of 100 women aged 15–19, and 23.8 out of 100 aged 20–24 were pregnant at first marriage. The shaming of women for sexual indiscretion was temporary; in mid-seventeenth-century Middlesex, Massachusetts, only 1 woman in 10 who was convicted of sexual misconduct failed to marry and obtain church membership. Six women convicted of fornication in the 1660s and 1670s married men other than their partners in crime, in the same parish that had convicted them.[80]

Still, physical danger stalked Anglo-American women. Sir Matthew Hale, author of the renowned *Pleas of the Crown* (c. 1680), defined rape simply but carefully as "the carnal knowledge of any woman above the age of ten years against her will, and of a woman-child under the age of ten years with or against her will."[81] Only a few publicists—like Gerrard Winstanley, spiritual leader of the Digger sect in England, who said in 1652 that such carnal knowledge amounted to "robbery of a woman['s] bodily freedom"[82]—strenuously objected to violence against women in streets, shops, and bedrooms. Most of the time, physical insecurity went unremarked. Alison Duncan Hirsch notes the "precarious situation of unmarried women" in white communities, even while living with parents, in an age of "unlocked doors" and rootless young men. Although the point is controversial, she also argues that an eighteenth-century rise in premarital sex resulted more from the "lifting of restraints" on boys than from the "rebellion of young women" against tradition.[83] Long stories of uninvited night visits to women's quarters, or of maids resisting advances and succumbing to force, fill court records. Men sometimes complained about the need to use force. One Marylander admitted in 1651 that if he had not "taken that Course of bearing with her" [force], the rape would have failed; another revealed that when a maid "woold not yeald quiatly," he had "plucked his handkerchif out of his pocket and stop[d] her mouth and forch her whether shee will or noe."[84]

In such cases, judges often believed women's accounts or at least weighed the reputations of parties and closely scrutinized moral character. Sarah Lepingwell, a Bay Colony servant, failed to cry for help when assaulted in her bed by her master's brother; she later said that she feared causing "scandal" in her master's house. The court believed her, even though another man occupying the same bedroom testified to the contrary. Nonetheless, women were at a distinct disadvantage in contests with powerful masters or, as in modern times, when defendants pointed to the possibility of their consent. In Massachusetts, jurors acquitted a good many men on the ground that women might have "invited the rape" by flirting or "requesting to smoke" with the men or failing to resist vigorously.[85] It may be, too, that judges decided not to convict men charged with raping artisanal, unattached, or black women on the ground that only "bad" women lived in rented rooms, earned wages for themselves, or walked alone on city streets.

Punishments for rape varied by colony. In Plymouth, lawmakers in 1636 put rape on the capital crime list but left the death penalty to judges' discretion. Connecticut Puritans initially urged men to square things, after the biblical rule, by marrying the victims; New Haven punished the rape of single women but not of wives. Only Rhode Islanders made rape and the molestation of young girls capital offenses from the outset. At least in New England, sexual violations of girls presented special problems. Perhaps because Mosaic law made marriage the penalty for violating an unbetrothed virgin, Puritans resisted the English practice of defining child molestation as rape. Beginning in 1641, however, when Daniel Fairfield and his cronies repeatedly ravished three girls, the Bay Colony began to punish such violations as sodomy ("unnatural" sex)—in Fairfield's case, with nostril slitting, whipping, and public shaming. In 1669, in response to a public outcry, jurors hanged the confessed rapist of an 8-year-old girl, although the precedent was later overturned.[86]

The modern concept of a right to privacy (in the sense of being free from the state's prying eyes and ears) was part of the early American sensibility only in limited ways and to different degrees in particular communities. Certainly, such a right was not called a "privacy right." Puritans seem to have walled off the mind and home from unwarranted snooping. Even outside patriarchal families, crimes that involved consenting adults behind closed doors may well have been underreported: New Englanders arrested only one woman, Mary Hammon, for lesbianism in the seventeenth century, and then because she had been indiscreet. But as Hutchinson's case shows, governors could and did intervene when activities threatened the commonweal. And even where "privace" was valued in a social sense, women usually could not insist on solitude; husbands and fathers, after all, had exclusive rights to women's company and labor.

Close proximity, of course, led to unwanted pregnancies. Women had access, often through midwives and other birth specialists, to contraceptive or abortifacient herbs, but these could be ineffective or toxic. Life-threatening abortions could be obtained only under the cloak of secrecy. Women bore the lion's share of risk, in no small part because physicians and quacks practiced dangerous procedures on their bodies. English and colonial law designated abortion a misdemeanor and punished abortionists alongside or instead of the patients. Yet men usually escaped permanent detriment. In early eighteenth-century Connecticut, a liaison between Sarah Grosvenor and Amasa Sessions led to pregnancy and death at the hand of a huckster. Jurors convicted the so-called doctor of endangering Sarah's life and ordered public shaming "with a rope visibly hanging about his neck." But no lasting shame attached to Sessions; only Sarah's family bore scars—from her death, the memory of her "shame," and the ruination of the life of her sister, who had participated in the abortion and whose conscience brought events to the magistracy's attention.[87]

Seventeenth-century farm women may well have been the most circumscribed of all. In the Chesapeake, women rarely got away from the farmstead; responsibility for domestic affairs kept them at home or within a few miles of it. Planters' wives depended on their husbands' contacts and links forged with other women for news; soon burdened with nursing and domestic duties, they rarely traveled, and in any case required spousal permission to do so.[88] This relatively closed world sometimes shielded drunken or abusive men from the magistracy; as slavery and patriarchal plantation governance crystallized in the early eighteenth century, the isolation of women and children, black and white, may well have worsened, particularly in the back country.

Thus, "privace" was a limited concept at best. And as Hutchinson's case makes clear, all bets were off when women's activities threatened domestic or political governments. Because theorists viewed the "husband's power over the wife" as the "source and origin of every human society,"[89] what happened at home *did* affect the public. Even after the clergy's affirmation in the 1648 Cambridge Platform of the old idea that courts punished only the "outward man" for unsafe speech, leaving the "inward" man in peace, Puritans reserved the right to reach into homes for evidence of treachery or to circumscribe women's speech harshly—particularly when renegades threatened the community's Errand in the Wilderness. In 1660, one of New England's best-known poets, Anne Bradstreet, registered both anger and despair at her sex's plight:

> I am obnoxious to each carping tongue,
> Who says my hand a needle better fits,
> A Poet's pen all scorn I should thus wrong,
> For such despite they cast on Female wits. . . .
> Let Greeks be Greeks, and women what they are
> Men have precedency and still excell,
> It is but vain unjustly to wage warre;
> Men can do best, and women know it well
> Preheminence in all and each is yours;
> Yet grant some small acknowledgement of ours.[90]

WOMEN IN COURTROOMS

Although colonists might not have recognized the term *due process of law,* they did insist on the evenhanded application of law when the Crown laid hands on subjects or their property. Legal rules, in turn, expressed the values and ongoing arguments of a rank-order, patriarchal, increasingly capitalist society. Britons did not view gender-specific rules and practices as a breach of what we now call *equal protection of the law.* Instead, the rules and procedures prevailing in courtrooms powerfully supported inequality, which the colonists usually took to be God given and inevitable, rather than unjust.

It is less than clear when and why gender-specific crimes entered Anglo-American law. Carol Smart suggests that the English constructed the idea of the "bad mother" between the 1630s and early nineteenth century, when parliamentarians criminalized evasions of motherhood (for instance, attempts to hide or abort pregnancies, refusals of marriage by pregnant women, or female abandonment of children).[91] Certainly in New England, criminal law and procedure expressed prevailing conceptions of men's and women's nature. There, only men could be convicted of perjury, sodomy, buggery, and idolatry (all capital offenses); in Massachusetts, although not in Connecticut, the tendency to color these crimes "masculine" persisted through several code revisions. In the case of perjury and idolatry, these practices departed from English tradition; Puritans may well have expected female carnality as well as duplicity and so could overlook them—or, in the case of buggery, assumed that female delicacy removed the possibility. At an early moment, moreover, Bay Colony legislators seem to have created woman-specific rules in relation to rebellious *speech* and women's marital inconstancy, thereby ensuring "safe" speech communities and sturdy families; laws punishing infanticide and witchcraft remained sex neutral into the Victorian age. In America, the systematic policing of maternity probably awaited the relative abundance of labor and body-centered medical discourses of the nineteenth century.

Everywhere, the criminal law affirmed married women's indentured status and supposed passivity. As a rule, English law courts held wives accountable for crimes undertaken alone, entirely beyond the husbands' ken. But when the *baron* was present or aware of a woman's actions, criminal courts usually punished him rather than her. In the eyes of the law, men supplied *mens rea* (or a culpable state of mind) and the will to act; the male will, embodied in the sovereign "head" during coverture, presumably swept women along in its wake. In 1765, the treatise-writer William Blackstone set out principles "at least a thousand years old" by which the criminal law relieved a wife of responsibility for "theft, burglary, or other civil offences" undertaken "by the coercion of her husband," by "his command, which the law construes a coercion," or simply "in his company, his example being equivalent to a command"; judges presumed her to be acting "by compulsion and not of her own will." Only when behavior constituted treason or a great evil in itself (*malum in se*), like murder, was the wife responsible as an individual. Because murder supposedly violated natural, rather than man-made, law, it was said to occur in the state of nature, where "no one is in subjection to another." In cases of treason, where the laws of mankind did apply, "no plea of coverture" could "excuse" the wife," and "no presumption of the husband's "coercion" would "extenuate her guilt." No wife could be expected to obey a husband in such cases. When a wife kept a brothel, moreover, she could be "set in the pillory with her husband." Such "intrigues of the female sex," said Blackstone, originated not within masculine society, but within the distinctly feminine domain, and spoke to slipshod "government of the house."[92]

Throughout British America, women were accused of crimes less often than were men. In the century before the French and Indian War, only 17.9 percent of 1,049 New Englanders who were charged with crimes were female. Of these women, two-thirds stood accused of crimes against persons; in contrast, 58.5 percent of the charges leveled at men involved property crimes. If court records can be trusted, seventeenth-century men committed burglary and theft twice as often as did women; they also counterfeited and forged about four times as often as women.

To some extent, these are empty statistics: Family, plantation, and parish governments often punished dependents of all kinds for misbehavior without resorting to formal legal processes. Crime statistics therefore understate female criminality and no doubt misrepresent female propensities for violence or resistance. We may never know the extent to which such crimes as absconding, damaging the master's property, refusing to work, bastardy, intemperance, fornication, or sedition—particularly when undertaken by wives or girlfriends without threatening the broader community—fell through the cracks. Infanticide flourished in secret, with women assuming responsibility for keeping it that way; Elizabeth Wells, for example, gave birth in Middlesex County, Massachusetts, and assured the child's father that she would "kil it or lay it to an other and you shal hae no blame at al for I haue had many children and none have none of them."[93]

Still, when read cautiously, criminal records shed light on early constructions of the "bad man" and "bad woman." When it occurred, female badness differed markedly from its male counterpart. Male criminality supposedly stemmed from a man's failure to discipline his proprietary, active nature or to respect the boundaries set by other freemen. In Massachusetts between 1673 and 1774, men made up almost 81 percent of those charged with serious crimes. They stood accused of 181 rapes, 268 of 301 instances of theft or burglary, and 166 out of 243 murders or manslaughters. Eighteenth-century Philadelphians thought of adultery less as a sex crime than as a political challenge to "the husband who was master of his wife"; much as the kidnapper of a man's wife had not violated her rights so much as "stolen another man's cargo," so the adulterous male undermined the husband's authority over his dependents. Prerevolutionary colonists tied manhood to household mastery; a man who could not control his wife or servants was "not a full member of the civil community of adult men." Hence, a man committed adultery "only when he seduced a married woman, not when he had sex with a single one"; it did not matter whether the accused man was married or single. In New England, courts intervened on the complaints of husbands or fathers to end unauthorized liaisons, and, to some extent, the magistracy's defense of the family aimed to prevent adultery and the sexual abuse of daughters. Thus, a New England judge intervened to prevent a man from "cohabitation and frequent keepeing company with Mrs. Freeman, under paine of such punishment as the Court shall thinke meete to inflict."[94]

"Bad women," unlike male felons, supposedly had succumbed to their sexual insatiability and penchant for disorder. When the minister of Boston's Brattle Street Church sought an image to embody Satan, he chose a woman. "So you twine your lusts about your breasts," he wrote, "and hang 'em as bracelets on your neck and arms."[95] Infanticide charges likely attached only to women, though men often abetted and presumably had a hand in pregnancy. Massachusetts women stood accused of 30 out of 38 cases of adultery and 34 of 36 witchcraft indictments, but only 77 of 243 homicides; officials hanged 19 of these women (about 10 percent of the male total), mostly for murder and infanticide. Connecticut jurors tried five times as many women as men for bastardy and fornication.

Gender distinctions also shaped public executions. The hanging of a woman brought crowds to a fever pitch with its novelty, thinly veiled misogyny, and sexual titillation. Seventeenth-century executioners sometimes stripped women to the waist before flogging and hanging; they might affix the sign "CHEAT" to the bare breast of a wife accused of adultery and infanticide. And, while such punishments happened rarely, only female adulterers stood beneath a gallows with a metaphoric noose around the neck, or—less commonly—forever wore a cloth "A." Such women had demonstrated a capacity not just for sexual misconduct, but for damaging society. A suspected witch, Hannah Gray, wore a "paper on her head" for long hours proclaiming, "I STAND HERE FOR MY LACIVIOUS AND WANTON CARRIAGES"; in Boston, a banner pinned to Ruth Read's chest said, "THVS I STAND FOR MY ADVLTEROVS AND WHORISH CARRIAGE."[96]

Maryland courts, on the other hand, penalized women as often for economic or political offenses as for immorality. During all the colonial years, 155 out of 701 criminal
prosecutions (or 24 percent) involved at least one female defendant. Of these, 38 percent
charged women with bastardy (compared to only 5.5 percent of male cases), 7 percent
with infanticide, and 11 percent with adultery or fornication. Husbands usually did not
lodge adultery charges; only one man did so during the entire period. When prosecutions
occurred, judges emphasized the public cost of rearing bastards, rather than immorality.
Marylanders evinced great interest in rebellious women; 15 percent of the cases brought
against women involved abandoning indentures or abusing servants, and only 12 percent
accused women of theft, assault, or homicide (compared to 22.8 percent of the male cases).
More than half Maryland's female defendants answered for sexual misbehavior, including bastardy and infanticide, compared to 11 percent of the male defendants. Magistrates
accused twice as many men as women of violent crimes against persons or property, and
women accused of property crimes seem to have been treated leniently. In Maryland,
moreover, the "hazard of bearing a bastard was a hazard of being a servant": Only a handful of free women were presented for bastardy in Charles County from 1658 to 1705.
Many planters sought wives, but servant women could marry only if they bought back or
worked off contracts or if would-be husbands reimbursed masters for their loss. Because
few women enjoyed a direct relationship with the state, judges cited mostly men for con-
tempt, treason, or neglect of duty (one-third of the male defendants); the list of masculine crimes also included drunkenness, killing other people's animals, profanity, and
blasphemy.[97]

In capital cases, felons who were eligible for holy orders (demonstrated after the reign
of Henry II by reciting the first line of the Fifty-First Psalm) might escape the noose by
claiming "benefit of clergy." Other than nuns, convicted women could not claim this exemption until 1624, when Parliament placed women who were accused of 10-shilling lar-
cenies on the same footing with men. Seven decades later, Parliament extended the benefit to women who were convicted of clergiable capital crimes, although confusion
remained about its applicability to the nobility. Some evidence suggests that Massachusetts women read the "neck verse" from the colony's founding; between 1699 and 1719,
Pennsylvanians gradually eliminated sex-specific applications of the benefit. Until 1732,
Virginians may well have transported (or sentenced to servitude) unclergiable female
felons alongside illiterate men; in that year, following a controversy about allowing a baptized African bondswoman named Mary Aggie to read, lawmakers extended the benefit
to women, slaves, and Indians. Far less is known about American use of "benefit of the
belly," by which English judges stayed the executions of pregnant women; in one study
of English Assizes well before 1624, an amazing 38 percent of the woman felons pleaded
pregnancy, which suggests that the "belly" was used as a surrogate for benefit of clergy.[98]
But beyond scattered mention in witchcraft trials, its New World career is mostly
uncharted.

Maryland records reveal other sex-specific practices. Men appeared in court on their
own behalf or through agents; husbands or fathers usually represented absent women. Men
filed complaints quickly; women postponed filing suit and sometimes decided to resolve
differences informally through religious groups, relatives, or petitions to officials. "No legal barrier prevented a woman from going to a constable or a judge with an account of
damage done to her," writes Mary Beth Norton, "but daughters, wives, and especially
maidservants nevertheless deferred to fathers, husbands, and masters." Women on the
eastern shore came forward mainly in desperation—to charge men with extreme physical

or emotional abuse, for instance, or to obtain economic help with bastards; for these acts, they risked a public whipping for fornication or, in the case of indentured servants impregnated or maimed by masters, on-the-job retaliation and countersuits for breach of contract. Servants therefore sued with great reluctance, and courts could do nothing for dead women. Alice Sandford was "beaten to a Jelly" repeatedly and then killed by her master; convicted of manslaughter, he was granted benefit of clergy and punished with a thumb brand.[99]

Deborah Rosen similarly finds that in seventeenth-century New York, women avoided courts with petitions to governors, legislators, and other officers—for protection of property, financial support, security against abusive men, license to beg, and permission to engage in otherwise illegal acts. "Finding themselves unprotected by the law, limited by societal expectations that women be passive and subordinate, and lacking in financial resources," Rosen concludes, "early American women regularly turned to less formal, and less rule-determined, methods of obtaining official justice." Rosen also suspects that these practices "helped mitigate women's lack of formal legal rights."[100]

SCOLDS, SHREWS, AND DOMESTIC SABOTEURS

As Hutchinson learned the hard way, magistrates punished women resoundingly for disrespectful, brazen, or treacherous speech—or, as in Hibbens's case, for refusing to speak on command. Included were verbal attacks on household heads. The scold had no male counterpart; when verbal brawling threatened male governance, it was punished swiftly. In some cases, noisy women were treated no differently than men; when Mistress Hog said in 1684 that the "Governor and the rest of the Gentlemen were a crew of pitiful beggarly curs," New Hampshire officials convicted her of sedition, much as they convicted lower-class men for similar insults. When Elizabeth Wilson of Maryland responded to an officer's attempt to seize her horse by brandishing a knife, promising to "cut his hand off," and advising the governor to "kiss her arse," judges charged her with sedition, as they did men who scandalized the magistracy.[101]

In other cases, though, gender stereotypes powerfully shaped outcomes, which, in turn, drove home linkages between threats to family government and female "badness." In 1626, for example, a fight broke out between Margaret Jones of Virginia and a neighbor, John Butterfield, over who could harvest peas from a garden. A witness "found her with her hair about her ears"; she also upbraided her husband as a "base rascal" for his "apparent lack of concern over her condition"—that is, for his ineffective governance. With Margaret "rumpled" and Butterfield "all bloodied over his face," another man tried to stop the fight; she beat him with a tobacco stalk. Constables tied Margaret "to the back of a boat" and dragged her "up and down the James River for her words and behavior," less for claiming peas than for refusing arbitration and challenging male headship.

In subsequent decades, fears about unruly women regularly seeped into Virginia law books. Forty years later, for instance, lawmakers noted that "brawling women . . . slander and scandalize their neighbours for which their poore husbands are often brought into chargeable and vexatious suites, and cast in greate damages"; a wife whose undisciplined tongue subjected her husband to a slander suit was to be "ducked in water for each five hundred pounds of damages adjudged against her husband if he refused to pay." But in the Chesapeake, the persistent scarcity of white women, combined with Cavalier-inspired protectionism, could help women; after Bacon's Rebellion, for example, legisla-

tors made special provision for female sedition or seditious libel. For the first two offenses, women would be whipped less harshly than men and spared the pillory. At the
third offense, however, the charge became treason; men and women alike could be hung.
Officials drew the line at speech that was likely to bring down constituted authority,
whether at home or in a city square.[102]

Certain kinds of anarchism implicated both the family and the polity. Theoretically,
for example, British wives or servants accused of murdering husbands, masters, or mistresses (or a servant falsifying a lord's seal, a manservant committing adultery with his
master's family's women, or a child killing his or her father) could be tried for petit treason—that is, for subverting the authority of the household's "little king"—and burned at
the stake. Burning had long been the punishment for witchcraft—in Catholic Europe, a
crime against both church and state—and continued to be the punishment, after drawing
and quartering, when men undertook high treason. Men who were convicted of petit treason, usually for killing masters, were not burned, but were "drawn to the place of execution on a hurtle, then hanged"; husbands convicted of murdering their wives were hanged
for garden-variety homicide. Several scholars have argued, following Blackstone, that
burning aimed to preserve the "natural modesty of the female sex." But whatever the punishment signified (Blackstone's reading was late and perhaps chivalric), the object seems
to have been to punish murderous household dependents with a vengeance. Colonists,
moreover, were less likely to charge black women with the "aggravated offense" of
petit treason when they killed husbands than when they eliminated white masters or
mistresses.[103]

Scattered evidence also suggests that judges in cases of infanticide were most strin-
gent when women resisted both authority and demands for contrition. Jane Kamensky
demonstrates that the "gendered meaning of public apology" emerged most vividly in
cases in which women did not defer to male governors—when they "misspoke in con-
frontational (male) styles" or "failed (immediately, privately) to mend the rifts their words
had caused." Punishments that were assigned "even to those female misspeakers whose
words and styles most closely resembled men's," she adds, "reveal a tension between the
association of women with submission, and their presumed unfitness for its expression in
public speech." Indeed, a demonstration of "regoverned speech" often consisted of "remaining silent in the face of onlookers."[104] In cases involving unrepentant women, courts
occasionally refused to extend discretionary elements of procedural due process—for example, the privilege of remaining silent or mitigation of punishment by reason of
insanity—to drive home the perils of aggression. Two cases make the point. Mercy Brown
of Wallingford, Massachusetts, escaped the gallows in 1691 after killing her son; the Court
of Assistants delayed passing sentence because she was "distracted" and then jailed her.
They may well have acted on the suggestion (as made by William Perkins in a 1592 argument *against* leniency for convicted witches) that women's confessed "weakness" could
"lessen both the crime and the punishment." In any case, Brown's acceptance of authority probably allowed the court to extend a measure of mercy.[105]

The trial of Dorothy Talbye of Salem, reported in detail by Winthrop, elicited a different response. Convicted of murdering her daughter in 1638, Talbye had been a church
member in "good esteem" until she began arguing with her husband. Given to "melancholy . . . delusions," she "sometimes attempted to kill him and her children, and herself,
by refusing meat." When the church "cast her out," she got worse; officials "caused her
to be whipped," and for a time, she "carried herself more dutifully to her husband." But,
finally, she resisted governance so completely that magistrates had to intervene: she was

"so possessed with Satan that he persuaded her (by his delusions, which she listened to as revelations from God) to break the neck of her own child, that she might free it from future misery."

> This she confessed upon her apprehension; yet, at the arraignment, she stood mute . . . till the governor told her she should be pressed to death, and then she confessed the indictment. When she was to receive judgment, she would not uncover her face, nor stand up, but as she was forced, nor give any testimony of her repentance. . . . The cloth, which should have covered her face, she plucked off, and put between the rope and her neck. She desired to have been beheaded, giving this reason, that it was less painful and less shameful. . . . [Ministers] went with her to the place of execution, but could do no good with her. Mr. Peter gave an exhortation to the people to take heed of . . . despising the ordinance of excommunication as she had done; for when it was to have been denounced against her, she turned her back, and would have gone forth, if she had not been stayed by force.[106]

INSTRUMENTS OF SATAN

Trials for witchcraft lay bare the precariousness of the notion of a redeemable woman. As Cornelia Hughes Dayton rightly observes, for the first few decades of settlement in New England, Puritans suspended "traditional suspicions about women's carnality,"[107] thus allowing women to test their spiritual wings. But with commercialization, erosions of religious orthodoxy, and traumas like the Antinomian Controversy, allusions to Eve and Jezebel resurged. Despite the sex-neutral language of statutes—in Massachusetts, "any man or woman" could be a witch[108]—sorcery was a gender-related crime; scattered male suspects usually were married or related to accused women.

The demonization of Hutchinson, Hibbens, and Talbye originated partly in the belief that women (and, in a different way, Indians) easily succumbed to "Satan's malignity"[109] or served as slates upon which God might inscribe messages to fallen-away Saints. New Englanders regularly noted God's use of witches to remind Christians of sin; some even indulged, in Cotton Mather's words, in a tendency to suspect "every old woman whose temper with her visage is not eminently good."[110] Indeed, years after Hutchinson's death, Winthrop toyed with the idea that she might have been a witch, as evidenced by her ability to sow discord and mobilize women against the clergy. On the one hand, as Puritan divine William Perkins noted in his 1590 *Christian Oeconomie*, woman (because derived from Adam) was a "mate" rather than a "servant"; on the other hand, original sin had been Eve's gift to man. As Perkins said in his *Discourse on the Damned Art of Witchcraft* (1596), "In all ages it is found . . . that the devil hath more easily and oftener prevailed with women than with men. . . . [T]he more women, the more witches."[111]

This was not a new view. Since at least the fifteenth century, theologians had linked witchcraft with woman's sexual insatiability; by the early seventeenth century, as historian Elizabeth Reis brilliantly demonstrates, links between demonism and femininity had worked their way into reformed Congregationalist doctrine.[112] Satan took advantage of female weakness and lust and used women to destroy men. "A woman," said the author of a 1486 text on witchcraft, "is beautiful to look upon, contamination to the touch, and deadly to keep." What was new was the possibility that women could be Saints as well. As historian David Leverenz notes, to the extent that men viewed women as "pure mothers accepting subjugation to the pure Father," they could be "exalted in fantasy and given

great range for their emotional and assertive energies," but when women sought "intellectual and non-mothering identities," they were seen as willful and "unsafe." Periodic reassertions of authority in response to defiant women effectively delayed the collapse of
an increasingly incoherent religious orthodoxy. Witchcraft trials probably represented, in
Jane Kamensky's words, "a way to reaffirm patriarchal authority" in societies under stress.
The actual harm done by suspected women mattered less than their mysterious methods;
harms included frightening children, sickening livestock, or allowing one's stomach to
grumble peculiarly in church. These women stood accused of moving beyond scolding
and railing. Their words had a dramatic impact taken to be *uncommon* for women; as
Kamensky puts it, they "burst the bounds of language and assumed material form. Put
simply, you could take witches at their word."[113]

After 1647, witchcraft trials became a recurrent feature of colonial life. These cycli-
cal sprees may well have been extensions of broader European witch-hunts: British American prosecutions were substantial, but European executions of women for witchcraft far
exceeded anything in the New World. Estimates of deaths range from 50,000 (the number accepted by most scholars) to 1 million over five centuries; one historian fixes the
number at 100,000 between 1500 and 1750 alone.[114] Massachusetts made witchcraft a
felony punishable by death in 1641; Rhode Island did the same in 1656, and Plymouth
Colony as of 1671 (amended in 1685), Connecticut in 1672, and New Hampshire in
1679–80. Between 1620 and 1725, New Englanders accused at least 344 people of witchcraft, by European standards a small number. Before 1647, Bay Colony magistrates per-
secuted a small number of suspected witches (notably, two of Anne Hutchinson's friends)
only informally, by means of church hearings and the rumor mill. Britons executed more
witches over two years' time in one English county than did Americans during the entire
seventeenth century. Bay Colony judges heard 27 witchcraft cases in the 1650s, 13 in the
next decade, and 9 in the 1670s; over the same decades, Connecticut tried 7, 24, and 2.
About 78 percent of the American victims were women; half the men accused of sorcery
were related to or publicly supported accused women. In Salem, Massachusetts, magistrates charged 141 women and 44 men with the crime during the 1692–93 outbreak there;
31 were convicted and 19 executed, 14 of them women.

Before the Salem debacle, judges probably respected English judicial procedures;
ironically, Puritan legalism may have spared dozens of women from the gallows. Magistrates opened a preliminary hearing to explore the merits of evidence; there followed a
grand jury indictment and a trial by a male petit jury, sometimes aided by midwives or
matrons' juries. Only in witchcraft trials did judges consider spectral evidence—that is,
testimony by the witch's accusers about visitations or torment by what Peter Hoffer calls
"otherwise invisible wraiths."[115] Although the rules required two witnesses of such phenomena, courts (except in Connecticut after 1669, where witnesses had to testify about
the same events) could create "acts" from different phenomena observed by disparate witnesses. In 1651, jurors acquitted Mary Parsons of Springfield, Massachusetts, along with
her "testy" husband, of witchcraft on procedural grounds, although they later convicted
her of infanticide; in 1665, a Connecticut appellate court overturned a verdict against Elizabeth Seager on the ground that the jurymen had exceeded the terms of the indictment.[116]

Conviction rates rose dramatically during the Salem witch-hunt, during which, in one
scholar's chilling phrase, Bay Colony judges presided over "judicial murders."[117] The
Salem trials initially sprang from a disagreement over the merits of a minister; factions
quickly formed around two warring families. The accusing girls lacked good marital or
inheritance prospects; David Konig wisely urges us to take seriously Mather's identi-

fication of witches *and* accusers with burgeoning resistance to "Poverty" and "Misery." Five decades after settlement, cultural and economic stress stalked New Englanders; yeomen and peasant farmers schooled in traditional relationships and work ways faced obsolescence.[118]

While witchcraft in New England can thus be seen as a "tool of the poor and those in servile or subordinate positions" against their oppressors, the public prosecution of witches probably represented a collective attack on hundreds of aging, discarded, or un-attached women who seemed to embody the reality of terrifying changes in the fabric of everyday life. In Salem, the devil apparently preferred women over age 40; in one way or another, every "witch" had challenged or vacated her assigned niche. In some cases, women had escaped dependence with inherited property, sometimes without male heirs. In others, cantankerous, poor women threatened to become public wards; perhaps 20 per-cent of the accused were impoverished or had collided previously with constables. Brid-get Oliver had been cited before 1692 for calling her second husband, Thomas, "many opprobrious names, as old rogue and old devil." She and her husband had stood "on a lecture day in the public market place, both gagged, for about an hour, with a paper fas-tened to each of their foreheads upon which their offence"—she had done it, he had al-lowed it—"should be fairly written." When Thomas died, Bridget sold property to pay his debts, leaving her poor and ill tempered; because visitors found "poppets" in her house, one scholar thinks that she did practice witchcraft. Tried unsuccessfully in 1679–80, she married Edward Bishop in middle age; twelve years later, convinced that she roamed the village as a black cat, Salemites executed her as a witch, depriving her (if she did prac-tice the craft) of a "powerful method of resistance."[119]

Witchcraft trials died out only in the early eighteenth century, coincident with a de-cision among Europeans and Americans to eliminate governmental reliance on "Christ-ian political ideology";[120] in Scotland, the scene of bloody witch scares in the 1620s, the crime became obsolete in 1736. Meanwhile, Quaker communities were the only sure havens against capital punishment for "crabbedness" or "spiritual independence." It did not help that the first generation of white women in New England lived longer than any-one (especially unmarried children waiting to inherit property) had planned. Under the best conditions, Europeans were ambivalent about aging, displaced women; it was a short step from social disorder to public catharsis at the gallows. Decades later, as Americans mobilized for war against Britain, a Loyalist correspondent in New Haven, Connecticut, accidentally put his finger on the nature of the association between unruly women and anarchism. A rebellion against "good and constitutional government, against the Magna-Charta of the British constitution," he warned his neighbors in 1775, "is as the sin of witchcraft, a transgression of an eternal law of nature, and incurs the penalty of that antient edict from heaven, '*He that sheds man's blood by man shall his blood be shed*.'"[121]

Chapter 2

Toward the Revolutionary Settlement

On May 15, 1793, Priscilla Mason delivered a salutatory oration to the trustees of the Young Ladies Academy of Philadelphia. She assured listeners that she sought only toleration of women's speech before "promiscuous assemblies," not the establishment of a right. Yet she energetically championed "the right of being heard on . . . proper occasions," the opportunity to address "the reason as well as the fears of the other sex," and the "right to instruct and persuade." Did not properly educated republican women possess the "power of speech, and volubility of expression . . . in eminent degree"? This self-described "young and inexperienced" speaker no doubt took a deep breath before adding these remarks: "Our high and mighty Lords (thanks to their arbitrary constitutions) have denied us the means of knowledge, and then reproached us for the want of it."

> Being the stronger party, they early seized the scepter and the sword; with these they gave laws to society; they denied women the advantage of a liberal education; forbid them to exercise their talents on those great occasions, which would serve to improve them. They doom'd the sex to servile or frivolous employments, on purpose to degrade their minds, that they themselves might hold unrivall'd, the power and pre-eminence they had usurped.

With every sentence, the ice under Mason's feet grew thinner. Suppose women educated in women's academies possessed oratorical talent: Where would they find "a theater for the display of them? The Church, the Bar, and the Senate are shut against us. Who shut them? *Man*; despotic man first made us incapable of the duty, and then forbade us the exercise. Let us, by suitable education, qualify ourselves for those high departments—they will open before us." Even the bar would embrace women. "I am assured," she said, "that there is nothing in our laws or constitutions to prohibit the licensure of female attornies; and surely our judges have too much gallantry to urge *prescription* in bar of their claim."[1]

Mason's complaint had deep roots in late colonial law and culture. A century after settlement, British Americans began to close the gap between the English law courts' relatively harsh treatment of women and early colonial liberality—which, in any case, had been partial and geographically specific. Although Americans eliminated titled aristocracies, the sovereign head of household survived the trans-Atlantic voyage and, as the eighteenth century advanced, tightened his grip on family government. By the 1750s, two related processes of change underlay a loss of ground for women, especially wives. Colonists witnessed, first, the masculinization of "important" work and the removal of much (although not all) paid labor from the home and, second, the gradual "reconstruction of womanhood" (to borrow Carol Karlsen's phrase)[2] in ideological terms as a domestic, private, noneconomic *condition* or status. On the eve of the Revolution, women's prospects for a public identity and cosovereignty had dimmed—notwithstanding a fiery religious revival that forced many Americans to rethink patriarchal claims to lawmaking authority.

During the revolutionary decades, American judges and lawyers sometimes gave thought to the implications of republicanism for women. But on the legal and constitutional level, they ultimately refused to meddle with tradition. Choosing to perpetuate the constitutional dependence of a majority of the adult population was problematic: A virtuous and independent citizenry supposedly distinguished republics from other forms of political association. Few themes were more central to the American rebellion than its condemnation (in the words of the Declaration of Independence) of any government that did not derive its "just powers from the consent of the governed"; constitutionally dependent subjects of George III had claimed the "right" and "duty" to throw off a tyrannical king and his ministers.[3] Still, by 1805–07, the vast majority of legislatures and several state courts had decided that key revolutionary doctrines need not be extended to women (particularly married women); despite its feudal character, they perpetuated the life of the supposedly indivisible petit king within families. In effect, republicans decided to embrace virtual representation and vestiges of feudalism in domestic government.

This decision, in turn, set the Sons of Liberty on a collision course with the Daughters of Liberty. Many women thought of themselves not as mere helpmeets, but as companions of men, producers of wealth, coforgers of revolution, and comembers of the constituent power—in no small part because republican men had entrusted them with the job of conserving the idea of the republic and conveying it into the next century. This mixed message—women are subject to men; women are keepers of the revolution—did not bode well for the future of the monarchical principle, whether in domestic or political governments. Consider the tensions embedded in a Columbia College commencement speech of May 1795. "Let us . . . figure to ourselves," said the male speaker, moving seamlessly from female domesticity to patriotism, "the accomplished woman, surrounded by a sprightly band,"

> from the babe that imbibes the nutritive fluid, to the generous youth just ripening into manhood, and the lovely virgin, blest with a miniature of maternal excellence. Let us contemplate the mother distributing the mental nourishment to the fond smiling circle. . . . See, under her cultivating hand, reason assuming the reins of government, and knowledge increasing gradually to her beloved pupils. . . . Contemplate the rising glory of confederated America. Consider that your exertions can best secure, increase, and perpetuate it. The solidity and stability of the liberties of your country rest with you, since Liberty is never sure, till Virtue reigns triumphant. . . . While you thus keep our country virtuous, you maintain its independence and ensure its prosperity.[4]

FLIRTING WITH FREEDOM

Between the 1680s and 1770s, British North America essentially reinvented itself in response to the apparent collapse of civil society, the failure of traditional Calvinism to control immorality, and the early stages of the so-called market revolution. Theologian Jonathan Edwards, with many others, noted the general inability of "family government" to stem "frolicks"[5] and other kinds of unseemly deportment. In the Bay Colony, a serious breakdown in social order appeared as early as the 1660s. People skipped town, brawled, lied, refused to confess criminality, and stopped spying on neighbors; by the 1680s, as Salemites geared up for witchcraft trials, courtrooms fairly burst with cases of bastardy, fornication, and marital infidelity. The proportions of women involved in crimes, and the nature of charges against them also changed. Serious female criminality shrank dramatically, from 33 percent of the total in the 1670s to 9.5 percent a century later. Moreover, while women in seventeenth-century Massachusetts were more apt than men to be involved in violent crimes resulting in death, by the 1740s most crimes by women involved property, rather than persons, and homicide become a male preserve. Laura Thatcher Ulrich shows that neighborhood supervision of sexuality and morality continued to be effective until the Age of Jefferson, but with few exceptions, courts steadily lost interest in sex and immorality after the 1680s. For better or worse, Americans had decided to keep indecent speech and family skeletons hidden in closets and to permit a certain amount of wickedness behind closed doors.[6] Maryland judges' interest in sexual misconduct waned after the 1710s, and in the Virginia Piedmont, magistrates stopped enforcing interracial moral and sexual codes. Such laws never had been implemented vigorously. Before 1755, only nine white servant women were indicted for having mulatto bastards; thereafter, only two women answered for interracial sex crimes—arguably, the lapses about which southerners cared most deeply. Eighteenth-century Virginia law codes zeroed in on the sexual activities and births of *black* women, not white, in keeping with a cultural decision to associate carnality with undisciplined, unchurched, or nonwhite women.

Social change and disarray need not have led to a dramatic loss of ground for women; indeed, for a relatively brief, magical time in the mid-eighteenth century, growing pains seemed to be *liberating* women—at least at the spiritual margins of society, in "free spaces" constructed by nonconforming Protestants during the Great Awakening. Within those spaces, women were catapulted into positions of real authority, and—the regular ministry aside—elevated to virtual equality with men. The Awakening swept the colonies with the force of a hurricane, shattering what remained of Puritan orthodoxy. Christians *"Ravished* with the discoveries of *another World"* swarmed over the countryside with wild, often sexualized abandon. As with antinomians a century earlier, preachers invited Christians to strike up personal relationships with God, without the aid or interference of law-bound clergymen and ossified parish bureaucracies. Circuit-riding lecturers urged converts to "come out and be . . . separate" in streets and open fields; to "reject the bonds of family, neighborhood, and society"; and to construct an ideal community purged of social and legal conventions, including African and female subjection.[7]

Women had been exercising rusty vocal chords in Protestant churches since at least the 1680s, when believers like Sarah Whipple Goodhue regularly urged women to "get a part and portion" of salvation and to secure a modest role for women in church government.[8] By 1700, women dominated New England church rolls; thirty years later, although men still governed churches, at least 40 percent of funeral sermons eulogized female members. Indeed, after the Salem witch trial debacle, the "bad woman" who was capable of unhinging the polity seemed to disappear in evangelical as well as mainstream Protestant circles; in her place, regenerate Christians erected a feminine "instrument of regeneration," capable of making her own spiritual contracts. In 1745, a Baptist woman resolved to leave a Connecticut parish because, by "Covenant," she was "not held here any longer than I am edified."[9] Within liminal speech communities, as historian Susan Juster puts it, Congregationalists sometimes encouraged women to follow God rather than their husbands: "Tho' we would ever avoid any just occasion of offence to any & particularly between husbands & wives," Baptist elders in Middleborough, Massachusetts, told Relief Hooper, whose husband disputed church teachings and ordered her to stay home, "yet when husbands commands interfers with Christs authority we ought to obey God rather

than man." For at least two decades, Baptist women chose ministers, elected parish officials, served as lay preachers and judges, and sat on committees; when Ezra Stiles, the
renowned Congregational minister, heard that women participated in Baptist affairs in
every capacity short of the regular ministry, he made a study of evangelical practices and
reported that it was "a Usage & practiced Principle among the Baptists of this Colony . . .
to admit the Sisters to equal Votes in the Ch[urc]h meetings, & this by *Lifting Up of
Hands.*"[10]

Pressing hard against tradition, divinely inspired women made important inroads into
public life and destabilized conventional understandings of God's "natural" order. The revivalist Sarah Osborn of Newport, Rhode Island, held mixed-race religious meetings in
her home; when slaveowners and her spiritual mentor, Joseph Fish, objected to her meetings (which in 1767 attracted 500 people weekly), she said that while she initially had
tried to "avoid Moving beyond my Line," she had God's permission to fill "a larger
sphere." She simply refused to "shut up my Mouth and doors and creep into obscurity."[11]

The Awakening's central instrument, the conversion experience, also eroded gender
stereotypes. For white men, conversion required humiliation, self-abasement, and giving
over of the self to community—all of which called to mind feminine traits. White women,
by contrast, shed relationships with kin and community to strike up an individualized,
erotic, unmediated relationship with God—experiences usually reserved for men. Within
these speech communities, bounded by little more than a shared language and a desire to
escape social conventions, members called one another "brother" and "sister"; women,
empowered by conversations with God, rose at meetings to speak and sometimes to teach.

THE INVENTION OF "WOMAN'S SPHERE"

Yet the Awakening's enchanted moment was fleeting. From the beginning, fainthearted
Christians objected strenuously to women's supposedly indelicate notoriety, especially exercises of authoritative varieties of speech through lay preaching. As a spokesman for the
Philadelphia Baptist Association put it in 1746, women "ought not to open the floodgate
of speech in an imperious, tumultous, masterly manner." Sometimes, female parishioners
objected to other women's speeches; in 1771, "Sister Lucy" told elders in Lyme, Massachusetts, that she opposed "Letting the Sisters Improve as they do which is contrary to a
divine Rule and I cant walk with the Church." Reformer Isaac Backus used St. Paul's admonition that women should "keep silence in the church" to strengthen gender lines; when
Paul forbade speech by women, said Backus, he gave "liberty to all men, . . . opposing
women to men, sex to sex."[12]

By the 1780s, and in some cases earlier, Baptist parishes in Massachusetts and Rhode
Island began to emulate the establishment, partly to compete in the spiritual marketplace.
Elders took out mortgages and created patriarchal governing boards; they also eased "brass
mounted" or "disorderly" women out of lecterns, committees, and electorates. Women
who complained were tried for disorderly conduct or otherwise censured. The disfranchisement of evangelical women took several decades, but by 1791, previously active
women throughout Massachusetts, Connecticut, and Rhode Island had been silenced. The
First Baptist Church of Providence—the most venerable Baptist community in New England—incrementally eliminated women from church government between 1786 and 1808;
after 1791, parish women voted only to confirm decisions made by men. The Waterford
Baptist Church, another old Baptist society, rewrote its covenant in 1786 to exclude women

from "matters of rule and Determination." Old associations between women and sinfulness resurged: During the revolutionary era, carnality, duplicity, irrationality, and other supposedly feminine attributes came to be synonymous with sin. In this revisionist view, only disciplined women escaped their nature; discipline, in turn, mandated pastoral supervision of relations between women and God and the relegation of women to singing and cake baking.[13]

Even revivalist "enthusiasm" (the opposite of "rationalism") came back to haunt women. Initially, revivalism seemed to reinforce the idea that men and women were equal in God's eyes. But enthusiasm also provided mortar for the bricks of an emerging "cult of true womanhood" in which religious *feeling* came to be seen as something that women understood more fully than did "rational" men. A parallel series of spiritual revivals emphasizing "tradition" (meaning "an altered tradition,"[14] in Joan Gunderson's phrase, deeply imbued with European values) overtook American Indian women. By 1800, men in many tribes had begun to wear nonfeminine, European-style dress and hairstyles; to exclude women from sacred spaces and from touching sacred objects; and to monopolize leadership positions. Among whites, the gradual sentimentalization of romantic love also helped to disfranchise beings who were deemed too soft-headed to lock horns with roughnecks. As Jonathan Edwards explained, a wife received her husband "as a guide, as a protector, a safeguard and defense, a shelter from harms . . . , a reliever from distresses, a comforter in afflictions, a support in discouragements."

> God has . . . made man of a more robust [nature] and strong in body and mind, with more wisdom, strength and courage, fit to protect and defend; but he has made woman weaker, more soft and tender, more fearful, and more affectionate, as a fit object of generous protection and defense. . . . Thus it is against nature for a man to love a woman as wife that is rugged, daring and presumptuous, and trusts to herself, and thinks she is able to protect herself. . . . And it is impossible a woman should love a man as an husband, except she can . . . sweetly rest in him as a safeguard.[15]

In economic life, women by the 1770s had been squeezed out of complex commercial transactions as traders and attorneys. Early American settlers had postponed the developmental process, afoot but incomplete in the British Isles, by which "home work" (poorly paid or unpaid, supplemental, mostly female) came to be divorced from "factory" or "shop work" (salaried, primary, usually male, and performed away from home). As the new century advanced, the dam of traditional economic relations burst, sweeping away many (not all) household industries. Frequently, women had kept books for family businesses or farms, as female traders, husbands' agents, or widows; in New Haven County, Connecticut, from 1666 to 1720, women sued in 15 percent of the debt cases brought to the county tribunal. Before the mid-eighteenth century, "attorney" had designated little more than a person assigned by another person the authority to do business in the assignor's name; men commonly granted power of attorney to women. As late as the 1710s, female merchants still pursued debtors in court, particularly in "book debt" cases; they also testified about commercial matters and served as attorneys.

In the late eighteenth century, the expanding demand for cloth in the Bay Colony may have allowed women to enter the textile field; entrepreneurs began to employ a large number of women in the last two decades of the colonial era, laying foundations for the nineteenth-century Lowell factory experiments. Country girls went to school; writing and calculating skills meant better jobs, which allowed workers to buy crockery, clothing, housewares, and privacy. Perhaps as a result of women's ability to take better care of themselves, female life expectancy rose (after several decades' reversal of first- and second-generation longevity), from 62 to 66 for women who married between 1760 and 1774 and then to 68 for women who wed from 1775 to 1800. These gains mattered. As one scholar reminds us, "comfort is no mean thing."[16]

Still, after 1720, beginning in the north, sex-based economic differences multiplied. Female "school dames," who could not attend college, charged half as much as college-educated schoolmasters. When woman-run home bakeries succeeded, men took over at higher wages in shops apart from home. Gender-specific fault lines also appeared in textile production: Women made thread and coarse weaves; men did fine work. Relatively well-paid male "tailors" made costly woolen suiting from fabric woven by men. Women spun thread and wove coarse cloth, from which poorly paid female "seamstresses" stitched gowns, shirts, and linens. Elaine Crane finds overwhelming evidence of persistent disparities between male and female wages even in New England seaports, where women had a certain amount of room to negotiate; in a single account book, a merchant might report paying a women 2 pounds and a man 2.5 to 6 pounds for a day's work. She concludes that despite an ongoing female presence in port city economies, "women's economic viability dissipated over the course of two centuries." The colonial era "began and ended with Salem women owning 9–10 percent of the total wealth," she points out. Even though "the pool of unmarried women who could own property in their own right increased dramatically," women as a class apparently had lost economic ground.[17] Another scholar notes that in 1777, the new state of Massachusetts posted wage ceilings by which "[m]aximum weekly rates for 'maid's work' equaled the maximum daily rates received by male farm laborers in the summer."[18]

Gradually, doors began to close. Many early colonial women had served as agents, executors, or attorneys in routine commercial and probate transactions; men had monopolized specialized exchanges (or tasks requiring professional training) in banks, mercantile houses, and law offices. Although lawyers and judges had never accepted female apprentices—the usual route to the bar—and courts had never enrolled female lawyers, women at least had acted in courtrooms, often on their own behalf. Now, fluency in law underlay commercial success and access to important legal and economic institutions. As eastern cities devoted collective energies to the Atlantic trade, women simply dropped out of mainstream economic life; only a handful braved the courtroom in self-defense. Because the marketplace was a vital civic space, women lost an important toehold in their struggle for public personalities.

Professionalization (to use a modern term) thus fostered a reception among lawyers and entrepreneurs of new divisions of labor by sex, as well as the marginalization of female economic contributions. In part, these changes reflected the general decline of the household economy in the Atlantic basin. Financial dealings came to depend less on personal relationships and knowledge of local markets than on impersonal connections between trading firms that organized and regularized an overwhelmingly masculine economic empire. At the same time, British Americans were caught up in what historian John Murrin calls the Anglicization of the bench and bar. As lawyers who were trained at the Inns of Court began emulating English ways in commercial, contract, and property law, many colonial jurists seem to have replaced old, variable practices with relatively inelastic English rules of practice and began reading other bodies of law (inheritance or marital law, for instance) in light of these new formulations. Men who had "read law," moreover, flourished as bankers, traders, and commercial planters because of their familiarity with the rules governing commercial paper (e.g., promissory notes or bills of exchange).

Slowly but surely, women vanished from the extra-familial economy. Cornelia Hughes Dayton shows that, amid a flood of litigation in the 1720s, which scholars associate with a surge in trade that lasted until the depression of the early 1760s, Connecticut women (and New York women during the earlier transition from Dutch to English rule) mostly vanished as parties to complex financial transactions. Indeed, as the scarcity of labor eased and the sex ratio righted itself, white middle-class women steadily lost the ability—in the northern and middle colonies especially but also in the plantation south—to hold, deal in, and protect all kinds of property. Numerous exceptions belied the rule, and many enterprising women resisted class-based restraints. But limitation was in the air. Then, in the 1770s, a flood of male immigrants poured into the Middle Colonies and Chesapeake, sharply lowering women's wages. Female migrants (barely one-quarter of newcomers between 1773 and 1776) thus confronted shrinking opportunities; one agent asked for "tradesmen and farmers" and "common laborers, *the fewer women the better*."[19]

For an increasing number of women, then, the market had become a foreign country, to be visited or occupied at the behest of men. To make matters worse, domestic women came to be eliminated from the category of "worker"; the term *work* increasingly called to mind labor validated by wages earned beyond the household. In a 1765 report on New York's productive classes, Cadwallader Colden listed the leading land proprietors, gentlemen of the bar, merchants, and "Farmers and Mechanics," omitting work ordinarily done by women and much of the labor undertaken by slaves, servants, or children.[20] By 1774, the number of women with property sufficient to be probated had declined to no more than 7 percent of the total population. In Newport, Rhode Island, a town of 8,000 people, 35 unmarried women constituted 3.6 percent of the taxpayers in 1760; two decades later, 44 made up 3.7 percent of the total. Attempts to exclude women from economic life could reach ludicrous extremes; for example, paternalism led Newport officials to excuse delinquent female taxpayers, which reinforced dependence and deprived the treasury of revenue. In a 1767 poll of 129 persons "at sea or sick" and thus exempt from taxation, 38 percent were women; another list of 140 whose delinquent taxes had been quadrupled was wholly male.[21]

Probate and other judicial records reveal similar patterns. Before 1720, for instance, husbands in Hingham, Massachusetts, regularly named wives with adult sons as executors; between 1761 and 1800, the figure dropped to 6 percent, with 85 percent of the wills written by men naming sons as the sole executors. In Bucks County, Pennsylvania, women's proprietary and testamentary capacities regressed; one historian attributes this change to the wrenching transformation of a family-centered economy into a market-driven economy observed elsewhere.[22] As communities tied their futures to commerce, moreover, many lawyers and judges seemed to view the once-sacrosanct widow's dower as a "dormant incumbrance on a title" and an impediment to economic development. In addition, English courts at midcentury apparently began reversing early, generous readings of women's contractual capacities. One after another, English jurists began to say in writing that wives were *not* "free individuals in marriage contracts" or fully constituted citizens.[23]

Southern women had it slightly easier. In mid-eighteenth-century Maryland, widows increasingly chose not to remarry, depriving sons of property but acquiring some degree of autonomy. While husbands and fathers increasingly left property to children (including daughters) rather than to wives, women may have benefited from income generated by home industry; and Marylanders' bequest of land and slaves to daughters increased during the Revolution, perhaps because sons had been (or would be) lost in battle. Furthermore, county courts seemed to be willing to honor parental wills even when the terms flew in the face of established practice. In the 1780 case of *Henry Britt v. William Godfrey Adams and Mary Adams*, for example, a Charles County judge decided that a daughter, Tabitha Britt, not her husband, would get the wages of a slave named Henry, as Tabitha's father had instructed.[24]

Nevertheless, wartime generosity signaled the beginning of the end for the region's relatively autonomous daughters and wives. Although southern women continued to bequeath what one scholar terms a "legacy of independence" to daughters well into modern times, it became progressively more difficult to do so. As the sex ratio righted itself, age at first marriage rose substantially, and white women—healthier, more numerous, and so less valuable—probably lost place in household economies. During the phenomenal eighteenth-century expansion of the Chesapeake economy, men could afford to reward women lavishly for loyalty, affection, and labor. But women's prospects came to be intertwined with the transition from indentured to slave labor and with the fact of arithmetic, rather than geometric, economic growth. By the 1770s, Chesapeake planters increasingly behaved like "little kings," partly as a consequence of the assumption of quasi-manorial mastership in relations with African laborers. In the decades between 1700 and 1770, Tidewater entrepreneurs imported over 100,000 enslaved laborers; black populations grew from 13,000 to 250,000. The revolutionary abolition of entail also hurt southern women, whose control over entailed property had augmented their political and domestic power. As a racialized plantation system took the place of relatively pliable, disorganized agricultural societies, women sacrificed a degree of freedom to a peculiar blend of "Georgian elegance and primitive savagery."[25]

SENTIMENTALISM AND DOMESTICITY

As middle- and upper-class Americans came to associate well-disciplined white women with virtue and domesticity and then to naturalize these traits (that is, to cast them as God given or inborn), they also moved to protect women from corrosive influences, among them, wage labor, the physical sciences (anatomical diagrams, for example, were said to scandalize women), and riff-raff gathered at polls on election day. William Hogarth's famous portrayal of the "Harlot's Progress" implied that women—Satan's favored targets, after all—could be tarnished with lightning speed. But, beyond post-Awakening evangelical churches in New England, where women's identification with Eve seems to have remained strong, few middle-class men doubted that their wives and daughters, while delicate and easily unhinged, possessed a moral authority and emotional understanding ordinarily denied to men and (in one educator's words) ought to function as "guardian angels" for men.[26] A wife-companion supervised household economies and child rearing; a male head of household "laid down the law" at dinner and waged economic, political, and military warfare in the broader world as his family's representative and defender.

At about the same time, Americans began to alter their conceptions of both the nature of marriage and government's role in policing sexual misconduct. New Englanders' contractual view of marriage and divorce was fast becoming the American Way: after the 1750s, as the colonies (and then many new states) reformed divorce laws and eliminated established churches, the number of dissolutions mushroomed. Other changes, while less sweeping, were equally portentous. As early as 1700, Connecticut judges—and probably other New England magistrates as well—gave up enjoining sexually active couples to marry; by the 1740s, they ceased prosecutions of young men for premarital sex. And dur-

ing roughly the same decades, colonists in New England (and perhaps elsewhere) institutionalized what Cornelia Dayton calls a "marked sexual double standard," exculpating
men from legal responsibility for seducing or impregnating women.[27]

In many critical respects—although not in every way and not irreversibly—eighteenth-century Americans had severed the traditional link between domestic and political
governments. In the process, families became less clearly "public" in a formal sense and
perhaps less effective as instruments of political socialization. Fewer and fewer Americans characterized "private" sexual offenses like infanticide or bastardy as threats to the
stability of the polity; as family government came to be viewed as qualitatively different
from the state and *sufficient* to its appointed tasks, the old assumption of a public stake
in the morality or regularity of home life seemed far less obvious. While this development signaled the beginning of the end in many communities (although, as Laura Thatcher
Ulrich shows, not in all) for socially sanctioned meddling by neighbors and constables, it
left unlucky women and children at the mercy of abusive men. Moreover, in the words
of Daniel Scott Smith and Michael Hindus, because modern parents typically "lack the
power to be oppressive in an effective way," privatization of domestic life probably underlay surges in premarital pregnancy after 1750. Certainly, by midcentury, young women
asserted an active interest in sex and resisted attempts to preserve female "delicacy" until marriage. A poet captured this mood in a 1785 celebration of the old practice of premarital bundling:

> Some maidens say [that if] . . . bundling should quite go out of fashion,
> Courtship would lose its sweets; and they,
> Could have no fun till wedding day.
> It shant be so, they rage and storm,
> And country girls in clusters swarm,
> And fly and buzz like angry bees,
> And vow they'll bundle when they please.[28]

Although a sharply bipolar conception of "private" and "public" realms probably did
not crystallize fully until the early nineteenth century, its emergence in the last half of the
eighteenth century powerfully altered women's lives. Women now were supposed to exert only an indirect influence on the state, forgoing direct participation and representation.
Wage labor was said to "unsex" white girls, rendering them unmarriageable, and because
the ability to deal in property still served as a springboard into public affairs, pure domesticity further lessened a woman's opportunity to weigh and discuss civic questions
with other citizens. More and more, women worked (if at all) to supplement men's primary wages, or to secure a foundation for marriage. As Carolyn Merchant notes, the capitalist revolution "split production and reproduction into two separate spheres"; dualities,
such as "male and female, head and heart, calculation and emotion," replaced a system
of relatively flexible gender boundaries. Homes became what Carole Shammas calls "centers of sociability." To the extent allowed by a chronic shortage of servants, middle-class
wives stopped serving at table and "ruled" a domestic realm purged of partisanship and
entrepreneurship—as a matter of obligation to their husbands and community. Children
encountered these ideas in primers: "When a woman quits her own department," said one,
"she offends her husband, not merely because she obtrudes herself upon his business, but
because she departs from that sphere which is assigned to her in the order of society, because she neglects *her* duty and leaves *her own* department vacant. . . . [T]he same rule

which excludes a man from . . . domestic business, excludes a woman from law, mathematics and astronomy."[29]

Without a doubt, working-class and rural women often ignored the strictures laid out in primers and advice books. Having secured beachheads of freedom in the marketplace by reason of economic necessity or having evaded the commercial revolution altogether on isolated farmsteads, thousands of women effectively escaped the ideological straitjacket of "woman's sphere." Meanwhile, middle-class creature comforts improved dramatically. American homes boasted crockery, silverware, and cooks or housekeepers. As colonists moved out of early, precommercial stages of settlement and development, men and women, even those with modest means, essentially invented luxury, leisure, and consumerism. In southeastern Pennsylvania, historian Lisa Wilson Waciega finds strong evidence of male respect (mirrored in generous, laudatory wills) for business partner-wives, as well as entrepreneurial acumen and initiative among more than a few widows, who not only ran husbands' firms capably but sometimes struck out on their own, educating their daughters to do the same. And at least until the 1750s, a number of married women in New York, apparently without female trading licenses, regularly entered courtrooms on their own behalf—perhaps as a residue of the civil law regime that prevailed during the Dutch era. New York lawmakers banned women only from working as surgeons. Myriad wives (many of Dutch lineage) flourished as importers; shipowners; fur traders; and keepers of houses, bawdy and otherwise.

But feather cushions, pots, and expanded autonomy where one might expect to find them (in the Chesapeake and in labor- and capital-scarce commercial cities) did not offset women's loss of ground after the midcentury. Even in New York and Virginia, the possibilities open to married women narrowed after 1750. In the words of two historians, "New York City women could no longer become freemen; the power of attorney was no longer a frequent tool for wives; husbands began to give their wives less control over property; widows found themselves forced to sue to gain the minimum bequests set by law; and women increasingly received smaller portions or life interests when their husbands died."[30] Everywhere, as a feminized private zone theoretically came to be walled off from a masculine public zone, women were locked out of lucrative professions, silenced even in nonconforming Protestant churches, denied equal pay for equal work, eased to the margins of the forum, and cut off from public help when abused by profligate or brutal men. Women could divorce more readily than earlier; in Massachusetts—because of revolutionists' preoccupation with "virtue" and "vice" and what Nancy Cott terms the "equalization of the consequences of adultery by either spouse" in divorce proceedings[31]— women could hope to escape disastrous marriages. Yet they lost custody of children in the bargain and rarely earned wages sufficient to maintain independent households.

For those who lived through these decades, especially those colonists who made gender relations a new topic for public discussion, the years after 1750 were, at best, unsettling. Mary Beth Norton puts it this way: "Americans not only became aware that women's lives were changing but also began consciously to promote or oppose those changes." The nature of womanhood and manhood in white society became the "subject of a heated debate that played an essential part in reshaping American society to fit a republican mold." Joan Hoff interprets the same events less dispassionately. In her view, the colonists had long been engaged in a "basic disagreement over power"; at some point in the eighteenth century, women simply "lost." The English poet Anne Finch might have agreed. Savagely attacked in Anglo-American newspapers for unwomanly writing, Finch saw how the winds were blowing as early as 1713:

Alas! a woman that attempts the pen,
Such an intruder on the rights of men,
Such a presumptuous creature, is esteemed,
The fault, can by no virtue be redeemed.
They tell us, we mistake our sex and way;
Good breeding, fashion, dancing, dressing, play
Are the accomplishments we should desire,
To write, or read, or think or to inquire
Would cloud our beauty, and exhaust our time . . .
Whilst the dull manage, of a servile house
Is held by some, our utmost art, and use. . . .
Marriage does but slightly tie men,
Whilst close prisoners we remain.[32]

REPUBLICAN MOTHERHOOD AND THE WOMAN-CITIZEN

Into the 1770s, a primary component of an emerging revolutionary settlement between men and women was the notion of Republican Motherhood (to use Linda Kerber's phrase). The revolutionary generation put well-educated, maternal women center stage in their new political community, vesting them with responsibility for transmitting civic virtue and republicanism to children. As Kerber explains, American patriots surmounted ancient aversions to the "learned lady" by constructing as the new republican ideal, not an unnatural bookworm squirreled away in her study, but an altruistic companion to man and teacher of youths.[33] Public work undertaken at home—or, as the occasion demanded, in forays beyond home to achieve feminine objectives—was not inconsequential. The philosopher Montesquieu warned that republics failed without a well-informed citizenry and a reservoir of virtue; the Daughters of Liberty could preserve these resources without unduly alarming men like John Trumbull, who asked, "[W]hy should girls be learnd and wise,/ Books only serve to spoil their eyes./ The studious eye but faintly twinkles/ And reading paves the way to wrinkles."[34]

At the same time, white women's world continued to be primarily domestic and maternal; to abandon that station was to jeopardize the republic. Thus, it was possible to mobilize revolutionary rhetoric in defense of, say, women's right to vote, but difficult to mobilize the cultural *heart* of the revolution toward that end, since revolutionaries situated women in a private, relational sphere and men in a public, individuated sphere. It was also difficult, if not impossible, for American Indian and black women to measure up to white middle-class standards. Both groups engaged regularly in manual labor and had been tarred with the broad brush of carnality. Hence, such women "could be mothers, but not of the republic."[35]

Answers to the related questions of whether republican women might shoulder public responsibility (yes), and whether they possessed sovereign authority equal to men's as part of the constituent power (no), affirmed the male monopoly of political government and repackaged (as patriotic) women's time-honored responsibilities for reproducing both culture and the human race. At the same time, republican mothers undoubtedly advanced the revolutionary project, both as moral anchors and as agents provocateur. Gifted writers like Mercy Otis Warren viewed themselves as soldiers armed, not with muskets, but with pens. When a friend asked Warren in 1774 to make a list of the "necessities of life" in preparation for boycotts, she urged women to "resolve on a small sacrifice, and in the pride of Roman matrons rise," to "quit the useless vanities of life. . . ."[36] In Boston and elsewhere, women joined in processions, circulated petitions, supplied troops with food "liberated" from shops, cooked and sewed, harassed Loyalist women, made ammunition, boycotted tea and other British goods, donned homespun, published inspirational poetry, occasionally took men's places on the front lines, spied, and eagerly talked politics at the dinner table. Women's political activism changed more than a few men's minds about what marriage could entail: Samuel Adams told his wife Betsy in 1776 that he could "see no Reason why a Man may not communicate his political opinions to his wife, if he pleases."[37]

Nonetheless, through no fault of their own, women's contributions to the rebellion never quite matched those of French women in their struggle against monarchism. Elaine Crane is surely right to say that, unlike their English and French sisters, North American women simply did not have a "militant tradition" of their own; their revolution, more-over, aimed largely to preserve the ancient English constitutional past, not to dismantle it. By the 1760s, European radicalism was "too remote from the American collective memory to stimulate activism." Nor were there female partisan clubs, as there were in England and France, through which women could identify with other women in a political sense.[38] The American Daughters of Liberty never circulated anything like the "Declaration of the Rights of Woman and Citizen," published in 1790 by the French playwright Olympe de Gouges, three years before her execution: "Woman is born free and remains equal to man in rights. O women! women, when will you stop being blind? What advantages have you received from the Revolution?"[39]

Instead, upper-class American women absorbed ideological lessons—women, after all, *had* acted politically, many for the first time; achieved a "reverence of self";[40] and questioned constitutional authority—and awaited a better moment. Lower-class women continued to labor without political representation, adequate wages, or (in the case of enslaved women) relational rights. Women sometimes scoffed at the terms of the settlement. Abigail Adams—who, according to her daughter, "loved her dish of politics"—promised a female rebellion if her husband, John Adams, failed to enable women to protect themselves from tyrants. But, in the end, women like Adams did not betray their class. Anne Willing Bingham blasted men like Thomas Jefferson for suggesting that American women (unlike their French counterparts) were content to "soothe and calm the minds of their husbands returned ruffled from political debate,"[41] but stopped short of rebellion. Mercy Otis Warren wielded her pen on behalf of the republic and, in a limited sense, of women; one reviewer damned her *History of the American Revolution* as "the product of a mind that had not yet yielded to the assertion that all political attentions lay outside of the road of female life." But she did not "soldier" explicitly against masculine government.[42]

Perhaps as a consequence of women's relative invisibility at the barricades or in places that were designated "public," male patriots swiftly embedded the terms of the settlement in constitutions, election laws, and other boundary-setting devices. By 1776, all the new states except Vermont had established some kind of property or taxpayer requirement for suffrage; Vermont followed suit in 1792. Equally important, framers in the several states replaced unwritten, relatively fluid "customs of the neighborhood" with male-only suffrage limitations, both statutory and constitutional. To the extent that black-letter law eliminated the possibility of informal grants of privilege from community leaders, women lost ground. Between 1776 and 1784, when New Hampshire revised its original constitution, every new state but New Jersey ruled out the possibility of women's political participation in constitutional texts. Virginia and Delaware carried colonial election laws into republican law codes; Virginia then constitutionalized its traditional male electorate. Georgia, New York, and New Hampshire enfranchised "male inhabitants" who met property or taxpayer requirements. Maryland, North Carolina, Pennsylvania, and Vermont extended ballots to freemen; and between 1776 and 1778, South Carolina abandoned an electorate composed of "persons having property" in favor of one that included "every free white man" possessed of the requisite property.[43]

Extraordinarily, lawmakers in New Jersey allowed women to vote; the state constitution read "all inhabitants," and a new election statute made provision for "he or she." More than a few women took advantage of this opportunity. But the state's experiment barely survived the eighteenth century. Critics such as "Friend to the Ladies," a correspondent to the *True American* in 1802, called women "timid and pliant, unskilled in politics, unacquainted with all the real merits of the several candidates," and susceptible to male influence. This "friend" complained about "whole wagon loads" of women at the polls, supposedly herded up like cattle; he envisioned not five or six independent voters per household and a division of sovereignty, but the traditional sovereign "head" voting five or six times, since women voters were "almost always placed under the dependence or care of a father, uncle or brother" and so "will of course be directed or persuaded by them." Another offended New Jerseyite called woman suffrage a "mockery." It was "evident" that women generally were "neither, by nature, nor habit, nor education, nor by their necessary condition in society, fitted to perform this duty with credit to themselves, or advantage to the public." In 1807, shortly after opponents of woman suffrage blamed "a throng of women" allegedly "herded to the polls" for defeating Federalist candidate William Crane, the assembly reestablished a male electorate. The "peaceful scene/ Of government in petticoats," as a Jersey wag put it, would not appear again for over a century.[44]

LOCKE, FILMER, AND THE SEXUAL CONTRACT

Political philosophers have come to see that the "he" and "him" of framing documents spoke literally to men, not to a generic humankind; women entered the compact as wives or proto-wives, subordinated to men (according to John Locke and others) by reason of their fragility and to ensure administrative clarity. During the War for Independence, in other words, sovereign authority passed not from a father-king to all children, but from a father to his sons.

Perhaps ironically, Locke's influential *Second Treatise of Government*—written before the Glorious Revolution in opposition to absolute monarchy—lent support to the American decision to transplant indivisible male family "heads" onto American soil. The *Second Treatise* conveyed several messages to readers, only one of which aided the cause of women.[45] First, and most helpful, Locke condemned monarchical conceptions of what he called "Paternal Power," which lodged authority over children "wholly in the *Father*, as if the *Mother* had no share in it." According to Locke, wives had "equal Title" to the labor of household dependents; even Genesis, from which monarchists derived "their Government of a single Person only," vested authority in "two Persons joyntly." He argued, too, that marriage was not a sacred, indissoluble arrangement but, rather, was a "voluntary Compact between Man and Woman" depending for its validity and continuance on the fact of an ongoing "Communion of Interest." Here, we see something of Lockean liberalism's potential power to remake the marital relation. The process of "reaching [to-ward] their common Interest and Property," said Locke, "leaves the Wife in the full and free possession of what by Contract is her peculiar Right, and gives the Husband no more power over her Life, than she has over his. The *Power of the Husband being* so far from that of an absolute Monarch, that the *Wife* has, in many cases, a Liberty to *Separate* from him; where natural Right, or their Contract allows it . . . ; and the Children upon such Separation fall to the Father or Mother's Lot, as such Contract does determine."

At the same time, however, the *Second Treatise* deftly shifted the primary allegiance of adults from familial "kings," limited by custom and interpersonal obligations, to political governments, limited by an impersonal, mechanical rule of law. Although fathers and mothers governed the household jointly, the family's role in *political* society (Locke called the family a "conjugal society") was potentially less consequential than in traditional, monarchical regimes. For theorists like John Filmer (the author of *Patriarcha* and others defenses of monarchism), the "little commonwealth" represented the broader realm in microcosm; for contract theorists like Locke, the family stood apart from the state, in many respects reduced to a legal fiction (the marital contract), apparently designed, to use Locke's unsentimental phrase, to facilitate "its chief end, procreation," and the sustenance and education of offspring. To be sure, the fiction carried with it the presumption of equality among contracting parties: parents no longer possessed "an Authority to make Laws and dispose as they please, of . . . lives and Liberties." It was "one thing," said Locke, to "owe honour, respect, gratitude, and assistance," and quite another to exact "absolute obedience and submission," as only the state could do under well-specified circumstances. The "temporary Government" of offspring, moreover, ended when the children came of age. But within the marital estate, the political power of *both* parents was diminished in the bargain: Neither parent acted as a direct agent of government, as husbands and well-born wives had done in the past; and "Law" stood apart from the family, to be hammered out by legislators in the public realm. Parents and children were "Subjects of the same Law together, without any Dominion left in the Father [or Mother] over the Life, Liberty, or Estate" of children, "whether . . . in the State and under the Law of Nature, or under the positive Laws of an Establish'd Government."

Having cut the family loose from its ongoing conversation with political government, Locke effectively marooned women in a private domestic space organized around reproduction, rather than the production of wealth. And even as he hammered home the wife's power to withdraw from an unsuitable union or demand equal rights to the custody of children at divorce, Locke gave the final determination within families to men, if only to ensure administrative clarity. Although parents had "but one common Concern, yet having different understandings," wrote Locke, they "unavoidably sometimes have different wills too." Because it was "necessary" that the "last Determination, i.e., the Rule, should be placed somewhere, it naturally falls to the Man's share, as the abler and the stronger." If these arbiters were no longer "little kings" at home, neither were wives cosovereigns or lawgivers. Rather, married women presided over separate, apolitical domains in a condition of relative freedom from abuse, and male heads "laid down the law."

Locke's subordination of women within an apolitical family, combined with the formalization of a masculine polity, hurt all women, at least until they could mobilize natural rights theory in self-defense. As Mary Beth Norton sees it, Locke's synthesis of English custom and the classical distinction between family and state mostly demolished women's ability to observe affairs of state at close range—that is, *within the household*— as aristocratic women had long done, since lords of every rank were part of the king's political "family." Nor could women benefit from the ancien régime's sense of masterly obligation to subordinates.[46]

The writer Mary Astell—one of a growing number of English women who were deeply suspicious of Locke's motives—disputed his treatment of women, zeroing in on the problem of unreconstructed monarchism within family government. "If the Authority of the Husbands so far as it extends," she wrote in 1706, "is sacred and inalienable, why not of the Prince? The Domestic Sovereign is without Dispute Elected, and the Stipulations and Contract are mutual. . . . [I]s it not then partial in Men to the last degree, to contend for, and practise that Arbitrary Dominion in the Families, which they abhor and exclaim against in the State?"[47]

The monarchical alternative, it must be said, was no bed of roses. For traditionalists like Filmer, the "natural" subjection of women and other dependents to men was a basic tenet; thus, many scholars think that women's best hope—at least into very modern times— lay with natural rights theory and the concept of possessive individualism, by which women could argue their way out of a position in which their identity depended upon relationships with men. Filmer reminded natural-law theorists of God's ordination of Adam "to rule over his wife," whose "desires were to be subject to his: and as hers, so all theirs that should come of her." This "original grant of government" was "the fountain of all power, placed in the father of all mankind"; surely, the "law for obedience to government" commanded subjects to "'honour thy father.'"[48]

The Tory law professor William Blackstone's characterization of female indenture ensured the persistence of medieval political thought in American courtrooms and (as part of republican domestic ideology) within domestic governments. Published during the Stamp Act crisis, Blackstone's *Commentaries* explored varieties of subjection, all analogous to the relation of king and subject (in order of presentation, "master and servant," "husband and wife," "parent and child," "guardian and ward"). These pairings were hardly novel; even Locke called many of them "natural" (in the *Second Treatise*, he listed a "Father over his Children, a Master over his Servant, a Husband over his Wife, and a Lord over his Slave"). Nor did Blackstone's synopsis accurately depict English law practice, as his critics noted repeatedly, in part because he distrusted the rules of equity. But in American law offices, few texts commanded more respect. "By marriage," Blackstone wrote in a much-plagiarized passage, "The husband and wife are one person in law: that is, the very being or legal existence of the woman is suspended during the marriage, or at least is incorporated and consolidated into that of the husband:"

> under whose wing, protection, and *cover*, she performs every thing; and is therefore called in our law-french a *feme-covert*; is said to be *covert-baron*, or under the protection and influence of her husband, her *baron* or lord; . . . Upon this principle, of an union of person in husband and wife, depend almost all the legal rights, duties and disabilities, that either of them acquire by the marriage. . . . [A] man cannot grant any thing to his wife, or enter into covenant . . . with her, for the grant would be to suppose her separate existence; and to covenant with her, would be only to covenant with himself.

Like John Winthrop, Blackstone insisted that a wife realized freedom through subjection and that even her "disabilities" were "for the most part intended for her protection and benefit. So great a favourite is the female sex of the laws of England."[49]

By embracing Blackstone's jurisprudence and Locke's vision of the social compact, Americans entrusted the soul of the republic to women and enhanced wifely authority within conjugal society while erecting new barriers to the sex's political freedom. On the one hand, a Lockean taste for natural law and the social equality of householders, when combined with sensitivity to connections between productive labor and civil rights, gave women a leg to stand on in relations with tyrannical men. On the other hand, Locke's hard-and-fast line between home and "the public" and the general degradation of family governments compared to political governments at least temporarily undercut women's ability to contend for a place in the *polity*. On this score, the American revolutionary fascination with Whig republicanism was perhaps fortunate. Lockean contractualism came to be leavened with doses of a political language tied closely to community- and family-centered visions of the polity. As a result, women's expressions of patriotism *through* homework at least temporarily destabilized the wall that had existed since midcentury between "public" and "private" life. And by virtue of their role as social conscience and ideological archive, women helped Americans to remember alternative societies in which queens governed realms and cottagers negotiated contracts to knit stockings or churn butter.

IMPLEMENTATION AND CONSOLIDATION

In keeping with the terms of the revolutionary settlement, written constitutions and law codes drew women under the political umbrella, not as full-fledged members of the constituent power, but essentially as wards of men. Nor did revolution alter women's economic condition. The proportion of wealth owned by American women remained more or less the same—from 1 percent to 11 percent of the total, depending on the location—throughout the era, and if Marylynn Salmon is correct, the revolutionary experience had virtually no effect on the property or contractual rights formally conceded to belong to women. When property- or economy-related law changed, it seems to have done so in response to alterations in the marketplace. In Pennsylvania, for instance, creditors' rights probably overtook the rights of married women and widows by the 1790s, but doctrinal changes had little to do with revolution. Hostility to courts of chancery mounted in the late eighteenth century, depriving women in every jurisdiction except South Carolina of a forum in which they might argue their right to keep their wages from irresponsible husbands or to insist on the validity of contracts struck between marriage partners. This development, like so many others, had less to do with revolution than with the need to ensure contract performance, protect creditors, and eliminate "unscientific" or antidevelopmental rules of law practice.

Three court decisions a few years after Jefferson's presidential victory illustrate the states' judicial reception of traditional constructions of the woman-citizen. In 1804, a Connecticut judge sitting as a chancellor in the case of *Dibble v. Hutton* refused to recognize as lawful an unwritten agreement concluded between Mary and Samuel Hutton during their marriage. Samuel had cajoled Mary into selling fifty-five acres of land on which they had long lived as tenants in common and in which she claimed a one-fourth interest by promising her "one-fourth part of the sum . . . for her separate use." In 1798, they jointly conveyed the tract to two men, who gave notes to Samuel for £192 10s. Samuel handed over a quarter of the notes to Mary for her own use; she stashed the money in a drawer. Meanwhile, he made a will giving her only the widow's "third" of *land*, apparently unaware of the fact that Connecticut, Pennsylvania, and South Carolina had adopted a new English rule allowing widows a third of real and personal property. When Samuel died in September 1799, Mary lodged her claim for the cache of notes with her husband's executor, Nehemiah Dibble, reminding him that she had not received a third of Samuel's personal property; that the notes represented payment for lands belonging to her; and that while Samuel's estate exceeded $20,000 after debt settlement, she was "dependent upon her friends for support." Dibble demanded the notes; she complied. The lower court and then the Supreme Court of Errors faced a disarmingly simple question: Was "a contract, by husband and wife, made during the coverture, and to be performed during coverture, . . . a legal, valid contract?"[50]

By Blackstone's rule, the answer was no: A man could not "grant any thing to his wife, or enter into covenant with her: for the grant would be to suppose her separate existence; and to covenant with her, would be only to covenant with himself." But the existence of separate rules of equity in Anglo-American practice muddied the case. Mary Hutton's attorneys contended vigorously and from sound authority for her right to separate property—a doctrine "too clear to be denied, or even doubted." Dibble's counsel thought it would be "impolitic" to introduce novel marital doctrines in America; the other side insisted that the cat was already out of the bag. "Admit the wife's right to property," said Hutton's lawyer, "and she will require for it the same protection, that she now has for her person; and no greater inconvenience will result from her going to law upon one subject, than upon the other." Here, doctrinal purity *departed from* English practice, since Londoners allowed separate estates. Why *not* "adopt the English law . . . ? Experience is our best guide," Hutton's lawyer added, "and more evils have arisen by departing from the English rules, . . . than have ever resulted from adopting them."[51]

Dibble's attorney, by contrast, urged judges to hold the line against unscientific departures from strict legal rules by courts of chancery, thus shoehorning *Dibble* into a debate within the scholarly community about undesirable competition between law and equity. The Supreme Court of Errors in *Adams v. Kellogg* (1788) had allowed a married woman to convey land inherited from a former husband to her present spouse. Yet counsel insisted that because chancery proceedings could never lead to a result impermissible at law, Hutton's claim must fall. He then focused—in a case that had nothing to do with divorce—on the perils of wifely independence: "In this state, but one divorce *a mensa et thoro* [from bed and board] has been granted."

> We happily have never heard of forming certain exceptions to the marriage contract, when framed, that the wife need not lose her independence; nor of relations giving property to married women, to their separate use. But the idea has here been, that lines of separation were not to be drawn between husband and wife; and the generosity of our females has not allowed them to wish to keep their property from those, to whom they have not refused their persons. Our customs . . . do not require the introduction of these new principles.[52]

The court agreed: Family governments must be preserved. New Englanders had not adopted the "manners, different ranks, and general state of society in England" that gave rise to equity; instead, they had received "principles of the common law . . . unqualified by . . . chancery." The "plain and simple" rule governing marital compacts won the day, even though the English and many colonists had abandoned it. The court aped Blackstone: "By the common law, the husband and wife are considered as one person in law. . . . As a consequence . . . the . . . husband and wife cannot contract with each other, nor the husband make a grant or gift to the wife, nor the wife have personal estate, to her sole and separate use. If these principles are to be received and applied . . . to this claim, they, at once, determine all the questions, that arise in considering the case." Complex British rules "ought not to be engrafted into our chancery system; but those of the common law remain unimpaired." In effect, Samuel's executor had lawfully relieved Mary of part of her legacy.[53]

Perhaps to eliminate inconsistency, the same court reversed its *Adams* decision in *Fitch v. Brainerd* (1805): No longer could a wife make a grant of property unless the assembly passed a private bill allowing her the privilege. Although "the common law of England hath not, *as such*, nor ever had, any force here," the court explained, it now was necessary, in order to avoid "arbitrary decisions, and for the sake of *rules . . .* to make that law our own."[54] Even after Connecticut's adoption of generous legislation in 1809 on women's right to will land and despite pressure exerted by Connecticut lawyers schooled in the rules of equity, the Supreme Court of Errors doggedly refused to endorse married women's right to make wills or actively use separate property well into the age of Jackson.

Also in 1805, a state appellate decision in *James Martin v. The Commonwealth of Massachusetts* further clarified the extent to which women had not benefited from the rebellion against English tyranny. Even more clearly than in the Connecticut cases, the *Martin* court considered and rejected the possibility of altering women's political and constitutional status. Anna Martin had followed her Loyalist husband, William, from Boston to England in 1776. Acting under a wartime confiscation law, a court of common pleas in 1781 declared both of them "absentees" who had "freely renounced all civil and political relation" to the United States. Massachusetts confiscated their lands; both Martins lost the ability to transmit real estate to their heirs.

In 1801, after Anna and William had died, their 48-year-old son James appealed the inferior court ruling just before the twenty-year statute of limitation ran out, asking the Supreme Judicial Court to recognize his right to inherit, not from both of his parents, but from his *mother*. William, after all, held the land for "his natural life" only; Anna had a dower portion that passed unimpeded to her heirs. The heart of the matter was this: Did *femes-covert* fall within the confiscation statute? The act referred to "every *inhabitant* and *member* of the state": Were not married women part of political society? If wives could freely choose to remain loyal to the Crown and if Anna Martin chose to leave Boston, then James had no claim to inherit from her. "Absentees" relinquished all power to pass title to children. But if only men could freely choose allegiance to Britain and women *lost* their national identity automatically when their husbands so chose, then Anna had not "freely renounced" her ties to the republic, and James could inherit her land, which the state had confiscated unlawfully.

Massachusetts solicitor-general Daniel Davis mounted powerful arguments in favor of Anna's volition. Certainly, she had been both a person and an inhabitant; the "real question" was "whether a *feme-covert* is capable of committing the offences, or any one of the offences, specified in the statute." If a wife could commit them and Anna could be said to have done so, the judgment should stand. Attorney General James Sullivan also defended the original judgment against James's attempt to unsettle it; in his view, it mattered not a whit that the "words" of the law were "in the masculine gender." Would anyone seriously argue that because "constitutions use the terms 'he' and 'him,' they do not extend to women?" By that measure, women would possess "no rights, no privileges." Did James think that his mother's rights hinged on the inclusion of "words in the feminine gender?" "Who are members of the body politic?" asked Sullivan. "[A]re not all the *citizens*, members? infants, idiots, insane, or whatever may be their *relative* situations in society? Cannot a *feme-covert* levy war and conspire to levy war? She certainly can commit treason; and if so, there is no one act mentioned in the statute which she is not capable of performing." If Anna's right to a separate identity were to be "scanned by the strict rules of the common law," he added, "we shall feel the consequences to our sorrow."

Nevertheless, Massachusetts' highest court reversed the lower court. In the process, it granted James his inheritance, affirmed married women's ongoing subjection to their husbands, and denied women the primary association with the state supposedly enjoyed by members of the constituent power. The English, it should be noted, held that citizenship, once conferred, could not ordinarily be lost; revolutionaries were scuttling settled practice. Women's obligations still lay first with domestic governors; their relationship to political government would be indirect and mediated, rather than direct and unmediated. In argument, James's attorneys had insisted repeatedly that when women were not named in legal texts, they were absent: Women were "members" of the polity, but not precisely "inhabitants," as the statute put it. "Had the legislature intended to include . . . wives, they certainly would have been mentioned." The lawyers had no doubt that the statute excluded "persons who have, by law, no wills of their own" in favor of "persons who have *freely* renounced their relation to the state."

> Infants, insane, *femes-covert*, all of whom the law considers as having no will, cannot act *freely*. Can they freely renounce? The statute meant such, and such only, as could. Is the state entitled to the *personal* services of a *feme-covert* to defend it in war? Can she render any? What aid and comfort can she give to an invading enemy? Has she the control of property? Is she ever required to take the oath of allegiance?

Even Anna's dower was "merely the donation of the state, giving to her a part of that which was absolutely its own."

In a series of seriatim opinions, the court agreed. The most influential opinion, written by Judge Theodore Sedgwick, refused to "suppose" a wife present in a text unless she was named. "Can we believe," wrote Sedgwick, "that a wife, for so respecting the understanding of her husband as to submit her own opinions to his, . . . should lose her own property, and forfeit the inheritance of her children? . . . Because she did not, in violation of her marriage vows, rebel against the will of her husband?" Surely not. "A wife who left the country in the company of her husband did not *withdraw* herself; but was . . . withdrawn by him. She did not deprive the government of the benefit of her personal services; she had none to render; none were exacted of her." In Judge Simeon Strong's view, wives could not "act" in any sense comprehended by the statute. "The law considers a *feme-covert* as having no will"; Anna remained "under the direction and control of her husband," obliged to "obey his commands." Said Chief Justice Francis Dana, wives had "no will" and so "could not incur the forfeiture"; no rational assembly would "oblige them either to lose their property or to be guilty of a breach of the duty, which . . . they owed to their husbands."[55]

A few years later, in the wake of New Jersey's decision to restrict the suffrage to male "inhabitants," a similar dispute over the confiscation of a widow's land reached the U.S. Supreme Court, where the justices turned back the appeal while signaling some amount of disapproval of a separate legal personality for married women. In *Kempe's Lessee v. Kennedy* (1809), a "tenant" (the term in this case denoted a legal fiction) of Grace Kempe, the widow of John Tabor Kempe, who had been the British Crown's last attorney general in New York City before the Revolution, disputed the confiscation and sale of land in New Jersey secured to her by premarital agreement. With her husband, Grace had moved to Great Britain just before the colonies' official declaration of independence and continued to live there after his death; in accordance with New Jersey's confiscation statute, the Court of Common Pleas for Hunterdon County, had judged Grace an "inhabitant" and sequestered her land. After a ruling by the County Court of Sussex County, the state's agent sold her land to a man named Kennedy. Some time later, Kempe's agent commenced an action of ejectment in the Circuit Court for the District of New Jersey, which affirmed the legality of the confiscation and, with it, Kennedy's title.

Together with another postrevolutionary case, *Kempe* affirmed federal judicial acquiescence in continued state control over revolutionary treason trials, as well as litigants' need to exhaust state remedies before approaching federal courts. But, for our purposes, its importance lies in arguments spread over the Supreme Court record about Grace Kempe's legal personality, and in Chief Justice John Marshall's apparent dissatisfaction with the confiscation order's imputation of autonomy. Citing the earlier Massachusetts decision in *Martin* as authority, the well-known Richard Stockton argued against Kempe's status as an "inhabitant" and in favor of her continuing title to the land; the authors of a standard textbook term his arguments "a classic statement of the disabilities of a woman under coverture."[56] A wife, said Stockton, could not be "properly called . . . an inhabitant of a state: the husband is the inhabitant." New Jersey had just concluded a controversial experiment with limited female suffrage; Stockton and others no doubt hoped to keep the lid on. "By the constitution of New Jersey," he said, "all inhabitants are entitled to vote; but it has never been supposed that a *feme covert* was a legal voter. Single woman have been allowed to vote, because the law supposes them to have wills of their own." Stockton argued, too, that the statute, which referred explicitly to "he" and "she" as potential traitors, must refer only to "single women." As in *Martin*, attorneys insisted that Kennedy's (and New Jersey's) interpretation of the confiscation statute to include Grace Kempe was grotesque and "unnatural"; no legislature could be "presumed to have intended to include persons in her situation; for that would have been cruel." Rational laws did not "legislate against the most important duties of social and domestic life, to cut asunder the bands of matrimonial union, to compel a wife to abandon her husband or forfeit her estate." Because Kempe lacked the "capacity voluntarily to commit the offense," she could not have been "an object of the law" and thus retained title to her property.

In the end, the court affirmed the confiscation and, by implication, Kempe's separate identity and inhabitant status. Yet the U.S. Supreme Court, with John Marshall at the helm, termed the Common Pleas decision "erroneous," although it mysteriously stopped short of saying why. Marshall simply upheld the right of the inferior court to sit on the case and refused to say more until the parties had exhausted state remedies. The result was to quiet controversy about the legality of confiscation while signaling doubts about the assumption of wifely autonomy on which it depended. We may never know why Marshall perceived "error" or whether, with procedural difficulties swept away, he might have brought *Kempe* into line with *Martin*; nothing like the *Kempe* appeal came before the Court until *Shanks v. DuPont* in 1830.[57]

For the Daughters of Liberty, everything and nothing had changed. On the one hand, American men and women had renounced kingship, fought a bloody civil war on and behind the lines, established a federated republic, and enshrined a popular sovereign in written constitutions. On the other hand, neither the Great Awakening nor the Revolution had restored much of the ground lost by many white middle-class women over the course of the eighteenth century, much less secured additional freedom for them. The republican mother, although venerated and charged with important work, could not yet claim cosovereignty and the right to make law alongside men, whether at home or in civil society. Instead, distinguished jurists seemed to be embracing a vision of domestic government that was archaic even for English tastes, and refused to establish unmediated relationships between all members of the constituent power and the governments they had struggled to create.

Scholars disagree as to when and where James Madison and other Federalists managed to solve the perennial problem in English constitutional theory of the indissoluble sovereign "Head." But few doubt that they *did* solve it before the end of the 1780s. In British practice, the King-in-Parliament embodied the sovereign power—a legitimating entity that theoretically could neither be removed from government nor divided without smashing it to pieces. Sovereignty could be relocated, but in the move from one place to another, it had to remain whole. It was this abstract difficulty, joined by several others, that prevented English acquiescence in the claims of colonial assemblies not just of remedial powers, but of a separate sovereign power potentially competing with that of the King-in-Parliament. By lifting sovereignty *out* of government and vesting it in the people, Madisonians made it possible, in John Murrin's words, for a radically decentralized sovereign ("the people") to "delegate some powers to one level of government, others to another level, and to insist that these powers were as full and ample as any that a just government could possess." Murrin views this move as the single "most important" innovation in American constitutional history.[58]

Yet, in the process, the framing generation reconstructed only *political* government, in no small part because Locke allowed them to distinguish clearly between "conjugal society" and the polity. Within the latter sphere, Americans managed to divide sovereignty without annihilating it, but they did not undertake a parallel decentralization of domestic governments—for instance, by declaring all adults corulers in the household or by giving over sovereign authority within families to political government (as continental theorists managed to do) for redistribution among parental cosovereigns. Instead, in postrevolutionary explorations of the impact of republicanism on gender relations, judges held that *barons* still governed the women, children, and bonded laborers in their households. Women were seen, however paradoxically, as members of the constituent power represented for most purposes by men. Moreover, despite the "private" and "public" distinction increasingly apparent in social theory, political governments continued to delegate important governing responsibilities to household heads. The bright line between the family and the state, in other words, did not put family governors out of a job; rather, it assumed their ongoing presence and increasingly put their families beyond the state's line of vision.

This retreat from the implications of republican doctrine seems to have retarded woman's progress for decades, but the dike could not withstand revolutionary floodwaters indefinitely. As Linda Kerber points out, even as social conservatives resisted change, the arguments for sovereign coequality sketched in *Martin* affirmed "the authenticity of the republican break with the past, pointed the way to a reconstruction of the relationship of women to real property, and explicitly claimed for women the responsibility of assuming the obligations of citizenship." While the path was "too rocky" for the first generation's taste, it had been blazed, and a number of patriots decided to follow it—some during the earliest years of revolution, as when the brilliant African American poet Phillis Wheatley denounced mastership in its various guises. In every person, wrote Wheatley just as Great Britian imposed the Intolerable Acts, God had "implanted a Principle, which we call Love of Freedom; it is impatient of Oppression . . . . I will assert, that the Principle lives in us."[59]

Judith Sargent Murray—perhaps the first widely read American women's rights theorist—furnished a particularly riveting example of the postrevolutionary rebel. Murray saw clearly that white men had undertaken the war against Britain largely for the benefit of sons and grandsons. Armed with the language of republican constitutionalism, she took dead aim and fired. "Yes, ye lordly, ye haughty sex," she wrote in a pungent 1790 essay, "our souls are by nature *equal* to yours; the same breath of God animates, enlivens, and invigorates us." Surely as many women as men "by *mere force of natural powers* have merited the crown of applause." Why, then, did the Sons of Liberty tolerate among the Daughters of Liberty "no other ideas, than those which are suggested by the mechanism of a pudding, or the sewing of the seams of a garment?"[60]

Part Two

"Talk Is the Fountain-Head of All Things"
Republican Speech Communities and Coequality

"A woman is nobody. A wife is everything."

—PHILADELPHIA *Public Ledger and Daily Transcript* (1848)[1]

"They had risen up from their church pews, their school-teacher benches, their parlor chairs, and they were standing erect on their own feet, avowedly out to secure their share of that liberty which was being so loudly cried as the American heritage. They had tried to speak for temperance, and found they first had to speak for a woman's right to open her mouth in public. They had tried to speak for the right of slaves to be free, and found that they had first to establish their own right to unmolested freedom of appearance on a public platform at an abolitionist meeting.

So by force of public pressure they came to the boiling point. If they were going to do effective work in school teacher assemblages, in churches, in sick rooms, for temperance, or for abolition of slavery, they must somehow get out from under these hampering insistences that their part in the world was to stay home and say nothing."

—MILDRED ADAMS for the National Woman Suffrage Association (1940)[2]

Agitation on behalf of women emerged in the wake of the American Revolution, with a rising tide of resistance to domestic "tyranny" and inequality. The Daughters of Liberty supposedly safeguarded revolutionary republicanism from loss or contamination; they were bound to notice a gap between theory and practice in their own lives. By the 1840s, a loosely knit women's rights movement appeared, determined to renovate marriage and remake the woman-citizen so that Americans might realize what Elizabeth Cady Stanton called a "GENUINE republic."[3]

The so-called first wave of modern American feminism was both a cause and product of a postrevolutionary remapping of culture to accommodate new ways of thinking about social relations, the marketplace, and political authority. By 1860, the United States had tripled in size; its economic center of gravity steadily shifted westward to Cincinnati and other bustling river towns. Northern European immigrants surged into eastern cities in response to reports of inexpensive farmland and relatively high wages. Entrepreneurs built canals and railroads at fever pitch. Settlers pressed through mountain gaps, routing native people and carrying both King Cotton and slavery beyond the Appalachians. Calls for universal manhood suffrage captured the public imagination as few things had ever done; stump speeches and campaign buttons proliferated.

As capitalism transformed American culture and politics, domestic life vanished ever more completely from public view. In the labor-scarce West, where settlers could ill afford to consign household "dependents" to drawing rooms, women often flexed muscles alongside men. But in better-developed states, white middle-class Americans increasingly committed surplus wealth to leisure and to the support of "workless" (that is, unpaid) wives and children. By midcentury, as the "culture of sentiment" swept the Atlantic basin, it was possible for unhappy couples to argue plausibly that emotional tyranny ("mental cruelty") ought to be grounds for divorce. The number of marital dissolutions increased, particularly in the late nineteenth century. Judicial divorce proceedings steadily replaced traditional legislative divorces, and women filed for divorce more often than in earlier decades. Family size shrank dramatically, from about 7 children per fertile woman in 1800, to 5.42 in 1850 to about 3.5 by the century's end. Although the modern family antedated industrialization, the two developments were mutually reinforcing: As Carl Degler explains, a domestic refuge can be useful in a "personally threatening industrial society," making modernization "endurable" for laboring classes and ensuring a steady supply of worker-citizens.[4]

These changes in the texture of society coincided with the Second Great Awakening, a fifty-year wave of revivalism no less unsettling than its colonial antecedent. As Protestants recast their spiritual lives, they also remade American culture to reflect a sense of physical and spiritual "boundlessness," to borrow John Higham's term.[5] If Jacksonian democracy symbolized equality and fair dealing among white men, "associationism" called to mind civic regeneration and the gathering of moral beings into fellowships, both small scale and continental. Reformers celebrated the emergence of new classes seeking liberation from various "masters," including corn whiskey. Preachers and visionaries spoke unblushingly about re-creating primitive Christianity on the Great Plains; gathering all Judaism onto Grand Island in upstate New York; and teaching every man, woman, and child in America to read Bibles and constitutions.

As during the late colonial awakening, spiritual ferment destabilized gender roles. Ann Douglas notes that the "feminization" of culture permitted women to be "aggressive, even angry, in the name of various holy causes" and men to be "nurturing" within parishes or families. Newly fluent in the language of benevolence, women began to invade civic spaces; male associators criticized patriarchal marriages and struck up affectionate friendships with other men. As Donald Yacovone explains, these men spoke a new "language of fraternal love," rejected "rigid definitions of gender," and set about remaking the republic to comport with God's conception of an ideal polity.[6]

Well past midcentury, the "proliferation of democratic publics" (in Mary Ryan's words) offset both the atomizing effects of rapid growth and the homogenization that accompanied nation building.[7] Virtually any group with shared objectives could declare itself a "public" and leap into the fray. Many of these new communities boasted large female memberships, and as had been the case during late colonial revivals, women inevitably rose to speak or preach. When excluded or "shouted down," they fought back— sometimes through sex-specific break-away groups within such mainstream reform movements as temperance and abolitionism, and sometimes through an emerging woman's movement and its quasi-revivalist conventions (which one scholar calls "the heart of the movement").[8] As in the 1750s, these communities came to be bounded by little more than fellowship and a shared language of emancipation; within them, women hoped to suspend the ways of the world long enough to call into being a new reality through structured conversation.

In the end, women's rights reformers fell short of achieving their goals. To be sure, thousands of activists publically articulated fears, aspirations, and opinions for the first time in their lives. By the mid-1850s, a distinctive women's rights discourse emerged, and politicians began to heed pleas for expanded economic freedom within marriage. Yet most Americans dismissed calls for a division of household sovereignty on the ground that a few "unsexed" women spoke only for themselves. Thus, women's rights activists usually found themselves relegated to "separate-but-equal" speaking platforms and the back pages of newspapers. To make matters worse, with the advent of the Civil War, divisions appeared within the movement. As citizens of speech communities, women often recommended discussion as an avenue to reconciliation. But when Republicans decided not to extend new civil rights laws and constitutional amendments to women, many activists concluded that their former allies had closed ranks against them. By 1869, disagreements about how to respond to an apparent erosion of women's constitutional standing tore the movement apart. At the same time, with the so-called New Departure, law-minded activists began to shift gears away from the notion of personal and civic regeneration through speech toward the pursuit of sex-neutral citizenship and direct, unmediated relationships between citizens and their governments.

The New Departure mostly failed. Lawmakers insisted that a class defined by physical traits (woman) could not be cracked apart to yield sex-neutral individuals (women), and common law judges regularly intervened to prop up household heads or to shepherd women into relations of dependence with the state. Moreover, the movement had yielded decisively—as had Atlantic civilization in general—to legalization and secularization. Increasingly, the language of law supplanted the movement's discourse, particularly among liberals interested in helping female citizens achieve direct relationships with political governments. Women settled *into* the world, absorbing the intellectual systems and prejudices of the broader society in a crusade for rights; even "first-wave" evangelicals, whose moral and communitarian interests ultimately found expression in social purification groups like the Woman's Christian Temperance Union, focused increasingly on suffrage as an avenue to moral reform. Convention resolutions bristled with talk about legal remedies for injustice. The idea of women's "voices" often came to be synonymous with relatively decorous utterances at the polls. With other Americans, women moved away from republican speech communities (some would call them "the public forum") comprised of middle- and upper-class citizen-reformers toward a mass electoral democracy and from actual to metaphoric political speech; women's electoral voices would merge with men's, and face-to-face debate would largely cease. Elizabeth Oakes Smith's expression of rage when an 1853 Massachusetts constitutional convention tabled a suffrage petition as "inexpedient" might as easily have been written in 1890: "The believers in the rights of woman . . . are entirely in the minority."

> The majority believe that their wives and mothers are household chattels . . . expressly created for no other purposes than . . . maternity . . . [or] passion. . . . [W]omen are sewers on of buttons; darners of stockings; makers of puddings; appendages to wash days, bakings, and brewings; echoes and adjectives to men for ever and ever. . . . *The idea of a true, noble womanhood is yet to be created.* It does not live in the public mind.[9]

Chapter 3

Law, Gender, and Domestic Culture

In an 1842 hearing before a panel of the New York Supreme Court headed by the well-known writer and judge Ezek Cowen, an obscure Englishman named John Barry managed—on his fifth attempt—to secure custody of his young daughter. With a handful of other state decisions, *Barry v. Mercein* contributed to the emergence of the modern "tender-years" (or "tender-age") doctrine in domestic relations law. More important, the *Barry* opinions provide a clear window into many of the tensions that gave rise to first-wave women's rights agitation in the 1840s. As the century advanced, family law came to express three related ideas—that women were by nature domestic and maternal; children were young innocents, rather than "little adults"; and either the male household head or the state had to retain undivided sovereign command within families. On the basis of the first two ideas, judges concluded that because children of "tender years" (or young girls) benefited from female nurturance, women ought to be awarded custody of them. But this small foot in sovereignty's door triggered anxiety. What would happen to paternal government if the sexes stood on the same ground as coheads of families and comembers of the constituent power?

THE CASE OF BARRY V. MERCEIN

In 1835, John Barry married Eliza Anna Mercein of New York City, and the couple parented a son and a daughter. Court records describe the daughter, Mary Mercein Barry, born in about 1837, as "frail" and subject to "attacks of dangerous illness." John and Eliza squabbled from the outset of their marriage. In 1838, after his business failed, John went to Nova Scotia in search of work; when he returned, he proposed "certain measures preparatory to their permanent settlement in Nova Scotia." Eliza told him "she never would consent to go," that he might "force her to go" by abducting their son, but that she would prefer to live in her father's home with both children.[1]

With the help of Eliza's father, Thomas Mercein, the couple signed an agreement amicably resolving their differences. Mary Mercein Barry would live with her mother, and John could visit her as he wished. After the first year, John would relinquish "all his right" to Mary. Meanwhile, their son would live temporarily with his mother, who agreed to hand him over at a later time. In June 1838, John Barry left New York City, only to return four months later, promising to remain for the winter if Eliza would come to Nova Scotia. When she refused, he threatened to take their son at once; she "acknowledged his power of doing so," but warned him that "such a step would seal their fate."

In May 1839, John applied to the recorder of New York City for a writ of habeas corpus—a usual device in custody and desertion cases—to force Thomas and Eliza to cease their "imprisonment" of Mary and deliver her to John. The court found that her mother and grandfather had "not improperly restrained" or imprisoned Mary and saw "no good reason" to remove her from the "care and protection" of her mother. John approached two more courts in search of a writ without success; in April 1840, Judge William Inglis of the Court of Common Pleas upheld the previous decision on the ground that Eliza's care might restore the child's health. Meanwhile, John kidnaped 2-year-old Mary and Eliza snatched her back, protesting that the girl's "nervous system had been very much deranged" by the appearance of a "stranger" bent on "violent abduction." To challenge Inglis's decision, John sought a writ of certiorari from the Supreme Court (*not* the highest state court), which reversed Inglis's dismissal, leaving John free to seek another habeas corpus writ. In reply, Thomas sued out a writ of error in 1840 to the Court for the Correction of Errors, seeking a reversal of the Supreme Court decision and affirmation of Inglis's ruling. The court complied.

As it moved through the system, *Barry v. Mercein* laid bare many of the undercurrents that gave rise to both a women's rights movement and antifeminist opposition. One member of the Court of Errors, Senator Alonzo Paige, thought that the issue was not custody per se but men's unitary authority as owners of the labor of household dependents, proprietors of marriage beds, and (much as English monarchs were sworn to preserve the realm) trustees of marital estates. Was a husband analogous to a king? Or was he a partner in the family enterprise? Leaning on Continental authorities, Paige argued (against Anglo-American practice) that the father had "no paramount right to the custody of his child." By the law of nature, the "wife and child are equal to the husband and father"; thus, the family head had "no authority over his wife and children." While primitive chieftains had possessed such power, sovereignty passed in modern nations to *political government*, which delegated administrative power to both parents. Because there was "no inequality between the father and mother," custody rights attached as easily to Eliza as to John.

In 1840–41, John applied for a fourth writ of habeas corpus, which Judge Oakley of the Supreme Court denied. A year later, however, Ezek Cowen's panel rewarded John's efforts. In his opinion, Cowen did not dispute new family law doctrines. With children of "tender years," he wrote, courts rightly intervened to assess whether strict adherence to law served their best interests. As Eliza's counsel had argued, in keeping with "the dictates of nature and humanity," a mother could be "regarded as the guardian, by nature and nurture, of young children, especially to females, and as better calculated than the father to nurse and protect them . . . in the years of infancy." In the abstract, Cowen saw nothing wrong with a decision to award custody of a toddler on the basis of her sex, her frailty, and her mother's supposedly innate maternalism.

Why, then, did Cowen summarily reject Paige's arguments and award custody to John? Against both law and custom, John and Eliza had settled questions of property and custody for themselves. John had agreed to transfer his paternal rights and obligations to Eliza, violating a public trust; neither judges nor marital partners were "at liberty to disregard" the father's "paramount right to the custody." Eliza had deserted John, for which she was "without a shadow of excuse." Nor could she charge John with abuse; she relied on a "highly wrought picture of their family jars, in which . . . there were faults upon both sides; and which . . . do not form a proper subject for judicial inquiry." Cowen thus refused to grant a legal separation after the fact, without which the Barrys' contract was unenforceable.

Cowen heaped special scorn on the Barrys' attempt to transfer inalienable rights willy-nilly from father to mother. Even though judges sometimes allowed lawfully separated couples to set out financial arrangements in writing, this agreement reached beyond questions of alimony or pin money. "Whatever latitude may have occasionally been allowed for the framing of bargains between husband and wife," Cowen denied that such leniency might be extended here: This contract paved the way for "the doctrine of conventional divorce in its worst form," by which spouses made their own arrangements. "The advocates of that doctrine"—among them, Elizabeth Cady Stanton—"carry out their system to its proportional consequences," helping partners to "evade" obligations and so to "defraud both the law and one another." In the process, the "sentiments of filial reverence are subverted," and the "conjugal relation itself . . . traduced."

Before all else, Cowen sought to preserve unitary male governance: "If the husband has a right to transfer the marriage bed to his wife, I deny that he has, therefore, the right still further to violate his duty by selling his children. . . . These he holds under the duty of a personal trust, inalienable even to another who is *sui juris*"—which a *feme covert* was not. Much as a monarch's sovereignty was indivisible, so the *baron*'s authority had to remain entirely with him. Were division or transfer permitted, the "general allegation that a daughter may be well in the hands of a mother who chooses to leave her husband, would . . . work an entire subversion of his right." Cowen directly confronted the specter of domestic equality. "The claim of the husband," he wrote, "has throughout been allowed to be paramount by everybody except the wife. It has not been denied that he is the legal head of the whole family . . . ; and I have heard it urged from no quarter that he should be brought under subjection to a household democracy. All will agree . . . that such a measure would extend the right of suffrage quite too far. Yet I do not see how this defense can be sustained unless we are prepared to go that length." Although marriage was "a mere civil contract," it could not be repudiated by "a majority of the family. . . . [I]ts obligations should be maintained in all their ancient rigor." At stake was husbandly control within marriage: Because "the prerogatives of the husband as they are announced by the common law" mirrored "the order of nature and providence," Mary would be packed off to Nova Scotia.

John's victory was short lived. The Court of Errors soon restored Mary to Eliza, and though a chancellor later refused Thomas's application to enjoin John from further suits, U.S. Supreme Court justice Joseph Story ended the drama by declaring habeas corpus petitions against private parties to be beyond his court's original jurisdiction.[2] Yet, for a brief moment, Cowen's bench had swept aside an amicable agreement and imposed the law of domestic relations with a vengeance. If John Barry was a man possessed, Cowen was a common law constitutionalist determined to preserve the family and its petit king— the main engines of patriarchal government.

MARRIAGE, THE INDIVISIBLE MALE HEAD, AND THE PUBLIC INTEREST

The lines of division in *Barry v. Mercein* mirrored deep fissures in American society. Citizens disagreed about whether they could afford to refashion the marital relation to comport with republican constitutionalism, whether and how to acknowledge women's membership in the constituent power, and whether to entrust married women with marital estates. On what theoretical ground, they wondered, did unitary male sovereigns preside over republican families? How could Americans square republicanism with the constitutional dependence of women?

The judicial tendency to award custody to mothers was a double-edged sword. Lawyers' advancement of a maternalist stereotype undoubtedly helped free women to retain their children after divorce. Not all women, however, were willing to role-play for the benefit of judges. And custody awards to women usually involved judicial acknowledgment only of a *possessory* right—lodged in mothers at the court's pleasure—rather than *title* (the "natural" or "bare" right), which many judges reserved for men. Reliance on the incidents of sovereignty still furnished a way for courts to preserve elements of medieval constitutionalism and insist on the inalienable character of husbandly authority. Even when granting custody to a woman, a judge could refuse to locate sovereign command in her until a man's title had been extinguished. Because Cowen could not imagine a divided sovereign, he could only surmise that John Barry had in mind transferring the *entire* indivisible right to Eliza. The attributes of sovereignty could reside in one or the other, but not in both at once.

In 1868, Thomas Cooley—a justice of the Michigan Supreme Court and author of the influential *Constitutional Limitations*—said much the same thing. "The father of an infant," he wrote, "being obliged by law to support his child, has a corresponding right to control his actions and employ his services during the continuance of legal infancy. . . . The mother during the father's life has a power of control, subordinate to his," unless he died or went to prison. As late as 1879, a Rhode Island court in *McKim v. McKim* affirmed the tender-years doctrine but reserved *title* for men. To be sure, Anne McKim gained custody of her infant, but, as in *Barry*, the object of the suit was a frail girl. Had the child been a boy of "riper age, in good health," judges would have thought it their "duty under the law to restore him to his father." More important, the court reminded Anne that its decision was "not necessarily definitive" and that she had been granted only possession, not title: Although custody had been "confided to her, the father's *right* had not been forfeited."[3]

Such apprehensions were commonplace. New York lawyer Charles O'Conor, a fierce oppponent in the 1840s of married women's economic empowerment, warned that household democracy was a "new and dangerous principle" tolerated only in degenerate countries. If spouses were "converted" into "mere partners, . . . a most essential injury would result to the endearing relations of married life."[4] The influential treatise-writer Joel Bishop also assumed the necessity of female subordination, albeit to better men than in past time. "The husband," he wrote, "is in law the head of the family. This implies a right to control its movements, including what the books speak of as government over the wife." To be sure, patriarchy was "not unlimited, nor at the present day is it precisely what it was in the ruder early periods of our law," but "obedience" still was woman's primary "duty."[5] Others were even less inclined to emancipate women. In denying an 1860 petition for major changes in family law, the chair of a New York legislative committee announced that families embodied the state and that husbands embodied the family: "Government has its miniature as well as its foundation in the homes of our country; and as in governments there must be some recognized head to control and direct"—if not a husband or father, then surely a judge—". . . [and] to act . . . as the embodiment of the persons associated."[6]

For proponents of the liberalization of domestic relations law and the conceptually distinct law of divorce, postrevolutionary America had been an auspicious moment. Before 1805, for instance, Maryland men usually lodged divorce petitions with the assembly; after 1806, women entered the fray, initiating petitions in 3 out of 5 cases. Historian Norma Basch finds that in the wake of a revolution in which Americans had "divorced" a despotic king and formed a new political family, lawmakers viewed divorce "as a wife's legal counterweight to her husband's conjugal authority."[7] While South Carolina retained old Anglican bans on marital exits, providing only for financial maintenance in permanent separations, other states allowed divorce—if only by surrounding old rules with myriad exceptions. They also expanded the grounds to include, in addition to adultery and desertion, extreme cruelty, drunkenness, and mental anguish. But as Cowen grudgingly acknowledged in *Barry v. Mercein*, many courts recognized "articles of agreement" by which a couple might agree to live apart with the man providing necessities; despite Cowen's rejection of the possibility, a husband could then renounce "marital rights to her person." As late as 1889, Justice Granger of the Iowa Supreme Court held as invalid a contract made between an adulterous man and his wife so that they might continue to live together, on the ground that the contract bred "discord."[8] Yet, in cases of total irreconcilability, courts often gave force to "unlawful" pacts. And as Michael Grossberg shows in his study of the *D'Hauteville* custody case, courts could recast legal rules in response to cultural pressure, particularly when domestic spats became public dramas, tried as much in newspapers as in courtrooms.[9]

Legislators, moreover, often sprang to the aid of abused women, most reliably when men failed to meet their obligations. In 1806, for example, Marylanders pronounced the six-year marriage of Catharine and James Dimmett "absolutely . . . null and void." In her petition to the assembly, Catharine claimed that James "lived on terms incompatible with the happiness of the conjugal union." She was "in hourly danger from his violence, as he not only attempted his own life, by cutting his own throat in the most barbarous and shocking manner, but he also threatened repeatedly the life of your petitioner, thereby shewing himself free from every moral restraint, and prepared for the commission of the most desperate and bloody deeds." James was "in one continual state of intoxication, and freely indulges in every species of irregularity." He also neglected economic obligations, leaving the family "entirely dependent" on charity.[10]

Nevertheless, early expressions of interest in remodeling marriage so that female citizens might throw off marital "tyranny" did not survive the Era of Good Feelings. While few Americans doubted that the public was deeply interested in marriage and divorce, they hotly disputed how, whether, and on what ground the state could meddle with family governments. As Norma Basch notes, liberalized domestic relations and divorce law—like the streamlining of law codes in general—facilitated commercial development, the efficient deployment of capital, and the orderly rearing of an educated labor force. Yet extreme liberalization amounted to "an attack on the legal outlines of the patriarchal family,"[11] eroding notions of marital sanctity and male sovereignty. Thus, public officials increasingly fashioned rules that allowed divorce in dire circumstances but continued to put state power behind the conservation of marriage, even if it meant blinking at serial unions, physical abuse, or bigamy. As Bishop argued, "Matrimony is a natural right, which can only be forfeited by some wrongful act. It would appear, therefore, to be incumbent upon the government to permit every person of mature years to be the husband or wife of another, who will perform, substantially, the duties enjoined by the marital relation." In the rush to divorce, the "permanence" of marriage should be remembered, but when unions had failed utterly, states had a "duty" to help the parties "form another alliance." After remarriage, society would enjoy "the fruits of . . . new alliances . . . ," and children would benefit from "matrimonial concord."[12]

Who would regulate marriage and divorce? Virtually no one argued that federal officials should administer family law. The idea certainly would have been anathema to proslavery judges, for whom the concept of "domestic relations" included slavery. Scholars have not yet determined whether pro-slavery fears of the diminution of the household head's constitutional authority to "make law" within his domain directly influenced domestic relations law—that is, how far it pressed judges to defend feudal notions of baronial indivisibility or, as is discussed later, of marriage as primarily a "status." But in *Barber v. Barber* (1858), a Supreme Court appeal from Wisconsin of an alimony suit, pro-slavery jurist James Wayne "disclaim[ed] altogether" any family law jurisdiction in federal courts and seemed more generally to advocate caution in judicial invasions of households. His court, he wrote, would not "assume to regulate the domestic relations of society" and, "with a kind of inquisitorial authority, enter the habitations and even into the . . . nurseries of private families."[13]

Americans therefore looked to the states to answer questions about marriage, divorce, and the extent of husbandly power—notwithstanding the states' inability to prevent bigamy across state lines or to stop men from evading alimony or child support payments simply by moving.[14] *Was* matrimony mostly a private or public institution? Did the sexes "rule" equally at home? In the case of bonded women, these questions were moot. The Southern states refused to recognize slave marriages, and female slaves at law were wholly owned vassals, "compelled to obey" their masters rather than their slave husbands.[15] But among free women, these questions mattered. If marriage was analogous to a civil contract, then legislators could register and affirm divorces, with the parties settling divisions of property for themselves. If, however, interests or rights in the marriage itself vested in the partners or if divorce involved fact finding, punishment, or the alteration of property rights, then a court—which alone offered procedural protections—was the proper forum.

By the 1850s, as antislavery agitation increased and women geared up for a rebellion, legal scholars had begun to recast the marriage contract primarily as a social institution, or "status." In so doing, they de-emphasized its relationship to the law of contract (which, after all, governed market relations), labored to distinguish it from slavery (in which workers also lacked both salaries and legal personalities and heads of households reigned supreme), and underscored its social consequences. In editions of his work published after 1850, Bishop insisted that marriage was mainly "an institution of society"— a "status of the parties, created and controlled by the law." Although marriage affected individuals, Bishop added, it was "treated by the law *as a public interest*, to be moulded, modified, or destroyed by the public command," rather than by private decision. Bishop distinguished between this public entity and the "drapery" surrounding it—that is, the "private rights of the married parties which exist . . . apart from the status and do not depend thereon."[16]

Such a formulation defeated radical attempts to keep the marital relation out of the state's line of vision. When possible, Elizabeth Cady Stanton and a handful of allies wanted to eliminate public involvement in the making and unmaking of marriage. This unsettling view, which moved well beyond early Protestant conceptions of marriage as a civil contract imbued with certain social attributes, formed the nub of Cowen's nightmare about runaway "conventional" divorces and radical contractualism. By constituting women and men as parties to contracts, radicals weakened men's claims to exclusive control of both the marital estate and dependents' labor; neither women nor their labor could be said to *belong* to "masters" if couples could strike up binding agreements as equals. As Amy Dru Stanley puts it, both moderate and radical women's rights activists "pronounced equal contract rights the negation of chattel status" and the foundation on which self-possession might be erected—and their opponents knew it.[17]

The decision to emphasize the "status" part of marriage and to downplay "contract"—which, it should be emphasized, was gradual, relative, and nonconspiratorial—coincided with an extended conversation among legal scholars about the constitutionality of legislative divorce (the usual practice in early America). The controversy not only propelled Americans toward judicial divorce and the notion of marriage as a social institution infused with vested rights and the public interest, but also advanced the career of what historians call "judicial patriarchy" or "state paternalism."[18] The initial question was whether legislative divorces violated the contract clause of the federal constitution, which barred legislative interference with contractual obligations. Although lawyers disagreed about the clause's application to public agreements, few doubted that it proscribed meddling with the rights enshrined in private contracts, of which marriage seemed to be one type. If divorce acts altered or destroyed property rights, moreover, they also might run afoul of constitutional prohibitions against "takings" and ex post facto (after the fact) legislation. Pennsylvanians, for example, regularly "discharged" marital partners "from all the rights and duties" arising under marital contracts, as if "they had never been joined in marriage."[19]

Prominent lawyers expressed concern about the constitutionality of legislative divorces as early as the 1810s. In his concurring opinion in the Supreme Court's 1819 *Dartmouth College v. Woodward* decision (which had nothing to do with divorce), Justice Story offhandedly put legislators on notice that private divorce acts might run afoul of the contract clause. While arguing *Dartmouth*, counsel for New Hampshire had observed in passing that legislative divorce threatened the rights inherent in marital contracts. Story seemed to agree: A married couple had property rights in their union. To the extent that legislators destroyed such rights, they violated the contract clause and perhaps the takings clause as well. Story wrote:

> If under the faith of existing laws a contract of marriage be duly solemnized, or a marriage settlement be made (and marriage is always in law a valuable consideration for a contract), it is not easy to perceive why a dissolution of its obligations, without any default or assent of the parties, may not as well fall within the prohibition as any other contract for a valuable consideration. A man has just as good a right to his wife as to the property acquired under a marriage contract. He has a legal right to her society and her fortune; and to devest such right without his default, and against his will, would be as flagrant a violation of the principles of justice as the confiscation of his own estate.[20]

On one side, legislative divorce allowed the popularly elected branch of government to decide whether a particular marriage harmed individuals and the community sufficient to justify ending it. On the other side, the framers of 1787 seemed to have put it out of the way of legislators to do what legislative divorces entailed; in 1826, in fact, Chancellor James Kent of New York concluded that Story had called legislative divorce an unconstitutional "violation of the principles of justice."[21]

Then, in his 1833–34 *Conflict of Laws* treatise, Story returned to the problem. While Anglo-American authorities saw marriage "in no other light than as a civil contract," it surely was more than a "mere contract between the parties" subject to "their mere pleasure and intentions"; it was also a "civil institution, the most interesting and important . . . of any in society."[22] Yet he did not say which aspect predominated. Meanwhile, other scholars continued to describe marriage as primarily a civil contract with secondary social attributes. In the *Law of Baron and Femme*, Tapping Reeve, a well-known judge and law school proprietor, noted that a marital agreement rested "upon the same footing as any other contract." This was the "doctrine of both the common and civil law," despite attempts by "Popish priests" to muddy the rule. Wedlock was a "mere civil transaction," governed primarily, although not entirely, by the law of contract.[23]

Finally, Bishop came to the rescue with his landmark *Commentaries on the Law of Marriage and Divorce* (1852). Unlike Story, who thought of marital contracts as unitary civil contracts with social implications, Bishop divided such contracts into two stages. The agreement to marry was indeed a contract. "A man and woman come together and agree . . . that . . . they will be husband and wife," wrote Bishop. During espousal, they entered into "a mere civil contract." But at marriage, the agreement transmutated into a "civil and political status"; the partners were "no longer governed by any contract . . . , but by the law." Legislators might encourage and regulate these civil institutions but could neither destroy nor fundamentally alter them. Only courts, with their complement of procedural guarantees, could do that. For these neat moves, Bishop claimed full credit, though he probably owed much to Continental European lawyers and a handful of state judges— among them, Judge George Robertson of the Kentucky Court of Appeals, who declared in *Maguire v. Maguire* (1838) that marriage was a variety of contract so remote from the ordinary kind that the framers of the contract clause could not possibly have meant to include it. "Marriage," wrote Robertson, "though, in one sense, a contract . . . [is] *sui generis*, and unlike ordinary or commercial contracts, is *publici juris*, because it establishes fundamental . . . domestic relations." Although it was "controlled by the sovereign power of the State," it could not, "like mere contracts, be dissolved by the mutual consent only of the contracting parties."[24]

What about legislative divorces granted in the past? In its 1888 ruling in *Maynard v. Hill*, the U.S. Supreme Court, while admitting that such divorces posed grave constitutional questions, chose to uphold them. It was important only that Americans cease the practice. David Maynard had gone to Oregon Territory (the portion that is now Washington) in 1850 and acquired property under the Oregon Donation Act, leaving Lydia, his wife of twenty-two years, and two children in Ohio. In 1852, without Lydia's knowledge, David successfully petitioned the territorial assembly for a divorce; a month later, he wed another woman, with whom he lived until his death. In 1856, to secure title to land cultivated during their marriage, the couple certified to the land office that Lydia was dead. But Lydia was alive and, after David's death, traveled to Oregon to claim her children's share of his property. Initially, officials voided the certificate tendered by David and his second wife, but, in the end, they decided that neither wife should prevail. Hill, Thomas Valentine, and others, who now owned land originally acquired by David in 1853, then filed various suits asking judges to confirm their titles.

When the territorial court ruled against Lydia's children, relatives appealed the decision to the nation's highest court. Their attorneys argued that the 1852 divorce and 1853 marriage had been invalid because Lydia had not agreed to the divorce and because legislative divorces violated the federal contract clause. Associate Justice Stephen Field affirmed the lower court's decision and rejected Lydia's claims. While he deplored David's "loose morals and shameless conduct," he refused to cast doubt on hundreds of acts, "bastardizing" thousands of children and tarring good citizens with bigamy charges. He incidentally summarized late-century views of marriage and its relationship to the public interest: Matrimony, he wrote, created "the most important relation in life" and had "more to do with the morals and civilization of a people than any other Institution." Although

an injunction preventing Charles from taking Emily's child out of Michigan. The injunction, Charles's attorneys contended, interfered with "the *marital rights* and *duties* of the husband in a way not to be tolerated." The court agreed. Unless life was threatened, equity could only follow the law, binding parties to good behavior. This left Emily "where the *law* leaves her, in the custody and under the protection of the husband"—even though Charles had abandoned her and "abused and ill-treated her," frequently resorting to "acts of violence upon her person" and treating his young child with "great cruelty" and "violence."[35]

Wives could be especially imperiled when states decided to honor both marriage and a privacy norm. Bishop thought that when a man tried to "burn his wife alive," no amount of "provocation on her part justifies it,"[36] but without such extreme violence, judges often refused to intervene. Another writer insisted that if a wife could "insure her own safety by lawful obedience and by proper self-command," she had "no right" to divorce an abusive man.[37] In *State v. Rhodes* (1868), state judges left "petty" violence to private resolution, underscoring the state's duty to defend family heads unless injuries were "permanent or malicious." Said Justice Reade, "family government is recognized by law as being as complete in itself as the State government is in itself, and yet subordinate to it"; great "evils . . . would result from raising the curtain, and exposing to public curiosity . . . the nursery and the bed chamber." Every home required a "government of its own, modelled to suit the temper, disposition and condition of its inmates," within which the *baron* was "supreme." From this rule, there could be "no appeal" unless women absolutely required "the strong arm of the law."[38]

THE IMPRINT OF SOCIAL THEORY

As these decisions suggest, jurists steadily read social theory into law—notably, ideas about separate male-female "spheres" and woman's "natural" maternalism. In the Massachusetts case of *Maria Wightman v. Joshua Coates* (1818), an action for breach of a promise of marriage, Wightman had offered the trial court as evidence of the promise "sundry letters" written to her and evidence of "attentions" paid to her; Coates argued that the material did not amount to "direct evidence of an express promise." When the court accepted Wightman's evidence, Coates appealed. Chief Justice Isaac Parker, in sustaining the lower court ruling, explained that a "promise on the part of the woman" might be proved "from such circumstances of acquiescence,"

> or tokens of approval, as ordinarily attend the acceptance of an offer of marriage—her presence when the offer was made, and the consent of parents asked without her making any objection; her subsequent reception of the suitor's visits and concurrence in the arrangements for the wedding; her carrying herself as one consenting . . . , for her consent in words is not necessary.

More was needed to "prove a promise by a man"; neither custom nor "considerations of delicacy" barred an "explicit declaration." Parker thus converted ideas about gender difference (female silence and passivity versus male verbosity and aggression) into legal rules and put state power behind their conservation. "When the female is the injured party, there is generally more reason for a resort to the laws than when the man is the sufferer. . . . It is also for the public interest, that conduct tending to consign a virtuous woman to celibacy, should meet with . . . punishment." The "delicacy of the sex . . . requires for its protection and continuance the aid of the laws."[39]

As the century advanced, judges and law scholars paid close attention to the governance of women and children. Perhaps because he disliked easy divorce and distrusted women, James Kent decided that "the adultery of the husband" need not be prosecuted as zealously as "that of the wife," since it was "not evidence of such entire depravity, nor equally injurious in its effects upon the morals, and good order, and happiness of domestic life." Others thought that because a *feme sole* might be "unaccustomed to bargains" and fail to "sufficiently guard her rights," she required superintendence. Indeed, Bishop claimed that the "chief object" of modern legislation was the "protection of the wife in her property-rights" in transactions with designing men. Thus, in an 1850 New York seduction case, the judges announced that "the female and her seducer do not stand on equal ground." She was "the weaker party and the victim of his acts" as well as his bad faith (the seduction followed a "promise of marriage which he never intended to perform"), and so merited judicial protection.[40]

Public opinion probably supported the paternalism underlying these decisions. Time and again, Americans contended that the family, not the individual, was society's basic social unit and a permanent social institution—unlike slavery because it was founded in love, but more than a business agreement, and thus unlike a contract. Sometimes, women so argued because the home afforded them a modicum of power. Others believed that male governance was divinely mandated. In 1847, Catharine Beecher analogized wives to apprentices and husbands to benevolent masters. "[W]ho shall take the higher, and who the subordinate, stations in social and civil life?" she asked. "This matter, in the case of parents and children, is decided by the Creator. . . . In most other cases, in a truly democratic state, each individual is allowed to choose for himself, who shall take the position of his superior. No woman is forced to obey any husband but the one she chooses for herself," much as an artisan selected "the employer to whom he is to accord obedience."[41] In 1873, Theophilus Parsons noted in his *Law of Contracts* that wedlock bore the marks of the "feudal system": "He is her husband; he is the stronger, she is the weaker; all that she has is his."[42]

In these discussions, social anxiety was almost palpable. What *about* revivalists' intimations of male-female spiritual equality? How could officials police the dependent classes in a nation migrating westward? Settlers not only disappeared behind the frontier, but fashioned new institutions and practices in response to social reality—many of them beneficial to women. *Could* Americans make use of women's labor and capital without jettisoning or damaging traditional family culture—in Antoinette Brown's judgment, "the nursery of the State and the Church?"[43]

ECONOMIC AND PHYSICAL INSECURITY

As of 1846, the answer was unclear. In that year, admirers of Tapping Reeve edited and posthumously republished some of his lectures as *The Law of Baron and Femme* (first published in 1816 under a different title). Reeve laid out the structure of four domestic relations—"*Baron* and *Femme*," "Parent and Child," "Guardian and Ward," "Master and Servant"—much as William Blackstone had done a half-century earlier. In the 1862 edition, the editors applauded "radical changes" afoot in the land, notably in married women's economic rights, which they thought would work "an entire revolution in the law," but in 1846, the "revolution"—much of which Reeve might have welcomed as an aid to economic growth—had not yet come to pass. Juries, for example, continued to be masculine, reflecting the electorate from which they were drawn, and matrons' juries had long since fallen into disuse, depriving women of an important slice of public power. But as economic and territorial expansion proceeded, Americans detected large pockets of instability.[44]

Neither the War for Independence nor the so-called market revolution had dramatically altered married women's capacity to deal in property. As in the 1750s, the law of coverture forced men and women to structure their lives around an arcane web of legal rules. Reeve affirmed the *baron*'s acquisition at the moment of marriage of "absolute title to all the personal property of the wife," such as "money, goods or chattels personal"; all these became the man's property "as completely as the property which he purchases with his own money" and could "never again belong to the wife . . . unless it be given to her by his will." On the husband's death, the property did not revert to the woman, but became part of his estate, to be distributed as his will (or, in case of intestacy, the law) dictated. Choses in action (bonds, notes, rights under contract, or rights to recover damages) held by the wife at marriage were entirely at the husband's disposal during coverture, but could not be devised by him and reverted to the wife at his death. If she died first, choses in action became part of her estate, not his. Chattels real (e.g., leases) were "at his disposal during coverture, liable to his debts, and on her death belong to him absolutely as . . . one of his marital rights," but could not be devised by him. Title to a woman's land remained with her, but her husband claimed the rents and other proceeds of her real property; when she died and for his lifetime, he might be entitled as tenant by curtesy to her land.[45]

Interestingly, Reeve disapproved of rules that injured creditors—as when a wife owed debts, for which the husband was responsible during the marriage. Only if a husband died before creditors had "collected from him the debts due from the wife" would a marital estate escape liability. But though a wife remained liable after her husband's death to her former creditors "as much as when she was a single woman," she might be unable to pay them. Reeve found no other instance in which "the property of one person is transferred to another, by operation of law, at the expense of creditors." Nor could he understand why women contracted marriage; "in point of property," they gained "nothing." Even the widow's dower had little value. At her husband's death, a wife in most jurisdictions was still entitled to dower ("one-third part" of the personal property remaining after payment of a man's debts or one-half if he left no children). The right, however, had softened: A husband easily could devise away the widow's portion of personal property. To be sure, a woman became entitled to the lifetime use of one-third of "the real estate of inheritance of which the husband had been seized" during coverture, and the husband could not deprive his wife of that portion by will. But if a wife did it in writing, she could trade dower for property or money, and at divorce, a woman's property rights in dower mysteriously disappeared. A man could not claim an interest in ordinary "paraphernalia" ("her beds and clothing, suitable to her condition in life") nor will away "ornaments and trinkets." But he could take paraphernalia away from his wife and dispose of it during marriage, and because courts treated women for such purposes as creditors of the estate ranking lower than others, trinkets could be lost at auction. Moreover, if a wife received property by will and the devisee did not specify that the property was for her "separate use," it belonged "absolutely to the husband."[46]

Inconsistencies abounded. The common law, for instance, typically refused to admit a wife's contracts as binding. Because the law presumed the wife to be "in the power of the husband," any contract made by her during the coverture "might be the effect of coercion" and so void, and a wife who was capable of contracting might be "arrested, taken in execution, and confined in a prison," depriving the man of her company, which "the law will not suffer." Yet in some situations in which a woman contracted as her husband's agent or in her own name, policy makers waived general rules. Reeve sharply criticized the rule declaring women's antenuptial wills invalid, so that a wife could only die intestate: "Has marriage caused her to lose her ability or her volition?" If she was "sufficiently discreet to devise when unmarried," how did wedlock make her less so? "Is it not enough," he asked, "that the law has given to her husband the whole of her personal estate . . . , and the entire disposal . . . of her personal property . . . without taking from her the power of devising that estate which is still her own, to which he has not any right, and never can have . . . merely because it is the sovereign pleasure of her husband that she should die intestate?"[47]

Ancient doctrines also compromised women's physical security, both directly and indirectly, especially (but not only) within marriage. Men's interests in the labor and conjugal services of wives gave rise to myriad rules that conserved the doctrine of marital unity and, with it, male custody of women's bodies. For example, although children or servants could be punished for crimes undertaken "in obedience to the command of their parents or masters, or by their coercion," a wife would escape punishment when crimes other than treason or murder were committed in a husband's presence; the law still presumed that, while in her husband's company, "whatever the wife does is done by coercion"—that is, under the influence of his dominant, *active* personality. In such cases, the constabulary could not seize married women's bodies without violating men's rights, although husbands who were charged with women's crimes paid a price for the right to make law at home. When a husband was absent, however, the presumption usually vanished, and in divorce cases in which women were charged with adultery, they were assumed to be capable of making independent choices.[48]

Nor would judges relieve husbands of marital obligations. Men still paid their wives' fines and business expenses, even when women had posed as independent traders, on the ground that husbands *ought* to be aware of wifely doings. Husbands had to provide "necessaries"—according to Bishop, food, clothing, medicine, medical attendance, means of locomotion, housing, furniture, and social protection. Without a signed agreement, however, men were not bound to maintain children from a woman's previous marriage. As long as husbands had not informed merchants to the contrary, wives living with their husbands acted as their agents, and men had to make good on their wives' agreements or purchases wherever it was usual for women to so act (e.g., in purchasing groceries). Even if a man treated his wife so badly that she left, he had to pay for household goods sold to her. It was his duty, in short, to maintain her and their children, even if she neglected some of her duties or was wealthy, unless property had been given to her for the express purpose or they lived apart and had agreed to be self-supporting (an agreement that judges could recognize, or not). If merchants did not trust a man's credit, Bishop added tartly, especially if he left town, a woman was "at liberty to starve"; although friends might waive the rule, a married woman legally could not buy goods on her own credit or contract in her own name.[49]

Common law rules also put women's bodies at risk while reinforcing male proprietorship. At least in theory, if an outsider harmed a wife's "person or reputation," the damages for battery or other wrongs belonged to her. But her husband joined her in the lawsuit and could bring a separate action of trespass for the loss of his wife's labor and company. In cases of sexual transgression, a husband could bring an action for "criminal conversation" with his wife. In form, this also was an action for trespass (actually an action "on the case," an offshoot of trespass) for seduction—that is, for the "alienation of her affections from the husband, and exposing him to shame, ridicule, and the hazard of maintaining a spurious issue" (having to rear another man's child). Bishop noted that because men held title to their wives' "society and services," they might sue for damages when anyone alienated "a wife's affections from her husband," brought "unhappiness to the domestic hearth," or rendered her "services less efficient and valuable."[50] Scholars sometimes lambasted feudal rules. Bishop scoffed at the idea that men "procured" adulterous favors. "A rigid adherence to a maxim," said an equally irate Reeve, "that has not the least foundation in common sense, that a wife has no will, occasioned the form of the writ [in adultery and rape cases] to be . . . trespass." But the rule held: A wife "could not have consented to commit adultery."[51]

By at least the 1850s, in response both to women's rights agitation and to the reception of what one writer calls the "rule of love" within marriages,[52] old doctrines allowing husbands to chastise wives as if they were apprentices had passed into disuse, along with benefit of the clergy, benefit of the belly, and other indications of the Crown's "benevolence." Notably absent was the idea that a man could whip a woman so long as the rod was no larger than his thumb or passed through a wedding ring. In Reeve's view, the "battery of the wife" could be justified only on the ground of "absolute necessity to repel an injury." The "nature of the connection between them" ruled out the possibility of a wife suing her husband for damages. Yet when a woman eloped "without cause," a man could "seize upon her person and bring her home"; he also could take their children, in whose labor he retained a property right and for whose upbringing he bore financial responsibility. As the case of *Shaw* suggests, women could not refuse sexual relations unless performance of the duty threatened their lives, nor could they withhold domestic services. A man controlled access to the home and could "imprison" his wife to prevent her from "going off with an adulterer" or "squandering his property." In Bishop's view, because a man was "criminally responsible for her acts of crime committed in his presence, and civilly for her torts whether he is present or absent," he needed "physical control over her" sufficient to "free himself " from liability.[53]

To be sure, by the 1870s, many judges sought to protect women from extreme violence. In 1871, for example, the Massachusetts Supreme Judicial Court rejected tradition in *Commonwealth v. McAfee*, in which a husband hit his drunken wife "several times on the cheek and temple" so that she died; wife beating "violently with the open hand" was "not one of the rights conferred on a husband by the marriage, even if the wife be drunk or insolent." In the same year, Alabama judges also abandoned old law, coincidentally laying out their sense of what the rules *had* been. In *Fulgham v. State*, an appeal of the indictment of a freedman for beating his wife, the court said, "The wife is not to be considered as the husband's slave."

> And the privilege, ancient though it be, to beat her with a stick, to pull her hair, choke her, spit in her face, or kick her about the floor, or to inflict upon her like indignities, is not now acknowledged by our law. . . . [I]n person, the wife is entitled to the same protection of the law that the husband can invoke for himself. . . . Her sex does not degrade her below the rank of the highest in the commonwealth.

The rationale for the decision in *Fulgham* was unusual, since the parties were black. As Reva Siegel shows, a good many judges were "more interested in controlling African-American men than in protecting their wives." At virtually the same time, courts were re-inforcing the wall between middle-class "private" domains and the state, and suggesting the existence of marital privacy. Although judges disliked wife beating, they often looked for it only within the so-called dangerous classes. Elsewhere, they saw moderate spousal violence as an element of the *baron*'s prerogative. A North Carolina judge in *State v. Hussey* (1852) refused to call a "slap on the cheek" or "any touching . . . in a rude or an-gry manner" a battery when it transpired between man and wife. Such a rule would dam-age "the great principle of mutual confidence and dependence; throw open the bedroom to the gaze of the public; and spread discord and misery." A few years later, the same court decided in a battery case that it was unwilling to take cognizance of "trivial com-plaints arising out of the domestic relations" because the "evil of publicity would be greater than the evil involved in the trifles complained of; and because they ought to be left to family government."[54]

Equally important, access to contraception and abortion diminished after the 1840s. This is not to say that Anglo-American women had enjoyed bodily freedom before then; plainly, they had not. Both childbirth and abortion carried serious risks of disability or death. But for the most part, custom, rather than law, had governed reproductive deci-sions. Married couples could and did resort to herbal remedies (called "abortifacients") that midwives, physicians, and mothers purveyed, and to the extent allowed by imperfect information, couples sought to control the size of their families. As in England, lawyers viewed only newborns as persons and their willful destruction as homicide. Short of birth, Americans adhered to the "quickening doctrine": In Blackstone's view, killing a fetus was a crime—but not murder or manslaughter—only when "a woman is quick with child" and the fetus "able to stir in the mother's womb."[55]

Although the English departed slightly from old doctrines after 1803, Americans kept them well into the nineteenth century. In *Commonwealth v. Bangs* (1812), the Supreme Judicial Court of Massachusetts (and, subsequently, other state courts) formally endorsed the idea, as Grossberg puts it, that so long as abortion occurred "before animation," it was "legally and morally justifiable." Isaiah Bangs had been indicted in 1810 for "assaulting and beating" Lucy Holman and for giving her a "dangerous and deleterious draught or potion, against her will, with intent to procure the abortion . . . of a bastard child" that he had fathered. The state dropped assault charges; when the jury found Bangs guilty of try-ing to abort Lucy's fetus, he appealed on the ground that "no indictable offence" had oc-curred because Lucy was not yet "quick with child." The appellate court agreed, in the process receiving the quickening doctrine: "[N]o abortion is alleged to have followed the taking of the potion; and if an abortion . . . ensued, the averment that the woman was quick with child at the time is a necessary part of the indictment."[56]

Between 1820 and the 1880s, every state made postquickening abortions illegal. But before the Civil War, legislators often punished abortionists, rather than pregnant women, on the ground that immoral practitioners preyed on desperate or soft-minded women. Con-necticut passed a law in 1821 severely punishing physicians, midwives, and quacks who "maliciously" administered "any deadly poison, or other noxious . . . substance" in order to cause the "miscarriage" of a quickened fetus. In 1830, Connecticut lawmakers expanded this prohibition to include the abortion of quickened fetuses with herbs or instruments, but reduced the penalty from life imprisonment to seven-to-ten years. Missouri and Illi-nois adopted statutes based on Connecticut's 1821 law in 1825 and 1827, respectively. In

1828, New York adopted a relatively complex abortion statute. It was the first to make what is now called a therapeutic exception to the ban on abortion when the procedure was necessary to save the mother's life or "advised by two physicians to be necessary for that purpose." After the New York law took effect in 1830, persons who killed quickened fetuses or their hosts were guilty of manslaughter; an attempt to induce an abortion at any stage of pregnancy was made a misdemeanor punishable by up to a year in jail. Legislators partly aimed to eliminate hucksters. One such quack advised women to inject "brandy and water, or water only. . . briskly into the passage by a female syringe" to prevent or end pregnancies; others prescribed toxic or worthless herbs and pills, caustic salves and douches, suction tubes, and bizarre physical exercises. But an 1845 revision of the New York statute—later followed in other states—made the woman who submitted to abortion guilty of a misdemeanor as well.[57]

TOWARD THE "FIRST WAVE"

By the 1850s, American women confronted a formalized system of rules and practices both like and unlike the ones that their grandmothers had known. The American Revolution had put women on a slightly different footing at home and perhaps inspired lawmakers to abandon obviously barbaric legal doctrines. But by at least the 1830s, revolutionary zeal had dissipated. Judges still enforced common law tradition, especially when women defied gender stereotypes or threatened unitary government within families; before 1845–50, when legislatures earnestly began to expand wives' capacity to hold property, the bundle of women's civil rights remained more or less what it had been in late colonial times. The contract clause dilemma, combined with other pressures, led republicans away from legislative divorce toward judicial proceedings that could be incongenial to women, if only because they were expensive. While legislators sometimes intervened to help women of modest means escape bad relationships, as with Tennessee's 1831 law waiving court costs when women sought judicial divorce, even wives with the "strong" cases required in Tennessee could be ruined if judges decided to preserve marriage rather than individual women.[58]

By urging officials to conceive of the marital estate as a prelegal contract, Elizabeth Cady Stanton's followers—who, it should be emphasized, were a minority within the women's rights movement—rowed against the current, openly challenging the drift toward judicial paternalism and formalization. To a significant degree, judicial decisions to act in place of collapsed male heads, treating spouses as parties to agreements with the state, ameliorated the stark inequalities inherent in coverture; in that sense, as Grossberg contends, contractualism helped women and other dependent classes. But Stanton had in mind wholly private agreements that could be terminated *by the parties*, followed by state approval of the result, not the supervision of marital relations by surrogate governmental "heads."

Nobody made the case for married women's right to self-possession more powerfully than Stanton. In her February 8, 1861, address before the New York Senate's judiciary committee on divorce reform, she underscored the persistent inequality embedded in marital contracts and the antirepublican character of family governments. "The law," she said, "takes it for granted that the wife lives in fear of her husband; that his command is her highest law. . . . An unmarried woman can make contracts, sue and be sued, enjoy the rights of property, to her inheritance, her wages, her person, her children; but in marriage, she is robbed by law of her natural and civil rights. . . . If the contract be equal, whence come the terms . . . 'obedience and restraint,' 'dominion and control'?" Why did lawyers still portray women as infants? "Woman, as woman, has nothing to ask of our legislators but the right of suffrage. It is only in marriage, that she must demand her rights to person, children, property, wages, life, liberty and the pursuit of happiness. All the special statutes of which we complain . . . fall on her as wife and mother. We have not yet outlived the old feudal idea, the right of property in woman." Divorce law was just as "unequal"; the "advantages seem to be all on one side, and the penalties on the other." Evoking the "culture of sympathy,"[59] she flirted with what we might now call equal protection ideas. "Are not young women . . . dragged into your public courts—into assemblies of men exclusively? The judges all men, the jurors all men! No true woman there to shield them . . . from gross and impertinent questionings."[60]

As a partial remedy, Stanton advocated voluntary marriage covenants—that is, "mere legal contract[s]" subject to the restraints and privileges of "all other contracts." In Elizabeth Clark's estimation, she aimed to remake the family "along the lines of the republican state," to consist of "independent individuals voluntarily contracting for a corporate existence" at the pleasure of the parties, who, in turn, would be protected in their autonomy by "inalienable individual rights." Why did republicans leave "all contracts . . . and partnerships" to "the discretion of the parties, except that which, of all others, is considered most holy and important?" Stanton especially criticized masculine insistence on a homogenous female *class*. "Thus far," she said, "we have had the man-marriage, and nothing more. . . . He has spoken in Scripture, and he has spoken in law."

> As an individual, he has decided the time and cause for putting away a wife; and as a judge and legislator, he still holds the entire control. In all history, sacred and profane, woman is regarded and spoken of, simply, as the toy of man. She is taken or put away, given or received, bought or sold, just as the interests of the parties might dictate. But the woman has been no more recognized in all these transactions, . . . than if she had had no part or lot in the whole matter. . . . I place man above all governments, . . . all constitutions and laws. . . . The best interests of a community never can require the sacrifice of one innocent being, of one sacred right. In the settlement . . . of any question, we must simply consider the highest good of the individual. It is the inalienable right of all to be happy.

Stanton demanded an "entire revision of your whole code of law on marriage and divorce," to "secure justice"—that is, "man's highest idea of right"—for every citizen in the republic.[61]

Chapter 4

Republican Speech Communities

On October 23, 1850, Paulina Wright Davis of Rhode Island—the first American woman known to have charged lecture fees equal to men's—convened an inaugural national women's rights convention at Worcester, Massachusetts. In her keynote address, Davis eloquently sketched the movement's goals: "The reformation we propose, in its *utmost* scope is radical and universal. It is not the mere perfecting of a reform already in motion, . . . but it is an epochal movement—the emancipation of a class, the redemption of half the world, and a conforming reorganization of all social, political, and industrial interests and institutions."

> [I]t is a movement without example among the enterprises of associated reformations, for it has no purpose of arming the oppressed against the oppressor, or of separating the parties, or of setting up independence, or of severing the relations of either. Its intended changes are to be wrought in the intimate texture of all societary organizations, without violence or any form of antagonism. It seeks to replace the worn-out with the living and the beautiful, so as to reconstruct without overturning, and to regenerate without destroying. Our claim must rest on its justice, and conquer by its power of truth. . . . [W]hatever had been achieved for the race belongs to it, and must not be usurped by any class or caste. The rights and liberties of one human being can not be made the property of another. . . . We claim for woman a full and generous investiture of all the blessings which the other sex has solely, or by her aid, achieved for itself.[1]

The activists who were drawn to the Worcester meeting (and to a more radical meeting in the same town a year later) came from many walks of life and vigorously disagreed with one another. But for all of their differences, they shared certain experiences, convictions, and habits of mind. At a jubilee fifty years later, Worcester veterans pronounced that meeting the clarion call of the postrevolutionary campaign for women's rights, and although Elizabeth Cady Stanton and others sometimes gave pride of place to the 1848 meeting at Seneca Falls, the Worcester convention was the first *national* gathering devoted to inaugurating a *movement*. Most of the delegates were experimental Protestants or utopianists, and many had lived through the American Revolution or had been raised by revolutionary republican parents. As reformers, they tended to rely upon a well-educated white elite to shape political agendas and forge change; in that sense, they were more "republican" than "democratic." Many had migrated to women's rights from abolitionism, the temperance movement, or health and educational reform, often after severe abridgments of speech freedom. A large number were circuit-riding lecturers or preachers, subjected repeatedly to ridicule, character assassination, muggings, and arson; many formed part of the phenomenon in the New World, stretching back to at least 1740, of revival-related female prophesying and preaching. Few doubted that the law of domestic relations and misreadings of the Bible lay at the heart of woman's oppression, although they failed to agree on a remedy. And while class and racial differences sometimes set them at loggerheads, all believed that speech could transform American culture as well as individual citizens.

NEW WOMEN, NEW LANGUAGES

Abigail Kelley, a brilliant Quaker from Massachusetts, followed a rocky path to the Worcester gathering. After a sporadic education, she taught briefly at the Society of Friends school at Lynn, where she discovered William Lloyd Garrison's abolitionist newspaper, the *Liberator*, and promptly joined the antislavery cause. By the late 1830s, she had become a well-known antislavery and pacifist writer and a cofounder with Garrison of the New England Non-Resistant Society. In 1838, she made her first speech before a mixed (or "promiscuous") audience at an antislavery meeting at Philadelphia's Pennsylvania Hall. In Lucretia Mott's telling, many delegates "considered it improper for women to address promiscuous members" and so shunted female orators off to a separate room. As Kelley and Angelina Grimké spoke, rocks and brickbats shattered the windows. Kelley later recalled what she had said: "I ask permission to say a few words. I have never before addressed a promiscuous assembly; nor is it now the maddening rush of those voices, which is the indication of a moral whirlwind; nor is it the crashing of those windows, which is the indication of a moral earthquake, that calls me before you. . . . But it is the 'still small voice within' . . . that bids me open my mouth." To leave, the women had to run a gauntlet of jeering men and boys. Then a mob torched the hall—ironically, a new building dedicated to "the right of free discussion."[2]

Because of her talent and courage, reformer Theodore Weld asked Kelley to become a full-time lecturer. Then, at a New England Antislavery Society meeting in Boston, Kelley made her first women's rights speech when the clergy moved to bar women from the podium. Engagements proliferated. After each appearance, journalists attacked her character and severe dress; because she often traveled with black male abolitionists, critics denounced her variously as a prostitute, an "unsexed" monster, and an agent of racial mixing. Audiences pelted her with rotten eggs. According to Stanton and Susan B. Anthony, she regularly encountered "scorn, ridicule, violence, and mobs" and "all kinds of persecutions." Everywhere, she insisted that whatever "ways and means are right for men to adopt in reforming the world, are right also for women to adopt in pursuing the same object."[3] Sarah Grimké, Angelina Grimké's sister, rejoiced that Kelley possessed the "strength" to "plead the cause of woman" and that she was "not dismayed at the opposition." What Kelley had done would "do more toward establishing the rights of woman than a dozen books."[4]

Until 1870, when poor health forced her to retire, Kelley moved restlessly from state to state, inspiring other women to do the same. In 1845, she married Stephen Foster, a flaming radical from New Hampshire; together, they waged war on behalf of "true" Christians, blacks, and women. In 1846, they openly brawled with officials of Oberlin College in Ohio over the meaning of scriptural passages; several years later, an Oberlin professor condemned Kelley and her kind as "women of masculine minds and aggressive tendencies . . . who cannot be satisfied in domestic life." By 1860, she had severed relations with the Society of Friends for their tepid position on slavery and with many abolitionists for support of the Republican Party. When Kelley died at age 75, Samuel May credited her with steeling a generation of women for battle at the podium; she "hewed out a path over which many women are now walking toward their equal political rights." Said Lucy Stone, "The world of women owe her a debt which they can never pay. The movement for the equal rights of women began directly and emphatically with her."[5]

Another Worcester delegate, Sojourner Truth, was born enslaved around 1797 near New Paltz, New York, as Isabella Baumfree. She was sold at about age 9 with "a lot of sheep"[6] to a family in Ulster, New York, resold to a saloon keeper, and then resold to another New Yorker, John Dumont, who persuaded her to marry a bondsman named Thomas. When Dumont refused to heed New York's emancipation act of 1817, Isabella fled with her infant daughter (the first of several children) to the home of Isaac Van Wagoner, a Quaker who had agreed to emancipate her and for whom she worked as a servant.

In the late 1820s, Isabella changed her surname to Van Wagoner and moved to New York City, where she gained a reputation as a prophetess. Eventually, she joined forces with Elijah Pierson (nicknamed "the Tishbit"), a street preacher who was determined to redeem New York's lowliest classes, with whom she established a new church and a home for prostitutes, Magdalene Asylum. In 1832, the church gave its assets to Robert Matthews, called the Prophet Matthias; the merged group founded Zion Hill, a communal society near Sing Sing. Rumors spread of cultish immoralities. When the Tishbit mysteriously died in 1834, Matthias stood trial for murder. Newspapers unfairly implicated Isabella in the scandal. To clear her name, she filed and won a slander suit against the *Commercial Advertiser*; once exonerated, she slipped away to live quietly in New York, tend her children, work as a domestic servant, and attend the African Church.

Around 1843, divine voices commanded Isabella to adopt the name Sojourner Truth and take up an itinerant ministry. In her own words, God named her Sojourner because she was supposed "to travel up an' down the land, showin' the people their sins, an' bein' a sign unto them." When she told God she needed a surname, he added "Truth, because I was to declare the truth to the people."[7] Thus reborn, she walked through the countryside speaking for small fees; urging blacks to throw off oppression; and selling pamphlets, including *The Narrative of Sojourner Truth* (1850). Increasingly, she joined whites at the podium—as at the 1850 women's rights meetings at Worcester and Rochester, New York. Eventually, she traveled west. Missourians mobbed and clubbed her; in Indiana, to counter allegations that she was really a man, she bared her breast. When racial violence overtook Kansas and Nebraska, Truth moved to Michigan; when civil war shattered the nation, she again took to the road, gathering food and clothing for black regiments and traveling on one occasion to Washington, D.C., for an audience with Abraham Lincoln.

Women's rights leaders may well have encouraged Truth and other black women to speak at mostly white meetings so that delegates might learn to empathize with them; for her part, Truth failed to see why reformers wanted to talk so much. Harriet Beecher Stowe and others later recalled Truth's reactions to the 1850 proceedings: "Well, honey, I's ben der meetins, an harked a good deal. Dey wanted me fur to speak. So I got up. Says I, 'Sisters, I a'n't clear what you'd be after. Ef women want any rights mor'n deys got, why don't dey jes' take 'em, an' not be talkin' about it?'"[8] Truth's famous "Ar'n't I a Woman" speech of 1851, delivered in Akron, Ohio, chided hostile clergymen for trying to impose delicacy upon laboring women. According to witnesses, every eye was "fixed on this almost Amazon form, which stood nearly six feet high, head erect, and eyes piercing the upper air, like one in a dream." Truth said something like this: "Well, chilern, whar dar is so much racket dar must be something out o' kilter. . . . [D]e white men will be in a fix pretty soon. But what's all dis here talkin' about? Dat man ober dar say dat women needs to be helped into carriages, and lifted ober ditches, and to have de best place every whar. Nobody eber help me into carriages, or ober mud puddles, or gives me any best place." Raising herself to her "full height," she added, "and ar'n't I a woman? Look at me!"

> I have plowed, and planted, and gathered into barns, and no man could head me—and ar'n't I a woman? . . . I have borne thirteen chilern and seen 'em mos' all sold into slavery, and when I cried out with a mother's grief, none but Jesus heard—and ar'n't I a woman? Dat little man in black dar, he say women can't have as much rights as man, cause Christ want a woman. Whar did your Christ come from?[9]

Truth hammered away at the movement's racism and classism. She identified bloomers, for example, as a reform not likely to appeal to blacks long deprived of skirts ("You see . . . , dey used to weave what dey called nigger cloth, an' each one of us got jes' sech a strip, and had to wear it width-wise. . . . Tell *you*, I had enough of bloomers in them days"). And she despised foppery, believing that silly dress trivialized women's social contributions. "When I saw them women on the stage at the Women's Suffrage Convention . . . , I thought, What kind of reformers be you, with goose-wings on your heads, as if you were going to fly, and dressed in such ridiculous fashion, talking about reform and women's rights? 'Pears to me, you have better reform yourselves first. Women," she continued, "you forget that you are the mothers of creation. . . . You rig yourselves up in panniers and Grecian bend-backs and flummeries." White reformers wore "high-heeled shoes and humps on their heads . . . and stuff them out so that they keel over when the wind blows. Oh mothers, I'm ashamed of ye! What will such lives . . . do for humanity?"[10]

Truth also urged an alliance of abolitionists and women's rights workers against white patriarchs of every stripe. In 1867, as movement leaders tried to persuade Republicans to include women alongside black men in civil rights statutes and constitutional amendments, Truth told delegates to the American Equal Rights Association convention that women's productive *and* reproductive work fully supported rights claims and that white men's theft of property (including property in rights) underlay civil strife. In her view, God's promise of spiritual equality mandated an end to patriarchy and authorized oppressed peoples to demand the restoration of rights taken unlawfully. She refused to bargain with men as to whether they would return property that had never belonged to them: "I want to see before I leave here—I want to see equality. I want to see women have their rights, and then there will be no more war. . . . All the battles that have ever been was for selfishness—for a right that belonged to some one else, or fighting for his own right. . . . [N]obody has any business with a right that belongs to her." As in 1850, she had little time for niceties: "I can make use of my own right. I want the same use of it. Do you want it? Then get it. If men had not taken something that did not belong to them they would not fear."[11]

Few upper-class whites could fathom the plight of black mothers, for whom arcane questions of "title" in (or "possession" of) children were meaningless. Bondswomen might have settled gladly for a possessory right in toddlers stolen from the slave quarters, for the right to be "private," and for an income. Thus, Truth's determination to speak for women unable to help themselves. "I pity the slave mother, careworn and weary," she sang in 1855,

Who sighs as she presses her babe to her breast;
I lament her sad fate, all so hopeless and dreary,
I lament for her woes, and her wrongs unredressed.
O who can imagine her heart's deep emotion,
As she thinks of her children about to be sold;
You may picture the bounds of the rock-girdled ocean,
But the grief of that mother can never be told.[12]

Antoinette Louisa Brown also followed a religious path to Worcester, albeit within established Protestant churches. The first woman ordained a minister by a mainstream sect, Brown was born in Henrietta, New York, in 1825, just as religious revivalism reached flood stage. Her old-line Calvinist family converted to evangelical Protestantism; at age 9, the precocious Antoinette persuaded Congregational elders to admit her to full membership. She garnered a better-than-average education at local schools, pursuing (with the exception of Greek studies) the boys' programs. But, in the end, her intellectual goals could not be addressed at home. In the mid-1840s, after amassing a nest egg as a teacher, Brown decided to attend Oberlin College, the first college to admit women to traditionally masculine fields in 1837 (the handful of other colleges that matriculated women usually did so into sex-segregated, "soft" programs).

The Oberlin experience indelibly marked Brown. Entering as a third-year student in the literary program, which did not award bachelor's degrees, she soon decided to follow her brother into theology and the ministry. For experimental Protestants, few colleges were more congenial: After 1835, the controversial evangelist-theologian Charles Finney had transformed Oberlin into a laboratory for the refinement of his creed. Brown's family and friends discouraged her. Women were not supposed to "combat a beneficent order tending to promote harmony in the family and in the commonwealth"; a male pastorate ostensibly reflected "the inmost fitness of things"—that is, God's natural order.[13] When Brown persisted, the faculty decided to allow her to acquire knowledge in theology and encouraged her to publish essays reinterpreting St. Paul's admonition, "Let the women keep silence in the churches," and related passages. But, when she completed the program in 1850, the college withheld her degree and license to preach, as well as the license of another successful woman. Twenty-eight years later, Oberlin granted the 53-year-old Brown an honorary master's degree; in 1908, it added a doctorate. But, when degrees finally appeared, she had little use for them.

Brown did not lack courage or grit. In 1848, she told her "best friend" Lucy Stone (who had addressed mixed-sex audiences at Oberlin and cofounded a women's debating club) about conversations with faint-hearted faculty about a woman's "right to public labors" and "*speaking* in particular." One critic said that women had "a right to speak in public [g]atherings," such as "social meetings, prayer meetings &c.," but "no right to preach & the thought of a womans . . . becoming a pastor over a church seemed to him perfectly absurd." Brown found "hardly . . . any one to *talk with*," and fewer still in agreement with her.[14] Finney initially had opposed female oration in his classes, even though students were "all required to tell their religious experience" in public. When he asked for volunteers, fellow students brought the women to his attention, but he ignored them. "Once he looked as though he did not know what to say," Brown recalled,

& the next time said "O we dont call upon the ladies." They had all told me we should have to speak & I felt so badly at what he said that I just began to cry & was obliged to leave the room. . . . After I went out they talked over the matter & it seems Prof Finney did not know we were members of the department. . . . He said he was willing any lady should speak if she wished to.

When Finney asked Brown to address a prayer meeting, she spoke of her "determination to preach & speak in public." Listeners "seemed surprised & pleased" that she was "speaking . . . views so plainly" and that she was "really expecting to speak."[15]

But Oberlin was a "free space" in which many social conventions had been suspended. Elsewhere, women like Brown regularly locked horns with religious and civic authorities. At the 1852 New York temperance convention, for instance, presiding officers decided that speakers who had "something else more at heart than temperance" should be excluded. Convention delegates apparently had resolved not to "listen to the voice of woman in legislating upon great public questions," on the ground that the "constitution of the female mind" rendered woman "incapable of correctly deciding upon the points involved" in the adoption of new temperance laws. When Kelley and others were ejected, the would-be speakers roundly condemned a reform society "in which woman is voted not of the world!"[16]

Then, in May 1853, Antoinette Brown presented her credentials to officials at the World Temperance Conference in New York City as the official delegate of two state temperance leagues. This was the same group that had misbehaved in 1852; Brown and others pressed the question to see what might happen. The convention's presiding officer, Neal Dow, accepted her letters; when she rose to address the audience at a "suitable time and in a perfectly orderly manner," he granted her the floor. But other delegates refused to let her speak. For two days, Brown's fellows shouted her down; on the third day, as William Henry Channing and others later testified, they "succeeded in silencing her voice." The Reverend John Chambers of Philadelphia reportedly "stood stamping until he raised a cloud of dust around him, pointing with coarse finger and rudely shouting 'shame on the woman.'" In the end, she was "crowded off the platform." When delegates voted to exclude women and a black delegate, James McCune Smith, the outcasts' supporters called an alternative "*Whole* World Temperance Convention" in another hall and dubbed the original meeting the "Half World Temperance Convention."[17]

Brown's account merits close attention. She had attended the convention, she later explained, to "assert a principle" that would "promote *all* good causes and retard *all* bad ones. I went there, as an item of the world, to contend that the sons and daughters of the race, without distinction of sex, sect, class or color, should be recognized as belonging to the world,"

and I planted my feet upon the simple *rights of the delegate*. I asked no favor as woman, or in behalf of woman; no favor as a woman advocating temperance; no recognition of the cause of woman above the cause of humanity; the indorsement of no "ism" and of no measure; but I claimed, in the name of the world, the rights of a delegate in a world's convention.[18]

Perfectionism merged seamlessly with republicanism. Brown did battle, not for women's rights alone, but for universal civic autonomy—for the natural human right to speak for a constituency ("rights of the delegate"), for the right to *be* and to speak authoritatively in a public place—that is, to be recognized as an individuated "item" in a place taken to be part of "the world." In this quest, she eschewed partisanship ("isms" and "measures") and instead acted as a citizen engaged in a search for rational as well as spiritual truth through public discussion.

Horace Greeley's antisuffragist New York *Tribune* predicted—wrongly, as it turned out—that the "*gentlemen*" responsible for Brown's ouster would "live to understand their own folly." They had managed a "very different thing" from what they intended. Had they aimed to "strengthen the cause of Woman's Rights, they could not have done the work half so effectively."

> Had Antoinette Brown been allowed to speak . . . , her observations would certainly have occupied but a fraction of the time now wasted, and would have had just the weight proper to their sense and appropriateness, and no more. But instead of this the World's Convention was disturbed and its orators silenced. The consequences will be the mass of people . . . who might otherwise not know of its existence, will have their attention called and their sympathies enlisted in its behalf.

"Many who question the propriety of woman's appearing in public," Greeley added, "will revolt at the gagging of one who had a right to speak. . . . There is in the public mind of this country an intuitive love of fair play and free speech and those who outrage it . . . bestow a mighty power on the ideas they . . . would suppress."[19]

Stanton later characterized the affair as a "great battle for free speech and human equality" won handily by Brown's allies.[20] But in 1853, activists knew that "gagging" (a politically loaded term because of Congress's long-standing antiabolitionist gag rule)[21] stripped her of essential attributes of citizenship and thus of influence in an important part of the forum. From her "separate but equal" podium, Brown spoke mainly to the converted; skeptics confronted her ideas in partial, often hostile newspaper accounts. The lesson was clear: As a delegate, orator, and teacher, she had no place in the "public" marked out by temperance reformers.

Shortly afterward, Brown was ordained minister of the First Congregational Church in South Butler, New York. But years of disappointment, lingering ambivalence about female pastorates, and a desire to be acting directly on social disease led her away from organized religion. In 1854, she gave up her pulpit, joined the Unitarian community, and began to work in New York slums, prisons, and asylums. In 1856, she married the reformer Samuel Charles Blackwell; Lucy Stone then wed Samuel's brother, Henry Blackwell. Antoinette also began to write, perhaps as a surrogate for speaking; publication of *Shadows of Our Social System* (1856) cemented her reputation as a social critic. In 1869, she produced *Studies in General Science*, an attempt to square social Darwinism with women's rights and Christianity; four years later, in an implicitly autobiographical essay, she labored to reconcile womankind's maternal responsibilities with individual women's divinely sanctioned right to pursue all interests. "The work nearest and clearest before the eyes of average womanhood," she wrote, "is work within family boundaries," within a "sphere which men cannot enter; surrounded by a still wider area of duties and privileges that very few of us desire to relinquish." It did not follow, however, that "no work equally imperative" awaited a woman elsewhere; the decision was "personal," not limited by membership in a "class."[22]

Nor should men and women come to blows. "The Cooperation of both sexes must reach everywhere," wrote Brown Blackwell, "into industries, science, art, religion, and into the conduct and government of the State. Family life would be ennobled . . . with the wider sympathies of a more enlightened motherhood"; man and woman should be "associates but not rivals." In *The Sexes Throughout Nature* (1875), she laid out what she took to be a divinely ordained coequality. The sexes were "always true equivalents—equals but not identical in development and in relative amounts of normal force." Both social theory and theology mandated a "broader field" for women's talents, though not necessarily a field identical with men's.[23]

Finally, in 1878, Brown Blackwell reentered the lecture circuit, in part to help her husband Samuel recover from financial woes. She aided Stone's American Woman Suffrage Association, accepted leadership posts in other women's rights associations, urged young women to study science, ordained two women in 1885 and 1893 at Unity Church in Cleveland, and helped found the liberal All Souls' Unitarian Church in Elizabeth, New Jersey, for which she served as pastor emeritus from 1908 until her death thirteen years later. Her principled (some would have said "inflexible") beliefs consistently attracted criticism. She refused to wear the alarming bloomer costume. She scandalized many movement stalwarts by insisting upon a Christian invocation at conventions. And her view of marriage always generated sparks. She simply refused to say that marriage *as envisioned by God* was like slavery or that the liberalization of divorce and the recasting of matrimony as a wholly private contract advanced woman's or the republic's cause. Brown Blackwell nevertheless entered the twentieth century a venerated figure. Into old age, she continued to publish books and essays; young women lauded her efforts to expand women's professional prospects and to secure universal suffrage. In 1920, at age 85 and nearly blind, she cast a ballot in the presidential election.

Not every female reformer took to the lecture circuit. Catharine Beecher, for example, grew weary of women's complaints. No less than Worcester delegates, Beecher championed both her sex and the republic. But she urged her sisters to extend Republican Motherhood into the neighborhood through the "Christian female teacher." A founder of the seminary movement, Beecher organized the Hartford Female Seminary in Connecticut to educate and employ female teachers, reverse illiteracy, and carry republicanism into ordinary homes. Like Brown Blackwell, Beecher espoused coequality, but with a difference: She believed that women who entered masculine realms had gone too far. Talented women surely had a right to "happiness" and to "equal advantages." But they violated nature when they undertook "the care of civil life." Men subordinated women only when a concern for the sex's "best interests demands it"; usually, they treated women as "superiors." In a letter written with Harriet Beecher Stowe for the *American Woman's Home*, Beecher condemned public women. Did the "ballot and the powers of office" offer any real benefits for women that men "would not grant to a united petition of our sex?" Surely, it would be "a wiser thing to *ask* for what we need," if only because the alternative promoted disharmony.[24]

For the most part, the movement's leaders disagreed. They doubted that women should *ask* for freedom hat in hand, that Republican Motherhood served all women equally well, or that an expanded female presence in public life threatened the republic. On the contrary, as Paulina Wright Davis suggested at Worcester, they sought harmony through equalization. At an 1852 meeting in Westchester, Pennsylvania, Ruth Plumbly proposed "not only to cure, but to prevent the diseases of the body politic; to place man and woman in such natural and true relations of equal and mutual development, and to so sanctify marriage that from their union . . . , a regenerate humanity shall not only cease to be violent . . . , but shall outgrow the[se] dispositions."[25]

SILENCE AND DISCONTENT

Silence and passivity figured large in time-honored images of woman. Europeans had long rewarded inobtrusive women with social privilege, simultaneously using silence to prove the sex's unfitness for public life—as when a sixteenth-century cleric dubbed it the "noblest ornament of a woman" and then disqualified women from lawyering and preaching on the ground of customary timidity.[26] Americans regularly insisted that girls and women were to be "seen and not heard." As the Seneca Falls *Democrat* put it in 1840, a "good wife" should be "like a snail, always keep within her own house. . . . Second, be like an echo, to speak when she is spoken to; but like an echo she should not always have the last word. . . . Third . . . be like a town clock, always keep time and regulation; but she should not, like a town clock, speak so loud that all the town may hear her."[27]

Discontent came to the fore as early as the 1780s, when the Daughters of Liberty began to chip away at the walls erected between home and forum. During the war, thousands of ordinary women had worked alongside men at the front. They sacrificed brothers, sons, and husbands; they also managed farms and shops, talked about English tyrants at mealtime, and fielded political ideas whenever they could find an audience. Virginia's Anne Terrel urged women to undertake "another branch of American politics" in place of soldiering. If they worked at "carding, spinning, and weaving . . . ," observers would see that "free" women as well as men were no longer subject to "lords" determined to bring "our posterity into . . . slavery."[28] Radical deportment also conveyed political and social messages: The Daughters of Liberty condemned the British in parades, boycotts, and raids, as when women ransacked shops to liberate coffee and food from Loyalists. And, by the 1820s, a new breed of woman had come to the fore in magazine articles about the frontier—among them, Trans-Appalachia's hard-laboring, horseback-riding Ann Bailey, whose rule-breaking deportment "spoke" eloquently to female possibilities in the new world.

Letter writing contributed powerfully to the groundswell of talk, although largely among free white women. Sometimes, letters remained unpublished, as did Abigail Adams's warning to her husband John about the possibility of female insurrection. While statesmen had been "proclaiming peace and good will to Men, emancipating all Nations," she wrote,

> you insist upon retaining an absolute power over Wives. . . . Arbitrary power, is like most other things which are very hard, very liable to be broken—and notwithstanding all your wise Laws and Maxims we have it in our power not only to free ourselves but to subdue our Masters, and without violence throw both your natural and legal authority at our feet.

She told John that he had turned her into a "politician"—not as a voter, but as a "writer of notes."[29] Other letters were published. "I won't have it thought," wrote the wealthy South Carolina widow Eliza Wilkinson shortly after independence, "that because we are the weaker sex as to bodily strength . . . we are capable of nothing more than minding the dairy." Women had "as just a sense of honor glory, and great actions, as the 'Lords of Creation'. . . . They won't even allow us the liberty of thought, and that is all I want." While she did not wish to "meddle in what is unbecoming female delicacy," she was "sure we have sense enough to give our opinions . . . without being reminded of our spinning and household affairs."[30]

Publication had long been an avenue into the public forum, so long as women avoided masculine topics and stopped short of scandalizing readers. Writers like Mary Astell had published poetry, stories, essays, and plays for centuries, some of them laced with social criticism; after 1780, American women followed the road a bit further. Judith Sargent Murray and other "scribblers" (as critics dubbed them) made clear that America was not Europe and that words were not a masculine preserve. In 1780, at the height of the war, Esther de Berdt Reed—the organizer of a successful drive for money ultimately used to buy shirts for soldiers—published a broadside entitled *The Sentiments of an American Woman* in which she contended for woman's right to "march to glory by the same paths as the Men." And while Mercy Otis Warren grudgingly accepted women's "appointed Subordination" for the "sake of Order in Families," she damned "that Part of the human Species who think Nature . . . has given them the Superiority over the other." Printed words often stood in for other forms of political action. Said the British journalist Harriet Martineau, "I want to be doing something with the pen, since no other means of action in politics are in a woman's power."[31]

Progressive female education similarly served as a springboard into the forum, if only because companionate marriages required familiarity with political economy, philosophy, law, and other "masculine" fields. An important shift toward female literacy can be seen as early as 1750, when the majority of women could sign their names; by 1775, three-quarters of the women who were required to sign legal documents in one Connecticut county did so without assistance.[32] The initial decision to educate girls and women probably reflected market pressures, but the republican mothers' responsibilities gave urgency to the impulse. Academically rigorous schools for young women (or campaigns to revise the curricula in established schools) proliferated in postrevolutionary America—particularly in New York, where the Troy Female Academy and other seminaries cracked through old barriers to female learning. Elsewhere, as if to stem the tide, academicians rigorously policed the borders between "masculine" and "feminine" knowledge well into the nineteenth century. In 1822, an Ohio newspaper republished a supposedly jocular essay called "Learned Ladies":

> "I should be glad to know," said angrily a learned lady, "how knowledge is incompatible with a woman's situation in life. I should like to be told why chemistry, geography[,] algebra, languages, and the whole circle of arts and sciences, are not as becoming in her as in a man." "I do not say," replied one of our celebrated wits, "that they are entirely unbecoming; but I think a very little of them will answer the purpose. In my opinion now a woman's knowledge of *chemistry*, should extend no farther, than to the melting of butter; *geography*, to a thorough acquaintance with every hole & corner in the house; her *algebra*, account of the family expenses; and as for *tongues*, heaven knows that one is enough . . . and the less use she makes of that, the better."[33]

But the tide was irrepressible. While teachers often reserved rational sciences and higher education for boys, the young republican woman of means—and, in different ways, girls enrolled in common schools—could study, among other subjects, moral philosophy, geography, literature, history, and languages. Founders of new schools (and curricular reformers at old schools) often justified their innovations on the grounds of women's expanded civic presence in a republic, mothers' responsibilities as children's teachers, and wives' roles as companions to men. In a 1787 speech at the Young Ladies Academy in Philadelphia, reformer-physician Benjamin Rush observed that educated women would be easier to rule: "If men believe that ignorance is favourable to the government of the female sex," he noted, "they are certainly deceived; for a weak and ignorant woman will always be governed with the greatest difficulty." But he argued as well that republican mothers required a serious, if not identical, education: "The equal share that every citizen has in the liberty and the possible share he may have in the government of our country make it necessary that our ladies should be qualified to a certain degree, by a peculiar and suitable education, to . . . [instruct] their sons in the principles of liberty and government." Education bred insurrection. In 1839, orators at the liberal Pierce School in Litchfield, Connecticut, wrote a parody entitled "Ladies Declaration of Independence" for a July Fourth gala: "When in the course of human events, it becomes necessary for the Ladies to dissolve those bonds by which they have been subjected to others, and to assume among the self styled Lords of Creation that separate and equal station to which the laws of nature and their *own talents* entitle them, a decent respect to the opinions of mankind requires, that they should declare the causes which impel them to the separation." Fifty years after the revolution, they noted, "all *mankind* are created equal."[34]

The Second Great Awakening also propelled women into public life. With dozens of others, Paulina Wright Davis apparently discovered spiritual freedom and the ability to think and act independently in the religious revivals that "burned over" upstate New York after 1800. On the question of women's rights, she had been "roused to thought," as her friend Elizabeth Cady Stanton later explained, by early exposure to parish debates of women's right to "speak and pray in promiscuous assemblies." When religious fervor abated, she and other newly vocal women were "not so easily remanded to silence."[35] Between 1800 and 1850, a staunch handful of female preachers stood their ground in the face of withering criticism; indeed, historian Catherine Brekus identifies the 1830s, when the Second Great Awakening started to wane and pastors began to worry about respectability, as the decade of the "fiercest attacks against women speaking in public," whether in pulpits or elsewhere.[36] At the midcentury, Antoinette Brown and Lucretia Mott were especially visible; but a significant number of less-prominent women responded to the pastoral call, often as itinerant lecturers. Among whites, Mary Howell and Clarissa Danforth (judged by many to be the most riveting preacher of her time) drew large crowds; successful African American ministers included Elizabeth, an ex-slave who confronted extreme hostility on the road, and Jarena Lee, converted by a leader of the African Methodist Episcopal Church in 1805 and the church's first female preacher.[37] The notion that woman embodied Christian, as well as republican, virtue led quickly to female majorities in many parishes and a modest but growing demand for woman preachers. In postrevolutionary New York, where women fanned the flames of revivalism, Mary Ryan shows that evangelical rural women carried the word into cities through tract societies and study or moral reform groups, in the process remaking themselves as citizens.

At every turn, uppity women scandalized tradition-minded members of their own sex. South Carolina's Alice Izard was one of many critics who condemned the English radical Mary Wollstonecraft (author of the influential *Vindication of the Rights of Woman*) as a "vulgar, impudent Hussy." Izard thought that a "good Woman" had little ground for complaint: "She frequently guides, where she does not govern, & acts like a guardian angel." In 1846, Catharine Beecher presented an address in Columbus, Ohio, by "sitting on the platform and getting her brother to read it for her." Even more dramatically, in an 1853 meeting of the Ohio Women's Temperance Society in Dayton, a group of "well-dressed ladies" marched in "two and two, and spread themselves in a half circle in front of the platform, and requested leave to be heard," ironically to protest women's public oratory. The visitors cited the "unseemly and unchristian" practice of calling conventions and "taking our places upon the platform, and seeking notoriety by making ourselves conspicuous before men." They shook "the dust from their own skirts of the whole thing," condemned the "disgraceful conduct" of Brown in New York, and "filed out of the low dark door."[38]

In the end, opponents of *"assemblages of rampant women"*[39] failed to stem the tide of words. Some years later, Stanton and Susan B. Anthony pointed to "a thousand pens and voices"—many of them fairly obscure—as catalysts of a "complete revolution" in American life and thought.[40] But, at midcentury, the battle for the podium and pulpit was far from won. Because the vast majority who rose to contest sex-based exclusion were comfortably situated white women for whom the problem was *not* what the critics of ambitious lower-class men called "ignorance," gender rather than class emerged unambiguously as the main bar to entry into the forum. Silence caused great pain. "I wish that I were as free as you and could stump the state in a twinkling," wrote Stanton in a poignant 1855 letter to Anthony. "But I am not, and what is more, I passed through a terrible scourging when last at my father's. . . . I never felt more keenly the degradation of my sex."

> To think that all in me of which my father would have felt a proper pride had I been a man, is deeply mortifying to him because I am a woman. That thought has stung me to a fierce decision—to speak as soon as I can do myself credit. But the pressure on me just now is too great. Henry [her husband] sides with my friends, who oppose me in all that is dearest to my heart. They are not willing that I should write even on the woman question. But I will both write and speak. . . . I have sent six articles to the *Tribune*. . . . I have promised to write for the *Una*.[41]

"THE SPEECH PRINCIPLE" AND CULTURAL TRANSFORMATION

In early modern Europe, female writers sometimes imagined what Peter Goodrich calls "a community of virtuous women kept separate from the world of men" so that they might cultivate virtue "in female commonality," free from the "demands and the degradations" of the male world. Christine de Pisan's *Boke of the Citye of Ladys* (1521) and Mary Astell's *A Serious Proposal to the Ladies* (1694) both described idyllic societies in which women withdrew from the world to reinvent society and promote a "philosophy of the feminine."[42] Something akin to these fictitious speech communities emerged among radical English women in the eighteenth century and again in the United States during the second third of the nineteenth, when revivalism made it possible for women's rights activists, abolitionists, temperance workers, and other reformers to imagine stepping out of the world long enough to change it. As suffragist Mildred Adams later explained, "It was an earnest age, and light language had as yet no place in great causes."[43] Through structured conversation and "radical remembrance," as James Epstein puts it, members of women's rights communities aimed to recover their own history, describe the sex's condition, propose remedies for injustice, and persuade opponents to join them in a regenerative "social revolution."[44]

Women described their fledgling communities as sacred spaces located beyond culture. "We must work out our own salvation," said publicist Elizabeth Oakes Smith, "and God grant it be not in fear and trembling! Women must henceforth be the redeemer, the regenerator of the world. . . . We must place women on a higher platform." Stanton envisioned "a transformation into nobler thought, some purer atmosphere to breathe, some higher stand-point from which to study human rights." Esther Ann Lukens of Ohio invoked Christianity leavened with republican constitutionalism. "Could his spirit look down upon us," she wrote in 1851, "he would see those synods . . . assembling all over the land, not to restore an age of semi-barbarism, but to hasten the advent of a new and far more golden era, when there will be no dangerous pilgrimage of years' duration to win back the Holy Sepulchre, but a far more divine and sacred inheritance . . . ; namely, freedom for woman to exercise every right, capacity, and power with which God has endowed her."[45]

Within female "synods," liberty of speech quickly emerged as a primary constitutional aspiration and norm, and though women typically did not claim a *right* to associate, they understood the power of assemblies. This was an age of verbal combat in newspapers and on the lecture circuit; republicans everywhere believed that speech acts would disseminate what Richard Brown calls "rational knowledge," lead speakers and listeners toward enlightenment, and help construct new social realities.[46] Women's rights activists (and perhaps other reformers) sometimes defined freedom of expression much more expansively than did judges and scholars. In lawyers' circles, liberty of speech, to lean on Jack Rakove, was "more . . . a privilege of legislators than of citizens," tightly controlled by community elites and therefore *not* viewed as an unabridgeable natural right; freedom of the press consisted mainly of protection from restriction or punishment in advance of publication ("prior restraint"). Early Americans did not especially prize freedom of assembly or the distinctly modern right of association, and after two centuries, the right to be where speech occurs in order to hear ideas or information essential to public life has yet to be fully recognized as an essential aspect of speech freedom.[47]

For many antebellum women, however, liberty of speech included not only a natural right to express ideas without governmental interference, whether aloud, in print, or symbolically (in street parades, demonstrations, exhibits, or banners). It also encompassed the freedom to *be* in forbidden spaces—as an active participant in proceedings or as a listener able by virtue of her presence to gather information essential to forming opinions or being powerful. White men of good reputation could traverse masculine spaces freely; entry with peer approval affirmed manhood. But women could never be men; to cross gender lines was to court condemnation as a contaminated, masculinized, or deranged person. In an 1860 convention, Philadelphia's Mary Grew said this: "Good men and true . . . believe, that if a woman . . . teaches in the public congregation, she can not act well her part in the family circle."[48] It followed, too, that men "unmanned" themselves by occupying feminized spaces or abetting "strong-minded" women. Witness an 1852 New York *Herald* editorial responding to the Syracuse women's rights convention: the speakers were said to be "old maids, whose personal charms were never very attractive, and who have been sadly slighted by the masculine gender in general; some of them women who have been badly mated. . . . [S]ome, having so much of the virago in their disposition, that nature appears to have made a mistake in their gender—mannish women, like hens that crow." Male delegates were "hen-pecked husbands, and all of them ought to wear petticoats."[49]

Opponents of female participation in political or professional life contested every aspect of the claim to speech freedom. When Harvard medical students objected to the college's decision to admit Boston's Harriot Hunt to lectures in 1844, the issue was not whether Hunt could speak in a lecture hall—all students were expected to absorb information passively—but whether she might "listen to the discussion" of the subjects at hand without "unsex[ing]" herself, destroying "respect for the modesty and delicacy of her sex," and (because her presence ruled out talk about body parts and other supposed obscenities) impairing male students' speech freedom.[50]

Movement leaders therefore characterized the right to gather, listen, speak, and be heard in civic spaces as an indispensable foundation for procuring other rights. Without such freedom, lawmakers might never come to see women as sovereign *individuals* who had moved from "silence and subjection" into "individualism" and public responsibility.[51] As Stanton explained, women had been "compelled" by virtue of their exclusion from male spaces to "defend the right of free speech for themselves"; the ability to claim and use liberty of speech thus prefigured the search (in Mariana Johnson's words) for "knowledge, sound judgment, and perfect freedom of thought and action."[52] In the first volume of the *History of Woman Suffrage* (1881), Stanton and Anthony highlighted female wordsmiths, the "clerical attempt to silence women," and women's dogged attempts to secure liberty of speech for all citizens; Lucretia Mott's mesmerizing lectures supposedly eliminated "padlocks on our lips." When all else failed, women resorted to humor—as in Maria Weston Chapman's popular 1837 poem:

Confusion has seized us, and all things go wrong,
The women have leaped from 'their spheres,'
And instead of fixed stars, shoot as comets along,
And are setting the world by the ears! . . .

They've taken a notion to speak for themselves,
And are wielding the tongue and the pen;
They've mounted the rostrum; the termagant elves,
And—oh, horrid! are talking to men!

Our grandmothers' learning consisted of yore
In spreading their generous boards;
In twisting the distaff, or mopping the floor,
And *obeying the will of their lords.*
Now, misses may reason, and think, and debate,
Till unquestioned submission is quite out of date.[53]

"WILD ANARCHY AND SHAMELESS VICE"

After 1837–40, female invasions of the forum multiplied. Editor and social critic Margaret Fuller viewed postrevolutionary "triumphs of Female Authorship" as a "sign of the times. . . . Women have taken possession of so many provinces for which men had pronounced them unfit," she wrote in 1844, "that . . . it is difficult to say just *where* they must stop."[54] Activists applauded the establishment of woman-owned journals, such as *Una* (dedicated in 1854 to elevating women's legal status), the *Lily*, the *Woman's Journal* (published by Lucy Stone and Henry Blackwell), and Stanton's *Revolution*. They also assailed mainstream papers for effectively tightening the "vise" of woman's sphere with derision and disinterest—as when the New York *Herald* trashed the 1850 Worcester meeting as a "motley gathering of fanatical radicals, of old grannies, male and female, of fugitive slaves and fugitive lunatics."[55]

But Americans could choose not to buy and read newspapers. Female lecturing and preaching in reform conventions, parish halls, and town squares were harder to avoid, and the response was commensurately hostile. When the utopian reformer Frances (Fanny) Wright came to the United States from Britain in 1818 and again in 1824, she created an uproar. Journalists assailed her for traveling alone, espousing free love, and addressing mixed audiences. The term "Wrightist" came to be hurled like a spear at transgressive women. The African American lecturer Maria Stewart, the first woman known to have addressed mixed audiences in the United States, demanded as early as 1831 that republicans remake their society so that the "fair daughters of Africa" did not have to "bury their minds and talents beneath a load of iron pots and kettles." She accused ministers of misreading the Bible and, despite taboos against public talk about sex and bodies, damned white men for compelling black women to "commit whoredoms and fornications." Had St. Paul known of "our wrongs and deprivations," she said in 1833, "I presume he would make no objections to our pleading in public for our rights. . . . [H]oly women ministered unto Christ and the apostles"; others had a "voice in moral, religious and political subjects."[56]

Indeed, black women so prized the right to speak freely that they gave it pride of place in the 1832 constitution of the Female Anti-Slavery Society of Salem, Massachusetts, the first such women's society in the United States. Members decided that "the meetings of this Society shall commence and conclude with prayer and singing. Any member who wishes to speak, is allowed the privilege: when any member speaks, there shall be no interruption." And, because African American men encountered many of the same difficulties that white women faced in the forum, they sometimes (although not always) faced down their own prejudices; in 1850, after men at an Ohio freedman's convention had debated the propriety of seating and hearing female delegates, they decided to distinguish themselves from whites and extend parliamentary freedom to women.[57]

Reform societies, including those created by women, served as training grounds for public women. In 1832, the New York Magdalene Society (the alliance of missionaries to which Sojourner Truth had been attached) revealed in its first annual report that 10,000 prostitutes worked the streets of New York City, providing sexual services for leading citizens. Working quietly, members created a network of reform clubs, linked to evangelical churches, to rescue victims of seduction and to remind New Yorkers of their obligation to oppose "sexual sin." Although their success was limited, the reformers defended prostitutes' *bodies* and threatened to name names in their newspaper, the *Advocate*, which by 1850 had come to support women's rights. Says one scholar, for ladies to "come into contact with the fallen" threatened to besmirch *them*. But they did it anyway, deploying the written word as a weapon. "We mean to let the licentious know," they wrote, "that if they are not ashamed of their debasing vice, we will not be ashamed to expose them. . . . It is a justice which we owe each other."[58]

By 1836–37, as Americans plunged into a catastrophic economic depression, opponents of female oratory increasingly tarred belligerent women with heresy, witchcraft, and promiscuity. In 1836, Wright was driven off a Masonic stage with cane pounding, stink bombs, and cries of "whore." Catharine Beecher entirely agreed. "[W]ho can look without disgust and abhorrence upon such an one as Fanny Wright," she said,

with her great masculine person, her loud voice, her untasteful attire, going about unprotected, and feeling no need of protection, mingling with men in stormy debate, and standing up with bare-faced impudence, to lecture to a public assembly. . . . There she stands, with brazen front and brawny arms, attacking the safeguards of all that is . . . sacred in religion, all that is safe and wise in law, all that is pure and lovely in domestic virtue. Her talents only make her the more conspicuous. . . . I cannot conceive any thing in the shape of a woman, more intolerably . . . disgusting.[59]

At a New York reform gathering the same year, the Polish-Jewish émigré Ernestine Rose rose to dispute the sexism and racism of a Kentucky minister, Robert Breckinridge. Shouts of "Throw her down!" and "Drag her out!" and "She's an infidel!" drowned out her remarks; she promptly joined the embryonic women's rights movement. Newspapers called her "lewd" behavior a "forewarning of some terrible calamity, that a woman should call a minister to account, and . . . in a church."[60]

Warfare escalated. In the wake of the stormy temperance convocations of 1837, one writer thought it not coincidental that "heretics" (especially Quakers) should be the first to demand male-female equality. Sarah and Angelina Grimké established the first white women's abolitionist society, the Anti-Slavery Convention of American Women. The city of Charleston formally exiled Angelina for her public oratory and her incendiary abolitionist and women's rights pamphlets. Publicists accused both women (alongside Anna Dickinson, suspected of sexual laxity because of her "coarse" speech) of moral turpitude; in a testament to the power of words, South Carolina postmasters publicly burned Angelina's *Appeal to the Women of the South*. Angelina had urged every woman to "do all that she can by her voice, and her pen, and her purse, and the influence of her example" to smash slavery *and* to secure "the right of women to unite in holy co-partnership with man" to regenerate the world.[61] Also in 1837, after the Grimkés caused a riot in Massachusetts by addressing a mixed audience, Angelina declared a victory: "It is wonderful how the way has been opened for us to address mixed audiences, for most sects here are greatly opposed to public speaking for women, but curiosity and real interest in the antislavery cause . . . [induce] attendance at our meetings."[62]

Criticism, far from destroying the movement, served as a catalyst for action. After the 1852 Syracuse convention, sympathetic writers noted that "daring women" held the platform with great skill; by contrast, a minister thought that the "infidel" affair was "tainted with the unholy doctrine of woman's rights." Four years later, hecklers in Rochester, New York, denied Anthony access to the podium on the ground that the "spirit" of their constitution forbade it. The abusive crowd made her feel like a latter-day Ann Hibbens: "If all the witches that had been drowned, burned and hung in the Old World and the New had suddenly appeared on the platform threatening vengeance for their wrongs, the officers of that convention could not have been thrown into greater consternation."[63] After Brown's famous ouster, women formed the Woman's New York State Temperance Society, which allowed both sexes to speak but reserved offices for women. In an 1852 address, Stanton linked temperance to women's rights; a year later, she made the speech connection: "We have been obliged," she told members of the new society, "to preach woman's rights, because many, instead of listening to what we had to say . . . , have questioned the right of a woman to speak on any subject. In courts of justice and legislative assemblies, if the right of the speaker to be there is questioned, all business waits until that point is settled. Now, it is not settled in the mass of minds that woman has any . . . right to stand on an even pedestal with man, look him in the face as an equal, and rebuke the sins of her . . . generation. Let it be clearly understood, then, that we are a woman's rights Society; that we believe it is woman's duty to speak whenever she feels the impression to do so; that it is her right to be present in all the councils of Church and State."[64]

Protestant clergymen led the assault. In the difficult year of 1837, the Reverend Jonathan Stearns of Massachusetts admonished women to seek "influence," rather than publicity. "*Society* is her empire, which she governs almost at will," he wrote. "It is her province to *adorn* social life, to throw a *charm* over the intercourse of the world, by making it lovely and attractive." He then addressed the speech problem: "That there are ladies who are capable of public debate . . . and who might speak to better edification than most of those on whom the office has hitherto devolved, I am not disposed to deny. The question is not in regard to *ability*, but to *decency*, to order, to Christian *propriety*."[65] A particularly vivid example of clerical outrage appeared in July 1837, when Hubbard Winslow, pastor of Boston's Bowdoin Street Church, delivered a discourse on the "Appropriate Sphere of Woman." Winslow fairly bludgeoned his audience: "[W]hen females undertake to assume the place of public teachers, whether to both sexes or only to their own";

> when they form societies for the purpose of sitting in judgment and acting upon the affairs of the church and state; when they travel about from place to place as lecturers, teachers, and guides to public sentiment; when they assemble in conventions to discuss questions, pass resolutions, make speeches, and vote upon civil, political, moral, and religious matters; when they begin to send up their names to gentlemen holding official stations, gravely declaring their own judgment . . . , and informing them, with solemn menace what they [will] do, if they do not yield . . . ; when they attempt the reformation of morals by engaging in free conversation and discussion upon those things of which the apostle says, "it is a shame even to speak;" . . . —in short, when the distinguishing graces of modesty, deference, delicacy, and sweet charity are . . . displaced by the opposite qualities of boldness, arrogance, rudeness, indelicacy, and the spirit of denunciation of men and measures, . . . —it is then no longer a question whether they have . . . violated the inspired injunction which saith, "Let the woman learn in silence with all subjection, but I suffer not a woman to teach, nor to usurp authority over the man, but to be in silence."

"The world," he concluded, "has had enough of Fanny Wrights. . . . [W]hether they appear in the name of avowed infidelity, or of civil and human rights, . . . their tendency is ultimately the same—the alienation of the sexes, the subversion of the distinguishing excellence . . . of woman . . . , the destruction of the domestic constitution, . . . [and] the reign of wild anarchy and shameless vice."[66]

Conservative pastors reminded their flocks of Ephesians, 5:22–24: "Wives, submit yourselves unto your own husbands, as unto the Lord. For the husband is the head of the wife, even as Christ is the head of the Church. . . . [A]s the church is subject unto Christ, so let the wives be to their own husbands in every thing." In August 1837, clerics who were scandalized by attempts to merge women's rights with abolitionism printed a pastoral letter in the *Liberator*: "The appropriate duties and influence of women are clearly stated in the New Testament. . . . The power of woman is in her dependence, flowing from the consciousness of that weakness which God has given her for her protection." Brazen hussies would be thrown to the wolves: When woman "assumes the place and tone of man as a public reformer, our care and protection of her seem unnecessary; we put ourselves in self-defence against her; she yields the power which God has given her for protection, and her character becomes unnatural." The clerics condemned the "mistaken conduct" of women who played "an obtrusive and ostentatious part" in reform or worked as "public lecturers and teachers," as well as the "promiscuous conversation of females" about "things 'which ought not to be named,'" such as rape, body parts, and contraception.[67]

Nor did resistance to women's authoritative speech end with the Civil War. As late as 1876, the Reverend Isaac See found himself hauled before Presbyterian elders in Newark, New Jersey, to answer charges that he had allowed two women to speak about temperance from his pulpit. In the galleries were Matilda Gage and a number of other female theologians. In prosecuting See (who lost the case), the Reverend Dr. Craven set out what Gage called "the general clerical and church view" and cast women's oratory as an attack on male sovereignty: "I believe the subject involves the headship and crown of Jesus." Dr. See had "admitted marital subordination," but refused to say that woman as a class had been subordinated to man. Craven called this condition the "created subordination . . . of woman as woman to man as man."

> The proper condition of the adult female is marriage. . . . Women without children, it might be said, could preach, but they are under the general rule of subordination. . . . Man's place is on the platform. It is positively base for a woman to speak in the pulpit; it is base in the sight of Jehovah. The whole question is one of subordination.[68]

Women responded to these tongue-lashings with more speech. And while scholars have long known that the "Woman Question" ultimately ripped organized abolitionism apart,[69] it is critical to note that women often described exclusion as a *constitutional* problem. Once evicted from halls, "lovers of free speech" (as one woman put it) lamented shortages of alternative spaces and civil leaders' disinterest in "protecting the right of free speech." Said another publicist, "What we want for women, is the *right of speech.*"[70] William Lloyd Garrison understood why the right mattered so much: If women were allowed to speak in public as a matter of right rather than by permission, "they might speak elsewhere for another object" and "proceed to occupy a pulpit and settle over a congregation." There was "no knowing where such a precedent might lead"; once Americans granted women equal access to the forum, they might have to confer "title" to a myriad of rights. Antoinette Brown confessed that she had attended the Half World Temperance Convention partly to test "the speech principle"; once there, she refused to "utter words of flattery" by which she might win the day's battle but lose the war.[71]

Even Frederick Douglass, for whom the right to vote was *the* badge of citizenship, saw the importance of speech freedom for women. In post–Civil War speeches urging universal suffrage, he recalled that, at midcentury, men had "shuddered at the thought of daughters, wives, sisters, and sweethearts standing before a multitude . . . and making themselves heard in speech. All manner of ridicule and ribaldry was poured upon women's conventions." What women wanted, he said, "first of all, and most of all, was that greatest of all rights, the right of speech, the right to utter their pent up feelings and . . . convictions . . . ; to make a fiery protest against the fetters with which custom, bigotry and superstition had . . . bound them." In woman's collective voice, he thought, men heard "the wild alarm cry of revolt. . . . It was the uprising of one half of the human race against the opinions and customs of the other half." In "the most stupendous revolution the world has ever witnessed," words served as what he called a "lever" to pry open the forum.[72]

At issue was the realization of the promise of the Revolution and Awakening, for women and for the republic. Could the female majority claim its rightful place in the constituent power? Share authority at home? Join men in civic undertakings? For many, the answer was no; as Stanton put it in 1856, in marriage and society as in business, the "silent partner loses everything."[73] Frances Gage recalled that during the ado over Brown, the Reverend Carey presented a resolution recognizing women "as efficient aids and helpers in the home, but not on the platform." Ernestine Rose underscored European despots' love of silence: Could it be that "here, too, there are tyrants who violate the individual right to express opinions on any subject? And do you call yourselves republicans? No; there is no republic without freedom of speech." At an Akron, Ohio, meeting in 1851, Gage explained why republican women needed access to the podium: "Let woman speak for herself, and she will be heard."

> Let her claim with a calm and determined, yet loving spirit, her place, and it will be given her. I pour out no harsh invectives against . . . our fathers, husbands, and brothers; they do as they have been taught; . . . they act as the law requires. Woman must act for herself. . . . Oh, if all women could be impressed with the importance of their own action, and with one united voice, speak out in their own behalf, in behalf of humanity, they would create a revolution without armies, without bloodshed, that would do more to . . . purify, elevate, ennoble humanity, than all that has been done by reformers in the last century.[74]

Occasionally, publicists interpreted women's demand for speech freedom as a simple assertion of the right to petition government or an attempt to secure the remedies available to citizens when government broke the law. Thus, in 1852, the Syracuse *Standard* affirmed that if "any of the natural rights belonging to women are withheld from them by the laws and customs of society, it is due to them that a remedy should be applied"; aggrieved citizens required "an opportunity to give free expression to their opinions."[75] But early feminists had in mind more than a hat-in-hand right to petition. Stanton viewed oratory and planned "disturbances" at men's meetings as avenues to social refabrication and steps toward self-ownership. However inexperienced or terrified speakers might be, however life threatening the arsonists and muggers gathered outside the hall, women were obliged to speak, literally to save their lives. Brown compared "enforced silence" to "slavery," and while many black reformers understandably argued that such comparisons slighted differences between white and black women's experiences, Brown thought that liberty of speech would empower *all* women in relations with all men.[76]

Nothing illustrates the belief in the transformative power of speech more completely than the proceedings of women's rights conventions: Once reason had won the day—both in new communities and in the broader society, where citizens might read and consider published debates—families would boast co-heads, men would open doors to women, and the republic would be reborn. In 1854, Rose asked "man to meet us . . . in the spirit of inquiry, in the spirit of candor and honesty, as rational human beings ought to meet each other, face to face, and adduce arguments, if they can, to convince us that we are not included in that great Declaration of Independence. . . . If they can convince us that we are wrong, we will give up our claims; but if we can convince them that we are right, . . . then we expect them in a spirit of candor . . . to acknowledge it."[77] Conventioneers encouraged women to speak often and fully. In 1853, for instance, Frances Gage asked delegates to the fourth national convention in Cleveland to extend "perfect liberty here to speak upon the subject under discussion, both for and against; and [to] . . . urge all to do so." She wanted *conventions*, not hostile newspapers, to become primary sites for talk about women's rights.[78] In 1860, the tumultuous national convention in New York urged "consciousness of responsibility" for increased "writing and speaking." When the collectively managed *Woman's Advocate* opened in 1855, Stanton and Anthony cheered both its economic value and its contributions to the movement's discourse. For many women, in fact, official newspapers were anathema because they might diminish the volume of speech. In 1854, leaders went toe to toe with advocates of a movement newspaper; Lucy Stone, Lucretia Mott, and others finally defeated the proposal, on the ground that while they valued "organization," they positively revered "individual freedom and responsibility." Women were *not* to be seen as a class that spoke sotto voce.[79]

Occasionally, activists disfranchised men. One woman recalled that, at the Salem, Ohio, convention of 1850, no man had been "allowed to sit on the platform, to speak or vote. *Never did man so suffer.*" When men tried to comment, they were ruled out of order and, for the "first time in the world's history . . . learned how it felt to sit in silence." The Woman's State Temperance Society of New York decided that although men could join their organization, only women could address the membership. But into the Civil War era, other societies maintained an open forum, sometimes with amusing results. During the seventh annual women's rights convention of 1856, women enjoyed a debate between a male theology student, who maintained that God had not "fitted" woman for "the pulpit, the rostrum, or the law court, because her voice was not powerful enough," and Thomas Higginson, who argued that the "capacity to speak indicates the right to do so." In 1863, when delegates tried to silence a man at a Loyal League meeting, Anthony intervened: "Some of us . . . have many a time been clamored down, and told that we had no right to speak, and that we were out of our place in public meetings; far be it from us, when women assemble, and a man has a thought in his soul . . . to retaliate upon him."[80]

Women's rights workers clearly viewed public speech as a vital ingredient in the shaping of new women; mere attendance at meetings had salutary but different effects. At the formative 1850 women's rights convention at Salem, Ohio, delegates resolved to regard "those women who content themselves with an idle, aimless life" as the cause of the "guilt as well as the suffering of their own oppression" and lauded "those who go forth into the world, in the face of the frowns and the sneers of the public, to fill larger spheres of labor, as the *truest preachers of the cause of Woman's Rights.*" When the organized clergy "place[d] its hands on woman's lips" and silenced her, women decided at Syracuse in 1852 that the antidote was more female preaching. At an 1860 meeting in New York City, the Reverend Samuel Longfellow of Brooklyn, New York, brother of the poet, made clear that speech *did* have the desired effect:

> When a woman speaks, and speaks well, speaks so as to interest and move and persuade men, there is no need of any argument . . . to prove that she has the liberty . . . , and that it is a part of her sphere to do it. She has done it; and that of itself is the whole argument—both premise and conclusion in one. And I think if there were none but men present here, it would be better that only women should speak.[81]

Margaret Fuller pointed to one of Abigail Kelley's performances to illustrate the *necessity* of female speech. Public speakers like Kelley, she wrote, "invariably subdue the prejudices of their hearers, and excite an interest proportionate to the aversion with which it had been the purpose to regard them." Orators walked through walls so that future generations might walk through doors. "The scene was not unheroic—to see that woman . . . a centre of rude eyes and tongues," one of Fuller's correspondents had written. Kelley sat "amid the great noise" and, after "tenderly open[ing] to the sphere around her, . . . did much good, more than the men in her place could do."[82]

Time and again, members of speech communities testified, as if in a revival, about conversions to the cause. Said Lucy Stone in 1867 after a pro-suffrage straw poll in a

Kansas meeting, "Verily there was a great turning to the Lord that day, and many would have been baptized, but there was no water."[83] Journalists marveled at the suspension of class and race antagonisms, the absence of dress codes, and (with exceptions) delegates' sensitivity to differences of opinion. As one writer noted, the convention officers were "all without bonnets. . . . Every variety of age, sex, race, color, and costume were here represented. Bloomers were side by side with the mouse-colored gowns . . . [of Quakers], and genteelly dressed ladies of the latest Paris fashion. . . . The colored people scattered through the audience seemed quite at their ease, and were evidently received on grounds of perfect equality, which was the subject of much comment."[84]

In an 1887 account of her life, Mary Livermore credited oratory with personal as well as professional victories. Head of the Civil War-era Sanitary Commission, a suffrage moderate, and an orator of "rare powers" and "magnetism,"[85] Livermore came to public speaking relatively late, while serving as a nursing administrator. In 1863, when she traveled to Iowa to encourage patriotic work among ladies' aid societies, she was appalled to learn that organizers had invited hundreds of men and women to hear her. "I am *not* a public speaker," Livermore told a dignitary. "I have never made a speech in my life, and never have addressed any but companies of women. I had something to say to you, ladies, . . . but it is not at all worthy to be presented as an address to the great audience that you have unwisely called together. *I cannot do it.*" Although the organizers persuaded governor-elect William Stone to speak in her place, he told Livermore that *her* voice would better advance the cause. "Tonight," he scolded, "God has prepared for you an opportunity to speak to all Iowa. . . . [H]ow dare you . . . say, 'I cannot do it'?"[86]

Suppressing terror, Livermore navigated the passage from sex segregation and public silence to integration and vocality: "I followed him down the aisle of the church to the platform, erected in front of the pulpit, where a seat was reserved for me. The ladies of the Aid Society looked their astonishment. As speedily as possible Colonel Stone presented me to the great gathering. I rose by a supreme effort, trembling in every fibre of my being, although outwardly appearing calm. Shutting out all thought of the expectant multitude before me, I concentrated my mind upon what I had to say. For the first ten minutes I talked into utter darkness. It was as if the house was unlighted. I did not even hear the sound of my own voice—only a roaring, as if ten thousand mill-wheels were thundering about me. . . . The physical tumult into which this effort plunged me was exhausting. . . . But gradually it began to grow light about me. I began to hear my own voice."

> I could, after a little, distinguish the faces of people whom I knew. I was aware that I was being heard all over the house. Then I lost all sense of fear, and after the first fifteen minutes I forgot the audience, the fact that I was a novice as a public speaker. . . . Once I was interrupted by long and loud applause. I was so absorbed that I did not understand it for a moment, and looked around to see what had fallen. I thought some of the seats had given way.

Thereafter, Livermore crossed the continent "in 'mud-spankers,' in stages, 'prairie schooners,' on railroads, and in every conceivable way. I held meetings," she wrote proudly, "and did whatever was necessary" to raise money for the war effort and to advance woman's cause.[87]

Hundreds more braved platforms to investigate what the Seneca Falls organizers called "the Social Civil and Religious Condition of Woman"[88] and to establish public personalities. Well into the Civil War, women acted on the knowledge that oratorical self-defense, especially when listeners *knew* the speaker, was at least as powerful as utterances at the polls. Indeed, when Stanton ran for Congress in 1866 (for which effort she received twenty-four votes), she offered a "creed" of *"free speech, free press, free men, and free trade—the cardinal points of democracy."* Without a "coeval" right to speak in mixed assemblies and to be where men gathered, women's citizenship would be a matter merely of "law," rather than of social "fact."[89] Nobody made the point more effectively than Wendell Phillips. "Why talk?" he asked at an 1860 women's meeting. " . . . [T]hirty millions of thinking, reading people are constantly throwing it in the teeth of reformers that they rely upon talk! What is talk? Why, it is the representative of brains. And what is the characteristic glory of the nineteenth century? That it is ruled by brains, and not by muscle; that rifles are gone by, and ideas have come in; and, of course, in such an era, *talk is the fountain-head of all things.*"[90]

Chapter 5

Toward Coequality and Self-Possession

Sometime in 1838, hard on the heels of the Grimké sisters' incendiary lectures about white mens' immoral and unconstitutional subordination of blacks and women, Harvard law professor Simon Greenleaf decided to mount his own lyceum series about the legal status of women. He had in mind cooling fevered brows. "The public ear," he said, "has been filled with declamation upon the wrongs of woman,—her political and legal non-existence,—her natural equality,—her inalienable rights, and her degrading servitude; as though the sex . . . had been conquered and subjugated by man, and were still held in a state of bondage." Not so, he argued: the doctrine of marital unity actually advanced human equality and women's best interests.[1]

Listening intently was 32-year-old "Keziah Kendall" (probably a pseudonym), who supposedly lived with two sisters on a dairy farm near Cambridge, Massachusetts. In "Kendall's" telling, the trio boasted a "good estate—comfortable house—nice barn, garden, orchard . . . and money in the bank besides." She had heard about one of Greenleaf's lectures from her milkman; afterward, she wrote a letter informing him that his talk had been useless. As a property owner liable for taxes but disfranchised, Kendall had hoped to learn *why* she was absent in government; Greenleaf's lecture shed no light. As she put it, the "whole responsibility" of the farm fell on her, and while she was "not over fond of money," she had "worked hard" for long years trying to "do all in my power to help earn, and help save." Would it not be "strange" if she did not value property more than "those who never earned anything?" She did not like the lecture: "[I]t was pretty spoken enough, but there was nothing in it but what every body knows. We all know about a widows' third, and we all know that a man must maintain his wife, and we all know that he must pay her debts, if she has any. . . . What I wanted to know," she added pugnaciously, "was good reasons for some of those laws that I cant account for. I do hope if you are ever to lecture . . . again, that you will give us some."[2]

The unmarried "Kendall" resented both disfranchisement and the long shadow of married women's disabilities. "Now we are taxed every year . . . taxes for land, for movables, for money and all," she said. "I dont want to go representative or anything else, . . . but I have no voice about public improvements, and I dont see the justice of being taxed any more than the 'revolutionary heroes' did." What *about* no taxation without representation? The law of coverture, moreover, had altered her life. Her indebted fiancé had feared that should they marry, his creditors would "get my property"; depressed and broken, he had gone to sea, never to return. "What I have suffered, I cannot tell you," she wrote; there was "more might than right" in the law of domestic relations. She did not "wish to go about lecturing like the Misses Grimkie," but she sensed in them a "call from humanity to speak" and judged *his* lecture "a onesided thing." Nor were the Grimkés troublemakers: "When the fuss was about Antimasonry, the women did nothing about it, because there were no female masons, and it was none of their business." This was different: "Women are kept for slaves as well as men—it is a common cause, deny the justice of it, who can!"[3]

By the mid-1850s, thousands of women had found "common cause." The woman calling herself Kendall was a full-time farmer and so wrote letters; others labored as canvassers, speakers, writers, and organizers—not only to advance the cause of women but also to *name* ideas and experiences never before broached in public. Mariana Johnson, president of the Westchester, Pennsylvania, convention of June 1852, dubbed the movement a "new thought . . . destined to work a revolution in human society."[4] As with all "new thoughts," agitation came to involve a certain amount of creative disorder. But by 1850, at least three styles of thought and argument could be discerned within the movement—a dominant evangelical approach to reform (linked over time with sex-conscious coequality, "social feminism," and late-century groups like the Woman's Christian Temperance Union); a legalistic approach (ultimately associated with sex-neutral equality, "liberal feminism," and what Aileen Kraditor calls the "justice" school of post–Civil War suffragism);[5] and dissenting or radical frames of mind (such as socialism and utopianism, which together made up a small but influential minority). From within their new communities, women forged distinctively feminine "constitutions of aspiration" from bits and pieces of evangelical Protestantism, republican constitutionalism, and an emerging culture of sympathy. In the process, they took long strides toward self-possession and self-rule.

GOD'S REPUBLIC, LAW'S REPUBLIC

As the careers of the Worcester delegates make clear, advocates of republican coequality carried experimental Christianity and perfectionism into women's communities, fundamentally altering their objectives and culture. Nancy Hewitt reminds us that one-fourth of the signatories at the 1848 Seneca Falls meeting were Quakers who likely responded not to Elizabeth Cady Stanton's call, but to that of Quakerism's leading figure, Lucretia Mott, and her coreligionists, who "took an alternate path to the public platform" and envisioned a radically different women's movement than did many of their confederates. Paulina Wright Davis's keynote address provides ample evidence of perfectionist inspiration. She proposed nothing less than the "redemption of half the world" without "arming the oppressed against the oppressor"—a transformation of the female class from a condition of subjection to full citizenship without resorting to "violence or any form of antagonism." How? Not only by securing "rights," but by replacing the "worn-out with the living and the beautiful, so as to reconstruct without overturning, and to regenerate without destroying." God's own justice would "conquer by its power of truth," which, in turn, would emerge in the course of structured conversation. This "radical joining of Heaven and earth," in Robert Abzug's inspired phrase, lay at the heart of attempts by Wright Davis and others to force men to make good on eighty-year-old promises of equality and deliberative self-government.[6]

In 1849, the charismatic Mott eloquently laid out the perfectionist vision of republican coequality in response to a speech by novelist Richard Henry Dana, who had charged activists with "mannish" neglect of Christian duties at home. "We would admit all the difference, that our great and beneficent Creator has made in the relation of man and woman, nor would we seek to disturb this relation," she said, "but we deny that the present position of woman is her true sphere of usefulness; nor will she attain to this sphere, until the disabilities and disadvantages, religious, civil, and social, which impede her progress, are removed out of her way." Man-made laws and customs, which posed as the work of God, "enervated her mind and paralyzed her powers." So long as republicans assumed that the "existing differences" between the sexes were "not arbitrary . . . but grounded in nature," woman would be unwilling to "make the necessary effort to obtain her just rights," in part to avoid the "scorn" of critics like Dana.[7]

Mott thus celebrated biological difference *and* criticized the relatively recent crystallization of sexualized "spheres," thereby challenging more than one tenet of the revolutionary settlement. Why not follow talents and interests wherever they might lead? Why should men have to be "mannish" and women "womanish"? With other advocates of a merger between "fundamental principles of Christianity and Republicanism," as one woman put it, Mott was ambivalent about female involvement in party strife—not because of some incapacity, but because of women's moral superiority. At Seneca Falls, Mott had opposed the suffrage plank; years later, she still abhorred the profanity and violence of political life. Perhaps women could ease the "turmoil of political life," as some claimed, but she doubted it. As early as 1838, Angelina Grimké likewise had advised women to avoid "the contention and strife of sectarian controversy" and the "intrigues" of parties. She rejoiced that woman did not "stand on the same platform which man now occupies in these respects"; indeed, she regretted that man would "thus prostitute his higher nature." She criticized the "fallacious doctrine" of separate "male and female virtues" and spheres and condemned the moral squalor inseparable from the halls and saloons in which men conducted public business. Mott and many other radical Protestants encouraged women to participate in conventions organized to advance "self-government on Christian principles." There, activists could pursue truth through conversation, renegotiate the social compact, and identify the proper balance between rights and duties. But Mott, for one, did not "encourage women to vote, or to take an active part in politics in the present state of our government." When a woman of conscience wanted to be "acknowledged a moral, responsible being" by casting ballots, the right should be "yielded"; in effect, Mott's faith in moral self-determination trumped her misgivings about partisan violence.[8]

Perfectionists appreciated the power of law in society and so advocated law reform. But like their antinomian forebears, they regarded the legal order as an imperfect expression of "truth"—a system to be scrutinized constantly for signs of decay. "In the intelligent ranks of society," said Mott, "the wife may not in point of fact be so degraded as the law would degrade her; because public sentiment is above the law. Still, while the law stands, she is liable to the disabilities which it imposes."[9] Religious women argued, too, that republicans should abolish legal fictions by which some citizens held others in subjection. In some ways, they walked a tightrope: Because many of them saw men and women as essentially different, they often thought of womankind as a *class* blessed with sex-specific gifts and responsibilities. Yet they also believed that women were self-sovereign agents capable of wresting their own salvation from a sinful world. As Wright Davis said in 1850, woman did not seek "either identity or likeness . . . of the two sexes" but rather an "equivalence of dignity, necessity, and use; admitting all differences and modifications which shall not affect a just claim to equal liberty in development and action."[10]

This community- and family-centered search for justice gave rise to breathtaking visions of cultural transformation in which impediments to freedom simply fell away. Wright Davis had sketched one such utopian future in her 1850 Worcester address. Four years later, delegates at Albany, New York, aspired to "take off burdens, to remove hindrances, to leave women free as men are free, to follow conscience and judgment in all scenes of duty."[11] In the 1852 meeting at Westchester, reformers sought "perfect freedom of thought and action"—that is, woman's "equal freedom with her brother to raise her voice and exert her influence directly for the removal of all the evils that afflict the race." Ruth Plumbly's vision was equally dazzling: "We think the first great step is to clear away the rubbish of ages from the pathway of woman, to abolish the onerous restrictions which environ her in every direction, to open to her the temples of religion, the halls of science and of art, and the marts of commerce, affording her the same opportunity for education and occupation now enjoyed by man."[12]

The use of a perfectionist idiom probably encouraged skeptical Christians to consider arguments they might otherwise have dismissed, and the knowledge that women might put on divine armor *before* they entered profane spaces likely eased some anxiety about contamination. In 1852, convention leader Ann Preston saw women occupying the polity alongside men in perfect safety, with both sexes shielded by a "sacred and beautiful covering" of faith. After an 1851 convention at Worcester, editor Henry Bellows of the deeply skeptical New York *Christian Inquirer* declared himself impressed by the piety and rigor of speeches delivered there. He had expected empty rhetoric; he had been wrong: "No more practical or tremendous revolution was ever sought in society, than that which this Woman's Rights Convention inaugurates." To "emancipate half the human race from its present position of dependence on the other half " was a change that surpassed "any other now upon the platform, if it do not outweigh Magna Carta and our Declaration themselves." Bellows even approved of women's methods: "In starting a radical reform . . . , it is expedient that it should be put, not on the basis of old grievances, but upon the ground of new light, of recent and fresh experiences."[13]

This infusion of tradition ("Magna Carta and our Declaration") with boundless faith in the human race's capacity for improvement ("the ground of new light") altered the meaning of old concepts. When Americans schooled in revolutionary constitutionalism talked about cultivating "voluntarism," "harmony," or "equality," they usually envisioned a virtuous polity comprised of male citizens unequal in society but equal at law, empowered to make bargains with other men and with the state as individuals, obliged to engage in public service, and responsible not only for self-discipline but for the ordering of "subject" classes. When Johnson spoke of a "true Harmonic Order," in contrast, she probably had in mind a society of divinely inspired, spiritually equal men and women who were free to discover their own paths, constrained only by irreducible physical differences. Republicans would govern families as coequals and would make decisions (and come to agreements) jointly, but, in the end, conscience dictated what individuals might contribute to society. If a godly woman wanted to vote, make hats, or run for Congress, the right had to be yielded, but nobody could force others to do these things. The sexes were "pillars in the same temple and priests of the same worship," in public as in spiritual life, but not in any other sense identical and free to follow whatever path God had marked out. Quaker physician Elizabeth Blackwell (the founder of the Woman's Medical College of the New York Infirmary in 1868) foresaw a "great work of human regeneration," the "full harmonious development" of woman's "unknown nature," and "Harmonic Freedom" for all republicans.[14]

A second frame of mind—spearheaded after 1837 by women like Stanton, Susan B. Anthony, and Ernestine Rose, and a minority view before the Civil War—also bore the imprint of religious enthusiasm. As Elizabeth Clark observes, this way of thinking about emancipation, like its evangelical kin, originated in "a liberal Protestant creed that celebrated the innate goodness of human nature and its ability to find its own right course once external regulation was lifted." But the languages of choice tended to be legal, not theological, originating mainly in what Stanton called "liberal principles of republicanism," the law of contract and property, and (to a lesser extent) European moral philosophy. Ultimately, and with important exceptions, these reformers envisioned sex-neutral equality rather than sex-specific coequality.[15]

In her keynote address at Worcester, Wright Davis had employed the evocative language of republican constitutionalism alongside religious tropes. As in 1776, women aimed to "achieve for the race" (that is, for human beings) everything that "belongs to it" as a matter of birthright. Just as the minions of George III had not been free to usurp the liberties of colonists, so the "rights and liberties of one human being" never could be pronounced the "property of another" without due process of law. Every lawyer knew that rights were a species of property carried into the polity by signatories to the social compact and that God wisely placed the natural rights of citizens beyond the reach of legislators. In the absence of a judicial hearing (such as a criminal trial) or adequate reimbursement (as with property seized for a public use), nobody ordinarily could create or abolish rights, or arbitrarily transfer one person's property to another, as happened to women's property at marriage. A man "owned" his bundle of rights, but only his own; the "blessings" of liberty that the woman-citizen claimed by dint of hard work, humanity, and membership in the constituent power belonged to *her*; the government's job was to keep her secure in the use and enjoyment of rights. In theory, abrogations of a woman's natural rights without judicial proceedings amounted to an unconstitutional "taking" of her property—and, with it, her security in liberty. As Davis said, woman sought a "full and generous investiture of all the blessings which the other sex has solely, or by her aid, achieved for itself"; the restoration of rights taken unconstitutionally; and recognition of a female presence in the constituent power.[16]

Stanton and other liberal constitutionalists tended to consider individuals, not families—and certainly not classes—as the republic's building blocks. They also hoped to surmount biological differences, emphasizing the shared humanity of men and women, blacks and whites. As Matilda Gage put it, "Woman has been legislated for as a class, and not as a human being upon a basis of equality with man, but as an inferior to whom a different code was applicable."[17] These women saw "contracts" where others found social relationships; they also toyed with the possibility that legal rules, when rightly conceived and executed, might embody "truth." To reiterate Clark's important point: Stanton and other liberals (as we now would call them) hoped that the family would develop "along the lines of the republican state" so that women might escape "obligations that had become unwanted bonds," akin to the debasing ties that bound medieval serfs to lords. Rights-bearing citizens would be tied directly to the state, identified first as sovereign individuals; no longer would women's public personalities depend on marital or kin relationships.[18]

Although caught up in legal norms and tropes, these rebels were anything but cautious. Metaphorically, the Sons of Liberty had committed regicide; now, the Daughters of Liberty aspired to smash kingship within families and renegotiate constitutions. Stanton told New Yorkers in 1867 that when they remade the state constitution, "ALL THE PEOPLE should be represented. . . . Woman and negroes, being seven-twelfths of the people," were a majority and the "rightful rulers of the nation."[19] To be sure, activists relied heavily on law reform and rejected violent upheaval, but the plan to liberate colonized women by remaking the social compact was no less radical than the 1776 decision to replace the Crown with a popular sovereign. Indeed, in 1854, Stanton proposed trying petit kings for treason, much as patriots had done with George III. "The tyrant, Custom," she said, "has been summoned before the bar of Common-Sense. His majesty no longer awes the multitude—his sceptre is broken—his crown is trampled in the dust—the sentence of death is pronounced upon him. All nations, ranks, and classes have . . . repudiated his authority." Now, the female majority refused to submit: "Yes, gentlemen, in republican America, in the nineteenth century, we, the daughters of the revolutionary heroes of '76, demand . . . the redress of our grievances—a revision of your State Constitution—a new code of laws."[20]

Only occasionally did God's republic and the republic of law collide head-on, but when they did, sparks flew. To give an example, when the 1860 National Woman's Rights convocation opened in New York's Cooper Institute, Stanton offered ten resolutions related to the law of marriage and divorce. Any "constitution, compact, or covenant between human beings," she began, "that failed to produce or promote human happiness" was without "force or authority," and woman's "right" as well as her "duty" was to "abolish it." Marriage, although divinely sanctioned, nevertheless was "only known by its results"; it could not be described as an inviolable estate, to be preserved even when unproductive, dangerous, or coerced. Said Stanton, when "society . . . by its laws or customs, compels its continuance, always to the grief of one of the parties, and the actual loss and damage of both, it usurps an authority never delegated to man, nor exercised by God himself." Were not social compacts bottomed on *voluntarism*? Why force women and children to live with tyrants?[21]

Antoinette Brown Blackwell disagreed. In an attempt to derail Stanton's resolutions, she delivered what one listener called a "sermon" against the idea that the republic would benefit from revised marriage and divorce laws. Delegates listened aghast as she moved away from the meeting's "equal rights" focus toward divisive social questions. In seven counterresolutions, Brown Blackwell pronounced wedlock a "voluntary alliance of two persons of opposite sexes into one family," which, because of its "possible incidents of children, its common interests, . . . must be, from the nature of things, as permanent as the life of the parties." She therefore seemed to be embracing the sacramental view of marriage still prevailing in many southern states. Yet, unlike many conservatives, she rejected the notion of "natural" marital inequalities. Although marriage had never been "merely a contract," spouses retained "sovereignty" within "true units"; inequality within marriage indicated a misreading of God's plan. Sovereign individuals were supposed to "co-work," seek a "higher idea of life," and collectively redeem "the whole human family."[22]

Thus, Brown Blackwell and sympathetic Christians parted ways with both Stanton *and* Joel Bishop. On the one hand, natural law rather than the law of contract supposedly created marriage, which made it a divine, permanent undertaking. On the other hand, the marital contract embodied *equality*, not female subjection; the villain was not marriage per se, but bad theology and law. A wife was "morally obligated to maintain her equality in human rights in all her relations in life"; if she consented to her "own subjugation, either in the family, church or State," she was "as guilty as the slave" in "consenting to be a slave." When caught in a "false relation," a woman was "bound to maintain her own independence . . . ; to assert herself . . . as the equal of man, who is only her peer." But having ensured her own safety, she had to work toward a true relation.[23]

Stanton and Brown Blackwell disagreed less about the importance of marriage per se than about the nature of the republic's building blocks. By 1860, Stanton saw relational views of women as symptoms of legal-cultural disease; to experience freedom, women as individuals had to strike up direct relationships with the state and escape the inequalities built into the law of coverture. Brown Blackwell contended, on the contrary, for the primacy of families governed by cosovereign "units"; without these building blocks, the moral fabric of society would unravel. Perfectionism led her to reject (as "false") conceptions of families as sites of oppression *and* to reject (as misguided) Stanton's radical individualism, with its condemnation of all "status" relations, including marriage.

INVENTING A COMMON LANGUAGE

Before the 1860s, such open warfare was exceptional, if only because evangelical and secularized approaches to change rarely existed in pure form. As Nancy Cott observes, feminists did not fasten on modern labels, such as "sameness" (or liberal) feminism and "difference" (or social) feminism, until well after adoption of the Nineteenth Amendment[24]—not because they were naive, but because they spoke the language of female emancipation (the *Woman* Movement) rather than that of modern suffragism or the broader strains of feminism that emerged after 1960 (*women's* movements). Citizens of antebellum speech communities shared more than a few convictions and habits of mind. As a group, they believed, for example, that rational conversation produced truth and social change; that most women, most of the time, *lived* freedom and government differently from men; that inherited legal, educational, and religious systems hurt women; that an aristocracy of sex pervaded American society; and that the wall between masculinity ("public" life) and femininity ("private" life) was both arbitrary and unnecessary. Women also evinced a remarkable command of the language of law. Like abolitionists, they usually grounded rights claims in natural law, rather than man-made law, especially when lawyers contended that the right in question could be limited or regulated. Treating rights as a form of property was problematic. On the one hand, because "the masculine element" lawfully asserted property rights in women's labor and society, to secure the modification of "bad law," reformers had to argue that such rights were not inviolable. On the other hand, since women had in mind asserting *title* to their own labor, bodies, and children, they could ill afford to erode popular reverence for property or for property in rights. Thus, much as the abolitionists did, they relied on natural law to cast doubt on claims to women's labor and property and to condemn (as "bad" law or "false" readings of texts) the common law doctrines supporting such claims.

Speakers and writers also condemned the idea of "rights-as-grants," even when such rights benefited women; Garrison's *Liberator*, for instance, won applause for noticing that women had long been viewed as "creatures of law—from which [they are] said to derive rights." To discredit the rule by which dower rights vanished on remarriage, Mariana Johnson averred that *none* of women's property, including dower rights, could ever be "held by sufferance, dependent for a basis on location, position, color, and sex, and like government scrip, or deeds . . . , transferable, to be granted or withheld, made immutable or changeable, as caprice . . . or the pride of power and place may dictate."[25] Time and again, women affirmed that the rights demanded were *not* merely "conventional," but were "inalienable" and "coeval with the human race." In 1848, framers of the Seneca Falls Declaration claimed on behalf of women the "equal station to which they are *entitled*"; and while the rights enumerated there included several that lawyers took to be limitable, Stanton noted twice—as did Garrisonians on behalf of slaves—that rights originated with "the laws of nature and of nature's God."[26]

In addition, women used rigorously empirical styles of argument, especially when challenging doctrines rooted in custom or "faith." To some extent, radical empiricism reflected the influence of European feminists, with whom Americans corresponded, but it also betrayed familiarity with legal science, philosophical skepticism, and the writings of William Sampson (who called the common law "judicial astrology") and other democratic law reformers.[27] The record bristles with compilations of fact, "true" histories of women's lives, and "corrected" accounts of church-state crimes against women. Stanton and Anthony called the massive *History of Woman Suffrage* (published in stages between 1881 and 1920) an "arsenal of facts" in the war against custom. Stanton's shining example of the virtuous skeptic was Matilda Gage, taught as a girl to "accept no opinion because of its authority, but to question the truth of all things. Thus was laid the foundations of her . . . non-acceptance of masculine authority."[28]

Nor did women doubt that the law governing marriage and divorce lay at the heart of women's powerlessness. Nothing touched daily life more constantly: All women had to deal with the expectation of marriage, law's power to shape cultural norms (for example, presumptions of incompetence), and social punishments meted out to "bad" women. Marital reform thus affected how all women would be governed and, by implication, how all household dependents would be treated by all masters; without it, man never would come to see woman "as a co-sovereign"[29] robbed of her freedom. Both Stanton and Brown Blackwell (who supported reform of the law of marriage, if not of divorce) clearly regarded domestic relations law as a key instrument of woman's subjugation. "I feel as never before," Stanton told Anthony in 1853, "that this whole question of women's rights runs on the pivot of the marriage relation, and, mark my word, sooner or later it will be the topic for discussion." She deplored the transmutation of marital contracts into Holy Writs and campaigned hard for demystification. "If you take the highest view of marriage, as a Divine relation, which love alone can constitute and sanctify," she said in 1854, "then of course human legislation can only recognize it. Man can neither bind nor loose its ties, for that prerogative belongs to God alone. . . . But if you regard marriage as a civil contract, then let it be subject to the same laws which control all other contracts. Do not make it a kind of half-human, half-divine institution, which you may build up, but can not regulate."[30]

Well beyond the Civil War, feminists insisted that emancipation began at home. In 1870, Stanton observed in *Revolution*, "We know that the ballot when we get it, will achieve for woman no more than it has achieved for man. . . . [T]he ballot is not even half the loaf. . . . [It] touches only those interests . . . which take their root in political questions. But woman's chief discontent is not with her political, but with her social, and particularly her marital bondage. The solemn and profound question of marriage . . . is of more vital consequence to woman's welfare, reaches down to a deeper depth in woman's heart, and more thoroughly constitutes the core of the woman's movement, than any such superficial and fragmentary question as woman's suffrage." Lucy Stone thought, too, that marital inequality underlay "the whole movement, and all our little skirmishing for better laws and the right to vote, will yet be swallowed up in the real question, viz., Has woman a right to herself? It is very little to me to have the right to vote, to my own property, etc., if I may not keep my body . . . in my absolute right." Two decades later, Anthony called wifely dependence "the tap-root of our social ills" and of woman's "subjection," lying "deep down at the very foundations of society."[31]

Male reformers often agreed. Henry Blackwell and the utopianist Robert Dale Owen, for example, signed contracts at marriage renouncing the "legal superiority granted to them at law"—precisely the kind of agreement that Bishop later condemned as being "against law." Owen divested himself in 1832 of "the unjust rights which in virtue of this ceremony an iniquitous law tacitly gives me over the person and property of another"; in 1855, Blackwell denounced the "whole system of coverture"—including male "custody of the wife's person," the "exclusive control and guardianship of . . . children," the "sole ownership" of a wife's earnings and property, and unequal treatment of widows and widowers. In their wedding protest, Lucy Stone and Blackwell further declared (against law) that "personal independence and equal human rights can never be forfeited, except for crime," which marriage presumably was not, and that wedlock should be "recognized by law" as "an equal and permanent partnership."[32]

A petition prepared in 1854 by Judge William Hay of Saratoga, which he and Anthony presented to a New York legislative committee, vividly illustrates the numbing rigor as well as the sweep of the war against coverture. Ernestine Rose thought that the document embodied the most pressing demands of the "second half of the nineteenth century." Hay demanded that spouses be made "tenants in common of property;"

> . . . that a wife shall be competent to discharge trusts . . . [like] a single woman; that the statute in respect to a married woman's property descend as though she had been unmarried; that married women shall be entitled to execute letters testamentary, and of administration; that married women shall have power to make contracts and transact business as though unmarried; that they shall be entitled to their own earnings, subject to the proportionable liability for support of children; that post-nuptial acquisitions shall belong equally to husband and wife; that married women shall stand on the same footing with single women, as parties or witnesses . . . ; that they shall be sole guardians of their minor children; that the homestead shall be inviolable and inalienable for widows and children; that the laws [of] . . . divorce shall be revised, and drunkenness made cause for absolute divorce; that better care shall be taken of single women's property . . . ; that the preference of males in descent . . . shall be abolished; that women shall exercise "the right of suffrage," and be eligible to all offices, occupations, and professions; entitled to act as jurors; eligible to all public offices; . . . that a law shall be enacted extending the masculine designation in all statutes . . . to females.[33]

Women relied as well upon the legitimating aphorisms of revolutionary constitutionalism and its political analogue, liberal republicanism. Indeed, the introduction to the *History of Woman Suffrage* tied emancipation firmly to basic constitutional maxims and to the struggle against slavery (at law, the erasure of civil identity). "Women's political equality with man," Stanton and Anthony averred, "is the legitimate outgrowth of the fundamental principles of our Government, clearly set forth in the Declaration of Independence in 1776, in the United States Constitution . . . , [and] in the prolonged debates on the origin of human rights in the anti-slavery conflict in 1840."[34]

These gestures were both expedient and deeply patriotic. While the framers had resisted extending the fruits of revolution to women, old English ideas *had* been put to subversive use after 1765, and the incongruity of women's situation occasionally had been recognized—as with arguments in *Martin v. Massachusetts* and the abolition of petit treason in the 1780s on the ground that monarchism had been abolished. It remained only for women to locate themselves in the sovereign people and use arguments fielded against British "lords" in the 1770s—as when reformers decried "taxation without representation" in dozens of convention speeches, letters, and newspaper articles. Lawmakers often re-

sponded positively to evocations of America's civil religion. In May 1856, Wisconsin legislators heard a minority report from a committee on the reenactment of election laws.
Wisconsin women apparently had asked that the "theory of our government . . . be reduced to practice"; a significant number of legislators had to agree that republicanism had
to be more than a "rhetorical flourish." While Europeans proclaimed "the divine right of
kings, and assume that man is the mere creature of the government, deriving all his rights
from its concessions," said the minority chair, Americans elevated "all men to an equality with kings" and made government "his creature instead of his master." "Man-mascu-
line" did not claim "certain inalienable rights because he is male, but because he is human"; when he denied basic human rights to "man-feminine," he exercised the same
"tyranny against which *we* felt justified in taking up arms."[35]

Stanton's 1848 keynote address at Seneca Falls showcased her mastery of republican
constitutionalism. "We have met here today," she began, "to discuss our rights and wrongs,
civil and political." She then demanded redress for those wrongs and a remaking of the
constituent power to include women: "We are assembled to protest against a form of government, existing without the consent of the governed—"

> to declare our right to be free as man is free, to be represented in the government which
> we are taxed to support, to have such disgraceful laws as give man the power to chastise
> and imprison his wife, to take the wages which she earns, the property which she inher-
> its, and, in case of separation, [her] children; laws which make her the mere dependent
> on his bounty. It is to protest against such unjust laws . . . that we are assembled to-day,
> and to have them . . . forever erased from our statute-books. . . . The great truth, that no
> just government can be formed without the consent of the governed, we shall echo and
> re-echo in the ears of the unjust judge.[36]

On its face, the Seneca Falls Declaration seemed to embrace rather than reject lawyerly
practices and basic constitutional texts. Women exercised their right to petition government whenever it broke the rules, much as colonists had peaceably protested the Stamp
Act. The preamble, like that of Jefferson's original declaration, sought to explain and justify behavior known to be treasonous in terms that lawyers might understand. It pointed
to certain "self-evident" truths, notably the unacknowledged fact of a female presence in
the constituent power. It alluded to the pursuit of "life, liberty, and . . . happiness" and it
listed "repeated injuries and usurpations" by which men maintained an "absolute tyranny"
over women—among them, "takings," the erasure of women's civic obligations, the government's failure to ensure all citizens' physical security, and male mediation between
women and both the state and God.[37]

Yet, in pointing to the inadequacy of social compacts negotiated during the revolutionary settlement, the Seneca Falls Declaration also subverted the constitutional order. It
reminded the Sons of Liberty that when a government destroyed freedom, citizens could
"refuse allegiance to it" and demand the "institution of a new government." Man, for example, had "so framed the laws of divorce" as to benefit himself first, and women and
children secondarily, which undermined promises of legal equality. Woman's "happiness"
mattered less than access to her property when it could "be made profitable," and preservation of the "supremacy" of a sex that "monopolized nearly all the profitable employments." Mankind withheld "all the avenues to wealth and distinction which he considers
most honorable to himself," including "theology, medicine, or law"; professional expertise, in turn, allowed men to "prove" female inferiority.[38]

Orators at Seneca Falls and elsewhere portrayed women as yet another formerly colonized population mobilizing at a preordained moment on the world stage. The women's rights movement was a "legitimate outgrowth" of republican political experience; in the 1850s, Americans were witnessing the "natural" evolution of yet another class from servitude and dependence to sovereignty and accountability. As in the 1770s, an entrenched aristocracy saw rebellion as the "willful outburst of a few unbalanced minds, whose ideas can never be realized under any form of government." If sex was America's main class distinction, as many women claimed, was not the "male element" obliged to abolish sex distinctions? Why perpetuate a "false sentiment" that burdened the female sex with moral responsibilities but let men off the hook? Having charged woman with preserving virtue, men had persuaded her that she could do *only* that, destroying "confidence in her own powers" and encouraging her to "lead a dependent and abject life."[39]

Stanton promised a flood of speech: Women would "employ agents, circulate tracts," petition various legislators, enlist the pulpit and press, and call a "series of Conventions, embracing every part of the Country."[40] Reformers did just that. After Seneca Falls, convention delegates pointed repeatedly to the fact of virtual representation—as in Syracuse, New York, in 1852, when women asked not for "rights as a gift of charity, but as an act of justice. For it is in accordance with the principles of republicanism, that, as woman has to pay taxes to maintain government, she has a right to participate in the formation and administration of it." In 1860, Rose observed ebulliently that she was *speaking* and then explained why republicans had to listen: "I am speaking in a democracy; I am speaking under republican institutions."

> The rule of despotism is that one class is made to protect the other; that the rich, the noble, the educated are a sort of probate court, to take care of the poor, the ignorant, and the common classes. Our fathers got rid of all that. They knocked it on the head by the simple principle, that no class is safe, unless government is so arranged that each class has in its own hands the means of protecting itself. That is the idea of republics. The Briton says . . . "I will protect you." And the American says, " . . . I had rather take care of myself!"—and that is the essence of democracy.[41]

Such talk reopened the revolutionary settlement to which most Americans had acquiesced after 1800. "Do we fully understand," asked Elizabeth Oakes Smith, "that we aim at nothing less than an entire subversion of the present order of society, a dissolution of the whole existing social compact? Do we see that it is not an error of to-day, or of yesterday, against which we are lifting up the voice of dissent, but that it is against the hoary-headed error of all times?"[42] If Victorians failed to facilitate "woman's free development," said physician Elizabeth Blackwell, "then society must be remodeled, and adapted to the great wants of all humanity." There was no mistaking the stridency of the much-repeated assertion that women already possessed the right to make law; the threat of "complete revolution" appeared in newspapers alongside pleas for "unity" and "social harmony." At the Broadway Tabernacle convocation in New York City in 1853, delegate Charles Burleigh noted that a woman was "under no moral obligation" to comply with "any laws which, wanting her assent, yet assume to control her every action, word, and even thought." Her "property, her person, all her rights, her most sacred affections, come within the province of those enactments; yet she can have no voice." Dr. Harriot Hunt and other prominent women withheld taxes pending a restoration of citizenship rights. Said Stanton in an 1854 address, "It is not enough for us that by your laws we are permitted to live and breathe, to claim the necessaries of life from our legal protectors—to pay the penalties of our crimes; we demand the full recognition of all our rights as citizens of the Empire State. We are persons; native, free-born citizens; property-holders, taxpayers." Because man denied woman "the most sacred rights of citizens," she was "theoretically absolved from all allegiance to the laws of the State." In effect, women challenged men to confront them in debate and voluntarily cede their monopoly on wealth, knowledge, and power. Otherwise, they risked a constitutional rebellion.[43]

William Lloyd Garrison therefore was right to say that women were simply "measuring the people of this country by their own standard."[44] At an early moment, the Litchfield Declaration had illustrated this sanctifying resort to "the Spirit of '76," as did the 1848 Seneca Falls Declaration and dozens of resolutions adopted at rights conventions after 1848–50. So thoroughly did Stanton's colleagues exploit the tradition's exhortative power in 1848 that the Reverend Asa Mahan, president of Oberlin College, condemned the resulting Declaration as an embarrassing "parody" of Jefferson's document.[45] Activists continued to make use of revolutionary imagery well into the Civil War era. When Stanton confronted New York lawmakers in 1867, for instance, she began by accusing them of betraying the principles of '76. White men were the "nobility" in America, a "privileged order" that had "legislated as unjustly for women and negroes" as had English lords for their "disfranchised classes." How could republicans tolerate such practices? "If the history of England has proved that white men of different grades can not legislate with justice for one another," she asked, "how can you . . . legislate for women and negroes, who, by your customs, creeds and codes, are placed under the ban of inferiority? If you . . . claim that woman is your superior, and . . . shield her by your protecting care from the rough winds of life, . . . your statute books are a sad commentary on that position. Your laws degrade, rather than exalt woman; your customs cripple, rather than free; your system of taxation is alike ungenerous and unjust."[46]

Stanton then made an important leap to women's property. Lawyers had long associated the capacity to deal in property with broader claims to a public personality; self-mastery and "freedom from dependence on the will of others" (as historian Jack Greene puts it) traditionally went hand in hand.[47] It mattered little whether all members of the female class owned property and paid taxes. The fact that *many* members of a class had property and supported the government implied that *all* possessed a latent capacity; conversely, demonstrations of a class's membership in the constituent power traditionally mandated access to economic rights. Indeed, as "independence" came to be severed from old moorings in real property, the exclusion of woman solely on the ground of economic dependence made less and less sense. Tenant farmers and male wage earners, who *could* vote and make contracts, were equally dependent on lordlike capitalists for survival. As Nancy Fraser and Linda Gordon observe, one of white men's shining achievements in the nineteenth century was their assumption of rights and obligations based solely on *wages*, which, in turn, gave cultural urgency to the old suggestion that wage labor "stigmatized" women.[48]

Perhaps because the idea of economic capacity as a springboard into political life was fraught with difficulty, William Hay, Anthony, and others toyed with emphasizing linkages between sovereignty and the right to engage in self-defense, rather than between economic and political rights. Old avenues to autonomy had been muddied by those who wanted access to women's capital without paying a political price. As Hay noted, critics worried less about property rights than about "unsexing woman," as if the "revolutionary maxim concerning taxation and representation going together is not a property rule." He suspected that "personal rights, secured by the right preservative of all rights [the ballot]," might be "more important" for the purpose than "mere property rights." Hay may have had in mind South Carolina Justice Nott's well-known ruling in the 1819 equity case of *Sturgineger v. Hannah.* In that case, the judge ruled that wives could "retain all their interest in personal as well as real estate," so long as retention did not impair male sovereignty: "I am sensible of the mischiefs which might result from a *divided empire. But the right of property is not necessarily connected with the right of sovereignty.* I am disposed, therefore, to protect . . . the rights of the wife, as far as we can consistent with the rules of law, and the decisions of our courts, provided we do not invade the prerogatives of the husband."[49]

Still, because the argument was time honored, leaders of the movement continued to posit a connection between economic capacity and the constitutional right to be represented directly in government—as when Stanton insisted in 1854 that the right to property would "of necessity, compel us . . . to the exercise of our right to the elective franchise, and then naturally follows the right to hold office." In many circles, these connections still had great force. As a Wisconsinite put it, because woman had "all the interests on earth that man has, [and] . . . all the interest in the future that man has," she ought to be enfranchised. If a man became "a better man . . . by the possession of his rights," so a woman inevitably would improve and progress.[50]

THE "FIRST WAVE" CRITIQUE OF PATRIARCHY

Within women's new communities of opinion, there emerged a powerful critique of "man-made creeds"[51]—among them, the common law, education, theology, and custom, which many reformers accorded the force of law. Having studied "facts," women resolved to see "clearly," to learn to recognize and eliminate mental cobwebs, and to escape what Stanton called the "triple bondage of the man, the priest, and the law." Delegates at Seneca Falls had announced in 1848 that women intended to identify *truth* by means of "writing and speaking" in "any assemblies proper to be held"; thereafter, any "custom or authority adverse to it, whether modern or wearing the hoary coat of antiquity," would be rejected "as a self-evident falsehood." Skepticism was pervasive. In an 1854 discussion of the movement's objectives, for example, Mott noted, "We too often bind ourselves by authorities rather than by the truth"; Garrison added that for women's rights activists and abolitionists alike, "texts and books are of no importance."[52]

Activists left few stones unturned. Because examinations of school curricula revealed a "masculine" pedagogy, women began to distinguish between convention-bound school curricula and republican education per se. Matilda Gage produced searching commentaries on biblical texts and church practices, exhumed women omitted from official accounts of the Christian church's development, and limned the historical partnership between church and state in controlling women. Such critics not only unearthed historical relationships between women's degradation and church policies, but between religious and common law doctrines. As Nancy Isenberg aptly observes, antebellum women "recognized that the church itself was a religious public that assumed political and moral duties": the much-touted "church-state" distinction, like the "public-private" one, has meaning only in a fairly recent and formal constitutional sense.[53]

The author of the controversial *Woman's Bible* wholeheartedly agreed. Having been taught that "father and husband stood to her in the place of God," said Stanton, womankind had been denied "liberty of conscience, and held in obedience to masculine will." She pointed out as well that without Eve and the serpent, there would have been "no need of a Savior. . . . [T]he bottom falls out of the whole Christian theology."[54] For all her life, she characterized much of human history as a war between the sexes, with churchmen presiding over woman's degradation: "The priestess mother became something impure, associated with the devil, and her lore an infernal incantation." The woman "as mother and priestess, became woman as witch," and witch trials, the "very real traces of the contest between man and woman."[55] Gage similarly concluded that the church-state leviathan was "essentially masculine" in its origin and development. All the evils associated with "dignifying one sex and degrading the other may be traced to this central error: A belief in a trinity of masculine Gods in One, from which the feminine element is wholly eliminated." Mott, whose belief in the primacy of "individual conscience" led to her excommunication from the Society of Friends, put it succinctly: "It is not Christianity, but priestcraft that has subjected woman as we find her."[56]

The common law and its votaries came in for sharp criticism. "Man can not represent woman," said Brown Blackwell at the 1852 Syracuse meeting. "They differ in their nature and relations. The law is wholly masculine; it is created and executed by men. The framers of all legal compacts are restricted to the masculine stand-point of observation, to the thought, feelings, and biases of man. The law then could give us no representation as woman, and therefore no impartial justice . . . ; for we can be represented only by our peers."[57] Rose insisted in 1853 that men per se were not the cause of woman's difficulties. "We do not fight men," she said. "[W]e fight bad principles. We war against the laws which have made men bad and tyrannical. Some will say 'But these are laws made by men.' True, but they are made in ignorance of . . . eternal principles of justice and truth . . . engrafted on society by long usage." Indeed, mindless adherence to "usage" was at least as important as bad law. Said Ohio's Elizabeth Jones in 1852, though the law deprived women of many freedoms, there were others which "no law prevents." Women could secure "rights as merchants and in other avocations . . . ; but we stand back and wait till it is popular for us to become merchants, doctors, lecturers, or [mechanics]. I know girls who have mechanical genius . . . but their mothers would not apprentice them. [Y]et there is no law against this!"[58]

Some women aimed only to force conversation. One hoped to "strike a hard blow, and if possible . . . shake the old systems of laws to their foundations, and leave it to other times and wiser councils to perfect a new system." Others had in mind laying "male sophistries" alongside republican principles and persuading legislators to eliminate rules that fell short. Still others ridiculed lawyerly preoccupation with the "harmony of the statutes" or explored alternatives to the common law—notably, the civil law-inspired rules predominating in states and territories influenced by Spanish, Dutch, and French practices. For many, the archetypal example of legal irrationality was "the old Blackstone code for married women"; speaking for delegates at the path-breaking 1850 convention in Salem, Ohio, Johnson condemned the "whole theory of the Common Law" as "unjust and degrading," in violation of "great principles of equality and justice."[59]

Criticism of "irrational" systems led, in turn, to talk about their function within society. Speakers, for instance, repeatedly urged women to read the Bible for themselves. "Ignorance of women in general as to what their Bibles really do teach," said Stanton, "has been the chief cause of their bondage."[60] For Abigail Kelley, false education underlay female incapacity: "We are what we are educated to be." Stanton similarly urged her comrades to break the "shackles of a false education." But, in the end, lawyers—especially "old lawyers"[61]—vied with the clergy for the title of chief antagonists. Dozens of women charged lawyers, legislators, and judges with ensuring female helplessness. Said one woman, "The law of the country creates *sentiments*"; wives and daughters internalized the "degraded position" described in law books. Rose feared that her sisters had "hardly an adequate idea how all-powerful law is in forming public opinion, in giving tone and character to the mass of society. . . . Such is the magic power of law." As Wendell Phillips explained on the eve of the Civil War, "all our social life copies largely from the statute-book."[62] Insights multiplied. Women decided, for instance, that blind faith in outmoded doctrine underlay both the sex's resistance to its own liberation and the portrayal of reformers as traitors. "This morning," reported a sorrowful Gage in 1853, "when I was leaving my boarding-house, some one said to me, 'So you are ready armed and equipped to go and fight the men.' I was sorry, truly sorry. . . . I have no fight with men. I am a daughter, a sister, a wife, and a mother. . . . What do we seek to overturn? The bad laws and customs of society. These are our only enemies, and against these alone is our hostility directed; although they be 'hallowed by time,' we seek to eradicate them."[63]

WOMEN'S "CONSTITUTION OF ASPIRATION"

Within this framework of criticism and renegotiation, women laid out many of the elements of an alternative social compact and bill of rights. They did not lack ambition. Delegates to the Massilon, Ohio, convention of 1852 sought "rights personal, social, legal, political, industrial, and religious, including . . . representation in the Government, the elective franchise, free choice in occupations, and an impartial distribution of the rewards of effort." In an 1853 issue of *Una*, Wright Davis—who thought of her colleagues as "the abolitionists of slavery among women"—demanded "equal opportunity for free development, equal access to advantageous positions, equal wages for equal work, and equal rights for equal capacities." Three decades later, Stanton said that the Seneca Falls Declaration encompassed "equal rights in the universities, in the trades and professions; the right to vote; to share in all political offices, honors, and emoluments; to complete equality in marriage; to personal freedom, property, wages, children; to make contracts; to sue, and be sued; and to testify in courts of justice."[64] For a good many convention participants, moreover, identifying the "mould of prejudice . . . gathered thick upon the common mind" was hardly enough: Women had to remake both themselves and the polity. Reformers proposed not only to change law and culture, but also to provide hands-on experience with what Stanton called "self-sovereignty." Only when women had claimed their "natural rights as human beings" would they be able to secure "civil and political rights as citizens of a republic."[65]

As they struggled to remake the republic, women framed hundreds of rights claims. Not surprisingly, economic freedom figured large. Theoreticians were certain that once married women possessed agency rights equivalent to men's, fictions of marital unity and female dependenc would explode. In fact, widespread disdain for women's economic contributions—and, even more fundamentally, linkages between economic dependence, the lack of political freedom, and physical insecurity, particularly among married women—sometimes persuaded women to join the movement. Amelia Jenks Bloomer, the popularizer (though not the inventor) of what came to be called the bloomer dress in her temperance journal *Lily*, attended the Seneca Falls meeting but withheld her signature from the Declaration. Then, when Tennesseans decided that women lacked "free and independent souls and therefore had no right to own property," Bloomer changed her mind. "Wise men these," she said, "and worthy to be honoured with seats in the hall of legislation in a Christian land. Women no souls!"[66]

Everywhere, conventioneers worried aloud about how unpaid woman's work (and its long shadow in the wage labor market) contributed to woman's "degradation"; said Frederick Douglass, while woman's "first demand was for speech," her "next was for education, and the next was for an enlargement of her industrial vocations." Time and again, women urged legislators to adopt the Continental idea of community property, as practiced in old Spanish, French, and (to some extent) Dutch colonies and territories, by which spouses held the marital estate jointly; as late as 1875, Anthony opined that matrimony would "never cease to be a wholly unequal partnership until the law recognizes the equal ownership in the joint earnings and possessions" of spouses. In strikingly modern terms, reformers demanded "equal pay for equal work"; at Seneca Falls, Mott insisted on a resolution to "secur[e] the woman an equal participation with men in the various trades, professions, and commerce." In 1859, a New Englander denounced "great evils" at the "foundation of depressed wages"—among them, the "want of respect for labor" which prevented "ladies from engaging in it," and disrespect for women, which "prevents men from valuing properly the work they do."[67] George Francis Train of Kansas (who ultimately embarrassed the cause in Kansas) damned the male monopoly of meaningful work. "Do you mean to say," he charged in 1867, "that the school mistress . . . should only receive three hundred dollars, while the school master . . . gets fifteen hundred?"

> All the avenues of employment are blocked against women. . . . Embroidering, tapestry, knitting-needle, sewing needle have all been displaced by machinery; and women speakers, women doctors, and women clerks, are ridiculed . . . till every modest woman fairly cowers before her Emperor Husband, her King, her Lord, for fear of being called "strong minded."[68]

Virtually everyone agreed that economic rights and autonomy were intertwined. Ultimately, women were able to make use of the writings of Harriet Taylor and John Stuart Mill, in circulation as early as 1861, which argued that the "power of earning" underpinned the "dignity of a woman," particularly if she had no "independent property."[69] But well before then, workers and activists alike connected freedom (both political and physical) to the production of wealth. In 1841, Betsy Chamberlain, a young operative at the experimental Lowell factories in Massachusetts, dreamed of seeing wages for women "equal to the wages of males" so that she and her friends might "maintain proper independence." In her 1850 introduction to Barbara Bodichon's *Women and Work*, Catharine Sedgwick wrote, "It is the Christian theory of our social organization, that no class among us is condemned to perpetual labor, and none (like the English Aristocracy) exempt from it. Labor—*work* should, therefore, have no plebeian brand among us. Qualification for work should be the stamp of citizenship—the badge of nationality. Our women of every class have a right to this qualification." New England's Caroline Dall condemned a system that "blots out the legal existence of a wife, denies her right to the product of her own industry, denies her equal property rights, even denies her right to her children, and the custody of her own person." Such practices "give men a slave but never a wife."[70]

Speakers and publicists also denounced unconstitutional treatment of the property rights of wives, widows, and divorced women. More than one pundit wondered why judges had created a new felony (marriage) to be punished, as if it were treason, with the loss of constitutional rights to make contracts, retain earnings, and manage property. And notwithstanding widespread support for married women's property acts (which partly aimed to offset the loss of dower rights), activists condemned both the erosion of the widow's "third" and governmental confiscation of dower rights at divorce. Said Clarina Howard Nichols at the 1852 Syracuse meeting: "It is a provision of our National and State Constitutions, that property rights shall not be confiscated for political or other offences against the laws. Yet in all the States, if I am rightly informed, the wife forfeits her right of dower in case of divorce for infidelity to the marriage vow." Howard Nichols claimed that "the laws which cut off the wife's right of dower . . . confiscate property rights, and hence are *unconstitutional*." Women protested sex-specific treatment of widows and widowers—the husband's right as a tenant in curtesy to use the "better part of his dead wife's property, the wife's life interest under the best conditions . . . a paltry third." In 1854, Stanton went so far as to demand equal rights to privacy: "Had she died first, the house and land would all have been the husband's still. No one would have dared to intrude upon the privacy of his home, or to molest him in his sacred retreat of sorrow. How . . . can that be called justice, which makes such a distinction . . . between man and woman"?[71]

Simultaneously, women sought personal security—again, especially (but not only) within marriage. Surely, they argued, the law's unsubtle suggestion of female subjection (such as in the *baron*'s claim of conjugal rights and domestic services) conditioned all men to view all women as providers of sexual pleasure and encouraged citizens of both sexes to mete out punishment when women violated the line between domestic and public spheres. Reformers touted the manhandling of Brown Blackwell as an example of both political retaliation and disrespect for women's bodies. They avidly pursued the Maine Temperance Law and new divorce laws to protect women from physical abuse and "imprisonment" by drunkards and tyrants.[72] They aimed to walk city streets without imputations of whoredom or masculinity. And in defiance of taboos, they demanded freedom from abuse during pregnancy, from "enslavement of the soul" by husbands authorized by law to "seize" runaway wives, and from the claustrophobia induced by a man's "common law right to a woman's society." Without often naming it, activists claimed the right of locomotion; indeed, lecturing often appealed to women precisely because it allowed "perfect physical freedom." One speaker relished "space to cut loose from the marital buttons, and go out into the world alone!" When officials exiled Angelina Grimké from her native city in 1836–37, she cast the problem in terms of a right to move about freely—to "exercise her right as an American citizen, and go to Charleston."[73]

Restrictive clothing contributed to a sense of confinement and insecurity. The amazing array of horsehair, metal, horn, and whalebone required to clothe a lady immobilized and weakened her; it was no small wonder that, for the relatively brief period in which she wore the bloomer costume, Stanton experienced a "sense of liberty."[74] In June 1857, a Michigan editor reprinted part of an essay by Fanny Dowling describing the process by which a young woman prepared for bed, thereby gaining a measure of freedom. "First, the little lace collar and ribbons were removed from the neck, and the bright merino dress laid aside";

> next the snowy skirts were lifted over the head, then a spring touched in front of the rounded waist when, with a clicking metallic sound, down came the wide expanse of crinoline, while [she] stepped out of its steel circle, considerably collapsed. . . . A somewhat similar operation was repeated and numerous springs and curls were sent in lively motion and then with a stretch upward of the plump white arms, and a long drawn sigh

of relief, off came the little French 'railroad' corsets, and the dimpled shoulders of the
wearer rose in *unrestricted freedom*. The snowy night gown was now slipped over the
head, and its delicate frills daintily adjusted at the throat and wrists. . . . And then drawing a low seat close to the fire, the young girl laid one pretty foot lightly on her knees
and began to unlace the tiny boot which incased it. . . . [75]

Corsets, layered garments, and contrived hairstyles not only jeopardized health and safety
(for instances, cinches and whalebone restricted the rib cage and lungs, making it impossible to work hard or run; long fingernails reduced manual dexterity; tiny shoes retarded
the development of the feet; beehive hairdos attracted bugs; and layers of cotton and wool
caused heat stroke, infections, and skin disease) but also made women appear idle and
frivolous. In 1838, Sarah Grimké warned that women who "submit to be dressed like
dolls" would never "rise to . . . stations of duty and usefulness"; the adoption of silly dress
set them apart from serious-minded, moral citizens. What would Americans do if they
saw "ministers of the gospel rise to address an audience with ear-rings dangling from their
ears, glittering rings on their fingers, and a wreath of artificial flowers on their brow, and
the rest of their apparel in keeping? If it would be wrong for a minister, it is wrong for
every professing Christian."[76]

Bloomers fostered health and physical freedom, or so the controversial army surgeon
Dr. Mary Walker maintained. "The greatest sorrows from which women suffer to-day,"
she wrote in 1871, "are those physical, moral, and mental ones, that are caused by their
unhygienic manner of dressing!" Walker donned a modified bloomer costume, consisting
(as historian Elizabeth Leonard describes it) of a "one-piece linen 'undersuit,' slacks 'made
like men's' and 'buttoned to the waist of the undersuit or . . . arranged with the usual sus-
penders,' and an upper garment resembling a knee-length dress, cinched in at the waist
and with long sleeves, a high neck, and a full skirt." So dressed, she experienced "freedom of motion and circulation," but became the butt of sexual slurs.[77] Stanton wore
bloomers to counteract the "tyranny of custom." Her cousin Gerrit Smith approved: Traditional dress signaled female's "inferiority"; were women dressed otherwise, mankind
would have to admit their "transmutation into his equal." In 1874, Stanton said, "Hang a
hoop skirt on a boy's hips, lace him up in a corset; hang pounds of clothing and trailing
skirts upon him; puff him out with humps and bunches behind; pinch his waist into a com-
pass that will allow his lungs only half their breathing capacity; load his head down with
superfluous hair . . . and stick it full of hair-pins; and then set him to translating Greek
and competing for prizes in a first-rate university. What sort of a chance would he stand
in running that race or any other!"[78]

Sexualized violence also figured prominently. During both the Revolutionary and
Civil Wars, soldiers had harassed and raped more than a few women, and peacetime did
not greatly increase women's physical security. "As you go down in the scale of manhood," wrote Stanton at midcentury, "the idea strengthens at every step, that woman was
created for no higher purpose than to gratify the lust of man. Every daily paper heralds
some rape on flying, hunted girls." She also set about tracing the "slender threads that
link these hideous, overt acts to creeds and codes that make an aristocracy of sex," whether
in slave quarters or middle-class homes.[79] Especially in talk about sexual crime, analogies between women's and slaves' plight proved irresistible for abolitionists and women's
rights reformers alike. Black women embodied in extreme form all the civil, political, and
physical disabilities visited upon the sex. The Grimké sisters, perhaps the best-known

southern abolitionists, encouraged white women to find slavery in every form of mastership, beginning with white men's sexual mastery of black women. This empathic strand emerged on the masthead of the *Liberator*'s women's department ("As I not a woman and a sister?"). But women also noted parallels in the treatment of sexual and racial *classes* at law and sometimes concluded that the shared problem was the "brutal cruelty" inflicted on women and black men alike by "their self-styled lords and masters."[80] Sarah Grimké made interesting connections. "A woman has no name!" she began. "She is Mrs. John or James . . . just as she changes masters; like the Southern slave, she takes the name of her owner." Coverture resembled the slave's loss of "self-possession, including the possession of one's own body." Was not the "very being of a woman, like that of a slave, . . . absorbed in her master" at marriage?[81]

Leaders frequently contended that women needed "rights and powers" sufficient to "control the conditions and circumstances of their own and their children's life."[82] Cosovereignty within households thus included women's ability not only to be coequals with men in civic matters, but to command their own bodies. Few things mattered more to Stanton's followers than what she called "self-sovereignty"[83]—that is, "the sacred right of a woman to her own person, to all her God-given powers of body and soul." Inherent in self-sovereignty or self-ownership was the idea (again in Stanton's words) that "to the mother of the race, and to her alone, belonged the right to say when a new being should be brought into the world." While pleading "for the right of woman to the control of her own person as a moral, intelligent, accountable being," Stone told of a wife who had not "set foot outside of her husband's house for three years" because he refused to let her leave when he was at home, and "lock[ed] her up when he is absent." Rose wanted to know how womankind could "have a right to her children" without a "right to herself."[84] Sarah Grimké condemned marital rape and the sexual abuse of pregnant women. "Man seems to feel," she said in an 1855 essay, "that Marriage gives him the control of Woman's person just as the Law gives him the control of her property. Thus are her most sacred rights destroyed by that very act, which under the laws of Nature should enlarge, establish & protect them." Once pregnant, a woman could be subjected to the "*unnatural* embraces of her husband," endangering "her embryo babe."[85]

In different ways, the reformer Lydia Maria Child and the religious mystic Elizabeth Parsons Packard thought that physical force or the threat of it effectively kept women indoors and compliant. "That the present position of women in society is the result of physical force, is obvious enough," wrote Child in 1843; "whosoever doubts it, let her reflect why she is afraid to go out in the evening without the protection of a man." In her view, "gallantry" was a "flimsy veil which foppery throws over sensuality, to conceal its grossness."[86] In 1860, Packard found herself incarcerated in an asylum when her husband, a Presbyterian minister, tired of her public opposition to his teachings. Ultimately, Packard escaped life commitment by seeking a writ of habeas corpus and persuading a Massachusetts jury of her sanity; she then wielded her pen in defense of married women's autonomy (*Marital Power Exemplified in Mrs. Packard's Trial . . .*).

To say the least, enslaved women did not enjoy personal security. Masters' ownership of women's bodies implied the legality of rape; black women who resisted sexual or disciplinary violence suffered incomparably. In 1855, a self-emancipated Canadian black, Mrs. James Seward, described her master's behavior: "A sister of mine has been punished by his taking away her clothes and locking them up, because she used to run when master whipped her."

He kept her at work with only what she could pick up to tie on her for decency. . . . I was beaten at one time over the head by my master, until the blood ran from my mouth and nose: then he tied me up in the garret . . . [and finally] brought me down and put me in a little cupboard, where I had to sit cramped up . . . all night, and . . . next day. The cupboard was near a fire, and I thought I should suffocate.

In the same year, another enslaved woman said that while she had been "treated tolerably well, compared with others," she had been "whipped with a wagon whip and with hickories, . . . kicked and hit with fists," and had a "bunch" on her head from "a blow my master gave me."[87] Harriet Jacobs, enslaved for twenty-seven years and the author (as Linda Brent) of an important autobiography, recounted her master's campaign to force her to be his mistress, in the process revealing how powerful law could be in shaping social reality. The obsessed man, she wrote in 1860–61, "met me at every turn, reminding me that I belonged to him, and swearing by heaven and earth that he would compel me to submit to him." To escape, she allowed an unmarried but duplicitous white man to seduce her. "You never knew what it is to be a slave," she wrote; "to be entirely unprotected by law or custom; to have the laws reduce you to the condition of a chattel, entirely subject to the will of another."[88]

As the women's rights community struggled to name its grievances and desires, the list of freedoms grew longer. Many of the freedoms so named, moreover, were unknown at law or known as something else. Rebecca Sanford, who became postmistress at Mt. Morris, New York, sought the right of "equal administration with men." Women discussed the "right to serve" (freedom to engage in community service without their husbands' permission), the "right to knowledge," the "right of conscience" and the related "right of volition" (conveying a right to "do one's own thinking and believing"), the "right of membership and association," and dozens more. Conventioneers and writers frequently demanded the feminization of criminal trials; in Stanton's words, because woman had been "forbidden to enter the courts" except as a felon, she had been "unjustly tried and condemned for crimes men were incapable of judging" (such as homicides by rape victims or battered wives).[89]

In this wish list, "freedom of action" (also called the "right to act") loomed large. Women often denigrated the right of petition as the antithesis of action, noting that it was the *only* freedom granted easily. There was ground for concern. When using the term *action,* reformers sometimes had in mind a right to pursue the ends toward which abstract rights aspired; as Frederick Douglass put it, "woman must practically as well as theoretically, assert her rights. She must *do* as well as *be.*" Temperance worker Mary Vaughan, who got caught up in the skirmish over female orators at the notorious meetings of 1852, noted simply that women "would act as well as endure." [90] Others associated the right of action with political freedom. In 1831, Tennesseans captured this idea in a law abolishing debtors' prison, especially for women. Having affirmed the old idea that "liberty of person like the liberty of conscience should not be restrained" unnecessarily, they termed "independence of thought and freedom of action" among the "most inestimable of our political rights." But, more often, women had in mind a general right of free agency. In Angelina Grimké's *Appeal to the Women of the Nominally Free States* (1838), she tied freedom of action—which, she believed, was protected by "our national Bill of Rights and the Preamble of our Constitution"—firmly to speech freedom and to a citizen's obligation to avoid enslavement. "The denial of our duty to act," she wrote, "is a bold denial of our right to act; and if we have no right to act, then may *we* well be termed 'the white slaves of the North'—for like our brethren in bonds, we must seal our lips in silence and despair."[91]

Women loudly condemned impediments to action. The business committee of the 1856 Broadway Tabernacle convention noted in a resolution that women were "taxed but not represented, authorized to earn property but not free to control it, permitted to prepare papers for scientific bodies but not to read them, urged to form political opinions but not allowed to vote upon them." Said Harriet Martineau in an 1851 letter, "Women, like men, must be educated with a view to action." She damned the idea that women could "study anything that her faculties led her to," so long as she agreed to "stop at the study." When she "entered the hospital as physician and not nurse; . . . took her place in a court of justice, in the jury box, and not the witness box; . . . brought her mind and her voice into the legislature, instead of discussing the principles of laws at home; . . . [and] announced and administered justice instead of looking at it from afar . . . , she would be feared." In Martineau's view, "an intelligence never carried out into action" could not be "worth much."[92] A few women tied "action" to natural law. Witness Pennsylvania attorney Carrie Burnham Kilgore's 1881 speech defending her right to practice law: "In natural rights there is no sex. . . . The right to life means the right to attain the object of life—that is the complete and perfect development of the entire capabilities of the human soul through physical organization. It means the right to sustain and defend life by individual effort. It presupposes freedom of action, and an equal right to life implies equal freedom of action."[93]

Many women thought that patrilineal naming, and the underlying transfer of property rights in a woman's labor and society from father to husband, greatly weakened claims to freedom of action. But social and legal penalties for noncompliance were severe; for example, because Lucy Stone retained her birth name at marriage, Massachusetts barred her from the polls when it extended school board suffrage to women. In 1852, Lucretia Mott announced, "Woman's rights women do not like to be called by their husbands' names, but by their own." But this was an overstatement. Only a small minority retained their fathers' surnames. Mott herself adopted James Mott's name; Stanton, as did many other middle- and upper-class women, used both her father's and husband's surnames.[94]

THE ROAD NOT TAKEN

What about ballots and ancillary political rights? Before the mid-1850s, rights to be exercised in nongovernmental domestic or civic spaces took center stage. "Keziah Kendall" and many others deeply resented disfranchisement, but before the Civil War, the right to cast ballots in periodic elections lacked the immediacy of speech freedom, marital and economic rights, and demands for physical security. Notwithstanding firebrands like Kelley, reformers often settled for partial suffrage (as in school board elections) even when it affirmed dependence because they had no choice in the matter and because other concerns pressed harder. Although women chafed under such restrictions, movement leaders (especially evangelical women) primarily aimed to secure female self-ownership, agency, and autonomy within marriage.

This is not to say that ballots were unimportant or, as some scholars contend, that Victorian matrons shied away from demands that might offend their husbands. Stone spoke for almost everyone when she announced in 1855, "We want rights"—by which she meant citizenship rights.[95] Rather, activists variously perceived that resistance would be impossibly fierce, that voting required a direct invasion of "profane" spaces and thus endangered both women and the republic, and that vassalage began at a more fundamental level—with enforced silence and passivity, the expectation of domesticity, and male sovereignty in families. Only by speaking, acting, and cracking apart the unitary domestic "head" would women be able to take their stations as members of the constituent power. As Elizabeth Clark once observed, suffrage did not "automatically take pride of place in the panoply of rights sought . . . before the Civil War, but stood as one goal among many," and much of the time "not the most important" goal.[96]

Stanton had long suspected that the right to vote would be *necessary* for admission to other aspects of public life—that structured conversation might not prevail. She had so argued at Seneca Falls; after 1860, she continued to make the case for the suffrage. But the plea was tempered by growing skepticism about the value of all political "gifts" in a masculine polity and by the certain knowledge that neither ballots nor bloomers *in themselves* would ameliorate woman's condition. "We who have spoken out," she told Gerrit Smith in 1855, "have declared our rights, political and civil; but the entire revolution about to dawn upon us by the acknowledgment of woman's social equality, has been seen and felt but by a few. The rights to vote, to hold property, to speak in public, are all-important; but there are great social rights, before which all others sink into utter insignificance."

> The cause of woman is . . . a broader and a deeper one than any with which you compare it; . . . It is not a question of meats and drinks, . . . but of human rights—the sacred right of a woman to her own person, to all her God-given powers of body and soul. . . . [W]hen woman shall stand on an even pedestal with men—when they shall be bound together, not by tithes of law and gospel, but in holy union and love, then, and not til then, shall our efforts at minor reforms be crowned with complete success.

As always, Stanton came back to the problem of the "true marriage relation," which had "more to do with the elevation of woman than the style and cut of her dress."[97]

Had the day come for republicans to "think less of sex and more of mind"?[98] Many women thought so. Consider the leaps of faith—from speech to wealth production to political freedom—in Elizabeth Oakes Smith's 1852 speech at Syracuse, which began and ended with women's voices: "We should have a literature of our own, a printing-press, and a publishing-house, and tract writers and distributors, as well as lectures and conventions; and yet I say this to a race of beggars, for women have no peculiar resources. Well, then we must work, we must hold property, and claim the consequent right to representation, or refuse to be taxed. Our aim is nothing less than an overthrow of our present partial legislation, that every American citizen, whether man or woman, may have a voice in the laws by which we are governed."[99]

Chapter 6

Capitalism and the New American Empire

In 1860, Mary Livermore attended the Republican convention at Chicago with her journalist husband; years later, she described a remarkable encounter between the press corps and convention officials. "It was my good fortune," she recalled, "to be present at the National Convention . . . which nominated Mr. Lincoln to the Presidency. It was held in an immense building . . . known as the 'Wigwam.'" She had agreed to report the proceedings for an "editor friend" and had been seated "near the platform" where "not one word could escape me."

> My place was in the midst of the great reportorial army. . . . I was fortunate above all women on that occasion, for the far-away gallery was assigned them, and they were strictly forbidden the enclosed and guarded lower floor, which was sacred to men exclusively. From the immensity of the "Wigwam," the proceedings could not be heard in the gallery, and seemed there like gigantic pantomime.
>
> I have never understood the good luck that bestowed me among the reporters . . . , nor how I succeeded in retaining my position when the official attempt was made to remove me. Women reporters were then almost unheard of; and inconspicuous as I had endeavored to make myself by dressing in black, like my brethren of the press, the marshal of the day spied me, after the lower floor was densely packed with masculinity. In stentorian tones . . . , while his extended arm and forefinger pointed me out, and made me the target for thousands of eyes, he ordered me to withdraw my profane womanhood from the sacred enclosure provided for men, and "go up higher," among the women. I rose mechanically to obey, but the crowd rendered this impossible. My husband, beside me, reporting for his own paper, undertook to explain, but was not allowed. The reporters about me then took the matter into their own hands, and in a tumult of voices cavalierly bade me "Sit still!" and the marshal "Dry up!" A momentary battle of words was waged over my head, between my husband and the reporters, the police and the marshal, and then I was left in peace.[1]

In 1860, the vision of male-female relations shared by a handful of journalists actually prevailed: Suddenly, "profane womanhood" exercised key elements of citizenship within "a sacred enclosure provided for men." To be sure, this was the Republican Party—a society as liminal as women's rights groups had been a decade earlier—and Livermore's husband sat beside her, effectively sponsoring her. But the tale still commands attention. In the Wigwam, where citizens gathered to make important public decisions, a handful of men beat back elements of a customary constitution and forged a new reality, for themselves as well as for Livermore. What is more, Livermore attended the convention as a publisher's agent; she earned her way in the world, initially as a nurse, then as an administrator, writer, and paid lecturer. By 1860, it was possible for civic groups to tolerate and even cultivate female participation—a change attributable, in part, to women's participation in economic development. To the extent that Americans still viewed the production of wealth as a ground for claims of right, the law of coverture and attendant practices seemed to be on a collision course with capitalism.

LIBERATING WOMEN'S CAPITAL

As antebellum women demanded greater freedom, politicians set about expanding the economic capacities of wives—sometimes in response to women's rights agitation, but usually not. As early as 1800, New Englanders provided for the descent of estates to widows and children when men died intestate. In the late 1830s, a number of states and territories that were originally governed by the civil law tradition, which made better provision for married women's economic power within marriage than did common law regimes, moved to restore some of the capacities lost in the transition from French, Spanish, or Dutch law to Anglo-American common law. Among them were Arkansas, Mississippi, and Florida, where statutes appeared in 1835, 1839, and 1845, respectively. These acts were inspired, however, mainly by two unsentimental policy goals: First, a desire to liberate capital and put it into circulation, and, second, a determination to close off women's nest eggs to husband-trustees, who sometimes transferred money into them to evade creditors. Not coincidentally, talk about expanding wives' economic autonomy coincided with the financial emergencies of 1819 (when legislators in Kentucky, for example, discussed reform without acting) and 1837 (after which, statutes began to appear across the nation).

Typifying the double-edged character of this kind of reform legislation was a statute passed by the Kentucky General Assembly in 1838 allowing "any person" to make an "annual provision for a resident female friend, relative, or connection" by transferring state bank stock to the woman. The act reserved interest income for her "exclusive use," and stock never could be deeded to the husband or used to pay his debts; a state-appointed trustee (who could not be the husband) guaranteed this arrangement. But even as public trusts ensured a separate income for a few lucky women and protected them, to some extent, from profligate husbands, they also advanced commerce by shoring up bank vaults that had been seriously depleted by the depression of 1837. The Kentucky act also reinforced women's dependence by inviting the "guardians of wards" to make similar investments and forbidding women and minors from converting stock to cash during their lifetimes or using it to pay debts. Thus, the capacity of women to *act* in the marketplace was not appreciably advanced.[2]

Invitations to affirm or expand women's competence that did not clearly advance economic interests usually met with indifference or hostility. In January 1830, for instance, Joseph Story opened a tantalizing doctrinal door—albeit in an international law case, and probably to advance legal science rather than the rights of women. In *Shanks v. DuPont*, on appeal from the superior court of South Carolina, he adopted the old English rule by which nationality ordinarily could not be eradicated. The facts of the case bore a striking resemblance to *Martin v. Massachusetts*; at least one scholar thinks that, at least until 1855, lawyers looked to *Shanks* rather than to state cases like *Martin v. Massachusetts* in disputes involving married women's political allegiance.[3] Ann Scott had married Joseph Shanks, a British officer, in 1781 during the British siege of Charleston; a year later, she went with him to England, where she stayed until her death in 1801. *Shanks* tested whether Ann's English-born children could inherit part of their American grandfather's estate. Had Ann by her marriage and removal assumed Joseph's allegiance? If so, her children inherited nothing. Did marriage alter women's *political* identity? No, said Story; Ann's children could inherit through their mother. Marriage had not erased her nationality (for Story, a political right, in keeping with the law of nations). Marriage to an alien, "whether a friend or an enemy, produces no dissolution of the native allegiance of the wife. *It may change her civil rights, but it does not affect her political rights or privileges.*"[4]

Story's idea might have altered the legal landscape, for good or ill. Even though civil rights changed at marriage, he seemed to be saying, political capacity need not be affected; the two aspects of a legal personality could be disentangled. By implication, perhaps married women could cast ballots despite civil incapacity. But policymakers did not leap into the breach and empower married women to act politically (as male voters without property had been able to do). Instead, *Shanks* governed only the narrow question of the right to retain a national identity after women married aliens, and then only until 1855, when Congress began to impose limits and affirm husbands' power to change the nationality of alien women by marriage—all of which reinforced the traditional "cover" on a wife's political and legal personality.

Meanwhile, Americans steadily expanded wives' ability to deal in property and ignored the political implications of their actions. In constitutional conventions at the mid-century, Michigan, Wisconsin, and Ohio inserted clauses permitting wives to defend their families against economic disaster, typically in articles establishing homestead exemptions. But the devices best calculated to restore limited economic rights were married women's property acts, which, by the end of the century, came to include earnings and contract acts as well as custody legislation (because of parents' property rights in children's labor). Many observers saw these acts as coverture's death warrant. As an optimistic law review writer put it in 1871, "The law of the status of women is the last vestige of slavery. Upon their subjection it has been thought rests the basis of society; disturb that, and society crumbles into ruins. By the married women's property acts, the first blow has been struck. . . . The huge idol will sooner or later be broken to pieces."[5]

Developments in Michigan show how parts of the "idol" came to be smashed. In 1844, legislators guaranteed a married woman's title to all property acquired before marriage (whether by "her own personal industry or by inheritance, gift, grant or devise"), ownership of property to which she might be entitled "by inheritance, gift, grant or devise," and control of income emanating from her property.[6] Lawmakers then retreated, in 1846 barring women's management even of separate property without husbands' consent and, in another act, permitting but not requiring court-assigned trustees (who could be husbands) to hand over control of separate estates to wives. At the 1850 constitutional convention, delegates protected married women's separate estates from husbands' creditors and made them susceptible to the claims of wives' creditors, but withheld the possibility that wives might act freely in the market. Historian Debra Viles concludes that delegates, recalling the depression of 1837, aimed to protect families from future devastation by creating nest eggs (trusts) in women's estates that neither men *nor* women could raid. Five years later, Michiganders codified the existing law and loosened men's hold on property that women brought into marriages. As earlier, the real and personal estate of a woman acquired before marriage, as well as all property to which she later gained title, remained her "estate and property" during coverture and would not be "liable for the debts, obligations and engagements of her husband." A wife also could manage separate property as if she were unmarried, but the marital estate itself was off-limits, unless a trustee deeded part of the estate to her. A wife still could be sued "in relation to her sole property" as if she were a *feme sole*, husbands' creditors could not touch separate property, and contracts made by women before marriage remained "in full force."[7]

In Michigan and elsewhere, economic legislation clearly improved women's prospects over fifty years' time. Legal scholar Carol Shammas estimates that by 1900, about one-third of the estates probated in American courts belonged to women who, in turn, owned about one-quarter of probated wealth; in her estimation, "more change in female wealth-holding occurred between the 1860s and the 1890s" than in the previous two centuries.[8] This quantum leap partly reflected women's increasing participation in the salaried work-force and growing wealth among single white women. In 1860, women constituted about 10 percent of paid workers, of whom about 90 percent were single; thirty years later, the figure was 17.1 percent, of which 40.5 percent were never-married women and an equal proportion were widowed or divorced. In cities, unwed "working girls" constituted 68.2 percent of the female laborers. But over time, the law altered married women's expecta-tions. It came to be *normal* for middle-class wives to deal in property, assume responsi-bility for contracts or debts, and (within limits) speak the language of commerce. Mar-ried women also ventured into the labor market. In 1890, they constituted 4.6 percent of all wage workers; by 1900, the figure increased to a modest but significant 5.6 percent and would have been larger if census takers had counted paid home work.[9]

The sheer volume of legislation astonished friends and foes alike. By historian Joan Hoff's count (and excluding separate estates, which some women always had been able to hold and devise, if not manage), in 1800, not one state permitted wives to make wills without some kind of male supervision; by 1900, almost three-quarters of the states and territories allowed women to pass virtually any kind of separate property to their own heirs. Given the dramatic decrease in fertility over the same decades, children benefited increasingly from women's wealth. In 1800, only 4 percent of the states permitted women to wall off separate assets from husbands' creditors or personally deal in such property; a century later, the figures were 85 percent and 60 percent, respectively. As of 1850, al-though not much before then, lawmakers in half of the states permitted wives to claim separate property during coverture, beyond assets brought into marriage; five decades later, 89 percent had done so. By 1860, 24 percent of the state legislatures had adopted earnings laws by which wives might lay claim to their own wages during marriage; by 1900, 61 percent had so moved. In 1850, slightly more than one-third of the states granted *feme sole* status to abandoned wives so that they might defend themselves and their chil-dren in the marketplace, which aided poor working mothers; fifty years later, about two-thirds of the state legislatures had adopted this rule.[10] Over the same period, public offi-cials continued to downgrade dower rights; by the 1870s, the "widow's third" was taken to be contingent upon the needs of the estate. In both *Stelle v. Carroll* (1838) and *May-bury v. Brien* (1841), Roger Taney's U.S. Supreme Court ruled that the claims of cred-itors and financially pressed heirs trumped dower rights, thereby federalizing rules artic-ulated first in state courts. But married women's property acts may well have offset the loss of dower, and many women believed, as Miriam Fish of Illinois told Susan B. An-thony in 1863, that they could "make better bargains . . . ourselves with our husbands."[11]

The reform impulse varied dramatically by region. The old plantation South resisted liberalization: In South Carolina, for example, legislators and judges aimed mainly (in Marylynn Salmon's words) to protect women from dangerous or profligate men; there was no commensurate movement to renovate the law of coverture or to "release women from their dependence upon the common law."[12] Instead, substantive legal change oc-curred primarily in the West, the Northeast, and (to some extent) the Midwest; indeed, lawyers in former Spanish and French colonies often paved the way for their fainthearted brethren. Beginning with Louisiana early in the century, community property territories and states generally adopted (at least for purposes of property management) the civil law conception of marriage as a joint venture between wholly merged yet equally vested eco-nomic partners. Beyond Mississippi and a few other states that had restored married women's rights in 1837, the list of community property jurisdictions came to include Arizona, California, Idaho, New Mexico, Texas, Nevada, and Washington. And civilian principles shaped women's rights consciousness—as with Elizabeth Packard's plea for wives' right to use separate property "as if it were our own, that is, just as we please, just according to the dictates of our own judgment."

> Do let us have a right to our own home—a right to our own earnings—a right to our own patrimony. A right, I mean, as partners in the family firm. We do not ask for a separate interest. We want an *identification of interests, and then be allowed a legal right to this common fund as junior partners of this company interest.* We most cheerfully allow you the rights of a senior partner; but we do not want you to be senior, junior, and all, leaving us with no rights at all, in a common interest.[13]

Meanwhile, in the wake of the financial panic of 1837, the common law state of Maryland forged ahead with 1842 and 1843 measures protecting married women's land from husbands' creditors; between 1844 and 1847, Alabama (for antenuptial obligations only), Connecticut, Iowa, Massachusetts, Maine, Ohio, New Hampshire, Indiana, and Vermont followed suit. By 1847–48, after twenty years' debate, New York finally passed its celebrated property act, followed over the next two decades by a series of lesser-known augmentations, retreats, and refinements. As Ray August and James Paulsen observe, New Yorkers borrowed many ideas from Louisiana and Texas, but the borrowings were well concealed, so that reformers could bill the result as "the product of American genius and not the offspring of foreign jurisprudence."[14]

In Texas, the tug-of-war between civilian and common law rules was particularly dramatic. As Mexico's former province commenced its long passage to statehood in 1840, legislators adopted a revision of the Spanish *Nueva Recopilación*, which had embraced community property principles; the new code merged elements of old Spanish practice with the Mississippi married women's property act of 1839, Louisiana statutes of 1808 and 1825, and aspects of the law of coverture. Texans asserted that although spouses jointly owned "common property," assets could be managed—that is, "sold or otherwise disposed of "—only by husbands. Men also managed land and slaves that women brought into marriages, and wives could make no contracts impairing "the legal rights of the husband over the person of the wife, or the persons of their common children." At the same time, the statute gave a wife a cause of action against a husband if he failed to support his family or failed to educate *her* children "as the fortune of the wife would justify."[15]

The mixture was unstable: On the one hand, Texans accepted the civil law's relative faith in women's economic and custodial competence; on the other hand, they embraced the common law insistence on masculine headship and agency. When Texas joined the Union, the framers of the state constitution removed some ambiguity, embedding marital communities and female economic competence (including limited rights to manage a homestead) in their 1845 text. Oppositionists denounced the idea both of constitutionalizing women's rights and of granting women equal rights with men as "heads of household." Said one delegate, homesteading sections advanced a "most mischievous principle" opposed to God's command that "the woman shall be subject to the man"; others insisted that Texans were "a common law people" averse to foreign ideas. But after weeks of wrangling, John Hemphill (later chief justice of the state supreme court) and other women's rights champions won the day. One delegate pointed to the "opinion of the age," that "women should be protected in their property." The day had "passed away," he said, "when women were beasts of burthen, and as intelligence increases they will be placed upon the high and elevated ground which rightfully belongs to them." Hemphill thought that a husband ought not to possess such "absolute control as to enable him to seriously injure or destroy the estate of the wife by wasteful expenditure or fraudulent misman-agement"; developing societies could ill afford to waste capital. But even Hemphill with-held managerial rights, liberating wealth for investment without inviting cultural insta-bility. Only when the marriage ended did a wife (or her heirs) realize her expanded power—for example, in her rights of devise and succession.[16]

The new Texas constitution included both community property and homesteading provisions; it guaranteed that the real and personal property that a wife brought into mar-riage, as well as all property acquired afterward, would be her "separate property." Del-egates provided as well for laws "more clearly defining the rights of the wife, in relation as well to her separate property, as that held in common with her husband." Texans also commanded legislators to provide for "registration of the wife's separate property," in ef-fect using state power to help women defend themselves. As elsewhere, reform was a double-edged sword: Because unregistered property belonged to the husband, estranged men could walk away with the property of homebound women or those without access to county seats, and neither the constitution nor registration provisions secured coman-agement of the marital estate. Nevertheless, Texas substantially enhanced married women's economic position. In 1849, moreover, legislators recognized female agency in land conveyancing; county clerks were permitted to "take the separate acknowledgment of Married Women to deeds executed by them"—an important power in a developing region.[17]

Californians adopted Texas's community property system more or less intact. Dur-ing the state's population explosion, from about 8,000 residents in 1848 to 76,000 two years later, delegates to the 1849 constitutional convention confronted a proposal to en-shrine the law of coverture in the state's organic law. Reformers aimed to secure for a wife "the benefit of all property owned by her at her marriage, or acquired by her after-wards, by gift, devise or bequest, or otherwise than from her husband"; to reserve man-agerial rights for the husband; and to repudiate the community property regime that Span-ish residents favored. The proposal's main advocate thought that Californians "tread upon dangerous ground" by abandoning the common law system that had "prevailed . . . for hundreds and hundreds of years" in Anglo-America. Another delegate found "no such provision so beautiful in the common law" as the "sacred" marital contract. He condemned "mental hermaphrodites" like "Fanny Wright, and the rest of that tribe." Still others pre-ferred to retain civilian rules. In the end, that view prevailed, although not out of defer-ence to Spanish American residents as much as to ensure "the security of property . . . of the wife" and attract female settlers; one delegate explained that he had chosen the "best provision *to get us wives.*" As in British North America, departures from old law reflected labor shortages, skewed sex ratios, the scarcity of capital, and men's poor bread-baking skills. Other westerners made similar choices: In the wake of another depression and partly to free up women's capital, Oregon and Kansas constitutionalized married women's eco-nomic rights in 1857 and 1859, respectively.[18]

The relatively widespread ownership of land by western women, combined with their contributions to economic growth, no doubt inspired legal reform. After 1850, photo-journalists produced a remarkable record of women branding and roping cattle, running saloons, panning for gold, raising barns, butchering cattle, and ploughing heavy sod. Dur-ing a post–Civil War trip to the Dakota Territory, an incredulous woman told of two home-steaders "hauling wood with a four-horse team. Elsie stands up on her load and touches up the leaders with the whip like any man. They have done almost all the work on their farm this season: plowing, seeding, and harvesting. I cannot understand how any female can do such work as they do; yet it is plain that they are females." Hence, as Mari Matsuda observes, in Wyoming and elsewhere, legislators anxious to attract and keep hard-working women "went beyond mere protection of family land holdings," giving women equal standing with men in commercial transactions and equal custody rights.[19] In 1846, lawmakers in Iowa Territory announced that a wife could own property "in her own right, and the same shall in no case be liable to the debts of her husband." In Minnesota and Wisconsin, generous rules encouraged unmarried women to establish homesteads. In 1876, the Supreme Court of Wisconsin laid waste to a venerable doctrine, deciding in *Brown v. Worden* that a husband was not liable for the cost of "necessaries" unless he consented to his wife's purchases. Henceforth, there would be "no presumption that she was . . . *ipso facto* the agent of her husband."[20]

At about the same time, in its only major nineteenth-century statement about women's right to hold land, Congress allowed female homesteading in the so-called Oregon Donation Act of 1850. In Richard Chused's words, legislators responded to "the perceived need to attract women to a distant territory" and to the arguments of an Oregon territorial delegate sympathetic to women's rights. During committee hearings, congressmen struck out language that would have extended managerial rights and deeded to women all lands "donated" to them in their own right.[21] But these limitations aside, the act at least allowed women to hold title to certain lands during coverture.

FEMINISM OR CAPITALISM?

First-wave activists justifiably took some credit for an apparent sea-change in public policy. Female lobbyists apparently persuaded Samuel Thurston, a prime mover behind the Oregon Donation Act, that women, no less than men, required "preparation" to defend themselves in a society obsessed with the marketplace. Instead of "suppressing the sciences and literary acquirements from the refining souls of the female sex," he wrote, "let them be favoured with the *means to obtain them*." Judge Thomas Hertell, the sponsor in 1837 of the married women's property act that New York legislators adopted eleven years later, claimed to have been influenced by women's rights orators; he apparently wanted a wife to be "respected as the equal of a good husband." And during adoption of the 1848 measure, other New Yorkers applauded the efforts of women like Elizabeth Cady Stanton and Ernestine Rose. When Massachusetts passed a comparatively generous property act in 1854, observers credited Mary Upton Ferrin, who had circulated petitions and "traveled six hundred miles, two-thirds of the distance on foot," gathering support for wives' economic freedom. In Ohio, incessant campaigning to persuade delegates to the constitutional convention to grant women "all the political and legal rights . . . guaranteed to men" led to passage of a married women's property law in 1861.[22]

Even so, observers realized that legislation was as much a stimulus *for* political action as it was the product *of* activism. In her autobiography, Stanton emphasized the power of new laws and related public debates to bring complacent or untutored women into the fold; the 1848 New York statute inspired "action on the part of women, and the reflection naturally arose that, if the men who make the laws were ready for some onward step, surely the women themselves should express some interest in the legislation."[23] It mattered little whether support followed or antedated statutory change; what mattered was women's participation in their own emancipation.

Activists knew as well that victories often had little to do with women or "women's work"—only their otherwise idle capital and children's security. Lawmakers certainly did not have in mind dismantling household governments or paying women for domestic services. Often, they aimed to reinstitute principles of equity that had been erased from the jurisprudential blackboard when states abolished courts of equity, and in New York, reformer James Humphreys opposed trusts and therefore supported adoption of the 1848 property act, which made separate estates unnecessary and made land easier to convey. His colleague, Edward Livingstone, hoped to purge the United States of an antirepublican reliance on judges, while the renowned David Dudley Field saw the act as a necessary accompaniment to commercialization: In his view, Americans wrongly retained "feudal tenures," which rendered land "inalienable" and women incapable of aiding economic development.[24]

Other limitations appeared as well. While women in antebellum Petersburg, Virginia, came to be less dependent on individual men and managed to devise property to heirs of their own choosing, they did not escape the demands of a patriarchal social system. In rural New York, the breakdown of patriarchy in response to capitalism ironically had the effect of reinforcing walls around feminized "cradles of the middle class."[25] Everywhere, officials ignored proposals for legal reform when such proposals seriously compromised male authority; as Richard Chused shows, antebellum acts mostly "created a special set of assets available for family use when husbands found themselves in trouble with creditors,"[26] without greatly expanding women's right of action. When lawmakers tried to augment managerial powers, judges typically rose to defend male sovereignty. Stanton was convinced that fathers who passed estates to daughters had in mind "securing to woman certain property rights that might limit the legal power of profligate husbands." Moreover, attempts to eliminate men's abuse of women's trusts could backfire. Husbands, for instance, frequently deeded separate property to wives "in times of prosperity" to keep it away from creditors, and then tried to persuade women to dispose of it in particular ways.[27] John Stuart Mill shrewdly observed in 1869 that because women's economic freedom admitted of "remedy without interfering with any other mischiefs," it had been augmented first. Why, if not for self-interest, did Anglo-Americans retain class legislation for women, exempting them from a general preference for individuated relationships with the state? "The social subordination of women . . . stands out," he wrote, "[as] an isolated fact in modern social institutions; a solitary breach of what has become their fundamental law; a single relic of an old world of thought and practice exploded in everything else, but retained in the one thing of most universal interest."[28]

Even in Texas, where Chief Justice Hemphill managed to preserve relatively lenient civilian-inspired property rules into the 1860s, the common law prevailed; after Hemphill's death, judges incrementally erased much of the autonomy that many women had come to expect.[29] Similarly, New York legislators and judges quickly recanted reforms that weakened unitary family governments. On March 20, 1860, lawmakers adopted one of the most generous earnings and custody acts in the country; a married woman could "bargain, sell, assign and transfer her separate personal property, and carry on any trade or business, and perform any labor or services on her sole and separate account"; the "earnings of any married woman, from her trade, business, labor or services" would be "her sole and separate property," to be "used or invested by her in her own name." Women had lobbied for a year to secure this remarkable measure. To be sure, the law pertained only to a wife's separate property, not to the marital community; in Reva Siegel's words, lawmakers basically invited judges to interpret it "in accordance with equitable traditions"—notably, the old doctrine of charging—"that traced a wife's capacity to her property, not her person,"[30] thus sidestepping the possibility of woman suffrage. But the law still represented a stunning advance. When husbands lacked competence or failed to consult, women could petition county courts for permission to sell or convey their own property. In addition, women who were burdened with "habitual drunkards" could bypass husbands to do business, and legislators made widows' rights of survivorship equivalent to widowers' rights. Finally, the act cast a mother as "the joint guardian of her children, with her husband, with equal powers, rights and duties." Reformers could say without exaggeration that the 1860 statute potentially granted married women "equal rights with their husbands, save simply the right of voting." Certainly, the act cast serious doubt on the unitary character of the *baron*.[31]

In 1862, however, a rescinding statute gutted the act, eliminating judicial bypasses and sex-neutral survivors' rights, and eradicating joint guardianship. In place of the latter was a ban on the apprenticeship of children without wives' consent. Only in 1871 did the legislature allow maternal custody of minor children, with the permission of a court-appointed surrogate; sixteen years later, it finally recognized mothers' right to use writs of habeas corpus, as Barry Mercein had done three decades earlier, to regain custody of children. In 1874, New Yorkers made special provision for widows, but not for presumptively self-defending widowers, in a revised homestead act setting aside household goods for the maintenance of what was assumed to be a *man's* family. Among the items not to be listed as taxable (or auctionable) assets were spinning wheels, looms, and sewing tools; stoves; the "family table, family pictures"; family books; ten sheep with fleeces; necessary "wearing apparel, beds, bedsteads and bedding, necessary cooking utensils, the clothing of the family, the clothes of the widow and . . . ornaments proper for her station; one table, six chairs, twelve knives and forks," and other domestic gear.[32] As late as 1884, the authors of a "dialogue" about woman suffrage astutely observed that in property and custody disputes, legislators still embraced the notion that the "father was the head of the family" and had "absolute power over all its members, even to life and death. The State finally deprived the father of this latter power. . . . But it maintained the complete authority of the father as against the mother."[33]

New York appellate judges directed the course of reform by the way they interpreted legislation. The only judicial test of the 1860 law's custody provision happened in an 1861 case much like *Barry v. Mercein*, in which Clark Brooks sought custody of a child living with his ex-wife, Lydia, who supposedly left him "without any just cause or provocation, and remained away without his consent." An inferior court ruled that under the 1860 law, Lydia had as good a right to the child as Clark, but the New York Supreme Court decried the statute's "radical" effect on family life and "grave consequences" for public peace. If lawmakers had intended to revolutionize the law of marriage, wrote Judge Allen, they would have said so in "very plain and explicit" language; "nothing should be taken in favor of social anarchy and domestic anarchy, by implication." If a wife could lawfully leave home "upon her own volition," seize children, and make it impossible for her husband to fulfill marriage vows, then "very great and sad changes" had been wrought by a "very short statute." Since the law did not expressly confer rights on a wife living apart from her husband, the court ruled that it applied only to cohabiting couples; an estranged husband (as Hendrik Hartog puts it) "regained his common law rights, including the right to custody over his children."[34]

Somewhat more positively, the Court of Appeals affirmed married women's "full promissory capacity at law"—that is, their ability to undertake binding notes and contracts—in earnings legislation. In *Frecking v. Rolland* (1873), the bench found a broad grant in the 1860 law of "power to carry on a separate trade or business," including the capacity to "borrow money, and to purchase, upon credit, implements, fixtures, and real or personal estate necessary or convenient for the purpose of commencing it, as well as the power to contract debts in its prosecution after it has been established." Five years later, the same court reversed a lower court ruling that denied a wife's liability for a mortgage. Because the court encouraged women in their own right to assume responsibility for business-related loans and commercial agreements, legislators picked up on the signal and passed another law in 1884 that repudiated the old charging doctrine and granted married women who were engaged in business "full capacity to contract with persons other than their husbands" as legal *individuals*.[35]

Yet, on the question of women's property right in *earnings*, which directly implicated husbands' property right in wives' labor, the same court was less generous. In the 1873 case of *Brooks v. Schwerin*, the court initially suggested that the earnings section of the 1860 law worked "a radical change of the common law": When a woman labored for another person and kept the proceeds, her husband no longer functioned as a "master" with title in her labor. In *Birkbeck v. Ackroyd* (1878), however, the court ruled that a husband could recover wages owing from a miller to his wife and children. The 1860 statute had not wholly abrogated common-law rules: "[A wife] may still regard her interests and those of her husband as identical, and allow him to claim . . . the fruits of her labor. The bare fact that she performs labor for third persons . . . does not necessarily establish that she performed it . . . upon her separate account. The true construction of the statute is that she may elect to labor on her own account, and thereby entitle herself to her earnings, but in the absence of such an election . . . , the husband's common law right to her earnings remains unaffected." Unless a wife was known to be a trader or explicitly invoked the privilege, the husband's rights trumped whatever the statute provided.[36] By 1895, the rule had hardened, so that a wife's acquiescence to the marital contract's laboring requirements allowed a husband to claim her earnings. As the New York Supreme Court said in *Lashaw v. Croissant*, "Undoubtedly, in the absence of any agreement [between spouses], the meals delivered and services rendered would give rise to a cause of action in favor of the husband . . . [because] all her services and earnings belong to her husband. . . . [I]n the absence of circumstances showing her intention to avail herself of the privilege conferred by the statute . . . , his common-law right is unaffected." Only in 1908 did the Court of Appeals recognize that laws passed since 1848 had affected "the complete commercial emancipation of married women."[37]

Illinois judges also interpreted earnings statutes ungenerously. In February 1861, assemblymen adopted a statute aimed at securing wives' separate estates. It provided, in part, that all real and personal property belonging to a married woman as her separate property or that she acquired during coverture "in good faith, from any person, other than her husband, by descent, devise or otherwise, together with all the rents, issues, increase and profits thereof," would remain her "sole and separate property, under her sole control, and be held, owned, possessed and enjoyed by her the same as though she was . . . unmarried." It would not be subject to the "disposal, control or interference of her husband, and shall be exempt from . . . attachment for the debts of her husband." But the courts intervened. In 1870, justices ruled in *Jesse Thomas v. City of Chicago* that the term *separate property* excluded money that Thomas's wife inherited from her mother because the mother's will had not designated it "her separate estate, or for her exclusive use"; unless the will imparted the "character" of separateness to the money, it belonged to Jesse. The same court concluded that even when a wife owned a firm in which a husband worked as managing agent, his contributions of "time, skill and labor" rendered the firm vulnerable to his creditors.[38]

FENCING AND GUARDING

Economically independent women posed special problems for defenders of American culture, which increasingly absorbed and advanced the values of both capitalism and patriarchy. On the one hand, the republic could ill afford to relegate over half the potential workforce to kitchens; the traditional exclusion of women's capital from the economy seemed both wasteful and anachronistic. On the other hand, the prospect of men and women scrambling willy-nilly after the same jobs played havoc with the notion of separate spheres, as well as with male control of wealth and household dependents. As Linda Kerber explains, "Capitalism required that men's and women's economic relations be renegotiated"[39]—a process visible but not manifest in the revolutionary era. If manhood (as Julie Matthaei reminds us) had come to depend increasingly on success as a "bread-winner,"[40] with its ripe competitive connotation, how would married women's augmented access to the marketplace affect "separate but equal" divisions of responsibility between "public" and "private" spheres? The male head of household's indivisible authority? Men's view of themselves?

Elements of this extended negotiation bear special notice. Women indeed gained access to the marketplace, but usually in support roles and without "family wage" recompense. At the same time, sex segregation of the workplace accelerated; more and more, women performed monotonous tasks in support of better-paid, highly skilled men. In the textile industry, the scarcity of labor initially led to the hiring of women and children in almost all phrases of production; as the labor pool deepened, women spun thread or stitched garments designed and marketed by men. The adoption of typewriters late in the century led to the replacement of prestigious male clerks, who could rise to managerial posts, with female secretaries hired for low wages and without career prospects. In the garment trade, the post-1850 adoption of scientific systems, including paper patterns, eroded what one scholar calls the "unique authority" of female dressmakers, who designed, cut, and sewed clothing without mechanical aids.[41]

Moreover, because the fiction of an ideal female "worklessness" persisted, at least among whites, motherhood and housekeeping emerged, more powerfully than in earlier times, as *the* avenues by which married women might achieve coequality without becoming "unsexed." The laboring poor came under extraordinary social pressure. As social theorist Thorstein Veblen noted in 1894, financially strapped women had to "supply not only the means of living, but also the means of advertising the fiction that they live without gainful occupation."[42] American Indian women from matrilocal cultures (such as the Dakota and Iroquois nations) who were seeking to preserve head-of-household status found themselves reduced to the white standard, on the ground that female supremacy and agricultural prowess were barbaric. In the years between the Jacksonian Indian-removal campaigns and congressional adoption of the assimilationist Dawes Act in 1887, judges repeatedly ruled that American Indian women could not be termed "heads," that children of mixed marriages could not inherit through Indian mothers, and that non-European marriages were unlawful. When agents took young girls on reservations off to school, they had in mind teaching them to be servants, not matriarchs.[43]

Links between the home and unpaid labor also encouraged widespread exploitation of women for commercial purposes. For example, in nineteenth-century Lynn and in other shoemaking towns in Massachusetts, household heads trained male apprentices in the art of making shoes for wages and gave the "sewing of the upper part of the shoe," in Mary Blewett's telling, to unpaid wives and daughters, thereby cutting labor costs and compounding women's workload. Such women were "barred from apprenticeships and group work" and isolated from the shop, the "center of artisan life."[44] Property laws had little to say about domestic labor, except to make it possible for workers to keep their earnings, as with farm women's "egg money." Margaret Fuller and other reformers interested in the sexual division of labor pushed hard throughout the century for recognition of women's unpaid contributions to economic growth. But such arguments usually fell on deaf ears. Indeed, Americans often penalized both spouses for women's attempts to earn money: Female wealth production supposedly revealed men's inadequacy and disqualified women for child rearing.

These developments, in turn, supported the incremental reception in state, federal, and eventually constitutional law of economic protection for women and children. The protectionist impulse, with its imputation both of the unfitness of the protected class and of gender-specific standards for strong and weak citizens, appeared across a broad range of legal heads—among them, contract and property law; family law; torts (that is, civil wrongs not involving breaches of contract), including the law of nuisance and negligence; agency; and the law of industrial accidents. After the midcentury, for example, prevailing views of "ladylike" behavior came to support disparate standards of blameworthiness for men and women, so that in a late-century Colorado case involving the injury of Anna Marie Lorentzen at a train depot, a judge could say that the jurors need not "exact the same degree of care and diligence from a woman that we would from a man under the same circumstances," since women were "not accustomed" to train stations.[45] The resulting polarization of the sexes closely resembled that used to justify white "protection" of the black race. As early as 1835, Thomas Dew contended that the "relative position of the sexes" originated in bodily "organization." The "greater physical strength of man," he wrote, "enables him to occupy the foreground. . . . He leaves the domestic scenes; he plunges into the turmoil . . . of an active, selfish world; in his journey through life, he has to encounter innumerable difficulties. . . . Hence, courage and boldness are his attributes." Such a man was "the shield of woman, destined by nature to guard and protect her. Her inferior strength and sedentary habits confine her within the domestic circle; she is kept aloof from the bustle and storm of active life."[46]

Overall, then, legislation for married women's benefit probably represented what Norma Basch has called "small islands in the vast ocean of the common law";[47] when women eschewed commercial activity or labor markets, the laws had scant effect, except in the long run. In an age given over increasingly to laissez-faire economic and social theory, public officials responded with alacrity to the apparent need to reassert the masculinity of the workplace and to affirm society's attachment to domestic traditions. Industrializing America managed to fit unitary family governments and female domesticity into industrial capitalism without renovating either system and without appreciably altering female *workers'* economic prospects. Women could work and hold property, but not too seriously, not as a rule, and not for "family" wages. Many wives and daughters still were encouraged to contribute, as in the past, to wealth production at home. And, in the South, bonded black women's unpaid labor supported a good part of the republic's rise to global power over the course of the century. Ex-slave James Curry's mother exercised a dazzling array of skills without hope of compensation. "My mother's labor," said Curry, "was very hard. She would go to the house in the morning, take her pail upon her head, and . . . milk fourteen cows."

> She then put on the bread for the family breakfast, and got the cream ready for churning, and set a little child to churn it, she having the care of from ten to fifteen children, whose mothers worked in the field. After clearing away the family breakfast, she got breakfast for the slaves. . . . In the meantime, she had beds to make, rooms to sweep, &c. Then she cooked the family dinner. . . . Then the slaves' dinner was to be ready at from eight to nine o'clock in the evening. . . . At night she had the cows to milk again. . . . This was her work day by day. Then in the course of the week, she had the washing and ironing to do for her master's family . . . and for her husband, seven children and herself. . . . She would not get through to go to her log cabin until nine or ten o'clock at night. She would then be so tired that she could scarcely stand; but she would find one boy with his knee out . . . , a patch wanting here, and a stitch there, and she would sit down by her lightwood fire, and sew and sleep alternately, often till the light began to streak in the east.[48]

Equally important, the long shadow of the law—call it "custom"—powerfully shaped women's lives. As Anthony and others sadly observed, unexamined assumptions underlying the "practical relations of men and women"[49] still caused wives to hand over wages to husbands and presented insurmountable bars to female heads of households in the search for subsistence. In the South, well beyond the Civil War, progressive women lamented a certain disinterest among white women in wage labor, perhaps (as Louisiana's Virginia Merwin explained) because "[l]abor and servitude were for so many years synonymous terms" and were "applied to a degraded class."[50] Throughout the century, poor women flocked to cities in search of work or charity; the typical pauper was a widow or deserted mother. In one study of early national Philadelphia, 498 of 549 out-of-doors paupers were female, 406 of them widows; Matthaei concludes that abandoned women, then as now, were "casualties of the sexual division under the cult of domesticity." Losing a male provider was "the worst tragedy a homemaker could experience."[51]

Siegel rightly notes that cultural evolution had a silver lining, for even as Americans (including many women's rights trailblazers) embraced elements of "difference," they elevated home work to the level of a profession, so that, within their coequal sphere, women at least could be "confident of the value of women's work" and of their own competence.[52] Yet women knew that their situation was precarious. Free-market boosters conceived of women and their children as dependents who were laboring either within the extended household of state-supported capitalism or within family economies. In his *Appeal of One Half the Human Race* (1825), the Irish reformer William Thompson (recently dubbed "the forgotten man of the woman's movement") warned that the "inclination of men to use power over [woman] beneficently" might be a "pretext set up to exclude women from political rights" and economic security; the "penalties of injustice" served as "the justification" for the same injustices.[53] American developments would not have surprised him. In 1886, when laissez-faire advocate Christopher Tiedeman set out exceptions to workers' constitutional right to make their own bargains ("liberty of contract"), he made clear that men still governed women. "The restrictions upon personal liberty . . . are either of a public or private nature," he wrote; because of "disabilities . . . in the law of domestic relations," the liberty of "certain classes" was "subjected to restraint" for their "own benefit." Restraints were imposed *"under the law by private persons* who stand in domestic relation to those whose liberty is restrained."[54]

What about women's "private" benefits and privileges as keepers of the hearth? In 1872, journalist Helen Jenkins wrote tartly, "This work of the home—this mother work, which men poetically praise (praise is so cheap!), is not recognized by the State as having any value whatever. Neither does society recognize a value in it, notwithstanding it never tires of lauding and flattering. . . . [The] estimated worth of a thing . . . is its money value. Law and society say this home work need not be paid in money; therefore, society and law value this work of the mothers of the nation at—how much? . . . [N]othing."[55]

Chapter 7

The Civil War Settlement

During the Civil War era, Americans decided emphatically that the polity, whatever else it might be, most certainly would be male. With ratification of the Reconstruction Amendments, race joined the freehold requirement as a discredited barrier to citizenship; at the same time, sex made its first appearance in the nation's organic law. The Thirteenth Amendment (1865) abolished involuntary servitude. The Fourteenth Amendment (1868), among other provisions, extended common-law citizenship to all native-born residents, threatened to reduce the representation in Congress of any state that denied the right of suffrage to loyal "male inhabitants," and (at least for those inhabitants) forbade policies that withheld equal protection of law, due process of law, and the privileges and immunities of citizenship. The Fifteenth Amendment (1870) promised federal intervention if states deprived citizens of the ballot by reason of race, color, or previous condition of servitude. The states, in turn, formally enfranchised black men. In April 1870, for example, New Yorkers made it unlawful for all "officers of election to reject the name . . . or the vote of any colored *man*."[1]

Such measures greatly altered women's prospects for equality across race and class lines. Lawmakers had constitutionalized, and to some extent federalized, old legal and customary bars to female participation in public life; by the war's end, as Richard Brown puts it, women were "more uniformly excluded from electoral politics than black men"— or, for that matter, than any other class of native-born adults. In the short run, moreover, legislators and judges largely blocked reformers' attempts to put new amendments to the task of cementing what Linda Kerber calls the woman-citizen's "connection to the political community."[2]

For women *were* citizens. In 1857, Roger Taney had affirmed the fact in *Dred Scott v. Sandford*, in which he pointed to womankind as a premier example of how states might exclude entire classes from "the political power" without denying citizenship to individuals within the class. Lawyers mostly agreed: Unlike slaves of both sexes, the unbonded female majority theoretically formed a part of "the people."[3] But unlike most white men, free women could be excluded lawfully from public life on the ground of economic dependence, unreliability, and unfitness for combat (political, economic, military, and rhetorical). In an age given over to securing autonomy for individual men, publicists urged women to suppress selfishness and political ambitions, identify their interests with those of the family, and agree to be relieved of civic obligations. In short, as one group put it, legislators refused to "bury the woman in the citizen."[4]

Governments regularly affirmed these decisions. A Kansas judiciary committee on woman suffrage told Clarina Howard Nichols in 1859 that women possessed equal rights to "protection of life, liberty, property, and intellectual culture," but to little else. "Such rights as are natural," by which committee members meant procedural and substantive liberties, augmented by a few economic rights, "are now enjoyed as fully by women as men. Such rights and duties as are merely political"—the suffrage, the right to hold office, jury service obligations, a wife's right to claim a nationality separate from her husband's—"they should be relieved from, that they may have more time to attend to those greater . . . responsibilities which . . . devolv[e] upon woman."[5] By 1883–85, judges and legislators had hammered out a new settlement between the sexes, alongside a retreat from racial equality. As in the 1780s, Americans confronted the implications of constitutional revolution for heads of households and decided that women would be included in the body politic primarily as dependents of husbands or of paternal governments.

THE BITTER FRUITS OF WAR

As Americans entered the wrenching decades of Civil War and Reconstruction, women continued to lobby—sometimes to good effect—for the elimination of disadvantageous statutes, common law rules, and customary practices. Isabella Beecher Hooker led successful drives in Connecticut for married women's property laws; in Illinois and elsewhere, activists doggedly pursued wives' right to retain earnings. By the early 1880s, statute books groaned with new laws, many of them unheralded. In April 1867, for instance, New Yorkers eliminated impediments to married women's service as executors or guardians and granted women the right to give bond "as though they were not married." Eleven years later, the same body empowered wives to "execute and deliver" powers of attorney.[6]

Moreover, as women entered the salaried workforce in larger numbers, protective societies swung to their defense. Between 1860 and 1880, for instance, New York legislators chartered a swarm of sex-specific leagues—among them the Ladies' Christian Union (for promoting "the temporal, moral and religious welfare of . . . young women who are dependent upon their own exertions for support"), the Working Women's National Association (one of Susan B. Anthony's projects, which addressed "every emergency and necessity" of women "thrown outside of homes" and provided "information and employment, and instruction to all the various industrial branches" as well as "aid, comfort and advi[c]e"), and the Working Women's Protective Union, which promoted the "interests of women who obtain a livelihood by employments other than household service," extended "legal protection from the frauds . . . of unscrupulous employers," helped women find jobs, and tried to pry open "suitable departments of labor" not yet available to female workers.[7]

The integration of the sexes often depended on reformers' ability to persuade universities and professional groups to adopt neutral admission standards and permit women to acquire specialized knowledge. A few professional schools opened their doors to female students. In the United States and England, moreover, a flush of sex-segregated institutions appeared after 1860, partly in response to claims that a female presence "lowered the value of . . . diplomas" and destroyed male students' property rights in lucrative occupations,[8] but also as a way to meet the burgeoning demands for advanced education for women. Elite women's colleges such as Barnard and Bryn Mawr are only the best-known examples. In New York alone, lawmakers chartered dozens of sex-segregated academies and vocational institutions during the war years. In 1870, Washington University in St. Louis, Missouri, adopted sex-neutral admission standards; in the same year, Ada Kepley graduated from Union College of Law (now part of Northwestern University) in Chicago. A year earlier, the Iowa Supreme Court had confirmed the legality of Arabella

Mansfield's admission to the bar; the law code of 1870 omitted the term *white male* as an admission criterion.

Equally important, war-related labor transformed women's lives, sometimes by affording avenues into public life. As Civil War nurse Hannah Ropes explained in December 1862, "I have given myself to this work, not as the strutting officers on the avenue have, for a salary, and laziness, but for love of country. . . . The cause is not of either North or South—it is the cause of . . . the nineteenth century, to take the race up . . . and on to broader freedom."[9] "Michigan Bridget" and other "irregular" patriots carried the flag, tended the wounded, put out fires, and fought. At least 400 female spies and soldiers slipped into service. Women stood in for dead husbands and lovers; a few—such as Jennie Hodgers, a.k.a. Private Albert D. J. Cashier, of the 95th Illinois Infantry, and Sarah Rosetta Wakerman, a.k.a. Private Lyons Wakerman, of the New York 153rd Regiment—cross-dressed and enlisted, evading detection for most or all of the war. Wakerman told her parents in 1863 that she stood "ready at a minute's warning to go into the field of battle" and proceeded to do just that.[10] Over 3,000 women risked life and limb as field nurses. Dr. Mary Walker enraged army officers by demanding titles equivalent to men's in hospitals, spying, and allowing herself to be captured by the enemy. Before tossing her into a Virginia jail alongside men, a Confederate officer claimed to be "amused and disgusted . . . at the sight of a *thing* that nothing but the debased and the degraded Yankee nation could produce—'a female doctor'—attired in the full uniform of a Federal Surgeon." He recommended that she be "dressed in a frock" and sent home, or admitted to a "lunatic asylum."[11]

Female contributions to the war effort changed more than one mind about proper womanly deportment. In late 1864, a Chicago *Tribune* writer applauded women's patriotism and suggested that they might be repaid with ballots. "The women, always loyal, are just as patriotic and enthusiastic as their lords," he wrote. "They attend the meetings, rain or shine, and they applaud as loudly as if they had the right to vote. I sometimes wish they could meet at the ballot box with the worser half of creation."[12] After grappling with "gentlemen" for the right to manage sanitary association work, Iowa's Annie Wittenmyer gained control of state programs and then took an unprecedented step. As a wide-eyed friend told it, in 1864, Wittenmyer "*addressed* the General Assembly" for more than two hours, "hall and gallery *crowded*, a *decided success*, unrestrained enthusiasm, applause, etc."[13] In the South, white women served as soldiers, farmers, nurses, cooks, and artisans and took government jobs, sometimes in arms factories targeted by Union forces. "Mothers, wives, and daughters," trumpeted a Virginia woman in 1861, "buckle on the armor for the loved ones; bid them, with Roman firmness advance, and never return until victory perches on their banners." In the Midwest, Livermore noted a "great increase of women engaged in outdoor work" and in provisioning "blue-coated boys in the hospitals"; they were "in the field everywhere, driving the reapers, binding and shocking, and loading grain, until then an unusual sight." This was *patriotic* work akin to soldiering. As a farmer named Annie told her, "as long as the country can't get along without grain, nor the army fight without food, we're serving the country just as much here in the harvest-field as our boys are on the battle-field." Livermore judged that these "hard-handed, brown, toiling" women were "peers of the women of the Revolution."[14]

In every region, public-spirited work raised ceilings, broadened horizons, and spawned economic independence. Among the 205,564 widows of Union and Confederate soldiers identified by census takers in 1890—a figure known to be low—as many as 20 percent earned wages; virtually all headed households for a time, often with children to raise.

"Everywhere there was a call for women to be up and doing," said Livermore, "with voice and pen, with hand and head and heart"; such a patriot developed "potencies and possibilities of whose existence she had not been aware, and which surprised her, as it did those who witnessed her marvelous achievement."[15]

Reform-minded Americans also began to rethink old ideas about girlhood and female education. In her popular postwar speech, "What Shall We Do With Our Daughters?," Livermore applauded the "great awakening of women" and urged "thorough physical training of our young girls" and "equal education—not necessarily the same—with young men" at universities. Now, republican mothers would be independent and healthy as well as virtuous. Girls would be equipped with "a remunerative vocation"; the "doors of trades . . . and suitable business" would be "open to them." They would "receive the most careful moral culture, and the wisest domestic training, as they were to be the wives and mothers of the future," and, Livermore added hopefully, they would be granted "equal legal status with young men by the American government."[16]

The most dramatic alterations of women's condition occurred within African American communities. With the abolition of slavery, freedwomen gained legal personalities that were theoretically comprised of all the civil rights claimed by white women of the same class; only on the suffrage question did new amendments and statutes take special notice of men. Some of these rights were wholly beyond the pale of Radical Republican concern. Among whites, for instance, it was usual to write letters; for ex-slaves, pen and paper were gifts from Abraham Lincoln. Masters often had forbidden or censored writing by literate slaves (whose very literacy was illegal), and postage required money. Indeed, in some areas, surveillance persisted into the 1860s. Said the enslaved Lucy Skipwith, writing to a friend from Alabama during the Civil War, "[T]he white people who have stayed on the plantation are always opposed to my writing to you & always want to see my letters and that has been the reason why my letter has been short." Only when there was "no white person . . . present" could she write at length.[17]

In addition, wartime experience augmented black women's political and defensive skills, propelling many of them into activism. Georgia's Susie King Taylor learned to "handle a musket" while traveling with her husband's South Carolina regiment. "There are many people," she reported, "who do not know what some of the colored women did during the war. . . . [H]undreds of them . . . assisted the Union soldiers by hiding them and helping them to escape." Black abolitionist Harriet Tubman shuttled homeless or self-emancipated blacks northward and helped to liberate people still held in bondage, in the process liberating herself from restrictive garments. Tubman asked a friend in Boston to buy bloomers for her; she had tripped over "long skirts" while running from pursuers "double quick" and resolved never again to be jeopardized by her clothing.[18]

THE LIMITS OF CONSTITUTIONAL REVOLUTION

Still, Americans were not prepared to eliminate sex as a category of exclusion and limitation. In the hard decades between Taney's decision in *Dred Scott* and the official withdrawal of federal troops from the South in 1877, women of every description confronted brick walls. The complex wartime settlement struck between women and men, blacks and whites, northerners and southerners, seriously weakened women's claims to constitutional equality, in many respects confirming and reinforcing the masculine (as well as white) character of public life.

Freedwomen's plight vividly illustrates the downside of the settlement: Their interests—indeed, their presence in the female population—often went unremarked. In Congress, "black" implied "male"; within organized suffragism, "female" usually called to mind white women. In the postemancipation South, whites' retaliation against ex-slaves jeopardized blacks of both sexes, but their experiences to some extent diverged. On the one hand, emancipation inspired some black women to take whites to court for slashing them with knives, invading their homes, harassment, and rape, much as black men (and some women) sued whites for slander or theft (including refusals to honor labor contracts). On the other hand, blacks fought a losing battle against whites who were determined to control freedwomen's reproductive and economic decisions and to police the border between white "ladies" and black "wenches."

The African American wish list commenced with physical security. In "Bury Me in a Free Land" (1858), the poet Frances Harper tied bondage directly to sexual slavery, the disappearance of children, and other feminine perils:

> I could not rest if I heard the tread
> Of a coffle-gang to the shambles led,
> And the mother's shriek of wild despair
> Rise like a curse on the trembling air.
>
> I could not rest if I heard the lash
> Drinking her blood at each fearful gash,
> And I saw her babes torn from her breast
> Like trembling doves from their parent nest. . . .
>
> If I saw young girls, from their mothers' arms
> Bartered and sold for their youthful charms
> My eye would flash with a mo[u]rnful flame,
> My death-paled cheek grow red with shame.[19]

Emancipation did not allay fears of brutalization, many of them borne of poverty, nor would ballots eradicate these concerns. The burdens of child care often devolved on black mothers. Among blacks especially, infant and childbirth-related female mortality remained high; if a black child survived infancy, southern laws mandating the apprenticeship of children meant the children's removal from their parental homes. In addition, employers often refused to consider hiring black women with children if any other kind of laborer could be obtained; in 1866, a federal agent in Virginia found "little call for female help, and women with children are not desired." Compared to ill-paid black men, moreover, freedwomen earned less for comparable work. As Sojourner Truth informed the American Equal Rights Association in 1867, "I have done a great deal of work—as much as a man, but did not get so much pay. I used to work in the field and bind grain, keeping up with the cradler; but men never doing no more, got twice as much pay. . . . We do as much, we eat as much, we want as much. I suppose I am about the only colored woman that goes about to speak for the rights of the colored woman. . . . *What we want is a little money.*"[20]

In addition, even as black men came to be accused of raping white women and were turned over to lynch mobs or all-white juries, southern white men continued to wage war (one scholar calls it the "sexual terrorism of race politics")[21] on and through black women's bodies. Ex-rebels supposedly emasculated by the loss of both the war and a subject class sometimes punished uppity freedmen by harassing, beating up, raping, or killing their wives and daughters. On one occasion, the Ku Klux Klan came to the home of George Band, took his wife, "hung her to a tree," and "hacked her to death with knives."[22] The story of Roda (or Rhoda) Ann Childs of Georgia differed only by degree. According to an agent of the Freedman's Bureau, Childs was "taken from her house, in her husband's absence, by eight white men who stripped her, tied her to a log, beat and sexually abused her." The Childs had fallen prey to one of many devices that whites used to deprive black people of wages. They had been employed as farmworkers; just as the job drew to a close, whites "visited" them by night. In an account transcribed by a bureau agent in 1866, Roda said this: "They . . . 'bucked' me down across a log, Stripped my clothes over my head, one of the men Standing astride my back, and beat me across my posterior, two men holding my legs. . . . "

> Then they turned me parallel with the log . . . and one man placing his foot upon my neck, beat me again on my hip and thigh. Then I was thrown upon the ground on my back, one of the men Stood upon my breast, while two others took hold of my feet and stretched My limbs as far apart as they could, while the man Standing upon my breast applied the Strap to my private parts. . . . Then a man, Supposed to be an ex-confederate Soldier . . . fell upon me and ravished me. During the whipping one of the men ran his pistol into me, and said he had a hell of a mind to pull the trigger . . . as my husband had been in the 'God damned Yankee Army,' and Swore they meant to kill every black Son-of-a-bitch they could find. . . . They then went back to the house, Seized my two daughters and beat them.[23]

Freedwomen who set out on foot to look for family members or who withdrew from the workforce to experience domesticity often ran afoul of whites determined to keep them at work. In August 1864, Union officer A. S. Hitchcock urged new rules that would keep laborers on the land and curtail the movements (and, to white eyes, the incipient immorality) of women who "flock back and forth to Hilton Head . . . simply to while away their time, . . . seek some new excitement, or . . . live by lasciviousness." In General Order No. 130, adopted a month later, military governors outlawed "the practice of negro women . . . wander[ing] about from one plantation to another, and from one Post or District to another . . . for no other purpose than to while away their time, or visit their husbands serving in the ranks of the Army." These activities were thought to be "subversive of moral restraint"; black women had to be "compelled to work at some steady employment."[24]

Mixed signals abounded. To help restore public order and black manhood, white southern legislators, as well as Freedmen's Bureau officials, encouraged African Americans to form families; husbands would ensure (in the words of a North Carolina statute) that their dependents were "industrious" and "honest." As Laura Edwards explains, before the war, both marriage and slavery provided lines of demarcation between families and the state; with emancipation, wedlock acquired "even greater importance in structuring southern society, because it was now the only institution that legally constituted households." And, although black communities continued to observe their own rules about marriage, divorce, kinship, and the nature of households with a doggedness that baffled whites, many blacks readily complied, associating wedlock with privacy and full citizenship. Mary Reynold proudly recalled that "after freedom, I gits married and has it put in the book by a preacher"; in the wake of the Emancipation Proclamation, black couples lined up to be married, partly to legitimate their children.[25]

But many whites also hoped that women would accept labor contracts or apprenticeships, thus confirming old associations between blackness and degrading manual labor; women who could "plough, drag, drive team, clear wild lands, [and] work on the highway" as capably as men supposedly relinquished all claim to ladyhood.[26] To complicate the situation further, many black women rejected marriage *and* fieldwork, refusing to trade one form of bondage for others. Suzanne Lebsock finds that, in Virginia, many black women refused to marry explicitly to retain autonomy. As self-divorced freedwoman Dink Watkins proudly told a judge, "I am my own woman and I will do as I please."[27] Sometimes, freedmen confirmed black women's fears; a bridegroom from Tennessee said of his new wife that he had "married her to wait on me." And black leaders strenuously encouraged female domesticity; in an 1869 letter to the National Convention of Colored Citizens of the United States in Washington, D.C., the African American bishop D. A. Payne, of Ohio, reminded delegates of "evils . . . to be corrected"—among them, a shortage of black republican mothers. "The domestic . . . relations of colored Americans," he wrote, "having been invaded and broken up by the *Lords of the lash*, have left the majority of us, in the most deplorable condition—so that we find ourselves destitute of *Mothers* . . . qualified to train our sons into a noble manhood, and our daughters into a noble womanhood!"[28]

The racialization of the lady was especially nettlesome. No matter how decorous, well-educated, or attentive to domestic concerns a black woman might be, many whites refused to *see* her as a lady; streetcar and railway conductors ejected African American women from ladies' cars, relegating them to unisex colored or smoking cars. And though courts often came to the aid of black women so treated, they did not do so invariably. In Mary Jane Chilton's 1870 suit against the St. Louis and Iron Mountain Railroad for relegating her to the smoker, the bench accepted the defendant's claim of "equality" between "seats covered with enameled cloth" and "seats covered with plush" and ignored the presence of two rude men in the smoker. The public career of Ida B. Wells began in 1884 when a Tennessee conductor shoved her from a ladies' car; the episode, combined with an appellate court's reversal of a $500 award for damages, pushed Wells into activism, including campaigns to integrate public transportation in southern cities. Journalists did not approve of such women. In 1860, the New Orleans *Picayune* derisively told of the crusade of a "Mrs. Putnam," the wife of a Massachusetts barber, to integrate sailing vessels for both blacks and women. Putnam, wrote the editor in a burst of racial and gender anxiety, "like a good many of her sex, white and black . . . has for some years acted as if she felt it to be her mission to keep herself in the public eye and ear, as the advocate of certain . . . [reforms]; such as the right of women, of whatever hue, to teach, preach, doctor, vote, and do anything and everything else they please; the perfect and unquestionable right of black folks to sit at the same public tables, to travel in the same public conveyances, to occupy the same pews in churches, the same beds . . . in steamships."[29]

What about white women? By the 1870s, campaigns for coequality within marriage seemed to be (in Linda Speth's phrase) "in abeyance."[30] Undoubtedly, some part of this apparent suspension of effort reflected first-wave achievements: Reformers *had* softened the law of coverture and engendered new ways of thinking about women. In 1867, the New York legislature made it lawful for a husband or wife to "be a witness for or against the other," preserving only their immunity from compulsory testimony about "confidential communication made by one to the other during their marriage." Six years later, it democratized the law of adoption so that a child could be adopted by "any adult" without the permission of a spouse and empowered women to defend themselves against sexual slurs that diminished their value in the marriage market. A woman (but not a man) could sue "to recover damages for words . . . spoken imputing unchastity to her." This provision reinforced notions of a woman's unique interest in sexual purity. Still, the same act allowed a wife to "sue alone" and keep damages as "sole and separate property," which compromised the doctrine of unitary male headship.[31]

As with married women's property laws, these reforms were relatively painless; legislators could be generous without intruding significantly upon husbands' prerogatives. And even as New Yorkers expunged sex distinctions in adoption law, they reinforced the indivisibility of domestic sovereignty—for instance, by using the word *persons* to mean men in an 1871 law punishing "all persons who abandon . . . their wives and children . . . without adequate support."[32] When reformers pressed for a division of authority within families or access to zones monopolized by men, resistance was fierce. Moreover, beyond the state's line of vision, a good many professionals simply closed ranks against female practitioners. Physicians insisted that women belonged in nursing programs, not in surgical theaters or anatomically explicit lectures; in 1870, a Columbia Law School trustee trumpeted, after denying admission to three females, that no woman would "degrade herself by practicing law in New York, especially if I can save her." In the workplace, the vast majority of salaried women undertook low-paid, boring jobs that men had rejected and that resembled, in Linda Kerber's disarming phrase, "what they do at home."[33]

BUMPS AND JOLTS

The decision to suspend women's rights agitation had less to do with its achievements than with leaders' decision to divert collective energies into the war effort. For five years, organizers suspended rights conventions in favor of Loyal League gatherings. By 1863–64, league workers of both sexes were bending their shoulders to the task of securing the adoption of an amendment (ultimately the Thirteenth) that would liberate "all persons of African descent held to involuntary servitude or labor."[34]

Even as the focus among northerners shifted to black emancipation and reunification, women found ways to advance the sex's cause; as earlier, *words* served as agents of change. Armed "with speech and pen,"[35] women demanded that Congress proclaim black freedom, in the process training themselves for public life; woman-centered newspapers such as *Una, Lily, Sybil*, the Pittsburgh *Visitor*, Stanton's *Revolution*, Lucy Stone and Henry Blackwell's *Woman's Journal*, the *Ballot Box*, and the *National Citizen* pushed hard for women's rights and other reforms. As New Hampshire's Clarissa Olds explained in 1863, "The right to take any responsibility in regard to [abolitionism] was denied to woman; it was out of her sphere; it ran into politics, which were unfit for woman. . . . But this painful hour of warfare crowds home upon us the conviction that woman's interests equally with man's are imperiled—private as well as public, individual as well as social."[36]

Yet the war took its toll. New York's recission in 1862 of the path-breaking 1860 earnings and custody act horrified Stanton's allies; women had given a "hard year's work" for nothing. Why could men not see that a woman possessed "the natural human desire to accumulate, possess, and control the results of her own labor"? Or did they see too well? In a society that pegged wealth to power, New Yorkers granted only "bare support" to wives. Even as organizers put women's crusade on hold to support the war effort, said Stanton, "dastardly law-makers, filled with the spirit of slaveholders, were stealing the children and the property of the white mothers." It was hard to imagine stronger "proof of woman's need of the ballot in her own hand for protection." The experience also lay bare women's complacency: While the "old guard sleep, the young 'devils' are wide awake, and we deserve to suffer for our confidence in man's sense of justice, and to have all we have gained thus snatched from us. . . . All our reformers seem suddenly to have grown politic."[37]

Reversals multiplied. In the South, activists learned that white women's wartime experiences of freedom would not lead to expanded citizenship rights. Underlying this phenomenon were at least two realities. First, even though female supporters of the southern cause engaged in such activities as spying and sabotage, they typically backed away from what they took to be male impersonation. In her riveting tale of death-defying activities behind Union lines, the courier-spy Belle Boyd claimed the "right to act, think, and speak" alongside men, but added an important caveat: "I do not set myself up as an advocate of the woman's-rights doctrine, but would rather appear in the character of a quiet lady expressing her sentiments, not so much to the public as to her immediate friends."[38] Second, many postwar southerners confronted extraordinary physical devastation of homelands and sought to reimpose social order, especially among freed blacks. Hence, although white women's benevolent societies and clubs persisted into and beyond the war, allowing women to participate in civic causes, they also helped to revive a race-centered patriarchy at war's end. In May 1870, inspired by Matilda Joslyn Gage's speech at a women's rights convention, Anna Whitehead Bodeker and others founded the Virginia State Woman Suffrage Association (VSWSA), the first such group in the state. Yet neither VSWSA nor kindred groups attracted a significant following until the turn of the century; as historian Elizabeth Varon explains, the "timeworn counterargument to the call for suffrage—that women could make meaningful contributions to electoral politics without the vote—proved extremely resilient." Southern whites simply could not imagine a New South without paternalistic relations with blacks; race-led reassertions of tradition, in turn, reinforced parallel systems of domestic paternalism.[39]

Setbacks appeared almost everywhere. In early 1867, when voters in Kansas decisively rejected black and female suffrage, the latter even more resoundingly than the former, activists worried that the cause had been lost. Undoubtedly, as Helen Elim Starrett maintained, "truths" spoken during that campaign forever altered Kansans' political consciousness, prospects for lucrative employment, and political aspirations. Women elected as superintendents of public schools survived a judicial test of their singular achievement. But the loss was profoundly unsettling. When New York also turned back woman suffrage in 1868–69, Stanton and Anthony were inconsolable. After a long debate of "universal suffrage," Horace Greeley—the well-known editor of the New York *Tribune*, chair of a committee of the whole in the state's constitutional convention, and an old school reformer—came down for "universal manhood suffrage" only, because federal policy seemed to require it, and because female ballots invited upheaval. "However defensible in theory," he explained, "we are satisfied that public sentiment does not demand . . . an innovation . . . so openly at war with a distribution of duties and functions between the sexes . . . and involving transformations so radical in social and domestic life." For her part, Stanton found it "amazing" that "Radical Republicans in the capital of the Empire State should repeat in the ears of the nineteenth century stale platitudes from the effete civilizations of the Old World—that to their starving wives and mothers, knocking at the door of the political citadel, instead of bread and the ballot, they should give stones and . . . degradation." George William Curtis hazarded to say that women ought to throw off government. "It is alleged," he said testily, "that woman are already represented by men. Where are they so represented? And when was the choice made? If I am told that they are virtually represented, I reply, with James Otis, that 'no such phrase as virtual representation is known in law'. . . . Nobody pretends that they have ever been consulted."[40]

Republicans revealed themselves to be a band of "devils": When party leaders refused to merge black and female emancipation, Democrats readily agreed. As they retreated from the radical possibilities of Reconstruction, politicians gave priority to conserving white male political power; Republicans defended elements of black male citizenship—for example, the right of locomotion, the capacity to work and deal in property, the right to serve as household heads, and suffrage (with its bundle of ancillary rights)—and assumed that freedmen, like their white brothers, adequately represented their wives. Said Democratic senator John Brooks Henderson of Missouri in 1866, whereas freedmen required ballots because the "weak must be protected with power to inspire fear . . . into the strong," white men's "pride" in their wives and daughters made woman suffrage unnecessary "as a means of self-protection." Black women were simply invisible. Moreover, when women predicated rights claims on wartime service, as men had done for centuries, Republicans turned a deaf ear. In 1870, Red Cross founder Clara Barton (whose unfeminine achievements prompted suspicions of loose morals) urged men to do for women what had been done for them: "Brothers, when you were weak, and I was strong, I toiled for you. Now you are strong, and I am weak because of my work for you, I ask your aid. I ask the ballot for myself and my sex, and as I stood by you, I pray you stand by me and mine." Congress was unmoved. Woman "makes the soldier," said Henderson, but "takes no musket to the battlefield."[41]

Many old-line reformers (among them, Gerrit Smith; William Lloyd Garrison; and, until 1875, Frederick Douglass) put distance between themselves and former comrades on the lecture circuit. Even as he lobbied hard for woman suffrage in the western territories, Henry Blackwell sought to weaken female opposition to Republican policies and, indeed, may have been the first reformer to suggest, in the form of a sustained political argument, that woman suffrage might help white southerners restore white supremacy. In his notorious "What the South Can Do" (1867), he reminded ex-confederates that 4 million white women would "counterbalance" the South's black men and women and ensure the "political supremacy" of the "white race."[42]

Congressional perfidy was especially troubling; at stake was women's constitutional standing in every state of the Union in relations with men of all races and classes. Stanton and Anthony decried the "wriggling, the twisting, the squirming" of congressional Republicans. Much as the "spider-crab walks backwards," so Congress refused to include the female sex in new amendments and civil rights acts and imposed fresh "legal disabilities upon women" by using the word *male* and by leaving behind a legislative record hostile to women's interests.[43] In debates of the Fourteenth and Fifteenth Amendments and in discussions of suffrage in the federal district, a few brave souls defended the constitutional theory underlying universal suffrage: Republicans *did* believe in government by consent; women *were* governed, taxed, and tried for crimes; and elections *were* the main avenue by which Americans expressed consent. But Republicans mostly temporized. The father of the Fourteenth Amendment, John Bingham, urged postponement of talk about women's rights. On December 11, 1866, Oregon Republican senator George Williams contended hotly that women, unlike "negroes" (by which term he meant black men), had "not been enslaved"; benefited from male protection; and, despite a few troublemakers, did not seek publicity. "Intelligence has not been denied to them," he said;

"they have not been degraded; there is no prejudice against them on account of their sex; but, on the contrary, if they deserve to be, they are respected, honored, and loved." Much as Taney had used the fact of slave codes to prove the naturalness of black degradation in *Dred Scott*, so Williams pointed to custom and law to justify women's exclusion from the polity: Women did not "bear their proportion . . . of the public burdens."

> Men represent them in the Army . . . ; men represent them at the polls and in . . . Government; and though . . . individual women do own property that is taxed, yet nine tenths . . . [is] controlled by the men. Sir, when the women . . . love to be jostled . . . [in] trade and business; when they love the treachery and the turmoil of politics; when they love the . . . blood of battle better than they love the affections . . . of home and family, then it will be time to talk about . . . women voters.[44]

Still others championed race- and sex-blind suffrage in order to frighten the horses. In 1869, congressmen literally giggled when a Delaware senator proposed abolishing all distinctions of race and sex in law; in J. R. Pole's words, such men invoked the "abstract claim that equality was in principle indivisible" to sabotage *all* expansions of the elective franchise beyond white men. Others proposed (after Blackwell) using white women's votes to offset black ballots; as one opponent of black suffrage put it, white women would "neutralize its poison if poison there be."[45]

Members of Congress typically resisted treating members of the female class as rights-bearing individuals or dispensing with lines traditionally drawn *within* the class (as between the *feme sole*, *feme covert*, and *relict*). During debate of the Fourteenth Amendment, Robert Hale insisted that equal protection of law required only that lawmakers "extend to one married woman the same protection you extend to another, and not the same you extend to unmarried women or men." In 1866 debates leading to black male suffrage in the District of Columbia, senators warned that while freedmen *and* women would taint elections with ignorance, woman suffrage also threatened male control of families. "[E]very man is king, every woman is queen," said one critic, "but upon him devolves the responsibility of controlling the external relations of his family, and those external relations are controlled by the ballot. . . . Within the family man is supreme; he governs by the *law of the family, by the law of reason, nature, religion.*" New Hampshire's James Patterson was not supporting household democracy when he asked "what the effect would be in case women were allowed to vote, if there were a difference of opinion between the husband and wife on some political question—where the authority of the family would rest?"[46]

As Reconstruction advanced, anxieties about speech freedom also resurged. Antisuffragists tied voting to female oratory and condemned them both, as when the Albany *Evening Journal* in January 1867 rued the transfer of women "from the drawing room and the nursery to the ballot-box and the forum." In the same year, Stone confided that she hoped men would not be asked to speak at an upcoming convention; she was tired of being on her "knees" begging them to keep their promises.[47] More than once, the Senate barred women from the hall—to some activists, a violation of speech freedom—as on January 11, 1875, when Senator Hannibal Hamlin of Maine, a former vice president of the United States, vetoed female observation of the proceedings.

MR. STEVENSON. I rise to offer a resolution admitting ladies on the floor of the Senate. There are a great many ladies who have come here to hear this debate. It has often been done before, and I ask that the Doorkeeper be instructed to admit ladies on the floor of the Senate in the lobbies beyond Senators' seats.

MR. HAMLIN. What is that?

THE VICE-PRESIDENT. The Senator from Kentucky moves that the Doorkeeper be instructed to admit ladies on the floor of the Senate.

MR. HAMLIN. That . . . requires the unanimous consent of the Senate. Well, sir, upon a former occasion I had the independence to interpose an objection. I know it is a most ungracious position, but I think it is one that I ought to interpose again, and I do it.

THE VICE-PRESIDENT. Objection is made to the motion of the Senator from Kentucky.[48]

The Republicans' complicity in such debacles not only caused pain, but also spurred the leadership toward suffragism and increased reliance on the language of law. In the 1867 Kansas campaign, said Stanton, studiously silent men "did not grasp the imperative necessity of woman's demand for that protection which the ballot alone can give; they did not feel for *her* the degradation of disfranchisement." As conversation across gender lines waned, references to speech multiplied. "The fact of their silence deeply grieved us," said Stanton for the National Woman Suffrage Association (NWSA), "but the philosophy of their indifference we thoroughly comprehended for the first time . . . , that only from woman's standpoint could the battle be successfully fought. . . ."

> Our liberal men counseled us to *silence* during the war, and we were *silent* on our own wrongs; they counseled us again to *silence* in Kansas and New York, lest we should defeat negro suffrage, and threatened if we were not, we might fight the battle alone. We chose the latter, and were defeated. But standing alone we learned our power; . . . and solemnly vowed that there should never be *another season of silence* until woman had the same rights . . . as man.

Only when woman "stands on an *even platform* with men," she concluded, "his acknowledged equal everywhere, with the same *freedom to express herself* in the religion and government of the country . . . can she safely take counsel with him."[49]

SUFFRAGISM AND THE "NEW DEPARTURE"

The worst was yet to come: After 1869, the movement itself began to unravel. Women of all political persuasions keenly felt the sex's loss of ground, but disagreed as to the best course of action. As early as 1866, leaders of the American Equal Rights Association (AERA) predicted that women would have to withdraw from the social compact. Such arguments terrified moderates. As radicals put it, the time had come for the polity to be "once more resolved into its original elements"; in the "reconstruction of our government we again stand face to face with the broad question of natural rights." As tumult grew, activists occupied the high ground of universal human rights: At the "baptism" of a "second revolution," they claimed to see clearly that "the peace, prosperity, and perpetuity of the Republic" depended on the restoration of "EQUAL RIGHTS TO ALL." Adoption of the Fourteenth Amendment and the prospect of a fifteenth to enfranchise freedmen exacerbated intramovement tensions. The 1869 call for an AERA convention linked war-related losses to political invisibility: "With every type and shade of manhood thus exalted above their heads, there never was a time when all women . . . should be so wide awake to the degradation of their position, and so persistent in their demands to be recognized in the government."[50]

During the disastrous AERA gathering in 1869, two camps emerged; these, in turn, developed into Stanton and Anthony's NWSA, established two days after the AERA's adjournment, and Stone's American Woman's Suffrage Association (AWSA). AWSA attracted old antislavery and temperance reformers, supported Abraham Lincoln's party, allowed male officeholding, attracted more black members than did NWSA, and softpedaled demands for women's inclusion in the Reconstruction amendments. Instead, the group doggedly pursued the enfranchisement of freedmen, supported a range of social reforms, and anticipated state-by-state enfranchisement of women at a later time. And AWSA typically characterized the incidents of citizenship (as did most post-1865 Republicans) not as natural rights, but as a bundle of common law rights and privileges superintended by states.

In contrast and as circumstances allowed, NWSA persisted with cultural criticism. It restricted officeholding to women, distrusted mainstream parties (and threatened to form its own), and inaugurated what came to be called the "New Departure." At the heart of this campaign was a single explosive idea: If women were citizens and suffrage was a natural right incumbent on citizenship, then women already possessed the right and needed only to seize it and demand congressional recognition of the fact in a declaratory act. For the moment, "rights talk" subsumed virtually all other discourses. NWSA leaders singlemindedly pursued federal guarantees of "equal rights to all," especially political rights, so that "the ideal republic of the Fathers" could be "made a fact of life." Stanton's *Revolution* made suffrage NWSA's "test of loyalty. . . . Do you believe women should vote? is the one and only question in our catechism." Much as abolitionists and associated suffragists had demanded universal enfranchisement on the ground of natural law and the essential divinity of all human beings, so NWSA hammered home the immorality and illegality of recent decisions to constitutionalize an aristocracy of sex.[51]

Not surprisingly, NWSA condemned AWSA's gradualism as political capitulation and moral cowardice; the group's rhetoric also betrays some amount of anger at AWSA's complicity in the silencing of women. Why should women who were barely admitted to lecterns heed "pathetic appeals to keep silent"? Why had questions about suffrage been resolved, not as a matter of natural right, but by statute and "on the narrow ground of class"? How could former abolitionists now say that state legislatures properly controlled elements of citizenship? And why had so many women succumbed to pressure? Said a disheartened Anthony, women were asking opponents "if they think we had better speak, or, rather, if they do not think we had better remain silent."[52]

NWSA's faith in the power of the federal government to affect needful change bears notice. Increasingly, the leadership invited Congress to create zones of safety within which women might experience political freedom. In the 1860s, even the increasingly anarchic Stanton urged Congress to make public policy "homogenous, from Maine to California," as it had done when it affirmed black citizenship. Matilda Gage made the case as well as anyone. "The centralization that fortifies and secures liberty," she declared at an NWSA meeting in 1873, "is National centralization. . . . Most persons who have been awake to the evils of State centralization, have applied the same rules of judgment to national centralization. The two are dissimilar as are darkness and light. State centralization is tyranny; National centralization means general laws" and "political equality," the "corner-stone" of the federation.[53]

NWSA tailored its arguments to meet the time-honored proposition that citizenship rights originated not in natural law but in acts of government. On one side, as Republican Senator Jacob Howard told the Senate in mid-1866, the franchise, while central to a democracy, continued to be "the creature of law. It has always been regarded . . . as the result of positive local law, not . . . as one of those fundamental rights lying at the basis of all society and without which a people cannot exist except as slaves." On the other side, Stanton and others, building upon old abolitionist arguments, claimed that a "majority" of statesmen and scholars viewed suffrage as a "natural right" that could be "regulated" but "not . . . abolished by state law."[54] In 1865, Anthony and Stanton looked as well to the so-called guarantee clause, as antislavery agitators had done, demanding that Congress "extend the right of Suffrage to Woman—the only remaining class of disfranchised citizens—and thus fulfill your constitutional obligation 'to guarantee to every State . . . a Republican form of Government.' "[55]

Initially, New Departure activists aimed simply to persuade Congress to universalize voting rights in a single constitutional amendment; to make the point, sex-specific amendments found their way into the House and Senate. In spring 1869, as congressmen moved toward black manhood suffrage, the *Revolution* applauded George Julian's March 15 introduction in Congress of a proposed Sixteenth Amendment, initially worded more strongly than the Fifteenth ("The Right of Suffrage in the United States shall be based on citizenship, and shall be regulated by Congress; and all citizens of the United States, whether native or naturalized, shall enjoy this right equally without any distinction . . . whatever founded on sex"). Simultaneously, women exercised the right of petition, pelting Congress with letters and memorials demanding a declaratory act, federal laws prohibiting state impositions of sex-specific disabilities, and eventually a Sixteenth Amendment. On one occasion, Iowans told Congress to expect a petition signed by more than 10,000 citizens, with "others . . . upon the way," and asked that it "not be sent to the waste-basket."[56]

Tensions increased when NWSA nervously formed a temporary alliance with Victoria Woodhull, a controversial champion of "free love" and woman's right to control her own body. Woodhull argued that if the right to vote was an element of federal citizenship embedded in both the original Constitution and the Fourteenth and Fifteenth Amendments, then women already possessed voting rights and could force Congress to pass a declaratory act restoring rights unlawfully confiscated, without further emendation of constitutional texts. The adoption of such an act would have been a godsend; as Frederick Douglass put it, the prospect of securing a separate amendment for woman suffrage put a "vast obstacle in the way of woman's cause."[57] But by 1871, the Woodhull connection threatened to tear NWSA apart. Social conservatives like Mary Livermore and Paulina Wright Davis wanted nothing to do with "free love"; in their view, Woodhull's presence on platforms with Lucretia Mott and other venerable figures lent weight to opponents' charges of suffragists' immorality. And Stanton sometimes fanned the flames: "Conservatism cries out we are going to destroy the family. Timid reformers answer, the political equality of woman will not change it. They are both wrong. It will entirely revolutionize it." When Woodhull published an essay assailing the hypocrisy of reformers on questions of sexual purity, NWSA leaders empathized with her interest in self-possession and refused to scrutinize her sex life. Anthony told Isabella Hooker in 1871 that she would not agree to interrogate women's purity until the republic agreed to "catechise and refuse men." It was "only that Mrs. Woodhull is a woman, & that we are women—all of an enslaved class—that we even dream of such a thing."[58]

The declaratory-act strategy required Congress to admit the unconstitutionality of past denials of women's birthright—in political terms, an unlikely possibility. But Woodhull put it to the test. In a well-publicized address delivered before the Judiciary Committee of the House on January 11, 1871, she contended that the Constitution in its original form empowered all citizens equally; Isabella Hooker, Stanton, and a number of reform-minded lawyers lent support. Woodhull distinguished between common law citizenship (aspects of which could be controlled by legislation) and the natural rights of the sovereign people, and included suffrage in the latter category. On what authority did legislators meddle with the constitutional rights of half the constituent power, when sex did not appear in the nation's original Constitution? For good measure, she linked suffrage to constitutionally protected political expression; noted that the disfranchisement of black women implicated race, a constitutionally-suspect category of exclusion; and condemned coverture as involuntary servitude.

Because Woodhull's address laid out the main arguments of NWSA constitutionalists, it bears close reading. "The public law of the world," she began, "is founded upon the conceded fact that sovereignty can not be forfeited or renounced. . . . The people in this republic who confer sovereignty are its citizens: in a monarchy the people are the subjects of sovereignty. All citizens of a republic by rightful act or implication confer sovereign power."

> The subject of a monarch takes municipal immunities from the sovereign as a gracious favor; but the woman citizen of this country has the inalienable "sovereign" right of self-government in her own proper person. Those who look upon woman's status by the dim light of the common law, which unfolded itself under the feudal and military institutions that establish right upon physical power, can not find any analogy in the status of the woman citizen of this country, where the broad sunshine of our Constitution has enfranchised all. As sovereignty can not be forfeited, relinquished, or abandoned, those from whom it flows—the citizens—are equal in conferring the power, and should be equal in the enjoyment of its benefits and in the exercise of its rights and privileges. One portion of citizens have no power to deprive another portion of rights and privileges such as are possessed and exercised by themselves. The male citizen has no more right to deprive the female citizen of the free, public, political, expression of opinion than the female citizen has to deprive the male citizen thereof.
>
> The sovereign will of the people is expressed in our written Constitution, which . . . makes no distinction of sex. The Constitution defines a woman born or naturalized in the United States, and subject to the jurisdiction thereof, to be a citizen. It recognizes the right of citizens to vote. It declares that the right of citizens of the United States to vote shall not be denied or abridged by the United States or by any State on account of "race, color, or previous condition of servitude."
>
> Women, white and black, belong to races, although to different races. A race of people comprises all the people, male and female.
>
> With the right to vote sex has nothing to do. . . . All people of both sexes have the right to vote, unless prohibited by special limiting terms less comprehensive than race or color. No such limiting terms exist in the Constitution. Women, white and black, have from time immemorial groaned under what is properly termed in the Constitution "previous condition of servitude."[59]

Between 1869 and 1872, as the nation entered the early stages of an economic depression, NWSA widened the intramovement rift with civil disobedience: If women already possessed the right to vote, they would storm the polls and reclaim it. The Republican Party apparently decided to await the results of the election before it moved decisively against the intruders. In a speech supporting Woodhull's resolutions, pro-suffrage attorney and judge Albert G. Riddle promised to test the reach of the Reconstruction amendments by presenting numerous "ladies for registration, two or three months hence. . . . If they are not registered, I propose to try the strength of the Supreme Court of the District of Columbia . . . to see if they will issue a mandamus. If they won't," he said, "I will take the case to the Supreme Court of the United States."[60] One of the primary tools in this effort was the Enforcement Act of May 1870, which seemed to extend federal protection to citizens' lawful attempts to vote in presidential and congressional elections. In South Carolina, the Freedman's Bureau reportedly encouraged black women to use the Enforcement Act as a shield at the polls. Women sometimes succeeded. In 1871, Nadine Gardner of Detroit persuaded a ward official to let her vote. A year later, she gave her ally a "banner of white satin, trimmed with gold fringe," bearing his name and this slogan: "By recognizing civil liberties and equality for woman, he has placed the last and brightest jewel on the brow of Michigan."[61]

Elsewhere, however, victories were few. Hundreds of women crowded registrars' offices and polling places in advance of the 1872 elections; when they actually cast ballots, authorities charged them with the federal crime of voting without a right to vote under Section 19 of the Civil Rights Act of 1870[62] (an act originally designed to prevent whites from casting multiple ballots to cancel out black votes) and sometimes jailed them. Pro-suffrage lawyers speculated that the Reconstruction amendments, despite the word "male," might have enfranchised all adult "citizens" of the United States, especially if judges and legislators could be persuaded to treat suffrage as a natural right and incident of federal citizenship, rather than as a state privilege regulated (as in England and early America) by representatives of the sovereign. California's Ellen Van Valkenberg went so far as to sue election officials under the Enforcement Act for refusing her ballot; other women soon followed her lead, buffeting courts with lawsuits. But almost to a man, judges held their ground, and the suits failed.

NWSA therefore swung decisively away from the New Departure and the declaratory act idea toward sex-specific emendation of constitutions—from opponents' vantage point, a tacit acknowledgment that women's constitutional right to vote could not be found in the organic law. In January 1878, Senator Aaron Sargent reintroduced Julian's woman suffrage amendment.[63] At the same time, as NWSA and AWSA languished (particularly compared to the burgeoning membership rolls of the Woman's Christian Temperance Union) and as the Republican Party began to move away from black voters, racism reared its head with uncommon fury. White women, in both the North and the South, had imbibed the antiblack sentiments that permeated antebellum society and were drawn easily into a vortex of racialized accusations and counteraccusations. Nor could they resist the competition with black men into which congressional Republicans seemed to be pushing them. The New York *World*, for example, cast AERA delegates in 1866 as "[m]ummified and fossilated females, void of domestic duties, habits and natural affections; crackbrained, rheumatic, dyspeptic, henpecked men, vainly striving to achieve the liberty of opening their heads in presence of their wives [and] self-educated, oily-faced, insolent, gabbling negroes." Women's rights groups often responded in kind, frantically trying to distinguish themselves from freedmen or to establish the historical credentials of sex prejudice as compared to racism.[64]

The apparent contest for rights between mostly white, upper-middle-class women and impoverished black men, combined with the periodic resort to racial slurs within the movement itself, drove many black suffragists (who had never been well represented in women's communities) into segregated suffrage societies. Beginning perhaps in 1880 with the establishment of Mary Shadd Cary's Colored Women's Progressive Franchise Association in Washington, D. C., black women began to construct a distinctively black feminist discourse. As educator Anna Julia Cooper later explained, "The colored woman . . . occupies . . . a unique position in this country. In a period . . . transitional and unsettled, her status seems one of the least ascertainable and definitive of all the forces which make for our civilization. She is confronted by both a woman question and a race problem, and is as yet an unknown or an unacknowledged factor in both."[65]

To some extent, white feminists were responding to the hard fact that the electorate *had* been expanded along gender lines. As politician Stephen Foster put it in 1866, universal suffrage should have been "the true basis of the reconstruction of our government. . . . Suffrage for woman was even a more vital question than for the negro; for in giving the ballot to the black man, we bring no new element into the national life—simply another class of men." But white women, noting a loss of ground in relation to all men as Congress pursued manhood suffrage, often lashed out against black men, and black women would have none of it. It was bad enough that the Democratic demagogue George Francis Train should embarrass suffragists in Kansas with his race-baiting election ditties: "Woman votes the black to save,/The black he votes to make the woman slave,/Hence when blacks and 'Rads' unite to enslave the whites,/'Tis time the Democrats championed woman's rights." But suffragists also contributed to the groundswell of acrimony. It was common enough to say, as did Stone in 1867, that "[t]hese men *ought not to be allowed to vote before we do*, because they will be just so much more dead weight to lift."[66]

A graphic example of this tug-of-war appeared at the 1874 NWSA convention in Washington, D. C., in response to the sweeping civil rights legislation then pending in Congress (eventually, the Civil Rights Act of 1875). During consideration of the sex's apparent decline into second-rate citizenship, Anthony asked, "What is the reason of this low valuation of woman? Because she is never to have anything to do with the State. It is a humiliating thing to ask, but I insist that the white women of this country be placed on the same civil and political footing with the colored men from the plantations of the South. . . . We want a civil rights bill that shall make every white woman just as respectable as a negro or a white man." Anthony supported a draft bill that would have secured to women "equally with colored men, all the advantages and opportunities of life;"

> open to them all colleges of learning; secure to them the right to sit on juries; to sue and be sued; to practice in all our courts on the same terms with colored men; to be tried by a jury of their peers; to be admitted to theaters and hotels alone; to walk the streets by night and by day, to ramble in the forest, or beside the lakes and rivers, as do colored men, without fear of molestation or insult from any white man . . . ; to secure equal place and pay in this world of work.[67]

Congress, however, passed the 1875 act without mentioning gender-based disabilities.

THE CIVIL WAR SETTLEMENT: WOMEN IN PUBLIC

One "advantage and opportunity of life" long denied to women had been admission to the bar. As pressure increased on law schools, legislatures, and bar associations to consider female candidates, resistance also increased—in no small part because talk about women at the bar brought to mind the woman voter, juror, and officeholder. Lawyers, after all, not only served as independent agents for clients, but embodied the law itself and the related promise of rational deliberation and argument. Antebellum critics of female lawyering had pointed to married women's inability to contract, sue, or be sued on their own behalf as a ground for refusing all women admission to the bar. With those impediments removed, critics pointed to the possibility of diminished income and prestige for male lawyers and to the specter of pregnant lawyers, ministers, or politicians. "How funny it would sound in the newspapers," wrote a New York *Herald* editor, "that Lucy Stone, pleading a cause, took suddenly ill in the pains of parturition, and perhaps gave birth . . . in court; or that Rev. Brown was arrested in the middle of her sermon . . . from the same cause. . . ." In Karen Sanchez-Eppler's words, female "delivery of arguments, sermons, and services" came to be suffused with images of "the delivery of children."[68]

The federal government's guarantee of the basic economic rights of freedmen (including the right to make contracts in the labor market) implied support for women's occupational choices. But federal courts laid waste to these hopes, beginning with cases involving white butchers in New Orleans. In June 1870, Supreme Court justice Joseph Bradley, in his capacity as a Louisiana circuit judge, rendered an opinion in *Livestock Dealers and Butchers Association v. Crescent City Livestock* and a number of associated suits; in the process, Bradley (who, in Albert Riddle's tart phrase, was "not preeminently in favor of . . . woman's right")[69] supplied a tantalizing Fourteenth Amendment weapon for the suffragist arsenal. New Orleans butchers had brought suit under the Thirteenth and Fourteenth Amendments as well as the Civil Rights Act, seeking to overturn a state law that required butchers to work in a monopolistic facility on the outskirts of town. When the state forced artisans to work under conditions not of their own choosing, they argued, it created involuntary servitude, which was prohibited by the Thirteenth Amendment; the due process clause of the Fourteenth Amendment forbade legislative meddling with entrepreneurial freedom, and the privileges and immunities clause barred the destruction of property rights, including the right to work.

Perhaps to underscore the amendments' potential radicalism, Bradley endorsed the butchers' Fourteenth Amendment claims, identifying a "fundamental right of labor" beyond the reach of state police powers. He noted that the privileges and immunities clause probably addressed "absolute rights" rather than mere "capacities," and barred a state from "abridging the privileges and immunities of the citizens of the United States, whether its own citizens or any others"—among them, the right of labor. Bradley speculated that this prohibition might be consistent with states' requirements of licenses to practice professions such as law or medicine—occupations "open to all alike," provided they met the licensing criteria. The Fourteenth Amendment thus mandated that "the privileges and immunities of all citizens shall be absolutely . . . unimpaired" unless states could show a public interest in regulation. Finally, Bradley pointed to shadowy "rights" in the amendment's interstices; it took scant imagination to find woman suffrage as well as lawyering there or to see that Bradley was rehearsing arguments that women might offer. "It is possible," he wrote, "that those who framed the article were not themselves aware of the far reaching character of its terms."

> They may have had in mind but one particular phase of social and political wrong. . . .
> Yet, if the amendment . . . does in fact bear a broader meaning, and does extend its protecting shield over those who were never thought of when it was conceived . . . , and does

reach social evils which were never before prohibited by constitutional enactment, it is to be presumed that the American people . . . understood what they were doing, and meant to decree what has in fact been decreed.[70]

Did those "evils" include gender inequality? Reformers decided to find out. Arguments for enfranchisement seemed to gain strength with the decisions handed down in Albert Riddle's 1872 test cases. In *Sara Spencer v. Board of Registration* (1873) and an associated case involving suffragist Sarah Webster's invasion of the polls, Chief Judge David Cartter of the Supreme Court of the District of Columbia echoed Bradley's *Crescent City* opinion: While "male citizens only can exercise the elective franchise in the District of Columbia" and suffrage probably was "not a natural right," as reformers frequently claimed, the "first clause of the fourteenth amendment" made "the plaintiff and all other persons born in the United States . . . capable of becoming voters." But the amendment was not self-executing; it required "legislative action" (a statute or declaratory act) to affect the reform. Thus, although Cartter rejected NWSA's (and Bradley's) "natural right" arguments, he affirmed both the Fourteenth Amendment's federalization of *citizenship* and Congress's ability to enfranchise women without a new amendment.[71] At NWSA's 1873 meeting in Washington, D.C., Virginia attorney Belva Lockwood presented a resolution demanding congressional recognition of women's right to vote, and Francis Miller berated Cartter's half-useful opinion: "It was said that the ballot was a creature of legislation, consequently not natural. This was an absurdity. There was no way in the world for a man to govern himself except by the ballot." The handwriting was on the wall: If judges refused to find women in constitutional texts, suffragists would have to "go through the States with a new amendment, and fight a battle in each."[72]

At almost the same moment, the U.S. Supreme Court delivered two body blows. First, it repudiated Bradley's speculations in *Crescent City*. For a majority of the Court, Justice Samuel Miller held in the *Slaughterhouse Cases* (a group of cases that included *Crescent City*) that the new amendments addressed only "the freedom of the slave race . . . and the protection of the newly-made freeman and citizen" from southern oppression, not the right of whites to be free from state health and welfare legislation. Nor had the amendments altered the states' traditional superintendence of the privileges and immunities of whites— including the right to labor, no longer characterized as an "absolute" right. Miller did not rule out the possibility that the amendments ultimately might be used to help other enslaved classes or that if the states attacked "other rights" that fell properly within the amendments' scope, they might be used to protect citizens "not . . . of African descent." But for the moment, the Court refused to say that the amendments mandated federal scrutiny of *all* state legislative attempts to abridge the citizenship rights of entire classes of citizens.[73]

The second blow arrived a day later, with the Supreme Court's decision in *Bradwell v. State of Illinois*. In the 1860s, Myra Bradwell—editor of the prestigious *Chicago Legal News*, a main force behind married women's property laws in Illinois, and a trained lawyer—had obtained certificates of good character, passed the bar exam, and applied to the state supreme court for a license to practice law. With her application, she included a brief reminding justices that state law did not explicitly rule out women. In 1869, however, the court denied her a license on the ground that a wife "would be bound neither by her express contracts nor by those implied contracts" struck up with clients and that judges had been authorized to exclude any "class of persons . . . not intended by the legislature to be admitted, even though their exclusion is not expressly required."[74]

The Supreme Court had considered *Slaughterhouse* and *Bradwell* together for more than a year; as legal scholar Barbara Babcock contends, it is "not farfetched to speculate" that the Justices crafted their *Slaughterhouse* opinions in light of Bradley's suggestion that expansive readings of the Fourteenth Amendment "would necessarily change the status of women."[75] Matthew Carpenter, a Republican senator from Wisconsin and a friend of woman suffrage, had served as a member of Louisiana's defense team in *Slaughterhouse*; in *Bradwell*, he appeared on the other side. In a terse brief, Carpenter insisted that professional law was "an avocation open to every citizen of the United States"; while legislators could "prescribe qualifications for entering upon this pursuit,"

> they cannot, under the guise of fixing qualifications, exclude a class of citizens from admission to the bar. . . . [A] qualification, to which a whole class of citizens never can attain, is not a regulation of admission to the bar, but . . . a prohibition. If the [privileges and immunities clause] does not open all the professions . . . to the colored as well as the white man, then the Legislatures of the States may exclude colored men from all the honorable pursuits of life.

On the other hand, if the clause protected emancipated blacks, it surely protected "every citizen, black or white, male or female," if only because half of all blacks were women.[76]

Justice Samuel Miller thought otherwise. Pointing to the Court's *Slaughterhouse* ruling of the previous day, he announced that the Fourteenth Amendment had not created a federal right to occupations. "We agree . . . ," wrote Miller, "that there are privileges and immunities [of] citizens of the United States, . . . and that it is these and these alone which a State is forbidden to abridge. But the right to admission to practice in the courts of a State is not one of them." In a telling concurrence on behalf of himself and Justices Swayne and Field, Bradley made clear that even his vision in *Crescent City* of a sweepingly inclusive Fourteenth Amendment permitted distinctions between the sexes pegged to "natural" sociobiological attributes. This concurrence, even more clearly than Miller's majority opinion, wrapped federal constitutional law around the twin ideologies of separate male-female spheres and Spenserian sociology. "It certainly cannot be affirmed, as an historical fact," wrote Bradley, "that [a right to practice law] has ever been established as one of the fundamental privileges . . . of the sex. On the contrary, *the civil law, as well as nature herself*, has always recognized a wide difference in the respective spheres and destinies of man and woman."

> Man is, or should be, woman's protector and defender. The natural and proper timidity and delicacy which belongs to the female sex evidently unfits it for many of the occupations of civil life. *The constitution of the family organization, which is founded in the divine ordinance, as well as in the nature of things, indicates the domestic sphere as that which properly belongs to the domain and functions of womanhood.* The harmony, not to say identity, of interests and views which belong . . . to the family institution is repugnant to the idea of a woman adopting a distinct and independent career from that of her husband.

Past experience justified the governance of women within a "family organization" with its own interests and constitution; from time out of mind, a woman had been accorded "no legal existence separate from her husband, who was regarded as her head and representative."[77]

What about the *feme sole*? Here, social theory operated with great force. Unaffected by marital "incapacities," said Bradley, spinsters formed "exceptions" to the rule; brides-in-waiting also inhabited a realm apart from the male realm, governed by scientifically validated "natural" laws. "The paramount destiny and mission of woman," wrote Bradley in a notorious passage, "are to fulfil the noble and benign offices of wife and mother. This is the law of the Creator. And the rules of civil society must be adapted to the general constitution of things"—in other words, to social structures consonant with the law of nature—"and cannot be based upon exceptional cases. The humane movements of modern society, which have for their object the multiplication of avenues for woman's advancement . . . have my heartiest concurrence. But I am not prepared to say that it is one of her fundamental rights and privileges to be admitted into every office and position. . . . In the nature of things it is not every citizen . . . that is qualified for every calling and position."[78] Ironically, in 1872, before the Supreme Court announced its decision in *Bradwell*, the Illinois assembly granted all citizens the right to choose an occupation. Bradwell never opened a practice, but in 1890, when she was 59, state judges acted on her original petition and admitted her to the bar.

Susan B. Anthony enjoyed a slightly different fate. On the last day of registration in 1872, Anthony (with sisters Hannah, Mary, and Guelma) marched into the local barber-shop and registered to vote in federal elections; almost fifty other women in Rochester, New York, did the same. When election judges contested their registration, Anthony presented documents, recited relevant constitutional clauses, brandished the name of Judge Henry Selden, and threatened to sue them "for large, exemplary damages." After consulting with John Van Voorhis (a pro-suffrage lawyer) and learning that punishments would fall on the women, the officials permitted them to register. On November 5, 1872, Anthony cast a ballot. "Well, I have been & gone & done it!!" she told Stanton. "Positively voted the Republican ticket—strait—this A.M. at 7 o'clock & swore my vote in."[79]

With Anthony's arrest (and the arrest of election inspectors and fourteen other women voters in Rochester) on November 28, 1872, just after the federal elections, the New Departure finally struck a public nerve. For many Americans, the imposing Quaker symbolized political integrity; even her opponents tempered criticism with grudging praise—as in 1873, when Alice Stone Blackwell, daughter of the AWSA's Lucy Stone, portrayed Anthony as "sharp, dictatorial, conceited, pugnacious & selfish," but "plucky, undoubtedly."[80] Anthony refused bail; when Selden sued out a writ of habeas corpus, the court released her to await action on the writ. On January 21, 1873, a federal district court judge denied the writ and set bail at $1,000. Anthony again refused to pay. Without her knowledge, Selden put up the bail, thereby sacrificing an opportunity to get the case before the Supreme Court. Anthony was livid: When Selden refused to bill her for professional services, she gathered money from friends and paid him anyway.

On January 22, a grand jury indicted Anthony under the 1870 federal statute; in March, she voted in a local election in defiance of the indictment, at the same time lecturing across the county to "educate any possible jurymen" and mobilize support. She urged women to defy unjust laws and chastised public officials for presuming to grant natural rights to the sovereign people. Had not Americans rejected monarchism a century earlier? "We throw to the winds the old dogma," she said, "that governments can give rights. The Declaration of Independence, the United States Constitution, the constitutions of the several States and the organic laws of the Territories, all alike propose to *protect* the people in the exercise of their God-given rights. Not one of them pretends to bestow rights."[81]

Perceiving that Anthony's speeches had prejudiced Monroe County jurymen, the authorities moved the trial to Canandaigua in Ontario County; Anthony and Gage promptly
moved the lecture series to the new site.

The trial began on June 17, 1873, with U.S. Supreme Court justice Ward Hunt presiding. The prosecuting attorney contended that Anthony was a woman and had voted il-
legally; Selden admitted his client's sex and the act of voting, arguing that he had advised
her to cast a ballot because the Constitution of the United States as amended in 1868 and
1870 authorized woman suffrage. In an opinion prepared in advance of the trial that leaned
heavily on *Slaughterhouse* and *Bradwell*, Hunt found Anthony guilty. The Fourteenth
Amendment indeed extended citizenship rights to all native-born adults in the United
States, but suffrage was not one of the privileges and immunities so conveyed. Hunt then
instructed the jury to convict her, without hearing all the evidence on Anthony's side.
When Anthony tried to testify on her own behalf, Hunt silenced her and ordered her to
sit down (critics later called it a "high-handed outrage"). She accused the judge of tam-
pering with her right to a trial by peers: Had he "submitted my case to the jury, as was
clearly [his] duty, even then I should have had just cause to protest, for not one of those
men was my peer; but, native or foreign born, white or black, rich or poor, . . . each
and every man . . . was my political superior; hence, in no sense my peer. . . . Even my
counsel . . . is my political sovereign." Despite admonitions to "sit down," Anthony continued. Hunt then ordered her to stand up and imposed a fine of $100, which she refused
to pay on the ground that "'resistance to tyranny is obedience to God.'" In January, 1874,
NWSA delegates in Washington, D.C., condemned Hunt's "grossly partial course," urging women to engage in civil disobedience; Congress spread over the record a petition
containing Anthony's constitutional arguments and, in lieu of a Supreme Court appeal, a
request for remission of the fine.[82]

Clearly, woman suffrage was in the wind, rearing its head directly in the civil disobedience cases and indirectly whenever female lawyers sought admission to the bar.
Matthew Carpenter outraged suffragists when he prefaced his entire brief in *Bradwell* with
assurances that a federal guarantee of a woman's right to an occupation need "not involve
the right of a female to vote."[83]

No sooner was the ink dry on *Bradwell* and *Spenser* than federal courts addressed
the suffrage question head-on. In November 1872, Virginia Minor—a woman suffrage
leader in Missouri and the source of many of Woodhull's and Anthony's arguments—
applied to Happersett, the registrar of voters, demanding the right to cast a ballot in federal elections; he refused on the ground that "she was not 'a male citizen of the United
States,' but a woman" and so could be excluded lawfully from the ballot box. Joined by
her husband, Francis Minor, Virginia sued Happersett in Missouri courts for "wilfully refusing to place her name upon the list of registered voters, by which refusal she was deprived of her right to vote." As early as 1869, Virginia and Francis had proposed testing
whether the Fourteenth Amendment invalidated sex-specific state election laws; women's
rights groups supported their efforts. When local judges affirmed the legality of the registrar's action, the Minors brought a writ of error to the U.S. Supreme Court.[84]

In *Minor v. Happersett* (1874), Francis Minor and two other attorneys argued, first,
that Virginia, a "citizen of the United States," was "entitled to any and all of the 'privileges and immunities' that belong to such position . . . ,'" which was to imply that property rights inhered in the "office" of citizen. Second, they contended that she might claim
all privileges "held, exercised, and enjoyed by other citizens of the United States"—an
equal protection point. The ballot, moreover, was a "privilege preservative of all rights

and privileges," especially "the right of the citizen to participate in his or her government." Nor could states tamper with the rights of federal citizens; the authority to exclude
whole classes from elements of citizenship lay with the U.S. Constitution. No "inferior
power . . . can legally claim the right to exercise it." They condemned sex-specific statutes
as unconstitutional bills of attainder and abrogations of the guaranty clause. Did not *republican* imply universal suffrage, as Republicans had argued on behalf of black men?
Finally, said the Minors, the Fourteenth Amendment expressly forbade states from making or enforcing "any law which shall abridge the privileges or immunities of citizens of
the United States."[85]

The Court unanimously disagreed. Chief Justice Morrison Waite conceded that
women were citizens as well as "persons." They had been part of political society since
the republic's inception; indeed, if the right of suffrage was "one of the necessary privileges of a citizen of the United States, then the constitution and laws of Missouri confin-
ing it to men are in violation of the Constitution of the United States, as amended, and
. . . void." The question, though, was "whether all citizens are necessarily voters"; the answer was no. Until Congress passed uniform rules preempting the states' traditional role
in shaping the electorate, state power was "supreme." The Fourteenth Amendment "did
not add to the privileges and immunities of a citizen. It simply furnished an additional
guaranty for the protection of such as he already had. No new voters were necessarily
made by it. Indirectly it may have had that effect, because it may have increased the number of citizens entitled to suffrage . . . , but it operates for this purpose, if at all, through
the States . . . , and not directly upon the citizen."[86]

Waite then looked to the intentions of the framers: In 1787, the right to vote had not
been "co-extensive" with either federal or state citizenship. The framers would not have
left such an important freedom "to implication"; instead, they expressly granted citizens
all the "privileges and immunities of citizens in the several States." So clearly did the
states control the polls that Congress felt compelled to adopt the Fifteenth Amendment,
to prevent state disfranchisement of black men. Nor did the guaranty clause alter women's
prospects; in the 1780s, "all the citizens of the States were not invested with the right of
suffrage," yet governments were taken to be "republican." It was "certainly now too late
to contend that a government is not republican . . . because women are not made voters."
Waite did not close the door entirely; if the "law is wrong," he said, "it ought to be
changed," but the "power for that is not with us." "No argument as to woman's need of
suffrage can be considered. We can only act upon her rights as they exist."[87]

Congress held firm against woman suffrage. A month after Woodhull delivered her
influential address, Senator John Bingham decided for the Judiciary Committee that the
Fourteenth Amendment did not "change or modify the relations of citizens of the State
and nation as they existed under the original Constitution." Rather, the constitution "uses
the word 'citizen' only to express the political quality of the individual in his relation to
the Nation; to declare that he is a member of the body politic, and bound to it by the reciprocal obligation of allegiance on the one side and protection on the other." The federal
government would not intrude upon the states' right to maintain reasonable distinctions
in election laws. Thus, he concluded, a declaratory act would be illegal—that is, neither
"authorized by the Constitution nor within the legislative power of Congress." When Gage,
Mott, Stanton, and a dozen other women demanded, in light of Cartter's *Spenser* opinion, the immediate enfranchisement of women (by enfranchising black men in the federal
city, they argued, congressmen had "made an unjust discrimination against sex"), the
House shuffled the petition off to the Committee on the District of Columbia.[88]

The Supreme Court eventually found federal protection for the privileges and immunities of black male citizenship on rather telling grounds: In *Ex parte Yarbrough* (1884), the justices confronted white intimidation of a freedman at the polls; state counsel cited *Minor v. Happersett*, claiming that Congress had no authority to regulate the polls during federal elections. Purporting to find the proposition "so startling as to arrest attention," the Court distinguished the case from *Minor* and held that although the Fourteenth and Fifteenth Amendments did not confer new rights on anyone, men always had possessed the right to vote. Hence, Congress could protect that sex's citizenship rights. In so constitutionalizing and federalizing the exclusion of women from the electorate, the Court dealt a blow from which women did not recover until ratification of the Nineteenth Amendment, which overruled *Minor*.[89]

Only once did Congress rise to the occasion, and then not in a suffrage case. The U.S. Supreme Court as well as the state of Virginia had denied Belva Lockwood admission to the bar; in an 1877 campaign led by Lockwood, members of the District of Columbia bar petitioned Congress for relief. Although Lockwood had been admitted to the District bar in 1873, she wrote, she had been "debarred from admission" to the nation's highest court "on the ground that she is a *woman*"; that fact had been "published over the country much to the detriment of her law practice, upon which she and her family are dependent for support; and for which profession she has duly prepared herself." Hence, she urged adoption of House Bill 4435, which required the Court "to receive as members of its bar your petitioners and all other women similarly situated."[90] Congress passed the bill, razing formal barriers to admission to the federal bar.

Into the new century, however, state lawmakers continued to resist female attorneyship. Only in 1920 did the last two holdouts (Rhode Island and Delaware) eliminate sex-specific admissions requirements. In 1881, Chief Justice Gray of the Massachusetts Supreme Judicial Court provided a window into the nature of the legal profession's resistance to women, as well as an illustration of the ongoing attempt to sever political freedom from economic capacity. Lelia J. Robinson, a qualified lawyer and applicant for admission to the Boston bar and (unlike Bradwell or Lockwood) an unmarried woman, challenged the state's authority to make sex-specific rules. Two members of the Boston bar submitted an amicus brief opposing her admission. In support of her application, Robinson cited the state law allowing a "citizen of this State . . . who is an inhabitant . . . of the age of twenty-one years and of good moral character . . . on the recommendation of an attorney" to be "examined for admission as an attorney." The statute ambiguously used the word *citizen,* as well as *his* and *he.* In what Gray called "elaborate briefs," Robinson pointed to rules of statutory construction by which the masculine pronoun encompassed both sexes; she seems to have argued, too, that women's economic disabilities had been eliminated and that legislators could not destroy property rights in occupations.[91]

Treating the case as if it involved claims to political freedom, Gray demolished the idea that the capacity to deal in property qualified women automatically for political rights, including the right to serve as an officer of the court. While "the word 'citizen' . . . in its most common and most comprehensive sense, doubtless includes women," Robinson was not, by virtue of either state or federal citizenship, vested with "any absolute right, independent of legislation, to take part in the government, either as a voter or as an officer, or to be admitted to practice as an attorney." A lawyer, while not "in the strictest sense, a public officer," came "very near it," and tradition strongly mitigated against female officeholding. Neither professional competence nor the ability to deal in property altered the case because sex alone barred women from the practice of law. "The statutes permitting a married women to hold and convey property, to make contracts, to sue and be sued . . . ," said Gray, "have in no way enlarged the capacity of any woman, married or unmarried, to hold office, and have no application to single women or to legal disabilities to which married and unmarried women alike are subject." In making changes, legislators had moved with "great caution, one step at a time"; nothing had been done by implication.[92]

As authority, Gray cited *Lockwood* and *Bradwell*, as well as an 1875 Wisconsin Supreme Court ruling in which Chief Judge Ryan denied the motion of the well-qualified, unmarried Lavinia Goodell for admission to that court's bar. Goodell had been admitted to the Janesville, Wisconsin, bar in 1874; after the debacle in Ryan's courtroom, she got the law changed and gained admission to the state supreme court in 1879. Ryan's *In Re Lavinia Goodell* decision warned that the admission of female lawyers would "emasculate the constitution," force legislators to extend the "constitutional right of male suffrage" to women, and trigger a "judicial revolution." The judge found no statutory basis for Goodell's admission; above all, he objected to violations of God's law:

> We cannot but think the common law wise in excluding women from the profession of the law. . . . The law of nature destines . . . the female sex for the bearing and nurture of the children of our race and for the custody of . . . homes. . . . And all life-long callings of women, inconsistent with these radical and sacred duties . . . are departures from the order of nature; *and when voluntary, treason against it.*

Though exceptions might appear, it was best to "provide for the sex, not for its superfluous members; and not to tempt women from the proper duties of their sex by opening to them duties peculiar to ours." Besides, he added, it would be "revolting" for women to sully themselves with "all the unclean issues" that came before courts—many of which involved women's bodies and lives—such as "sodomy, incest, rape, seduction, fornication, adultery, pregnancy, bastardy, legitimacy, prostitution, lascivious cohabitation, abortion, infanticide, obscene publications, libel and slander of sex, impotence, divorce: all the . . . indecencies . . . [of] society."[93]

THE CIVIL WAR SETTLEMENT: MARRIAGE AND WOMEN'S BODIES

During the same decades, public officials subjected maternity to heightened scrutiny, entrenching in law the idea that women (especially white middle-class women) best expressed patriotism through monogamous marriage, child rearing, and homemaking. Not coincidentally, the Victorian family had come under heavy fire. Fresh policy mandates coincided not just with the end of Reconstruction, but also with a period of increasing divorce rates, heavy migration from southern and eastern Europe, anti-Chinese and anti-Mormon agitation in the West, and women's growing involvement in a wage economy. Many women simply refused to toe the line and, by amassing independent wealth, sabotaged one of the main engines of subjection. Louisa May Alcott was one of many self-supporting women who decided that "liberty" might be "a better husband,"[94] and so rejected marriage in favor of spinsterhood or same-sex relationships.

Immediately after Mormon Utah adopted woman suffrage and before the Mormon Church officially abandoned polygamy in 1890, Americans held a public "trial" of polygamy; before it was over, it lay bare many of the elements of late-century social conservatism. Plural marriage had been a centerpiece of Mormon religious and social practice since 1843, when Joseph Smith, founder of the Church of Latter Day Saints, resuscitated what he took to be a biblical practice; in 1852, Mormon theologians publically made polygamy incumbent on all believers, defining its practice as the salvation of the family and society. Without actually naming it, Utah legislators sought to protect polygamy by carefully framing legislation so that neither male participants nor their children were penalized. When Utah became a territory in 1850, Brigham Young and other Mormon leaders secured control of the territorial government, including the office of governor. Indeed, when legislators declared in 1854 that territorial courts were not to follow the common law, it was widely understood that they aimed to preserve plural marriage, which the common law prohibited. But victory was short lived; on July 1, 1862, Congress adopted the Morrill Act, outlawing polygamy (conceptualized as a species of bigamy for purposes of criminal punishment) in American territories and invalidated the act of the Utah territorial assembly incorporating the Church of Latter Days Saints (1851) to the extent that it encouraged polygamy.[95]

The Mormons held fast, using probate and ecclesiastical courts to police and protect local practices. In February 1870, in an effort to prove to the rest of the nation that Mormon patriarchs respected women, the territorial legislature granted women the right to vote, although not the right to hold public office. Observers were scandalized. In novels, pamphlets, newspaper essays, and eventually appellate courtrooms, citizens mobilized to eliminate Mormon patriarchy and harems of brain-washed wives. Plural marriage seemed to epitomize antirepublican tyranny and patriarchal abuse of women; as Sarah Barringer Gordon points out, the controversy forced Americans to look closely at bedrock constitutional values, notably the doctrine of government by consent. Utah women voted and thus seemed to be consenting to degradation. Did women's complicity in their own debasement mean that other citizens had to respect those choices? Was the problem perhaps woman suffrage as well as polygamy? If polygamy made a "mockery of marriage," asks Gordon, did its presence also "make a mockery of woman suffrage"?[96] Members of Congress certainly thought so. In 1882, they provided that no male "polygamist" or "bigamist" and no female "cohabiting with any polygamist, bigamist, or man cohabiting with more than one woman" could register to vote or hold office in federal territories.[97]

Federal judges also took action. In 1878, the U.S. Supreme Court heard arguments in the case of George Reynolds, a Mormon and Brigham Young's secretary, who had been convicted of bigamy under the Morrill Act. Counsel for Reynolds contended that the federal government could not regulate territorial institutions; the prosecutor and then the Court brought up the possibility that the 1862 act might violate First Amendment rights to the free exercise of Mormonism, which mandated polygamous marriage, and then denied that it had any such effect. In *Reynolds v. United States* (1879), the majority, speaking through Chief Justice Waite, not only sustained Congress's power to intrude upon religious practice in the name of public morality, but also explained—more fully than at any other moment in the Court's history—why marriage and the family mattered.

The majority offered an argument eventually consonant with Justice Field's ruling in *Maynard v. Hill* (1888), in which he proclaimed marriage and the social harmony it fostered indispensable to the republic. Waite noted that the legal framework of marriage, while undeniably a "sacred obligation" and therefore a part of spiritual life, was also "in most civilized nations, a civil contract, and usually regulated by law. Upon it society may be said to be built, and out of its fruits spring social relations and social obligations and duties, with which government is necessarily required to deal." Whatever else republicans might come to value, they had to defend monogamous marriage and the family as indispensable social rudders. "[P]olygamy leads to the patriarchal principle," said Waite, "which, when applied to large communities, fetters the people in stationary despotism, while that principle cannot long exist in connection with monogamy." Polygamy embodied the patriarchal, monarchical principle and monogamy, the egalitarian, republican principle. If Mormonism damaged women and the republic, monogamy preserved them and so merited state protection; otherwise, Mormon children would "multiply and spread themselves over the land," infecting the body politic.[98]

A similar argument appeared in *Murphy v. Ramsey* (1885), a suit brought against the Utah Board of Commissioners by a number of Mormons who were turned away from the polls in 1882 for polygamous practices. Justice Matthews decided that Congress had the authority to regulate territorial elections. In finding that several of the plaintiffs maintained "bigamous" or "polygamous" relationships at the time of registration, the Court underscored its opposition to unconventional families. Surely, "no legislation can be supposed more wholesome and necessary in the founding of a free, self-governing commonwealth," wrote Matthews, ". . . than that which seeks to establish it on the basis of the idea of the family, as . . . springing from the union for life of one man and one woman . . . ; the sure foundation of all that is stable and noble in our civilization." The Court applauded a statute that withdrew "all political influence" from the enemies of republicanism.[99] In 1890, the Supreme Court increased the stakes in two decisions linking Utah statehood to monogamy. In *Late Corporation of the Church of Jesus Christ of Latter-Day Saints v. United States*, Bradley affirmed Congress's considerable authority to regulate territorial institutions. Then, in *Davis v. Beason*, Justice Field dealt summarily with a "conspiracy" of polygamists in Idaho Territory, affirming both the power of territorial lawmakers to disfranchise Mormons and the Court's commitment to monogamous households: "Bigamy and polygamy," he wrote, destroyed "the purity of the marriage relation" and "debase[d]" both men and women.[100]

In 1885, a pamphleteer found it "curious" that the main objection to both woman suffrage and polygamy was that they would "*destroy the home!*"[101] Yet, as Gordon clearly shows, Americans associated both monogamy and benificent male headship with republicanism itself; all else was unnatural and pernicious. Monogamy was "both essential to civilization, and the only possible marital form in a democracy. . . . The argument for the relationship between democracy and monogamy mirrors the traditional argument that the state reflects and is dependent upon the individual families that make up its constituents. In this view, a tyrannical husband (like a slaveholder, a man who has too much power over those dependent upon him) would be unfit to participate in the reasoned debate of democratic politics," because he would replicate "the tyrannical politics of his home in the political arena." If republican social health depended on "respect for women, polygamy by its very nature was anti-social, but so were individual husbands who indulged their passions indiscriminately." The crusade thus merged a "profound political critique of marriage" with talk about the need to restrain men, respect women, and put state power to the task of restoring the "true" republican family.[102]

During the same decades, new legal rules emerged to discourage women from suing for divorce. In North Carolina, as divorce rates mushroomed and women sought marital dissolutions in record numbers, lawmakers as early as 1870 began to revise family law dramatically (in historian Victoria Bynum's words) "in a way that favored husbands"; new statutes encouraged women to remain in marriages by allowing them to sue for alimony without obtaining divorces. The grounds for divorce also changed; while adultery and impotence continued to be the sole grounds for dissolution, male "adultery" came to be defined as sexual misconduct *combined with* abandonment. Elsewhere, although "mental cruelty" came to be included as a ground for divorce in a number of jurisdictions, legislators sometimes yielded to conservative pressure and scaled back statutes that had permitted judges to exercise considerable discretion. As a result, many white women could not file for divorce unless they had been deserted or (in some jurisdictions) emotionally terrorized, and courts helped black men retain control over "bad" wives ("Sapphires") simply by refusing to grant divorces to such women.[103]

In cities, reform-minded boards and agencies zeroed in on "delinquent" teenagers—a category that included abused, sexually active, rebellious, or simply unhappy young women. Authorities took girls into protective or punitive custody in response to complaints by parents, friends, or disapproving neighbors. Young people found themselves policed by state and municipal employees. "Homes" and refuges opened in major cities. And when states rewrote vagrancy laws, they distinguished between prostitution and other forms of immoral or unruly behavior. As Amy Dru Stanley persuasively contends, the late-century streetwalker not only took the place of the female slave as the leading symbol of masculine depravity, but also seemed to illustrate the perils of "wage slavery" in women's lives. It was better to stay home than to risk such humiliation. In postwar Detroit, the House of Corrections carved out a special women's section to transform women at risk of prostitution into employable "ladies."[104] Dozens of benevolent associations labored to purify or remodel women. In 1870, for example, New Yorkers chartered the Society for the Aid of Friendless Women and Children to "aid destitute and friendless women and children to help themselves by providing a temporary home, where they may receive proper moral and intellectual culture" and prepare for honorable employment. A month later, reformers established the Ladies' Helping Hand Association of New York City to "advance the social and moral condition of women . . . ," convey marketable skills, and "elevate them in the social scale to self-respect and *true womanhood*."[105]

The policing of women's bodies thus figured large in an emerging settlement between men and women. On the antiabortion and anticontraception front, the war years also brought unprecedented victories. In 1868, just as the Fourteenth Amendment made its way through Congress, Horatio Robinson Storer and Franklin Fiske Heard published their influential antiabortion brief, *Criminal Abortion: Its Nature, Its Evidence, and Its Law*—one of many such tracts. They observed that law codes seemed "almost wholly to ignore foetal life, to refuse it protection, to insure their own evasion, and by their inherent contradictions to extend the very crime they were framed to prevent." They insisted, too, that abortion at any point during a pregnancy should be made a felony rather than a misdemeanor.[106]

Even as federal courts beat back attempts to secure women's political and occupational equality, legislators completed the process, begun in the second quarter of the century, of outlawing trade in and information about abortion and contraception, and though the American Medical Association (AMA) had been laboring since its founding in the 1840s to "medicalize" the regulation of maternity, physicians began more seriously to urge legislators to heed expert advice. By the 1880s, most states had passed restrictive abortion laws which punished physicians who performed post-quickening abortions. In some states, abortion at any stage of pregnancy was made a crime and women were pun-

ished for procuring abortions. By one scholar's count, eight states "forbade the adver-
tisement of abortion-inducing drugs"; three others outlawed ambiguous ads—as when sell-
ers signaled abortifacients with the phrase "caution to the married." Medical crusaders
usually had in mind protecting women and exerting "scientific" control over childbirth.
In the process, they drove out midwives and deprived poor women of care; and, as Leslie
Reagan notes, a policy to limit reproductive choices inevitably "forces women into
maternity."[107]

New York provides a good illustration of the proliferation of maternity-related laws.
In 1868, legislators adopted a statute suppressing the "trade in and circulation of obscene
literature, illustrations, advertisements, and articles of indecent or immoral use, and obscene advertisements of patent medicines," including anatomy books, birth control pamphlets, and abortifacient ads; punishments included one-year jail terms and thousand-
dollar fines. In 1869 and 1872, they recast the abortion laws and encouraged abortionists
to turn state's evidence; in 1875, they declared the "dying declarations" of women upon
whom abortions had been performed to be irrefutable evidence at trial. Five years later,
even as they granted women the right to serve as school trustees and vote in school elections, lawmakers again beefed up antiabortion and anticontraceptive laws.[108]

After 1850, demand had skyrocketed for advice books, safe abortions, and "miracu-
lous" birth control potions. Many Americans preferred to buy sex-related materials by
mail, avoiding red-faced encounters with shopkeepers—although, as a pregnant Idaho
woman told a friend in 1878, she would "face anything," even shaming, to avoid the "inevitable result of Nature's methods."[109] Women knew that, so long as men retained a sex
right within marriage, unwanted pregnancies were unavoidable. Then, on March 3, 1873,
at virtually the same moment that Myra Bradwell lost her case, Congress adopted the
Comstock Act, named for evangelical Christian reformer Anthony Comstock, as of 1872
the salaried agent of the New York Committee for the Suppression of Vice and, after passage of the act, special agent for the Post Office.

The Comstock Act criminalized the manufacture, exchange, and possession of "obscene" material in the District of Columbia and federal territories; it also prohibited mail
trafficking anywhere in "any article" for the "prevention of conception, or for causing unlawful abortion." The act made it a misdemeanor punishable by up to five years of hard
labor or steep fines for residents of federal districts to "sell, or lend, or give away, or
. . . exhibit,"

> or . . . offer to sell, or to lend, or to give away, or in any manner to exhibit, or . . . oth-
> erwise publish or offer to publish in any manner, or . . . have in his possession for any
> such purpose . . . any obscene book, pamphlet, paper, writing, advertisement, circular,
> print, picture, drawing or other representation, figure or image on or of paper or other ma-
> terial, or any cast, instrument, or other article of an immoral nature, or any drug or med-
> icine, or any article whatever, for the prevention of conception, or for causing unlawful
> abortion, or shall advertise the same for sale, or write or print . . . any card, circular, book,
> pamphlet, advertisement, or notice . . . stating when, where, how, or of whom, or by what
> means any of the articles . . . can be purchased or obtained, or shall manufacture, draw,
> or print, or . . . make any of such articles.

The act also forbade importation of prohibited articles, except for drugs shipped in
bulk for medical purposes. Dragnet language encompassed—to give a few examples—
advertisements for birth control devices (such as diaphragms), abortifacients, and instru-

ments; "free love" prints, including tracts urging women to refuse unwanted sex; anatomy books; packets of herbs; pamphlets describing "natural" birth control methods; and descriptions of the reproductive cycle or the symptoms of venereal diseases.[110]

To some extent, the Comstock Act (and the so-called mini-Comstock acts adopted in twenty-five states) expressed a nativist desire to prevent a takeover of American society by non-Teutonic immigrants. The move to imbue maternity with a public interest also fit into a general move by lawmakers to assume responsibility for work and moral choices previously undertaken within families. Physicians and churchmen took dead aim at moral laxity and "amateur" medical practices. Witness the "Memorial" circulated by the AMA in 1859–60 to state and territorial governors. The flier found its way into the statehouse in remote Washington Territory. "The moral guilt of Criminal Abortion," wrote the AMA, "depends entirely upon the real and essential nature of the act. It is the intentional destruction of a child within its parent; and physicians are now agreed . . . that the child is alive from the moment of conception. . . ."

> In many States of the Union, abortion is not yet legally considered an offence, and is unprovided for by statute; in others, the statutes are so drawn as to be easily evaded, or indeed, by their inconsistencies, directly to encourage the crime they were framed to prevent. This is the case also with the Common Law, which, by a strange contradiction, fails to recognize the unborn child as criminally affected, whilst its existence for all civil purposes is nevertheless fully acknowledged.[111]

By the 1890s, even female physicians joined and sometimes led campaigns against amateurism. Dr. Elizabeth Jarrett of New York, for example, condemned midwives as "ignorant, unskillful, [and] dirty"; the "woman doctor and the midwife," she said, "have nothing in common."[112]

Nor did women manage to escape the "prison" of restrictive clothing. As Barbara Welke notes, women still wore "tight corsets, still dragged long, heavy skirts after them, and were still severely constricted . . . by dresses or shirts with tight armholes, by multiple layers of undergarments, and by high-heeled shoes." When mainstream reformers thought about dress as a problem in liberty, they usually underscored the sex's inability when so attired to compete in the marketplace, not a woman's lung capacity or her ability to run from a rapist. Social theorist Thorstein Veblen, who was not in any sense a feminist, could not fathom why women were "encumbered with garments specially designed to hamper their movements and decrease their industrial efficiency."[113]

"SPEAKING" AT THE POLLS

Small wonder that organized feminism tilted in the direction of suffragism and the direct occupation of "profane" realms. To some extent, this shift reflected changes in the movement's leadership. Survivors of the 1850 Worcester Convention shared the stage with younger, college-educated social workers, lawyers, lobbyists, businesswomen, labor organizers, and journalists. Trained to work within established systems, such women often rejected old-fashioned rabble-rousing. Yet even first-wave women concluded that as sites of collective liberation, republican speech communities had failed. Said Mary Livermore, "I firmly believed it was only necessary to present [men] the wrongs and injustice done to women, to obtain prompt and complete redress. . . ."

[W]hen we lay before them our need of enfranchisement, they will be prompt to confer on us the ballot. . . . Alas! Experience has taught me a very different lesson. In the present composition of political and legislative bodies, no cause, whose claims are based *only* on eternal right and justice, need appeal to politicians, legislatures, or congresses, with expectations of success.

Livermore then put her husband's newspaper to the task of securing woman suffrage.[114] Stanton feared, too, that no amount of talk would win the day. "A moral power that has no direct influence on the legislation of a nation," she wrote in 1881, "is an abstraction, and might as well be expended in the clouds as outside of codes and constitutions, and this has too long been the realm where women have spent their energies fighting shadows. The power that makes laws, and baptizes them as divine at every church altar, is the power for woman to demand now and forever."[115]

Women's rights champions thus embraced the spirit of the times—typified by Americans' increased reliance on mass democracy, elections, and law to organize public life—and tacitly acknowledged that the Age of Revolution had passed. In liberal theologian Amory Dwight Mayo's words, republicans had witnessed "the radical transformation of an Anglo-Saxon, semi-aristocratic into an American, democratic order of human affairs."[116] Within democratic suffrage communities, women would dance with the wolves—as voters, jurors, politicians, lawyers, and lobbyists.

Not surprisingly, as women began to move from the political margins to the center, antisuffrage jeremiads grew more shrill. The opposition especially condemned feminist dissatisfaction with a divinely mandated domesticity and household representation. As woman's rights champion Charles Burleigh explained in 1867, "One objection to our claim is, that the right of voting should not belong to human beings as individuals, but rather to households of human beings." Such an argument was "not a denial of equality . . . , but an allegation that the right belongs neither to the man nor to the woman, but to the household; and that for the household, as its representative, the man casts the ballot."[117] Said antisuffragist Orestes Brownson in 1869 and 1873, female balloting would "weaken and finally break up and destroy the Christian family. The social unit is the family, not the individual; and the greatest danger to American society is, that we are rapidly becoming a nation of isolated individuals, without family ties or affections. The family has already been much weakened, and is fast disappearing"; when the "family goes, the nation goes too." The villain was the suffragist-wife who espoused "one political party, and the husband another." At stake was both male *authority* and male *power*. "We do not believe women . . . are fit to have their own head. . . . Revelation asserts, and universal experience proves that the man is the head of the woman, and that the woman is for the man, not the man for the woman." Man's "greatest error . . . is that he abdicates his headship, and allows himself to be governed by a woman."[118]

The postwar shift toward woman suffrage was a matter of degree and preponderance. Always, there had been women who had argued for the centrality of suffrage, in both universal and sex-specific terms. Rose, for one, insisted in 1856 that the ballot was "the focus of all other rights, . . . the pivot upon which all others hang," and the only way that woman would be able to "protect her person and her property." Four years earlier, Stone had dubbed "the right to vote, the right to our own earnings, [and] equality before the law" the "Gibraltar" of the cause. On the other side, even after 1920, many otherwise generous women insisted that the sex's peculiar attributes precluded suffrage; as society became more complex, they argued, maternal vigilance would determine the fate of the republic. In 1882, on behalf of a thousand signators, "Mrs. General Sherman" and "Mrs. Admiral Dehlgren" read a petition in Congress contending that woman suffrage would shatter "peace and happiness," add to the sex's burdens, undermine the position of "the working women of the country," introduce "discord in the existing marriage relation," further increase the divorce rate, and damage children. As an alternative, they proposed a constitutional amendment federalizing the law of domestic relations so that Congress could superintend "the transfer and descent of all kinds of property," marriage and birth registration, the rights and obligations of married people, and both divorce and alimony. The amendment also would have limited divorces to cases of adultery and prohibited divorced people from remarrying.[119]

Suffragism nevertheless gained adherents. Even Catherine Beecher decided by 1870 to support woman suffrage, albeit as an extension of her vision of public motherhood. To be sure, single-minded crusades for ballots were not without critics. Well before the war, Woodhull and other radicals insisted that suffrage was a "simple question of political privilege" rather than a powerful engine of social reconstruction. With other anarchists and socialists, Emma Goldman suspected that suffrage was a trap that would lead women away from one another into straitjackets fashioned by men. What good were ballots if candidates and party leaders were men, all of whom were in capitalists' pockets? Former allies on the reform circuit similarly worried about the law's apparent seduction and taming of the old movement. "I . . . hope," wrote Gerrit Smith to Anthony in 1874, "that [you] will not tolerate the idea of measuring the rights of woman by a man-made constitution. . . . Constitutions are useful in settling ten thousand subordinate questions. But the great question of primary and inherent human rights are to be submitted to no lower decisions than those of God's . . . justice."[120]

Gradually, law prevailed. As early as 1860–62, convention resolutions situated suffragism and "equal rights" alongside demands for cosovereignty at home. Increasingly, speakers and writers blasted recalcitrant judges, proposed amendments and statutes, condemned particular legal doctrines, and urged ambitious sisters to bang at the doors of law schools. Most of all, they demanded the right to vote. Delegates at the 1869 National Woman's Rights Convention in Washington, D.C., devoted seven of their nine resolutions to suffrage and related questions; the tumultuous AERA meeting of that year declared that "any party professing to be democratic in spirit or republican in principle, which opposes or ignores the political rights of woman, is false to its professions, shortsighted in its policy, and unworthy of the confidence of the friends of impartial liberty." As a disheartened Stanton later explained, it was finally necessary to secure woman's political freedom: "In an age when the wrongs of society are adjusted in the courts and at the ballot-box, material force yields to reason and majorities." Women hoped, sometimes against hope, that ballots would open college doors, secure equal pay for equal work, and make woman an equal partner in both public and private life; surely, the sex had been disregarded during war-related deliberations for want of political illegitimacy. "Having *failed* to secure her legal rights by virtue of her disfranchisement," said Clarina Nichols, "a woman must look to the ballot for self-protection."[121]

In all this, the old vision of cultural change through conversation had been altered, if not entirely lost. By 1880, women's voices resounded mainly in separate debating halls; as Mary Ryan shows, Americans mostly admitted symbolic women to public life—the bronze Columbia atop statehouses, the white-gowned Liberty on war posters. Women's newspapers sometimes stood in for public lecturing: Stanton thought of *Revolution* as a "mouthpiece" for feminist argumentation.[122] For better or worse, thousands of suffragists fell behind goals advanced in the 1850s by law-minded reformers and a good many abolitionists; surely, political power would allow women to remake society from the inside out. Old warriors from the antislavery battle wholeheartedly agreed; their hearts had been with suffrage all along. Said Frederick Douglass at the first meeting of the AERA in 1867, "[T]he ballot . . . means bread, intelligence, self-protection, self-reliance and self-respect; to the daughter it means diversified employment and a fair day's wages for a fair day's work; to the wife it means the control of her own person, property and earnings; to the mother it means the equal guardianship of her children; to all it means colleges and professions, open, equal opportunities, skilled labor and intellectual development."[123]

Others, while equally determined to achieve justice and freedom, were decidedly melancholy. The brutally honest Declaration of Rights for Women, read by 56-year-old Anthony at Independence Hall on the occasion of the nation's centennial, synthesized many of the postwar movement's intellectual strands—its turn to law, its debt to revolutionary constitutionalism, and its interest in securing citizenship rights. "It was the boast of the founders of the republic," warned the grande dame of American suffragism, who died without casting a lawful ballot in a presidential election, "that the rights for which they contended were the rights of human nature. If these rights are ignored in the case of one-half the people, the nation is surely preparing for its downfall. *Governments try themselves.* The recognition of a governing and a governed class is incompatible with the first principles of freedom."[124]

The decision to pursue a disembodied electoral "voice" fundamentally altered the course and character not only of women's rights agitation, but also of American constitutional culture. No longer would citizens meet *as men and women* at the lectern; on election day, the mixing of male-female voices would be metaphoric rather than actual, ritualized rather than spontaneous. In the 1870 convention celebrating the twentieth anniversary of the first Worcester meeting, Paulina Wright Davis lamented the movement's miscalculations. It was a "fitting question to ask," she said, "if there has been progress; or has this universal radical reform . . . been . . . but a substitution of a new error for an old one; or like physical revolutions, but a rebellion? Has this work, intended . . . to change the structure of the central organization of society, failed and become a monument of buried hopes? . . . We answer, in many things we have failed, for we believed and hoped beyond the possible. . . . Women are still frivolous. . . . Men are still conceited, arrogant, and usurping, dwarfing their own manhood by a false position toward one half the human race. In commencing this work we knew that we were attacking the strongholds of prejudice, but truth could no longer be suppressed, nor principles hidden." In 1850, women had known that "it would take a generation to clear away the rubbish, to uproot the theories of ages." Few had been "brave enough"; hence, the demand for direct "participation in government."[125]

To some extent, women sacrificed community on the altar of political individualism; indeed, for some women, ballots became an end in themselves, rather than instruments of change. But, to vote, women had to think of themselves as part of the sovereign power, and judges had to agree to divide the supposedly indivisible "head of household"—an undertaking no less radical than it had been in 1776. Few doctrines have exhibited such resilience. As late as 1981, Georgians retained an 1855 statute which stated that "the head of the family and the wife is subject to him; her legal [and] civil existence is merged in the husband, except so far as the law recognizes her separately, either for her own protection, or . . . benefit, or for the preservation of public order."[126] Republican Senator James Rood Doolittle of Wisconsin knew that woman suffrage entailed a division of male sovereignty. In a republic, he reminded fellow congressmen in 1866, "every man is king, every woman is queen; but upon him devolves the responsibility of controlling the external relations of this family, and those external relations are controlled by the ballot; for the . . . vote which he exercises goes to choose the legislators who are to . . . govern society. Within the family man is supreme; he governs by the law of the family, by the law of reason, nature, religion. Therefore . . . I am not in favor of conferring the right of suffrage upon woman."[127]

To an important degree, ballots represented an alternative way of speaking in public. It was common enough for women to use the term *voice* to mean all kinds of public expression, including suffrage. During the Revolution, Abigail Adams had warned that women would not be bound by laws in which they had "no voice, no Representation." Decades later, Anthony used the term as a metaphor for women's utterances at ballot boxes and in courtrooms, noting that her sex had never had "the slightest voice" in the making of laws that regulated relations between the sexes; men alone decided who had committed such crimes as "adultery, breach of promise, seduction, rape, bigamy, abortion, [or] infanticide," with "judge, jury and advocate all men," and with "no woman's voice heard in our courts, save as accused or witness."[128] Suffragists increasingly characterized the ballot as a way to "speak" in public with some hope of success and without making women "conspicuous"[129]—a shift, in turn, that signified the absorption of the ideal of rational, face-to-face debate *by* and *into* a mass democracy. At the first woman's rights convention ever held in Pennsylvania in June 1852, meeting president Mariana Johnson suggested that ballots might be a way for woman to "raise her voice." In a petition read in the Senate in January 1877, 202 Californians demanded ballots for women so that they might "express opinions upon public affairs" and get a fair hearing. In 1888, Frederick Douglass lambasted the idea that a woman, simply because she did not have large biceps, should be denied the "right to express her thought, and give effect to her thought by her vote."[130]

Antifeminists and many judges understood the importance of speech for excluded classes, and occasionally linked oratory to self-liberation. When Roger Taney tried to explain in *Dred Scott* how he knew that the patriots of 1776 could not have meant to include blacks in the constituent power, he thought first of the power of free men's speech. Much the same reasoning applied to white women, who already enjoyed social access to white men and might be expected to exploit it. Citizenship supposedly allowed people to "enter every other State whenever they pleased, . . . to go where they pleased at every hour"; it gave them "full liberty of speech in public and in private upon all subjects upon which its own citizens might speak; to hold public meetings upon political affairs, and to keep and carry arms." Speech freedom among the unfree would "inevitably produc[e] discontent and insubordination," jeopardizing "the peace and safety of the State." In 1867, Horace Greeley said that he supported female "influence" in politics, but opposed the blending of electoral voices; the female sex should "speak and be heard distinctly as woman, not mingled and confused with men." As an alternative to such confusion, he proposed "separate-but-equal" assemblies to be comprised of women. These bodies would consider legislation "related to the family . . . , the control and maintenance of children, education, the property rights of married women, inheritance, dower, etc. . . . A female legislature, a jury of women, we could abide; a legislature of men and women, a jury promiscuously drawn from the sexes we do not believe in."[131]

Nothing captured the late-century elision of oratorical and electoral voices more completely than the First Amendment argument set out in Virginia and Francis Minor's *Minor v. Happersett* brief. Only when read as an artifact of the speech-centered discourse in which the Minors had been schooled does the brief make sense. "The first amendment to the Constitution declares," they wrote,

> that Congress shall make no law abridging freedom of speech or of the press, thus incorporating into the organic law of this country absolute freedom of thought or opinion. We presume it will not be doubted that the States are equally bound with Congress by this prohibition. . . . [I]n the very nature of things, freedom of speech or of thought can not be divided. It is a personal attribute, and once secured is forever secured. To vote is but one form or method of expressing this freedom of speech. Speech is a declaration of thought. A vote is the expression of the will, preference, or choice. Suffrage is one definition of the word, while the verb is defined, to choose by suffrage, to elect, to express or signify the mind, will, or preference, either *viva voce*, or by ballot. We claim then that the right to vote, or express one's wish at the polls, is embraced in the spirit, if not the letter, of the First Amendment, and every citizen is entitled to the protection it affords. It is the merest mockery to say to this plaintiff, you may write, print, publish, or speak your thoughts upon every occasion, except at the polls. There your lips shall be sealed.[132]

Part Three

"Governments Try Themselves"
Democratic Suffrage Communities and Equality

THE SUFFRAGISTS

Lady robed in light,
    At our harbour standing,
Equal law and right
    Promising, demanding,
Can you tell us, do you know,
Why you treat your daughters so? . . .

THE STATUE

Be not deceived, my daughters, I'm not she—
The wingèd Goddess, who sets nations free.
I am that Liberty, which when men win
They think that others' seeking is a sin;
I am that Liberty which men attain
And clip her wings lest she should fly again:
I am that Liberty which all your brothers
Think good for them and very bad for others.
Therefore they made me out of bronze, and hollow,
Immovable, for fear that I might follow
Some fresh rebellion, some new victim's plea;
And so they set me on a rock at sea,
Welded my torch securely in my hand
Lest I should pass it on, without command.
I am a milestone, not an inspiration;
And if my spirit lingers in this nation,
If it still flickers faintly o'er these waters,
It is your spirit, my rebellious daughters.

—ALICE DUER MILLER, "An Unauthorized Interview Between
the Suffragists and the Statue of Liberty" (1917)[1]

D espite wartime reversals, suffragists pressed forward. By 1890, when the American Woman Suffrage Association and the National Woman Suffrage Association merged to form the National American Woman Suffrage Association (NAWSA), the movement seemed to have surmounted internal strife. The first NAWSA president was 75-year-old Elizabeth Cady Stanton—a lifelong critic of those who would "protect" women out of a public voice. "No matter how much women prefer to lean, to be protected and supported," she said in her now-classic "Solitude of Self " speech in 1892, "nor how much men prefer to have them do so, they must make the voyage of life alone, and for safety in an emergency they must know something of the laws of navigation. . . . Whatever the theories may be of woman's dependence on man, in the supreme moments of her life, he cannot bear her burdens. . . . [In] the tragedies and triumphs of human experience, each mortal stands alone."[2]

Increasingly, however, a new generation of women supplanted the Old Guard. By the year of her unsettling address, Stanton had alienated many reformers with her sharp criticisms of conventional marriage, the Bible, and state paternalism. As early as 1867, she told Kansas legislators, "We ask you literally to do nothing for us. Take our names out of your constitutions and statute books. . . . Let your codes be for persons, for citizens, throw all the Negroes and women overboard."[3] More and more, Stanton seemed to be out of step with both the movement and American culture; in 1896, a majority at a NAWSA convention voted to censure her *Woman's Bible* and related statements in support of "free love" and against organized Christianity.

Underlying Stanton's marginalization were sweeping changes in American society. The mostly rural landscapes of 1848 had given way to urban congestion and squalor. Depressions rocked the nation in 1873 and 1893, prompting pay cuts and labor unrest. As white southerners disfranchised black voters, the race question mostly vanished from party platforms; in its place were economic and "social purity" questions. Social scientists championed social Darwinism (a marriage of evolutionary biology and sociology), laissez-faire economics, and state paternalism toward workers and other "dependent" classes. African American leaders struggled against steep odds to combat both racism and sexism. In 1896, Mary Church Terrell helped to found the National Association of Colored Women; two years later, she noted laconically that, by any measure, the "progress made by colored women" was a "veritable miracle of modern times."[4]

Increasingly, white reformers took on railroad cartels, corporate exploitation of workers, and other fruits of industrial capitalism. Urban Progressives and agrarian radicals mounted searing critiques of monopolism and political corruption. Angry citizens formed rescue and self-improvement societies. When African American nurse-educator Jane Edna Hunter sought work in Cleveland in 1905, she found the city inhospitable and, as part of the "club movement," founded the Working Girls' Home Association to aid "the poor motherless daughters of the race."[5] Elsewhere, settlement workers labored to "equalize" access to wealth and power among natives and immigrants; Jane Addams, founder of Chicago's Hull House, thought that the task laid upon her generation was not to smash capitalism or republicanism, but to adapt old ideas and institutions to the "peculiar problems" of the day.[6]

By 1900, legions of women pushed hard against law and custom. A handful of colleges and universities joined Oberlin and Antioch in admitting women to regular programs; elite women's schools like Vassar and Wellesley flourished. Notwithstanding hostile professional societies, a small number of graduates pursued careers in medicine, law, and university teaching. White women, many of them self-described feminists, formed artistic and political societies; black women followed parallel, often segregated paths into public life, determined to hone intellect and to enlarge the zone of freedom for other African Americans.

Because both Gilded Age reformers and the later Progressives aimed to pit government against corruption and to assign vital public work to the home, they challenged both laissez-faire economic theory and the idea of a male "public," which, in turn, destabilized elements of the Civil War settlement between the sexes. As suffragists began to think of "social mothering" as a civic duty, ballots seemed increasingly pivotal. Victorian legal scholars had tried to sever political rights from economic capacity, arguing that the real measure of a class's qualification for suffrage ought to be its "natural" fitness. The suffragists met the challenge head on. The question became not whether women were fit to govern, but how their "separate but equal" competencies might be put to public use. As in the 1850s, women established what one scholar terms "a female dominion in American reform."[7] And in keeping with the globalization of reform culture, feminists reached out to their European counterparts, who also wanted to create a "new, humane state, identified with the values of the home rather than those of the marketplace."[8]

Thousands of Americans also changed their minds about sexuality and female attire. Even as Freudian analysts portrayed women as defective men, they fostered a certain candor about sex and bodies. Images of apple-cheeked, buxom girls appeared on flour sacks. Kodak cameras and wiretaps obscured the line between "public" and "private" life, inspiring talk about privacy as a social and legal value. The "New Woman"—a bicycle-riding, uncorseted figure in shortened skirts—took America by storm, despite pastoral warnings that the "ungraceful, unwomanly, and unrefined game" of bicycling violated "the canons of womanly dignity and delicacy."[9]

These developments reflected the fact of a growing female presence in factories, classrooms, and sports arenas. Yet women's prospects were still quite limited. Although late Victorian women sometimes voted in local elections, their voices usually did not resound beyond the polls, where, in any case, citizens said yes or no to decisions made elsewhere. As social theorists embraced new ideas about the origins of racial and sex differences, female ambition came to be regarded as a sign of moral and biological degeneracy. Both law and custom still barred women from occupations taken to be masculine or immoral, and because of persistent wage inequities, sex-specific trade associations multiplied. Perhaps most important, despite statutory reform and dramatic changes in women's economic power, marriage still entailed the loss of key elements of citizenship, even in community property jurisdictions. And, for the most part, judges resisted dividing the sovereign head of households so that women might exercise authority as voters, jurors, and public officials.

The question, then, was not whether to pursue political freedom, but how. Although first-wave activists had initiated the demand for ballots, their Gilded Age daughters refashioned the women's movement to include lobbies, political campaigns, and lawsuits in a single-minded campaign for ballots. NAWSA and Alice Paul's National Woman's Party (or NWP, initially the Congressional Union) lent powerful aid to the suffrage cause, particularly after 1913–15, when NAWSA had perfected pressure-group techniques and had been "galvanized," in Sara Hunter Graham's word, by NWP radicalism.[10] So did Frances Willard's Woman's Christian Temperance Union (WCTU) and state suffrage leagues. Indeed, into the new century, it was the well-supported WCTU, not NAWSA,

that carried the suffrage ball into western towns with multiple saloons, large male populations, and a handful of women who were determined to purge their communities of
corruption.

Simultaneously, feminists expanded their vision to include problems not only of marriage and citizenship rights, but also of the workplace. In response to both the new social
sciences and antisuffragist attempts to use domesticity as prima facie evidence of feminine incompetence, many suffragists situated their arguments in "woman's sphere" rather
than in the language of universal human rights. If mothers and their children were going
to work in factories and politicians meant to regulate activities previously overseen at
home, then mothers had to "speak" at the polls about such topics as child welfare, sani-
tation, and public morality. As the new century dawned, Progressive reformers (including women later called "social feminists") also pursued sex-specific economic legislation
and therefore collided head-on with "equal rights" feminists associated by 1920–23 with
the NWP, which advocated an Equal Rights Amendment (ERA) and the elimination of
sex-based legal classifications. Within a third camp (which Ellen DuBois calls "left feminism"),[11] women like Harriot Stanton Blatch tried to bind women together across class
lines on the basis of shared experiences in the labor market.

The Nineteenth Amendment yielded half a loaf: Women cast ballots, but for candidates chosen by male-centric parties. For many ex-suffragists, the half-loaf was reward
enough. Others watched with mounting rage as judges in half the states refused to "find"
ancillary political rights in the amendment and then as the Great Depression and World
War II pushed their unfinished agendas onto back burners. To some extent, appearances
were deceptive: Trailblazing women held office, waged war over the merits of statutory
protection for women and children, and secured important social programs. And into the
1930s, women's groups wielded decisive influence in securing the repeal of the Eighteenth Amendment, largely on the ground that federal prohibition had been ineffective
and immoral. But a full-scale resurgence of the movement awaited the 1960s, when several developments converged to produce the "second wave" of modern feminism.

The American polity after World War II barely resembled its 1920s counterpart. Elements of a new regime had been in the wind for decades. The Civil War transmutation
of the federal government into an instrument of liberation for oppressed classes suggested
that it might be mobilized on woman's behalf; the 1920 federalization of woman suffrage
underscored this impression. Into the 1930s, intellectuals gradually discredited scientism
across many disciplines—a process that Morton White once called "the revolt against formalism";[12] at the same time, the natural law foundations of first-wave feminism collapsed,
leaving black-letter law and judicial reinterpretations of old law as women's main hope
for advancement. Increasingly, feminists debated what *kind* of legal reform to pursue, not
whether to go to law, with ERA serving as a flashpoint for conversation and disagreement.

Other elements of law-centered rights agitation were even newer. By 1919–20, partly
because of the altered political cast of evangelical Protestantism, the women's movement
had been significantly (though not entirely) secularized; feminists usually acted *upon* organized religion, rather than the other way around. When women adopted the rhetoric of
religious crusaders, they often did so to create what Evelyn Kirkley calls "a climate of
respectability."[13] More and more, theological arguments emanated from the antifeminist
camp. Americans also came to see women's wartime contributions as patriotic acts worthy of reward. "We have made partners of the women in this war," said Woodrow Wilson in 1918. "Shall we admit them only to a partnership of suffering and sacrifice and

toil and not to a partnership of privilege and right? This war could not have been fought
. . . if it had not been for the services of the women," at home and at "the very skirts and
edges of the battle itself."[14] Most important, in the wake of the New Deal's judicial "revolution" of 1937, as federal judges began to see themselves as defenders of the rights of
"discrete and insular minorities"[15] against popular majorities, activists turned increasingly
to lawsuits and statutory reform as avenues to emancipation. It is small wonder that modern feminist accomplishments often seem to be synonymous—whether rightly or not—
with the history of sex-related litigation.

After 1964–65, cracks appeared in the wall of tradition. But deeply rooted ideas about
the nature of women blocked advancement, particularly when women pursued goals that
were taken to be transgressive. When judges refused to subject many sex-specific laws
and practices to the highest level of constitutional scrutiny, feminists concluded that courts
had to be forced onto new ground. The National Organization for Women (NOW) and
other liberal groups pushed the ERA with a vengeance so that claims of equality might
rest on firm constitutional foundations. Feminists also encouraged women to organize new
speech communities, epitomized by NOW's consciousness-raising groups and women's
studies programs in universities. Involvement in (and disappointments within) the black
civil rights movement further honed women's political skills, as did demonstrations against
the Vietnam War. These experiences exerted leftward pressure on organized feminism,
greatly complicating and enriching its racial, ideological, and class composition.

In the 1980s, however, the second wave began to crack apart. Modern feminists had
erected their movement on a foundation of universal suffrage, an expanding female economic presence, and the galloping legalization of American life; campaigns for individual rights coexisted uneasily with calls for sisterhood and governmental recognition of
class grievances. Feminists struggled to find "voices," to identify what Betty Friedan called
the "problem that has no name,"[16] and to remake the woman-citizen. Yet women did not
always agree on how and whether physical differences mattered, where constitutional
equality might help their sex, and whether sisterhood implied a primary allegiance (no
matter what a woman's race, class, or sexual orientation might be) to the female tribe, as
many "cultural feminists" had come to argue. Radicals accused liberals of running with
the wolves; women of color formed their own liberation groups.

In addition, many influential feminists had come to think that equal rights jurisprudence was less than a magic bullet. This was true especially as activists turned from their
post-Reconstruction preoccupation with industrial democracy toward reproductive freedom, physical security, and domestic support—to some extent, a reversion to the antebellum agenda. Equal protection doctrine could be expanded to encompass women only
if men already possessed the right in question. What *about* women's unique capacities
and responsibilities? In the past, women had been ill served when lawmakers noticed biological differences. Yet their liberty interests differed from men's. Often, equal protection law fell silent on questions that were vital to women, or forced women to adopt male
standards. Reproductive freedom, moreover, had been tied not to male-female sovereignty
and government's responsibility for guaranteeing it, but to a constitutional right of privacy that depended for its life on judges' willingness to defend a line of cases leading to
Roe v. Wade. Nor could law address customary impediments to experiences of freedom.

In effect, critics of the second wave zeroed in on a new settlement between the sexes
that had been emerging since the 1970s. To achieve social peace, lawmakers had forged
a "separate but unequal" compromise with women's rights activists in which governments
(against the wishes of many liberals) retained certain class-based legal categories, partic-

ularly when public policy addressed women's bodies. Few Americans doubted that organized feminism had altered the social fabric. As Anna Quindlen wrote in 1994, "[I]t's important to remember that feminism is no longer a group of organizations or leaders. It's the expectations that parents have for their daughters, and their sons, too. It's the way we talk about and treat one another. It's who makes the money and who makes the compromises and who makes the dinner. It's a state of mind. It's the way we live now."[17] The question was whether change was sufficient or excessive, good or bad. Left feminists criticized the liberal tendency to preserve male privilege; they also insisted that Americans look again at the traditional family's role in perpetuating inequality and violence. Antifeminists damned the unnatural blurring of the sex line, neglect of motherhood, and inattention to men's rights. By their lights, the enemy was organized feminism, not entrenched sexism. Said an *Economist* writer, the "real backlash" is "not so much against feminism as against its excesses"; at the millennium, the women's movement called to mind only stale slogans, "humourlessness," and "hairy legs."[18]

Chapter 8

Democratic Suffrage Communities

In the wake of Reconstruction, the drive to secure what Susan B. Anthony termed "our full equality with man in natural rights" seemed to portend not just a doubling of the electorate, but a social revolution that would pit mothers against their own husbands and children.[1] Antisuffragists therefore fastened on the supposedly endangered family as their movement's ideological anchor. In an 1878 letter to the Senate Committee on Privileges and Elections, novelist Madeleine Vinton Dahlgren issued a warning: "Marriage is a sacred unity. The family, through it, is the foundation of the State. Each family is represented by its head, just as the State ultimately finds the same unity, through a series of representations. Out of this come peace, concord, proper representation, and adjustment—union."[2] The primary stumbling block remained: Women were not coequal constitutional sovereigns. Said a frustrated Anthony in 1902, "Woman never will have equality of rights anywhere, she never will hold those she now has by an absolute tenure, until she possesses the fundamental right of self-representation. . . . Had this right been conceded at the start, the others would have speedily followed; and the leaders among women . . . might have contributed their splendid services to the general . . . strengthening of the government." Instead, women confronted "the obstinate prejudices . . . of the ages" and "the still more stubborn condition of its hard and fast intrenchment in constitutional law."[3]

But all was not lost. As Alice Duer Miller saw clearly, although women were not precisely "people" in a constitutional sense, their patriotism, support of economic development, and taxable wealth served as wedges in the political door, notwithstanding late Victorian attempts to unhinge connections between economic and political power. Miller introduced a book of rhymes, *Are Women People?* with this fictitious conversation between a father and son:

> Father, what is a Legislature?
> A representative body elected by the people of the state.
> Are women people?
> No, my son, criminals, lunatics and women are not people.
> Do legislators legislate for nothing?
> Oh, no; they are paid a salary.
> By whom?
> By the people.
> Are women people?
> Of course, my son, just as much as men are.[4]

THE BEGINNINGS OF SUFFRAGISM

By 1900, thousands of women voted alongside men in local elections. Initially, however, grants of partial suffrage had little to do with women's rights. The Kentucky Assembly's well-known decision in 1837–38 to grant school suffrage to a limited number of women makes the point. The law establishing common schools (actually a reenactment of a statute that first appeared in 1829 but failed for want of funding) granted school suffrage to "any widow or *feme sole*, over twenty-one years of age, residing and owning property subject to taxation for school purposes," excluded married women and—more important—granted ballots to "any infant residing and owning property" and the agents of "all banking corporations." Lawmakers plainly had in mind representing all *property* at the polls—the entity that Theophilus Parsons in 1778 called "the whole body politic, with all its property, rights and privileges."[5] Both in the exclusion of wives and in a section of the statute distinguishing between the classes enfranchised by the law and fully empowered "inhabitants," lawmakers reinforced images of female inferiority. As late as 1899, Thorstein Veblen could say quite accurately that although many Americans were reconsidering their views, the majority "still felt that woman's life . . . is essentially and normally a vicarious life" in which her faults and accomplishments were "imputed to some other individual who stands in some relation of ownership or tutelage" to her. Judges usually refused to extend the constitutional principle of equal protection to women, black or white, reasoning that the framers of the Reconstruction amendments had intended no such result. Women thus fell between constitutional cracks—and they knew it. As Stanton explained in 1881, Republican principles virtually mandated inequality:

> [Women] applied to Congress for protection against the tyranny of the States in depriving them of the right of suffrage, but they were remanded to the States, and were told that Congress had no jurisdiction in the matter. . . . [W]hen women claimed the rights of citizens as tax-payers who helped to support the Government, they were told that neither the fathers nor their sons ever thought of women in framing their Constitutions, and that some special legislation was needed before their rights of citizenship could be recognized or accorded.[6]

Westerners made the first moves toward political equality. On the frontier, female wealth production and skewed sex ratios tended to enhance women's bargaining power; lawmakers also hoped to attract female settlers with promises of freedom. As during the Second Great Awakening, moreover, many western women gained political experience within Populism, the Grange, and other radical communities. Western activist Elizabeth Barr described a Farmer's Alliance campaign as a "religious revival, a crusade, a pentecost of politics. . . . Women with skins tanned to parchment by the hot wind, with bony hands of toil, dressed in faded calico, would talk in meeting and could talk right straight to the point."[7] In 1869, Wyoming Territory permitted women to vote and sit on juries. A skeptical cartoonist portrayed female jurors with babies in their laps and the slogan, "Baby, baby, don't get in a fury; Your mamma's gone to sit on the jury,"[8] and, in 1887, the law was rescinded. Two years later, however, Wyoming became the first universal suffrage state; its constitution provided that the "rights of citizens . . . to vote and hold office shall not be denied or abridged on account of sex. Both male and female citizens . . . shall equally enjoy all civil, political and religious rights and privileges."[9]

Not counting antebellum attempts to represent property at the polls, sixteen states and territories moved before 1890 to enfranchise women *as women* (that is, not merely as bearers of property), if only in municipal and school elections. Kansas adopted limited suffrage in 1861; rejected universal suffrage in 1867; and, after a turbulent election two decades later, again included women in city and school elections. In 1875, Minnesota and

Michigan adopted partial suffrage; by 1890, thirteen other territories and states had so moved. In its 1898 constitution, Louisiana granted female taxpayers the right to vote in property tax elections; legislators in Washington Territory adopted universal suffrage in 1883, retreated from it a few years later, and adopted partial suffrage in 1889–90.

In repeated attempts to persuade skeptical Americans of the value of a female presence at the polls, NAWSA, the WCTU, and other groups pointed to the absence of turmoil in partial suffrage jurisdictions: By 1902, after all, twenty-six states had adopted some kind of school suffrage without revolution. But the example was problematic. Only in Kansas did women cast ballots in school elections as a matter of constitutional right. Well before 1900, it was clear to observers of the western scene that partial suffrage, far from empowering women, emphasized their dependence. Female balloting sometimes ceased when counties were reorganized (a common event in new states); the "mother's vote" could be, and often was, lost at the whim of politicians. Dakota Territory ended the practice when North and South Dakota entered the union in 1889. Thirteen years later, Kentuckians reversed a seven-decade tradition because black women had begun to vote in significant numbers, and in the mid-1890s, school suffrage failed constitutional challenges in New Jersey and Michigan. Some states even tightened their constitutions to prevent radical emendation—as when Minnesota and Nebraska decided to require not a simple majority of ballots cast on new articles, but a majority of all votes cast in the entire election. Minnesota women decided in 1902 that their "only hope" lay with a federal amendment.[10]

At the same time, the old guard suffragists lost place to a growing army of professional women. In 1892, the aging Stanton ceded her NAWSA post to Anthony—perhaps the most consistently venerated first-wave personality—who, in turn, gave over the position in 1900, first to educator Carrie Chapman Catt (who also headed the organization after 1913, spearheading the successful drive toward a federal amendment) and, in 1905, to the Methodist minister-orator Dr. Anna Howard Shaw. NAWSA's membership rolls expanded from 13,150 in 1893 to over 2 million in 1917. As the new century advanced, moreover, the women's movement developed roots and branches. By the 1910s, suffragism's main engine may well have been little-known workers allied with the NWP, state suffrage groups, and WCTU chapters. Colorado adopted full suffrage in 1893; Idaho and Utah followed suit in 1896, and Washington State did so in 1910. Between 1867 and 1917, suffragists conducted 480 state campaigns to secure constitutional amendments, 55 popular referendums, 19 congressional lobbying efforts in pursuit of declaratory acts or a federal amendment, and almost 300 campaigns to persuade party leaders to include woman suffrage in election platforms.

Through 1916, however, only nine state amendment campaigns bore fruit; as Aileen Kraditor reminds us, between the 1896 decisions in Utah and Idaho and Washington's pro-suffrage decision in 1910, "not one state enfranchised its women."[11] To a great extent, woman's constitutional *authority* at the ballot box (as distinguished from political *power*) depended on public officials' willingness to divide domestic sovereignty so that female citizens might claim direct relationships to the state and experience full membership in the nation. Cosovereignty, however, posed an administrative problem to which John Locke and others had alluded—notably, the seeming need to entrust decisive power to one adult in the household, typically the man. Without acknowledgment of equal constitutional authority, women (and especially wives) acted without legitimacy. Mary Johnston, a novelist and committed left-feminist, made the point clearly in an NAWSA-sponsored address to Virginia lawmakers in December 1912. "Every man here was born of a woman and man," she said, "and every woman here was born of a man and a woman, and we inherit equally from each. . . . [W]e are each . . . co-heirs, we are kings and queens—not kings with a queen-consort walking behind, but fellow sovereigns—Williams and Marys, Ferdinands and Isabellas!"[12] Many Americans knew, too, that uncontested exercise of the suffrage implied cosovereignty. Thus, men's claims to sovereign command at home seemed to depend on keeping women away from the polls.

THE CASE OF WASHINGTON TERRITORY

Developments in Washington Territory vividly illustrate how these fears could affect women's lives. The 1853 organic act by which Congress created the territory limited voting in the first canvass to "every white male inhabitant" over twenty-one years; voters' qualifications for "all subsequent elections" would be determined by the territorial assembly.[13] In 1867, a territorial statute authorized "all white American citizens above the age of twenty-one" to vote. Several Republican politicians insisted that the assembly intended to enfranchise women. Nonetheless, in 1867–68, women remained at home, lacking (in suffragist Mary Olney Brown's words) the "courage to go to the polls in defiance of custom."[14] In 1870, partly in response to Brown's agitations, a small number of women did vote. Then, after a visit by Anthony and a "statesman-like argument" before the assembly in support of woman's right to vote under both national and territorial law, legislators took flight, providing in a second statute that "no female shall have the right of ballot" until Congress nationalized woman suffrage.[15]

Later in the 1870s, women's prospects seemed to improve. The territorial supreme court mounted more than one defense of female autonomy. In 1877, for example, Associate Justice Roger S. Greene upheld an award of damages directly to Mary Phelps, a wife injured severely when she tumbled headlong into a ship's hatch. A married woman, wrote Greene, "retains, in the eyes of the law, a personality of her own. She does not, in marrying, barter her very self away. She does not go into utter slavery. . . . She has, as distinct from her husband, the rights of 'life, liberty and the pursuit of happiness,' rights inalienable even by nuptial bargain."[16] More important, in 1879, legislators formalized the territory's community-property system (enshrined two years later in a new territorial law code). Under the new rules, each spouse retained property owned before marriage, as well as assets accumulated during marriage by gift or inheritance, with all "rents, issues and profits," as separate property; each could dispose of personal property as he or she pleased. All other property acquired during marriage became part of the marital estate. As in Texas, legislators invited wives to list separate personal property and record it with county authorities. Also as in Texas, elements of English law practice survived. A husband would manage the separate *real* property of the wife during coverture, for instance, but could not "sell or . . . in any way dispose" of it without her permission. He similarly could dispose (except by will) of personal and real property that was part of the marital estate, but, again, could not sell *land* without his wife's agreement. Following an 1869 statute, the 1879 law disallowed dower and curtesy, but made the *earnings* of a married woman her separate property.[17]

At virtually the same time, the assembly adopted a law to "establish and protect the rights of married women" (also incorporated into the 1881 code). It abolished all laws that imposed civil disabilities on wives "which are not imposed or recognized as existing as to the husband," withholding only political rights. For any "unjust usurpation of her natural or property rights," a wife had the "same right to appeal, in her own individual name, to the courts of law or equity . . . that the husband has." Lawmakers also established sex-neutral earning and custody rights.[18] In *Holyoke v. Jackson* (1882), Roger Greene, newly installed as chief justice, explored the implications of the 1879 community-property statute and had little trouble saying that a man could not sell part of the marital estate without his wife's permission.[19]

Then, in November 1883, Washingtonians eliminated all mention of gender from territorial election laws. The main forces behind this dazzling move apparently were Mary Olney Brown and Oregon's Abigail Scott Duniway. Under the 1883 statute, "[a]ll American citizens, above the age of twenty-one years, and all American half-breeds over that age, who have adopted the habits of the whites," as well as loyal aliens, were to be "entitled to hold office, or vote at any election." Legislators added: "Wherever the word 'his' occurs . . . , it shall be construed to mean 'his or her.' " They also purged masculine language from the 1881 code's provisions governing jury selection; commissioners would identify "persons qualified to serve in their county" as petit jurors and grand jurors without regard to sex.[20]

The forces of resistance were not far behind. In July 1884, even as the territorial supreme court in *Hamilton v. Hirsch and Hayden* affirmed the constitutionality of the assembly's "radical" legislation (as the court put it) abolishing dower and curtesy,[21] justices also heard an appeal in the case of Mollie Rosencrantz, who had been found guilty of "keeping a house of ill fame." At the trial, Rosencrantz's attorneys had objected to the presence of five married women on the grand jury. On appeal to the supreme court, they challenged not only the legality of the indictment, but also the constitutionality of the territory's jury selection, property, and election statutes. According to Rosencrantz's lawyers, the 1883 statute violated the territory's organic law, which allowed legislators to alter the composition of the electorate, not the pool of candidates for juries. It also violated the command of the organic act that Washington Territory follow the rules of common law, including the law of coverture. In addition, the code of 1881 still allowed only "householders" to serve on grand juries; married women "residing with their husbands and maintained by them" could not be householders. Was not the husband "the head of the family, and the only householder therein?"[22]

Speaking for the majority of the court, Associate Justice John Hoyt (a reform-minded Republican and former governor of Wyoming) rejected this argument. The organic law authorized legislators to change the composition of the electorate. The 1883 election law extended the ballot to all "citizens," including women. Under the 1881 code, moreover, "all electors and householders" were potential grand jurors. Since married women were both, they could be empaneled on grand juries. Hoyt conceded that, at common law, a wife was "not . . . a householder" as contemplated by the statute; coverture eliminated her "right to be heard as to the disposition of the property or children that resulted from the marriage." But this "harsh rule" had been "gradually changing"; the division of sovereign authority in households had been "more and more recognized by the laws of nearly all of the States and Territories of this Union." The "radical legislation" of 1879 had replaced common law rules with a "new relation between husband and wife, as members of the family" characterized by "absolute equality before the law."[23]

Since others found it impossible to divide the sovereign "head" without smashing it—either the lord was whole or there was no lord at all—Hoyt painstakingly explained how the division might be accomplished. "[I]t is said, that if they are thus equal, then neither of them is the head of the family, and therefore not the keeper of a house, as each is only a half of a housekeeper. This, however, does not follow, as each of them has the absolute right to control the family and household in the absence of the other, and each has all the responsibilities and rights growing out of such control." At common law, the *baron* "had sole control, and was therefore properly treated and held as the head of the family; by our statute the two . . . acting jointly, have like sole control, and are, therefore, jointly the head of the family." A wife had "exactly the same measure of control over the children . . . as her husband, with the same right to any or all of their earnings, and the same voice in directing all things connected with the family government."[24]

In dissent, however, Associate Justice George Turner denied that women were competent jurors or that wives "living with their husbands" could be termed householders. He drew a sharp distinction between civil and political *rights*, such as the right to vote, and jury service, which was not a right but an *obligation*. The 1883 law expanded the right to vote, but could not at the same time affect the jury-service obligation, since the organic act specified that a law could not "embrace two objects." He thought, too, that mixed-sex panels deprived citizens of their constitutional right to be indicted by a legitimate grand jury. One of the historical "incidents" of juries was their masculinity. Turner expressed "repugnance" at seeing woman "exposed to influences which . . . [must] shock and blunt those fine sensibilities, the possession of which is her chiefest charm, and the protection of which . . . is her most sacred right." And he was incapable of imagining a division of sovereignty within the family. If, as the majority contended, husband and wife were "equal as to rights and obligations in the household," the "logical deduction would seem to be, not that the law had created two heads of the family, but that it has deposed from the position of superiority what was formerly the one head, and that now there is no head, as understood by the common law term. The idea of a *double head in nature or in government is that of a monstrosity*." The unitary head embodied "the idea of legal supremacy." Local law could not obliterate the fact that a man was "the head of the family at common law" and "had the right to be obeyed by all the family."[25]

Also in 1884, a Supreme Court majority turned back other challenges to female grand jurors,[26] and territorial legislators responded to Turner's hostility with a volley of new statutes reaffirming woman suffrage and declaring that words used in election laws "indicating persons of the masculine gender, shall be construed to include persons of the feminine gender."[27] But Turner won the day. Between 1884 and 1888, Grover Cleveland's administration had been replacing territorial judges; on February 3, 1887, a reconstituted bench heard the appeal of a criminal indictment in the case of Jeffrey Harland and other perpetrators of a "swindling game called bunko, or twenty-one." Harland challenged the validity of seating five married women as grand jurors. In his opinion, Turner made quick work of *Rosencrantz*, announcing that a majority was "unable to agree" with the views expressed there. Greene and another judge adhered to *Rosencrantz*, but two votes hardly mattered. In *Harland v. Territory of Washington*, Turner not only eliminated female jurors, but elaborated on his *Rosencrantz* dissent to purge women from the electorate. In his view, all the statutes in which legislators had affirmed or reaffirmed woman suffrage had other objects as well and so violated the rule laid out in the organic act that "every law shall embrace but one object," to be "expressed in the title." Nor should lawmakers have adopted a "measure of such a character, involving changes in our social and political structures so momentous, and . . . so disastrous" to society without overwhelming public support. Women therefore were "not voters in this territory, and not being voters they are not competent to sit on juries." Eleven months later, the court made clear that it objected not just to wives, but to a *female* public presence. In *White v. Territory of Washington* (1888), Chief Justice Jones reversed a manslaughter conviction on the ground that one of the grand jurors, an *unmarried* woman named Maggie Farr, had been empaneled unconstitutionally.[30]

In 1888, the legislature and the governor moved swiftly to shore up female balloting, in part by making jury service optional, but to no avail. In a feigned suit brought by Nevada Bloomer, an antisuffragist married to a saloon keeper, the Supreme Court again rejected woman suffrage. During city elections in April 1888, Bloomer had persuaded three election judges to reject her ballot, although witnesses claimed that other women at the same poll voted without impediment. Bloomer then sued the election judges. In *Bloomer v. Todd* (1888), her lawyer—a pro-suffrage man deeply suspicious of his client—relied on the assembly's constitutional authority to alter election laws and offered a new argument rooted in common law tradition. As in Wyoming, where Congress's "failure for many years" to intervene had tacitly validated woman suffrage, so Congress had acquiesced in and validated Washington's practices.[31]

Newly retired from the Supreme Court, Turner appeared with two other lawyers as counsel for the election judges. He argued that the new election law of January 1888 violated the organic act. Reiterating his *Harland* position, he noted that the word *citizen* meant *male citizen* because it had been so defined in the 1850s. Woman suffrage was "entirely inconsistent" with the "government of men" envisioned by the framers of the organic act. Citing *Minor v. Happersett*, *Bradwell v. Illinois*, and state decisions against woman suffrage and admission to the bar, Turner pronounced the new law unconstitutional, adding for good measure that woman suffrage deprived *men* of their constitutional right to execute a public "trust" as voters.[32]

For the majority of the court, Chief Justice Jones embraced Turner's views. While the 1888 statute expressly granted the right to vote to "all citizens of the United States, male and female," the term *citizen* could mean only what Congress had meant in the 1850s; another construction might "carry the state out upon a sea of revolution, with only passion for a guide." Jones nearly excluded the female sex from citizenship. "In 1852," he wrote, "when [the organic act] was passed, the word 'citizen' was used as a qualification for voting and holding office, and . . . the word then meant and still signifies male citizenship, and must be so construed."[33]

Women were outraged. In an eloquent front-page essay printed in Olympia's pro-suffrage *Washington Standard*, activist May Sylvester objected to the notion (set out by another correspondent) that the adoption of woman suffrage was an "insult to the manliness of men" and a "confession on their part that they are not competent to wield the strong arm of government."[34] But all such protests fell on deaf ears. The draft of a state constitution approved by an 1888–89 constitutional convention at Olympia specified male suffrage. When Washington men voted to approve the draft in 1889, they confronted two amendments—one banning alcohol, the other reintroducing and constitutionalizing woman suffrage—and handily rejected both. Shortly after statehood, the legislature adopted partial suffrage and education-related officeholding for women, but nothing more. Said Anthony in 1902, "There never was a more unconstitutional decision than . . . [*Bloomer*]. Congress should have refused to admit the territory until women had voted for delegates to the constitutional convention and on the constitution itself."[35] Only in 1910 and 1911, after a decade-long campaign, did Washington women regain full access to the polls and, by separate enactment, to jury service.

ANTISUFFRAGISM

Washingtonians were not the only Americans fearing shipwreck on a "sea of revolution." Everywhere, critics portrayed New Women as unnatural monsters who were bent on destroying themselves, their children, and the republic. "Despairing of herself as a woman," wrote one scholar, "she asserts her lower rights in the place of her one great right to be loved. . . . Failing to respect herself as a productive organism, she gives vent to personal ambitions, seeks independence . . . [and] becomes intellectually emancipated."[36] As when abolitionists threatened to remake "slaves" as citizens within southern households, a sex-blind electoral system portended a redistribution of sovereign authority and an end to male-centric governments. In the late 1880s, University of Wisconsin president John Bascom argued that because women had an undoubted right to the elective franchise, the state "in withholding this right, puts itself in AN ATTITUDE OF TYRANNY to its subjects, and of resistance to social growth." He then confirmed the antisuffragists' darkest fears: "A UNION OF REPRESSION is at bottom a union of force. . . . The progress on which we congratulate ourselves is a small occasion of pride, if we cannot, in the household, where we are sustained by family interest and family affection, accept the first principles of liberty—a free and equal use of powers. . . . We believe, that THE HOUSEHOLD IS PREPARED FOR JUSTICE."[37]

In response to such claims, antisuffragists raised a clamor. As early as 1869, in a debate on the merits of woman suffrage, Senator John Tyler Morgan of Alabama made clear that the issue was the unitary head of household, not sentimental pap about the "soiling" of women. To be sure, that "head" could be female, but because the head could not be divided and men monopolized the polls, prospects for female coheadship were remote. Noting the substantial "relief" of married women already extended in property acts, Morgan reported that Alabamans had "not thought it wise or politic . . . to go further and undertake to make a line of demar[c]ation between the husband and wife as politicians. On the contrary, . . . we look to the family relation as being the true foundation of our republican institutions. Strike out the family relation, disband the family, destroy the proper authority of the person at the head of the family, either the wife or the husband, and you take from popular government all legitimate foundation."[38]

Others agreed. In a 1910 speech before the Ladies' Congressional Club of Washington, D.C., retired Supreme Court justice Henry Billings Brown (the author of the Court's "separate but equal" opinion in *Plessy v. Ferguson*) deployed virtually every weapon in the oppositionist arsenal. First, he looked to past practice to "prove" the merits of the male monopoly of government. "From time immemorial," he argued, as Roger Taney had done in *Dred Scott* to "prove" the justice of slavery, "the power to govern has been devolved upon the male population." While men elsewhere had reduced women to a status "little above that of slaves," such debasement had not happened in America, where women were venerated.[39] Second, he assailed suffragists' constitutional arguments—the idea, for instance, that nonvoting women held property and paid taxes but were not represented in government, or that legislative confiscation of rights (including the right to vote) might be unconstitutional. In his view, the representation complaint was "more fancied than real." Women typically did not have occasion to deal in property; law existed for "the great mass of the people," not for "exceptions." Although women had "a natural right to protection in their persons, their property and their opinions," they had "no natural right to govern or to participate in the government of others." Brown insisted that the law was "even *more favorable to women* than to men": Wives kept their own earnings and spent money "as they please," whereas a man devoted his wealth to "the support of his wife and family."[40]

In essence, Brown's objections to universal suffrage were cultural rather than legal, grounded—as had been the majority opinion in both *Plessy* and *Bradwell*—on the fashionable idea that rules of law that were hostile to the order of nature would rip society to shreds. Brown did not doubt that societies evolved toward democracy; he doubted only that social advancement required the comingling of the sexes in public life. According to Brown, the "chief *objections to woman suffrage*" originated in its neglect of "*differences*" (the "physical distinction"), which determined the role each sex would play in "the economy of nature." Men had "physical strength," a talent for ensuring "public order and safety" and for imagining "great undertakings," and a "dispassionate view of important questions" (or "judicial temperament"), whereas women excelled in child rearing, a "superior vitality and patient endurance of suffering," a "natural refinement and delicacy," and "intuitive perceptions." Because suffragism ran afoul of "nature," it was a "*danger*." Nor was it constitutionally required. Although America boasted a "government of the people," lawmakers never spoke directly for "all persons constituting the people." Surely "children or persons of defective intelligence" were not "entitled" to direct representation. The sovereign power was presumptively male: "Formerly [suffrage] was only extended to property owners . . . ; then to those able to read and write—finally to *everybody*, or what is called *manhood suffrage*."[41]

Others made the case a bit differently. In 1909, Emily Bissell published (under the auspices of the New York State Association Opposed to Woman Suffrage) what she called a "talk to women on the suffrage question," showing how ballots would undermine both women's happiness and the republic. "There are three points of view from which woman to-day ought to consider herself—as an individual, as a member of a family, as a member of the state," she wrote. "Every woman's duties and rights cluster along those three lines; and any change in woman's status that involves all of them needs to be very carefully considered." In Bissell's judgment, woman suffrage—unlike purely "individual" questions, such as whether to go to college—affected "each one of these three relations deeply" and so had "hung fire" for decades. Americans wisely resisted a practice hostile to "human nature and . . . human government"; women performed "public work without it better than they could with it," considered it "a burden," and saw it as "man's duty and responsibility." If the *class* were enfranchised, individuals would feel obliged to vote, further limiting women's freedom.[42]

In the end, though, Bissell mainly regretted the loss of maternalism and relationalism; as she put it, "no good woman lives to herself. . . . God created man, not as an individual, but as a family." The home was the "foundation of American strength and progress"; woman had "her own place and her own duty to the family." Women's workplace experiences made the point: Although they often acted as "business women, professional women, [or] working girls, who are almost like men in their daily activity," most chose to marry, leaving "the man's place for the woman's." When spouses acted against nature, disaster ensued: A couple had "no children; or the children go untrained; . . . The woman, who might be a woman, is half a man instead." Suffragism thus damaged the republic by inviting women to misdefine themselves as free agents vested with all the badges of manhood. "The vote is part of man's work," she concluded. "Ballot-box, cartridge box, jury box, sentry box, all go together in his part of life. Woman cannot step in and take the responsibilities . . . of voting without assuming his place."[43]

Like Justice Brown, Bissell predicted that woman suffrage would lead either to an electorate degraded by gangs of uninformed voters or to elections in which men unconstitutionally cast two ballots instead of one. "Where would the state be," she asked, linking women to aliens and black men, "with a helpless, unorganized vote, loaded on to its present political difficulties? Where would the state be with a double Negro vote in the Black belt [or] . . . a doubled immigrant vote?" Why did suffragists romanticize politics, deluding women into thinking that their only obligation would be to visit the polls? Elections were decided not by isolated voters, but by parties, officers, and publicists. Did women mean to ignore "primaries and conventions, and caucuses and office-holding?" Because a good wife had no time for politics, she would ape her husband's views, giving him "a double suffrage." Why not express patriotism by rearing children as "citizens of the state?" At stake was republican motherhood and household-based democracy: The "individualism of woman" posed a "threat to the family" and to natural divisions of labor; suffragism abetted "[a]narchist and socialist and communist" schemes to destroy "the civilized family and the private home."[44]

SUFFRAGISM AND CIVIC HOUSEKEEPING

Suffragists of the Progressive cast typically stood on the same "natural difference" ground—often as a strategic choice, but also in response to contemporary sociology, which assumed both the steady growth of democracy and the existence of unbridgeable differences between the races and the sexes. Despite a common reliance on natural law, however, their conclusions differed from Brown's and Bissell's. According to the "new" social science, political communities evolved according to discernable laws ("social statics"). Emergent classes (conceptualized not as individuals, but as homogeneous groups) periodically demanded access to public life; women were one such class. Attempts to thwart evolutionary progress violated natural law and triggered social violence. As May Collins, a champion of the enfranchised New Woman, explained in 1896, "[T]he general drift of human society, during its different stages of development, is towards democracy. Of course, there are smaller . . . laws that operate against the larger and more powerful ones, and thus impede human progress, but . . . their influence gradually diminishes, and in the sweep of evolution is very nearly . . . lost sight of; while the general current of human affairs, controlled by those larger and more unvarying laws, never recedes, but continues always upward and onward."[45]

Progressives also argued that women ought to vote precisely because they mothered the human race. This was not a new idea; such notions dominated the first wave, especially among evangelical Christians. But although late nineteenth-century reformers often assumed that a feminine presence would neutralize profanity in public life, they usually cloaked their arguments in scientific, not biblical, garb. Theology, in other words, reinforced, rather than generated, the idea that women, exercising the rights of political individuals as voters, would move in concert to preserve the natural ("separate but equal") social order in areas of life beyond the polls. Women did not want to impersonate men; they would exercise citizenship rights en masse in order to defend family and community against corrosive social and economic forces and then return home to do what women did "naturally."

Post–Civil War suffragism thus embodied two discourses—the race- and sex-blind discourse of equal citizenship rights, integration, and individualism and the "separate-but-equal" discourse of protectionism, social segregation, and relationalism. Casting ballots as individuals, women would contribute their peculiar wisdom sotto voce. As Jane Addams put it,

> Insanitary housing, poisonous sewage, contaminated water, infant mortality, the spread of contagion, adulterated food, . . . ill-ventilated factories, . . . juvenile crime, unwholesome crowding, prostitution and drunkenness are the enemies which the modern cities must face. . . . Logically, its electorate should be made up of those who . . . have at least attempted to care for children, to clean houses, to prepare foods, to isolate the family from moral dangers. . . . To test the elector's fitness to deal with this situation by his ability to bear arms is absurd.[46]

At the heart of the matter was a promise, laid out in 1896 by freethinker Susan Wixon: "Woman will be always woman, whether she performs her part of life's work as lawyer, editor, doctor, banker, broker, president of corporations, ship-captain, mine-operator, stock raiser, teacher, merchant, or manufacturer; . . . or remains simply the housekeeper and regulator of the family, venturing not beyond the boundaries of home, she will remain distinctively and essentially woman. She will be always tender, solicitous, sympathetic, loving, and lovable. She will always be the principal factor of the household, the home-maker, the heart-sweetness, the true lover and comforter of man."[47]

In 1894, an eloquent group of women allied with the New York Political Equality League tried to persuade state legislators of the merits of their cause. In the process, they revealed much about the character of mainstream suffragism. League women leaned (as had many of their antebellum forbears) on basic constitutional principles, disavowing innovation or extremism. "We have no new arguments to present . . . ," said one speaker. "Every successful reform has proceeded upon fundamental and well-recognized principles. Any novel argument is a sign of weakness." Yet these women also pressed hard for cosovereignty. While Americans had lodged "sovereign power in the will of her people," election laws still reflected "the mediaeval theory of household representation. The family is the unit of the State, and the husband, as head of the household, casts the ballot for the family," marking the wife as "one who has no opinion worthy of consideration." If the "family is the unit of the State," they noted, "only a married man is entitled to the ballot. . . . [Yet] the citizen, not the family, is the unit of the State." Had not the founders sought direct representation? Said Brooklyn's Mary Craigie, New York's 1.5 million women deserved a "voice in the government." Could men explain "by what law, divine or human, they have usurped the entire control of government and withheld from one-half the people the privileges that should be equally shared?" The idea that a "part of the people is equal to or greater than the whole people" did not deserve to be enshrined in a state constitution.[48]

Patriotic garb barely disguised the radicalism of these demands: Remaking the sovereign power implied major redistributions of power and changes in male-female deportment. Suffrage publicists regularly fanned the flames—as in the drama *Melinda and Her Sisters,* produced at the Waldorf Astoria Hotel in 1916. In her strikingly militaristic pro-suffrage song, "Girls, Girls, Put Away Your Curls," author Elsa Maxwell explicitly rejected male governance and female "graces":

For a thousand years or so,
Since many moons ago,
Men have ruled us women East and West. . . .
To keep us women down they thought was best.
But turned now is the tide,
And we cannot be denied,
We are coming in our millions to enhance; . . .

So girls, girls, put away your curls,
Put away your petticoats and frills!
Step right into line;
Cease now to repine;
We'll show them that we all can learn to drill.
Left! Right! We can stand the pace.
'Tention! Halt! Right about face!
But we've done with teas and balls;
We've forgotten how to dance;
We'll show what we can do if we've the chance![49]

    Still, many suffragists hesitated to push political individualism too far or to demand legal "sameness" beyond the ballot box. Although members of the New York Equality League spoke in 1894 of what they called a "revolt of the soul" against outmoded "customs" and sought access to "larger opportunities," they affirmed the value of a separate womanly sphere; even as they proposed cracking apart the female class into voters, they pointed to the class's natural attributes as mothers and social moralizers as justification for universal suffrage. Such women often insisted as well that their political ambitions did not extend beyond balloting: Women would "speak" mainly on election day; they would be helpful rather than contrary, flag-waving rather than subversive. League women said, for example, in sentences reminiscent of Paulina Wright Davis's Worcester speech, that they did not aim to "antagonize the relation of the two sexes," but hoped to make them "more truly sympathetic and congenial."[50] The prominent Illinois writer Elizabeth Boynton Harbert said much the same thing. "We accept our woman's sphere," she wrote in 1885, "glorious almost infinite in its opportunities and responsibilities, but by all the sacred rights of womanhood we demand, that *the hand that rocks the cradle* shall help to rule the world." Years later, she promised to bring a "God-given woman nature" to bear upon public life, as a matter both of obligation and right.[51] In other words, while women would vote as individuals, they "spoke" in a feminine cadence that men could neither understood nor duplicate. Said a New Yorker, "The fundamental idea underlying the suffrage movement is the recognition of the fact that women are not men . . . ; therefore men cannot justly and adequately represent them."[52]

    In linking women's "separate but equal" natures (and home-based labor) to political and social modernization, suffragists tacitly embraced the idea of expanded state intervention in reproduction and other "private" concerns; in so doing, they contributed powerfully to the emergence of the modern welfare and surveillance state. Time and again, they insisted that they sought only the right to "speak" alongside men as to the *nature and extent* of governmental interventions, especially in areas of special expertise. "Many earnest, thinking women everywhere," said members of the New York Equality League, "are beginning to recognize the fact that the womanly element finds no expression in the politics of the town or State. . . . This thoughtful interest is as essential a part of true womanhood as of true manhood." Surely the "best argument" for enfranchisement lay with "the mother instinct, an older, deeper, more persistent trait than the paternal in man." Women's experiences could be "applied to every sphere of activity"; a woman could improve "the condition of not only her own children, but the children of the State."[53] And because elections were infrequent, women could participate in public life without unmanning men. Such fears were common enough. During Mary Olney Brown's first trek to the polls in Washington, a man had blurted out, "Well! If the women are coming to vote, I'm going home!"[54] These tensions were not easily resolved. Witness Miller's wry list of "Twelve Anti-Suffragist Reasons" to deny votes to women:

1. Because no woman will leave her domestic duties to vote.
2. Because no woman who may vote will attend to her domestic duties.
3. Because it will make dissension between husband and wife.
4. Because every woman will vote as her husband tells her to.
5. Because bad women will corrupt politics.
6. Because bad politics will corrupt women.
7. Because women have no power of organization.
8. Because women will form a solid party and outvote men.
9. Because men and women are so different that they must stick to different duties.
10. Because men and women are so much alike that men, with one vote each, can represent their own views and ours too.
11. Because women cannot use force.
12. Because the militants did use force.[55]

Sometimes, the image of cosovereign householders migrated into discussions of political office or jury service, as when NAWSA delegates resolved in 1893 to secure "as many official mothers as fathers" on school boards. Even more often, the notion of a mixed-sex megahousehold came to be synonymous with "the state," so that the walls between "public" and "private" zones of concern utterly collapsed. New York's Cornelia Hood averred that the "radius of our home is not bounded by the four walls of our dwelling place but by the nation, the State, and the municipality." At the 1912 meeting of the National Medical Association in Tuskegee, Alabama, the African American educator-reformer Adella Hunt Logan offered a verse (to be sung to the tune of "Coming Through the Rye") the last stanza of which vividly captured the idea that the government was an extended household with coequal parents at the head:

> Every man now has the ballot;
>   None you know have we,
> But we have brains and we can use them
>   Just as well as he.
>
> If a home that has a father
>   Needs a mother too,
> Then every state that has men voters
>   Needs its women too.[56]

Suffragists sometimes anticipated a cultural revolution—as when Carry Nation predicted that an enfranchised woman would stop wearing "mops at the bottom of her dress to sweep up the filth of the earth" and shoes "that injure her" and instead would address "important topics of the day."[57] Left feminists like New York's Harriot Stanton Blatch portrayed suffragists as "a vast army of all classes," capable of surmounting social distinctions as wage earners and voters. One scholar concludes that for such women, the "bonds of family were being displaced by the wage relationship," radically altering both the republic and female self-perceptions.[58] But, in the end, suffragists did not insist on radical change. Arguments rooted in women's sphere often formed part of a post–Civil War strategic shift toward what Aileen Kraditor calls "expediency"[59]—that is, a decision to use "woman's sphere" for constructive social purposes. Activists surely preferred to sidestep the charge that the act of voting would transform women into men and destroy the republic; civic leader Henry Wood, for one, predicted that "[s]ocial decay, moral deterioration, and the demise of the Republic" would ensue. Women also needed to attract male allies. Such support was difficult to obtain when critics persistently linked suffragism to emasculation (as when Wood warned men not to dilute "with the qualities of the cow, the qualities of the bull upon which all the herd's safety must depend") and when many women plainly wanted to eliminate fictive boundaries between the family and the polity, ironically in the *name* of home.[60]

Still, expediency per se does not fully explain this development; in addition, putting a group's special attributes to social use was good science. Many, perhaps most, of the participants in the woman suffrage crusade had imbibed cutting-edge social theory; changes within organized suffragism after the 1890s reflected (in Steven Buechler's words) "a more fundamental ideological change" in Atlantic basin reform culture. Social reformer Florence Kelley, the African American publicist Mary Church Terrell, and other influential Progressives perceived unbridgeable physical and cultural differences between whites and blacks, men and women, and (in some circles) criminals and their victims. Frances Willard, president of Evanston College for Ladies from 1871 to 1874 and of the WCTU after 1879, articulated an *enlightened* view when she promised that "motherliness in sympathy . . . shall exalt public station. Indeed, if I were asked the mission of the ideal woman, I would reply: IT IS TO MAKE THE WHOLE WORLD HOMELIKE." Rochester's Mary Lewis Gannett also spoke the language of science as well as of republican motherhood: "We come to ask you to give to women political equality with men. You have heard a great variety of reasons urged for this. I ask it because I am a happy wife, because I am a mother. . . . I say, let us share the duties and responsibilities of the larger home—the city, the state, the nation. . . ."

> Rather than less[er] wives and mothers we shall thereby be the better wives [and] . . . better fit our sons and daughters for true citizenship. By reason of its wider horizon of *large outlooking interests*, the home will be . . . worth more to the State. The women need the ballot and the State needs the women's vote. The State needs the powers developed in the home. . . . Politics is simply national and municipal housekeeping; is simply national and municipal child-rearing.[61]

The radical Emma Goldman thought that suffragists quite sincerely had made "a political fetish" of the ballot box, could not see that it had "only helped to enslave people," and had submitted all over again to male governance. Why not insist on social *revolution*? "Not only is suffrage a hoax," she concluded sadly, "but American women believe they will purify politics."[62]

WOMEN'S VOICES, WOMEN'S VOTES

As the new century advanced, feminists continued to exhibit a keen interest in speech freedom and to recognize (in Susan Wixon's words) that the movement's successes owed much to "a free and liberal press, to the free schools, to free thought and free speech."[63] Women testified often and eloquently to the power of speech communities to remake individuals, the sex, and the republic. The black club woman Estele R. Davis, for example, served in the Republican Party's Speakers' Bureau during the Coolidge campaign of 1924. Later, she reflected, "How little have we realized in our club work for the last twenty-five years that it was God's way of preparing us to assume this greater task of citizenship. I often wonder what would have happened without our organized club work which has not only trained us for service, but has created a nation-wide sisterhood."[64]

Increasingly, Americans tolerated female oratory, if officially sanctioned and "feminine." In Kansas in 1890, during the ultimately triumphant Populist (or People's Party) pro-suffrage campaign, Kansas orator Mary Lease took to the podium with what William Allen White called a "deep, rich contralto, a singing voice that had hypnotic qualities." But the party's general message was radical, and her deportment was suspect. Harsh criticism ensued, including suggestions of harlotry and mannishness. "All we know about her," wrote an editor, "is that she is hired to travel around the country by this great reform People's party, which seems to find a female blackguard a necessity in its business, spouting foul-mouthed vulgarity at $10 a night. . . . The petticoated smut-mill earns her money, but few women want to make their living that way." Even White complained that she stood "nearly six feet tall, with no figure, a thick torso, and long legs. . . . She had no sex appeal—none!"[65] In contrast, because the speaker was polite but also because female oratory was no longer synonymous in all circles with promiscuity, the Nashville *Democrat* praised novelist Mary Johnston's 1913 address to Tennessee lawmakers: The fact that "a young Southern woman of Miss Johnston's type [and] rearing . . . should become an ardent advocate of equal suffrage" was one of the "most marked evidences of the growth of the sentiment." Such a speech "twenty-five years ago would hardly have been conceivable."[66]

Although they sometimes walked a fine line between decency and condemnation, women made effective use of speech to sell suffragism. Witness Gertrude Foster Brown's description of oratorical soldiering: "In the days of trailing skirts and picture hats," she recalled, "to see a woman mount a soap box on a street corner, or stand on the back seat of an automobile, and begin to orate, was so startling that men could not help but stop and listen. The street meetings were so effective that soon, all over the state, women held their meetings on street corners or public squares, wherever traffic was heaviest, with gay banners and much literature. They haunted every place where men gathered. His clubs, his conventions, his amusement places, were never safe from the danger of a speech demanding votes for women."[67] Women's newspapers continued to publicize the movement's activities and ideas; gifted writers also published woman-friendly articles and fiction in scientific, reformist, and popular journals. Antisuffragists rarely doubted the power of speech; one group warned "MEN OF THE SOUTH" to "Heed not the song of the suffrage siren! Seal our ears against her vocal wiles."[68]

But more and more, balloting came to be seen as *the* way to speak politically. In a 1912 article in the *Ladies Home Journal*, which characterized the vote as a civic obligation, Jane Addams urged women to "be informed in regard to . . . grave industrial affairs, and then to *express the conclusions . . . reached* by depositing a piece of paper in a ballot-box."[69] Well into the new century, unpopular or strident expressions of opinion delivered in old-fashioned ways met stiff opposition. The silencing of National Woman's Party (NWP) picketers is perhaps the best known example. Because President Wilson and his administration resisted universal enfranchisement, the NWP adopted resistance techniques that had been used to good effect in England. In 1917–18, picketers ringed the White House, threatening to embarrass the war effort with bluntly worded picket signs. Reformer-lobbyist Lucy Burns and a Philadelphia woman together lofted a banner that read, in part:

> TO THE RUSSIAN ENVOYS
> PRESIDENT WILSON AND ENVOY
> ROOT ARE DECEIVING
> RUSSIA WHEN THEY SAY "WE ARE A
> DEMOCRACY. . . ."
> WE THE WOMEN OF AMERICA TELL
> YOU THAT AMER-
> ICA IS NOT A DEMOCRACY. TWENTY-
> MILLION AMERI-
> CAN WOMEN ARE DENIED THE RIGHT
> TO VOTE. PRESI-
> DENT WILSON IS THE CHIEF OPPO-
> NENT OF THEIR NA-
> TIONAL ENFRANCHISEMENT.
> HELP US MAKE THIS NATION REALLY
> FREE. . . .[70]

After a boisterous 1918 suffrage parade in the nation's capitol, NWP women burned copies of presidential speeches, as well as their own messages to Congress, in a ceremony at the White House. Harriot Stanton Blatch later explained that although picketing triggered "a storm of protest and hostility," suffragists chose to stand pat. "The suffragists of Civil War days had given up their campaign to work for their country, expecting to be enfranchised in return for all their good services, but when the war was over . . . [t]hey were told . . . their turn would come next." In 1917, women were "still waiting" and would "wait no longer."[71]

Sometimes, onlookers applauded militancy. A Washington correspondent said in early 1917 that he had "seen no more impressive sight" than the spectacle of White House picketing. "[T]o see a thousand women . . . marching in a rain that almost froze as it fell; to see them standing and marching and holding their heavy banners . . . against a wind that was half a gale—hour after hour, until their gloves were wet and their clothes soaked through . . . was a sight to impress even the jaded senses of one who has seen much."[72] Others, however, accused the NWP of undermining Wilson's credibility in Europe; the president himself said that the timing was "not opportune." Fearing a backlash, NAWSA and a number of left-feminists disavowed all connection with the demonstrators; NAWSA also cooperated with the Wilson administration to control press coverage of radical activities. Tennessee's Kate Burch Warner, president of Nashville's Equal Suffrage League, lambasted in the name of "all true Suffragists" the "ingratitude and lamentable indignity" of the NWP protesters.[73] Mobs jeered the picketers, and constables hauled the women off to jail. When arrested and incarcerated for obstructing traffic, Alice Paul and others went on hunger strikes, only to be manhandled, forcibly fed, and occasionally put in solitary confinement.

Other instances of state-sponsored silencing are less familiar. Particularly in the South, NWP organizers confronted repeated attempts to muzzle circuit-riding speakers. In Dallas, just as the United States prepared to enter World War I, NWP speaker Maud Younger and several companions met with what suffragist Inez Haynes Irwin called "the cry of 'Treason' "—in her judgment, an "incredible" development *in these days of free speech.*" According to Irwin, NWP organizers in Texas could not engage a hall or hotel room for Younger; the mayor refused to allow her to hold a street meeting. When she "offered to submit her speech for censorship," city officials "refused her even that." In Tennessee, agents of the War Association and Home Defense League supposedly went "to all hotels, or meeting-places, to ask them not to rent rooms for Miss Younger's meetings, and to mayors to request them not to grant permits for street meetings." At least one woman, Sue White of Jackson, Tennessee—editor of the NWP newspaper *The Suffragist*—decided to support the lecture series not because she agreed with the speakers' positions or even to secure "equal suffrage," but because the visitors had been denied "freedom of speech, which is not only essential to our cause but to every other step in human progress." In the end, organized labor came to the rescue: In Chattanooga, union members offered NWP orators their hall. In Knoxville, a labor leader "saw at once that it was a free speech fight" and resolved that "Labor would make the fight for the suffragists." NWP speakers spoke from the courthouse steps, fully expecting "to be shot"; deputies barricaded the building while "*eighty armed Union men*" guarded the speakers.[74]

Why such violence? To some extent, militant suffragism had come to be synonymous with political radicalism and opposition to the war and so fell prey to the same repressive impulses underlying the Red Scare and related curtailments of civil liberties. But perceptions of an attack on male suffrage by supposedly incompetent or treasonous classes raised hackles in distinctive ways. As entire regions of the once-commodious republican forum disappeared and a mass democracy emerged, voting came to bear a heavy load. Democratic decision making came to be synonymous with balloting; few Americans of either sex resolved public controversies in the old face-to-face way. Mainstream political parties articulated the terms of patriotic discussion; on election day, citizens responded subvocally at the polls. For antisuffragists, an attack on male suffrage was an attack on rational political deliberation and thus an attack on the republic. On the other side, to be heard politically, women had to vote, but on terms that promised to strengthen, not weaken, the polity—hence, the suggestion that the two sexes "spoke" in different but equally rational voices. "What personal influence may be exerted by tongue or pen," wrote Mary Putnam-Jacobi in 1894, "can be done by the unenfranchised full as well as by those who possess the . . . ballot." Women needed to *rule*: "Where rests the Sovereign Power? . . . According to the theory of a Republic, the sovereignty lies, with such Public Opinion as shall prove itself, through superior virtue and intelligence, to be not only the best, but the strongest. For intelligence must be stronger than ignorance, and virtue than vice." Among the inequities in "present distributions of Sovereign Power" was the fact that men ruled merely by "physical force"; Putnam-Jacobi demanded "the association of women with men for such functions of sovereignty as they are able to exercise."[75]

Highly decorous symbolic speech proved to be one of the movement's most effective tools, especially in the war against stereotype. On May 2, 1914, for instance, women and men in Minneapolis staged a suffrage march involving at least 2,000 people who silently paraded in single file through the city's streets. Seeing suffragists en masse in their great variety quickly shattered a number of myths. As a Minneapolis *Tribune* reporter wrote, "Equal suffrage put herself on parade today. . . . The parade was a revelation and a bump for those who have formed their ideas of suffrage . . . from the cartoonist. . . . The chap who had formed the idea that hopeless spinsters were in the majority in suffrage ranks, that girls with plenty of suitors were absent from their roster, was terribly jolted. . . . Perhaps this is the predominant feature of . . . the parade, this exploding of the entire popular conception of the personal appearance, motives and manners of the American suffragist." Minnesotans noted, too, that the walls between home and polity had crumbled: "Woman needs the ballot for her own individual and collective benefit almost as much as man needs woman's assistance. She cannot be denied full and equal participation in the multiplying activities of our political and social life without impairing her usefulness. Even her influence in the home must suffer, because her household has become a part of government."[76]

Historians sometimes condemn suffragists' apparent willingness to jettison woman-centered communities and cultural criticism in favor of suffrage communities and lady-like deportment; in retrospect, women did relinquish what Estelle Freedman calls the "strengths of the female sphere" without much hope of experiencing equality in a male-centric society.[77] But in clinging to the idea of "separate but equal" citizenship beyond the suffrage, women hoped to preserve female solidarity in areas of life beyond the insular experience of balloting. The question was not whether women should forsake face-to-face communities in favor of impersonal suffrage communities—short of eliminating a suffrage-based democracy, the handwriting was on the wall for everyone—but whether group solidarity could be married to political individualism, whether female voters would be allowed to "speak" loudly on questions of real moment, and whether lawyers and judges would concede that the division of domestic sovereignty that was implied in grants of suffrage had placed men and women on an equal footing in adjacent regions of the public, so that the ballot box could be a springboard into political life rather than a trap.

To some extent, suffragists weakened the case for "suffrage as springboard" by deciding not to insist that voting was a natural right accompanied by a bundle of ancillary rights. This decision reflected genuine social distress: Women could not be expected to provide full-time childcare *and* sit on juries for several weeks. American culture had not yet adapted to political change. But, equally important, suffragists, no less than their opponents, often suspected that the polity was peculiarly susceptible to attack by force of numbers. White suffragists basically promised to join men in the battle against political contamination—a threat that seemed to include not only rapacious corporations and urban machines, but the Chinese, black men, and "swarthy" (meaning Italian, Greek, and Jewish) European immigrants. Time-honored stereotypes about soft-headed women made such negotiations an uphill battle. In 1887, Missouri's Democratic Senator George Vest made the point this way: "The great evil in this country to-day is in emotional suffrage. The great danger to-day is excitable suffrage. If the voters of this country could think always coolly, . . . if they could go by judgment and not by passion, our institutions would survive forever . . . ; but massed together, subject to the excitement of mobs . . . , what would be the result if suffrage were given to women of the United States? . . . Women are essentially emotional." Americans needed "more logic" in public life and "less feeling."[78]

Attempts to present (presumptively white) women as men's allies in patriotic battle took several forms. Sometimes, suffragists portrayed electoral speech acts as the least offensive way for women to express opinions in public. In 1884, a Kentuckian asked lawmakers merely for the right to approve or disapprove of decisions made by others: "Why should women not vote, since voting is *merely an authoritative expression of an opinion of how those affairs of life should be managed in which women have as deep a personal interest as men?"*[79] Years later, Virginians circulated a catechism portraying ballots as a decorous way to "speak" in public:

> I believe that it is my inherent right to express my opinion directly and effectively through the ballot.
> I believe that it is not only my right but my *duty* to use my influence for the betterment of the world . . . and that my influence depends on my personality and the opportunity to express my character—an opportunity that the ballot will give me.
> I believe that suffrage is the quietest, most dignified, and least conspicuous way of exerting my influence in public affairs.[80]

Others depicted women as the least dangerous of the "new" classes and an antidote to nonwhite, non-Protestant groups. The racism and xenophobia that were so much a part of American society powerfully shaped the movement; women simply failed to see, as Rosalie Jonas wryly explained in a 1912 poem, that when it "comes ter de question er de female vote,/ Der ladies an' der cullud folk is in de same boat."[81] Suzanne Lebsock argues that Virginia antisuffragists' suggestions of feminist dalliances with blacks (and black men's supposed lust for white women) often forced movement leaders who were not otherwise inclined to racism to respond in racist terms. But without a doubt, women's rights supporters also dished out racial slurs, especially to obtain southern or nativist support. In the process, they alienated black women, as well as hundreds of white reformers active in the battle against racism. Said Mississippi's Belle Kearney in a speech at the NAWSA convention in New Orleans in 1903, "The enfranchisement of women would ensure immediate and durable white supremacy, honestly attained; . . . The South is slow to grasp the great fact that the enfranchisement of women would settle the race question in politics."[82] Among many southern women, in fact, racial difference operated less as a reason to *want* suffrage—the majority probably did not want it—than as a "*reason to expect that they could win it.*"[83] In 1916, a suffrage league in Greenville, North Carolina, reprinted a speech by Chief Justice Walter Clark. Noting that women would eradicate civic "dirt" ("The men put it there . . . , and we need the women to give us a good housecleaning"), the league's editors then played the race card: "In North Carolina the white population is 70% and the negro 30%, hence there are 50,000 more white women than all the negro men and negro women put together." Woman suffrage would not "jeopardize White Supremacy, but would make it more secure."[84]

Such tactics failed to convert Dixie to suffragism. The number of southern women prepared to work for enfranchisement gradually increased. But below the Mason-Dixon line, the pro-suffrage camp did not reach a critical mass before the 1910s. There, powerful antisuffrage clubs had persuaded a large majority that feminists were manly Bolsheviks and that a "vote for federal suffrage is a vote for organized female nagging forever."[85] In 1916, at the Dixie Night session of the Atlantic City NAWSA convention, Tennessee's Anne Dallas Dudley provided a telling glimpse of white upper-class perceptions of ideal gender relations, coincidentally affirming the importance of the Civil War for women's self-emancipation: "The awakening of southern women . . . has been slow. . . . Our laws were bad, . . . but then our men were so much better than our laws, so why worry? . . . Southern chivalry was so real that it was almost impossible to convict a woman in court. . . ."

As long as it was a question of woman's rights; as long as the fight had any appearance of being against man . . . , the Southern woman stood with her back turned squarely toward the cause. . . . But when she awoke slowly to a social consciousness, when eyes and brain were at last free after a terrible reconstruction period, to look out upon the world as a whole; . . . when she realized that through the changed conditions of modern life so much of her work had been taken out of the home, leaving her to choose between following it into the world or remaining idle; when . . . she saw that man needed her help in governmental affairs, particularly where they touched her own interests, she said, "Oh, that is so different!"[86]

But not "different" enough: After the late-century rash of western electoral experiments, the suffrage juggernaut came to a halt, stymied by antisuffragism east of the Mississippi and in the old South.

UNIVERSAL SUFFRAGE FEDERALIZED

Only with the state of Washington's pro-woman suffrage decision in 1910; California's a year later; and the adoption of full suffrage in Kansas, Arizona, and Oregon by 1912 did the logjam finally began to break. In 1913, Illinois became the first state east of the Mississippi to allow women to vote during regular elections, albeit only to help choose presidential electors; ambivalent legislatures and voters gradually followed. When New York adopted woman suffrage in 1917 with a state constitutional amendment, suffragists breathed more easily: now, it would be harder, though not impossible, for "anti's" to say that Congress had run roughshod over the states. Still, the war over what would become the Nineteenth Amendment raged for three more years. Southerners continued to deploy states' rights arguments against federal interference with local election laws, often as a proxy for white supremacist arguments. Led by the indefatigable Carrie Chapman Catt, NAWSA twice brought the amendment to Congress, only to see it narrowly defeated. Finally, in August 1920, after months of anxiety about congressional and presidential opposition and despite last-ditch attempts by antisuffragists to sway ambivalent lawmakers with good whiskey and warnings about tainted mothers, Tennessee became the critical thirty-sixth ratifying state. The article read in its final form, "The right of citizens of the United States to vote shall not be denied or abridged by the United States or by any State on account of sex. The Congress shall have the power to enforce this article by appropriate legislation." Neither the Nineteenth nor the analogous Fifteenth Amendment created new rights, except to the extent that both articles implied the right to vote in federal elections; rather, Congress promised federal intervention if states excluded women from the polls by reason of sex. The hero of the moment was legislator Harry Burn of Tennessee, who, inspired by his mother's fervent plea that he do something to help women, cast the deciding vote for ratification, in his own words "free[ing] seventeen million women from political slavery."[87]

Why did suffragism prevail after decades of disappointment? Clearly, the NWP's highly visible civil disobedience had its effect. But, equally important, as Canada, Australia, and other democracies granted the vote to women and the Wilson administration organized foreign policy around the idea of making the world "safe for democracy," antisuffragism had become a political liability. From the 1840s into Reconstruction, women's rights activists had pointed regularly to the spectacle of virtual representation of women in a land that had revolted against Britain to secure direct representation for men. Women, moreover, had become an economic force with which politicians had to contend. After 1910, old connections between property and direct representation resurged; despite late Victorian attempts to divorce property from balloting, economic power still seemed to be "central to the expectation of political liberty."[88] As Catt put it in 1902, propertied women enjoyed "self-government in the home and in society. The question now is, shall all women as a body obey all men as a body? Shall the women who enjoys the right of self-government in every other department of life be permitted the right of self-government in the State?" Ten years later, Virginia's Mary Johnston demanded that citizens who "pay a very considerable portion of the taxes of the State and of the country" be given "a voice in the apportionment of those taxes. We are asking that we who work may have a say as to the conditions which, even now, are largely under political control." Chief Justice Walter Clark of North Carolina thought that it was "enough" that women were "taxpayers and of equal intelligence and character with men, and hence, are entitled to a voice of the government which they do so much to support. . . . Women own probably one-half of the property in every State." Furthermore, although historians have not closely examined its influence, the World War I-related decision to impose a federal income tax made it more difficult to justify ongoing disfranchisement. Said Congressman John Baer of North Dakota, "For the first time in our history Congress has imposed a direct tax upon women and has thus deliberately violated the most fundamental and sacred principle of our Government, since it offers no compensating 'representation' for the tax it imposes. Unless reparation is made it becomes the same kind of tyrant as was George III." The many women "earning their incomes under hard conditions of economic inequality" harbored a "genuine grievance" against the federal government.[89]

Traditionalists did not go down without a fight. After federalization, for example, opponents filed a number of lawsuits challenging the ratification procedures used with both the Eighteenth and Nineteenth Amendments; battles raged in Tennessee, Vermont, Connecticut, West Virginia, Missouri, Ohio, Maryland, and elsewhere. The prospect of entrusting the amendment's future to the institution responsible for the *Minor* ruling deeply worried more than one suffragist. Critics argued basically that many of the requisite thirty-six states had ratified unlawfully (for example, by referring the question to groups that were not a part of the sovereign power in 1791 or by failing to do so). But state judges turned back these challenges, and in *Fairchild v. Hughes* and *Leser v. Garnett* (1922), Supreme Court justice Louis Brandeis spurned attempts by the American Constitutional League and others to "have the 19th Amendment declared void."[90]

SPRINGBOARD OR TRAP?

The enfranchisement of women did not automatically secure political freedom in the broadest sense. Suffragists' tacit acceptance of the notion that votes were a privilege (extended by the government and revocable at will), rather than a natural, inviolable right, made it difficult to insist on the full bundle extended in the previous century to new classes of male voters. Ancillary freedoms probably were a good deal more important to antisuffragists than historians have seen; in Washington Territory and elsewhere, "anti's" often worried less about voting per se—controlled, after all, by male-dominated parties—than about female invasions of courtrooms. When Abraham Kellogg, a Republican delegate to the New York Constitutional Convention of 1894, tried to defend the "sanctity and purity of the fireside" against the threat of woman suffrage, he listed everything *but* the act of voting. "No," he said, " . . . the true glory of womanhood is not in sitting upon the jury, not in being clothed in judicial ermine, not in being sent to the halls of legislation, not in following the example of the publican, . . . but rather by such fond devotion in that sacred place where she stands as a queen in the eyes of all mankind."[91]

Like Washington Territory's Judge Turner, judges commonly refused to "find" ancillary political rights in the Nineteenth Amendment without express statutory authorization. The most notorious examples involved jury service. In 1881, U.S. Supreme Court justice Harlan had held in the landmark *Neal v. Delaware* that the Fifteenth Amendment extended the jury service obligation to men of African descent and that an all-white jury could not decide the fate of a black man accused of rape. In contrast, in 1926, thirteen years before the state finally admitted women to jury service, the Illinois superior court provided a fairly typical argument against automatic extensions of the obligation to women. Mrs. Hannah Beye Fyfe, a registered voter and resident, sought to be included on jury lists as a consequence of enfranchisement; she relied on both the Nineteenth Amendment and Illinois's 1921 statute enfranchising women. In *People v. Barnett* (1926), Justice Heard ruled (much as Jones had done in *Bloomer v. Todd*) that because neither the federal amendment nor the new election law named jury service explicitly, women were relieved of the obligation. State law provided that jurors would be selected from "legal voters" and "electors," but the controlling legislative intent was that of the assembly responsible for the old jury law, which contemplated only male jurors. Women would have to seek new legislation.[92]

Similarly, in *Commonwealth v. Welosky* (1931), Chief Justice Rugg of the Supreme Judicial Court of Massachusetts pointed to understandings of the word *person* (the state election law specified that a "person" qualified to vote could sit on juries) before adoption of the Nineteenth Amendment. Women's prospects for jury service again came down to a question (as in prestatehood Washington) of proper "title": Because neither the amendment nor statutes mentioned female jury service, the court refused to infer it. With other judges, Rugg distinguished between the freedom of women and black men: Unlike (presumptively male) blacks, women had "not been enslaved," supposedly had been "recognized as citizens and clothed with large property and civil rights," and had long been seen as "the equal of man intellectually, morally, socially." Yet Rugg also characterized woman suffrage as massively destabilizing. Women were an entirely new "class" of voters (black men, after all, were *men*); a feminized electorate was "radical, drastic and unprecedented." Voting was one thing, and direct occupation of jury boxes quite another. The new amendment would be "given full effect in its field" but could "not . . . be extended by implication."[93]

Well into the 1970s, federal and state courts mostly agreed, particularly in states where female jury service had not been addressed in election or jury laws. In a rash of cases after 1920, the U.S. Supreme Court ruled that when states used the word *person* in old jury statutes, they had in mind a man. The National Woman's Party's struggle during the New Deal era to secure a federal right to jury service did not succeed.[94] By the early 1940s, only twenty-eight states allowed female jury service—among them, Washington (1911), Indiana (1926), Michigan (1920), Nevada (1918), Ohio (1928), Pennsylvania (1921), and Iowa (1921)—of which number, fifteen allowed voluntary exemption for causes, such as child care, that were assumed to be peculiar to women. The remaining states either refused to find jury service in the Nineteenth Amendment or denied any necessary connection between the right to vote and jury obligations. In Illinois, lawmakers inserted the words "of both sexes" into an old jury law in 1929, allowing "legal voters" and "electors" to serve on juries—whereupon women bowled over the opposition. "At first," wrote lawyer Matilda Fenberg in 1930, "they were treated with an air of amused tolerance or of skepticism by many lawyers and others connected with the courts. But as the women demonstrated their eager interest in jury service and their fitness for it, the attitude of the men changed and women jurors soon were accepted. . . . The number of women serving in Cook County has considerably exceeded the number of men. The reason [is] . . . that fewer women than men are seeking exemptions from the Jury Commissioners or are asking to be excused by the judges."[95]

Nonetheless, women often claimed exemption—perhaps because the jury box seemed "mannish" or because economic and domestic obligations were overwhelming. When Washington State's women regained access to jury boxes in 1911, for example, only six of the dozens of women who were empaneled in the rural counties of Walla Walla and Columbia between 1911 and 1913 actually served; most were excused "by reason of sex."[96] And even when women wanted to serve, men sometimes dug in their heels, refusing to do "women's work" while soft-headed wives and daughters sat on juries. In a 1937 debate of a bill extending the obligation to Hawaiian women, territorial senator David Trask quipped, "I have a wife and 9 children and if my wife went on a jury I would have to stay home and do the work. And my wife would feel sorry for every accused person."[97]

On other occasions, resistance wore black robes. North Carolina judges ruled in *State v. Emery* (1944)—a case involving three men convicted of violating prohibition laws who appealed on the ground that two female jurors were not jury*men*—that, at least in their state, where jury service was distinguished by law from voting rights, it was a "far cry from elector to juror," since the "qualifications of the one are quite different from those of the other."[98] In its 1946 decision in *Ballard v. United States*, the U.S. Supreme Court overturned an indictment on the ground that women had been excluded systematically from a California jury. Its decision was predicated, however, not on a citizen's right to assume jury service obligations, but on the accused person's right to trial by a cross section of the community and, secondarily, on the ground that women contributed a unique "flavor, a distinct quality" to courtroom deliberations.[99] A year later, in *Fay v. New York* (1947), the Court ruled that women did not have a constitutional right as citizens to sit on juries and that sex-based classifications therefore might be deemed "reasonable."

But "reasonable" in what sense? And who would say? As the Cold War heated up, two legal scholars described prevailing understandings of "equal protection of law" and the conditions under which courts might approve of statutory classification schemes. "The equal protection of the laws is a 'pledge of the protection of equal law,' " they wrote in 1949. But it was in the nature of legislation to "create classifications" and therefore "inequality"; every law imposed "special burdens" or granted "special benefits" to some person or group. In tackling this paradox, the Court had "neither abandoned the demand for equality nor denied the legislative right to classify. . . . It has resolved the contradictory demands of legislative specialization and constitutional generality by a doctrine of reasonable classification." At the heart of the matter was the fact that the Constitution did not seem to require judges to treat "things different in fact . . . as though they were the same." Rather, it required "in its concern for equality, that those who are similarly situated be similarly treated. The measure of the reasonableness of a classification is the degree of its success in treating similarly those similarly situated. . . ." A "reasonable" classification was "one which includes all who are similarly situated and none who are not" and that either prevented a public mischief or achieved "some positive public good."[100]

Well into the 1970s, state and federal courts permitted legislators to exclude women from jury lists, either by an outright ban or by exemption laws. When courts did extend the obligation to women, they often aimed to ensure the right of the *accused* to a trial by peers, rather than to ensure the political equality of would-be female jurors. Most famously, the nation's highest court decided in *Hoyt v. Florida* (1961) that Gwendolyn Rogers Hoyt, a battered wife convicted of "killing her husband by assaulting him with a baseball bat," did not have a constitutional right to a trial by a mixed-sex jury and that Florida reasonably could exempt women from jury service unless they registered a "desire to be placed on the jury list" with the clerk of the circuit court. The focus was on Hoyt, not on the trivialization of female citizenship that accompanied exemption from public obligations. In response to an *amicus* brief filed by the American Civil Liberties Union that emphasized women's obligation to assume all the rights and responsibilities of citizenship, counsel for the state underscored maternity and women's primary obligation to family governments. Nothing could alter "material reasons for the differences in responsibilities assigned to men and women in our society. . . ."

> Though many eons may have passed, the gestation period in the human female has likewise remained unchanged. . . . The rearing of children . . . remains a prime responsibility of the matriarch. . . . [T]he husband is still . . . the breadwinner, child's hurts are almost without exception, bounded and treated by the mother. . . . *The only bulwark between chaos and an organized and well-run family unit is our woman of the day.*[101]

The Supreme Court agreed. Relying on *Fay*, Associate Justice John Marshall Harlan ruled that the Fourteenth Amendment granted a defendant not the right to a "jury tailored to the circumstances of the particular case," but simply a right to a jury "indiscriminately drawn from among those eligible in the community for jury service, untrammeled by any arbitrary exclusions." Florida's statute employed a "reasonable classification"; it did not engage in racial or administrative discrimination. Nor did judges dispute the idea, set out by counsel for the state, that women could hardly quibble with all-male juries when they themselves had been trying to impersonate men since the nineteenth century: "If we again accept the appellant's argument, we find that women have sought for many, many years to achieve the ultimate—the status of men. This appears, over the years, to have been based on their sincere belief in themselves as the equivalent of men. . . . [I]n many respects, truly they are. That being so, must we not assume that inasmuch as she was tried by an all-male jury, she has attained the ultimate pinnacle to which she (as a member of our female body politic) had aspired?" Despite the "emancipation of women from restrictions and protections of bygone years," wrote Harlan, "and their entry into many parts of the community life formerly reserved for men, woman is still regarded as the center of the home and family life."[102]

The bench thus reasserted the ancient idea that a woman's first obligation was to her family—indeed, that "woman" still called to mind a mother not quite synonymous with the constituent power—and that the state should encourage that primary allegiance. As Ruth Bader Ginsburg observed some years later, Chief Justice Earl Warren's brethren could not imagine that "differential treatment of men and women in the jury-selection context" was "in any sense *burdensome* to women."[103] In an interesting departure, federal judges in Alabama did condemn the exclusion of women from juries as a denial of the prospective jurors' right to equal protection of law, but other courts generally followed

Hoyt. In 1966, the Supreme Court of Mississippi decided in *State v. Hall* that jury service was a legislative grant of privilege, not a right, and that lawmakers could reasonably "exclude women so they may continue their service as mothers, wives, and homemakers and also to protect them . . . from the filth, obscenity and noxious atmosphere" pervading a criminal trial. Chief Justice Ethridge filed a flaming dissent: "Jury service is not just a privilege," he wrote, "but a form of participation in the processes of government. It is a responsibility and right possessed by all citizens, regardless of sex." When a statute excluded half the citizenry from jury service merely on the ground of sex, it lacked a "reasonable basis" for classification. Four years later, however, Judge Walter Mansfield of the U.S. District Court for the Southern District of New York noted in *Leighton v. Goodman* (1970) that because jury service disrupted family culture, voluntary exemption was both permissible and desirable: "Granted that some women pursue business careers, the great majority constitute the heart of the home, where they are busily engaged in the 24-hour task of producing and rearing children, providing a home for the entire family, and performing the daily household work, all of which demands their full energies. Although some women now question this arrangement, the state legislature has permitted the exemption in order not to risk disruption of the basic family unit. Its action was far from arbitrary."[104]

At virtually the same time, a New York State court decided that, while racial and class exemptions were sufficiently "offensive" to be termed violations of the Fourteenth Amendment, sex-based exemptions were not. In *DeKosenko v. Brandt*, Justice George Stark derisively told the plaintiff, who had challenged the state's exemption statute, that she was "in the wrong forum. Her lament should be addressed to the 'Nineteenth Amendment State of Womanhood' which prefers cleaning and cooking, rearing of children and television soap operas, bridge and canasta, the beauty parlor and shopping, to becoming embroiled in plaintiff's problems." Despite the Civil Rights Act of 1957, which guaranteed women a place on federal juries, into the 1960s slightly more than twenty states continued to refuse to seat female jurors. As of 1973, although women could demand the right to jury service in all fifty states, nineteen allowed voluntary exemption for such reasons as pregnancy, a fear of public life, or maternal responsibilities.[105]

Attempts to use the Nineteenth Amendment to eliminate other badges of oppression or to claim ancillary political rights beyond the jury service obligation sometimes succeeded. One such badge was the requirement that, under certain circumstances, married women had to adopt their husbands' nationality. In 1915, well before the federalization of suffrage, Ethel Mackenzie, with other California suffragists, decided to test the validity of a 1907 statute requiring an American women who married a foreigner to "take the nationality of her husband"—the culmination of developments since 1855, when Congress first acted to penalize women for marrying aliens—and to require that they surrender their property to a federal agency.[106] Mackenzie argued that citizenship could be eradicated only as punishment for a crime. In *Mackenzie v. Hare* (1915), however, Supreme Court justice Joseph McKenna affirmed the validity of both the statute and the marital-unity doctrine. "The identity of husband and wife," he wrote, "is an ancient principle of our jurisprudence. It was neither accidental nor arbitrary and worked in many instances for her protection." McKenna conceded "much relaxation" of the old rule. But spouses' "intimate relation and unity of interests" made it a matter of "public concern . . . to merge their identity, and give dominance to the husband. It has purpose, if not necessity, in purely domestic policy; it has greater purpose, and, it may be, necessity, in international policy."

In response to the idea that Congress had divested Mackenzie of citizenship against her will, McKenna noted that *marriage* was voluntary; if a woman did not wish to renounce her citizenship, she could remain single.[107]

In 1922, Congress passed the Cable Act, which provided that "the right of any woman to become a naturalized citizen of the United States" would not be denied or abridged by reason of sex or marriage. Nor did marriage to an alien erase a woman's American identity or marriage to an American automatically confer citizenship upon an alien woman. An unpopular remaining restriction—that women married to aliens who were not eligible for American citizenship lost their nationality at marriage—was repealed in 1931. The Cable Act thus set the wheels in motion for putting an end to coverture's stranglehold on nationality law. Observers rightly credited the Nineteenth Amendment with forcing change: A member of the 87th Congress noted that there had been "no particular force in the demand for this bill" until its adoption.[108] Still, federal officials decided only in 1989 that children could claim birthright citizenship through an American mother living abroad.

Public officials also conceded women's right to hold public office—perhaps because, after decades of partial suffrage, women had attained more than a few elective and appointive posts. Officials had long since acknowledged female lawyers' right to serve as officers of the court, and periodic, entry-level public service did not seem to threaten male control of law making. Indeed, as early as 1869, Congress had turned back a proposed amendment to the federal constitution limiting officeholding to men "until the ladies have the privilege of electors of the United States."[109] Attorney Belva Lockwood ran for the presidency in 1884 and 1888 on the National Equal Rights Party ticket; in 1884, she almost won the electoral vote in Indiana and took great pride in the fact that 4,000 American men had voted for her.

Perhaps the strangest judicial statement about female officeholding came from the Supreme Court of New Hampshire, which held in 1927 that because the right to vote, rather than sex, formed the basis for a right to public office, women could hold elective but not appointive offices. But curiosities aside, the states had little trouble finding the right to hold office in the bundle of rights accompanying suffrage. In a 1921 advisory opinion, the Supreme Judicial Court of Maine easily located the right in the federal amendment; six out of eight justices further indicated that the citizenship rights embedded in the text were "precisely the same" as those conveyed to black men in the Fifteenth Amendment—one of the few decisions consonant with Supreme Court Justice Brandeis's prediction in *Leser v. Garnett* (1922) that the similarly phrased Fifteenth and Nineteenth Amendments would follow identical jurisprudential paths. A year later, North Carolina jurists sanctioned female officeholding; also in 1922, and in contrast to *Weloskey*, the high court of Massachusetts decided that the Nineteenth Amendment implicitly qualified women for public service.[110]

Elsewhere, though, the amendment's path was rocky. In reviewing a Florida case, *United States v. Hinson*, federal judges held in 1925 that the federalization of suffrage nullified old common law rules about husbands' responsibility for wives' criminality; when spouses collaborated, each would be tried as an individual.[111] And into the 1930s, state courts generally agreed that age and literacy qualifications for suffrage had to be identical for both sexes. Ohio judges decided in *State ex rel. Klein v. Hillenbrand* (1920) that women, like men, had to state their ages before casting ballots. A dozen years later, in *Prewitt v. Wilson*, the Kentucky supreme court invalidated all old statutes that made special provision for female voters, including a law permitting women to vote if they were literate and possessed the same civil capacities as men. In *In re Graves* (1930), Missouri judges rejected a law mandating separate ballots for female voters. The courts disagreed, however, about poll taxes. In Alabama, judges decided that both sexes had to pay. The U.S. Supreme Court thought otherwise. In *Breedlove v. Suttles* (1937), it upheld a Georgia law that exempted blind people and women from poll taxes. Georgia's tax had been levied to raise money for public schools; because it was "the father's duty to provide for education of the children," men might be expected to shoulder school expenses. The court also deemed it unfair that husbands (still household "heads" at law, to whom women were "subject") should pay poll taxes for wives who chose *not* to vote.[112]

The courts also defended old rules about marital residence. In 1913, a New Jersey court ably summarized tradition when it said that, at marriage, the "domicile of the wife merges with that of the husband" as a "legal consequences of the nuptial contract," unless a wife acquired a home elsewhere "by the husband's consent." And, as law scholar Kevin Paul observes, even when the law of coverture began to show signs of wear, there was "no shortage of 'policy reasons'" for conserving the domicile rule. In a 1900 California Supreme Court opinion (*In Re Wickes' Estate*), justices had stated that the "subjection of the wife to the husband was not the only reason" for maintaining the old doctrine; in practical terms, a husband had to be able to fulfill his obligation to feed, clothe, and house her.[113] In 1938, the Alabama Supreme Court in *Wilkerson v. Lee* decided that the Anthony amendment had not unsettled the "covering" of a woman's original domicile with her husband's. An election judge had refused to count the votes of two recently married women who had moved away from their hometown to live with their husbands, only to learn that they could no longer vote where they had registered. The judges ruled that "[w]hen a woman marries and enters in the family relation at the domicile of the husband, this domicile becomes the domicile of the wife." Judges conceded only that when a husband offered his wife a temporary, rather than permanent, home, thus depriving her of residency, she retained the right to vote.[114] As late as 1974, only four states permitted wives to claim a legal residence apart from their husbands; another fifteen allowed separate addresses for electoral purposes, six in order to run for office, five each for jury service and probate, and seven for taxation purposes.

For much of the twentieth century, moreover, the overwhelming majority of states either barred married women from retaining their own surnames or failed to tell them that they could use their fathers' names. In a 1945 decision, the Illinois Court of Appeals declared it a "well settled" point that "a woman upon marriage abandons her maiden name and takes the husband's surname." In 1971, the Burger Court affirmed without opinion the validity of an Alabama law requiring women to adopt their husbands' names when applying for driver's licenses; that decision, in turn, convinced the Sixth Federal Circuit bench in 1976 to reject a constitutional challenge to an analogous Kentucky statute. In addition, well into the 1980s, states sometimes refused to allow married women to change their surnames; for instance, before 1981, husbands had to "join in the petition" of Iowa women who were seeking to do so. Kevin Paul concludes that although such "overtly sexist practices" largely have fallen by the wayside, the fact that American law for "*most* of its history affirmatively assigned women the status of 'objects' in their relationships to and with men ought not to be entirely overlooked in contemplating the contemporary legal landscape."[115]

Furthermore, after 1920, political parties did not zealously pursue female activists, except as canvassers, demonstrators, and propagandists. Only minor parties regularly included female delegates in conventions or caucuses; a handful of women served in party bureaucracies, and even fewer ran for office on mainstream tickets. The situation was more disappointing than surprising. In a speech celebrating the Anthony amendment, Carrie Chapman Catt warned new voters about stiff opposition to ambitions beyond suffrage, urging them nevertheless to press forward. If they looked closely, they would see "a little denser group," the "umbra of the political party," where they would "not be welcome."

> Those are the people who are planning the platforms and picking out the candidates, and doing the work which you and the men voters will be expected to sanction at the polls. You won't be so welcome there, but that is the place to be. And if you stay there long enough . . . , you will see something else—the real thing in the center, with the door locked tight, and you will have a long hard fight before you get behind that door, for there is the engine that moves the wheels of your party machinery. . . . If you really want women's vote to count, make your way there.

Women faced "the prejudices of the male politicians, who, having been compelled to accept woman suffrage, set up a whole new system of defenses against a female invasion of their prerogatives."[116]

Others found even less ground for optimism. Emily Newell Blair, a Missouri suffrage leader and vice-chair of the Democratic National Committee in the 1920s, noted in 1931 that women had put too many eggs into the suffrage basket "in an age where politics counted less than before"; as political "individuals," they had "won little power" and had sacrificed their considerable influence as a class. "It continues to all effects and purposes," she concluded, "a man's world." Some years later, Eleanor Roosevelt asked whether a woman could be president of the United States: "[T]he answer is emphatically 'No'. . . . As things stand today, even if an emotional wave swept a woman into this office, her election would be valueless, as she could never hold her following long enough to put over her program. It is hard enough for a man to do that, with all the traditional schooling men have had; for a woman, it would be impossible because of the age-old prejudice. In government, in business, and in the professions there may be a day when women are looked upon as persons. We are, however, far from that day as yet."[117]

Nor did middle-class white women find common ground with black and working-class women. Historian Ann Gordon notes the "persistent discrimination and recurrent denial by white women of an equality with black women,"[118] as well as ambivalence about working women of all description. Classism and racism alienated many Americans who otherwise might have supported enfranchisement. Working women might have welcomed support; as of 1910, only about 77,000 women (or 1.5 percent of all female laborers and 5.2 percent of factory women) belonged to trade unions. The majority of working women were unorganized and without a political voice—although, it should be noted, women of color had an easier time finding common cause. In 1862, black female agricultural workers staged a strike; in 1881, the year of the American Federation of Labor's founding with a white male membership, 3,000 black members of the Atlanta Washerwoman's Association also went on strike. In emergent western states, fear of enfranchising thousands of Asian and Mormon women also limited suffragism's appeal. Despite periodic attempts to resolve such problems, women of color (and, in different ways, white working-class women) who were interested in joining NAWSA or the NWP typically felt like visitors in a foreign land. After 1920, moreover, feminists rarely intervened to assist disfranchised blacks. Jessie Ashley, treasurer of NAWSA and a leader in the Women's Trade Union League, rightly noted in 1911 that "handsome ladies as a class," in refusing to couple suffragism with "outside issues," fostered a "narrow view of what the suffrage movement really stands for."[119]

When whites back-pedaled on the race question, many black leaders (joined by a number of white left-feminists) reminded suffragists of basic democratic principles. As Adella Hunt Logan wrote in 1912, the "colored American believes in equal justice to all, regardless of race, color, creed or sex, and longs for the day when the United States shall indeed have a government of the people, for the people and by the people—even including the colored people." When W. E. B. DuBois said that any "reopening of the problem of voting must inevitably be a discussion of the right of black folk to vote in America and Africa," NAWSA's leaders collectively shivered.[120] Although whites typically claimed to be interested in mobilizing the "best" women to redeem the republic, they meant women like themselves. For blacks, the doxology that suffragists sang in Boston to celebrate the ratification of the Nineteenth Amendment was at best ironic:

> Praise God from whom all blessings flow,
> Praise Him all women here below,
> Now we can raise our voices high
> And shout hosannas to the sky.
> For we have won the mighty fight—
> Long did we labor for the right.
> And now in solemn thanks to Thee,
> We sing Thy praises. We are Free![121]

In the words of the National Council of Negro Women's Dorothy Height, suffragists' moral failures ensured that it would take "lynching, bombing, the Civil Rights movement and the Voting Rights Act" to secure basic political rights for African American citizens of both sexes.[122]

Chapter 9

Economic Protection versus "Equal Rights"

A s the twentieth century dawned, thousands of women had planted their feet firmly in the hardscrabble world of wage-earning and public affairs. Even as many Americans tried to reinforce distinctions between "private" and "public" life, many Progressive reformers and women's rights activists pushed in the opposite direction, insisting that home life impinged upon "the public" and so could be a proper object of state and municipal concern. At the same time, they sought to transform home work, including reproduction, into a species of community labor, to be regulated and dignified by the state. Social welfare experts argued, for example, that public schools should provide compulsory domestic training—later called home economics—for girls, not to cut them off from public life, but, in the words of Sarah Louise Arnold of Simmons College, to teach home work's "relation to the community."[1] Such arguments comported nicely with the idea, then current in lawyers' circles, that states could regulate "private" activities imbued with a "public interest" (such as the railroad industry). Progressive reformers like Florence Kelley insisted as well that unionization and passage of protective industrial statutes were as essential as the ballot—indeed, that they were interdependent. In response, "equal rights" feminists (represented mainly by the National Woman's Party) advocated sex neutrality in law codes, "equal chances" in the workplace, and an Equal Rights Amendment (ERA). Only by eliminating sex as a legal classification, they argued, would female workers escape the taint of legal and social dependence. In trying to forge a better world for worker-citizens, postsuffrage combatants gave form to the practical and theoretical questions around which second-wave feminism would coalesce several decades later.

FLORENCE KELLEY AND THE PROTECTIONIST VANGUARD

Born in Philadelphia in 1859, Florence Kelley grew up surrounded by Quakers, legal scholars, and suffragists. Her father, a self-taught lawyer and judge, promoted women's rights; shared his extensive library with his daughter; and urged her to attend Cornell University, from which she earned a bachelor of arts degree in 1876. Six years later, the University of Pennsylvania denied her admission to its graduate school on the ground of sex. While touring Europe in 1883, however, Kelley encountered the brilliant L. Carey Thomas, who had enrolled at the University of Zurich, the only European medical school that was willing to admit women. Kelley also matriculated at Zurich and developed an appetite for what a friend called "the new wildfire of socialism."[2] In 1887, she published an English edition of Frederich Engels's *Condition of the Working Class in England*; for the rest of her life, she relied on his analysis of social relations in capitalist societies, enriched by correspondence with him.

While in Germany, Kelley married Lazare Wischnewtzky, a Russian physician and socialist; in 1886, with son Nicholas in tow, the couple moved to New York, where they joined the Socialist Labor Party, parented two more children, and battled poverty. Although she lectured extensively for the party in New York City and elsewhere, her ideas and national loyalties prompted socialist leaders to expel both Florence and Lazare in 1887. Three years later, Florence moved to Chicago, obtained a divorce and custody of her children, resumed her original surname, and moved into Hull House—in her own words, a "center of hospitality for people and their ideas"[3]—and began path-breaking studies of "sweating" in urban tenements. Kelley wrote extensively about industrial abuses of workers; in 1889, she published "Our Toiling Children," which led to an offer the next year of a job with the Illinois Bureau of Labor Statistics to investigate sweatshops in the garment trade. Jane Addams later said that the newcomer had "galvanized" Hull House residents into a "more intelligent interest in . . . industrial conditions."[4]

Kelley espoused a tenuous mixture of socialism and liberalism. Early on, she had decided to reject "bourgeois philanthropy" and embrace "the philanthropy of the working class." If women failed to criticize their upper-class origins, she wrote in 1887, their charitable work would "bear its stamp, being merely palliative, saving one girl while the system sacrifices tens of thousands. . . . Women to be rescued, men to be reformed, whatever the form of the social wreckage, it all comes from the class of the plundered."[5] She therefore began to study laborers' approaches to self-defense—their "sick benefit societies, reciprocal help in times of strike and lockout, and, most of all, the trades organizations." There, she found widespread "sharing" of "poverty and savings"—in other words, the "social idea, 'each for all and all for each,' the principle of active brotherhood." Educated women merely apologized for the social system, ignorant of working-class practices. "To cast our lot with the workers," she wrote, "to seek to understand the laws of social and industrial development, . . . to spread this enlightenment among the men and women destined to contribute to the change to a higher social order . . . —this is the true work for the elevation of the race, the true philanthropy."[6]

Kelley struggled tirelessly to expose capitalist exploitation of workers through fieldwork, public education, journalism, and litigation. As a result of her work, the Illinois legislature in 1893 adopted a law prohibiting child labor, limiting the hours that women might work in factories, and regulating sweatshops; Governor Altgeld made her the state's head factory inspector—a position that had never been held by a woman. With a staff of twelve, Kelley studied industrial abuses to lay the facts before the public; her office also had responsibility for enforcing new laws in state courts. The work was perilous: On one occasion, a critic tried to shoot her during a factory inspection.

Dissatisfied with her office's track record, Kelley enrolled in an evening law program at Northwestern University; in 1894, she graduated and gained admission to the bar. When Altgeld's successor fired her in 1897, she continued to live at Hull House, wrote for the progressive and socialist press, and lectured extensively. Finally, in 1899, she accepted a post as general secretary of the National Consumer's League (NCL) in New York—an office she held for the rest of her life—where she hoped to mobilize citizens against industrial abuse; with her children, she took up residence in Lillian Wald's Henry Street Settlement, again to be near fellow reformers. Universities, labor groups, and women's clubs clamored for speeches. Legislators solicited her testimony on proposed child labor and truancy laws, factory legislation, consumer protection, and other welfare-related topics. Few lobbyists were so effective: Franklin Delano Roosevelt's labor secretary, Frances Perkins, said that she had "the voice and presence of a great actress, although she was far from theatrical in her intentions."[7]

Kelley's objectives (as described in her 1905 *Some Ethical Gains Through Legislation*) included the adoption of wage and hour laws and tight regulation of child labor, although she thought of factory legislation as a temporary substitute for unionization and child labor laws as a prelude to the abolition of child labor. And because of these interests, she was a staunch suffragist: Women required political legitimacy before they would take *themselves* seriously and reject "two standards of work and wages." Disfranchisement, she said in 1898, placed "the wage-earning woman upon a level of irresponsibility. . . . By impairing her standing in the community, the general rating of her value as a human being, and consequently as a worker, is lowered."[8]

In *Ethical Gains*, Kelley explored remedies for industrial abuse in terms of workers' and consumers' "rights"—the right to childhood, the right to leisure, the rights of purchasers, the right of women to the ballot—that were both public and private, individualized and social. She then wove exercise of these rights into a fabric that she called "ethical gains," and tied these gains to the public interest, notably society's interest in maintaining social interdependence. The public, for example, had a collective right to consume goods and services without fear of supporting unethical business practices. "The more closely the rights of purchasers are scrutinized," wrote Kelley, "the more clearly it appears that they are social rights. However much they may present themselves to the mind as individual, personal rights, the effort to assert them invariably brings the experience that they are inextricably interwoven with the rights of innumerable other people."[9]

Kelley thus aimed to raze barriers between individual and communal experiences of modern society. She thought, too, that women promoted ethical gains more effectively than did men because they valued human relationships. Because "an ethical gain" was made whenever the "intelligence of women" was made available to the public, women should be enfranchised; woman suffrage would help "close the gap between public and private interest," neutralizing social toxins with "moral power."[10] In all this, Kelley soft-pedaled her socialism. But Engels's analysis of the sources of working-class oppression powerfully shaped her thought: Women were a *class* in search of collective consciousness, and working women were the republic's main hope for the future.

Yet the same women produced wealth at home without recompense and undercut men in the labor market. What could be done? In the short run, Kelley urged the passage of compensatory factory legislation. She made clear, however, that wage, hour, and safety laws—which aimed to protect women from night work, pitiful wages, dangerous machinery, and sixteen-hour days—were at best a temporary solution to industrial abuse. Reformers who touted them as *the* solution lived in a "fool's paradise"; the laws encouraged speedups on the shop floor and did nothing to close the gap between men's and women's wages. The only permanent remedies were enfranchisement and unionization. Female workers needed a statutory safety net until they could defend themselves effectively on the shop floor, at home, and at the ballot box; an unorganized woman "presse[d] upon the wage scale of her competitors as the subsidized or presumably subsidized worker must always do," even as she endured the "twofold strain of home maker and wage earner."[11]

To secure protective measures for women and children, Kelley collaborated with liberals; she also struggled to square her radical politics with frequent capitulations to the legal profession and to industrial capitalism. Vivien Hart argues that Kelley was "caught in the contradictions between traditional views on women and the family, experience of women's working conditions, knowledge of the impact on women of the social and economic changes of recent decades, and her own socialist training and legal expertise. She endorsed the nuclear family and the woman's role as wife and mother, and she spoke of her preference for a family wage. But she advocated a minimum wage that recognized and legitimated the working woman and sought to give her an adequate income."[12] Rather tellingly, Kelley was as interested in the abuse of working children as in cut-rate female labor; at issue was the moral economy of *families*. Between 1902 and 1904, Kelley helped Wald establish the New York Child Labor Committee and its national equivalent; she then served as a board member for the latter. Particularly after the death of her daughter from heart disease in 1905, she lobbied for a new federal children's commission—an idea that bore fruit by 1912, when Congress established Julia Lathrop's Children's Bureau.

Kelley's protectionist allies certainly exhibited the "consciousness of elite reformers seeking to limit the rights of parents and enlarge the rights or powers of the state"; yet, as Eileen Boris reminds us, they also manifested a "needs consciousness," always trying to improve the "material conditions of women and children."[13] Without a doubt, the idea of "social mothering," which was at the heart of the mothers' pension and factory laws Kelley so avidly supported, undergirded the modern "maternalist welfare state"—in a limited sense, the embodiment of the notion of ethical gains.[14] Kelley vigorously defended this vision of a caring polity, and with her NCL colleague Josephine Goldmark, she collected and organized the social and biological information that Boston attorney Louis Brandeis (Goldmark's brother-in-law) used in preparing his fabled "Brandeis Brief" in *Muller v. Oregon* (1908), in which the Supreme Court validated Oregon's sex-specific maximum-hours law. Addams and others thought that Kelley single-handedly had brought the plight of exploited workers to the public's attention and had persuaded at least nine legislatures to adopt protective legislation by 1913. But her efforts did not stop there. Kelley supported the Keating-Owen Child Labor Act of 1916, bewailed the Supreme Court's 1918 and 1922 decisions invalidating both the 1916 measure and a later version, moved the Sheppard-Towner Maternity and Infancy Act of 1921 through Congress, and led campaigns to support victims of industrial toxins. She also worked closely with Felix Frankfurter and others to secure a pro-protectionist "saving clause" in the ERA.

Unlike some Progressives, Kelley supported a range of liberation movements and actively combated racism; in 1909, she helped found the National Association for the Advancement of Colored People (NAACP). She also maintained a presence in socialist and antiwar groups and formally joined the Society of Friends in 1927. Yet, for all Kelley's charisma and influence, her signal victories were few. Her socialist leanings occasionally hurt her, as when a senator tarred her child labor proposals as part of an "Engels-Kelley program." Judicial unwillingness to meddle with wages, combined with powerful ties between men and the "family wage," militated against advances for working women, and the NCL was only a lobby, not a bureau with coercive powers. As protectionists lost their footing in the 1930s, Kelley's legendary rages multiplied. Frances Perkins said that her friend was "[e]xplosive, hot-tempered, determined, . . . [and] no gentle saint," but also a "terrifying opponent" possessed of "humane passion" as well as the "gift of moving speech."[15]

Kelley ultimately despaired of statutory remedies, leading drives to secure constitutional amendments for woman suffrage and against child labor. With the latter, she lost resoundingly. But adversaries carefully weighed the costs of disagreement; for instance, she damned her own "rabbit-hearted" National Child Labor Committee, dismissed labor leader Samuel Gompers as an "aged dodo," and considered the ERA a death warrant for compassionate legislation. To the bitter end, Kelley insisted that equal rights jurisprudence disregarded inequalities that were inseparable from both the employment and the marital relation; Americans would be able to invoke mantras like "equal rights" and "liberty of contract" with safety only when they had managed to place workers and employers, husbands and wives, on an equal footing. In 1921, she submitted a list of twenty difficult questions to Ohio Congressman Simeon Fess, who was slated to present the ERA in the House. Kelley's document caused Fess to change his mind. Among other things, she asked him to consider what would become of the Mann Act (which outlawed white slavery), child support, maternity legislation (including the popular Mother's Pensions adopted in many states into the 1920s), bars against female military conscription, penalties for seduction and rape, and dower rights (where they still existed). "*Why*," she asked, "should wage-earning women not be permitted to . . . get protective laws for their own health and welfare, and that of their unborn children, and to carry on labor unions . . . ? Why should their activities be subordinated to the preferences of wage-earning men"?[16]

Historians often criticize Kelley's acceptance, especially in the drive toward factory laws, of time-honored views of women's biological weakness. Yet, in so doing, Kelley was relying on the progressive social theories of her day, and her innovative linkages between female maternalism and the public interest seriously threatened laissez-faire economic doctrines, many of which gravely injured working women. Nor was Kelley interested in sending women back to the kitchen; as she explained in 1910, the "woman question" would not be resolved until Americans adopted a cooperative economy, at home and elsewhere. She sometimes echoed conservative fears about childlessness among working women and downward pressure on wages attributable to the presence of "a throng of unorganized and irregular workers." But she rejected conservative remedies. Why should women stay home in poverty? Why not *organize* the "throng," teach women to value their own labor, and elevate wages for everyone?[17]

"SAMENESS" VERSUS "DIFFERENCE"

In 1923, just as the NWP mobilized around a new ERA, NWP leader Doris Stevens and Harvard professor Alice Hamilton squared off in *Forum* magazine. The question was whether factory laws helped or hurt working women. Stevens spoke for the "equal rights" camp: "There is not a single State in the Union in which men and women live under equal protection of the law. There is not a State which does not in some respects still reflect toward women the attitude of either the old English Common Law or the Napoleonic Code. Woman is still conceived to be in subjection to, and under the control of the husband, if married, or of the male members of the family, if unmarried." Why should all women be forced to "set their pace with the weakest member of their sex"? Stevens then listed the rights that women might possess alongside men, once sex-specific legislation had been eliminated:

- Equal control of their children
- Equal control of their property
- Equal control of their earnings
- Equal right to make contracts
- Equal citizenship rights
- Equal inheritance rights
- Equal control of national, state, and local government

- Equal opportunities in schools and universities
- Equal opportunities in government service
- Equal opportunities in professions and industries
- Equal pay for equal work[18]

On the "separate but equal" side, Hamilton urged state protection of working women, in keeping with republican tradition, so that they eventually might achieve parity with men. Outlawing sex-specific legislation could only harm women by encouraging them to compete head-on in settings where, through no fault of their own, they were sure to fail, and by ignoring grave inequalities in bargaining power between employers and employees. The NWP simply did not fathom working-class life. "We are told by members of the Women's Party," she wrote, "that if we 'free' the working woman, allow her to 'compete on equal terms with men,' her industrial status will at once be raised. She is supposed now to be suffering from the handicap of laws regulating her working conditions . . . and longing to be rid of them. But such a statement could never be made by anyone familiar with labor." Until woman was able "equally to compete, to earn, to control, and to invest her money, unless in short woman's economic position is made more secure, certainly she cannot establish equality in fact"; she possessed only "the shadow of power without essential and authentic substance." If forced to compete with men to make her own bargains with employers, she would surely fail, thereby fulfilling the antifeminist prophecy.[19]

By 1923, fissures had appeared in the wall of organized feminism. The question was not whether women and children suffered injustice at work, but whether and how to put government to the task of advancing economic growth *and* the public welfare. Across the nation, activists debated the merits of legal "sameness" beyond the ballot box, especially the sex-specific protective legislation to which Kelley had given her life. As the National American Woman Suffrage Association mutated into the moderating League of Women Voters (LWV), the NWP emerged as the main champion of both sex neutrality in law codes and an ERA—steps that the LWV, the American Association of University Women, Kelley's NCL, and other groups firmly opposed. Equal rights (or, as they came to be called, "sameness") feminists thought that the sustained exercise of the right to vote, combined with workers' education, organization, and the eradication of sex distinctions in law, would eventuate in economic and political equality. As labor expert Gail Laughlin told a congressional committee in 1902, "If woman is to be protected at all, she must protect herself. She can not protect herself while the man by her side competing with her possesses a power . . . to make conditions less favorable for her than for himself, and thus obtain for himself an unfair advantage over her. This, however, is the situation to-day."

> Men, through their right of suffrage and . . . power over legislation, have the right to handicap their women competitors. Already there has been some . . . restriction on the hours and occupations of women which do not apply to men. . . . Some of the restrictions made may be for the benefit of women workers, but women should be the ones to decide what is for their benefit rather than to have it decided for them by their business rivals, whose advantage it is to further their own interests.[20]

The NWP had its work cut out for it. The legal landscape was more like a patchwork quilt than a blanket. On the positive side, in Colorado, women had been voting since 1893 and dealing in property for considerably longer. At the turn of the century, the Reform

Department of the Women's Club of Denver reported a dazzling array of rights and privileges, tantamount in many (though not all) respects to civil equality for married men and women. The compiler, Adeline Harrington, noted that marriage was a simple "civil contract," to which both parties had to agree for its continuance; grounds for divorce were numerous and woman-friendly. A wife was "joint guardian of her children, with her husband, with equal powers, rights and duties . . . with the husband"; any unmarried person of either sex could petition for "leave to adopt a minor child." Wives had formidable managerial powers. "All property," she continued, "both real and personal, of which a woman is possessed on marriage, together with all property . . . which comes to her by devise, gift or purchase after marriage, are her sole and separate property,

> and not subject to the control and disposal of her husband, or liable for his debts. She holds an absolute legal estate as if unmarried. She may bargain, sell or convey her real and personal property, sue and be sued in all matters pertaining to property, person or reputation, and her property may be taken on any execution against her; she may carry on any trade or business; perform any labor or service on her sole and separate account, and her earnings shall be her sole and separate property, and be invested in her own name. She may execute any promissory note or other instrument for direct payment of money, and if it shall be proved that the consideration thereof went to the benefit of her estate, she will be liable thereon in an action at law. . . . The husband is not liable for any debts contracted in her business. . . . The expense of the family and the education of the children are chargeable upon the property of both husband and wife, or either of them, and in relation thereto they may be sued jointly or separately.

Inequalities remained: Husbands were liable for their wives' nonbusiness debts. When a woman resided with her husband, he was assumed to be the owner of their home and personal property; she had "the burden of the proof to show title in herself." But, on the other side, any man or woman, if the "head of a family," was entitled to a "homestead . . . exempt from attachment or execution," and husbands were required to obtain their wives' consent to mortgage their homesteads.[21]

Elsewhere, campaigns to secure a rough equality for married people had been markedly less successful. In her heated 1924 exchange with the NCL's Hamilton, NWP leader Stevens capably summarized the state of affairs. In most states, she wrote, parents had been made "equal guardians of their children." But many states still denied mothers "equal rights to the earnings and services of the children." In New York, fathers were "preferred to mothers as controllers of the services, earnings, and real estate of the children." In two states, a father could "will away the custody of the child from the mother" and demand his wife's earnings. In forty states, a husband owned "the services of his wife in the home." This provision usually meant that the man could recover damages for the loss of services when his wife was injured and that a wife could not "collect for her own suffering, for in the eyes of such laws, it is not the wife who is injured, but the husband . . . through the loss of her services to him. . . . In only a third of the States is prostitution a crime for the male as well as the female."[22]

At the core of the NWP's vision was a neo-Stantonian faith in the individual's capacity for self-defense, so long as gender-specific roadblocks had been removed. But unlike the late-life Elizabeth Cady Stanton, NWP stalwarts believed that equality was a "natural" sociological condition—that inequality signaled the presence of "unnatural" corporate or regulatory forces. They thought, too, that untrammeled competition in labor markets and elsewhere benefited everyone, so long as competitors lined up as equals at the starting gate. "Equal rights" feminists therefore focused less on the plight of industrial women than on the structure and content of American law as it affected *all* citizens, lobbying for the elimination of sex-specific laws or, failing that, for their neutralization to include all working people. Time and again, NWP publicists emphasized the ways in which sex-based legal classifications constrained women and distorted the labor market. Because they aimed primarily to get law off women's backs, their objectives fit comfortably into the laissez-faire paradigm that a good many legal and social reformers were struggling to dismantle.

Kelley's friends, in contrast, saw the ballot as a vital but limited instrument of self-defense in a polity characterized by *inequality*, and sex neutrality in law codes as a positive menace to working women's well-being. What *about* the effect on a woman's body and family of a job that required standing at a loom for sixteen hours a day? How exactly did ballots equalize the power positions of a garment worker and factory owner or of union men and their unorganized female coworkers? Kelley minced few words: "So long as men cannot be mothers," she argued, "so long as legislation adequate for them can never be adequate for wage-earning women; and the cry Equality, Equality, where Nature has created Inequality, is as stupid and as deadly as the cry Peace, Peace, where there is no Peace."[23] In 1923, the LWV, in a checklist of accomplishments since adoption of the Nineteenth Amendment, expressed a keen interest in securing "specific legislation to remedy legal discriminations against women," but not omnibus statutes or amendments. "BLANKET LEGISLATION ON THESE SUBJECTS IS DISAPPROVED," it noted emphatically. Why? Because such measures caused "serious confusion in the civil law," taking from women "existing rights such as right of dower," jeopardizing laws that aided working women, and "preventing passage of beneficial legislation" in the future. The LWV particularly objected to laws akin to Wisconsin's statute of 1921, which provided that women would have "the same rights and privileges under the law as men in the exercise of suffrage, freedom of contract, choice of residence for voting purposes, jury service, holding office, holding and conveying property, care and custody of children, and in all other respects." The law commanded judges to "construe the statutes where the masculine gender is used to include the feminine gender unless such construction will deny to females the special protection and privileges which they now enjoy for their general welfare," thus preserving state protectionist legislation. But the conservation clause was not strong enough to mollify the LWV.[24]

Protectionists maintained a neo-Perfectionist faith in neighborhoods and families as primary social units. They emphasized the need to strengthen human relationships through public policy, confront the essential *inequality* of marketplace transactions, and use social scientific expertise to eradicate social disease and danger. They also put great stock in parental (including state) authority as an antidote to corruption. Thus, Kelley's friends unselfconsciously harkened back to early American communitarian and moral reform traditions, rejecting the tenets both of laissez-faire constitutionalism and of "pure" electoral democracy. One scholar rightly notes that an elite rights consciousness led them to "limit the rights of parents" and expand the powers of government. Yet, as another scholar reminds us, they also sought improvement in the "material conditions" of women and children, as well as limitations of entrepreneurial freedom.[25] Industrialists *did* jeopardize workers' health in both general and sex-specific ways; many women labored from dawn until midnight six days a week without seats or sanitary facilities. As with limitations of political speech in wartime, reformers thought that the social advantages of state intervention outweighed losses of freedom, and they knew full well that women paid a steep price for a measure of security—notably, imputations of infancy and dependence. As the University of Chicago's Ernst Freund observed in 1910, British factory laws (the model for many American statutes) had applied "only to those who were not free agents, namely to children" and to wives. The "separate and distinct" treatment of women, became "an established feature of English factory legislation" and hence of its American stepchild, and though the imputation of childlike incapacity troubled him, he supported such measures as a temporary expedient.[26]

To achieve protectionist ends, activists organized watchdog and self-help groups—among them, the influential National Woman's Trade Union League, founded in 1903 to help women organize unions; the General Federation of Women's Clubs, led by prominent settlement house workers; and Kelley's NCL, which boasted dozens of branches and affiliates nationwide. Once women had been organized as voters and laborers and their children were enrolled in school, lawmakers elected by both sexes could worry about the workers' freedom to contract for wages and hours; until then, women's health, and perhaps the future of the human race, seemed to require the assignment of a handicap to women. Law would ensure *fairness* rather than a fictitious legal equality—the latter belied whenever a worker tried to obtain a rest period. As a character named Barbara Manning explained in a 1915 play, "It isn't just to compete with men that our factories and shops are filled with women and girls. It's to earn their living and not for fun that they are there."[27]

COMPLICATIONS

Feminists also participated actively in transnational discussions of women's economic and political status. Between 1890 and 1913, economic protectionists convened six international meetings—analogous in function to American women's antebellum speech communities—in Berlin, Brussels, Zurich, Basel, Bern, and Paris. During roughly the same period, feminists who were allied with the Second Socialist International held nine global conferences, all in Europe; and between 1878 and 1914, reformers organized nineteen general International Women's Congresses—three of them in North America (Washington, D.C., in 1888; Chicago in 1893; and Toronto in 1909).

Globalization profoundly influenced American feminism. On the one hand, international gatherings worked to homogenize thinking about the sexual division of labor; Ulla Wikander's analysis of the proceedings of the International Congress shows "widespread acceptance of social conventions that assigned different jobs to men and women" and reinforcement of the idea that men and women were "different but complementary."[28] On the other hand, transnational exchange sometimes upset mainstream applecarts. Moderates hobnobbed with unionists and socialists, who insisted in various ways that patriarchal marriage, suffragism, and protectionism were cruel traps, and that neither ballots nor statutory relief got to the taproot of capitalist and patriarchal exploitation: Women worked long hours at low wages (or no wages) because ruling classes mandated such practices and because entrepreneurs had captured the legal system, not because certain husbands or employers were more wicked than others.

Radical proposals, whether international in origin or homegrown, defy pigeonholing. In the United States, writers like Charlotte Perkins Gilman and Zona Gale advocated public kitchens to improve nutrition; eliminate household drudgery; and, in Gilman's words, help working women distinguish between "sex-interest" (time-consuming attempts to please men with unhealthful food) and "self-interest" (the human need for sound nutrition and honorable work). Labor organizer Mary Harris Jones ("Mother Jones") noted with disgust that she had never required a ballot to force social change and had "no confidence" in suffragists. She wanted women to sabotage capitalism not by hiding under protectionist bushels, but by storming the mines and factories and raising children to be unionists: "I don't care about your woman suffrage and the temperance brigade or any other of your class associations, I want women of the coming day to discuss and find out the cause of child crucifixion." Emma Goldman lambasted capitalism *and* matrimony— for robbing workers of the fruits of their labor and for crippling half the sovereign people. Marriage, she wrote in 1910, "makes a parasite of woman, an absolute dependent. It incapacitates her for life's struggle, annihilates her social consciousness, paralyzes her imagination, and then imposes its gracious protection, which is in reality a snare, a travesty on human character."[29]

Women of color further complicated the picture. American Indian women labored against heavy odds, in cities and on hardscrabble reservations, to raise families and preserve their indigenous cultures. Because many American Indians (prior to blanket grants of citizenship after World War I) were classified as "wards," rather than as citizens, and because native peoples usually did not form a large part of industrial workforces, debates among urban whites about protectionism were irrelevant. In the West, Chinese women struggled to defend their culture—including such practices as concubinage—against Christian "rescuers"; moreover, into the 1930s, revolutionaries in China belittled what Peggy Pascoe calls "the steps toward individual autonomy" made by Chinese immigrants as they navigated between Chinese and American gender systems.[30] Everywhere, black women continued to battle racism as well as sexism, abandonment, and poverty. South Carolinian Mamie Garvin Fields recalled Mary Church Terrell's appeal in Charleston for black women's help: "We have our own lives to lead. . . . We must care for ourselves and rear our families, like all women. But we have more to do than other women. Those of us fortunate enough to have education must share it with the less fortunate of our race. We must go into our communities and improve them. . . . Above all, we must organize ourselves as Negro women and work together."[31]

In addition, working-class women sharply criticized middle-class romanticization of the home. Sometimes, hostility appeared in odd places—as in public discussions of sweatshops. Since the 1880s, New York reformers had been struggling without success to regulate homework in tenements that came to involve entire families. In 1885, the New York Court of Appeals had struck down an 1884 statute, adopted on health and welfare grounds, outlawing cigarmaking at home; judges could not perceive how "the cigarmaker is to be improved in his health or his morals by forcing him from his home and its hallowed associations and beneficent influences, to ply his trade elsewhere."[32] On other occasions, laborites invited state intervention in home life. Mary Kingsbury Simkhovitch of Greenwich House urged legislators to subject "the private home to public action," outlawing most home manufacture and regulating the rest—a campaign that bore fruit in 1913, when New York adopted a limited home-work statute.[33] Like Kelley, Simkhovitch thought that the future lay with blue-collar understandings of home and work, not with NAWSA's or even the more militant NWP's vision. To achieve a "real social adjustment," a new generation of working women would infuse family life with sound management principles so that it might withstand industrialization. What about the sanctity of the home? "The woman movement," Simkhovitch wrote, "has sometimes been interpreted by . . . the re-

spectable middle class as furnishing a means of dignifying leisure. Among working
women, however, it has made little headway."

> [T]he working woman in New York . . . still retains the tradition of home life as her most
> cherished sentiment, expecting to return from industry to a home of her own. And the
> very beauty and power of this old ideal obscures the fact that the home of the future must
> be strong enough to stand all the strain to which . . . it will be subjected. To stand its
> ground it needs not the negative submission of dependents, but the co-operation of strong
> independent individuals. The new working women's movement . . . will have within it
> certain sounder elements than the movement among middle-class and wealthy women.
> For in industry one learns . . . efficiency. Bringing back this business sense into the home
> and enlarging it by those spiritual enthusiasms which give a sense of roominess and free-
> dom . . . , the working woman, when once this new social adjustment has been made, will
> be a new kind of new woman in whose consciousness the destinies of home, industry and
> society will be seen as fused into one.[34]

Only a handful of labor unions aided woman's cause. Groups like the American Federation of Labor (AFL) resisted the prospect of mixed-sex memberships; women could
pursue "independence" and "self-respect" to their heart's content, but not at the expense
of male workers. Connections between statutory limitations on female workers and the
interests of unionized men were of long standing. In 1879, to give one example, President Strasser of the International Cigar Makers explained why his union supported protective legislation for women: "We cannot drive the females out of the trade," he admitted, "but we can restrict this daily quota of labor through factory laws. No girls should
be employed more than eight hours per day, all overwork should be prohibited, while married women should be kept out of factories at least six weeks before and six weeks after
confinement."[35] Three decades later, AFL leader Samuel Gompers proclaimed that laboring men could do without the "competition of the unorganized, defenseless woman
worker, the girl and the wife," who exerted downward pressure on men's wages, so that
"the combined wages of the husband and wife" too often were "reduced to the standard
of the wages earned by the father." A woman best contributed to "the support of the family" as a "beloved wife" and through "the holiness of motherhood."[36] Radicals (and, to
some extent, Theodore Roosevelt's Progressive Party) broke ranks to support women, and
by the 1920s, AFL resistance had softened appreciably. A number of other groups—such
as the glove-makers unions, the International Ladies Garment Workers Union, the Amalgamated Clothing Workers of America, and several teachers' unions—boasted dues-pay-
ing female members and officers. But as male-dominated unions gained legitimacy, they
often maintained a gender line; unionists and employers alike insisted (in Alice Kessler
Harris's words) that "women did not need incomes equal to those of men because they
could rely on families to support them. . . . For men, the wage encompassed family support; for women, it tended to incorporate only the self-support of a single person."[37]

Female workers therefore gathered in ever-larger numbers in "separate-but-equal"
unions and self-help leagues—a process given real urgency in 1910 when the Triangle
Shirtwaist fire in New York City, on the heels of a thirteen-week strike in the dead of
winter, claimed dozens of lives, underscoring women's vulnerability to bad working conditions without powerful unions. Settlement worker and Women's Department editor Alice Henry called the strike and subsequent fire "an awakening for working women in many
industries" as well as for middle-class professionals, who finally saw "the necessity for
organization among working women." By the 1920s, it was common enough for the LWV

and other relatively cautious groups to assert the need to unionize industrial women. As Mollie Ray Carroll, an economics professor at Goucher College and an officer of the LWV's Women in Industry Committee, explained in 1923: "The labor movement has gradually attracted a large body of woman workers because of the obvious benefits it offers them. . . . The idea that woman's place is in the home has had a marked effect upon the industrial progress and organization of women workers. Since her sphere has been deemed the home, [woman] has been considered a casual amateur, temporarily occupied. It has not seemed worth while to remedy her wages or conditions of pay. . . . Men workers have only too readily accepted women's own estimation of their positions." Men saw women as "cheap, casual, temporary laborers competing for their jobs" and so resisted their admission into "the already successful men's unions."[38]

THE PROTECTIONIST HEYDAY

From an early moment, protectionism held sway in most state legislatures and state appellate courts. Helen Sumner, the main engine behind the nineteen-volume *Women and Child Wage-Earners in the United States* (1908–11) that led by 1920 to the creation of the Women's Bureau within the U.S. Department of Labor, mounted a critique of what she called an incomplete "industrial readjustment" linked to changes in women's work. "The history of women in industry," she wrote in 1910, "is . . . the story of the transfer of women workers from the home to the factory, from labor in harmony with their deepest ambitions to monotonous, nerve-racking work. . . . It is a story of long hours, overwork, unwholesome conditions of life and labor and miserably low wages. It is a story of the underbidding of men bread winners by women, who have been driven by dire necessity . . . or by the sense of ultimate dependence upon some man . . . to offer their services upon the bargain counter of the labor market." But all was not lost; in certain industries, she added, reform had improved working conditions for everyone. Industrial evils had been ameliorated with factory laws—the "only force" capable of saving lives and families.[39]

The idea that dependent classes ought to be protected from harm was anything but novel. According to Linda Gordon and Ellen DuBois, economic protectionism followed logically from first-wave preoccupations with danger, whether from sexual predators in cities, plantation masters, or tyrannical husbands. In legal circles, the impulse in its Progressive form harmonized with earlier sex-specific rules, not only in *Bradwell* and other notorious federal cases, but also in ordinary divorce, custody, and breach-of-promise suits. It is telling but not surprising that Washington legislators, having scaled back women's political and civil rights in 1885–86, adopted a protective hours law after statehood. In 1912, moreover, Justice Crow of the Washington Supreme Court affirmed in *State of Washington v. Somerville*—a suit brought by Henrietta Somerville, the owner of a box factory, to test the constitutionality of the statute—that women in their new relation to paternal government were "minors" requiring "especial care" so that their "rights may be preserved," albeit "not [minors] to the same extent" as children.[40] By 1908, nineteen states had banned night work or established maximum hours for women. Massachusetts adopted the nation's first minimum wage law in 1912; within eight years, fourteen other states had done the same thing.

Courtroom battles over industrial protection were fierce. In 1895, the Illinois high court sat on the case of *Ritchie v. People of Illinois*, which challenged that state's sex-specific hours law, threatening one of the results of Kelley's research. Section 5 provided that no woman could be employed "in any factory or workshop more than eight hours in any one day or forty-eight hours in any one week." Justice Magruder ruled that the law denied equal protection of law and the right to contract freely. It arbitrarily restrained only women in the garment industry; those employed "as saleswomen in stores, or as domestic servants, or as book-keepers . . . are at liberty to contract for as many hours of labor in a day as they choose." State and federal constitutions disallowed a "purely arbitrary restriction upon the fundamental right of the citizen to control his or her own time and faculties." In Magruder's view, liberty included "the right to make contracts, as well with reference to the amount and duration of labor . . . as concerning any other lawful matter. Hence, the right to make contracts is an inherent and inalienable one, and any attempt to unreasonably abridge it is opposed to the constitution." The legal classification existed solely "to protect woman on account of her sex and physique," even though statutes passed in 1872 and 1874 had eliminated the unitary family head and with it, the notion of female dependence:

> As a citizen, woman has the right to acquire and possess property of every kind. As a "person," she has the right to claim the benefit of the constitutional provision that she shall not be deprived of life, liberty or property without due process of law. Involved in these rights . . . is the right to make and enforce contracts. The law accords to her, as to every other citizen, the natural right to gain a livelihood by intelligence, honesty and industry in the arts, the sciences, the professions or other vocations. Before the law, her right to a choice of vocations cannot be said to be denied or abridged on account of sex.[41]

Nevertheless, in *Holden v. Hardy* (1898)—a year after it formally added the liberty of contract doctrine to its constitutional arsenal in *Allgeyer v. Louisiana*—the U.S. Supreme Court affirmed the constitutionality of an 1896 Utah statute that regulated the hours of underground miners and smelters, on the ground that mining entailed serious danger. The court did not question the fact that the same law outlawed the hiring of women and children for work in "any mine or smelter" in the state on the same health and welfare ground.[42] In his January 1915 decisions in *Bosley v. McLaughlin* and a companion suit, Justice Oliver Wendell Holmes upheld a California law limiting the hours of female pharmacists and nurses working in hospitals, calling it reasonable that legislators would make an exception of "graduate nurses," required on all shifts to keep hospitals running. A few days later, Justice Hughes decided in *Miller v. Wilson* that the same state's 1911 eight-hour statute created classifications based on the type of business, rather than the type of work, for employers' convenience and other reasonable purposes. Thus, women could be permitted to work long hours in canneries, where seasonality determined the workday, but not in hotels.[43]

State courts mostly upheld sex-specific hours laws. To be sure, in 1907, New York appellate judges contended in *People v. Williams* that an "adult woman is not be regarded as a ward of the state, or in any other light than the man is regarded, when the question is related to the business, pursuit or calling." She was "entitled to enjoy unmolested her liberty of person and her freedom to work for whom she pleases, where she pleases, and as long as she pleases. . . . She is not to be made the special object of the paternal power of the state." But this was an exception. Melvin Urofsky clearly shows that, except where unions lurked in the wings, state courts mostly embraced economic protection, in keeping with "the best common-law tradition, attempting to meet the new social and economic conditions of the country." Massachusetts judges accepted an hours law for women and children in 1876 and again in 1895; so did those in Pennsylvania, Nebraska, and Washington in 1902.[44]

Still, laissez-faire constitutionalism exercised great power. In 1905, in one of the U.S. Supreme Court's most consequential rulings, justices threw out New York's hours law of 1897 as violative of the Fourteenth Amendment. *Lochner v. New York*—the first case in which the Court used the doctrine of substantive due process to strike down a protectionist law—tested whether the statute (which prohibited work in excess of sixty hours per week) applied to male bakers. State courts had approved of the act on three separate occasions, but the Court balked. This was not a health law, wrote Justice Rufus Peckham, but an "illegal interference with the rights of individuals, both employers and employees, to make contracts regarding labor upon such terms as they may think best." Legislators had assumed the role of "supervisor or *pater familias*, over every act of the individual," crippling the "ability of the laborer to support himself and his family."[45]

In dissent, Justice Holmes pointed out that a "large part of the country" entertained a different idea about the laissez-faire assumptions at the heart of *Lochner*. A constitution, he said famously, was "not intended to embody a particular economic theory, whether of paternalism and the organic relation of the citizen to the State or of *laissez faire*." Rather, it was "made for people of fundamentally differing views." Also in dissent, Justice Harlan pointed out that bakers' work was known to be "among the hardest and most laborious imaginable" and that sixty-hour weeks affected their health. He noted, too, that the law reflected the common belief that employers and bakers were "not upon an equal footing." But, in the end, male bakers' right to bargain freely and to inhale as much flour as they chose joined *Ritchie* and *Allgeyer* in the growing body of Fourteenth Amendment jurisprudence devoted to preserving the right to contract for employment without interference. In effect, the Court concluded that the public did not have an interest in regulating that relationship or the health of men laboring in bakeshops—even though many of them were actual or prospective fathers.[46]

Three years later, however, the Supreme Court admitted the concept of sex-specific economic protection into federal practice, in the process asserting a public interest in regulating the employment relations of women (assumed to be mothers or would-be mothers). Writing for the majority in *Muller v. Oregon* (1908), Justice Brewer affirmed the constitutionality of an Oregon law that barred women from working in laundries for more than ten hours a day. Several state courts had decided, well before *Muller*, that the rule in *Lochner* applied to men and need not prevent the adoption of hours laws for women. Indeed, the "liberty of contract" fiction always had presupposed male rather than mixed-sex competition in the labor market. Ordinarily, *Lochner* would have controlled in *Muller*; William Fenton, the attorney for Portland hand-laundry owner Kurt Muller, certainly thought that it should. "Women, equally with men, are endowed with the fundamental and inalienable rights of liberty and property," he argued, "and these rights cannot be impaired or destroyed by legislative action under the pretense of exercising the police power of the State. Difference in sex alone does not justify the destruction or impairment of these rights" unless the "public health, safety or welfare is involved." The court disagreed, refusing to assume, as in the bakers' case, that "the difference between the sexes does not justify a different rule."[47]

In support of the protectionist view, Kelley and Goldmark had amassed what the Court called "copious" evidence of women's susceptibility to workplace hazards, which Brandeis presented to the court in *Muller*. The Brandeis Brief included European and

American testimony about likely damage to women and their progeny. Massachusetts labor bureau experts had concluded in 1875 that "the back . . . gives out. Girls cannot work more than eight hours, and keep it up." Women suffered from "general female weakness" and watery muscles; nursing mothers laboring for long hours supposedly provided milk "unfit for a child's nourishment," causing "spasmodic diarrhea, . . . convulsions and . . . death." A French expert reported that women "employed in the manufacture of tobacco and of matches are subject to gastric, intestinal troubles, and affections of the respiratory tract, necrosis of the jaw, and are liable to miscarriage." Female workers in paper factories were "liable to smallpox or carbuncle." British scientists attributed nervous disorders to "over-action." Others explained that a woman's knee was a fragile "sexual organ" damaged by standing and urged states to heed the "close relationship which exists between the health of its women citizens and the physical vigor of future generations." Women would "unfit themselves by excessive hours of work . . . for the burden of motherhood which each of them should be able to assume"; states should defend "the physical well-being of the community by setting a limit to the exploitation of the improvident, unworkmanlike, unorganized women" who would become the mothers of the "coming generation."[48]

The brief had its effect: The Supreme Court decided that the public had a compelling interest in maintaining women's (a term more or less synonymous with "mothers'") health and welfare. Justice Brewer referred to a factory inspector's report listing the "physical organization of women," their "maternal functions," the "rearing and education of the children," and "the maintenance of the home" as reasonable grounds for interposing state power. Surely, women's bodies and maternal obligations placed the sex "at a disadvantage in the struggle for subsistence," especially when "the burdens of motherhood are upon her. Even when they are not, by abundant testimony of the medical fraternity continuance for a long time on her feet at work . . . tends to [have] injurious effects upon the body, and as healthy mothers are essential to vigorous offspring, the physical well-being of woman becomes an object of public interest and care to preserve the strength and vigor of the race." The court noted, too, that woman had "always been dependent upon man." Despite advances, the sex was "not yet upon an equality."[49]

Muller represented a signal victory for protectionists and, in a curious way, for laissez-faire theorists as well. By taking Kelley's suggestion and constructing maternity as an activity imbued with a "public interest," courts could regulate maternity without disavowing their attachment to a free market in masculine labor. The NCL and other groups promptly mounted what William Chafe calls a "national crusade to place a floor under women's wages as well as a ceiling over their hours."[50] In 1916, it should be noted, neither Kelley nor her allies pitched arguments in old common law terms—that is, as a matter of married women's legal dependence; rather, judges translated the "ethical gains" argument into retrogressive legal language when they were confronted with particular cases. In a 1916 NCL pamphlet, Kelley listed five "advantages" to hours legislation, only one of which called to mind "women's work," and none of which invoked the law of coverture:

1. Where the working day is short, the workers are less predisposed to diseases arising from fatigue. They are correspondingly less in danger of being out of work, for sickness is in turn one of the great causes of unemployment.

2. Accidents have diminished conspicuously wherever working hours have been reduced.

3. They have better opportunity for continuing their education out of working hours. Where they do this intelligently they become more valuable. . . .

4. A short working day established by law tends automatically to regularize work. The interest of the employer is to have all hands continuously active, and no one sitting idly waiting for needles, or thread, or materials. . . .

5. For married women wage-earners it is especially necessary to have the working day short and work regular. For when they leave their workplace it is to cook, sew, and clean at home, sometimes even to care for the sick.[51]

Between 1908 and 1917, while some state courts adhered to *Lochner*, others sustained hours laws, sometimes for the benefit of both sexes. The NCL circulated its potent brief to lawyers around the country, prompting Felix Frankfurter to say in 1953 that Kelley "had probably the single largest share in shaping the social history of the United States during the first thirty years of this century."[52] On several occasions—as in the Ohio case of *Ex Parte Anna Hawley* (1911) and in the 1915 Supreme Court hearings of *Miller v. Wilson* and *Bosley v. McLaughlin*—Brandeis again participated in arguing the cases and preparing the briefs. Partly in response to such a brief, the Illinois Supreme Court in *Ritchie and Company v. Wayman* upheld a 1909 minimum wage law; to avoid formally reversing its decision in *Ritchie v. Illinois*, the court drew strained lines between the plight of 750 female paper factory workers in 1909 and the industry's condition in 1895. And in another chapter in Oregon's protectionist drama, the state supreme court, officially noting a 207-page Brandeis-Goldmark appendix, ruled in *State v. Bunting* and *Stettler v. O'Hara* (both 1914) that the state's hours and wage legislation passed constitutional muster. Legislative commissioners had outlawed the employment of female (and certain male) factory workers for more than ten hours a day unless employers agreed to pay as much as three hours' overtime daily; later, they mandated nine-hour workdays in Portland factories, extended lunch breaks, and wages of at least $8.64 per week for women. Both Stetler and Bunting refused to comply, arguing that the rules interfered with their right to bargain freely with workers.

In *Bunting v. Oregon* (1917), an appeal of *State v. Bunting*, the U.S. Supreme Court affirmed the state's judgments. Brandeis and Goldmark, with Frankfurter as lead counsel, submitted a two-volume amicus brief and appendix with over 1,000 pages of factual information documenting the harmful effects of long hours for all workers. For a slim majority, Justice McKenna upheld the Oregon law, refusing to question legislative reasoning even though the law affected male and female workers; it was sufficient that it fell within the boundaries of "an admitted power of government." Although he later changed his mind on the point, Frankfurter optimistically predicted on the eve of *Bunting* that, in time, the "whole problem" of factory laws would be seen in a different light; Americans would stop viewing "the regulation of women in industry as exceptional, as the law's graciousness to a disabled class," and begin viewing it as the regulation of "*industry* and the relation of industry to the community."[53]

Mythic images of ideal men, it should be noted, were as tenacious as stereotypes of women. Courts, for instance, used gender norms to penalize Asian men for being unmanly. In Montana, legislation required Chinese laundries to be licensed. In *Quong Wing v. Kirkendall* (1912), the Supreme Court decided that it was reasonable to impose special licensing fees on men who did women's work. Hand laundry was a "widespread occupation of Chinamen in this Country while on the other hand it is so rare to see men of our race engaged in it that many of us would be unable to say that they had ever observed a case." Justice Holmes thought that if legislators could "put a lighter burden upon women than men," they could burden Asian men who did work "commonly regard[ed] as more appropriate" for women. The Fourteenth Amendment did not require the court to impose a "fictitious equality where there is a real difference."[54]

THE ERA TUG-OF-WAR

After the adoption of the Nineteenth Amendment and long months of reorganization, the NWP mobilized to achieve (as historian Susan Becker puts it) "complete legal equality between men and women." In the process, the party allied itself firmly with free-market Republicans, so that social welfare worker Ida Tarbell could describe an ERA supporter as someone engaged in "Making a Man of Herself."[55] Particularly after the NWP's 1921 convention, Doris Stevens, Alice Paul, Mrs. O. H. P. Belmont (the party's major funder), and other party stalwarts single-mindedly championed the ERA and two international instruments, the Equal Rights Treaty (a global equivalent of ERA) and the narrower Equal Nationality Treaty (which emphasized citizenship rights). Indeed, the 1921 convention and subsequent NWP policy decisions persuaded many women to go their own ways—among them, the radical peace activist Crystal Eastman, who found NWP's rhetoric too polite and implicitly racist, and Kelley, who distrusted Paul's promises to conserve factory laws in otherwise sweeping demands for equality.

By 1922, ruptures had developed between NWP libertarians, protectionists like Kelley, liberals, and left feminists. These differences could be seen clearly in the increasingly frantic attempt to find acceptable language for use in a draft of the ERA. At least thirty-five versions of a proposed ERA moved back and forth among NWP leaders (especially Paul) and Kelley, the Harvard Law School's Roscoe Pound, Frankfurter, and other experts in a fated struggle to achieve agreement. Over a two-year period, Paul increasingly embraced the tenets of laissez-faire constitutionalism; for her part, Kelley began to couch her sense of a link between women's health and the public interest in language familiar to lawyers—that is, in the time-honored language of coverture. As the debate continued, the draft ERA changed remarkably. By 1923, an early focus on married women, as well as various "saving clauses" designed to preserve the NCL's factory laws, had vanished. As Joan Zimmerman demonstrates, negotiation steadily drove the two sides apart, cloaked arguments in wholly incompatible legal language, and severed ERA supporters from elements of their own history.

A few examples make the point. The first substantive section of a July 1921 version (based on the Thirteenth Amendment prohibition of involuntary servitude) provided, "Neither political nor legal disabilities on account of sex or coverture shall exist within the United States or any place subject to its jurisdiction." By autumn of 1921, after laborious negotiations, Paul had abandoned the "saving clause" but not the married woman: "No political, civil or legal disabilities or inequalities on account of sex, or on account of marriage unless applying alike to both sexes, shall exist within the United States." A year later, married women as a class had disappeared; the draft said simply, "No distinction between the rights of the sexes shall exist within the United States." In 1923, just as Paul finished law school, she wrote a final version of the amendment without further consultation, hitching the ERA's wagon to equal rights jurisprudence: "Men and women shall have Equal Rights throughout the United States and every place subject to its jurisdiction." The NWP approved this version at its 1923 convocation at Seneca Falls; in the same year, Senate whip Charles Curtis and Representative Daniel Anthony (a nephew of Susan B.) introduced it into Congress. Paul counseled against a state-by-state approach, warning Seneca Falls delegates that they would "not be safe, until the principle of equal rights is written into the framework of our [federal] government." She also confirmed social feminists' fears: The measure applied to women working in factories as surely as to other citizens.[56]

Kelley was livid: Was not the "proposed amendment somewhat like a great army tank sent out to crack walnuts"? ERA was "cunningly framed," she argued as early as 1921, "to attract women voters unacquainted alike with the intricacies of constitutional law and the daily experience of their wage earning sisters. It appears to the uninitiated to carry forward the process begun in the Nineteenth Amendment, and to contribute towards establishing more perfect equality between men and women. How misleading this appearance is." Many labor and civil rights groups agreed. The National Federation of Business and Professional Women's Clubs refrained from openly criticizing the amendment. But in January 1923, the *New York Times* listed a myriad of organizations that were standing firm against ERA, among them, the LWV, the NCL, "the Women's Trade Union League, the Charity Organization Society, the Girls' Friendly Society, the National Council of Catholic Women, the Council of Jewish Women, the National Association for Labor Legislation, the Women's Christian Temperance Union, the American Association for Organizing Family Social Work, the National League of Girls' Clubs, the Parent Teachers' Association, the National Federation of Federal Employees, and the National Congress of Mothers." Other opponents included the AAUW, the ACLU, the General Federation of Women's Clubs, the YWCA, and the AFL.[57]

A no-holds-barred debate in 1920 between journalist Marguerite Mooers Marshall and labor activist Rose Schneiderman, printed in the journal *Life and Labor*, set the two camps in sharp relief. Marshall chided the National Women's Trade Union League for adopting what she termed "the typical anti-suffragist, anti-feminist attitude—i.e., that women must 'be protected,' that they must 'shrink' from meeting men on the level ground of equality, that the dear, delicate creatures must be 'shielded against themselves, if necessary, for their own welfare and that of the race.'" At issue was an amendment eliminating exceptions (including one for female journalists) to New York's 1919 night work law, which outlawed women's wage labor after ten o'clock. Marshall condemned the "unfair, old-fashioned, and distinctly short-sighted advocacy of special privilege for self-supporting women," which would only give "new life" to the idea that "a newspaper office is no place for women." Schneiderman, in turn, damned Marshall as a "strong individualist" unfamiliar with working-class life and a "highly paid professional women" unqualified to speak for laborers. Marshall erred especially in thinking that "there is a career in industry or in the department store. Those of us who have worked in the factory or store know that there is only room for one at the top and the rest must struggle along until they get married or die." The average laborer did "not want a factory career, as there is no such thing. She is looking forward to getting married and raising a family."[58]

The U.S. Supreme Court ruling in *Adkins v. Children's Hospital* (1923) provided an occasion for even sharper disagreement. *Adkins* and a companion case, *Adkins v. Lyons*, originated in four suits brought in the Supreme Court of the District of Columbia in 1920 to test the constitutionality of a 1918 federal law designed to protect women and children in the district from "conditions detrimental to their health and morals" by establishing a minimum wage and ensuring "decent standards of living." By implication, these suits also challenged minimum wage laws in thirteen states, many of which submitted amicus briefs in support of wage regulation. The suits pitted Jesse Adkins and other members of the District of Columbia minimum wage board against the directors of Children's Hospital and assorted workers at the hospital and elsewhere. *Adkins v. Lyons* featured Willie Lyons, a young woman employed by the Congress Hall Hotel Company as an elevator operator for $35 per month and "two meals a day." Lyons supposedly found her work "light and healthful, the hours short, with surroundings clean and moral," and was "anxious to continue it for the compensation she was receiving." Yet the hotel had fired her, allegedly because the board's wage requirements and penalties made her an expensive luxury. Lyons's wages were said to be "the best she was able to obtain for any work she was capable of performing and the enforcement of the order . . . deprived her of such employment and wages." She could "not secure any other position at which she could make a living, with as good physical and moral surroundings, and earn as good wages." A minimum wage meant no job at all—and, in the eyes of the Court, that was unfair.[59]

The *Adkins* suits challenged the main weapons in the Progressive arsenal, as well as the twin notions, deeply embedded in reform culture, that women required state protection outside the home and that substandard wages by definition exploited workers. As in *Muller*, Brandeis (now a member of the Court) had collaborated at an earlier moment with Frankfurter, Goldmark, and Mary Dewson (secretary of the NCL) on a 1,000-page statistical brief submitted to the Court on the District's side. The hospital's lawyers conceded the fact of working-class poverty, but denied employers' responsibility for ameliorating it and termed the wage law an unconstitutional interference with the "freedom of contract" supposedly embedded in the due process clause of the Fifth Amendment. The battle raging beyond the courtroom between "equal rights" feminists and protectionists had its effect. Counsel pointed to Carrie Chapman Catt's statement that "every human being who is obliged to earn his or her living" ought to have "absolute freedom to find any employment which seems suitable and profitable, without discrimination or restrictions of any kind." They noted, too, that the NWP called for "equality between men and women in . . . laws affecting the position of women in industry, as well as other laws." The statute, they argued, was an unconstitutional "price-fixing law, directly interfering with freedom of contract, which is a part of the liberty of the citizen," in a "private business, not affected with a public interest, and as a permanent measure." It was also an unconstitutional "taking" of property without due process and "not even for a public purpose." On the other side, Frankfurter pointed to the Court's own rulings in *Muller* and elsewhere, and pronounced the hospital's position "wholly at variance with the decisions of this Court in numerous cases." The state *was* deeply interested in protecting the health of women; because an employer received "the benefit of the woman's working energy . . . , he ought to pay for its cost."[60]

In the end, with Justices Taft, Sanford, and Holmes dissenting and Justice Brandeis recused, a bare majority ruled that wage laws disrupted labor market competition. The court generally ignored the question of whether women *could* strike up fair bargains without state assistance, setting itself against state legislatures as well as much of the voting public (wage and hour laws for women and children were widely popular). Interestingly, Justice Sutherland referred to what antebellum activists had called a "right to action"; in his view, federal lawmakers had dictated "what will be necessary to provide a living for a woman, keep her in health and preserve her morals." The contested statute applied to "any and every occupation in the District, without regard to its nature or the character of the work. . . . To sustain the individual freedom of action . . . is not to strike down the common good but to exalt it; for surely the good of society as a whole cannot be better served than by the preservation against arbitrary restraint of the liberties of its constituent members."[61]

Sutherland understood that the Kelley-Frankfurter position, endorsed by virtually every major architect of sociological jurisprudence, posed a serious threat to laissez-faire doctrine. He therefore portrayed ratification of the Nineteenth Amendment as a radical event, termed the Court's contrary rule in *Muller v. Oregon* obsolete, and declared women the competitive equals of men in the marketplace. In view of "the great—not to say revolutionary—changes which have taken place since [*Muller*] in the . . . status of women, culminating in the Nineteenth Amendment," he wrote, "it is not unreasonable to say that . . . differences have now come almost, if not quite, to the vanishing point." Women no longer needed state assistance with wages—although, he added, legislators properly reserved the right to intervene in other areas. While "physical differences must be recognized in appropriate cases,"

> and legislation fixing hours or conditions of work may properly take them into account, we cannot accept the doctrine that women of mature age . . . may be subjected to restrictions upon their liberty of contract which could not lawfully be imposed in the case of men. . . . To do so would be to ignore all the implications to be drawn from the present-day trend of legislation as well as that of common thought . . . , by which woman is accorded emancipation from the old doctrine that she must be given special protection or be subjected to special restraint.

Sutherland objected most strenuously to the demand that an employer pay a living wage. Such a wage would reflect not the value of the service rendered, but the "extraneous circumstance that the employee needs to get a prescribed sum of money to insure her subsistence." Nodding to Kelley's idea, Sutherland conceded the "ethical right of every worker . . . to a living wage," but objected to governmental coercion and to the assumption that employers were "bound at all events to furnish it." Securing a good wage was one of the "purposes of trade organizations."[62]

Political cartoonists had a field day. One depicted Sutherland handing a sheet of paper (headed "Minimum wage decision") to a well-dressed "Woman Wage Worker" and saying, "This decision, madam, affirms your constitutional right to starve."[63] The dissenters also understood that the ruling had little to do with support for "sameness" feminism. Justice Holmes chastised the majority for allowing fads in economic theory to erode the rule of *stare decisis*, adding that it would take "more than the Nineteenth Amendment to convince me that there are no differences between men and women, or that legislation cannot take those differences into account." Justice Taft thought that *Lochner* had been overruled silently by *Bunting*, that *Muller* should have controlled in *Adkins*, and that the woman suffrage "revolution" had been limited. Certainly, it had not altered "the physical strength or limitations of women" as they bore on economic life. It gave women "political power," ensuring that "legislative provisions for their protection will be in accord with their interests as they see them." But courts were not "warranted in varying constitutional construction based on physical differences between men and women, because of the Amendment."[64]

Adkins did not help women any more than *Muller* had. Enfranchised women were not transformed into men's equals in the workplace. After *Muller*, the disgusted laundry owner replaced women with a Chinese crew and then with "deaf and dumb" workers.

Hours limitations, in other words, led directly to unemployment. The effect of *Adkins*, as Judith Baer observes, was to aid women in industries where they already enjoyed considerable bargaining power and to hurt them in occupations where they were poorly represented or absent. Despite Justice Sutherland's declaration that the sexes stood on the same economic ground, women continued to encounter an array of impediments to employment in many male-centric professions. In the 1930s, Emily Newell Blair observed that although thousands of women worked in the business world, men still dominated the field. With "rare exceptions," women were "underlings"; men occupied "positions that decide policies of any importance," while women labored "only as assistants or secretaries," playing the part of "servants, not equals."[65] In law enforcement, women boasted their own organization, the International Association of Policewomen, from 1915 to the mid-1930s. In 1910, Alice Stebbins Wells of Los Angeles became the first female police officer with arrest powers; eight years later, over 200 cities had hired policewomen. But the numbers increased slowly. By 1949, only 1,000 women worked as officers in American police departments, and then mostly as clerical workers, jail matrons, or juvenile workers. An Ohio deputy chief reported that, well into modern times, the "average male officer considered women in policing a fad and their entry an unjustified excursion" into an overwhelmingly male profession. In 1961, Lois Lundell Higgins, a police officer and president of the revived and renamed International Association of Women Police, noted in a handbook: "Both men and women police officers . . . have their proper roles and it is most obvious that routine police work is principally a man's job. . . . The idea that policewomen are social workers is still widely held."[66]

Similarly, women lawyers and law students continued to meet with obstacles in courtrooms, classrooms, and elsewhere. In the 1870s, for example, two women apparently were refused admission to the Harvard Law School; the reason "privately assigned" was that it was "not considered practicable to admit young men and women to the Law Library at the same time" and "not considered fair to admit to the Law School without giving the privileges of the Library." Fifteen years later, the *Chicago Law Times* noted that Harvard had "not yet found any way to get around or over this mountain of difficulty";[67] as it turned out, the problem confounded the law school until 1950. In an early experience at the bar, California's first woman lawyer, Clara Shortridge Foltz, listened aghast as the district attorney tried to discredit her in his address to the jury: "She is a WOMAN, she cannot be expected to reason; God Almighty decreed her limitations. . . . [T]his young woman will lead you by her sympathetic presentation of this case to violate your oaths and let a guilty man go free." Outraged, Foltz demolished the state's case and won, but the experience was devastating. And, as Supreme Court Justice Ruth Bader Ginsburg reminded an audience in 1981, her alma mater, Columbia Law School, refused to admit women until 1927, partly on the ground that the "choicer, more manly and red-blooded graduates of our great universities would turn away from Columbia and rush off to the Harvard Law School."[68]

Moreover, despite confident judicial assertions of female equality in economic transactions, observers of the industrial labor scene thought otherwise. In 1900, the division of labor into "men's work" and "women's work" that had been apparent since the first third of the nineteenth century was largely intact. The vast majority of salaried women congregated in a handful of occupations, most of them related in some way to women's presumptively maternal or sentimental nature; as in the 1830s, women's work supposedly required "nimble fingers, patience, endurance, and delicacy," whereas men's work called to mind "muscular strength, speed, and skill." Critics of protectionism hastened to point

mechanistic, rights-centered approach more consonant with legal formalism (including "equal rights" theory) than with sociological jurisprudence and the American reform tradition.[75] For whatever reasons, by 1935–37, federal and state lawmakers were steadily constructing a sex-neutral "safety net" and partially dismantling old connections among free labor, liberty of contract, and masculinity. These developments, in turn, lent support to feminism's "equal rights" camp and eventually facilitated the building of a bridge between ERA supporters and anti-ERA liberals.

On the "woman question," New Dealers were oddly constrained. Three factors contributed to this arm's-length treatment. First, women's rights clearly took a backseat to economic recovery and mobilization against fascism. To be sure, Franklin Delano Roosevelt took on Frances Perkins and a number of other female advisers; in 1934, he nominated the first female Article III federal judge, Florence Ellinwood Allen of the Ohio Supreme Court, who was eventually confirmed as judge of the Sixth Circuit Court of Appeals. But feminists waited until 1949 for another woman, Judge Burnita Shelton Matthews, to be seated on a federal bench.

Second, social welfare experts increasingly contended that sex neutrality would improve the lot of *all* Americans; by 1936, state paternalism was a flourishing enterprise, epitomized by passage of the landmark National Labor Relations Act, which posited the essential *inequality* of all parties to labor contracts and established federal superintendence of employment relations. In factory legislation, sex distinctions mostly vanished; in the place of *male* and *female* were *workers* and *employers*. In 1933, New Dealers proposed the nation's first sex-neutral program to secure minimum wages and maximum hours for industrial workers. The National Industrial Recovery Act (referred to as both NIRA and NRA) set out standards of fair competition and established boards within industries that were charged with drafting wage and hour codes for themselves. Because NRA required separate codes for each industry, it tended to reinforce race, gender, and class divisions in the workforce: Industries that employed mostly women and had paid their workers relatively less than men earned in other industries were not forced to increase wages to meet a national standard. The object was not to remake capitalism, but to forge an alliance between entrepreneurs and federal officials to increase employment, eliminate unfair pricing and wage practices, and allow capitalists to volunteer for service in Roosevelt's peacetime "army."

After the Supreme Court decimated sections of NRA, sex-neutral conceptions of industrial democracy rapidly gained ground—in the Walsh-Healy Public Contracts Act (1936), which required an eight-hour workday, overtime pay, and the abolition of child labor in all government contracts in excess of $10,000, and two years later, in the hotly contested Fair Labor Standards Act (FLSA), which equalized wages in certain classes of work (not all) without reference to sex. The Supreme Court seemed to be inviting these moves—as when it suggested in *Morehead v. New York ex rel Tipaldo* (1936) that although New York's sex-specific minimum wage law violated "liberty of contract," a sex-neutral measure might pass muster. "While men are left free to fix their wages by agreement with employers," wrote the majority, "it would be fanciful to suppose that the regulation of women's wages would be useful to prevent or lessen the evils . . . listed in the . . . act. Men in need of work are as likely as women to accept the low wages offered by unscrupulous employers."[76] At the same time, trade organizations like the Congress of Industrial Organizations (CIO), the Amalgamated Clothing Workers of America, and the Ladies' Garment Worker Union grew dramatically, partly in response to New Deal policies. In *U.S. v. Darby* (1941), the U.S. Supreme Court embraced sex-neutral public regulation of the terms of labor contracts; their constitutionality was "no longer open to question." Laissez-faire assumptions were conspicuously absent; now, judges assumed the *inequality* of parties to labor agreements and marshaled state power on the side of the weaker, whether male or female.[77]

Third, and no less important, post-World War I feminism lacked the organizational and ideological power to oppose these developments. As Nancy Cott points out, as early as 1926, *Survey* (a leading reform magazine) noted the curious disappearance of prewar radicalism; to a great extent, the radical strands of the women's movement had been forgotten in a rush to embrace its apparent success. By presenting feminism as a historically situated response to an industrial "readjustment" and pegging it to certain policy changes (wage and hour legislation), women like Kelley effectively put themselves out of business for those who believed that the "adjustment" had been made or that the New Deal's supposedly sex-neutral safety net had improved upon the notion of state paternalism by extending it to both sexes. As the NWP's Ida Clyde Clarke explained in 1929, "The modern feminist does not assert her equality with men, she assumes it, and proceeds accordingly" as a "well-rounded, perfectly balanced, thoroughly informed and highly intelligent person." The mother-worker could "manage her home" *and* "hold a job" without further ado.[78]

POSTWAR INDIRECTION

During and after World War II, many reformers continued to say that bargaining power varied by sex and that the Roosevelt administration had simply institutionalized sexist practices under the guise of equality. But, well into modern times, Congress repeatedly amended the FLSA to include a minimum wage for all adults; courts accepted the result, rejecting attempts to reintroduce gender-specific wage and hour distinctions unless they were related directly to a product or business interest; and liberal feminists generally applauded. In 1942, Helen Elizabeth Brown, president of the Women's Bar Association of Baltimore, pointed to the heart of *Darby*—the idea that a law was not objectionable if it "applies alike to both men and women"—and marveled that such a statement had been "made at all." Although women had "repeatedly been read out of the United States Constitution by judicial decree," they now had "gained equal working rights . . . through definite legislation which the courts have been unable to . . . misinterpret."[79]

Given the Supreme Court's "zigzag course,"[80] however, Brown urged vigilance, and her fears were well founded. In 1948, the Court heard arguments in *Goesaert v. Cleary*, which challenged the constitutionality of a Michigan law forbidding any woman to be a bartender unless she was "the wife or daughter of the male owner" of a licensed saloon. The plaintiffs contested the statute on Fourteenth Amendment grounds. Why could women take low-paying waitress positions without being related to a saloon owner, but not work as better-paid bartenders? How did carrying drinks differ from dispensing drinks? Justice Frankfurter found the subject "beguiling" ("We meet the alewife, sprightly and ribald, in Shakespeare") but made quick work of it. What could be more self-evident than the state's power to protect women and children from the liquor trade? "The Fourteenth Amendment," he wrote, "did not tear history up by the roots, and the regulation of the liquor traffic is one of the oldest . . . of legislative powers." Nothing prevented the states from forbidding "all women from working behind a bar"—not even the "vast changes in the social and legal position of women. The fact that women . . . now indulge in vices that men have long practiced, does not preclude the States from drawing a sharp line between the sexes . . . in such matters as the regulation of the liquor traffic." Invoking the lowest level of constitutional scrutiny, Frankfurter ruled that lawmakers' belief in the necessity of "oversight" by male kin was an "entertainable" ground for intervention. Nor was the court persuaded by evidence (accurate, as it turns out) that the "real impulse" behind the law was "an unchivalrous desire of male bartenders" returning from military service to squeeze women out of well-paid work. In dissent, Justice Rutledge and two others argued only that because a hypothetical *female bar owner* could "neither work as a barmaid herself nor employ her daughter," the law violated the equal protection clause.[81]

After World War II, in keeping with informal practices, Congress also removed married women from public payrolls to make room for unemployed men, even when female employees were better trained and needed incomes. Many women's groups protested these policies; the LWV's Edith Valet Cook argued, for instance, that each "human being has the right to develop himself by work he enjoys and can do well. To deny that right to women, because they marry, is not only unjust but wasteful." Firing married women caused "further unemployment" and discouraged rather than encouraged marriage, which was "against public policy."[82] But working wives' plight did not spark widespread protest, in part because many women accepted their situation. One female riveter later testified that she had quit work to get married. "Personally," she said, "I don't think it was right for the women to be pushed out of their jobs when the men came home. But on the other hand, I think most of them expected to be, to take a back seat to the men."[83] The unions were mostly unhelpful. The Ford Motor Company colluded in 1945 with the United Auto Workers (UAW) to lay off dozens of women and rehire men returning from war service, even when women had greater seniority. In 1945, female factory workers staged a "Women's Revolt" in Detroit; in 1946, women from Local 600 threatened to picket the union office if it continued to stonewall. Said Minnie Jones of Local 600, "We know we have been put out on the streets and people have been working on our jobs that have less seniority than we have. Some of our own Union men . . . say, 'You should go back into your homes and cook on your stoves.' Some don't have a stove to cook on. . . . [W]e are entitled to a decent wage and a decent living." But, for the most part, company hiring policies prevailed.[84]

As to the rest of Kelley's industrial project, well into the 1930s, federal judges greeted child labor legislation with hostility, refusing to allow legislative bodies to dictate how entrepreneurs might use their property or what kinds of bargains might be struck between minors and employers. Nor did lawmakers recognize the economic and social importance of home work. Despite attempts to regulate sweatshops, lawmakers tended to allow needlework and related home labor. Such work occupied a murky zone between wage labor and unpaid home work, perhaps because Americans understood home work to be largely nonwhite mothers' work. "Those of us who have been studying home-work conditions . . . ," said delegates to a 1936 conference, "know that [home work] is a menace to factory conditions: that the woman—and it usually is a woman who works at home—is least able to bargain for the maintenance of her labor standards." Eleanor Roosevelt said this after a 1934 trip to Puerto Rico: "I . . . saw the homework done by the women. . . . I am sure if the women of the United States knew the conditions under which those handkerchiefs, nightgowns and slips were embroidered they would want to boil them before putting them on or using them." The wages paid for home work were "unbelievably small. Little girls sat all during their lunch hour in school embroidering handkerchiefs to augment the family income."[85]

But New Dealers failed to ban these practices; in 1939–40, Congress rejected FLSA amendments to ban home work, agreeing only to regulate it in Puerto Rico. This left the Labor Department with relatively weak administrative weapons. In the 1940s, Secretary of Labor Frances Perkins managed to use the FLSA to eliminate home work in seven industries. In *Gemsco v. Walling* (1945), the Supreme Court upheld her efforts, but only on the ground that home workers undercut the wages of other industrial workers.

Beyond wage and hour laws, other highly restrictive practices and policies survived into the mid-twentieth century. In most cases, courts refused to question legislative judgments about "reasonable" interventions in economic relations or the enforcement of customs that severely harmed working women. In the air were best-selling Freudian-inspired works, such as *Modern Woman: The Lost Sex* (1947), which warned readers of the imminent "masculinization of women" and "enormously dangerous consequences to the home." As the "rivals of men," women would have to "develop the characteristics of aggression, dominance, independence and power"; the resulting "distortion of character" supposedly drove women "steadily deeper into personal conflict soluble only by psychotherapy."[86] Because employers anticipated that women would marry and become pregnant, they actively discriminated against female applicants; once hired, women had to choose between families and promotion or increased pay. Firms rarely, if ever, provided maternity leave, medical insurance for maternity costs, or child care facilities, and housework mostly fell on women. In addition, well into the 1960s, married women in many states still could not retain their original names for business purposes, transact business on their own authority, or develop separate credit histories, and statutes still barred them from occupations that required heavy lifting or that were traditionally masculine, like bartending and mining.

THE INVISIBLE DOMESTIC WORKER

Notably absent from the reform agenda were African Americans and the nation's least visible producers of wealth: domestic workers and farm laborers. For housewives, wage and hour laws were useless and even insulting: The state would "protect" women from exploitation only if they earned wages. Until recently, moreover, the wages, hours, and circumstances of paid domestic servants—many of them black, Asian, or Chicano—lay beyond the scope of labor legislation. In 1870, more than half the working women earned wages in private homes; as late as 1930, approximately 2 million women (about 18 percent of the female labor force) did so. Within black populations, domestic and agricultural work made up about 65 percent of all paid labor; by Evelyn Nakano Glenn's count, in the 1930 census category "servants and laundresses," only 2.5 percent of the enumerated women were white.[87] Yet, apart from Mothers' Pensions and the maternity and widow's benefits inaugurated in social security legislation, such women fell beyond the purview of regulators. Indeed, because New Dealers had excluded domestic and agricultural work from the Social Security Act of 1935, partly on the ground that it would be difficult to police, the law harmed blacks disproportionately. Certain women's groups and agencies, such as the YWCA and the U.S. Women's Bureau, urged policy makers to recognize domestic work as a bona fide occupation, but to no avail; into the 1950s, groups like the National Committee on Household Employment were domestic workers' only insider friends, and such groups had little or no governing power. As a result, women who labored at home (whether for their own families or for others) could not expect the government to defend their economic interests or draw pensions based on their own (rather than their husbands') achievements.

Servants, cooks, and other providers of home services had not been silent. During the Great Depression, domestic workers and groups claiming to represent them fruitlessly lobbied the Roosevelt Administration for inclusion in economic legislation, beginning with the NRA. Serena Elizabeth Ashford, a cook, told the president in 1934 of her keen disappointment "that the large and unprotected class of Domestics were not thought of." Why had he spoken of "the robbery of the Banker" but not "the robbery of the Housewives? . . . [W]e are called upon to do three and sometimes four Domestics work by one person for less than half of what they formerly paid one. And it is a case of try and do it or starve. When you mention a code for Domestics, they arrogantly tell you it . . . can never be done." In the 1940 census, household labor still occupied first place among female occupations. Only World War II-related industrial, technological, and demographic shifts ended women's main reliance on such work, as the once-male realm of clerical work (the stated occupation of 4 percent of working women in 1890, 21 percent in 1890, and 50 percent by 1920) came to be feminized and, in economic terms, cheapened. Meanwhile, for live-in domestics especially, the hours could be long and the wages abysmal, well into modern times. Said Dolethia Otis of Washington, D.C., in 1982: "The living-in jobs just kept you running; never stopped. Day or night, you'd be getting something for somebody. . . . It was never a minute of peace. . . . But when I went out days on my jobs, I'd get my work done and be gone. . . . This work had an end."[88]

Still, few Americans thought of domestics, farm women, housewives, or unsalaried children as serious workers. Family farm laborers usually were unpaid, homebound, and out of the state's line of vision, even though they produced vital commodities and contended with dangerous machines, toxic chemicals, and poor medical care. One woman reported in 1936 that before the purchase of a tractor, she had "four or five hired men to cook for all summer long and one, sometimes two, all winter," in addition to the care of "30 or 40 head of horses and mules."[89] Feminist writers sometimes cast such women as unsung heroines. But few analysts explored the process by which "women's work" *as a species of labor* came to be ignored. As Anna Garlin Spencer wrote in 1912, "The whole course of evolution in industry, and in the achievements of higher education and exceptional talent, has shown man's invariable tendency to shut women out when their activities have reached a highly specialized period of growth," so that women became generalists and men the better-paid specialists. She pointed especially to the medical profession, where the "process of differentiating and perfecting intellectual labor" during "acute periods of specialization and advance" had shut women "out of their own ancient work" as healers.[90]

At the midcentury, then, domestic work continued to be conceptualized not as a *labor problem*, but as a *social situation*. Boosters of domesticity regularly urged women to stay home, where men could protect them from harm, and where they could "rule." A Detroit journalist wrote in 1923, just as the ERA began its long career in Congress, that women might kill "two birds . . . with one stone" by "buckl[ing] right down to sweeping and scrubbing"; it was "not only good for the floor, but the best kind of exercise for women who dread excess poundage." A floor scrubber could be slim, safe, even regal. The writer quoted a female educator in New Jersey: "I recall one woman [who] dressed beautifully and walked gracefully. She filled my youthful heart with admiration when I passed her home . . . and saw her sweeping her front porch, with a smile and a manner that was nothing short of queenly."[91]

Others disagreed. As early as 1886, the *Washington Standard* in Olympia printed an essay about "Uncomplaining Labor." Housework was a "constant recurrence of tasks," the editor noted, "which, however congenial as a pastime, or in accord with the thrifty, persevering nature of womanhood . . . must . . . appal the stoutest heart with the magnitude of a responsibility that never ends." Did housewives "receive their fair share" of social and financial rewards?

> Is working fifteen hours a day, cooking over hot stoves, scrubbing over washtubs, exposing the body to every change of our fickle climate, bearing on an average one child a year, and making both ends meet after the rent is paid and the husband's beer money is spent, in return for food, shelter and the plainest clothing—is that a fair half of the working partnership? Is this an equal division of labor with an equal distribution of the profits?

What would men do if they were "bound to employers by a tie that could not be dissolved, while their work was made a thousand times more laborious and the hours nearly doubled?"[92]

Change was glacial. Seventy years later, the New York-born writer Edith Stern inserted a want ad in *American Mercury*: "HELP WANTED: DOMESTIC: FEMALE. All cooking, cleaning, laundering, social secretarial service, and complete care of three children. Salary at employer's option. Time off if possible." She noted that while no woman "in her right senses would apply for such a job," the ad correctly described the average wife's situation. Stern condemned "bilge" in the popular press about the sex's pampered existence; in 1949, woman's lot was boring, demeaning, and hazardous. A woman could enjoy domesticity or equality, but not both: "As long as the institution of housewifery in its present form persists, both ideologically and practically it blocks any true liberation of women. The vote, the opportunity for economic independence, and the right to smoke cigarettes are all equally superficial veneers over a deep-rooted, ages-old concept of keeping woman in her place. Unfortunately, however, housewives not only are unorganized, but also, doubtless because of the very nature of their brain-dribbling, spirit-stifling vocation, conservative. There is therefore little prospect of a Housewives' Rebellion. There is even less, in the light of men's comfortable setup under the present system, of a male-inspired movement for Abolition!"[93]

Chapter 10

Physical Protection versus Self-Sovereignty

On June 8, 1881, the Michigan Supreme Court sat on a novel case appealed from Gratiot County in which Alvira Roberts, a married woman and mother, had sued Dr. John De May and his friend, Alfred Scattergood, for monetary damages. The Supreme Court report describes the action as one for "intrusion upon [a] case of confinement." On January 3, Roberts had given birth to a child in a small, physically remote dwelling, which measured only "fourteen by sixteen feet," with a curtained "partition" across one end forming a "place for a bed or bedroom" but without a door. There was evidence to show, in the words of Chief Justice Marston, that when Roberts and her husband summoned Dr. De May to attend the birth of her child, the "night was a dark and stormy one"; the roads over which he had to travel to get to the plaintiff's house "were so bad that a horse could not be ridden or driven over them." The doctor was "sick and very much fatigued from overwork, and therefore asked the defendant Scattergood to accompany and assist him in carrying a lantern, umbrella and certain articles deemed necessary upon such occasions. . . . [U]pon arriving at the house of the plaintiff the doctor knocked, and when the door was opened by the husband of the plaintiff, De May said to him, 'that I had fetched a friend along to help carry my things'; he . . . said 'all right,' and seemed to be perfectly satisfied. They were bidden to enter, treated kindly and no objection whatever made to the presence of defendant Scattergood."[1]

Once inside the cabin, De May and Scattergood found that Roberts was not laying behind the partition, as she had been on De May's visit that morning, but had moved to a "lounge near the stove"; it was, after all, a January night in rural Michigan. The doctor found no evidence of labor. He told his patient that he "had been up several nights and was tired and would like to lie down awhile"; the Robertses provided supper and urged both visitors to go to sleep. The doctor removed his pants, hung them "by the stove to dry," and retired to a cot behind the partition; the fully dressed Scattergood dozed in a seat near the stove with "his feet on a pile of wood," his face turned to "the wall of the house" and his back turned "partially toward the couch on which Mrs. Roberts was lying." Some hours later, when labor commenced in earnest, De May "jumped right up," got dressed, and went to his patient. Roberts's husband "stood at her head to assist her"; a female neighbor, Mrs. Parks, stood beside her. The doctor "went to the foot of the couch." At one point during labor, the patient kicked Mrs. Parks in the stomach, and Mrs. Parks went outside to catch her breath. Before the woman had returned, Roberts began "rocking herself and throwing her arms"; the doctor asked Scattergood to leave his station by the fire and "catch her." Scattergood obliged, holding her hand until Mrs. Parks came back. He then resumed his seat. After the baby was delivered and mother and child "properly cared for," De May and Scattergood departed.[2]

Sometime later, the Robertses learned that Scattergood was not a trained medical assistant, as they had imagined him to be, but an "unprofessional young unmarried man" who had simply come along to help the exhausted doctor. Overwhelmed by the shame of having been heard, seen, and even touched during childbirth by a stranger and complete amateur, Alvira Roberts sued both De May and Scattergood, charging them with "deceit" and Scattergood with "assault." The Supreme Court, in affirming the lower court's judgment for the embarrassed woman, moved well beyond "deceit" and "assault" to emphasize the emotional distress caused to the plaintiff by the invasion of her "privacy" upon what Justice Marston called a "most sacred . . . occasion." The plaintiff, wrote Marston, had "a legal right to the privacy of her apartment at such a time, and the law secures to her this right by requiring others to observe it, and to abstain from its violation." It made no difference that she knew of Scattergood's presence or even that he had been helpful. The harm lay in her subsequent feelings of "shame and mortification" at discovering his "true character"—sensations wholly interior and private, as were womanly modesty, childbirth, and, more generally, the feminine realm itself.[3]

The *De May v. Roberts* decision occupies a jurisprudential watershed: After about 1880, law scholars and judges gradually began to construct what is now called the right to privacy, which came to protect men and women alike from a range of state intrusions into private spaces and choices. In its eventual form, the constitutional right to privacy embraced both control over the accessibility of the individual to others (including control over personal information) and freedom of choice in the conduct of private life. But, before the 1960s, questions about women's immunity from physical indignity and onerous regulation arose in a variety of contexts, some of which were ultimately gathered under the privacy umbrella, others not.

Common to all these situations was a tension between the desire to protect women from physical harm and countervailing pressures toward self-determination. On the side of protectionism: Just as fin de siècle reformers used law to assign a "separate but equal" handicap to salaried women, so they constructed legal-political cocoons within which women's bodies would be protected from danger. Because sovereignty attached most fully to men and because wives relinquished key elements of physical security at marriage, women's personal boundaries often were taken to be permeable and provisional. As in economic life, public officials made decisions *for* women as to which dangers they could face. They regulated female sexuality, aiming not only to punish violent men, but also to control women's "promiscuous" or extra-marital sexual activities, innoculate women with middle-class virtues, and warn them away from immorality. On the side of self-possession: "Equal rights" reformers and many nonactivist parties to lawsuits struggled to liberate women from familial cocoons and to eliminate "separate but equal" legal practices.

The experiences of two rather unladylike Kansans illustrate key elements of the "separate but equal" protective impulse, as well as women's impatience with what lawyer Beverly Blair Cook calls "encapsulation."[4] In 1917, Progressive legislators in Kansas adopted two new statutes that together forced the state supreme court to review penal policies as they affected female offenders. In one measure, lawmakers forbade the manufacture and sale of alcohol. In another, they established the State Industrial Farm for Women, described in the statute as "an institution for the detention and care of women convicted of criminal offenses, providing for the government of the same." By the provisions of the state's 1901 penal code, all adults convicted of crimes and sentenced to jail terms were supposed to serve fixed terms at county jails or the penitentiary. Men and women shared these facilities. Delinquent children, by contrast, served indeterminate sentences at a reformatory. As of 1917, however, women older than age 18 who were "convicted of any offense . . . punishable by imprisonment" were to be sentenced to the sex-segregated farm.

No longer would judges "fix the . . . duration of the sentence"; rather, as with children, women's sentences would be "terminated" at the pleasure of a state board, provided that inmates were not detained longer than the "maximum term provided by law" for their crimes. In addition, officials could parole first offenders aged 18–25 before they had served minimum terms, whereas older women or repeat offenders had to serve at least minimum sentences.

Sometime in 1918–19, constables arrested Josie Dunkerton of Coffeyville, Kansas, for defying the state prohibition (or "bone-dry") statute; the Montgomery District Court sentenced her to a fine and to an indefinite term at the Industrial Farm for Women. Dunkerton did not go quietly. Probably in 1919, she hired a lawyer and appealed the fine, arguing that the multiple punishments set out in the 1917 penal statute conflicted with the 1901 penal code. In a terse opinion filed in November 1918, Justice Burch of the Supreme Court of Kansas affirmed the lower court's judgment: Nothing in the penal act suggested that "punishment for crime shall be limited to detention."[5] Undeterred, Dunkerton applied for a writ of habeas corpus. Her attorney argued that in the case of older women and repeat offenders, the 1917 measure contravened the equal protection clauses of state and federal constitutions by eliminating hope of an early parole and mandating differential treatment of men and women. But in its 1919 hearing of *In Re Josie Dunkerton*, the Kansas Supreme Court found the law constitutional. Before 1917, Kansans had redirected a few incorrigible children by sending them to the state reformatory; now, women as well as children could be remade in "separate but equal" facilities devoted to "[r]eformation and education." The 1917 act also aimed to keep women out of harm's way. No longer would they be "subjected to the debauching influence of the county jail and . . . penitentiary"; they were "placed in a field where labor is pleasant and restraint is limited, and where the evil influence of other persons convicted of crime is minimized. The act seeks to improve, to educate, and to build up; not to punish."[6]

At the next term, the same court confronted another unhappy resident of the Industrial Farm for Women—a married woman listed only as Mrs. L. O. Heitman, convicted in 1918–19 of "keeping a liquor nuisance." Burdened with an indeterminate sentence of up to six months' reeducation at the farm, Heitman had decided that she preferred to be in jail with men for a fixed term. On appeal, her lawyer pointed out that a man in Heitman's place would have been sentenced to the Shawnee county jail for "some definite period within the maximum and minimum limits" established by the 1901 code, and challenged the 1917 statute establishing the industrial farm as violative of the Fourteenth Amendment's equal protection and privileges and immunities clauses. He cited what the court called "familiar decisions" to show that in the "administration of criminal justice, no different or higher punishment shall be imposed on one than that which is prescribed for all, for the same offense." Old authorities had based "justice on equality"; new sex-specific institutions and sentencing guidelines perpetuated both inequality and injustice.[7]

Supreme Court Justice Burch rejected the appeal, noting (after the influential German legal philosopher Rudolf von Ihering) that, to be meaningful, equality had to redound to the "welfare of society"; an "equality of misery" helped no one. Would it not "revolt justice" if children were "subjected to the same penal regimen" as mature criminals? Did not the same rule apply to women? The state could make sex distinctions, so long as they advanced worthy public purposes. Said Burch, "It requires no anatomist . . . or psychiatrist to tell the legislature that women are different from men" and that the ability to bear children prefigured "differences in personality between men and women," which, in turn, were the "predominant factor in delinquent careers."

> It was inevitable that, in the ages during which woman has been bearer of the race, her unique and absolutely personal experiences, from the time of conception to the time when developed offspring attains maturity, should react on personality, and produce what we understand to be embraced by the term womanhood. Woman enters spheres of sensation, perception, emotion, desire, knowledge, and experience, of an intensity and of a kind which men cannot know . . . and the result is a feminine type radically different from the masculine type, which demands special consideration in the . . . treatment of non-conformity to law.

The new farm was basically a safe house run by and for the female sex. "The superintendent," Burch explained, "is a woman. The farm is in fact a farm, and the buildings are constructed on the cottage plan. . . . The discipline is educative and reformative, and the work includes agriculture, . . . manufacturing, and practice of domestic arts and sciences." In addition, officials could prevent "promiscuous association of the sexes in prison." A woman "not merely requires, but deserves, on account of matters touching the perpetuation and virility of the human species, correctional treatment different from the male offender."[8]

Kansans were hardly alone. Beginning in the 1860s, prison reformers began to scrutinize mixed-sex correctional institutions and to advocate "separate but equal" havens for delinquent women. The number of female prisoners had escalated, as had examples of the sexual abuse of incarcerated women. In 1891, social reformer Susan Hammon Barney observed that female prisoners typically were "arrested by men, given into the hands of men to be searched and cared for, tried by men, sentenced by men, and committed to our various institutions for months and even years, where only men officials had access to them, and where, in sickness or direst need, no womanly help or visitation was expected or allowed."[9]

Talk about how to deal with incarcerated women's bodies inevitably converged with talk about economic dependence and moral reform. What should happen to female prisoners? Should their treatment be equal to or different from that of men? Should officials act to prevent harm to women while in state custody? Punish the sexes differently? Should women learn marketable skills? Or should female reeducation include only the skills and virtues associated with "ladyhood"? If the latter, how would women support themselves upon release? After the Civil War, men in the Detroit House of Corrections made chairs for sale; women studied domestic arts and worked as servants. Did such practices help or hinder impoverished women? What if they could make more money as prostitutes? By the 1910s, prison reformers had coalesced into "protectionist" and "equal rights" camps. Opponents of sex segregation greatly feared the reinforcement of stereotypes about women's sentimental nature, "soft" bodies, and economic failure beyond prison walls. In contrast, protectionists pointed to rape statistics and fundamental biological differences between men and women. What *about* pregnancy and menstruation? The children of female prisoners? What if a tradition of female dependence encouraged men to abuse women in mixed-sex facilities? Would women end up darning socks simply because men were present? Said reformer Jessie Hodder in 1922, "It is not humanly possible to avoid making women subservient to men so it results that women prisoners treated on this principle major in mending, washing, ironing, and sewing for men prisoners."[10]

Progressive and "social purity" reformers also took aim at male lust and undisciplined female sexuality. As immigrants surged into early twentieth-century cities, xenophobia ran rampant; much as antipolygamists aimed to save the West from the contagion of Mormonism, so urban reformers worried incessantly about prostitution and "sexual slavery," whether voluntary or involuntary—metaphors that sometimes expressed broader concerns about the purity of northern European racial stock and the coarsening of women. Poor working girls seemed to be especially vulnerable. In 1890, Jacob Riis cited a report of the Working Women's Society of New York: "It is a known fact that men's wages cannot fall below a limit upon which they can exist, but woman's wages have no limit, since the paths of shame are always open to her. It is simply impossible for any woman to live without assistance on the low salary a saleswoman earns, without depriving herself of real necessities." Members had been "shocked" to learn of a poor but "gentle and refined" woman who "threw herself from an attic window, preferring death to dishonor."[11]

These fears, in turn, fed into deeply racist and sexualized suspicions about alien conspiracies and "infections." Cities acted quickly to outlaw prostitution, even where "red light districts" had been tolerated for decades; driven underground, sex workers found themselves at the mercy of pimps, gangsters, and abusive customers. In 1907, Chicago's reformist *McClure's Magazine* published a lurid exposé of a "loosely organized association . . . largely composed of Russian Jews" that supposedly supplied "white slaves" (that is, young girls kidnapped and thrown into prostitution) to brothels. Within weeks, white slave hysteria swept the nation. A federal agency warned that unless a "girl was actually confined and guarded, . . . no girl, regardless of her station in life, . . . was altogether safe." In 1909, Chicago Congressman James Mann, relying on what David Langum calls the "ravings" of crusading journalist Edwin Sims, introduced a bill (predicated on both the interstate commerce clause and a 1904 international treaty devoted to the suppression of the trade) to "protect women and girls against *this criminal traffic.*" The Mann Act, passed virtually without opposition in 1910, augmented an already substantial Progressive arsenal of weapons that were available for use in the defense of women and children; as amended and expanded, it remained fully in effect until 1962, when weak enforcement and a series of limiting amendments derailed it.[12]

To the extent that prostitutes had chosen an occupation and wished to continue with it, reformers rendered their lives much less secure and—in the name of purification and "rescue"—subjected hundreds of them to virtual or actual incarceration. Few Americans considered the possibility that the criminalization of prostitution might deprive women of income and property rights in an occupation. Although undeniably demeaning, sex work usually paid considerably more than did many other occupations that were open to women, particularly those who lacked an education, capital, or social connections. Then, as now, a significant number of prostitutes told survey workers that they preferred to be self-controlling and even that they liked the work; but—often for good reason—reformers could not believe that women might choose to commercialize their own bodies.

Gilded Age and Progressive campaigns against prostitution, however, did little to protect women from sexual assault, at home and elsewhere. Until recently, battering was grossly unreported or underreported: Husbands, after all, could discipline their wives, even if much less severely than in the past. When a woman filed charges against a male companion or husband, courts frequently exhibited skepticism and—as in rape trials—sometimes put victims on trial for possible transgressions of gender norms (that is, for being a bad wife or a loose woman). The WCTU's Frances Willard, one of many fin de siècle reformers to protest sexual violence, thought that the states' failure to ensure women's physical security was scandalous. In 1890, she publically read a petition then being circulated across the nation that, in its sexual frankness, violated prevailing norms of civil discourse: "The increasing and alarming frequency of assaults upon women,"

and the frightful indignities to which even little girls are subject, have become the shame of our boasted civilization. A study of the Statutes has revealed their utter failure to meet the demands of that newly awakened public sentiment which requires better legal protection for womanhood and girlhood. Therefore we do most earnestly appeal to you to enact such statutes as shall provide for the adequate punishment of crimes against women and girls.

Willard asked not only for "heavier penalties," but also for the "total prohibition" of alcohol ("leagued with every crime . . . perpetrated against the physically weaker sex") and the ballot, so that "law and law-maker may be directly influenced by our instincts of self-protection and home protection."[13]

Rape law provides the classic example of unequal protection of citizens' bodies. Throughout the twentieth century, lawyers have relied on William Blackstone's 1769 definition of rape as the "carnal knowledge of a woman forcibly and against her will."[14] Modern criminal codes usually provide for the rape of men, but, generally, legislatures resisted reforming the law of rape well into the 1980s. Because rape victims have been overwhelmingly female and perpetrators male, trials typically have expressed and affirmed widely held views of proper womanly deportment. Cases of "real rape" (to borrow legal scholar Susan Estrich's important term) have occasioned the least difficulty: "A stranger puts a gun to the head of his victim, threatens to kill her or beats her, and then engages in intercourse." In such cases, even hidebound judges and juries have acknowledged that a serious crime has been committed. But, in Victorian America, as in the twentieth century, women's experiences were rarely so stark. "Where less force is used," notes Estrich, "or no other physical injury is inflicted, where threats are inarticulate, where the two know each other, where the setting is not an alley but a bedroom, where the initial contact was not a kidnapping but a date, where the woman says no but does not fight," the social and legal "understanding" of events typically has been far different, especially in cases involving nonwhite or lower-class women. In this gray zone, law and legal administration "reflected, legitimized, and enforced a view of sex and women" that effectively affirmed male aggression and punished "female passivity."[15]

Science has not always been woman's ally. Modern legal scholars and psychologists—after the teachings of Sigmund Freud and his disciple, Helene Deutsch—have insisted that masochism is an essential part of femininity, that rape stimulates female genitalia, and that women secretly enjoy violent sex. "Although a woman may desire sexual intercourse," wrote one such expert in 1966, "it is customary for her to say 'no, no, no' (although meaning 'yes, yes, yes') and to expect the male to be the aggressor."[16] As a number of scholars have pointed out, common law judges traditionally permitted an exculpating argument of self-defense when men who were subjected to forcible sodomy killed their assailants; no such firm right of self-defense attached to female rape victims. And when women kill rapists, juries have been known to retaliate. In 1977, after the first of two pathbreaking trials of Inez Garcia in Monterrey, California, in which she was convicted and then acquitted of killing a man who allegedly had helped another man rape her and then threatened to rape her again, a juror said: "You can't kill a man for trying to give you a good time."[17]

Throughout the twentieth century, moreover, judges and juries typically have tried both the accused rapist and his victim, scrutinizing the degree and sincerity of a woman's (or girl's) refusal to engage in an otherwise lawful act. Sex researchers have concluded that juries tend to convict men for rape less often than strict application of law might require: In one sample, judges said that they would convict a rapist in 22 out of 42 cases; juries voted to convict only in 3. Here, as nowhere else, tensions between governmental protection of the "good" or redeemable women, on the one hand, and the state's interest in controlling the "bad" or unrepentant woman, on the other hand, have emerged with real force. The "trial" typically has begun at the police station, with skeptical police officers grilling women for evidence of complicity. In the 1960s, one woman described the process this way: "I went to the police station and said, 'I want to report a rape.' They said, 'Whose?' I said, 'Mine.' The cop looked at me and said, 'Aw, who'd want to rape you?'"[18] Angry voters in Madison, Wisconsin, recalled Judge Archie E. Simonson from office when, during the sentencing in 1977 of a fifteen-year-old boy to a year's detention at home for raping a sixteen-year-old girl, he went so far as to admonish women to "stop teasing" men with provocative clothing: "[W]hether they like it or not, women are sex objects."[19]

This is not to say that rape law and law enforcement agencies have not changed. Since the 1980s, police treatment of rape victims has improved dramatically. And, as women have come to be seen as self-possessed members of the polity, the presumption of man's right as a class to the sexual services of all women has weakened appreciably. By the 1930s, it was no longer usual for a man to accuse a rapist of diminishing the value of his daughter as a future wife or of trespassing on his wife's body. A federal judicial decision in 1901 to award damages to a New Jersey father for the seduction of a daughter—for the loss of domestic services (as would be the case for any child) and as recompense for his (not her) "mental anguish, anxiety, permanent sorrow, dishonor, and disgrace"—was perhaps anomalous.[20] But as Ann Coughlan clearly shows, the law has required courts to find either that the accused man had committed a crime or that his victim had done so by failing to keep her sexuality in check; in that sense, rape law has taken the place of the old law of adultery and fornication in policing sexual behavior beyond marriage. Throughout the twentieth century, the test of acceptable levels of resistance greatly resembled the test for duress—a defense that can be used at trial to exculpate an otherwise guilty person. In other words, to secure a conviction, the law required rape victims—especially unmarried, nonwhite, or lower-class ones—to prove that they did not ask for it and that they had an excuse akin to duress "for engaging in sexual intercourse outside of marriage." To establish the excuse, a woman traditionally had to show that a "reasonable man" (not a "reasonable woman") would have found the rapist's behavior malevolent and that she resisted "to the utmost."[21]

Nor have wives been able to charge alienated or violent husbands with rape—a principle virtually unchanged until recently. Sir Matthew Hale laid out a rule on the point in the seventeenth century: "[T]he husband cannot be guilty of a rape committed by himself upon his lawful wife, for by their mutual matrimonial consent and contract, the wife hath given up herself in this kind unto her husband, which she cannot retract."[22] In 1903, the U.S. Supreme Court ruled in *Tinker v. Colwell* that the husband of an adulterous woman indeed had "certain personal and exclusive rights . . . to the person of his wife which are interfered with and invaded by criminal conversation with her"; that the wife was legally "incapable of giving any consent to affect the husband's rights" so that adultery might be termed an "assault"; and that the act injured "the personal rights and property of the husband," remediable with money damages.[23] In intervening decades, legislators and judges have clung tenaciously to the exclusivity doctrine. Only since about 1980 have the states moved to recognize the possibility of marital rape.

Women's clothing had contributed powerfully to the sex's physical insecurity; despite widespread fear of the appearance of "looseness," many post-Victorian women resolved to dress differently. In 1900, social critic Kathleen Norris offered this grim account of a woman's dress: "She wore a wide-brimmed hat that caught the breezes, a high chok-ing collar of satin or linen, and a flaring gored skirt that swept the street on all sides. Her full-sleeved shirt-waist had cuffs that were eternally getting dirty, . . . and her skirt was a bitter trial. Its heavy 'brush binding' had to be replaced every few weeks, for constant contact with the pavement reduced it to dirty fringe. . . . In wet weather the full skirt got soaked and icy."[24] By the 1920s, women increasingly opted for unrestrictive garments, sometimes inviting danger in the process. For centuries, women had tried to discourage sexual marauders through dress; among other functions, corsets, tight laces, girdles, and stiff brassieres held sexualized parts of the female body in check and kept them away from inquisitive eyes and hands. As women literally loosened up, they risked public cen-sure and hostile interrogation in courts of law when they accused men of improper sex-ual behavior; nevertheless, thousands of girls and women rejected corsets and heavy wool in favor of lightweight skirts, trousers, and short-skirted "flapper" dresses. They defiantly chopped off long, weighty hair and bared arms and legs at the beach. Some women cross-dressed to gain access to masculine spaces or to declare their independence from social constraint. Salaried women increasingly wore nondescript black or brown frocks to work, in keeping with what journalist Mark Sullivan called an "unwritten law governing the style of dress adopted by . . . self-supporting women." Fragile fabrics and beehive hair-dos were expensive, drew unwanted attention to the worker and, compared to working men's comparatively severe attire, conveyed frippery and sexual competition rather than seriousness. Corsets sharply reduced a woman's lung power. Sleeves and skirts got caught in machines; tight shoes and spindly heels made it hard to walk, stand, and run; and long fingernails (a symbol of leisure) decreased typing speed.

Into the new century, feminists labored long and hard to force public reconsideration of time-honored linkages between women's dress or deportment and violence (the "she asked for it" phenomenon). To ensure "self-sovereignty," they also demanded increased access to reliable, safe contraception and, in different ways, abortion. Americans had man-aged by the end of the nineteenth century to exercise better control over conception; in a 1933 study, 91.5 percent of the women at a clinic in New Jersey had used such techniques in the past; a year later, 93.3 percent of New York clinic patients reported the previous use of birth control "beyond abstinence."[25] But contraceptive information was still hard to obtain, and safe abortions were harder still to find and afford. Virtually every state had outlawed advertisements for contraceptive potions or devices. Between the 1860s and the 1910s, every state except Kentucky had criminalized abortion and abortifacients, allow-ing pregnancies to be terminated by physicians only when delivery threatened women's lives and, in scattered states, when pregnancies had resulted from criminal acts like rape or incest.

Before the 1970s, self-induced or clandestine abortions were the rule, when they could be done at all, especially for women or girls of limited means. Older women passed lore about abortifacients and contraceptive methods to daughters or granddaughters, often to the chagrin of physicians, whose control over women's fertility ended at the grandmoth-ers' kitchen door. Folk remedies could be dangerous. A coat hanger could puncture the uterus; desperate women forced lye and other caustic liquids into their wombs with catheters. Other procedures were less reliably fatal. "The older ladies of the community are prolific in advice," said one Chicago physician in 1900. "Hot drinks, hot douches and hot baths are recommended. Violent exercise is suggested and jumping off a chair or rolling down stairs is a favorite procedure." Women proudly told of boiling their own catheters to avoid infection during self-induced saline abortions. Before the 1950s, respectable abortionists operated at the edge of the law; magistrates often blinked, on the ground that clinics offered valuable services. "Best friends," mothers, and boyfriends often tried to help young women find abortionists, to avoid dishonor or forced marriages. In turn-of-the-century New York, one mother swore, "Death before dishonor, my daughter is not going to be disgraced all her days, and the man to go scot-free." Mary Colbert of Chicago was not the only pregnant woman to choose abortion over an offer of marriage. After her death, an aunt said, "She did not want to get married then. She did not want to marry anyone."[26]

Debate about the merits of reproductive freedom, as it later came to be called, swept over the nation in the second quarter of the twentieth century, cresting in the 1960s. The timing reflected profound alterations in Americans' sexual behavior, the rise of a powerful medical profession, and sex radicals' reading (at least one historian calls it a "misreading") of the works of Freud and other students of the human psyche. One study, conducted in the 1930s among 777 college-educated women, revealed that only 13.5 percent of the women who were born before 1890 had experienced premarital sex, compared to 68.3 percent of the women born after 1910.[27] Sometimes, male sex reformers joined with feminists to protest the sexual abuse of women. English author and healer Edward Carpenter thought that sexual liberation depended entirely on *women's* freedom; men were incapable of securing social peace. In 1911, Carpenter lambasted "men so fatuous that it actually does not hurt them to see the streets crammed with prostitutes by night, or the parks by day with the semi-lifeless bodies of tramps; men, to whom it seems quite natural that our marriage and social institutions should lumber along over the bodies of women, as our commercial institutions grind over the bodies of the poor."[28]

Well before the 1960s, changes in social and economic expectations triggered a sexual revolution. Suddenly, women were claiming many of the freedoms and sexual imperatives historically reserved for men—many of which had been expressed in old saws like "men will sow wild oats." The automobile, lurid tabloids, amusement parks, pool halls, pop music, and movies fueled the fire and carried a depoliticized revolution into rural and working classes. As the number of salaried unmarried women mushroomed, from 1.9 million in 1870 to about 8 million in 1910, and as thousands of girls moved away from parents' homes into relatively private quarters, municipalities were hard pressed to control extramarital sexual activity. In communities like Muncie, Indiana, Great Depression-era citizens began to register dismay at the number of glossy sex magazines at newsstands with articles like "She Wanted a Caveman Husband" and "Indolent Kisses." They also worried about the number of girls impregnated in the backseats of cars.[29]

How could a new generation of sexually active women exert greater control over their reproductive capacities? In previous centuries, abortion probably had been the most commonly used technique for controlling fertility, but during the nineteenth century, as expertise and experience with contraceptive medications and devices grew, the procedure lost place as a birth control technique. Better to control impregnation at the start than to risk injury or death with chemicals or surgery. Small, underpublicized "voluntary motherhood" societies had appeared in the United States as early as the 1840s; over the next seventy years, a few activists defied Comstock-era legislation and promoted access to contraception, abortifacients, and remedies for sexually transmitted diseases—such as Compound 606, also called Salvarsan, available after 1909 for the treatment of syphilis. Most especially, they championed the idea that fertile girls and women ought to be able to control their own bodies and did not want or need to be protected from information about birth control.

By 1915, an American birth control movement had coalesced around radicals like Emma Goldman, Margaret Sanger, Crystal Eastman, and Mary Ware Dennett—many of them working class and almost all of them inspired by or formally trained in European political and social theory. Sanger, a trained nurse and journalist, is perhaps the best known of the group, if only because she popularized the term *birth control* and repeatedly defied New York authorities by establishing birth control clinics and distributing information to women. Sanger tried to reach working-class women by appearing at workers' rallies, distributing leaflets to their homes, and writing for leftist periodicals. To increase newspaper coverage of her efforts, she welcomed raids of her clinics, complete with photographs of ordinary women being stuffed into paddy wagons, and endured both criminal conviction and jailing for the cause. In 1918, she was sentenced to thirty days in the workhouse for violating Section 1142 of the New York Penal Law. That law made it a misdemeanor to "sell, or give away, or to advertise or offer for sale, any instrument or article, drug or medicine, for the prevention of conception; or to give information orally stating when, where or how such an instrument, article or medicine can be purchased or obtained." In *People v. Sanger* (1918), the judges noted that the perpetrator was "not a physician" and had given "promiscuous advice" to women; not even physicians could dispense such information except to "cure or prevent disease," into which category pregnancy did not fall.[30]

Yet Goldman, a socialist and advocate of free love, more fully expressed the birth control movement's social objectives than did Sanger, and Dennett was a better lobbyist. Eastman and others went so far as to link "voluntary motherhood" with state funding of maternal labor and the achievement of economic autonomy for women. In 1920, Eastman insisted that the "immediate feminist program must include voluntary motherhood. . . . 'Birth control' is just as elementary . . . as 'equal pay.'" Women should be *paid* for reproductive work: "It seems that the only way we can keep mothers free, at least in a capitalist society, is by the establishment of a principle that the occupation of raising children is . . . a service to society, and that the mother . . . is entitled to an adequate economic reward from the political government. It is idle to talk of real economic independence for women unless this principle is accepted."[31]

Advocates of birth control conveyed a mixed message. On the one hand, as Linda Gordon explains, they united women's "personal experience and emotional understanding with political thought and action," creating "a politics based on women's shared experience" capable of uniting "masses of women." They did not lodge a "reform proposal" so much as a "revolutionary demand." They thought of birth control not primarily as "a sexual or medical reform," but as "a social issue with broad implications." They hoped as well to transform the meaning of "human rights" and "women's rights" to include "free sexual expression and reproductive self-determination."[32] On the other hand, voluntary motherhood came to be intertwined with talk about "social purity," eugenics, and the control of fertility among lower-class, immigrant, or black women, about whose sexual habits white middle-class women were decidedly squeamish. A turn-of-the-century placard, created by Mary Ware Dennett for the Voluntary Parenthood League, carried this slogan: "JOYOUS AND DELIBERATE MOTHERHOOD, A SURE LIGHT IN OUR RACIAL DARKNESS."[33] Sociologist James Bossard was even more explicit about class-based population control. "The demand for unskilled labor has been declining . . . ," he wrote in 1935, but it is in this group . . . that the reproductive rates are highest. . . . As the demand for unskilled, low intelligence labor decreases, corresponding readjustments must be made in the supply of this type of labor, if we are to avoid the crystallization of a large element in the population who are destined to become permanent public charges. This points again directly to birth control.

Indeed, as her career advanced, Sanger increasingly called on poor women to take command of their own bodies and defeat "destitution linked with excessive childbearing."[34] She thought, too, that women supported war by producing armies of sons. During the Great Depression, moreover, she sharply criticized New Dealers for extending relief to everyone and failing to distinguish between worthy and degenerate classes. "As long as the procreative instinct is allowed to run reckless riot through our social structure," she said in 1935, "as long as the New Deal and our paternalistic Administration refuse to recognize this truism, grandiose schemes for security may eventually turn into subsidies for the perpetuation of the irresponsible classes of society."[35]

Still, Sanger had in mind *personal*, rather than *state*, control of female bodies, albeit under the rubric of professional medicine; her ideas therefore could empower even those women whom she seemed to distrust. And despite marked divisions within the movement over Sanger's medical approach to birth control, which increasingly put midwives and other traditional caregivers out of business and subjected women to professionals who often opposed abortion and family limitation, her high profile attracted much public attention. Conservative physicians and the Catholic Church certainly viewed Sanger and the birth control movement as dangerous, even Satanic forces. During the battle in the 1920s to legalize clinics in Massachusetts, Cardinal O'Connell said that the proposed statute was a "direct threat . . . towards increasing impurity and unchastity not only in our married life but . . . among our unmarried people." When all else failed, opponents resorted to red-baiting, as when the chief of obstetrics at a Catholic hospital condemned the bill as "the essence" of "that putrid and diseased river that has its headquarters in Russia."[36]

Leslie Reagan concludes that the Great Depression helped to legitimate birth control and, to a lesser extent, abortion among working-class men and women, since unemployed or underemployed Americans simply could not afford children. A leading abortion expert, Frederick Taussig, opined that increased rates of illegal abortion, particularly among black and poor women, were "due less to [a] laxity of morals than to underlying economic conditions." Condoms sold by the gross at gas stations and grocery stores. In 1930, the American Birth Control League operated fifty-five clinics in fifteen states; eight years later, over five hundred dotted the landscape. Hostility toward "welfare babies" encouraged physicians to prescribe contraceptives, and throughout the 1930s, the federal government quietly supported birth control among welfare recipients. In 1937, a poll revealed that more than 80 percent of all women approved of contraception.[37]

But during and after World War II, the climate shifted: Population-control impulses shared space with family stabilization crusades. Governmental and extra-governmental efforts to restore social stability by reestablishing conventional family relations bore different meanings for sexually active married and unmarried women. Once married, white women reported what Elaine Tyler May calls "enormous discontent"—a sentiment more or less synonymous with Betty Friedan's "problem that has no name." Yet, because there was "no place for this discontent to go, it remained contained in the home." Women adapted, raised admirable children, and rarely abandoned their families. Men "put up with stress at work and struggled to earn enough income to provide 'the good life.'" For them, writes Tyler May, "viable alternatives to domestic containment were out of reach."

> The cold war consensus and the pervasive atmosphere of anticommunism made personal experimentation, as well as political resistance, risky endeavors with dim prospects for significant positive results. So they made the choices they believed they had to make. Most thought that the gains were worth the sacrifices. With depression and war behind them, and with political and economic institutions fostering the upward mobility of men, the domesticity of women, and suburban home ownership, they were homeward bound. But as the years went by, they also found themselves bound to the home.

This "ambiguous legacy of domestic containment," she adds, was "not lost on their children"; when baby boomers came of age, they made "different choices."[38]

For unmarried pregnant women, however, especially those who were poor or non-white, policies based on "domestic containment" were cruel at best. African American women suffered inordinately from state decisions to police motherhood: In 1939, for example, in the wake of congressional adoption of Aid to Dependent Children in 1935 (ADC, later called Aid to Families with Dependent Children, or AFDC), states passed so-called surveillance laws that charged special units of government with identifying and punishing (with the loss of benefits) all recipients who were actively involved with men. In 1951, Georgia moved to eliminate ADC payments for women with more than one "illegitimate" child (that is, a child born out of wedlock), and though the federal government required no such regulations, Congress was not inclined to question state practices. Into the 1960s, states increased their vigilance. Nineteen states decided around 1960 to eliminate welfare payments for the children born of unmarried couples; in Louisiana alone, 23,000 children (more than 6,000 unwed mothers, most of them black) suddenly lost all support. Many other states passed or tried to pass laws mandating the sterilization or imprisonment of ADC recipients with more than one "illegitimate" child. Into the 1990s, such laws reflected the long life of a presumption among whites of blacks' essential immorality and of black citizens' "soft" claims to privacy. At its inception, however, as an Urban League writer noted in 1960, the decision to single out black women for special disapprobation also reflected fears of a black rebellion as the civil rights movement gained momentum. In his view, Louisiana's policies were acts of "reprisal or intimidation against a Negro population which has been insistently pressing for an end to racial segregation in education and other areas of living."[39]

After the Great Depression, hundreds of homes for unwed mothers (by which their operators usually meant white mothers) flourished; as with "separate but equal" women's prisons, the idea was to rehabilitate "fallen women" and persuade them to give up their children for adoption so that they might start over. Rickie Solinger contends that because unwed mothers as a class had "violated multiple rules concerning femininity and sexuality," conservatives and liberals alike saw them as "a threat to the integrity of the family." Americans simply could not tolerate a large number of women choosing to *be* sexual, much less pregnant, outside marriage; as a post–World War II director of a large New York maternity home explained, society regarded illegitimacy as "an inroad on the family's stability and permanency" and dealt with it by "ostracizing the unwed mother."[40]

As early as the mid-1930s, moreover, in response both to the popularity of the birth control movement and to the severity of legal-professional punishments for physicians and participating clinics or hospitals, women began to lose access to herbs, personnel, and instruments capable of inducing abortions. By the 1950s, these shifts in direction effectively shut ordinary women (that is, women who could not afford to fly to Europe) out of the clean facilities to which word-of-mouth might have led them two decades earlier. As legislatures targeted "irregular" abortionists—including a good many skilled midwives—hospitals and clinics implemented ever-more-stringent rules, in effect assisting the government by forming therapeutic committees to supervise abortions. One committee warned Chicago administrators in 1935 of their "duty" to "prevent . . . illegal operations." By 1940, hospitals regularly required physicians to consult with their colleagues before they undertook abortions. In 1942, the factions associated with the birth control movement, including Sanger's Birth Control League, joined forces to create the Planned Parenthood Federation of America (PPFA, commonly called Planned Parenthood)—a move to which Sanger herself objected. A family- rather than a woman-centered organization, Planned Parenthood was determined to stabilize families and advance the goal (supported by eugenicists into the 1940s) of limiting population growth within unruly classes. One PPFA member advocated "a sound parenthood, in all economic classes, as a major means by which this nation can be maintained strong and free."[41] In 1954, the Joint Commission on Accreditation of Hospitals issued guidelines for mandatory consultations in advance of sterilization, cesarean sections, and all procedures that "interrupted" pregnancies. The fact that women, some of whom had tasted economic independence for the first time during World War II, were remaining in salaried jobs in record numbers added urgency to the century-old public interest in supporting family formation.[42]

The immediate result of the medical profession's lockdown was a dramatic increase in injuries and mortality. Women—especially poor women—resorted to back-alley abortionists and harsh chemicals, many of them peddled by unscrupulous entrepreneurs. In the early 1950s, for instance, a "vaginal pill" severely burned hundreds of women without inducing abortions. In 1939, hospitals in Cook County, Illinois, treated more than one thousand women for complications arising from abortion; in 1962, the same hospitals reported treating nearly five thousand women for the same problem—an increase that cannot be explained in terms of overall population growth. Hospitals opened special wards to deal with the influx of septic infections and abortion-related injuries. In New York City, postabortion deaths dramatically increased, from 27 women per year in 1952 to 51 in 1961, rising steadily in subsequent years until the federal courts legalized abortion. As Leslie Reagan wryly observes, abortion-related deaths increased as childbirth became less dangerous; at midcentury, the loss of life was "almost completely preventable."[43]

Into the 1950s, the racialization of health care and public policy also accelerated, so that when hospitals began to clamp down on abortions, black women in cities like Chicago and New York were four times more likely to die from abortion-related injuries than were white women. Whereas maternity homes and social workers energetically sought to rehabilitate white unwed mothers and to cure them of the "disease" of wanting to keep their babies, they typically treated black girls and women as criminals. As Solinger puts it, whites were "shamed" but encouraged to begin life anew, whereas blacks were "blamed" for pregnancy and forced to live with the fruits of their supposed sexual appetites. Said the Children's Bureau's Ursula Gallagher in the 1950s, "In some courts, it is almost impossible for a Negro unmarried woman to give up her baby for adoption. . . . [T]he courts believe the girl should be *made* to support her children and should be punished by keeping them."[44]

With the advent of oral contraceptives in the early 1960s, the question came to be whether taxpayers should subsidize the distribution of "the Pill." State legislators now could choose to prevent unwelcome increases in the African American population, rather than merely punish illegitimacy. Funding contraceptives had the disadvantage of seeming to tolerate extramarital sex, and the returns were not yet in on the long-term health effects of the Pill. But lawmakers typically believed that inner-city population growth, unlike suburban expansion, amounted to "overpopulation." In discussions of whether to withhold information on contraceptives from welfare recipients, Michigan state legislator William Ryan noted competing evils—"excessive illegitimacy at public expense on the one hand, and the idea that the State sanctions sexual promiscuity by providing birth control information to unmarried women on the other." Into the 1960s, state and federal officials often decided that what Solinger calls the "moral strain" of subsidizing sexual activity was less onerous than the public costs of illegitimacy. One television personality termed the decision a "triumph of pocketbook over principle"; cities were said to be "overpopulated" by fertile African Americans and therefore seedbeds of social instability. Federal and state agencies thus began paying for oral contraceptives to advance what President Lyndon Johnson called "population control."[45]

Into the 1970s, white women gradually escaped the "shame" paradigm; Americans came to think that sexual repression was unhealthy and that white unwed mothers (now taken to be "sexual and accidentally pregnant") could terminate pregnancies or retreat with their babies behind the privacy veil. But impoverished women—especially those of African American, Chicano, and American Indian descent—enjoyed no such reprieve and still cannot easily shut the door on intrusive public officials unless they forgo public assistance. Although studies of black society have confirmed overwhelmingly that most black mothers accept full responsibility for their children, the notion of a "population bomb"—the title of a widely read Hugh Moore Fund pamphlet—still undergirds policy. In 1965, *The Population Bomb* warned of "300 million more mouths to feed in the world four years from now—most of them hungry. Hunger brings turmoil—and turmoil . . . creates the atmosphere in which the communists seek to conquer the earth." These sentiments, in turn, reinforced links between black fertility and "unacceptable welfare expenditures, unacceptable demographic changes in the big cities," and high levels of juvenile delinquency and poverty.[46]

Talk about white women's power to make reproductive choices without state supervision ultimately converged with talk about privacy. Mention of the "right to be let alone" antedated the Civil War, appearing occasionally in cases having to do, for instance, with state interference with the mails and (as we have seen) with white men's authority to govern households—as when Joseph Story suggested in 1833 that the First Amendment sought to secure the rights of "private sentiment" and "private judgment."[47] In decisions like *DeMay v. Roberts*, however, judges increasingly associated privacy not only with state intrusions, but with private incursions into private spaces and feelings. Many such rulings in state courts involved nongovernmental invasions of women's bedchambers or other private spaces and some kind of sexual affront. In 1880, to give one example, shortly before the Michigan Supreme Court considered Alvira Roberts's complaint, Vermont judges heard the appeal of an action in trespass brought by "an unfortunate girl, blind from birth," who had sued the owner of a house in which she had been retained to teach piano lessons. Her employer had entered her bedroom at night, sat on the bed, and propositioned her. Despite the fact that the house belonged to him, she filed suit. In *Newell v. Whitcher*, the Vermont Supreme Court decided that her "right to her private sleeping-room during the night . . . was as ample and exclusive against the inmates of the house, as if the entry had been made into her private dwelling house through the outer door."[48]

Two years before *Newell*, Justice Thomas Cooley (a member of the Michigan Supreme Court in 1881) had published an influential treatise on the law of torts in which he speculated that "the right to one's person may be said to be a right of complete immunity: to be let alone" and tied it to an action in tort.[49] Nine years later, Louis Brandeis and Samuel Warren would publish a pathbreaking article in the *Harvard Law Review* in which they elaborated on Cooley's idea, citing *De May* and other state decisions as illustrations of what an actionable "right to privacy" might look like. In 1890, privacy had not yet found its way into constitutional law, nor had courts connected hurt feelings to bodies. But in its way, the privacy tort was already woman-friendly; an entering wedge had been the feminine world of sentiment and private experience—women supposedly confessed more readily to "hurt feelings" than men did—that Freudians had been mapping and that sex radicals as well as movie moguls eventually popularized. The fact that lawyers had abandoned the old writ system and *could* imagine new forms of action added fuel to the fire.

A constitutional right to marital privacy gradually emerged in federal law, beginning with *Poe v. Ullman* (1961). In that case, the Supreme Court dismissed a suit challenging Connecticut's late nineteenth-century "mini-Comstock" law prohibiting the use of contraceptives, brought by a physician and a married couple with several congenitally abnormal children. But in one of the *Poe* dissents, John Marshall Harlan noted that the law was an "intolerable and unjustifiable invasion of privacy in the conduct of the most intimate concerns of an individual's personal life." Harlan also criticized his colleagues' attachment to a distinction between "an intrusion into the home" and into "the life which characteristically has its place in the home."[50]

Then, in its 1965 *Griswold v. Connecticut* ruling, the Court began to make the leap from a right to be "let alone" in one's castle to a right to be secure in the "intimate concerns of . . . personal life" discussed or practiced in such spaces. *Griswold* straddled two worlds. It marked a transition from a privacy tort to the modern constitutional right of privacy, but even as it set the Supreme Court on a fresh path, it also struggled to avoid an impression of radical disregard for tradition. Justice William Douglas provided a marriage-conserving opinion that was capable only in its deepest recesses of destabilizing traditional gender relations within families. This opinion comported with the temper of the times: In 1963, President John Kennedy's Commission on the Status of Women, chaired by Eleanor Roosevelt, published a landmark report advocating expanded educational and job opportunities for women, rejecting the Equal Rights Amendment, and urging women to fulfill family obligations (the report called them "givens"). In its discussion of education, the report warned that "career opportunities should not displace traditional responsibilities of women in the home and in the local community."[51] Yet, in the same year, Friedan offered her now-classic *The Feminine Mystique*—a powerful feminist manifesto aimed expressly at the same white suburban women to whom the commission's report had been addressed.

In *Griswold*, the majority connected domestic spaces to the choices made within those spaces, largely on the strength of Justice Brandeis's capacious definition of privacy in *Olmstead v. United States* (1928). There, Chief Justice William Howard Taft had held that the Fourth Amendment did not prohibit federal governmental wiretapping of bootleggers' telephone lines; the amendment prohibited invasions of homes, not eavesdropping on conversations. Wrote Brandeis in dissent, "The makers of the Constitution undertook to secure conditions favorable to the pursuit of happiness. They recognized the significance of man's spiritual nature, of his feelings, and of his intellect. They knew that only a part of the pain, pleasure and satisfactions of life are to be found in material things. They sought to protect Americans in their beliefs, their thoughts, their emotions and their sensations. They conferred, as against the Government, the right to be let alone—the most comprehensive of rights and the right most valued by civilized men. To protect that right, every unjustifiable intrusion by the government upon the privacy of the individual, whatever the means employed, must be deemed a violation of the Fourth Amendment."[52]

Griswold pitted two executives of birth control clinics against the same Connecticut statute at issue in *Poe v. Ullman*—an act that citizens regularly disregarded, but that still exerted pressure on suppliers of birth control paraphernalia and publications. Estelle Trebert Griswold, the executive director of the Planned Parenthood League of Connecticut, and Helen Buxton, a physician and professor at the Yale Medical School as well as the medical director of New Haven's league, regularly gave out what Justice Douglas called "information, instruction, and medical advice *to married persons* as to the means of preventing conception." They had been fined $100 each under the terms of the law, which penalized both users and purveyors of contraceptive drugs, "medicinal articles," and "instruments."[53]

On appeal, the Connecticut Supreme Court of Errors affirmed the original judgment against Griswold and the league; Douglas's opinion reversed that court, in the process establishing a constitutional right to privacy in the choice and use of contraceptives. The U.S. Supreme Court's most iconoclastic civil libertarian emphasized that his brethren did not "sit as a super-legislature" to determine the wisdom or necessity of statutes. But in his view, Connecticut's law operated directly on "an intimate relation of husband and wife and their physician's role in one aspect of that relation." Douglas suggested that many constitutional rights had "penumbras, formed by emanations from those guarantees that help give them life and substance." Of particular moment were "penumbras" of the First, Third, Fourth, Fifth, and Ninth Amendments, which created constitutionally protected "zones of privacy" throughout the document and barred unwarranted state invasions of friendships and associations, minds, and dwelling places—especially bedrooms, which state courts had long accorded special protection. Much as the Court would not let the police "search the sacred precincts of marital bedrooms" for contraceptives, so it would defend a couple's right to be let alone when making birth control decisions. Interference was not only "repulsive," but would have a "maximum destructive impact" upon the marital relation.[54]

Griswold has elicited strong criticism from political conservatives, in part because it provided foundations for the eventual expansion of the constitutional right of privacy. Judge Robert Bork fulminated in 1971 that Douglas's "derivation of the principle" of privacy was "utterly specious"; in this "unprincipled decision," he wrote, multiple zones of autonomy would "add up to an independent right of freedom, which is to say, a general constitutional right to be free of legal coercion, a manifest impossibility in any imaginable society."[55] Yet Douglas intended no such anarchic result. *Griswold* did not purport to allow all women to control their own bodies in every way; rather, it erected an imaginary wall at the bedroom doors of married heterosexuals, beyond which the state could not intrude to dictate reproductive choices. Douglas did not address Connecticut's power to ban the making or sale of contraceptive devices—only the use of them. The decision protected spaces rather than individuals, homes rather than feelings or thoughts. It therefore evoked traditional Fourth Amendment preoccupations with a man's "castle" more completely than Brandeis's generalized "right to be let alone," which extended beyond the "sanctities of a man's home" to the "privacies of life" and an "indefeasible right of personal security, personal liberty and private property."[56] Nowhere did the majority say that citizens carried a right to privacy *beyond* the sacrosanct bedroom or that unmarried couples had expectations of privacy. Indeed, in affirming the federal government's obligation to protect marital relations from political, social, and economic upheaval or contamination, Douglas effectively used the state as a hedge against social instability; he also set marital spaces apart from unconventional alternatives (such as the bedrooms of unwed or homosexual couples) and tacitly embraced the suppression of radical alternatives. On the front pages of newspapers in 1965, after all, were feminists, hippies, and campus protesters. Marriage, wrote Douglas tersely, was "an association that promotes a way of life, not causes; a harmony in living, not political faiths; a bilateral loyalty, not commercial or social projects."[57]

Nevertheless, *Griswold* empowered thousands of married women by keeping the state away from private deliberations about fertility. "Voluntary motherhood" was now federal policy, at least for heterosexual, middle-class married couples. The opinion also cast such women as "bilateral" agents in reproductive decisions—a move that drew the Supreme Court closer to Elizabeth Cady Stanton's vision than to Blackstone's or George Turner's, particularly when men supported the idea of egalitarian marriages. In addition, *Griswold* provided a foundation for the formal overruling of *Olmstead* and the constitutionalization of the right to informational privacy in *Katz v. United States* (1967). Of course, *Griswold* offered no help to women whose husbands took advantage of the veil of privacy to abuse or tyrannize them; governments had been told to defend family formation by steering clear of private spaces, which reinforced old boundaries between the family and the polity. Douglas thus provided ammunition for antifeminist cannons whenever states tried to protect women from domestic violence. Yet, for all of its circumspection, *Griswold* triggered a crucial debate in legal circles and elsewhere about the extent of a woman's right to personal security—her right to enforce personal boundaries, to control what might be done with her body, and to demand a remedy at law when another citizen or the state disregarded her fundamental right to be secure in her person.

Chapter 11

The Civil Rights Settlement

In 1973, the Equal Economic Opportunity Commission (EEOC), the agency responsible for enforcing the Civil Rights Act of 1964, opened an investigation of Sears, Roebuck and Company, the world's largest retail firm and the nation's second largest employer of women.[1] Several years later, after fact-finding and conciliatory efforts, EEOC filed five lawsuits against Sears in federal district courts in Alabama, Tennessee, New York, Illinois, and Georgia. Four of the suits (later dismissed) charged the company with racial and ethnic discrimination in specific stores. The fifth suit, filed in 1979 in Chicago, the location of Sears's national headquarters, alleged nationwide sex discrimination. EEOC especially targeted discriminatory practices in the hiring and promotion of commission sales personnel, who usually dealt in "big ticket" items, such as appliances and roofing; noncommission people sold "small ticket" goods like clothing or toys. Sears's 1980 attempt to have the suit dismissed on the ground that EEOC members involved in the investigation had been cooperating unethically with the National Organization for Women (NOW) did not succeed.[2]

As Judge John Nordberg of the U. S. District Court in Chicago explained in 1986, EEOC sought to prove that Sears had engaged in "a nationwide pattern" of sex discrimination by failing to hire women for commission selling on the same basis as men and to promote female noncommission employees into commissioned jobs on the same terms as men. Between 1973 and 1979–80, full-time and part-time commission personnel on average earned "substantially more," to use the court's term, than did full-time and part-time noncommission workers. EEOC also alleged that the firm had paid women in some managerial posts lower salaries than it paid men in similar jobs.[3] The commission made its case primarily from statistical information and leaned heavily on the so-called disparate treatment theory of equal protection of law, rather than on the disparate impact theory— although, as the trial advanced, EEOC seemed to be using both theories at once. Within a disparate treatment paradigm, complaining parties need to show that a company intended to discriminate, not just (as would be the case under the disparate impact standard) that its policies had different effects on male and female employees. EEOC lawyers argued, on the basis of a comparison of Sears's employment statistics and numbers purporting to show what its labor force ought to look like, that Sears' highly "subjective"[4] employment practices failed to meet statistical expectations for the hiring and promotion of women and therefore discriminated against them in violation of Title VII of the Civil Rights Act. EEOC lawyers especially criticized Sears's seemingly biased employment manuals, hiring guidelines, and interview techniques. Implicit in EEOC's strategy was the idea that sex discrimination alone explained the gap between a statistical model of the labor market and Sears's actual hiring and promotion history.

Sears admitted that in 1980, women made up 83.5 percent of store cashiers and 81.8 percent of noncommission clothing salespersons, but only 7.8 percent of the staff selling motor vehicles and boats, 25 percent of the staff in hardware and building supplies, and a minute portion of employees selling durable goods in homes. EEOC argued that interviewing techniques led women away from commission sales by failing to mention the possibility and imposing masculine selection criteria. The firm's "Retail Testing Manual" described the ideal commission salesperson as a "special breed of cat" with a "sharper intellect and more powerful personality than most other retail personnel." A good "Big Ticket Salesman" was "active" with a "lot of drive," "considerable physical vigor," and a "liking for tools." The "Vigor Scale" (a test given to sales applicants) asked such questions as, "Do you have a low-pitched voice?" "Do you swear often?" "Have you ever done any hunting?" "Have you participated in wrestling?" "Have you played on a football team?"[5]

Although EEOC submitted the testimony of a number of expert witnesses, including Alice Kessler-Harris, a well-regarded labor historian, it did not put victims of employment discrimination on the stand. In the court's unsympathetic reading of her deposition, Kessler-Harris argued that "numerical differences between men and women within jobs in the workforce can only be explained by sex discrimination by employers" and that women sought economic advantages and opportunities, not jobs compatible with "interests." She took issue particularly with the notion that commission sales jobs were "different in kind" from noncommission jobs and that the only legitimate applicants should be those who indicated an interest on application forms. Because EEOC invited only a handful of experts to take the stand, Kessler-Harris' testimony bore a heavy load. It is unclear whether EEOC assumed that statistics provided sufficient proof of a discriminatory pattern or whether (as the *Washington Post* reported) President Ronald Reagan and his new EEOC commissioner, Clarence Thomas, had sabotaged the proceedings in midtrial. Administration officials categorically opposed affirmative action programs and, said the *Post*, had "privately made little secret of their desire to lose the . . . case, and lose it in a way that would explode any chance for future EEOC officials to bring class-action suits on the basis of statistics."[6]

On the other side, Sears conceded gender imbalances, but castigated EEOC's statistical techniques and emphasized the firm's heroic attempts to hire and promote women. After 1973, Sears had implemented affirmative action programs; even if the company had acted in response to the EEOC inquiry, as Kessler-Harris later suggested, their existence was indisputable. Sears pointed out that it tried to promote its own employees from noncommission to commission sales but had found few women willing to accept promotion. It also brushed aside the biased tests, manuals, and interview practices as a "minor consideration" in employment decisions, arguing that EEOC had not proved either intentional or unintentional sex discrimination. In the company's view, Sears's employment patterns originated in the fact that the sexes were not "equally interested" in high-paying, high-risk sales jobs or even in management positions. "[T]he one single most important factor intentionally excluded by EEOC is the applicant's interest in commission sales and in the product to be sold," wrote the judge. Sears had shown that men and women tend to have different interests and aspirations" and that these differences largely explained gender imbalances in commission sales. Nordberg agreed, interpreting testimony about women's *social segregation* as evidence of entrenched differences in work *"interests"*:

Female applicants who indicated an interest in sales most often were interested in selling soft lines of merchandise, such as clothing, jewelry, and cosmetics, items generally not sold on commission at Sears. Male applicants were more likely to be interested in hard lines . . . which are more likely to be sold on commission at Sears. . . . Women usually lacked interest in selling automotives and building supplies, men's clothing, furnaces, fencing and roofing. Women also were not as interested as men in outside sales in general, and did not wish to invest the time and effort necessary to learn to sell in the home improvements divisions. . . . [I]nterests of men and women often diverged along patterns of traditional male and female interest. . . . This lack of interest . . . was confirmed by the number of women who rejected commission sales positions. . . . Many expressed a preference for noncommission selling because it was more enjoyable and friendly.[7]

Kessler-Harris vigorously disputed the validity of "interests" analysis, which tended to confirm women's "natural" domesticity. Sears's position, she wrote in 1998, "rested on a prior categorization of applicants into those who could do the job and those who could not," conditioned powerfully by an anachronistic vision of the mother-worker as hobbyist. Sears then solicited "testimony about these differences, which obscured the contemporary reality of a diverse female population that might well lead many women to want the jobs in question," had they known about them. The real issue was "not whether women and men are different," but whether "the preferences of employers or those of women themselves best explain the under-representation of women in specific jobs."[8]

Unlike EEOC, Sears offered dozens of witnesses to buttress its case. Among the experts who were asked to submit written testimony was historian Rosalind Rosenberg, who found ample support in the social history of women for Sears's disparate interest argument. Although it was hard to avoid the suggestion that Sears had used the fruits of sexism (women's relative lack of familiarity with tools, for example) to "prove" women's lack of interest in promotion and good wages, Rosenberg's position commanded the court's attention. It was clear, too, that Nordberg empathized with Sears and partly misconstrued Rosenberg's testimony. Rosenberg had not said, for example, that "women generally prefer to sell soft-line products . . . and are less interested in selling products such as fencing, refrigeration equipment and tires." Rather, she contended that women and men had not always had "identical interests and aspirations regarding work" and that these differences, while diminishing, had "persisted into the present." The judge read this statement to mean that women as a class were "more interested than men in the social and cooperative aspects of the workplace," that they were less "competitive," and that they preferred "social contact and friendship" and "less stress." Such an interpretation was supposedly consistent with the "uncontradicted testimony of Sears' witnesses regarding the relative lack of interest of women in commission selling."[9]

In 1986, Judge Nordberg ruled in favor of Sears, praising the firm for its good-faith attempts to advance women while addressing the disparate interests of the sexes; he also chastised EEOC for bringing unsubstantiated charges. When EEOC appealed, Sears counterappealed, citing the trial court's failure to dismiss the original suit after learning of conflicts of interest. In 1988, the U.S. Court of Appeals for the Seventh Circuit affirmed the judgment of the district court. Justice Harlington Wood, Jr., took the occasion to reprimand EEOC for collusion: "In seeking to eliminate alleged discrimination at Sears," he wrote, "the EEOC was itself guilty of discrimination against Sears." Judge Cudahy, however, submitted an opinion concurring in part and dissenting in part, chiding both courts for ignoring firm evidence of sex discrimination. Why had Sears not publicized the availability of commission sales posts in advance of interviews? Nordberg and Wood had wrongly dismissed the "inexorable numbers," resorting instead to "highly dubious assumptions about the disparate levels of 'interest' of men and women in commission selling."[10]

The battle between "sameness" and "difference" at the heart of the *Sears* case was anything but new. Gilded Age and Progressive reformers had disagreed pointedly about whether governments ought to surround women with a protective arm, if only to prevent mindless applications of formulas to complex human situations. Consider Mrs. William J. Carson's warnings in 1931 on behalf of the National League of Women Voters: "We are not seeking a mathematical equality to be always measured and balanced, making sure that neither men nor women have one thing more or less than the other." Rather, the league sought "justice and human happiness and opportunities for the most useful development of citizens of the country regardless of sex—an end to which equality is only a means."[11] From 1920 well into the 1970s, legislators, judges, and feminists hotly disputed whether governments should retain legislative classifications that were rooted in physiological differences or replace them with what Carson called a "mathematical" sort of equality. Indeed, after four decades, the only point of agreement seemed to be the efficacy of woman suffrage. By 1964–65, as the second wave began to coalesce, "equal rights" liberalism seemed to be winning the day. But despite gains, women did not secure political equality, economic parity, or personal security. Liberal feminism succumbed to mounting social anxiety and to invidious comparisons with the liberty interests and experiences of black men; in the end, policy makers managed only guarded and partial affirmations of women's equality and sovereignty.

TOWARD POLITICAL AND SPIRITUAL EQUALITY

Given widespread satisfaction with (or at least indifference to) woman suffrage, the full bundle of political rights and obligations should have been relatively easy to attain. And, in some areas, the transition to universal suffrage proceeded uneventfully. The Twenty-fourth Amendment, combined with the Supreme Court's decision in *Harper v. Virginia State Board of Election* (1966),[12] put an end to sex-specific poll taxes. The polls themselves metamorphosed from masculine spaces into neutral or femininized spaces; elections moved from bars and barber shops into schools and churches. And, after a slow start in the 1920s—a characteristic of every group of new voters—women moved steadily toward equal participation in elections. In 1928, new female voters suddenly appeared and remained at the polls, drawn by Democratic presidential candidate Al Smith and the issues that animated what would become the New Deal coalition. Equally important was the entry of immigrant-stock voters on the side of the Democrats after 1927–28, especially in Irish and Italian neighborhoods. According to political scientist Kristi Anderson, women in Philadelphia represented 32.3 percent of the electorate in 1927 and 41.6 percent a year later; in Baltimore, the number of Republican male registrants increased by 13 percent between 1924 and 1928, whereas female registration rose by 62 percent.[13] Furthermore, as voter turnout has declined into the modern era, women have exhibited greater sticking power, often turning out more reliably than men.

In a stream of developments running alongside political changes, moreover, religious women managed to obtain increased access to church lecterns. And while many twentieth-century Americans no longer thought of churches as part of "the public," religious women disagreed; in their view, the ability to interpret biblical texts and to hold pastoral or rabbinical posts alongside men spoke to *political* power and public authority. Within Judaism, Reconstructionist, Reform, and Conservative congregations not only have drawn girls into the community as bat mitzvahs on equal terms with boys, but have permitted women to form part of the minyan, read the Torah, and—since the 1980s, even in Conservative synagogues—serve as rabbis. Among Christians, the old-line ecumenical churches have advanced women fairly rapidly, much as past generations of Quakers, Congregationalists, and Unitarians managed to do during periods of spiritual renewal. To be sure, Catholics continue to oppose abortion, contraception, and a female pastorate, and a number of evangelical Protestant sects periodically move to restore unitary male governance of women, at home and in public life. But in the last third of the twentieth century, the Anglican, Evangelical Lutheran, Methodist, and other old-line Protestant denominations gradually opened their doors to female pastors, often in response to feminist agitation within church ranks. Mary Daly, Gloria Steinem, and other influential feminists began their careers as Catholic dissenters or members of egalitarian Jewish families. Moravians—the early fifteenth-century followers of Czech "heretic" Jan Hus, and perhaps the first Protestants—decided in August 1998 to appoint Dr. Kay Ward the first female bishop in the history of modern Christianity. "We never know what will happen," said Ward in an acceptance speech, "when men . . . choose to break open tightly bound fists of power and authority. And so I understand that what is happening here today takes place in a much wider context, a much longer journey."[14]

Securing the full bundle of political rights and obligations, however, has proved to be difficult at best. In the wake of *Hoyt v. Florida*, judges and social conservatives resisted extending jury-service privileges that seemed to smash women's traditionally primary allegiance to husbands and families and to place women in positions of public judgment and command. It is interesting that the 1964 Civil Rights Act did not immediately affect the judiciary's "separate but equal" readings of women's jury-service obligations. In 1966, an Alabama federal judge did pronounce the exclusion of women from juries a violation of the equal protection clause. But other courts disagreed, usually on the ground of women's domestic and maternal obligations; Judge Mansfield's opinion in *Leighton v. Goodman* was typical. Only in 1975 did the Supreme Court grudgingly reconsider *Hoyt*; in *Taylor v. Louisiana*, the justices, on Sixth Amendment grounds, invalidated a statute denying a man accused of rape a jury composed of a cross-section of the population. *Taylor* did not declare sex a suspect classification under the Fourteenth Amendment—that is, a classification automatically subjected to the highest level of scrutiny in constitutional cases. Nor did it address a would-be female *juror's* right to serve alongside men; at issue were the rights of the accused, not women's obligations as citizens. But the Court did invalidate laws limiting jury service to men and four years later reiterated the *Taylor* rule in *Duren v. Missouri*.

Judges have been even more reluctant to acknowledge women's equal obligation to provide military service. Indeed, on such questions, judges and members of Congress rather than military personnel have held the line against sex integration. Abolition of the draft in 1973 provoked a sweeping reconsideration of rules within the armed services. As of 1974, men and women could enlist at the same age; a year later, military academies began to admit women, albeit in small numbers and amid controversy. After 1970, the armed services pursued uncommonly successful affirmative action programs. The army had desegregated basic training, and every service required weapons training for women. In 1979, the Department of Defense (DOD) asked Congress to repeal laws barring women from combat duty, pointing out (in Kenneth Karst's words) that "the combat exclusion prevented the effective use of personnel, limited opportunities for women, and limited the total number of women who could serve in the armed forces."[15]

Following the DOD's lead, during 1980 hearings of the House Committee on Armed Services, President Jimmy Carter proposed the sex-neutral registration of all men and women. He billed his decision as a "recognition of the reality that both women and men are working members of our society. It confirms . . . that women are now providing all types of skills in every profession. The military should be no exception. In fact, there are already 150,000 women serving in our armed forces. . . . There is no distinction possible, on the basis of ability or performance, that would allow me to exclude women from an obligation to register." But with the advent of the Reagan Administration, the DOD changed its position, and Congress (including a number of liberal women) refused to budge, deciding in 1981 to limit draft registration to men. When the Burger Court upheld the constitutionality of this decision, antifeminists cheered. Kathleen Teague of Phyllis Schlafly's Eagle Forum, for instance, noted that draft exemption was a right that every woman had "enjoyed since our country was born"—that is, the "constitutional right to be treated like American ladies."[16]

Thus, while the armed services have not resolved serious problems with gender and sex inequality (including sexual harassment, policies disadvantaging gay soldiers, and in-adequate child care), on the narrow question of promotion and fair employment, imped-iments to sex equality often have been external to the military rather than internal. For all practical purposes, the pro-maternal decision of the U.S. District Court for the Southern District of New York in the 1968 case of *U.S. v. St. Clair*, which sustained women's ex-emption from military obligations, is still the law of the land. James St. Clair, who had been charged with violating the Military Selective Service Act of 1967, argued that the draft system amounted to "invidious discrimination on the basis of sex" in violation of the Fifth Amendment. In his opinion rejecting St. Clair's motion for a jury hearing, Judge Bonsal embraced the "home and family" imagery in *Hoyt v. Florida*: "In the Act and its predecessors, Congress made a legislative judgment that men should be subject to invol-untary induction but that women [should not], presumably because they are 'still regarded as the center of home and family life.' . . . In providing for involuntary service for men and voluntary service for women, Congress followed the teachings of history that if a na-tion is to survive, men must provide the first line of defense while women keep the home fires burning." Because Congress did permit women to volunteer for certain military du-ties, if not for combat, the "distinction between men and women" was "not arbitrary, un-reasonable or capricious."[17]

At the center of the political stage, moreover, the number of female officeholders has barely increased. To be sure, as of 1991, 7.4 percent of federal judges were female. Women also made up 18 percent of state legislators, 17 percent of state and local executives, 14 percent of mayors and city council members, and 6 percent of the members of Congress. On September 26, 1981, Arizona legislator and judge Sandra Day O'Connor became an associate justice of the U.S. Supreme Court, and Ruth Bader Ginsburg—long a major fig-ure in feminist jurisprudence and a prime mover in post-1964 attempts to expand the reach of the Fourteenth Amendment to include women—joined her in 1996. Given the absence of women from high office a century earlier, these developments were significant. Yet, in 1983, Judge Miriam Goldman Cedarbaum of the Federal District Court for the South-ern District of New York noted that, of the 801 judges sitting on federal benches, only 62 were women—even though (in her words) between "one-third and one-half of the stu-dents in the entering classes of most law schools are now, and for the last fifteen or twenty years have been, women."[18]

Because women constitute an electoral majority and typically work harder (and with less money) than do men to win elections, these numbers are disheartening. Moreover, within party ranks, the number of African Americans, Latinos, Asian Americans, and lesbians is miniscule. As Justice O'Connor put it in 1991, "Until the percentages come closer to fifty percent . . . , we cannot say we have succeeded."[19] Journalist Gail Collins said bluntly that Geraldine Ferraro's 1984 vice-presidential nomination was "the high point for the women's movement." As of 1998, only three states (Arizona, New Jersey, and New Hampshire) boasted female governors—one more than in 1925, when Nellie Taloe Ross of Wisconsin and Miriam Ferguson of Texas took office. In Arizona, Jane Dee Hull came to the statehouse only after the conviction of the elected governor, Fife Symington, for fraud. In 1990s New York, to borrow Collins's words, a large number of promising women had "crashed and burned." Ann Richards of Texas had been edged out of politics, and though the number of women in Congress slowly increased, no woman in the House had come "within a mile of a real leadership role." In New Hampshire, women have gained a substantial toehold with a female governor and heavily feminine legislature (30 percent). But the exception makes the point, since the legislative job pays $100 a year. Says former Congresswoman Pat Schroeder, "It almost looks like it could be the end of the [nineteenth] century, except no one's taken our right to vote away."[20]

Commentators think that women's modest day on the political stage ended partly because of widespread perceptions of women as single-issue candidates with little interest in "hard" topics such as foreign relations, the military, and the budget. Campaign managers have reinforced this impression by portraying women as "Moms" in tennis shoes— as advocates mainly of child protection, education, and reproductive freedom or as representatives mainly of women and children. To some extent, these stereotypic representations reflect the fact of an electoral gender gap. In the 1980 presidential election, a significant difference emerged in male-female voting behavior. While women's voting patterns showed little change from the 1976 election (45 percent for Jimmy Carter, 47 percent for Ronald Reagan), Reagan got 55 percent of men's votes and Carter got only 36 percent. A few years later, women reported a "loss of confidence" in Reagan's willingness to defend women's interests. By 1983, 34 percent of the women who were included in a poll approved of presidential achievements and priorities, compared to 51 percent of the men. In subsequent elections, women's electoral behavior continued to differ significantly, in some cases dramatically from men's, leading many experts to think that the gap may become a permanent feature of the political landscape.[21] Managers seem to have concluded, to some extent wrongly, that women constitute a special-interest group with homogeneous, "soft" interests. In any case, as Collins also noted, issues to which women gravitate (or are seen to gravitate) "do not attract a lot of big donors. Women might benefit from a campaign-finance system in which candidates got matching funds and were prohibited from taking huge donations." But the same process might kill EMILY's List ("Early Money Is Like Yeast"), a major source of money for chronically underfunded female candidates.[22]

TOWARD ECONOMIC EQUALITY

In the post–World War II marketplace, two forces intruded aggressively on the struggle for constitutional equality—first, the lawyers' taste for what Sylvia Law calls "legal assimilationism" (that is, the drawing of as many classes as possible under a particular constitutional umbrella), and, second, lingering unease among conservatives and liberals alike about the implications of legal "sameness" for family life, social peace, and traditional gender ascriptions. In legal constructions of blacks and women (the two main groups around which case law in this area has developed), biological difference cuts in two directions. On the one hand, ineradicable physical differences set both blacks and women apart from whites and men, respectively; the two groups share marginalization and oppression. On the other hand, women's reproductive capacities set them apart from men of all classes and colors, and the class "woman" includes members of the "black" class, which introduces additional, equally ineradicable divisions *within* difference. As Law correctly observes, because legal assimilationism "builds upon analogies between race- and sex-based discrimination," in Fourteenth Amendment cases especially, perceptions of female uniqueness *as a class* have led to findings of "difference" and then to "soft" readings of *individual* women's right to be free from state-sponsored limitation. This has been particularly true when the case at hand implicated women's bodies or pregnancy.[23]

Postwar shifts in women's behavior and in workplace organization lent urgency to demands for economic equality. Despite attempts to remove women from the workplace and resituate them at home, female workers increasingly sought permanent places as wage earners. Women typically undertook relatively low-paying positions (as secretaries and sales clerks, for example) or jobs defined by their physical attributes and social or domestic skills (for instance, automobile upholstery stitchers, airline hostesses, and front-lobby receptionists). Women also clustered in sex-segregated fields, supervised by a handful of male managers, at lower wages than men earned for comparable work; cleaning women, file clerks, and waitresses were paid less than janitors, mail boys, and waiters. As the Cold War dawned, moreover, women's labor seemed increasingly essential to maintaining a strategic edge in relations with the Soviet Union. Hence, tensions between the ideal of female domesticity and the reality of the working woman were not resolved. While Rosie the Riveter had been a critical wartime worker, she had been tolerated rather than welcomed, and often denied essential support services. Day care centers implied social acceptance of decisions against full-time domesticity and perhaps against the patriarchal family; many Americans resisted making such a decision.

Perhaps ironically, both postwar feminism and sex-related economic policy came to be framed by the phantomlike presence in Congress of the unapproved, unratified Equal Rights Amendment (ERA); in federal courts, judges sometimes referred to ERA as if it were a jurisprudential reality and allowed it to shape legal outcomes. In all this, the National Woman's Party (NWP) was a main engine, keeping the amendment before congressional committees and lobbying for its passage. On the eve of World War II, NWP efforts almost paid dividends. In May 1936, a House subcommittee offered the first favorable report on it; a year later, subcommittees of both the House and Senate reported positively. But in 1938, senators ultimately sent it back to committee; the same pattern recurred from 1939 until 1946, when the Senate suddenly called a vote, producing a slim majority (38–35) in favor of adoption, which was not quite the requisite number for a constitutional amendment.

Evasive maneuvers were Herculean. Beginning in the 1940s, state lawmakers repeatedly introduced alternatives to a national ERA in the form of civil rights and equal pay acts, amendments to state constitutions, and proposals for boards of inquiry. In Congress, manifestoes like the protectionist "Women's Charter" of 1943 suggested "full political and civil rights" for women, as well as "full opportunity for education" and for "work according to their individual abilities," but with "safeguards against physically harmful conditions of employment and economic exploitation." By this proposal, Congress would guarantee women's "security of livelihood, including the safeguarding of motherhood"; wherever "special exploitation of women workers" existed, including "low wages which provide less than the living standards attainable, unhealthful working conditions or long hours of work . . . , such conditions shall be corrected through . . . legislation, which the world's experience shows to be necessary."[24]

Moreover, ERA periodically mutated (or threatened to mutate) in response to a complex tug-of-war between the NWP and kindred laissez-faire Republicans, post–New Deal liberals, and protection-minded laborites and social reformers. In 1943, Democratic Senator Harley Kilgore introduced an amendment that read, "Equality of rights under the law shall not be denied or abridged by the United States or by any State on account of sex. . . . This amendment shall not require uniformity of legislation among the several States, the District of Columbia, the Territories, and possessions of the United States." The same year, Republican Senator Warren Austin of Vermont proposed a text—widely supported by other Republicans—that dropped Kilgore's protectionist section and added a clause delaying implementation of the amendment for five years after ratification, to facilitate an orderly revamping of state law codes. Two years later, the United Automobile, Aircraft, and Agriculture Implement Workers of America sponsored an ERA rider: "Nothing in this article shall be construed as to invalidate or prevent legislation improving the working conditions of women." In 1950 and again in 1953, the Senate adopted an ERA with yet another rider drafted by Democratic Senator Carl Hayden of Arizona. It read in part: "Equality of rights under the law shall not be denied or abridged by the United States or by any State on account of sex. The provisions of this article shall not be construed to impair any rights, benefits, or exemptions now or hereafter conferred by law upon persons of the female sex."[25]

Such proposals competed with "women's status bills" for Congress's attention. In 1950, for instance, just as Alice Paul regained control over the NWP in the wake of a divisive lawsuit, lawmakers considered the Wadsworth-Taft bill to "establish a commission on the legal status of women" that would fasten upon a "policy as to distinctions based on sex." Senator Estes Kefauver's alternative to the Wadsworth-Taft bill provided for "the investigation of discriminations against women on the basis of sex" and adoption of "policies for the removal of such discriminations." Kefauver also advocated use of the "reasonableness" test articulated in cases like *Goesart*:

> Be it enacted by the Senate and House of Representatives of the United States of America in Congress Assembled, That it is the declared policy of the United States that in law and its administration no distinctions on the basis of sex shall be made except such as are reasonably justified by differences in physical structure, or by maternal function.[26]

Into the Cold War era, the ERA continued to attract riders and clauses as if it were flypaper. Consider several riders among many proposed in 1950—by Helen Hill Weed ("The provisions of this article shall not be construed to invalidate special legislation conferring benefits or exemptions on legally defined classes of men and women"), Paul ("This article shall not be construed to impair any rights, benefits, exemptions, or protection conferred upon men and women equally, or conferred upon one sex alone when inaplicable to both sexes"), and Ethel Ernest Murrell ("This article shall not be construed to impair any rights, benefits, exemptions, or protection conferred upon men and women equally or conferred upon one sex alone when inapplicable to both sexes, or any special consideration given to women on grounds of motherhood"). In 1953, senators resolved to support an amendment that would declare the words "person, persons, or people" where they appeared in constitutional texts to include both sexes and that would automatically amend state or federal laws to the contrary—whereupon Senator Hayden's alternative appeared, effectively scuttling the ERA for another decade.[27]

After 1962, Congress adopted a bundle of antidiscriminatory measures as possible alternatives to the ERA—especially the Equal Pay Act of 1963, but also the better-known Civil Rights Act of 1964. Neither statute owed much to President John Kennedy, whose support for "equal rights" was lukewarm at best. Historian Cynthia Harrison notes that Kennedy made only desultory attempts to locate female candidates for his administration's positions, disliked working with women, and—perhaps most important—preferred to entrust "women's issues" to the Women's Bureau and its new head, Esther Peterson, a labor activist, avid protectionist, and staunch opponent of ERA. To a great extent, the achievements of the 1960s had less to do with feminism than with an infectious liberalism in the air during and immediately after the Kennedy years, which political scientist Michael Walzer calls "an openness to new ideas probably unlike anything since the thirties."[28]

The Kennedy Administration quickly put equal pay legislation—a staple of the Eisenhower Administration and a widely favored alternative to ERA—at the top of its agenda. Peterson's Women's Bureau skillfully pasted together a coalition of supporters, including various labor unions, Business and Professional Women, the American Association of University Women, and (less enthusiastically) the NWP. During House debates, New York Representative Katharine St. George quipped that a vote against equal pay for men and women would be "like being against motherhood."[29] Over many months, however, St. George and other laissez-faire Republicans managed to replace a key clause ("equal pay for comparable work") with "equal pay for equal work," a change that invited employers to evade the law by rewriting job descriptions so that workplace segregation by sex might be retained. Lobbyists also persuaded Congress to remove language forbidding employers from achieving equality by lowering men's wages. By 1962, a main concern was that the bill might be useless, since wage discrimination was most egregious when work assignments were "comparable" rather than "equal." The much-altered Equal Pay Act finally passed both houses of Congress in May 1963, in the form of an amendment to the Fair Labor Standards Act, and became law several weeks later.

The resulting measure satisfied almost no one. Liberals found it too diluted to be useful, and many ERA supporters openly sneered. The measure applied only to workers who were subject to the minimum wage laws and so excluded professional women; it also exempted pay discrimination based on merit or seniority systems, as well as differentials "based on any factor other than sex."[30] Still, the new law put the federal government into the business, in Harrison's words, of "safeguarding the right of women to hold employment on the same basis as men."[31] And in more than one case, women have found the statute useful. In *Marcoux v. State of Maine* (1986), for example, judges of the first federal circuit ordered corrections officials to equalize retirement benefits for female and male guards working at sex-segregated prisons.

Peterson's Women's Bureau also succeeded in persuading the Kennedy team to create the President's Commission on the Status of Women (PCSW), to be chaired by Eleanor Roosevelt, again as a way to focus attention on women's issues without risking further, contentious debate of ERA. Established in December 1961, the twenty-six member commission was charged with assessing woman's condition and making policy recommendations by October 1963. Although it was supposed to be neutral on the ERA question, only one member—the NWP's Marguerite Rawalt—was known to support the amendment.

The PCSW moved swiftly to contain highly divisive talk about ERA, handing it over to a rump group (the Committee on Civil and Political Rights) for discussion, fact-finding, and resolution. When the committee met in May 1962, Pauli Murray (a prominent African American lawyer, member of the PCSW, and eventually an Episcopalian minister) suggested that commissioners surmount the ERA controversy by forcing the Supreme Court to expand the Fourteenth Amendment's equal protection umbrella to include women—a strategy also adopted in the 1970s by Bader Ginsburg (then a leader of the American Civil Liberties Union's Women's Rights project) and other prominent civil rights lawyers. Implicit in this strategy was Murray's sense that women's subjugation to men, if laid beside blacks' subjugation to the white race, would be found to be roughly comparable, and half of all blacks, after all, were women. In a widely circulated memorandum, Murray argued that policy makers ought to begin distinguishing between laws that were "genuinely protective of the family and maternal functions" and those that discriminated "unjustly" against individuals. In her view, the line of cases running from *Muller v. Oregon* had entrenched "separate but equal" doctrine in the law affecting women's economic and educational prospects—the very doctrine rejected in *Brown v. Board* when the Supreme Court brought the equal protection clause to bear upon racially segregated schools and declared "separate but equal" education to be unconstitutional. Why not get federal courts to declare an identity between sex- and race-based distinctions and condemn both on Fourteenth Amendment grounds? Murray did not have in mind eliminating all sex distinctions. She noted, for example, that state legislators might retain statutes that benefited "women of childbearing age." In her view, "maternity legislation" was not "sex legislation" because its benefits were "geared to the performance of a special service [reproduction of the race] much like veterans' legislation." But, for the most part, ERA would be moot, and women of all races and classes would have constitutional standing equal to that which courts had formally extended to black men.[32]

Initially, bitter disagreement engulfed the PCSW, but its members soon concluded that they could trust appellate judges to preserve laws that were truly beneficial to women and to eliminate merely discriminatory ones. When the Labor Department, Peterson, and Congress itself began pressing for a statement about ERA, the commission hammered out a compromise saying, in part, that given the existence of Fourteenth Amendment and state options, a new amendment did not "appear to be necessary to establish the principle of equality," unless "at some future time, it appears from court decisions that a need for such action exists." In effect, ERA had been closeted, but a door had been left open for future action, should federal courts drop the ball. As Harrison points out, the PCSW had at least affirmed women's right to "equal treatment under the Fourteenth Amendment to the Constitution" and moved constructively toward a compromise on the ERA question. The PCSW had also articulated the need for a *program* encompassing not only "equal rights" but also the "many problems that constitutional equality would not rectify."[33]

Despite the maternalist tenor of its final report, the PCSW's positive influence is undeniable: As a result of its insistence on systematic planning, a range of new agencies emerged that were devoted to the problem of male-female equality. Feminists and community leaders also initiated conversations on a broad range of topics—among them, education, child care, employment, and financial security. Although the PCSW's successors often rejected many of its proposals—for example, the idea (highlighted in its final report) that in light of women's childbearing contributions, men ought to bear primary responsibility for families' economic support—it set an important ball in motion. Pressure from the PCSW and NAACP underlay a wave of Kennedy Administration executive orders that established equality within the federal civil service, the creation of a Citizen's Advisory Committee on the Status of Women, and the elimination of sex quotas in the military. Although not immediately useful to all women, Executive Order 10925, issued shortly after Kennedy's inauguration in January 1961, created the Presidential Commission on Equal Employment Opportunity and required federal contractors to take "affirmative action" to prevent discrimination by "race, creed, color, or national origin."[34]

Perhaps the most consequential postwar attempt to secure equality through federal legislation was the Civil Rights Act of 1964, with its critical Title VII language. When Congress first considered Representative Emanuel Celler's civil rights bill in the summer of 1963, sex was nowhere mentioned. Although the NWP preferred an ERA to ordinary legislation, it promptly moved to include sex discrimination in Celler's bill. If the inclusion defeated the proposed legislation, all the better; if it did not, then women would stand on an even footing with African American men. Indeed, Michigan's Representative Martha Griffiths argued for including the word *sex* to help African American women compete with men of both races: As drafted, the law would have encouraged employers to define such women as "female" rather than "black." Said Griffiths,

> Supposing a little 100-pound colored woman arrives at the management's door and asks for the job of driving a haulaway truck and he says, "Well you are not qualified," and she says, "Oh, yes, I am. During the war I was the motorman on a streetcar in Detroit. For the past 15 years I have driven the school bus." . . . Of course, that woman is qualified. But he has only white men drivers. Do you know that that woman is not going to have a right under this law? Merely to ask the question is to answer it.[35]

On February 8, 1964, Representative Howard Smith, a Democrat from Virginia and ERA supporter, proposed an amendment adding discrimination by reason of sex. Because the bill threatened to unhinge protectionist laws across the country, the Women's Bureau and many other women's groups opposed it. Smith's proposal triggered laughter; Celler himself pointed out that he usually had the last two words in his "household of women, and they were 'yes, dear.' " Congressmen joked that, with Title VII on the books, men at long last could sue to become *Playboy* bunnies.[36] Beneath the jokes, however, lay weeks of discussion and lobbying. Historian Jo Freeman thinks that the jocular tone aimed to disarm opponents on the House floor, that Smith may well have supported the "sex" amendment, and that Republicans and southerners (who voted for the "sex" addition) probably viewed it as an appealing alternative to ERA.[37] Other scholars argue that Smith added the word "sex" to ensure the bill's defeat. Whatever the case may have been, when the Johnson Administration lent support alongside Griffiths, Margaret Chase of Maine, and other prominent women, the bill slid through Congress in July 1964. The Civil Rights Act established the EEOC to administer and enforce its provisions. Title VII called for "affirmative" attempts by employers to fill jobs with blacks and women and to eliminate socioeconomic "imbalances," which introduced a strong echo of protectionism. The act also outlawed practices that "deprive or tend to deprive any individual of employment opportunities or otherwise adversely affect his status as an employee" by reason of sex. This tough-minded provision shared space, however, with the bona fide occupational qualification (BFOQ) section, which allowed employers to exclude women or any other protected group on the basis of a qualification "reasonably necessary" to the "normal operation" of a business or other economic enterprise—that is, a distinction inherent in the work itself.[38]

The Civil Rights Act did not automatically eliminate protectionist legislation in the states. Liberal feminists were outraged to learn that EEOC did not mean to unsettle state protection of women and would treat sex classifications mandated by state law as BFOQs unless challenged in court. The first EEOC director, Herman Edelsberg, dismissed the sex provisions of Title VII as a "fluke,"[39] emphasizing racial discrimination. In December 1965, EEOC commissioner Richard Graham explained, in a letter to an NWP member, "There seems to be a widely held misconception that this Commission can or would overturn state protective legislation. This is not the case. . . . If there is a clear conflict between the laws, we would not ask that [an employer] violate the state law. Rather, we would suggest that this conflict be brought to the attention of the Governor or the State Legislature or the state commission for remedy."[40] In 1966, EEOC ruled that laws regulating minimum wages, overtime, and the physical attributes of the workplace had to apply to both sexes. All other single-sex laws (among them, hours legislation, restrictions on lifting heavy objects, laws excluding women from such occupations as mining or bartending, and bans on night work) would be left to the decision of state courts. The United Auto Workers triumphantly declared the age of protectionism at an end. But pro-protectionist lobbies, including many other unions, refused to cede the point, insisting that hour and weight restrictions helped the least powerful and that "equal rights" could only hurt working women.

EEOC foot-dragging did trigger one important development—the founding of NOW, a mid-twentieth-century analogue to the National American Woman Suffrage Association. As feminism resurged in the 1960s, and in keeping with women's long-standing sensitivity to words, post–World War II feminists had begun to establish new speech communities within the broader American suffrage community; these included woman-centered professional societies, study groups, political parties and caucuses, religious sects, food and health cooperatives, utopian communities, consciousness-raising groups, and women's studies programs and courses in academic institutions. In 1953, an American edition of Simone de Beauvoir's somewhat cerebral *The Second Sex* appeared; a decade later, Betty Friedan published the more accessible *Feminine Mystique*, which swept through both academic and lay circles like a firestorm. In academic circles, "free spaces" proliferated. The Radcliffe Institute for Independent Study, for instance, aimed to help gifted women, especially married women, confront a "sense of stagnation." The New Woman of the 1960s, like her counterpart in the 1850s, sensed "the new expectations the world holds for her"; increasingly, she thought of the "early years of marriage as offering new freedom and an unparalleled opportunity to experiment intellectually."[41]

By 1962–64, thousands of lawyers, educators, students, and political activists had joined the women's rights vanguard. When the ever-cautious EEOC decided in 1966 that Title VII allowed firms to publish sex-specific job advertisements, a number of disgusted women met in Friedan's Washington, D.C., hotel room to discuss how to deal with governmental inaction. The result was NOW. As Murray told the story, at a conference luncheon the next day, "Betty Friedan scribbled the new group's purpose on a napkin: 'To take the actions needed to bring women into the mainstream of American society *now* . . . in fully equal partnership with men.' " When thirty-two women held an organizational meeting in the autumn of 1966 and named Friedan NOW's first president, they scarcely imagined that, two decades later, it would boast more than 200,000 members and become a "potent force in American politics." NOW's 1966 statement of purpose closely resembled the resolutions issued by "first wave" women's rights conventions; it even took on the job of *speaking* for women. "We, men and women . . . believe," said the founders, "that the time has come for a new movement toward true equality for all women in America, and toward a fully equal partnership of the sexes, as part of the world-wide revolution of human rights now taking place within and beyond our national borders."

> The purpose of NOW is to take action to bring women into full participation in the mainstream of American society. . . .
>
> There is no civil rights movement to speak for women, as there has been for Negroes and other victims of discrimination. The National Organization for Women must therefore begin to speak.
>
> We believe, that the power of American law, and the protection guaranteed by the U.S. Constitution to the civil rights of all individuals, must be effectively applied and enforced to isolate and remove patterns of sex discrimination, to ensure equality of opportunity in employment and education, and equality of civil and political rights and responsibilities on behalf of women, as well as for Negroes and other deprived groups. . . .
>
> We believe that this nation has a capacity at least as great as other nations, to innovate new social institutions which will enable women to enjoy true equality of opportunity and responsibility in society, without conflict with their responsibilities as mothers and homemakers. . . . We do not accept the traditional assumption that a woman has to choose between marriage and motherhood, on the one hand, and serious participation in industry or the professions on the other.[42]

NOW urged child care facilities for working women; a "different concept of marriage" and an "equitable sharing" of household responsibilities; full sex integration of political party bureaucracies; educational campaigns to dispel the "false image" of women as lesser or subservient creatures; and an end to practices that, in the "guise of protectiveness," undermined women's self-confidence and blocked economic advancement. Delegates to the 1850 Worcester convention might have applauded the final paragraph's emphasis on speech, the right of action, and self-constitution: "We believe that women will do most to create a new image of women by *acting* now, and by speaking out in behalf of their own equality, freedom, and human dignity—"

> not in pleas for special privilege, nor in enmity toward men, who are also victims of the current half-equality between the sexes, but in an active, self-respecting partnership with men. By so doing, women will develop confidence in their own ability to determine actively, in partnership with men, the conditions of their life, their choices, their future and their society.[43]

Subsequently, over 300 women who were interested in political, rather than legal, action called a national conference in 1971 to establish the National Women's Political Caucus—the embodiment of attorney Eleanor Holmes Norton's call in 1970 for a "women's political coalition equal in its competence, professionalism, and drive to any lobby the Congress has ever seen."[44] Three years later, a different group founded the National Campaign Fund to help women run for public office.

As in the 1850s, in other words, women struggled to find "a voice" (though mainly as a personal and cultural goal rather than as a constitutional aspiration); to name their oppressors; to construct new vocabularies of freedom; and to reconstitute individuals as active, self-possessed citizens. Women's experiences of public oratory sometimes bore an eerie resemblance to Mary Livingstone's. Witness journalist Susan Faludi's account of a speech at the Smithsonian Institution in Washington, D.C.: "The dreaded evening . . . finally arrived. I stood knock-kneed and green-gilled before three hundred people. . . . I cleared my throat and, to my shock, a hush fell over the room. . . . It was as if their attentive silence allowed me to make contact with my own muffled self. I began to speak. . . ."

> My voice got surer, my delivery rising. A charge passed between me and the audience, uniting and igniting us both. . . . Afterward, it struck me that in some essential way I hadn't really proved myself a feminist until now. Until you translate personal words on a page into public connections with other people, you aren't really part of a political movement. I hadn't declared my independence until I was willing to declare it out loud. I knew public speaking was important to reform public life—but I hadn't realized the transformative effect it could have on the speaker herself.

"Women need to be heard not just to change the world," she added, "but to change themselves."[45]

In the new movement, as in its antebellum predecessor, calls to action proliferated on a number of fronts. Historians moved aggressively to recover the words and contributions of past women and then to remake the male-centric narratives of American and world history. Into the 1970s, radical feminists schooled in the civil rights and antiwar movements joined (and sometimes locked horns with) liberals in the struggle for "women's liberation," as the radical wing of the movement came to be called. Black power activist-professor Angela Davis's studies of racial and sexual subjugation began to appear, including *If They Came in the Morning* (1971). Increasingly, activists confronted sexism in the civil rights movement: In 1967, at the mixed-race "New Left" National Conference for New Politics in Chicago, a women's caucus asked permission to read a resolution denouncing sexism. The chairman shoved the resolution through without a reading and moved on to "more important issues"; a week later, caucus members formed their own liberation group. "We hope our words and actions," read their manifesto, "will help make women more aware and organized in their own movement through which a concept of free womanhood will emerge." By the early 1970s, black feminists responded in much the same way to Black Nationalist exclusions of women. The following statement triggered the formation of the Combahee River Collective: "We understand that it is and has been traditional that the man is the head of the house."

> He is the leader of the house/nation because his knowledge of the world is broader, his awareness is greater, his understanding is fuller and his application of this information is wiser. . . . After all, it is only reasonable that the man be the head of the house because he is able to defend and protect . . . his home. . . . Women cannot do the same things as men—they are made by nature to function differently. Equality of men and women is something that cannot happen.[46]

During the same period, the ERA became a central fixture in NOW's constitutional strategy, notwithstanding tension between the laissez-faire arguments at the amendment's heart and liberal feminists' faith in government as an agent of social change. In 1971, pro-ERA lawyers persuaded the *Yale Law Journal* to devote an issue to the legal and constitutional implications of ERA; Martha Griffiths and Senator Birch Bayh spearheaded its distribution and insertion into the *Congressional Record*. In the *Journal*, Yale law professor Thomas Emerson and three law students (Gail Falk, Ann Freedman, and Barbara Brown) offered an unambiguous brief for ERA. "[T]he principle of the Amendment," they wrote, "must be applied comprehensively and without exceptions. . . . [T]he prohibition against the use of sex as a basis for differential treatment applies to all areas of legal rights. To the extent that any exception is made, the values sought by the Amendment are undercut. . . . [T]he constitutional mandate must be absolute." They also captured a prevailing sense of woman's imminent escape from maternal expectations: "The structured legal and social discrimination against women is now being challenged by the demand for women's liberation. This movement for equality is made possible by relative affluence, broader educational opportunities for women, and mechanization of industry. It has been given impetus by the weakening of family ties,"

> the growing participation of women in the labor force, increasing life expectancy, and widespread concern about over-population. It accompanies more enlightened and flexible attitudes towards relations between the sexes. And it is allied with the struggles of minorities, youth, and other forces seeking new ways of life, and new ways for people to relate to one another.[47]

Congress batted the ERA back and forth until 1970, when the amendment finally passed the House with a two-thirds majority (350–15), but with a seven-year ratification clause and language granting concurrent enforcement powers to Congress and to the states. In October 1970, the Senate failed to get beyond the question of whether women would have to be drafted and instead adopted a bill outlawing a mixed-sex draft. One participant later said that she regretted NOW's failure to say more loudly that assignment of women to combat duty was discretionary with the military, not mandatory. Historian Jane Mansfield concludes, in fact, that the draft problem single-handedly determined ERA's fate in the court of public opinion; certainly, antifeminists seized on and exploited the image of innocent daughters and sisters raped by enemy soldiers before NOW could organize a defense.[48] In 1971, the House Judiciary Committee recommended an ERA to the full House with an amendment promising that it would "not impair the validity of any law of the United States which exempts a person from compulsory military service or any other law of the United States or any State which reasonably promotes the health and safety of the people." The House passed the amendment without the rider by a vote of 354–23. The Senate Subcommittee on Constitutional Amendments (chaired by Senator Bayh) recommended another rider providing that "neither the United States nor any State shall make any legal distinctions between the rights and responsibilities of male and female persons unless such distinction is based on physiological or functional differences between them."[49] In March 1972, however, both the full Senate committee and the requisite number of senators approved an unencumbered ERA and sent it to the states for ratification. The final version—basically Paul's handiwork—was a model of clarity:

> Section 1. Equality of rights under the law shall not be denied or abridged by the United States or by any State on account of sex.
> Section 2. The Congress shall have the power to enforce, by appropriate legislation, the provisions of this article.
> Section 3. This amendment shall take effect two years after the date of ratification.[50]

WHY THE ERA?

After the ERA had gone to the states for approval and as Americans began to take sides on the question, feminists continued to pursue civic equality in the courts and elsewhere, without benefit of a sex-specific equal protection clause. An AFL-CIO study, released in September 1997, revealed that 94 percent of American women saw "equal pay for equal work" as their top workplace priority and that a full one-third did not get equal pay on the job.[51] Within the professions, well-educated, capable physicians, lawyers, and professors still encountered sex-specific hurdles, many of them embedded in corporate or professional culture. In the 1980s, the American Bar Association commissioned a disturbing *Report on Women in the Profession*. Researchers found that although the number of female lawyers had increased, women regularly faced "overt and subtle barriers to complete integration into the legal profession." Witnesses had testified eloquently to what one female practitioner called a "dirty little secret"—that sexual harassment pervaded the profession. Women lost promotions for rebuffing sexual advances; men regarded female grievances as "trivial." Judges and lawyers addressed women by their first names, while calling male colleagues "Mr." A Texas judge asked a diminutive woman to face the courtroom and said, "Ladies and gentlemen, can you believe this pretty little thing is an Assistant Attorney General?" The report also confirmed what professional women had known all along—that women had more trouble than did men balancing private and professional responsibilities; indeed, women lawyers were much less likely to have children than were their male peers. Firms still thought of the ideal lawyer as a man with a wife; attorneys were described as "breadwinners and professionals with little or no responsibility for childcare."[52]

In the mid-1960s, groups organized by professional women (such as women's caucuses within bar associations) did battle for equal opportunity and equal pay in old male bastions of power and privilege. And at virtually the same time, the executive and judicial branches of government entered the fray. In 1965 and 1967, President Lyndon Johnson signed two executive orders, Nos. 11246 and 11375, respectively, that reaffirmed Kennedy's "affirmative action" order and added sex to the list of groups singled out for special scrutiny and protection. Johnson's view of race-based "affirmative action" extended by analogy to sex-based programs: "You do not take a person who for years has been hobbled by chains, and liberate him," he said in a 1965 speech at Howard University, "bring him up the starting line of a race, and then say, 'You are free to compete with all the others,' and . . . believe that you have been completely fair. Thus, it is not enough just to open the gates of opportunity; all our citizens must have the ability to walk through the gates."[53] If that decision meant instituting preferential hiring policies until the workplace could be purged of racism and sexism and temporarily perpetuating race- and sex-based classifications, so be it.

Federal courts began to throw their weight behind women's economic emancipation—although not at once and not completely. With few exceptions, feminism did not inspire the "liberal" Warren Court to interpret constitutional texts more generously; instead, in historian Judith Baer's estimation, judicial "passivity" probably "reinforced patriarchy."[54] While still sitting on the District of Columbia Court of Appeals, Bader Ginsburg noted that the court responsible for *Brown v. Board* did not "see" women within the African American minority and was "tied tightly" to the "breadwinner-homemaker dichotomy: It was man's lot, because of his nature, to be breadwinner, head of household, representative of the family outside the home; and it was woman's lot, because of her nature, not only to bear, but also to raise children, and keep the home in order." In contrast, the "conservative" Burger Court stood out "in bold relief" as "comparatively unrestrained, one might even say modestly revolutionary," in sex discrimination cases.[55]

As in the previous century, conversations about how and whether to deal constitutionally with sex classifications emerged first in the states. By 1971, for instance, the California Supreme Court had struck down part of the state's Business and Professional Code, which, like the Michigan law that gave rise to *Goesart*, banned female bartenders. Although it invalidated protectionism on due process ground, the bench compared sex-based classifications to their race-based counterparts and found both practices wanting. Said the majority in *Sail'er Inn, Inc. v. Kirby*, "Laws which disable women from full participation in the political, business and economic arenas are often characterized as 'protective' and beneficial. These same laws applied to racial or ethnic minorities would readily be recognized as invidious and impermissible. The pedestal upon which women have been placed has all too often, upon closer inspection, been revealed as a cage."[56]

At about the same time, the federal judiciary began to subject sex-specific economic legislation to more rigorous scrutiny—not the highest available level of constitutional scrutiny, but one step beyond the level employed in *Goesart*. Between 1949 and 1971, federal courts had eradicated virtually all mention of race from law codes and imposed a strict level of constitutional scrutiny on attempts to distinguish between blacks and whites in the workplace and elsewhere. With sex-specific laws, in contrast, governments needed only to demonstrate a *reasonable* public interest in maintaining "separate but equal" classifications. This was to demand relatively little: The test required states to demonstrate only that a "reasonable man" might find a sex distinction plausible or useful. Now, courts had to determine whether a sex classification served an *important* state interest. Judges were not yet willing to say that sex- and race-based discrimination were equivalent. But post-1970 rulings nevertheless reveal a marked shift in federal judicial readings of the Fourteenth Amendment's scope.

To some extent, this shift reflected civil rights agitation, the pressures exerted by organized feminism, and dramatic economic and technological changes in American society. By the 1960s, after decades of slow growth and recession, the American labor force grew rapidly, with women constituting a major segment of that growth. By 1968, a year marked by great tumult on college campuses and elsewhere, women constituted 37 percent of all citizens employed for wages. As a group, they remained in the workforce longer than in previous decades, worked largely by reason of economic or professional necessity, and were older than their 1920s counterparts (a median age of 45 instead of 25). By the early 1960s, women's wages (in the words of one scholar) had "climbed to 60 percent of men's wages."[57]

Gradually, the U.S. Supreme Court began to unravel the long sleeve of economic dependence, including residual elements of the law of coverture. In effect, justices put legislators on notice that they would be scrutinizing assumptions about the sexes embedded in pension, welfare, and other social policies. Did "woman" mean "wife" or "mother"? Was economic dependence a usual female condition? Did men necessarily wield managerial, executory, and administrative powers? Here, perhaps more clearly than anywhere else, feminists could examine the protectionist and antiprotectionist faces of constitutional law at close range. As Vivien Hart says of contests over minimum wage laws, campaigners for economic equality "saw constitutional interpretation as an obstacle to overcome but also as a political resource to contest and control. The prize was authority and legitimacy in defining the functions of the state and the public standing" of women, whether salaried or not.[58]

How far could constitutional tradition be pushed? In its 1965 report, the PCSW highlighted the possibility that, as Pauli Murray and many opponents of ERA contended, judges would be willing (if given the right cases) to "interpret the Fourteenth Amendment as prohibiting unreasonable discrimination based on sex."[59] Initially, the Burger Court seemed to be doing just that. In 1971, with Bader Ginsburg as counsel for the plaintiff, the Court heard an appeal from Idaho involving the decision of a probate court to appoint Cecil Reed rather than his wife, Sally Reed, as administrator of their son's estate. At issue was a section of the Idaho Code that required what Chief Justice Warren Burger called "a preference for Cecil Reed because he was a male." While a main section of the code listed the "father or mother" as possible administrators, an adjacent section instructed courts to prefer "males" wherever "several persons" claimed the right to serve. In such cases, Idaho had even dispensed with hearings to determine which person ought to serve. In its equal protection decisions, wrote Burger for the majority, the Court had "consistently recognized that the Fourteenth Amendment does not deny to States the power to treat different classes of persons in different ways." Nevertheless, he reminded Idaho legislators that the equal protection clause denied states the power to treat citizens differently when the criteria for exclusion were "wholly unrelated to the objective" of a statute. Classifications had to "rest upon some ground of difference having a fair and substantial relation to the object of the legislation," so that "all persons similarly circumstanced" would be "treated alike." Idaho's attempt to eliminate probate court hearings and avert "intrafamily controversy" did not bear a *substantial* relationship to a worthy state objective. Legislators had made "the very kind of arbitrary legislative choice forbidden by the Equal Protection Clause."[60]

As two legal scholars wryly observe, although *Reed* was "not the legal equivalent of the 'shot heard 'round the world,' it did get the attention of the government community."[61] *Was* sex analogous to race and therefore subject to the strictest level of constitutional scrutiny? In 1973, the Court provided a tentative answer—this time with Justice William Brennan announcing a plurality judgment (which, unlike majority opinions, do not bind the Court) in *Frontiero v. Richardson*. Sharron Frontiero, a lieutenant in the United States Air Force, had claimed her husband, Joseph Frontiero, as a "dependent" to obtain increased housing allowances and medical insurance, just as male soldiers regularly did with their wives. Officials denied her request on the ground that she had not shown that Joseph depended on her for "more than one-half of his support"—a demonstration not required when men made identical applications for spousal benefits.[62]

Counsel for Frontiero contended that sex-based classifications, like those based on race or national origin, were "inherently suspect" and so had to be subjected to "close judicial scrutiny." Justices Brennan, William Douglas, Byron White, and Thurgood Marshall found "at least implicit support" for heightened constitutional scrutiny in *Reed v. Reed*. Said Brennan, there could be "no doubt" that the United States had a long history of sex discrimination, justified in terms of "romantic paternalism." He also found ground for analogizing women's condition to that of enslaved blacks. Statute books groaned with "gross, stereotyped distinctions between the sexes and, indeed, throughout much of the 19th century the position of women in our society was, in many respects, comparable to that of blacks under the pre–Civil War slave codes." Although the situation had improved markedly, it could "hardly be doubted" that women still faced "pervasive, although at times more subtle, discrimination in our educational institutions, in the job market, and, perhaps most conspicuously, in the political arena." Because sex was an "immutable" trait determined at birth, discrimination violated "the basic concept of our system"—that "legal burdens should bear some relationship to individual responsibility." Sex classifications, like those based on race, were "inherently suspect" and subject to "strict judicial scrutiny"; the statutes at issue clearly ran afoul of the due process clause of the Fifth Amendment (the ground on which suit had been brought).[63]

Still, only three other justices shared Brennan's sense of an equivalence between race and sex and a consequent need to subject the latter to intensive scrutiny—even though, as attorney Donna Lenhoff pointed out in 1997, the Court's own criteria seemed to make the comparison irresistible. In tests of race classifications, the justices had elevated race to a suspect class because (1) race was an "immutable characteristic, with no relationship to ability"; (2) blacks were "under-represented in the political process"; (3) people of color had a "long history of discrimination even unto the present"; and (4) blacks were a discrete "minority."[64] The first three criteria applied with equal force to women and blacks (some of whom *were* women), and beyond a presumption of women's greater political power, it was hard for feminists to see why subjugated minorities should be protected more fully than subjugated majorities.

In *Frontiero*, Justices Lewis Powell, Burger, and Harry Blackmun also agreed with the result, but would not say that "all classifications based upon sex" were inherently suspect and took the occasion to administer a tongue-lashing. It had been "unnecessary" for the Court to make such a "far-reaching" pronouncement; *Frontiero* should have been decided using the middle-tier standard applied in *Reed v. Reed*, reserving for the future "any expansion of its rationale." Justice William Rehnquist dissented: The statutes at issue worked only "an invidious discrimination," the nature and severity of which he did not specify. Were his brethren trying to beat state legislatures to the punch, as the PCSW had recommended, mooting the ERA question? The unratified amendment had been approved by Congress and submitted for ratification by the states; if adopted, it would "resolve the substance of this precise question" in a manner "prescribed by the Constitution." By acting "prematurely," Rehnquist argued, Brennan's plurality had "assumed a decisional responsibility at the very time when state legislatures, functioning within the traditional democratic process, are debating the proposed Amendment." In his view, judicial preemption of a "major political decision which is currently in process of resolution" denigrated the legislative process, particularly with "issues of broad social and political importance."[65]

Through the 1970s, as Congress adopted other beneficial legislation (like the Education Amendments of 1972, which banned sex discrimination in federally funded educational programs, and the Equal Employment Opportunity Act of the same year, which extended Title VII coverage to state and local governmental employees and lent congressional support to several lower federal court decisions in favor of affirmative action), the Court repeatedly defended the right of men and women to be free of irrational sex-based burdens. In *Weinberger v. Weisenfeld* (1975) and *Califano v. Goldfarb* (1975), the justices moved decisively to reconstruct women as self-possessed individuals. Both cases involved the Social Security Act of 1935 and disparate benefits for men and women, rooted in the assumption that a man was responsible for his wife and family. In *Weisenfeld*, Justice Brennan agreed that men were more likely than women to be "primary supporters" of a family, but would not permit administrators to impose a rule that denigrated the "efforts of women who do work and whose earnings contribute significantly to their families' support."[66] In *Stanton v. Stanton* (1975), moreover, the Court invalidated a Utah statute requiring the provision of child support for girls until they were 18 (the age of legal majority for girls) and for boys until age 21 (boys' majority age). Legislators had assumed that women, unlike men, married at a relatively early age and did not require independent financial support for education beyond high school as often as did men. In a departure from much of the Court's tradition, the majority termed these distinctions a violation of the equal protection clause. "A child, male or female," they wrote, "is still a child."

> No longer is the female destined solely for the home and the rearing of the family, and only the male for the marketplace and the world of ideas. . . . Women's activities and responsibilities are increasing and expanding. Coeducation is a fact, not a rarity. The presence of women in business, in the professions, in government and, indeed, in all walks of life where education is a desirable . . . antecedent is apparent and a proper subject of judicial notice.[67]

Antidiscriminatory rulings multiplied. In the landmark case of *Craig v. Boren* (1976), the Court struck down a law allowing saloons to sell beer to women at age 18 but not to men until they were 21, and announced that it would subject all gender classifications to an intermediate or "heightened" degree of constitutional scrutiny—although not the highest available level, which would have required legislators to show that state goals were *compelling* rather than merely *substantial*.[68] Then, in *Califano v. Westcott*, the justices voided yet another social security guideline permitting payments to families with dependent children only when the father was unemployed. In *Orr v. Orr* (1979), the Court struck down a state law requiring only men to pay alimony; in *Kirchberg v. Feenstra* (1981), in a major blow to the law of coverture, the justices condemned another law permitting men to deal in marital property without their wives' consent. These rulings, which coincided with the advent of no-fault divorce in many states, seemed to place married women's claims to equality on firmer constitutional foundations and to ensure sex neutrality in family law.

At almost the same moment, however, the Supreme Court began to draw lines in the sand. In *Personnel Administrator of Massachusetts v. Feeney* (1979), the majority decided that a state law granting veterans a lifetime preference in public employment did not discriminate unfairly against women. Applying a higher-than-usual constitutional standard, Justice Potter Stewart insisted that Feeney had to show a discriminatory intention, rather than merely a discriminatory result, particularly when a statute was neutral on its face and rewarded citizens for patriotic service. Most war veterans were male; if employment pools were overwhelmingly masculine, the solution might be to persuade more women to enlist in the armed services. Two years later, in a plurality opinion in *Michael M. v. Superior Court of Sonoma County*, Justice Rehnquist applied the *Craig* standard to resolve another equal protection question. *Michael M.* tested the constitutionality of a California statutory rape law, which prosecuted only boys, not their female partners, when teenagers aged 14–17 engaged in sexual intercourse. Five justices upheld the law on the grounds that a sex-neutral law would be hard to enforce and that the prevention of pregnancy among children was an "important" state objective sufficient to override concerns about gender.[69] Meanwhile, Justice O'Connor had made intermediate scrutiny into a personal crusade. In *Mississippi University for Women v. Hogan* (1982), for instance, she used the standard to strike down a nursing school program that excluded women and suggested (as she would continue to do in later opinions) that the question of an appropriate level of constitutional scrutiny was still open.[70]

At first blush, a wave of lower federal judicial hearings of EEOC cases—many of them well before the *Sears* decision and the advent of Presidents Reagan and Bush—seemed to confirm the value of the EEOC for women. *Weeks v. Southern Bell Telephone and Telegraph Company* (1969) tested whether Southern Bell, invoking a Georgia law on the subject, could deny Weeks a position as a telephone company "switchman" on the ground that physical labor and lifting heavy weights were too "strenuous" for women. Judges in the Fifth Circuit decided that both company policy and the law violated Title VII. "[Company lawyers] introduced no evidence concerning the lifting abilities of women," said the judges. "Rather, they would have us 'assume,' on the basis of a 'stereo-typed characterization,' that few or no women can safely lift 30 pounds [a limit established in another Georgia statute], while all men are treated as if they can. . . . [I]t is not clear that any conclusions about relative lifting ability would follow. . . . What does seem clear is that using these class stereotypes denies desirable positions to a great many women perfectly capable of performing the duties involved." The "promise of Title VII," added the court as it effectively junked *Goesart*, was that as long as the statute remained on the books, the sexes were on an "equal footing" unless employers could show that discrimination served a compelling (that is, not merely "reasonable") business interest.[71]

After *Weeks*, the EEOC published new weight regulations. Commissioners now would assume that sex-specific restrictions had "ceased to be relevant," given the expanded role of women in the economy. No longer could employers "take into account the capacities, preferences, and abilities of individual females" when such considerations worked to "discriminate rather than protect." A chance soon arose to apply the new rule. Southern Pacific Company had denied Leah Rosenfeld an opportunity to be an agent-telegrapher on the ground that women were unsuited "biologically" for the job and that her employment would violate California's weight and hour legislation. In *Rosenfeld v. Southern Pacific* (1971), the Ninth Circuit embraced the new EEOC position, rejected the railroad's BFOQ claim, and awarded the job to Rosenfeld. Judges held that the capabilities of individual women, not "subjective assumptions and traditional stereotyped conceptions regarding the physical ability of women to do particular work," should determine how jobs would be allocated. Still, the court left a major loophole: When a company had relied on state law, it need not pay damages; employers could not be faulted for trying to adhere to the law. This exception, in turn, led employers to hide behind protective legislation until someone filed suit.[72]

Even when EEOC complaints implicated maternity, the U.S. Supreme Court applied a strict standard of scrutiny. In *Phillips v. Martin-Marietta* (1971), the first sex discrimination suit per se brought under Title VII, ex-waitress Ida Phillips claimed that child care responsibilities got in the way of promotion (she had young children and had missed some work as a result), whereas men with families got promotions and pay increases. A lower court had ruled that a distinction could be made between being female (which Title VII named explicitly as an improper ground for discrimination) and having children (which Title VII did not mention). Thus, the bedrock issue was motherhood: To what extent could businesses deny women "equal chances" when maternal responsibilities led to work disruptions unlike those experienced by men? The High Court ruled that *parents* should be treated similarly, referred the case back to the lower court for fact-finding as to whether the burdens of motherhood exceeded the burdens of fatherhood, and warned that the idea of not hiring women "similarly situated" as compared to men probably violated Title VII. Henceforth, employers would have to defend such policies as BFOQ exceptions. In *Hishon v. King and Spalding* (1984), the Court also held on Title VII grounds that as long as a law firm offered partnership to employees, it could not make sex-based distinctions within a pool of candidates.[73]

Was the glass half full or half empty? Political scientist Leslie Goldstein thinks that justices in the mid-1970s adopted an intermediate, rather than a strict, standard of constitutional scrutiny because they realized that ERA and the idea of race-sex equivalence would fail. Still, to pass constitutional muster, a classification at least had to be related *substantially* to an *important* public goal, not just related *reasonably* to a *permissible* one. As the years passed, egregiously paternal state laws and administrative practices fell by the wayside; a number of scholars have argued, in fact, that the unusually broad degree of judicial discretion involved in intermediate scrutiny has worked overall to the advantage of women. Certainly, when the classification is palpably irrational, the constitutional "mezzanine" (to use Judith Baer's term)[74] seems to suffice. And in Title VII suits involving employment practices that make gender a BFOQ, existing rules have proved to be adequate. As early as 1970–71, for instance, justices announced in *Diaz v. Pan American Airways* that under Title VII, airlines could not exclude men from positions as flight attendants. The airline argued that because women soothed nervous passengers, sex-specific hiring practices reflected a bona fide business interest. The Court decided that discriminatory practices did not substantially address the substance of Pan Am's business: The firm provided not nursing or psychotherapy, but transportation services, which men could deliver as readily as women.

In cases involving compensatory legislation and in EEOC rulings during the Reagan-Bush years, the track record is less impressive. In 1974, to give one example, Justice Douglas ruled in *Kahn v. Shevin* that Florida's exemption of widows from property taxes did not violate the equal protection clause because, as the state contended, the law bore a "fair and substantial relation" to an important state objective—in this case, a reduction of the "the disparity between the economic capabilities of a man and a woman." Who could dispute the fact that the "financial difficulties confronting the lone woman" exceeded those faced by men? When sex distinctions benefited women, courts need not invalidate them; and judges alone decided whether benefits to the class outweighed costs to individual women. In dissent, Justice White argued that the state had "not adequately explained" why it had lumped women with disabled and blind citizens. But he stood alone. In both *Califano v. Webster* (1977) and *Heckler v. Mathews* (1984), moreover, the Court permitted discriminatory pension offset plans, ostensibly so that women might receive compensation for past discrimination.[75]

The tables tipped sharply toward "protection" and workplace exclusion in cases involving pregnancy—the archetypal gender "difference." To be sure, in *Cleveland Board of Education v. LaFleur* (1974), the Court struck down a law that required schoolteachers to quit their jobs after the fifth month of pregnancy and forgo benefits. In that year, it should be noted, all states had laws forcing women to quit midpoint in pregnancy; some even required women to prove when they returned to work that they had made child care arrangements. Justice Powell, however, did not base the decision on equal protection doctrine, as the lower court had suggested; instead, he transformed *LaFleur* into a privacy case. Freedom of personal choice in family life, he wrote, was one of the liberties protected by the due process clause; punishing a woman for pregnancy placed a "heavy burden on the exercise of these protected freedoms." Hence, while Powell managed to invalidate the statute, he also suggested that pregnancy was a personal rather than an employment problem and evaded equal protection questions.[76]

"Hard" cases involving women's bodies filled judicial dockets. In its 1977 *Dothard v. Rawlinson* opinion, the Court decided that states might assert a BFOQ and hire only male guards in maximum security prisons where sex offenders posed a threat to women; as with "separate but equal" prison reform schemes, governments would judge when the risks were more than women could bear. And in *Geduldig v. Aiello* and *General Electric Co. v. Gilbert*, the justices dealt a serious blow to feminist lawyers in cases involving the exclusion of pregnant women from employment benefits. In *Aiello*, the majority held flatly that a California plan excluding pregnancy from insurance coverage while including disabilities specific to men was not sex discrimination. In a footnote, Justice Stewart said that the legislative scheme did not involve "gender as such"; rather, it drew a line between "pregnant women and non-pregnant persons." Many of the latter were female. Thus, while it was "true that only women can become pregnant," it did not follow that "every legislative classification concerning pregnancy is a sex-based classification" because women fall on either side of the line. In *Gilbert*, the Court confronted a disability plan that excluded pregnancy and decided that because "discrimination" was not defined in Title VII, they had to look to Fourteenth Amendment jurisprudence for the meaning of the term. In the end, the Court decided that although pregnancy posed an "additional risk, unique to women," its exclusion was not discriminatory.[77] A year later, Justice Rehnquist ruled in *Nashville Gas Company v. Satty* that while pregnancy imposed a "substantial burden" on women that "men need not suffer," a company did not have to accord benefits (in this case, pregnancy leave) unless both sexes were eligible. Only the denial of accumulated seniority to mothers returning to work violated Title VII.[78]

In response to such rulings, Congress passed the Pregnancy Discrimination Act in 1978, which declared pregnancy discrimination to be a form of sex discrimination. A decade later, in an apparent repudiation of both protectionism and the public's interest in maternity, the Court decided in the landmark *UAW v. Johnson Controls* (1991) that the firm did not have a bona fide business interest in keeping fertile women away from high-paying jobs working with lead alongside men in a battery plant. Women, no less than men, should be allowed to confront danger and evaluate employment risks; companies could not try to sidestep lawsuits by protecting female employees, thereby keeping them away from better wages. But, as in *Adkins*, the decision probably expressed the Rehnquist Court's taste for laissez-faire economics, rather than nascent feminism.

The years 1988 to 1990 may have marked a watershed for second-wave feminism and progressive law reform. Amid widespread attacks on liberalism and "political correctness" in American culture, the Bush Administration turned back a major civil rights act (finally adopted, in response to electoral pressures and public outcry over the Clarence Thomas–Anita Hill controversy, as the Civil Rights Act of 1991) that aimed, in part, to give statutory foundation to non-quota affirmative action programs and claims of workplace harassment or stereotyping. The act was a response to a cluster of Supreme Court retreats in employment discrimination cases in 1988–89, epitomized by *Price Waterhouse v. Hopkins*. Ann Hopkins had been passed over for promotion on the ground of her "masculine" appearance and demeanor; a supporter at the firm had advised her to "walk more femininely, dress more femininely, wear makeup, have her hair styled, and wear jewelry." When the firm turned her down the second time, she sued under Title VII. Without noticing that gender stereotyping in itself might be a form of sex discrimination, the Court ruled against Hopkins, in the process lightening the employer's burden of proof in EEOC cases. As of 1989, corporations did not have to provide "clear and convincing evidence" of nondiscrimination (the old rule); rather, they had to show only that they could have made the same decision on legitimate grounds.[79]

Such a climate severely chilled women's economic prospects. It is perhaps telling, as Leslie Goldstein once observed, that the Supreme Court has not sat on a Constitution-based sex discrimination case since 1984;[80] the bench typically confines itself to EEOC cases. To the present, moreover, affirmative action hiring and training programs have been subjected to harsh criticism, retrenchment, or (as in California) abolition. Courts have had to decide whether race or sex could be noticed lawfully when corporations, universities, and other bodies make admissions, employment, or scholarship decisions, and then whether the preferential treatment of individuals, set-asides, quotas, and similar policies pass constitutional muster. When the Court held in its 1978 *Regents of the University of California v. Bakke* decision that universities could not use numerical quota systems if they excluded equally well-qualified whites, affirmative action programs seemed to be in trouble. But in *Steelworkers v. Weber* (1979), justices laid out criteria (programs, for instance, had to be temporary) to be used in assessing the constitutionality of affirmative action plans. And in *Fullilove v. Klutznick* (1980), Chief Justice Burger concluded for a majority that race-conscious set-aside programs passed constitutional muster.

Would the Court do the same for sex-conscious practices? In Melvin Urofsky's words, because the Court seemed to view gender discrimination as "somehow more acceptable" than racial discrimination,[81] it was unclear whether it would adhere to its own criteria. In the 6–3 decision in *Johnson v. Transportation Agency, Santa Clara County* (1988), Justice Brennan provided an answer. As in the *Sears* case, 76 percent of the women who worked for Santa Clara County's Transportation Agency clustered in traditionally feminine occupations; only 7.1 percent of its administrators, 9.7 percent of the technicians, and 22 percent of the road personnel were female. In 1978, the agency had instituted a rigorous affirmative action program designed to make the labor force comport with the surrounding community. When it posted a job as a dispatcher in 1979, Diane Joyce and Paul Johnson applied; both were judged to be qualified, although Johnson had scored two points higher on written tests and had more of the requisite road experience. The agency initially hired Johnson, but changed its mind and took on Joyce instead; Johnson promptly filed suit, arguing that he had been denied promotion by reason of sex in violation of Title VII. In evaluating the merits of an affirmative action program, wrote Justice Brennan, his colleagues had to be "mindful" of the value of "voluntary efforts" to eliminate race and sex discrimination. In *Johnson*, the agency had mounted a permissible program. It had earmarked "no positions for anyone"; sex was but "one of several factors . . . taken into account." Nor did Santa Clara County intend to create a workforce according to "rigid numerical standards." Employers appropriately had considered sex "as one factor" in determining who would be promoted to road dispatcher.[82]

ECONOMIC RETREATS

As foreshadowed in the *Sears* decision, the more conservative federal judiciary since the 1990s has exhibited less patience with affirmative action and has steadily dismantled all but a handful of programs. Similarly, courts and legislators have retreated steadily from aggressive aid to poor, working-class, often black women. For such women, the "mezzanine" standard, combined with white middle-class stereotypes of the "good mother," have imposed extraordinary hardship. At midcentury, feminized poverty haunted American cities and, to a lesser extent, rural communities; in 1960, for example, the average woman-headed household generated about 61 percent of the income of its male-headed counterpart and 51 percent of the income of households headed by married couples. By 1981, the situation had deteriorated: Female-headed households earned 55 percent of the income of a male-headed family and only 44 percent of the income of married couples.[83]

The vast majority of female-headed families have been the product of divorce. By the end of World War II, divorce had become commonplace; historian Glenda Riley sardonically speaks of the "revolving door" conception of marriage.[84] As of 1945, South Carolina and New York still retained certain traditional limits on divorce, but South Carolina submitted to liberalization in 1949, and New York did so in 1966. By 1970, then, the year in which California adopted the first "no-fault" divorce system, every state permitted permanent marital dissolution, albeit with varying rules about grounds, child custody, the allocation of property, and legal procedure. Between 1970 and 1980, the divorce rate doubled, to more than one million annually. As of 1981, one out of every two marriages ended in divorce, which, in turn, left women economically disadvantaged compared to their ex-husbands, particularly when they were not white, not well educated, and retained custody of their children. Scholars like Susan Moller Okin have discovered that no-fault divorce—one of the fruits of "equal rights" agitation—did not increase the rate of divorce, as critics warned, but dramatically affected the *outcome* of divorce. "Many studies show," writes Okin, "that whereas the average economic status of men improves after divorce, that of women and children deteriorates seriously." In one study encompassing the years 1968 to 1977, men's standard of living rose by 42 percent during the first year after divorce, whereas women's declined by 73 percent—an example of what Okin terms "precipitous downward mobility."[85]

Relations between black women and federal welfare administrators have been especially perplexing. When indigent women accept public assistance in raising families, rights of privacy and other freedoms can be lost in the bargain. In 1972, Johnie Tillmon, the National Welfare Rights Organization's first chair and a powerful advocate for black women, characterized the Aid for Families of Dependent Children program (AFDC) as a "supersexist marriage" between mothers and the state, with the latter functioning as an austere household head. "You trade in a man for *the* man," she said. "But you can't divorce him if he treats you bad. He can divorce you, of course, cut you off anytime he wants. But in that case, he keeps the kids, not you. *The* man runs everything. In ordinary marriage, sex is supposed to be for your husband. On A.F.D.C., you're not supposed to have any sex at all. You give up control of your own body. . . . You may even have to agree to get your tubes tied so you can never have more children. . . . *The* man . . . controls your money. He tells you what to buy, what not to buy, where to buy it, and how much things cost."[86]

In lawsuits, black women find themselves in a kind of constitutional limbo. When a suit involves a woman's race, courts have applied the highest level of scrutiny; when gender is at issue, they use the intermediate standard. When a suit addresses more than one element of personal identity—the so-called intersectional or sex-plus claims, where (to give an actual example) an employer calls a black woman a "nigger bitch"—judicial confusion and inconsistency have been marked. Because Title VII suits are supposed to involve race *or* sex, black (or Chinese or American Indian) women can fall through the cracks. Federal judges sometimes have said, on the one hand, that black women cannot represent all black people and, on the otherhand, that black women cannot represent all women. In *DeGraffenreid v. General Motors* (1976), five black women sued General Motors (GM), alleging that its seniority system perpetuated past discrimination not against blacks, but against black women. The district court granted summary judgment for GM, on the ground that it could find no past decisions in which black women had been termed a special class. In *Moore v. Hughes Helicopters, Inc.* (1983), by contrast, a district court ruled that because Moore had not claimed to be a "female" but "only . . . a Black female," it doubted her ability to "adequately represent white female employees."[87] Worse, in a 1995 "reverse affirmative action" case, *Adarand Constructors, Inc. v. Pena*, the U.S. Supreme Court decided that because discrimination against blacks called to mind strict scrutiny, the same standard should apply in cases of discrimination against whites. Thus, "women" (over half of whom are white) merit intermediate scrutiny, whereas "whites" (half of whom are female) enjoy the highest available standard.[88]

Nor have Americans embraced the idea of comparable worth (for example, paying a cleaning woman the same wage as a male street sweeper) as a way to achieve a rough equality in sex-segregated workplaces—perhaps because of lingering associations between men and the "family wage," but also because female ghettoes serve the interests of employers. Without male competition, labor costs remain low—although the likelihood of comparison across corporate hallways renders the arrangement unstable. As early as 1931, Emily Newell Blair of Missouri observed that equality did not "necessarily mean identity with men. . . . It means," she said, "that what women do shall have the same quality, worth, power, effect, as what men do." Yet, in the 1990s, comparable worth has yet to take American industry by storm. Indeed, the Reagan administration called it "the looniest idea since Looney Tunes came on the screen."[89]

Sometimes, workers themselves raze walls between male and female ghettoes. In 1978, Wendy Robinson Brower, a clerical worker and organizer by 1980 of Minnesota Working Women, got a job at a local university. "In the basement of my building," she recalled, "there were job postings. . . . At that time there was a secretarial shortage. And there were lots of qualifications to be a secretary. Grammar and spelling, post-secondary education, three to five years experience, type 60 words a minute. . . . My job paid about $800 a month. And right across on the other side of the job board, they were looking for janitors. It only required an eighth grade education, and it paid $200 a month more. For starters." Brower got another job and set about organizing women.[90]

To some extent, women's workplace experiences reflect the downward pressure of female domesticity on wage scales. For the most part, Americans still refuse to value domestic (and, by extension, women's) labor—even though the Chase Manhattan Bank estimated housework to be worth $13,391 per year in the mid-1970s and $46,000 ten years later.[91] Two decades after implementation of the Civil Rights Act of 1964, a National Consumer's League representative could say, without fear of seeming to be anachronistic, "While men may also require protection from overtime hours, as a group their need is often less than women, who usually spend more time on family and home responsibilities."[92] Modern women have clamored for salaried positions, but as late as 1984, when 54 percent of adult women worked for pay, over half of them plied sex-segregated trades. Because the sexes rarely inhabited the same rooms or departments, it was hard to think of them as "similarly situated" for purposes of pay comparison or litigation. Thus, in 1984, women earned 65 cents for every dollar earned by men, and black women earned considerably less. Even with five years of college, the earning gap in 1989 was 69 percent.

The Economist hit the nail on the head. In a special July 1998, "Survey of Women and Work," the editors concluded that even in developed countries, where "three out of four mothers of school-age children have jobs," fathers had become only "slightly more helpful around the house than they used to be." The social consequences aside, such behavior made no economic sense: "Some pundits . . . continue to argue that if lots of women pour into the labour market, there will be fewer jobs to go around for men. But most governments now understand that the larger the share of the population at work, the better it is for the economy." Why did women not flourish? If they now made up "nearly half the labour force, you might expect them to be doing a broad range of jobs, similar to those done by men. Instead, a disproportionate number are stuck with the sort of 'women's work'—low status, often insecure, and poorly paid—which a modern service economy seems to create in ever-growing quantities." Women simply could not escape the long shadow of domesticity. Those who try to get ahead in "high-flying professional and managerial jobs continue to find it a struggle as men close ranks against them. . . . Career women drily note that their efforts would be greatly eased by a supportive wife." While women were pioneering a new "dual-earner family," the "world around them was designed for the traditional model of male breadwinner [and] female homemaker. . . . Model and reality have got out of synch."[93]

TOWARD EDUCATIONAL AND ASSOCIATIONAL EQUALITY

Rights to educational and associational equality have been secured slowly and enforced sporadically. A century ago, first-wave feminists pointed out that the Latin root *educere* means "to lead out" or "away," perhaps from danger or darkness. Education, as Baer observes, has long been an avenue by which oppressed classes have been "led" toward personal power; the possession of "specialized knowledge—of law, for example, or science, or languages—gives people access to even great power." As men returned from World War II service, GI Bill funding led to a surge in male attendance at American universities and a relative diminution of the female student population; in 1950, women earned only one-fourth of all bachelor's degrees awarded in the United States, the lowest percentage since the 1920s. In the 1940s, beauty pageants provided the only reliable source of scholarship money for female scholars; in 1995, the Miss America Pageant still was the largest grantor of scholarships for college-bound women.[94]

By the late 1980s, however, the situation had begun to change. Women constituted half of all beginning law and medical students. More important, the number of female lawyers increased from 6 percent of all attorneys in 1970 to 17 percent in 1990; the population of female physicians doubled, from 11 percent of all physicians in 1970 to 22 percent in 1990. Although women earned only 34.7 percent of all doctorates in American history in 1991–92, the figure increased to 57 percent in English and 59 percent in foreign language studies. Elsewhere, the proportions showed steady, if small, improvement: In 1981 and 1991, for example, women earned 2 percent and 14 percent of engineering doctorates; 9 percent and 11 percent of physical science doctorates; and 23 percent and 28 percent of life science doctorates. Although the total number was modest, African American women earned 43 percent more law degrees in 1990 than in 1981, and while women continue to be concentrated in lower ranks of college faculties, earning less than similarly situated men, they constituted 32 percent of all faculties in 1991, up from 10 percent in 1980.[95]

A large part of these increases can be attributed to legal change since 1970. The most pertinent judicial rulings before 1970 both involved Texas A & M University's long-standing exclusion of women on the ground that graduation required two years of military training; women were invited to attend Texas Women's University, a less well-known institution. In 1958, Lena Bristol and Barbara Tittle challenged the statute incorporating Texas A & M as a sex-segregated institution. Citing *Muller v. Oregon* and other "separate but equal" Supreme Court rulings, the Court of Civil Appeals affirmed the law's constitutionality. In 1960, the university again found itself in court, this time in a class-action suit brought by several women who had been denied admission, and again, the women lost.

Finally, in 1970, when four women sued the University of Virginia (then a sex-segregated institution), old rules began to soften. In *Kirstein v. University of Virginia* (UVA), a federal district court ruled on the basis of old "separate but equal" doctrines that because no other institution in the state rivaled UVA's quality, women denied admission were effectively deprived of equal educational opportunities. But because the plaintiffs in *Kirstein* claimed only to represent prospective UVA students, the court did not broaden the net to include the all-male Virginia Military Institute (VMI) or three publically funded all-female universities. Applying the equal protection rule promulgated in *Reed v. Reed*, a federal district court judge in Massachusetts decided in *Bray v. Lee* (1970) that Boston Latin School (a public all-boys academy) could not force ninety-five girls who had scored as well or better than boys on entrance exams to attend Girls Latin School, even though the two schools were roughly equal in academic terms.[96]

Two years later, Congress passed the Educational Amendments Act (Title IX), which basically outlawed sex segregation in both public and private educational institutions receiving federal money. It also set standards against which unaffected private schools could measure their performance. The act banned (to give a few examples) "sex-plus" discrimination against pregnant women, wives, and parents, as well as the use of separate grading, admissions, or financial aid standards for the two sexes, and pushed private schools toward integration. Certainly, the introduction of many new female athletic programs can be attributed to Title IX pressure; although the law did not require mixed-sex teams, it mandated equal access to athletic facilities, scholarships, and opportunities unless a school could show cause why it could or need not comply.

"Equal," however, could mean "separate but equal." In 1976, Judge Joseph Weis of the U.S. Court of Appeals for the Third Circuit held in *Vorchheimer* v. *School District of Philadelphia* that as long as educators offered "similar" programs of "equal quality," Philadelphia could maintain two segregated high schools, Girls High and the all-male Central High School.[97] A year later, a badly divided Supreme Court affirmed the decision. Only in 1983 did the Court of Common Pleas in Philadelphia reconsider *Vorchheimer* in light of the state's ERA, concluding in *Newberg v. Board of Public Education* that the facilities were not equal according to the criteria set out in *Brown v. Board*, and, in any event, that Pennsylvania's ERA disallowed a "separate but equal" system.[98]

Pro-integration decisions in the states did not impress the U.S. Supreme Court. In 1984, the majority in *Grove City College v. Bell* limited the reach of Title IX, holding that it extended only to programs that actually benefited from public money, not to the entire institution. Thus, if a college accepted a federal subsidy for academic scholarships, it was free to discriminate in, say, its athletic programs. In response, large majorities in both houses of Congress passed the Civil Rights Restoration Act of 1988, which again prohibited discrimination on the basis of race, sex, disability, and age. Lawmakers took the extraordinary step of identifying *Grove City College v. Bell* as the bill's target. When Ronald Reagan refused to sign the bill, both houses overrode the veto.[99]

In addition, federal courts ordered the sex integration of VMI and the Citadel in South Carolina. Since at least 1990, VMI had ignored Justice Department inquiries about the absence of young women on campus. In 1995, the U.S. Court of Appeals for the Fourth Circuit permitted VMI to retain its sex-segregated program, provided it created a "women's leadership institute" at nearby all-female Mary Baldwin College. Meanwhile, Shannon Faulkner successfully sued for admission to the Citadel. To preempt sex integration, the college tried desperately to create a "separate but equal" program like Virginia's. But, in the end, the Supreme Court seized the reins, holding in *United States v. Virginia* (1996) that VMI's exclusion of women (and, by extension, the Citadel's policies) ran afoul of the equal protection clause and that the "women's leadership institute," which used a co-operative, rather than a competitive, pedagogy deprived women who were interested in VMI's unique program of equal educational opportunities.[100]

Unfortunately, neither Title IX nor equal protection law have leveled the playing field for female athletes. According to the *New York Times*, in 1997, women made up half the students participating in athletic programs at nearly 300 Division 1A colleges. In 1997, 34 percent of all athletes were women—an increase of 5 percent from 1992. An NCAA report, published in May 1997, revealed yawning gender gaps and widespread noncompliance with Title IX. The money actually spent on female athletic programs had increased substantially: Between 1992 and 1997, the average amount spent by Division 1A colleges on female athletics increased from $263,000 to $663,000 annually, compared to $1.5 million and $2.4 million for male programs. Linda Grant, a Title IX expert at the University of Iowa, called the result "pathetic," perhaps because the increase, while substantial, did not match the increase of women in the sporting community. Many universities, moreover, have satisfied statutory requirements by showing either that they are "moving in the right direction" and have "a plan to get there" or that there is "no unmet need" among students. Enforcement has been sluggish, and implementation often is left to ambivalent or underpaid athletic program directors. Arthur Bryant, a lawyer involved in a successful 1997 Title IX lawsuit against Brown University, put it this way: "There is no question that if the Federal Government said we want compliance and we want reports from each and every university in the country in the next two months, the schools would come up with a plan and get into compliance." But no such pressure has been exerted. Recalcitrant schools tend to comply only when sued and only to the extent required in particular cases.[101]

What about women's right of association? For professional women, economic success can depend on access to bars, clubs, and raquet ball courts where powerful men congregate to socialize and cut deals. When female lawyers and entrepreneurs sought entrance to all-male, often private enclaves, they met stiff resistance. In 1969, two members of NOW's board of directors tried to buy drinks at one of New York's oldest all-male bars, McSorley's Old Ale House; when the bartender refused service, they sued, claiming that the bar's policy violated the Civil Rights Act of 1866. State and federal judges agreed. In *Roberts v. U. S. Jaycees* (1984), the U.S. Supreme Court ordered the Jaycees to admit female applicants; three years later, in a 7–0 decision, the justices spurned an attempt by Rotary International to defend male-only membership decisions as private matters not unlike intimate conversations between husbands and wives. Then, in a 1988 decision involving an association of private clubs in New York City, the Court affirmed the constitutionality of a law requiring "the admission of women to large, private clubs that play an important role in business and professional life." At stake were the long-standing policies of the prestigious Century Club and several other organizations. Across the nation, a number of clubs resisted integration, but by 1990, the Court's hard line had encouraged many cities to pass and enforce ordinances like New York's forbidding sex discrimination in private facilities.[102]

WOMEN'S BODIES AND REPRODUCTION

Reproductive freedom continues to present grave difficulties. In this area, a tradition of state scrutiny of maternity and women's sexuality exerts an almost irresistible pressure on the public imagination, precluding nonprotectionist policy choices. Comstock-era bans on birth control information and devices have proved to be the most amenable to change. In 1967, the Massachusetts Superior Court convicted William Eisenstadt for "exhibiting contraceptive articles" while delivering a lecture about birth control to students at Boston University and then for "giving a young woman a package of Emko vaginal foam" after his address. Eisenstadt seems to have invited arrest to challenge the local law. On appeal, the Massachusetts Supreme Judicial Court set aside his conviction for "exhibiting contraceptives" on First Amendment grounds, but sustained his conviction for distributing the foam. In *Eisenstadt v. Baird* (1972), the Burger Court extended the privacy umbrella articulated in *Griswold* to encompass all women. With Justices Powell and Rehnquist recused and Chief Justice Burger dissenting, Justice Brennan held for the majority that the state's mini-Comstock law violated the rights of single persons under the Fourteenth Amendment's equal protection clause. Citizens similarly situated could not be treated unequally unless the state had a rational ground for the distinction; only Burger found it rational to allow medical professionals to control contraceptive information and distribution. In *Eisenstadt*, the majority looked beyond the bedroom door to the rights of individuals to make decisions inside the room. "If under *Griswold*," wrote Brennan, "the distribution of contraceptives to married persons cannot be prohibited, a ban on distribution to unmarried persons would be equally impermissible."

> It is true that in Griswold the right of privacy in question inhered in the marital relationship. Yet the marital couple is not an independent entity with a mind and heart of its own, but an association of two individuals each with a separate intellectual and emotional makeup. If the right of privacy means anything, it is the right of the individual, married or single, to be free from unwarranted governmental intrusion into matters so fundamentally affecting a person as the decision whether to bear or beget a child.[103]

Thus, even as it held that the government ought to be absent, the Court asserted its presence within private spaces as a kind of custodian of individual citizens' rights; in *Griswold*, the government had been required simply to be absent from certain spaces.

Abortion rights have proved to be far less tractable. When Congress debated the 1964 Civil Rights Act, every state in the union still banned abortion except as a way to save a woman's life. In the late 1960s, NOW and other women's groups set about trying to persuade emergent pro-abortion coalitions that the procedure was not to be understood solely as a medical problem. In February 1969, Betty Friedan attended a convention of the National Abortion Rights Action League (NARAL), where she presented an amendment to NARAL's constitution (which did not mention women's rights) asserting the "right of a woman to control her own body and reproductive freedom as her inalienable, human, civil right." Although NARAL finally adopted the amendment, many delegates thought that abortion was "not a feminist issue." Feminists disagreed. Across the nation, women redoubled efforts to create networks to help women find safe abortions. Chicagoans, for instance, organized "Jane," a code name for the illegal Abortion Counselling Service of Women's Liberation, accessible by telephoning "Jane Howe." A "Jane" pamphlet read, "We are women whose ultimate goal is the liberation of women in society. One important way we are working toward that goal is by helping any woman who wants an abortion to get one as safely and cheaply as possible under existing conditions."[104]

The American Law Institute's Model Penal Code (MPC) of 1962, to which states have often turned when revamping laws, recommended the legalization of abortion for victims of rape and incest, in cases of severe fetal deformity, and when necessary to save a woman's life *or health* (a departure from tradition). *Griswold* added fuel to the fire. Then, Justice Blackmun handed down his now-classic opinions in the associated cases of *Roe v. Wade* (1973) and *Doe v. Bolton*. These rulings—arguably the Supreme Court's most controversial policy decisions in modern times—did not appear in a vacuum. By 1973, nineteen states had revised their abortion laws. Most of these states adopted MPC language. Four states (Alaska, Hawaii, New York, and Washington) went further and removed all limitations on the reasons for which abortions would be performed. Hence, *Roe* was less a bolt out of the blue than the expansion, federalization, and constitutionalization of policies quietly adopted in a growing number of states. Indeed, some critics charge the Court with redirecting and politicizing that trend by making abortion policy more visible. For social conservatives and others who saw abortion primarily as a moral or theological question, rather than as a problem in women's right to control their own bodies (or as a problem in the competing rights of a woman and a fetus), the Court also had usurped the community's (or family's) responsibilities.

In a nutshell, Blackmun expanded the right of privacy articulated in *Griswold* and *Eisenstadt* to encompass a woman's decision to terminate a pregnancy. The Jane Roe of the case was actually Norma McCorvey, a Texan who had been denied an abortion because of a state law allowing abortion only to save a woman's life. Blackmun navigated a mine field. He acknowledged the "sensitive and emotional nature of the abortion controversy," the "vigorous opposing views, even among physicians, and . . . the deep and seemingly absolute convictions that the subject inspires." Roe's lawyers contended that Texas law was unconstitutionally vague and, more important, that it invaded a pregnant woman's right "to choose to terminate her pregnancy"—a fundamental right embedded in the "concept of personal liberty," which, in turn, originated either in the Fourteenth Amendment's due process clause, or in the "personal, marital, familial, and sexual privacy" that the Court had declared, in *Griswold* and elsewhere, to be protected by the Bill of Rights and its penumbras.[105]

In *Roe*, Blackmun repeatedly invoked common law tradition. He emphasized time-honored rules by which "persons," not fetuses, were said to possess rights and noted that the common law had imposed less onerous restrictions on abortion than nineteenth-century statutes had done. He conceded that the state had an "important and legitimate interest" both in the health of the pregnant woman and in the potential life of the fetus. But during the first trimester, these interests were not sufficient to override a woman's right to make a decision privately, in consultation with her physician and family, to terminate her pregnancy. This conclusion reflected abundant evidence from medical science about the safety of abortion during this early period, as compared to carrying the fetus to term. After the first trimester, a state might regulate abortion in ways reasonably designed to promote maternal health. Toward the beginning of the third trimester, once the fetus became "viable"—that is, was "potentially able to live outside the mother's womb, albeit with artificial aid"—a woman's autonomy diminished and the state's interest in protecting the fetus permitted it to ban abortion. Thus, as Blackmun recognized, the right to marital privacy and the right advanced in *Roe* differed appreciably: In the justice's words, a pregnant woman "cannot be isolated in her privacy." Because she carried "an embryo and, later, a fetus," she was susceptible by degrees to public scrutiny.[106]

Justice Rehnquist vigorously dissented. The fact that a "majority of the States reflecting . . . the majority sentiment in those States" had restricted abortion for at least a century," he raged, was a "strong indication" that the "asserted right to an abortion" was not as deeply rooted in tradition as Blackmun claimed. How could the majority so easily dismiss a tradition of community regulation of maternity? Why did the state have to absent itself altogether from the first trimester, leaving the fetus at the mercy of women and their doctors?[107]

Other critics leaped into the fray. Feminists castigated Blackmun for relying on the law of privacy rather than equal protection law. They worried especially that the "privacy" framework did not obligate the government to ensure access to abortion rights and (as had been the case in *Griswold*) failed to protect women from husbands, fathers, and physicians. Legal scholars objected to Blackmun's reliance on rapidly changing medical technology, the slippery concept of "viability," and more talk about constitutional "penumbras." Bader Ginsburg, head of the ACLU's Women's Rights Project in 1973, regretted the opinion's focus on a "medically approved autonomy idea" and "exclusion of a constitutionally based sex equality perspective." In her view, Blackmun should have "placed the woman alone" as a sovereign individual with a right to governmental protection, rather than "tied to her physician."[108] In an influential essay, John Hart Ely argued that *Roe* had been a "mistake," that abortion could be regulated by statute because no legitimate constitutional issues beyond due process of law were at issue, and that although an "unwanted child can go a long way toward ruining a woman's life," a fetus's life (which Hart took to be as important as a woman's) was utterly ruined. He reminded legal practitioners that "no fetuses sit in our legislatures" to defend the interests of other fetuses.[109] In 1981, Senator Orrin Hatch offered a "Human Life Federalism Amendment" to overturn what he called an "act of raw judicial power."[110]

The executive branch also stepped up its antiabortion crusade. Rayman Solomon notes that the Reagan and Bush Administrations' dogged screening of candidates for federal judgeships to ferret out abortion rights supporters was "without precedent in the nation's past."[111] Meanwhile, an increasingly conservative Supreme Court encouraged states to regulate pregnancy and fertility more closely, so long as regulation did not create insurmountable obstacles to exercise of the right articulated in *Roe*. In 1976, the Court seemed to be standing firm on the essential components of Blackmun's opinion. In *Planned Parenthood v. Danforth*, it rejected Missouri's attempt to outlaw "saline amniocentesis" (then used in most second-trimester abortions), to force women to sign affidavits swearing that they had not been coerced into having abortions, to require physicians (on penalty of manslaughter charges and monetary damages) to exercise "professional care to preserve the fetus' life and health," and to secure the consent of husbands or parents.[112]

In 1977, however, the Court began to chip away at *Roe v. Wade*. In *Maher v. Roe* (1977), just as "right to life" activists had begun a fierce initiative in Congress to eliminate Medicaid funding for abortions, Justice Powell overturned a federal circuit court opinion that had invalidated, on equal protection grounds, a Connecticut abortion law under which state Medicaid funds could be used to pay the costs of childbirth, but not abortions, for indigent women. Powell concluded that lawmakers had expressed a "strong and legitimate interest in encouraging normal childbirth."[113] At the same term, in a *per curiam* decision in *Poelker, Mayor of St. Louis v. Doe*, the Court ruled that the city had not violated poor women's constitutional rights when it provided hospital services for childbirth but not for elective abortions. Beginning in 1981 with *H. L. v. Matheson*, justices began to accept parental notification and consent laws, particularly when they contained a "judicial bypass," by which pregnant girls could seek permission from a judge in lieu of parents. In 1982, Solicitor General Rex Lee filed a brief in *Akron v. Akron Center for Re-*

productive Health, signaling increased executive involvement in abortion politics; while the majority upheld *Roe*, Justice O'Connor submitted a dissent critical of Blackmun's trimester scheme.

Finally, in the Court's 1989 decision in *Webster v. Reproductive Health Services*, Justice Rehnquist not only jettisoned trimesters, but also expanded state regulatory authority, and seemed to be scaling back Blackmun's "fundamental right" to a lesser "liberty interest protected by the Due Process Clause." In *Webster*, the Court confronted a Missouri law proclaiming the existence of life at conception. The law also vested unborn children with protectable interests, and mandated tests to determine viability. Only Justice O'Connor's refusal to join Rehnquist in a formal reversal saved *Roe v. Wade*. Rehnquist had to be satisfied with affirming the constitutionality of the statute and condemning *Roe*'s "rigid" trimester framework, insensitivity to "democratic process," and insistence on a woman's autonomy before quickening. In dissent, Blackmun accused the majority of "cowardice and illegitimacy."[114] For the conservative *National Review*, Bruce Fein praised the Court's "withdrawal from constitutionalizing abortion policy in upholding a state law giving preference to childbirth over abortion. . . . The hallmark of a healthy democracy is citizen participation in forging public policy."

> It is a grave act when the Supreme Court shuts off the benefits of self-government with a constitutional decree in a search to end heated controversy. Thus, the Court's 1857 *Dred Scott* ruling aimed to supersede longstanding compromise and legislative rancor over slavery . . . , but the unintended result was calamitous. The High Court's 1973 *Roe v. Wade* abortion mandate fares no better than *Dred Scott* in the annals of judicial history.[115]

A few years later, however, in *Planned Parenthood v. Casey* (1992), pressure from the executive branch backfired. At issue were five provisions of the Pennsylvania Abortion Control Act of 1982. The law provided that a woman seeking an abortion "give her informed consent prior to the procedure," that she be provided with "certain information" at least twenty-four hours before the procedure so that she could make an informed choice, that minors obtain the consent of one parent (or, as an alternative, get permission from a judge), that married women get permission from their husbands unless the procedure was a "medical emergency," and that abortion clinics should undertake elaborate reportage of the details of their business. Five Pennsylvania clinics sued for injunctive relief, arguing that the statute was unconstitutional on its face.[116] The Court's opinion, jointly delivered by Justices O'Connor, Anthony Kennedy, and David Souter, rejected antiabortionist demands that the Court overrule *Roe v. Wade*. A concern for the stability of the constitutional system seemed to require a defense of the rule of *stare decisis*, if not the particulars of *Roe*. "[O]nly the most convincing justification under accepted standards of precedent could suffice to demonstrate," said the opinion, "that a later decision [to overrule] . . . was anything but a surrender to political pressure, and an unjustified repudiation of the principle on which the Court staked its authority in the first instance. So to overrule under fire in the absence of the most compelling reason to reexamine a watershed decision would subvert the Court's legitimacy beyond any serious question." The justices, however, did subject Blackmun's "outdated" trimester apparatus to criticism and announced a new review standard. Only when regulation imposed an "undue burden" on women would the Court say that it violated the "heart of the liberty" protected by the due process clause. The mere fact that a law made abortion "more difficult" or "more expen-

sive" would not be enough to invalidate it. By this new standard, only the spousal notification section of Pennsylvania's statute failed to pass constitutional muster.[117]

In the 1990s, destabilization of *Roe*'s intellectual structure triggered repeated tests of
judicial resolve. In 1996, Congress tried to ban so-called "partial-birth" abortions—a move
widely recognized as an attempt to narrow abortion rights by eliminating third-trimester
and, ultimately, second-trimester abortions. Among other provisions, the bill declared the
terms *fetus* and *infant* to be "interchangeable."[118] Kate Michelman of the National Abortion and Reproductive Rights Action League called the vote "an unprecedented intrusion
into medical practice." President Bill Clinton vetoed the bill; when antiabortion House
members voted to override the veto, senators rallied behind the president. Revised bills
on "partial-birth" abortion await congressional action; in May 1998, a lawyer for the National Right to Life Committee said, "We're optimistic. When we have the three more
votes we need in the Senate, that's when we'll bring it up."[119]

Meanwhile, more than two dozen states have adopted bans on "partial-birth" abortions, with other states poised to follow. In April 1998, in a move that terrified women's
groups, the Wisconsin legislature banned "partial-birth" abortions (a term invented by antiabortion forces) with a sweeping statute that defined the fetus as a "child" from the moment of conception; prohibited abortions of "living" children—defined as fetuses with
discernable heartbeats—except to preserve the life (not the health) of a pregnant woman;
and, unlike other "partial-birth" acts, proposed life imprisonment (Wisconsin's punishment for murder) for providers of abortions. The "heartbeat" rule was worrisome, since
hearts can be detected during the first trimester. All of the state's six abortion clinics
closed temporarily to seek legal advice. Said one doctor in Madison, "We called patients
and told them that we could not perform any procedures . . . because the law threatened
the physician with life imprisonment, and I'm not enough of a martyr to risk it."[120]

In June 1998, the same six Planned Parenthood clinics sought to enjoin enforcement
of the act; a federal district court judge in Madison refused the injunction, concluding that
lawmakers had an interest in protecting unborn children and that the law did not impose
an "undue burden" on women. On appeal, Chief Judge Richard Posner of the Seventh
Circuit Court of Appeals reversed the decision and allowed the injunction. Posner condemned the law's vague and overbroad incursion upon the "constitutionally recognized
right to an abortion." In his view, lawmakers not only aimed to terrorize abortion providers
and their clients, but also violated the requirements (set out in *Casey* and elsewhere) that
they allow abortions before viability and, when necessary to preserve women's lives *and
health,* after viability. In dissent, however, one judge insisted that the statute clearly banned
only one particularly repellant variety of abortion, that it did not create a constitutionally
impermissible hurdle over which women would have to climb in order to procure necessary abortions, and that the state's legitimate interest in "rescuing the unborn" permitted
intervention, so long as the mother's life could be preserved. And in 1999, Posner's opinion was overturned by a 5–4 decision of the Seventh Circuit sitting *en banc* in the case
of *Hope Clinic v. Ryan*—although enforcement of that decision was stayed pending the
U.S. Supreme Court's resolution of the question of the validity of "partial-birth" abortion
laws in *Stenberg v. Carhart.*[121]

Federal and state lawmakers, moreover, have tried to put reproductive control beyond
the reach of poor women. In 1976, after several years of delay and disputation, Congress
passed a rider to an appropriations bill, informally called the Hyde Amendment, denying
the use of federal Medicaid funds to obtain abortions "except where the life of the mother
would be endangered if the fetus were carried to term."[122] Congressional debate of the

measure moved far beyond the question of federal expenditures, implicating traditional female social responsibilities and the family itself. As Mississippi's Senator John Stennis put it, "I do not think [abortion] is a political question. . . . I do not think it is a question of money."

> I do not think . . . it is just strictly a legal question either. . . . I do not see how the Supreme Court of the United States could properly wander into this field and lay down the predicates and guidelines . . . and restrict the States and the Federal Government in this field which is not a legal question. It is murder, the wrongful taking of human life, which is to be condemned, and . . . [so it] is a question of old-fashioned morality. . . . I believe this trend that we have drifted into . . . strikes at the very basic foundations of the family, which is not just an isolated institution, but the . . . basic concept of our present civilization. . . . I am talking about the basic concept of the family and family life. As I understand human nature there is no doubt in my mind that this drifting trend we have taken . . . is leading us over the abyss on the basic question of what does the family mean and what is its place and how essential and necessary and indispensable it is.[123]

The Supreme Court apparently agreed. In *Harris v. McRae* (1980), Justice Potter Stewart upheld the Hyde Amendment; a decision to withhold federal money supposedly did not deprive poor women of equal protection of law—only of publically funded abortions. In a fierce dissent, Justice Marshall reminded Stewart, to no avail, that the legislation upheld by the Court had been "the product of an effort to deny to the poor the constitutional right recognized in *Roe v. Wade*"; the majority ignored the "undeniable fact that for women eligible for Medicaid—poor women—denial of a Medicaid-funded abortion is equivalent to denial of legal abortion altogether."[124]

The ban continues. Until 1993, except for occasional shifts in the Hyde Amendment's language, periodic attempts to restore funding for Medicaid abortions failed, initially because of President Carter's ambivalence on the question and then because of Republican resistance to both abortion and federal subsidies for low-income women. As President George Bush explained in a 1989 memorandum promising to veto any attempt to restore Medicaid funding, "My position on the issue of abortion is clear. I support a constitutional amendment that would reverse the Supreme Court's decision in *Roe v. Wade*. I also support a human life amendment with an exception for rape, incest, or where the life of the mother is threatened. I do not support Federal funding of abortions except where the mother's life is threatened."[125] Congress has reenacted the amendment annually since 1976. After 1993, even the Clinton Administration accepted a liberalized Hyde Amendment—one that funded abortions for victims of rape and incest, as well as for women apt to die from pregnancy.

In 1988, moreover, the Reagan Administration moved to restrict what clinics receiving federal money for family planning services could tell prospective parents about reproductive choices. Abortion was not to be mentioned. Many physicians and other medical professionals were incensed: Federal officials were interfering with their ability to advise patients fully and honestly. Then, in *Rust v. Sullivan* (1991), despite First and Fourteenth Amendment challenges to the administrative guidelines, the U.S. Supreme Court affirmed the constitutionality of the "gag rule," as it came to be called, asserting that the federal government, far from discriminating "on the basis of viewpoint," had merely "chosen to fund one activity to the exclusion of the other."[126] The restrictions continued until 1993, when the Clinton Administration summarily put an end to them.

Advocates of physical security for both sexes note optimistically that, in the main, *Roe v. Wade* still stands. Nevertheless, in response to federal disarray, several states have taken administrative action in defense of reproductive freedom, and Clinton appointees have been encouraging states to deal creatively with the Hyde Amendment's restrictions. One expert thinks that, for better or worse, the "future of abortion rights seems to hinge on state politics."[127] Equally important, while a good many scholars worry about *Roe*'s shaky doctrinal foundations, especially its association with privacy, others find ample ground within privacy law for energetic state intervention on behalf of women. In 1993, for example, legal philosopher Ronald Dworkin pointed out that the right to privacy endorsed in *Roe* is "plainly privacy in the sense of sovereignty over particular, specified decisions." In his reading, the right "not to be raped or sexually violated is another example of a right to control how one's body is used"—an essential attribute of sovereignty. Nor does it follow (as some scholars have contended) that states have "no responsibility to assure the economic conditions that make the exercise of the right possible and its possession valuable. Recognizing that women have a constitutional right to determine how their own bodies are to be used is a prerequisite, not a barrier, to the further claim that the government must ensure that this right is not illusory."[128]

Since 1998, and without much fanfare, a few state courts have begun to interpret state constitutions and civil rights laws as requiring the use of state Medicaid money for abortions; in November 1998, the New Mexico Supreme Court ruled unanimously that the state's ERA mandated such payments when "medically necessary for poor women." The court explicitly framed its decision in terms of equal protection of law, concluding (in the words of one journalist) that the state's human services department had "discriminated against women by denying money for abortion to poor women while paying for any medically necessary procedure for poor men." New Mexico was the sixteenth state to so move, and one of several to suggest that a denial of abortion rights implicated equal protection jurisprudence. Abortion opponents immediately saw the breach in the doctrinal wall, condemning the decision as a "sign of what could happen if a Federal Equal Rights Amendment for women should be enacted."[129]

In this ideological tug-of-war about who will control women's bodies and maternity, the real targets have been feminism and the specter of female autonomy (Dworkin's "sovereignty"). Since at least the 1850s, women's rights activists have sought to emancipate women from cultural expectations of maternity and from the consequences of healthy sexual desire. With rare exceptions, women have borne the social and economic burden of reproduction; men typically have not sacrificed health and economic advancement to become parents. As feminists and allied lawmakers began to shift the costs to both sexes, social conservatives and religious fundamentalists fought back. In a 1992 speech at the Republican Party's nominating convention, Pat Buchanan promised to deliver Americans from Hillary Clinton and other advocates of "radical feminism"; the Democrats supposedly wanted "abortion on demand, a litmus test for the Supreme Court, homosexual rights, discrimination against religious schools, [and] women in combat units."[130]

Attempts to reassert the public's interest in maternity have not been limited to abortion. Between 1985 and 1992, twenty-seven states as well as the District of Columbia imposed new restrictions on the habits and practices of pregnant women. Although few Americans would urge childbearing women to smoke, drink, or use cocaine, the idea that the state may dictate what pregnant women consume or do certainly gives pause. Such a construction recurs. A number of women in Congress have noticed a willingness to regulate women's bodily functions, but not men's. Said Patricia Schroeder, the former Democratic representative from Colorado, in 1997, "It seems to all go back to our reproductive organs, You know why? We're just not smart enough to deal with this by ourselves. We need Congress's help. Now, if we did this [t]o their health, they would be nuts."[131]

Courts also trump women's decisions about their own bodies. In 1987, Angela Carder—a cancer patient in her sixth month of pregnancy—was hospitalized with a lung tumor. She and her doctor planned an aggressive chemotherapy program, even if the fetus died; when she seemed to grow worse, and against her express wishes, a three-judge panel in Washington, D.C., authorized a Caesarean section, ignoring the fact that she had survived earlier bouts with cancer. The child lived for a few hours; two days later, Carder died in a coma. In 1990, another panel reversed the original decision, noting that her "right to bodily integrity" had been "subordinat[ed]" unjustifiably to "the state's interest in potential life." But, for Carder, it was too late.[132]

Since the 1990s, antiabortion radicals have resorted increasingly to violence. So-called "right to life" groups regularly mobilize small armies to picket abortion facilities, block doorways, and harass women with pictures and pamphlets; states' attempts to halt violence with "buffer zones" have not succeeded. The Supreme Court has been less than firm in maintaining a "balance" between freedom of speech and privacy rights. In *Schenck* v. *Pro-Choice Network of Western New York* (1997), Justice Rehnquist ruled that the police could enforce a fifteen-foot buffer zone between picketers and "clinic doorways, driveways, and driveway entrances." A few years earlier, however, in *Jayne Bray v. Alexandria Women's Health Clinic*, Justice Antonin Scalia decided that antiabortion organizations that had mobilized expressly to prevent women from exercising the fundamental rights described in *Roe* did not constitute a "private conspiracy" akin to the Ku Klux Klan. He ruled as well that the denial of a federal right to choose an abortion could not serve as a proper object of a "purely private conspiracy," and that women were not the issue. Invoking a strict Fourteenth Amendment standard in a case not involving the Fourteenth Amendment, Scalia insisted that the "goal of preventing abortion" did not qualify as "invidiously discriminatory animus directed at women in general." In dissent, Justice O'Connor argued to the contrary that when people organize to prevent women from "exercising their legal rights," they satisfy the requirements of conspiracy statutes. She also rejected Scalia's distinction between women per se and procedures performed only on women's bodies. "If women are a protected class . . . ," she wrote, "then the statute must reach conspiracies whose motivation is directly related to characteristics unique to that class." Surely, women's "ability to become pregnant" and to "terminate their pregnancies" was "unique to the class of women."[133]

Murders and injuries at abortion clinics have filled newspaper columns. In 1994, after an especially violent episode, the Senate adopted a resolution praising the executive branch for providing enhanced security at abortion facilities and promising to defend the "900 clinics in the United States providing reproduction health services." Senators condemned shootings at two Massachusetts clinics and another in Virginia, four murders, and one attempted murder; they also noted reports of "over 130 incidents of violence or harassment directed at reproductive health care clinics and their personnel in 1994 such as death threats, stalking, chemical attacks, bombings and arson." Violence, they warned, was "not a mode of free speech and should not be condoned as a method of expressing an opinion."[134] But terrorism continued. In late January 1998, a homemade bomb exploded a few feet from the front door of the New Woman All Women Health Care Clinic in Birmingham, Alabama. The blast killed a police officer and severely wounded a nurse. The FBI speculated that the explosion might have been related to others in Atlanta,

Georgia—two at the Northside Family Planning Services center in 1997, which injured seven people; one at a lesbian nightclub in 1997; and yet another at the Olympic Games in 1996. At the time of the Birmingham episode, the federal Bureau of Alcohol, Tobacco and Firearms (ATF) could point to 199 attacks on abortion clinics since 1982, when it first began to keep track of them. President Clinton condemned the Alabama attack. "This bombing," he said, "was an unforgivable act that strikes at the heart of the constitutional freedoms and individual liberties all Americans hold dear." Mayor Richard Arrington of Birmingham called it a "despicable incident"; even the National Right to Life Committee condemned "any form of violence to fight the violence of abortion." In November 1998, however, another physician was shot and killed, this time in his home.[135]

WOMEN'S BODIES AND PERSONAL SECURITY

If Dworkin is right, at the heart of the argument for reproductive freedom lies a woman's right, originating in personal sovereignty, to control how her body is used. Similarly, a woman has a right (again in Dworkin's terms) "not to be raped or sexually violated" on much the same constitutional ground. Government also has an obligation to make her secure in her liberty, as with all citizens. Yet threats to physical autonomy and safety persist, despite heroic efforts to stem violence. Since the 1970s, women's groups have established rape crisis centers and hot lines in virtually every American city and more than a few rural areas; attorneys have volunteered time to move battered women and their children to safehouses and to see rape victims through the agonizing process of reporting assaults, getting medical help, filing suits, and testifying in court. Feminists also have been instrumental in securing reform of criminal codes.

Concerns about physical and economic security sometimes converge in lawsuits alleging sexual harassment in the workplace. Female workers understand, in Vicki Schultz's words, the "power of men to harass, belittle, ostracize, dismiss, marginalize, discard, and just plain hurt them as workers." They know, too, that the legal system cannot protect them from abuse.[136] One study of engineers' views of gender differences found that male engineers associated manhood with technological proficiency; they also saw themselves as "striving, achieving, engaging in the public sphere of work," whereas women were "static, domestic, private people"—that is, "nonworkers." Because these men saw women as "aspect[s] of the decor" who "create a pleasant atmosphere," they could discredit female engineers as "performing seals" especially trained for the occasion, incapable of what one engineer called "*man*handling." They also jealously guarded an occupational culture riddled with "sexual stories, references and innuendo."[137]

Sexual harassment suits threaten that culture by revealing it to be a primary fount of male–female inequality. The term *sexual harassment* likely was invented in 1975 by Lin Farley, the instructor in a course called "Women and Work" at Cornell University. Farley organized a "speakout" on sexual misconduct at work and elsewhere that about 100 women attended. Then, in her pathbreaking book, *Sexual Harassment of Working Women* (1979), legal scholar Catharine MacKinnon laid further conceptual foundations for recasting gender-based harassment as a form of sex discrimination. First, she persuasively framed harassment as a problem of inequality—a position that many courts have adopted. Second, in a line of argument that has not yet been accepted by the courts—indeed, that the Supreme Court seemed to reject in 1998 in affirming Joseph Oncale's Title VII claim against male coworkers for repeated sexual assaults[138]—she distinguished between the abuse of working women and all other kinds of harassment. In the *Oncale* case, for example, the alleged victim of on-the-job harassment was male; MacKinnon's principles would rule out such a suit on the ground that men never experience sex "inequality" exactly as women do. When a woman is harassed, in other words, the object is less to control an individual than to affirm a power relation between all men and all women—a relation that permeates society and that women agree not to resist. A waitress made some of these connections: "[Men think] they have a right to touch me, or proposition me because I'm a waitress. . . . You aren't in any position to say 'get your crummy hands off me' because you need the tips. That's what a waitress job is all about." In contrast, women's harassment of men or same-sex harassment aims to intimidate an individual, not a class; it cannot affirm the dominance of all women over all men because no such relation exists in the world. In MacKinnon's words, men's harassment of female workers "uses and helps create women's structurally inferior status."[139]

In several key decisions, federal courts have given jurisprudential life to the idea of harassment as sex discrimination, in the process confirming the utility of Title VII for working women. In *Meritor Savings Bank v. Vinson* (1986), the Supreme Court permitted suit whenever employers tied a demand for sexual favors to continued employment (the so-called quid pro quo rule). The justices later elaborated on *Vinson*, holding in *Harris v. Forklift Systems* (1993), for instance, that plaintiffs need not demonstrate psychological injuries. Lower federal courts also have contributed bricks to the antiharassment wall. In *Bohen v. City of East Chicago* (1986), the Seventh Circuit decided that sexual harassment by a public employer could violate the equal protection clause. Five years later, in *Ellison v. Brady*, the Ninth Circuit allowed a Title VII remedy whenever unwelcome sexual advances or other kinds of sex-related hostility were "severe or pervasive" enough to create a "hostile environment" for female employees.[140] In 1995, an EEOC complaint against a cosmetics firm for harassment of fifteen female employees resulted in an award of $1.2 million. And in a 1996 complaint against Mitsubishi Motor Manufacturing of America, the EEOC claimed that "hundreds" of women might have experienced "'gross and shocking sexual discrimination.' Junior managers had fondled them and made physical threats. . . . One man had placed an air gun between a woman's legs and pulled the trigger."[141]

Perhaps because judges retain enormous discretion in saying what constitutes a hostile environment or a serious threat to continued employment, a certain plasticity runs through the cases. In a 1990 ruling, the First Circuit decided that five mild sexual overtures by a supervisor constituted an insufficient cause of action; another court decided not to allow suit against a firm employing a supervisor who stroked a woman's leg, kissed her, and then refused to speak to her after she rejected him. Yet another granted relief when a man called a woman "honey" and "dear," touched her, asked about her birth control practices and undergarments, and promised eventually to bed her.[142] An important 1998 refinement of harassment law illustrates the plasticity problem: In *Burlington Industries v. Ellerth* and *Faragher v. City of Boca Raton*, the Supreme Court held that an employer is subject to vicarious liability anytime a supervisor sexually harasses an employee, even though the employer was not otherwise at fault and the employee never suffered adverse job consequences. At the same time, the Court allowed employers to raise a defense if they could show that they used reasonable care to discourage sexual harassment or that the employee unreasonably failed to use remedial opportunities that they had provided.[143]

To the extent that discretion allows judges to wage vigorous war against harassment, the practice aids women; on other occasions, however, judges' commodious sense of what constitutes "fair play" has encouraged men to test the limits of the law. Fear of retaliation and an unsympathetic hearing prevents women from reporting episodes of harassment for years and even decades—and such fears can be warranted, as the wrenching "trial" of Anita Hill during Justice Clarence Thomas's Senate confirmation hearings made clear. When dozens of military women in the wake of the notorious Tailhook Association Convention in 1991 finally decided to go public with stories of harassment at such events, the armed services confronted detailed stories of systemwide abuse and silencing. In March 1994, Assistant Secretary of Defense Edwin Dorn conceded that field commanders "still may not say, loudly enough or often enough, that sexual harassment will not be tolerated." Stories are legion. A lieutenant assigned to a submarine testified that she received "suggestive cards and letters at home" from her superior officer ("That uniform does not show your body in a just light"). In 1992, a military police officer in the air force told of a supervisor who "explicitly described the benefits of my having a sexual relationship with him"; he "made me understand that if I refused, my career would suffer." When she refused, the tires on her car were slashed and the wheel bolts loosened. A staff sergeant wept as she described a gunner sergeant's "unwanted overtures" at a marine base. At a hearing in response to her complaint, defense lawyers had asked her "whether she wore provocative clothing or had sex" with men in her command. "Looking back on it now," she said, "it is not surprising that I felt like I was the one on trial."[144]

Women cannot always count on unions to help them. Consider the story underlying *Chrysler Motors Corporation v. International Union* (1993): "Ronald Gallenbeck, a factory forklift operator, put down the phone, walked up to a female co-worker from behind, grabbed her breasts while she was inspecting a door panel, walked back to the phone, and said, 'Yup, they're real.' The woman filed a complaint. After an investigation, the company discharged Gallenbeck. He filed a grievance through his union, which triggered an arbitration hearing. Despite evidence that the man repeatedly had abused women, the arbitrator found his discharge groundless and ordered him reinstated. Chrysler Corporation sued in federal court, urging the bench to vacate the arbitration award as contrary to public policies against workplace harassment. But the court upheld the arbitrator, and Gallenbeck was back on the job."[145]

The sexual abuse of female athletes vividly reveals the relationship between women's violations of gender norms and violence, and the perils of trying to force legal change *against* culture. Leslie Heywood, the well-known track star, observes that while "sports-minded young girls" as well as women's professional athletic teams and leagues now form an "everyday part of our culture," athletic women still confront trivialization and harassment, in part because they have succeeded on masculine turf. In such cases, Title IX is impotent. As Heywood tells it, "unethical" relationships include verbal taunting, rape, and "serial marriages" in which coaches marry and then divorce athletes. When Heywood first filed a complaint, she was a high school runner. The coach's lawyer accused her of "making it all up" and of "implicitly consenting" because she "went around with a lot of boys." In the 1990s, sexual harassment still undermines female athletes, "communicating to the women that they are of little value." When women do tell their stories, Heywood adds, they sometimes are cast "as victims or met with indifference. . . . We emphasize the importance of girls' and women's self-esteem and then treat them as victims, liars, or objects of prurient speculation when, despite formidable obstacles, they do muster enough courage to speak."[146]

Violent men also lurk in the nooks and crannies of private life, where—despite feminist attempts to recast sexual abuse as a problem in equality—the Bill of Rights and the Fourteenth Amendment (which restrict governments, not private persons) are largely useless. As Linda Hirshman wryly observed in 1994, equal protection law as presently applied, far from abolishing violence, provides that "a man could beat his wife only if she could beat him, too."[147] As of 1989, husbands could be prosecuted for raping their wives in 42 states, in the District of Columbia, and on federal property. But 26 states allowed exemptions or exceptions: A husband could be prosecuted for rape only if the couple were living apart, or if he used a weapon or caused severe physical injury. As of the same year, 8 states—Kentucky, Missouri, New Mexico, North Carolina, Oklahoma, South Carolina, South Dakota, and Utah—still refused to say that husbands could rape wives. In Maine, legislators and the supreme court recognized a "voluntary companion" defense when a woman "permitted . . . sexual contact, short of the sexual act itself," on a date. Not surprisingly, opponents of the reform of marital rape law have sometimes pointed to the sanctity of marital spaces, evoking Douglas's *Griswold* opinion. In 1980, for instance, Representative Tom Bush objected to the state of Florida's invasion of "the sanctity and intimacy of a relationship"; in the same year, Florida legislator John Mica decried "meddling in your bedroom," with the state deciding "what you can do and what you can't do." Other critics made tasteless jokes. Senator Bob Wilson of California remarked in 1979, "But if you can't rape your wife, who can you rape?"[148]

Why do so many Americans still think of male-female interaction as a contact sport like football or wrestling?[149] The Boston *Globe* reported in 1993 that men who beat wives or companions think that they are allowed to control "their" women with brute force.[150] After the fact, rapists say that the sight of a beautiful woman in itself provoked an attack; one man explained that his victim had been "a real fox, a beautiful shape. She was a beautiful woman and I wanted to see what she had." Said a gang rapist, "We were powerful, we were in control. . . . She wasn't like a person, no personality, just domination on my part." At some misogynist extreme are rapist-murderers, one of whom told a female researcher in 1980–81 that women exist to be raped: "Rape is a man's right. If a woman doesn't want to give it, the man should take it. Women have no right to say no. Women are made to have sex. It's all they are good for. Some women would rather take a beating, but they always give in."[151]

The U.S. Department of Justice's Bureau of Justice Statistics reported in 1991 that between 1973 and 1987, about 155,000 women were raped each year; Deborah Rhode notes that "[b]y even the most conservative estimates, the United States has the highest rate of reported rape in the Western industrial world."[152] In 1995, the Justice Department's National Institute of Justice found two gender gaps: Although men experience more non-sexual assaults in their lifetimes than do women (66.4 percent of men versus 51.9 percent of women), 18 percent of women compared to 3 percent of men experience completed or attempted rape. Furthermore, women's "castles" do not protect them; as of 1991, about two-thirds of all completed rapes occurred at night, most of them in the victims' own homes (4 out of 10) or in the homes of friends (2 in 10), and 3 out of 10 attempted rapes happened at home, and another 1 out of 10 occurred at a friend's house. Also as of 1991, young women, whether black or white, were three times more likely to be raped than were older women—indeed, from 13 to 23 percent of American *girls* experience childhood sexual abuse—and women who lived alone were more likely to be raped than those with housemates. About half of all rape victims (and three-quarters of all black victims) were in the bottom third of income groups. About 8 out of 10 women confronting rapists tried to defend themselves. More than half of all victims received medical care for the rapes or related injuries; a full 60 percent of all completed rapes included serious injuries beyond the rapes. Women reported about 53 percent of all completed or attempted rapes to the police. When a woman decided not to report the crime, she typically explained that rape was "a private or personal matter"; that she feared reprisal; or that the police would be "inefficient, ineffective, or insensitive."[153]

Experiences of rape redirect women's lives. For many victims, rape marks the moment at which they became aware for the first time of their sex's physical insecurity. In 1969, a photographer had this to say: "Somewhere along the line society had told me that if you're a woman and you stick your neck out by being conspicuous you're going to get it. The rape confirmed it. Before the rape I used to go all over the city with my cameras, I was never afraid for my safety. Afterwards I stopped taking pictures, or if I did go out into strange neighborhoods, I made sure that I had a male companion. But at some point you have to say that you're not going to be stopped by it. . . . Otherwise you'd just have to stay indoors."[154] A victim's sense of the passing of innocence can be profound. Some years after "date rape" at age 17, Andi Rosenthal wrote a *noir* poem:

> Afterwards, I walk to the edge of the silent
> pond, where strands of water lay entwined
> in the grass. The night is warm and thick
> with summer; the voices from the house, the lights
> hang in the air like overripe fruit. The sounds
> pervade my mouth, my skin like some sick fog,
> like my tongue rotting inside my throat. The house—
> Someone is playing music, and the sound
> has burned my eyes. I am the only dead thing here,
> kneeling beside the water's edge without a mouth
> to pray, without hands to clasp or implore, without
> the eyes that mutely screamed, and were ignored.
> A swan glides, rageless, through my reflection.
> Blood trickles down my thigh, and the party goes on.[155]

What interests does violence serve? Most obviously, physical abuse expresses patriarchal force and is therefore as much a proclamation of "title" in women's bodies as it is an attempt to hurt particular women. The numbers are staggering. Each year, according to the American Bar Association's Commission on Domestic Violence, 2 to 4 million American women are battered by their husbands or male partners. Judge and legal writer Richard A. Posner speculates that as women continue to seek and find salaried jobs, "husbands' diminished economic power over wives might result in a greater likelihood of a husband's resorting to force against his wife to get his way."[156] Sociologist Anthony Giddens similarly warns that the "sexual control of women by men" is "much more than an incidental feature of modern social life." As patriarchal control erodes, the "compulsive character of male sexuality" comes to the fore, generating a "rising tide of male violence toward women."[157]

In much the same way, pornography expresses and affirms both inequality and men's control over women's bodies. Disagreements about pornography have revealed important divisions within organized feminism and within society in general about how to ensure citizens' physical security and eliminate violent, sexualized depictions of women's bodies without jeopardizing other freedoms that are central to a democratic society—among them, liberty of speech, to which suffragists and feminists have long paid special homage. Susan Brownmiller's *Against Our Will* (1975)—a searing attack on the culture of rape and pornography—drew attention to the fact that most pornography, like rape, is essentially misogynistic: By presenting scenes of domination and violence in which women appear under conditions of sexual subordination, it devalues women, links female sexuality to subordination, and makes such subordination a source of male pleasure. It encourages men to regard women as complaisant, available sexual objects who exist for the purpose of gratifying their lust and thus eroticizes and perpetuates male power and violence against women. Acting on this insight, women's groups across the country began in the late 1970s to organize "Take Back the Night" marches, designed to mobilize public opinion against degrading representations and uses of women's bodies.

In 1983, Catharine MacKinnon and Andrea Dworkin (then teaching a course on the subject at the University of Minnesota) provided a legal focus for the antipornography campaign by drafting a model ordinance that banned pornography on the ground that it perpetuates inequality and therefore constitutes a form of sex discrimination in violation of municipal civil rights laws. The mayor of Minneapolis twice vetoed the adoption of this draft by the city council. Pushed by an odd coalition of feminists, religious fundamentalists, and right-wing Republicans, the city of Indianapolis actually enacted the MacKinnon-Dworkin ordinance in 1984. In *American Booksellers Association v. Hudnut* (1985), a suit that was supported by an equally odd coalition of booksellers, pornography producers, anticensorship feminists, and civil libertarians, the Seventh Circuit upheld a lower court's invalidation of the ordinance as an unconstitutional abridgment of the First Amendment. In 1986, the U.S. Supreme Court summarily affirmed this decision, effectively putting an end to efforts to enact the ordinance in other cities. Into the 1990s, however, Mackinnon and others argued forcefully that because pornography embodies and perpetuates inequality, it violates (among other constitutional provisions) the Fourteenth Amendment's equal protection clause.[158] Indeed, both MacKinnon and Andrea Dworkin see pornography as the lynchpin in a system of male supremacist violence. According to Dworkin, purveyors of misogynist representations of women and physical violence—among them, rapists, pornographers, pimps, and batterers—posit "a female nature that is essentially fulfilled by the act of violation, which in turn transforms violation into merely using a thing for what it is and blames the thing if it is not womanly enough to enjoy what is done to it."[159]

In the pornography wars, contestants form two camps—opponents of all kinds of censorship and foes of what Lynn Chancer calls "hegemonic pornography." Among the questions raised, but never fully answered, are these: Does the distribution of pornography really advance the First Amendment freedoms of speech and press, or does it merely encourage viewing women as natural objects of male lust and domination? Does the existence of pornography allow *women* to express themselves more imaginatively and erotically, or can it only address men's prurient interests? Should women try to silence pornographers, thus running the risk that censorship ultimately may be turned against feminists and other political dissenters? Or, borrowing a page from antebellum feminists, should they invade the citadel (in this case, the pornography industry and mainstream media), seeking to influence, control, and perhaps profit by pornographic representations of both sexes? Between the two factions lies an excluded middle position, which sees both cen-

sorship and pornography as problematic. Chancer suggests exploring that position, transforming the debate about pornography, and perhaps pornography itself, into discourses of
value to women.[160]

Discussions of pornography and prostitution sometimes intersect; as Dworkin points
out, the term *pornography* originally meant "writing about whores": the *porne* was the
cheapest . . . of all women, including slaves. She was . . . a sexual slave. *Graphos* means
writing. . . . In ancient Greece, not all prostitutes were considered vile—only the
porneia."[161] In recent years, COYOTE and other sex worker lobbies have tried to defend
women's right to ply their trade without police harassment and with state protection (in
the form of health examinations and insurance). But for wildly different reasons, conservatives and some feminists have resisted legalization. The Supreme Court has not had
cause to change its mind about its 1908 denunciation of prostitution in *United States v.
Betty*: Women who have "indiscriminate intercourse with men," said the majority, " . . .
are in hostility to the idea of the family . . . [and] the holy estate of matrimony; the sure
foundation of all that is stable and noble in our civilization."[162] Political conservatives
take much the same line. In contrast, Take Back the Night marchers condemned the com-
modification of women's bodies. As Brownmiller wrote in 1975, "[M]y horror at the idea
of legalized prostitution is not that it doesn't work as a rape deterrent"—although it does
not—"but that it institutionalizes the concept that it is man's monetary right, if not his divine right, to gain access to the female body, and that sex is a female service that should
not be denied the civilized male. Perpetuation of the concept that the 'powerful male impulse' must be satisfied . . . by a cooperative set of women, set aside and expressly licensed for the purpose, is part and parcel of the mass psychology of rape."[163]

In the 1960s and 1970s, feminists who were interested in empowering sex workers
labored to address some of Brownmiller's concerns. In the past, reformers had emphasized the ease with which *women* could be lured into sexual slavery, *women's* power to
seduce innocent fathers and husbands, and *women's* carnal natures. By 1960, police departments, legislatures, and social researchers had begun to rethink their assumptions and
to cast a broader net. Although sex-specific laws against prostitution treat "fallen women"
as primary agents and a central threat to public morality, as Barbara Meil Hobson points
out, a close examination of urban street life tells a different story. In one California experiment, female decoys attracted 150 propositions by men and made eight arrests a week;
male decoys arrested only 3 women per week.[164] Recent discussions of the possible licensing of sex workers, or statutory reform to eliminate sex-specific language and punish male entrepreneurs (among them, pimps and procurers) whose profits greatly exceed
women's, at least recognize the fact of male-female involvement in the trade.

LOSING THE EQUAL RIGHTS AMENDMENT

As the 1980s dawned, liberals faced full-scale attacks on campaigns to secure bodily freedom, some of which emanated from self-described feminists. The causes were not hard
to find. Alice Kessler-Harris's explanation bears repeating: "Home and work roles," she
wrote in 1982, "seemingly complementary in the preindustrial period, and tightly regulated thereafter, had by the 1980's burst their constraints. As long as women's social virtue
was clearly attached to their home roles, they could go out to work without threatening
the assumptions on which family and labor market rested. But when the majority of women
moved into wage work—albeit as a way of helping out in the home—the contradictions

between the two soon threatened the traditional organization of the family and the power relationships that derived from it."[165] Social anxieties bubbled to the surface not only in anti-ERA campaigns, but in constitutional decision making and legislation. In Congress and elsewhere, Americans determined to contain an uncontainable social revolution tacitly and awkwardly took the side of wife beaters and other exploitative men. Antirape campaigns were said to represent the hysterical machinations of "simpering prom queens" with "neopuritan preoccupations" determined to "transform the act of seduction into the crime of rape." What is most revealing about such talk, as Rhode notes, "is not that it offers new and persuasive insights, but rather that it builds so successfully on old and unfounded prejudices"[166]—that feminism is a symptom of female hysteria; that women invite male violence; and that wives, dates, and perfect strangers really like to be manhandled, even when they claim otherwise.

In addition, second-wave feminists confronted the limits of liberal legalism—in a myriad of judicial reversals and, perhaps most graphically, in the eleventh-hour battle over the adoption and ratification of the ERA. Cynthia Harrison surely is right in saying that, to friend and foe alike, ERA required a "reordering of the world,"[167] particularly if judges gave it full effect. A good many Americans, rightly sensing a connection between constitutional and cultural change, took flight. Conservatives argued that ERA threatened the protections and privileges that women (by which they meant middle-class mothers and wives) richly deserved. Even though courts have found an abortion right in privacy doctrine rather than in equal protection jurisprudence, and—much to the chagrin of many progressives—have refused to draw same-sex relationships under the equal protection umbrella, the antifeminist lawyer Phyllis Schlafly and others contended by 1972–73 that ERA would enshrine abortion in American law and mandate unisex bathrooms. They also accused feminists of stupidity and extremism. "The Equal Rights Amendment," said Schlafly in 1973, "will not give women anything which they do not already have, or have a way of getting, but it will take away from women some of their most important legal rights, benefits and exemptions. It is like trying to kill a fly with a sledgehammer; you probably won't kill the fly; but you surely will break up some of the furniture." Opponents argued that ERA would legalize homosexuality and foster its "spread," as if it were smallpox. The Eagle Forum circulated a pamphlet in 1993 entitled *ERA = Gay = AIDS Connection*, in which it not only smeared both gays and the amendment, but attempted to link them (ERA would give "homosexuals everything they ever asked for in the name of gay rights"). Critics also hoisted the states' rights banner, worrying with Schlafly about a federal "grab of power" in areas traditionally reserved for the states.[168] As in the 1850s and 1910s, "anti's" tarred feminists with the broad brush of treason—against families and motherhood, the republic, the womanly woman, and the manly man. In 1972, George Wallace's American Party damned ERA as a "socialistic plan to destroy the home," and the John Birch Society linked it to "communist plans . . . to reduce human beings to the level of animals."[169] In the Reverend Jerry Falwell's view, ERA was a "delusion" promulgated by a "minority core of women who were once bored with life, whose real problems are spiritual problems. Many woman have never accepted their God-given roles. They live in disobedience to God's laws and have promoted their godless philosophy throughout our society." Such women needed to "know Jesus Christ," to be "under his lordship" and "part of a home where their husband is a godly leader."[170]

But such critics, though well funded and often better organized than were the proponents of ERA, were not the only source of opposition. As in the 1920s, working-class men and women—many of them people of color—perceived in NOW's drive toward ratification of ERA an arrogant disdain for their relatively powerless situation in relations with employers and whites. In their experience, only women of privilege survived toe-to-toe competition with capitalists and politicians. What about affirmative action programs, which surely violated strict "equal protection" readings of the Fourteenth Amendment and relied for their success—as in Florence Kelley's day—on public recognition of the fact of racism and sexism in American life and thought? How could black women become CEOs when they attended inferior high schools and could barely afford tuition at state universities, much less Harvard? How would poor women survive without alimony in "no fault" divorce states, given the lingering, yawning gap between male and female earning power and the states' failure to help women collect child support awards?

From different quarters altogether, "essentialists" and some "cultural feminists"—that is, women's rights supporters persuaded of their special role *as women* in social purification—sometimes made arguments redolent of Antoinette Brown Blackwell's. From their vantage point, complete equality implied the eradication of cultural and even genetic differences; a denial of sex; and a disastrous corruption of womankind, and, with her, republican society. As Jane DeHart and Donald Matthews discovered in ratification-era North Carolina, antifeminists and "social feminists" alike decided that ratificationists "wanted—and wanted them—to be men." ERA supporters seemed to be "angry, foul mouthed, lesbian (masculine), mean, arrogant, elitist, self-centered, or aggressive," and a threat to the "sisterhood" of women. "Female solidarity," in other words, "depended on women's being feminine," whereas ERA seemed to promise universal manliness.[171]

From another camp, radical feminists argued that NOW's long waltz with the NWP's laissez-faire amendment largely ignored the extent to which law itself (including, but not only, affirmative action programs) expressed and affirmed patriarchal, heterosexual, and entrepreneurial values. Lesbians noticed that NOW had downplayed and even denied the fact that "equal rights," properly understood and implemented, probably mandated the restoration of gay rights—an argument that ultimately persuaded Hawaiian legislators to legalize same-sex marriages. What if judges decided to read the amendment narrowly? The law, after all, was an artifact of the same structures and practices within which sodomy has been outlawed and women and blacks had been traditionally subjected to mastership, and ERA would be interpreted in the courts, perhaps by analogy with the Fourteenth Amendment. In 1979, Bader Ginsburg concluded that the sex-specific intentions of the framers of ERA would ensure broad (if not sweeping) application, particularly compared to the Fourteenth Amendment alternative. "The equal status and dignity of men and women under the law is the animating purpose of the proposed Equal Rights Amendment (ERA)," she wrote. "By contrast, the framers of the fourteenth amendment did not contemplate sex equality. Boldly dynamic interpretation, departing radically from the original understanding, is required to tie to the fourteenth amendment's equal protection clause a command that government treat men and women as individuals equal in rights, responsibilities, and opportunities." But the judiciary's studied silence about the comparability of sex and race as constitutional categories gives pause: What if judges decided cases brought under the ERA in light of analogous Fourteenth Amendment cases? ERA then could be interpreted much less dynamically.[172]

From NOW's point of view, the closing chapters of the ERA story were heartbreaking. In 1972, Congress had placed a seven-year limit on ratification, in keeping with the limit attached to the Eighteenth Amendment and with the Supreme Court's ruling in *Dillon v. Gloss* (1921), which affirmed Congress's power to impose reasonable limits on the ratification of amendments. As resistance to the ERA increased, the clock seemed to tick more loudly. Detractors hammered away at the likelihood of a male-female draft and the imminent defilement of American girls. One mother wrote Senator Sam Ervin, an opponent of ERA, that she was "ashamed and terrified at what the future holds for my three little girls. Will my shy, sweet Tommy be drafted in six years? So modest I can't even see her undress. Oh God! . . . I can't stand it. I just can't bear it."[173]

By 1978, thirty-five states had ratified the ERA, but a number of legislatures had rescinded or had threatened to reconsider their original decision to ratify. ERA supporters therefore secured an extension until June 30, 1982, organized powerful coalitions in shaky or recalcitrant states, and took up the question of whether states could reverse their vote, largely in response to political alarmism and—because, year after year, at least 60 percent of Americans told pollsters that they supported ERA—against the wishes of popular majorities. Antifeminists argued that ERA had expired with the seven-year limit and that parties always could withdraw from contracts if the terms had not been clear. NOW insisted that the time limit (in keeping with the history of Article V of the Constitution) was a guideline, not a fixed rule, and that, to be meaningful, ratification had to be final.

In the end, feminists lost. By 1980, as Mary Frances Berry points out, the "tide had turned definitively"; NOW's decision to seek an extension "only made matters worse." In all-important Illinois, neither a Mother's Day march in Chicago of 100,000 ERA supporters nor a flood of mail nor an impressive lobbying effort (in Berry's words) by "saleswomen, teachers, housewives, nurses, executives, union members, [and] NOW leaders" had the desired effect. In July 1980, Illinois legislators rejected the ERA for the seventh time; two months later, a new roll call came out no better. The Republican Party, long a sponsor of ERA, eliminated its pro-amendment plank in 1980, largely in response to Reagan's opposition to the amendment; in its place, Reaganites inserted a compromise statement: "We acknowledge the legitimate efforts of those who support or oppose ratification of the Equal Rights Amendment." In 1981, Nevada legislators rejected ERA less than a minute after its introduction; Virginians killed it in committee. Despite feminists' efforts in virtually every state either to secure ratification or to prevent rescission, legislators refused to budge; in three years' time, not a single state joined the pro-ERA roster. By January 1982, in the face of a Gallup poll showing a 63 percent majority nationwide in favor of ERA, the Supreme Court effectively took itself out of the controversy by refusing to rule on the validity of rescission in the case of *Idaho v. Freeman.* Thereafter, Congress—standing on *Coleman v. Miller* (1939), in which the Court had granted that body the exclusive right to pass on the validity of state ratifications—decided to allow rescission, extinguishing the last glimmer of hope among ERA stalwarts.[174]

Anti-ERA forces immediately proclaimed victory over bra-burning feminists. Schafly vowed, for instance, to eliminate every scrap of the dread "ism" from public schools: "The way it is now," she noted with remarkable inaccuracy, "you can't show a picture of a woman washing the dishes."[175] In effect, groups like Stop ERA had successfully portrayed NOW and other feminist groups as the enemy of women, persuading nervous Americans (especially in rural areas, where anti-ERA campaigns were especially effective) that talk about "equality" was really talk against the family and women's much-touted social privileges. To destabilize traditional gender relations was to call into question many of the hallmarks of white middle-class society—among them, heterosexuality, female "modesty," Christian piety, male headship, and maternalism. It was simply unimaginable that the democratization of some people's families might result in a stronger society and better marriages. Instead, talk about equality triggered waves of cultural terror. Once again, hens would crow. Feminists allied with gays—many of whom pointed out that NOW had abandoned them in the rush to ratify ERA—would taint public schools with unnatural doctrines. The amendment and "women's lib" came to be synonymous with unmanly men pushing brooms, unwomanly women in air force fatigues, sexual promiscuity, high divorce rates, and (when both parents held salaried jobs) plummeting birthrates and juvenile delinquency. To the extent that Americans still preferred to think of women as Queens of the Home, obliged first to husband and family and only secondarily to the state, the very idea that "rights and *responsibilities*" might be "extended to all citizens without discrimination" triggered a stampede away from absolute equality.[176]

In all this, many Americans failed to notice that ERA aimed only to secure for women equal protection of the law because the Constitution of the United States made no such provision. As Bader Ginsburg explained, "There is in our Constitution no identifiable provision directed to the specific and recurring tendency to treat men and women unequally."

> Insofar as the fourteenth amendment is said to be such a provision, there is nothing on the face of the amendment to suggest that the propriety of this tendency is of any greater constitutional concern than the acknowledged discretion of legislatures to favor some kinds of business activity over other kinds, [or] to distinguish between minors and adults. . . . In brief, unlike most of the Bill of Rights, which register a concrete solicitude for specific concerns such as freedom of speech or religion, there is nothing is our fundamental law concretely committing us to the determination that "[e]quality of rights under the law shall not be denied or abridged by the United States or by any State on account of sex."[177]

"It will always take all kinds of women to make up the world," wrote Eleanor Roosevelt in 1940, "and only now and then will they unite their interests. When they do, I think it is safe to say that something historically important will happen."[178] One such moment occurred in the 1850s; another appeared a century later, when second-wave feminism appeared—most visibly in the tumultuous 1960s, but also well before then, in the day-by-day struggles of men and women who were dedicated to women's advancement. Into the 1970s, amid this extended conversation about male-female relations and the nature of the modern family, feminists and their allies made important strides toward both equality and equity. A growing number of academics powerfully aided these efforts in both classrooms and courtrooms. But, in the end, women secured only a much-diluted citizenship in many areas of public life. Political governments remained ambivalent about women's claims to state protection, and a good many citizens stumbled over maternalist stereotypes, as well as a perceived public interest in regulating motherhood.

The compromises and defeats at the heart of the civil rights settlement occurred in spite of, and in some respects on the foundation of, the Nineteenth Amendment. After 1920, men and women were constitutional cosovereigns. Despite marked resistance to women's exercise of ancillary political rights, Americans managed to integrate women into democratic suffrage communities. Notwithstanding widespread anxiety about women sitting in judgment over men, they managed as well by the 1980s to admit female voters to jury service and elective office. Yet, in economic and social life, feminists and antifeminists alike often framed "advances" in reactionary rather than constructive terms—variously as a contest between blacks' experience with the law of slavery and women's experience with the law of coverture, or as a way to evade or trump the ERA. Thus, in areas of law fundamental to women's day-to-day well-being—including economic freedom, reproductive autonomy, marital equality, and personal security—the female rights basket was filled not to the male or black standard, but to the level a deeply sexist society would tolerate. Statutes and case law, not constitutional clauses, secured women's right to be free from state and individual intrusions on basic rights to earn, to be safe, to be private, and to serve the republic in crisis times alongside men. Especially after the defeat of ERA, women stood on unstable constitutional ground, well beyond "wardship" but well short of equality and self-possession. Into the 1990s, women were said to be obliged to provide children and future soldiers rather than service on battlefields; and many men have no sense of a civic obligation to honor women's sovereignty by refraining from harassment and rape.

As a new settlement between men and women took shape in the 1980s, liberals had reason to celebrate. Only a handful of sex-specific statutes remained in state law codes, and both federal and state lawmakers had included "sex" in civil rights amendments and legislation. Sometimes, state laws provided greater protection than their federal counterparts—as with Michigan's remarkably sweeping Elliot-Larsen Civil Rights Act. Harrison concludes, in fact, that women in the year 2000 formally enjoy "equal rights" in most legal categories—albeit without an ERA and thus at the pleasure of legislators and judges fully capable of amending, repealing, or reinterpreting doctrines not yet constitutionalized. But even when the equality concept has been tied to constitutions, judges have been unwilling to subject violations of "equal rights" or physical security to the highest level of constitutional scrutiny, largely on the ground that society does not require and would not tolerate a sex-blind legal order that would draft mothers (or proto-mothers) alongside men. And as Elizabeth Cady Stanton might have said, statutes are a slender reed upon which to hang fundamental rights and liberties.

For Americans who support equal rights as an avenue to social peace, the signs are inauspicious. On Sunday, April 19, 1998, in the *New York Times* crossword puzzle—a cultural bellwether if ever there was one—the answer to the clue "Bygone political cause" was "ERA."[179] At roughly the same moment, old impulses—notably, but not only, the tendency to think about gender and race as purely biological phenomena—resurged in the popular press and elsewhere. Much as the notorious sociobiological study, *The Bell Curve*, explained racial differences and chronic black-white inequalities in terms of immutable genetics, so commentators began to posit wholly biological explanations for sex differences and the gap between male-female earning power—as social scientists and Darwinists had done a century earlier in the heyday of the "social purity" movement. Opinion makers sometimes parcel out thinly veiled threats. In a 1998 issue of *Currency* (a magazine aimed at high-income Americans), a financial writer said this in response to a question about whether "men find successful women sexy": "The truth is—often they don't. Money is one of the top three reasons that relationships have a hard time, and changing gender roles contribute to that. Men's primary need is to be needed—"

> to feel that they can contribute something to a woman's happiness. When a woman is self-sufficient, it keeps some men away. So although it's not impossible for an independent women to be in a romantic relationship, it's a lot easier for a woman who isn't so independent; men know she needs a male provider, or co-provider, and that gives them confidence. It gives her a much larger group of men to choose from.

The interviewer then asked *why* he thought "men need to be needed." "It's a biological drive," he replied. "Men need to feel competent. . . . How can he prove he is competent if she has the money? At the same time, most women want to feel taken care of. If a woman is out-earning a man, she may feel that he's dependent, and women don't do well with that." If a woman "does earn more, she shouldn't be encouraged to think that she's supposed to share her money equally. A man is expected to share—he wants to share. By nature, he's a provider. With a woman, sharing can actually cause dissatisfaction." A woman should "keep a big portion of her money separate"; a man should "always earn enough to support himself, whatever the woman's income." A man, he added plaintively, "needs to feel there is some arena in which he makes a crucial contribution."[180]

Chapter 12

Afterword

> The true representation of power is not of a big man beating a smaller man or a woman. Power is the ability to take one's place in whatever discourse is essential to action and the right to have one's part matter. This is true in the Pentagon, in marriage, in friendship, and in politics."
>
> —CAROLYN HEILBRUN, *Writing a Woman's Life* (1988)

This book began with Radcliffe College president Mary Bunting's announcement in 1961 that despite appearances to the contrary, woman's cause had been "won." In many respects, of course, she was right. Well before Bunting's time, women cast ballots. They traded on the New York Stock Exchange, held public offices, and made contracts on their own authority. At the beginning of the twenty-first century, two women sit on the U.S. Supreme Court. Yet evidence also accumulates on the other side. Are women permanently stuck several notches below men on economic and political ladders? If so, the problem lies as much in culture as in law. In 1934, Mary Beard pointed to that possibility in a letter to Harriot Stanton Blatch about "equal education" for women: "[I]f we are to *hold* any steps in equality, I have the hunch that we shall have to offer more to the community than straight 'justice' and 'right' since justice and right are never the basis of economic and political action."[1] Human beings and the legal systems they created were creatures of culture and language; it was there, Beard insisted, rather than in the realm of constitutional abstraction, that the battle for equality would be fought and won.

The historical record supports this view. On the one hand, there is little doubt that rights-based legal change has benefited the female sex and all of American society in the bargain. It is surely an exaggeration—borne partly of lawyers' infatuation with their own productions and partly of misreadings of nineteenth-century developments—to say (as scholars regularly do) that the "legal status" of women in the United States "changed more rapidly in the last twenty-five years than in the previous two hundred."[2] Surely the *constitutional* status of women began to mutate much earlier, as society began to respond to campaigns to secure basic constitutional rights and liberties—among them, the right to speak in public, to share power within family governments, to experience an unmediated relationship with one's God, to deal in property, to control access to one's body, and to move about freely. Before there could be ballots and law firm partnerships, in other words, women had to know that they were *not* just like servants, debtors, idiots, and children and that they, too, belonged to the constituent power. In a sense, modern judicial decisions like *Frontiero* are embroideries upon Victorian fabric: Until very recently, the question was not whether women and men received equal military benefits, but whether women could enlist in the armed services at all, shouldering citizens' obligations alongside men. Arguably, women's passage from public silence to vocality—a move embodied to some extent in suffragism—was the most important move of all, without which citizenship would have been imponderable. As Susan Bickford puts it, "Although democratic partic- ipation can take a variety of forms, political 'talk' among citizens is central to political action in 'strong democracy'; citizenship is not merely a legal status, but a practice that involves communicative engagement with others in the political realm."[3]

With so much else, the momentous shift from economic dependence to civic com- petence occurred well before the twentieth century. Married women's property acts, how- ever limited in scope, strengthened women's position in the marketplace as well as in law books, contributing by the 1890s to a public presence too substantial to ignore; in re- sponse, judges ultimately divided the supposedly indivisible male head of household—a constitutional development no less important then it had been in 1765, when colonists de- manded a division of sovereignty between the King-in-Parliament and colonial assem- blies. It was woman's growing economic strength, not her weakness, that spurred frantic attempts at the dawn of the twentieth century to sever the traditional Anglo-American connection between economic and political capacity, so that the female majority might aid in the great project of economic growth without upsetting patriarchal applecarts. Judges and legislators in Washington Territory took flight not merely from woman suffrage, but from domestic coequality and feminized systems of public judgment that followed in the train of economic power. Nor was it an accident that Congress approved a woman suffrage amendment at virtually the same time that it embraced a federal income tax amendment, which attached to nonvoting women's fortunes just as surely as to men's.

Equally important, since at least the 1770s, women have remade themselves as agents of change and self-defense, often in the face of pitched opposition and typically as a con- sequence of shifts in constitutional culture. The fact that women now represent a major- ity at American colleges and universities testifies eloquently to the sex's ongoing inter- est in self-possession; the parallel disappearance of men at these schools—the New York Times recently asked, "Where Have the Men Gone?"[4]—also suggests lingering discom- fort with the feminization of old bastions of male power. In this reshaping of both the woman-citizen and society, rights agitation (including the much-maligned suffrage move- ment) has been nothing short of critical. Into the twenty-first century, thousands of women and men have shown that activities as disparate as lecturing, demonstrating, selling a house, and sitting on a grand jury can remake individuals as well as the modern world.

Consider this fictive discussion of a revolution in legal consciousness: Barbara John- ston's feminist novel Hagar, published in 1913, featured an exchange between the novel's namesake and a boorish young suitor named Coltsworth who blamed feminism—what he termed "this fog of damnable ideas that has arisen in the last twenty years"—for Hagar's lack of interest in his proposal of marriage. "If it wasn't for that," he charged, "you would marry me." In his old-line family, Johnston explained, "men dominated women. To them God was male. They would have agreed . . . that the feminist movement was an auda- cious attempt to change the sex of the Deity." Suddenly, the enraged young blade ex- claimed, "All this rebellion of women is unthinkable!"

> Hagar looked at him somewhat dreamily. "However, it has occurred."
> "Things can't change like that—"
> "The answer to that is that they have changed."
> She sat and smiled at him. . . . "Do you think that only mind in man rebels? Mind in woman does it too. And it comes about that there are always more rebels, men and women. We are quite numerous today. . . .

". . . There is being drawn a line. Some men and women are on one side of it, and some men and women are on the other side of it. There is taking place a sorting-out. . . . [I]n the things that make the difference you are where you were when Troy fell. I cannot go back, down all those slopes of Time."[5]

As Johnston saw clearly, first-wave feminism generated changes that were central to the emergence of modern democratic suffrage communities. The architects of republican speech communities cannot be accused of faintheartedness: Women's pursuit of social and personal reconstitution through speech, and their successful assaults on the household *baron*, were radical undertakings. Mary Livermore's epiphanic movement from privacy to publicity and journalists' decision to support her intrusions reveal profound alterations in the texture of American life. Keziah Kendall dared to chastize Simon Greenleaf, a high priest of the law. Elizabeth Packard publically disputed her husband's theology as well as his right to commit her to an asylum; Maria Stewart and Abigail Kelley braved hostile crowds to establish woman's right to make decisions alongside men about pressing public questions. The steady dismantling of the law of coverture, beginning with the augmentation of married women's property rights, represented one of the most portentous reforms undertaken in American history—so portentous, in fact, that it matters little why legislators decided to change statutory systems. Despite judicial, clerical, and legislative opposition to drastic change in the marital relation, policy changes (and female resistance to old law) eroded the authority of the male head of household; women supported a century of economic and territorial expansion with their labor and (in the case of upper-class white women) with their pocketbooks, emerging by 1880 with an irreversible taste for independent action. Incrementally, and to varying degrees, women of all races and classes seized control of their own bodies; persuaded judges to extend possessory rights to mothers in custody disputes; hauled brutal men into court; and took the occasion of war to further hone their communicative, professional, and managerial skills.

On the other hand, women's experiences with liberty and with various governments amply confirm Beard's important insight. Before the 1830s, it is clear that middle-class white women gradually lost ground compared to the vast majority of respectable white men; it goes without saying that when black women were enslaved, they lost ground as well. If British North America was never, in any of its regions, quite the Golden Age that historian Richard Morris and others once described, demographic and economic conditions encouraged an initial flirtation with female autonomy; as conditions changed, women's situation became more straitened. And when Americans finally confronted the implications of republican revolution for gender relations, they postponed the implementation of full equality, moving instead to transplant and preserve medieval conceptions of unitary family governments, which, in turn, kept women out of polling places, pulpits, and, to a lesser extent, the marketplace.

As activists moved beyond a bloody Civil War, moreover, words literally failed them. Republican constitutionalism always had been most powerful when put to the task of defending sacred rights to property or confronting despotism. As in the 1770s, first-wave women sought to establish the reality of direct representation for all citizens and division of the indivisible petit king—problems in constitutional theory about which Anglo-American practice had much to say. They also demanded restoration of constitutional rights to property in revolutionary terms, arguing against virtual representation or unconstitutional takings. At such moments, the shining tropes of republican constitutionalism, long a powerful antidote to feudalism and monarchism, served the movement well, particularly when combined with perfectionism and utopianism. But, in the shift from a multifaceted antebellum rights agenda to single-minded talk about suffrage and election-centered social reform, women entered a new discourse that was severed in critical respects from old moorings in property, civic obligation, and the fear of arbitrary government. In the process, classical referents lost force. This shift was neither sudden nor pervasive. A major battle over the role of the New Woman in modern American life would be waged from 1860 to 1920, sometimes in remarkably old-fashioned terms. Nevertheless, by the 1880s, reformers increasingly were asking not whether "aristocratic" men would continue to tyrannize women within domestic and political governments, but how the sexes could mingle and compete equally in public places without losing their essential character as men and women, and how the government might help women achieve these goals.

This is not to say that campaigns to revise the marital relation had been unimportant. On the contrary, antebellum reformers saw clearly that the rules surrounding conventional marriage—indeed, women's expectation that they *would* be subject to the law of coverture—had been a formidable bar to direct participation in political and economic life. Arguably, dealing with the marital relation and the law of coverture has been the hardest nut to crack for organized feminism; as first-wave feminists and their modern sisters learned the hard way, tinkering with legal machinery has been tolerated only when it does not impinge on family culture and patriarchal power. The early movement's emphasis on domestic tyranny and speech freedom represented not a warm-up exercise for the "important" work of suffragism and equal rights, as historians often imply, but a tough-minded reading of woman's actual situation—that is, of how the sex was governed and what had to be done before women might claim constitutional *authority* alongside men as cosovereigns. Only then could women experience the many rights and obligations of citizenship. As war-torn Americans decided again to exclude women in a refashioned polity, an emerging discourse of republican feminism dissolved and reformed—first into a "pure" discourse of constitutional rights and then into competing discourses of "equal rights" and "separate but equal" protectionism.

Why did revolutionary republicanism lose force? To some extent, lawmakers saw the handwriting on the wall and shifted ground, whereupon women did the same; the influential treatise writer Thomas Cooley and many others decided, a century after the American Revolution, to sever relations between property and direct representation, in an effort perhaps to render eighteenth-century constitutional imagery less potent. Surely, a good many late Victorian reformers thought about emancipation in classical republican terms well beyond their expiration date, only to discover that democratization, legalization, industrialization, and evolutionary social science had changed the rules of the game. Whatever the case, into the 1910s, when old slogans like "No taxation without representation" resurged in the push to secure a federal woman suffrage amendment, revolutionary arguments seemed merely *old*. In the 1770s, political governments had been the enemy of freedom, and speech acts were the primary instruments of reconstitution. Now, governments were taken to be generators and guardians of freedom—as when Congress liberated black people from bondage—and face-to-face communities of opinion were considered a relic of the old republic.

Most important, whether for good or ill, a new generation of suffragists decided that first-wave speech communities had mostly failed and set about resituating women within democratic suffrage communities. To be sure, women could deal increasingly in their own property and sometimes in the marital estate alongside husbands. But as the Civil War settlement took concrete form, many propertied or salaried women found themselves decisively shut out of elite political, professional, and commercial circles, solely on the ground of sex or marriage. These developments, in turn, drove home the hard fact, in Nancy Cott's words, that the institution of marriage has long been "the vehicle for the state's part in forming and sustaining the gender order."[6] Black women experienced a cruel and dispiriting "emancipation," and, more completely than in the 1780s, lawmakers enforced a bright line between male-female spheres, encouraging women to express patriotism through maternity. Nonconforming women risked castigation as traitors, hermaphrodites, and, when they strayed into public spaces without permission, immoral "whores."

Suffragists and feminists moved swiftly to secure political freedom, partially collapsing the demand for a "voice" into a quest for ballots. Even within a reconfigured movement, old rallying cries persisted—as in 1873, when Carrie Burnham, chair of the Committee on Suffrage of the International Workingmen's Association and (as Carrie Burnham Kilgore) a pioneering lawyer in Pennsylvania, evoked the past to justify rebellion. "Whatever qualifications you place upon suffrage let them be applicable to both sexes and attainable to human effort," she warned delegates to a state constitutional convention. "You may treat our demands lightly . . . , but, gentlemen, republics have not been long lived. . . . That defect in our organic law, by which one citizen can be deprived of this most sacred right, will disfranchise every one of you whenever it is thought convenient. There is but one step from the elevation of one class of citizens above another to the elevation of one citizen above all others, either as Dictator or King." A year later, Elizabeth Cady Stanton and Susan B. Anthony summoned the spirit of the Stamp Act Congress to announce a convention of the National Woman Suffrage Association (NWSA): "The fact that women are already voting, holding office, and resisting taxation . . . should warn the Government that the hour . . . has come. It must now determine whether woman's transition from slavery to freedom shall be through reformation or revolution, whether she shall be permitted to express her interest in national questions through law [with ballots] . . . , or outside of law by indirect and irresponsible power; and thus, by a blind enthusiasm, plunge the nation into anarchy."[7]

Yet because women increasingly looked to the state for help, old warnings about the government's power to eradicate liberty rang hollow. The Declaration of 1876, written by Stanton and Matilda Gage, seemed in its deepest recesses a quaint echo of an age that had *known* kingship and African bondage; by 1900, women rarely compared themselves to "vassals" or damned the law as the "modified code of the slave plantation."[8] Instead, they assumed the fact of citizenship and began the job of articulating exactly what women might contribute to public life. Said Josephine Griffing, the corresponding secretary of NWSA, in 1871: "It was now clearly seen by the leaders of the movement that the agitation of woman's wrongs and oppressions was no longer a necessary part of the discussion. . . . [U]nder the supreme law of the land her right to person, property, children, and . . . equal citizenship must be pronounced and admitted; and, finally, her duty to vote, and . . . to assume a share of the responsibility of the States, as she has already of the home, are . . . to be the legitimate themes of discussion till woman is emancipated."[9] Acting as voters and "speaking" for the entire female sex, individual women would extend the moral economy of the home into the polity; at the same time, first-wave preoccupations with the marital relation gave way to increased scrutiny of the wage relation and demands for state intervention on behalf of "disorganized" classes. Proponents of equal rights in the marketplace did battle with protectionists. Would female laborers enter factories and offices as free agents, empowered to strike their own bargains without patriarchal assistance? Or would a paternal state take the place of the increasingly defunct head of household, in effect transforming women into precocious children?

Americans responded by federalizing woman suffrage and interposing state power between female workers and capitalists. Thus, when second-wave feminism finally appeared after World War II, it both benefited from and chafed under the constraints of democratic suffrage communities. Ballots and economic protectionism had been joined at the hip; after 1920, and in some cases earlier, tribunals like the Washington Supreme Court characterized women basically as enfranchised "minors" incapable of economic self-determination. A modern lawyer might say that such arguments were merely tactical, that protectionists said what they had to say to save statutes and win cases. But it was simply not possible to make such arguments about working men. Equally important, once the old culture of coverture had been fused to protectionist political ideology (as in *Muller v. Oregon*), it became more difficult and politically unnecessary for judges to make good on Florence Kelley's promise of an eventual end to protectionism. In effect, men and women occupied "separate but unequal" constitutional ground, and while the female majority clearly formed a substantial political force and (in the case of white women) had been admitted to the constituent power, political individualism mitigated against the formation of organic communities of opinion. Suffragism encouraged competition and disputation rather than solidarity and consensus; electoral "speech" also lacked the spontaneity and creativity of actual *talk*.

In keeping with the post–Civil War legalization of both culture and republican government, feminists leaned hard on the state, promising to help conserve the conventional family in exchange for ballots and "separate but equal" protection in the marketplace. Only in the years after World War II, as women's rights activists gradually shifted the focus from workplace coequality toward the domestic realm, did lawmakers (and especially judges) begin to reconsider Progressive-era policy choices. Slowly, feminists and their supporters traded in the state's "helping hand" for greater privacy and agency; into the 1970s, liberals answered old questions about the relative merits of "difference" (protectionism) and "sameness" (legal equality) in favor of the latter, inviting recrimination from many quarters. Social conservatives feared the loss of traditional family culture and masculine prerogatives; nonwhite and working-class women knew that they could only lose if they posed as "equals" in relations with capitalists; and lesbians were outraged at the imposition of white, middle-class, heterosexual legal standards.

At the millennium, the feminist dilemma is clear: Social justice seems to depend on public conversations about the fairness of class legislation and stereotype, universalized maternalism, and "separate but unequal" conditions and experiences, which, in turn, trigger charges of unnaturalness and ungodliness. Wherever feminism gains ground, the defense of patriarchal traditions grows more strident. Some critics of "women's lib" recommend holding men's feet to the marital fire. As Lisa Schiffren, an aide to former Vice President Dan Quayle told a *New York Times* reporter, "[F]eminist achievements"— notably abortion rights and "absolute sexual equality"—"make intimate relations more convenient for men, by releasing them from traditional obligations and considerations toward women."[10] Other critics say, with conservative writer and Catholic priest Andrew Greeley, that feminism hurts women as they search for husbands: "[S]ome of the social changes in the name of 'sexual revolution' and 'feminism,'" Greeley said in 1990, "have had the unintended . . . consequence of victimizing women. When men can obtain easy sex from a woman without having to marry her, there will be fewer marriages, with resultant unhappiness for women."[11]

At the root of such warnings is an accurate assessment of feminism's power to alter American life, for the idea of the sovereign individual is as radical in the twenty-first century as it was in 1776. In Mary Johnston's words, it affirms a "common humanity" and blasts the idea that a woman should be "thought of only in terms of relationships—as some one's wife or daughter."[12] Moreover, as Aileen Kraditor remarked in 1968, it is increasingly difficult for feminists *or* antifeminists to argue seriously that "women are relegated to the domestic sphere by either law or the need of a wife to keep house while her husband works to support the family." On the contrary, it may well be that in an era in which "there is no longer a rational basis for allocating either remunerative work or homemaking tasks according to sex," the patriarchal family "as popularly conceived, stands revealed as the obstacle to full sex equality. As long as the man engages more in the work of the world and the woman spends a large proportion of her time and energies in the isolated family circle, men will continue to lead in government, the professions, and all the other fields that provide us with our criteria of human achievement."[13]

Thus, when it finally swept the American landscape, second-wave feminism indeed posed a significant threat to unitary family governments and therefore to traditional social and cultural forms. For better or worse, the movement breached white women's century-old promise to defend a "separate but equal" domestic sphere—indeed, to make such a defense their primary civic obligation—in exchange for limited political and economic freedom and ongoing male protection on battlefields and elsewhere. Feminism's power to remake individuals, families, and traditional social relations has long been an open secret. Yet, precisely because many Americans see feminist criticism of patriarchy not as an attempt to ensure social harmony and democracy, but as an open attack on "family values," feminist leaders often have been forced to choose between political safety and political integrity. In addition, even though only one-fourth of all families have no wage-earning women, Americans have been spared an unflinching look at the division of labor by sex—the main impediment to female achievement and gender equality. Many citizens continue to assume, often against the evidence of their own lives, that women prefer to be dependent on men, that they work unseriously or "femininely," and that the married couple is the nation's basic social unit. Unresolved tensions between domestic fact and public policy continue to be off-limits during elections; "serious" politics means foreign affairs and tax cuts, not child care and domestic labor.

Can men and women find a way to surmount the swinging of the pendulum between "sameness" (a legal construct) and "difference" (a biological construct)? Why does public policy still burden all women with domestic and maternal expectations? Can Americans construct equality on foundations of difference without imputing female inferiority or powerlessness? To what extent is a woman's body public or social property and to what extent her own domain, to be governed as she sees fit? Why exactly do governments not take steps to ensure women's physical security in equal portion to men's? And how will women ever dignify citizenship if they cannot assume every public obligation incumbent on men and acquit them directly to the state, rather than to husbands and fathers? Linda Kerber puts it best: "[T]he basic obligations of citizenship have always been demanded of women; it is the *forms* and *objects* of that demand that have varied over time."[14] Is the answer perhaps to synthesize equal rights, equal obligations, and the culture of motherhood, so that (as Crystal Eastman recommended in 1920) women who choose to be mothers may be rewarded concretely for reproductive labor as a *public service*? In a 1997 article about the apparently widening wage gap between men and women, Journalist Tamar Lewin pointed to the civil rights settlement ("the new equilibrium") and identified its main engine: "[I]t's all connected to political and social change. The social movements that led to women's advances came in with great force. It was an enormous tide. Now we're coming into a new equilibrium. I see this as a household issue, and the new equilibrium is that all those strollers are still being pushed by women."[15] Sadly, Lewin might have been writing in 1902, when socialist Adeline Champney challenged readers to think about and deal with the big question: "It is the Baby Question, it is the Woman Question, it is the Social Question. It is peremptory, it is insistent, it will not be ignored, it must be answered, and you, men and women, must together find the answer."[16]

Whatever the solution, and for better or worse, Catharine MacKinnon was surely right to say that post-1960s feminism "identifies sexuality as the primary social sphere of male power,"[17] inequality as an artifact of life within that sphere, and law as a carrier of inequality. The problem of the patriarchal family as the main "social sphere" of sexualized power has been recognized for centuries; Anne Hutchinson, after all, brought it to John Winthrop's attention. As psychologist Olga Knopf noted in *The Art of Being a Woman* (1932), "The place where real equality must begin is where it is least looked for yet most obviously to be found: in the home."

> The institution of marriage and family life needs to be reorganized on the basis of an unconditional recognition of the equality of men and women. . . . Interests and capacities will be allowed to develop freely, without any limit except the welfare of others. . . . The moment one member of a family has a position of a special consideration, the others, and especially the members of the other sex, will feel their inferiority. . . . If this too prominent individual is the father, the girls will continue to meet the general underestimate of their sex outside of their homes. . . . [I]f even the mother is subordinated to the father, what can the girls expect for themselves?[18]

Almost seventy years later, bedrooms, factories, and city streets still function as sexualized combat zones. As Cynthia Grant Bowman reminds us, a "woman walks down the street," and a "man whom she does not know makes an obscene noise or gesture." For such men, this is harmless sex play, a compliment, an invitation; for many women, the encounter affirms power imbalances, physical insecurity, and the sexualization of ordinary exchanges—that is to say, inequality.[19]

Perhaps another negotiation between the sexes lies ahead. Meanwhile, women *are* better off than they were in 1776 or 1876. Both Ruth Bader Ginsburg and Phyllis Schlafly went to law school as a result of suffragism and feminism. More important, as a consequence of legal-cultural change and activism, millions of women have come to think of themselves not as drudges, sex objects, and second-class citizens, but (to use Antoinette Brown Blackwell's term) as autonomous, self-respecting "items of the world." Laborite Rose Schneiderman knew that legal change alone would liberate no one and castigated liberal legalism on exactly that ground. Advocates of ERA, she said in 1931, had "the grandiose idea of bringing about through the stroke of a pen this marvelous thing called equality. We know that equality is not brought about that way. Equality has to happen first within yourself. You have to regard yourself as a human being, and that can not be done by passing a law."[20] As women struggled to enter the world as sovereign *persons*, constitutionalism has been a foe as well as an ally. But without reliance on America's sanctified constitutional texts, organized feminism (to say the least) would have followed a different path. On the one hand, it would have been unconstrained by law's paternalism; on the other hand, it might have languished at the margins, condemned for its illegitimacy and profanity.

For women like Barbara Johnston, moreover, what *did* happen was plenty good enough. In 1913, her fictitious heroine described women's rights agitation as an open-ended excursion into foreign lands where the new woman-citizen might rise to fill any occasion. At center stage were speech freedom and the right of action; women would "belong to the world," in Brown Blackwell's memorable phrase, as well as to themselves. "In the last analysis," Hagar explained, "it is a metaphysical adventure—a love quest if you will. There is a passion of the mind, there is a questing soul, there is the desire that will have union with nothing less than the whole. I will think freely, and largely, and doing that, under pain of being false, I must act freely and largely, live freely and largely. Nor must I think one thing and speak another, nor must I be silent when silence betrays the whole. . . . And so woman no less than man comes into the open." Hagar's friend entirely agreed. "There is something that broods in this time," she replied. "I do not know what it will hatch. But something vaster, something nobler."[21]

Notes

PREFACE

1. Mary Bunting, "Radcliffe Institute for Independent Study" (1961), in Aileen Kraditor, ed., *Up From the Pedestal* (Chicago, 1968), 355.
2. Abigail Adams to John Adams, March 31, 1776, in L. Butterfield et al., eds., *Adams Family Correspondence*, Vol. 1 (Cambridge, MA, 1963–), 369.
3. Bonnie Watkins and Nina Rothchild, eds., *In the Company of Women: Voices from the Women's Movement* (St. Paul, MN, 1996), 88.
4. "Cyber View: Access Denied," *Scientific American* (August 1998): 38.
5. John Murrin, "The Great Inversion . . . ," in J. G. A. Pocock, ed., *Three British Revolutions* (Princeton, NJ, 1980). Murrin used the term *revolution settlement.*
6. Victor Turner, *The Ritual Process: Structure and Anti-Structure* (Ithaca, NY, 1969), 96. For sociolinguists' understandings of *speech community,* see, for example, the essay by sociolinguist Patricia Nichols, "Women in Their Speech Communities," in Sally McConnell-Ginet et al., eds., *Women and Language in Literature and Society* (New York, 1980), 140–149; and J. Gumperz, "The Speech Community," in Pier Paolo Gigliogi, ed., *Language and Social Context* (New York, 1972), 219–231.
7. Linda Kerber, "The Paradox of Women's Citizenship in the Early Republic: The Case of *Martin vs. Massachusetts,* 1805," *American Historical Review* (April 1992): 378.
8. Dorinda Outram, "*Le Langage Mâle de la Vertu*: Women and the Discourse of the French Revolution," in Peter Burke and Roy Porter, eds., *The Social History of Language* (Cambridge, England, 1987), 131.
9. I prefer to use the word *feminist* only after it entered American English, in the late Victorian era; if Nancy Cott is right, mainstream women's rights reformers adopted the term as a non-pejorative self-descriptor only in the first quarter of the twentieth century. See Cott, *The Grounding of Modern Feminism* (New Haven, CT, 1987), 14–16.
10. Judith Shklar, *American Citizenship: The Quest for Inclusion* (Cambridge, MA, 1991), 101.
11. Cott, *Grounding of Modern Feminism,* 49.
12. Sara Evans, "Women's History and Political Theory: Toward a Feminist Approach to Public Life," in Nancy Hewitt and Suzanne Lebsock, eds., *Visible Women: New Essays on American Activism* (Urbana, IL, 1993), 119–139, esp. 128–129.
13. For Norton and Norton quoting Sabean, see Mary Beth Norton, "Gender, Crime, and Community in Seventeenth-Century Maryland," in James Henretta et al., eds., *Transformation of Early American History* (New York, 1991), 125.
14. Susan Bickford, *The Dissonance of Democracy: Listening, Conflict, and Citizenship* (Ithaca, NY, 1996), 162.
15. Hendrik Hartog, "The Constitution of Aspiration and 'The Rights That Belong to Us All,' " in David Thelen, ed., *The Constitution and American Life* (Ithaca, NY, 1988), 353.
16. Pipefitter, quoted in Vicki Schultz, "Telling Stories About Women and Work," in Katharine T. Bartlett and Rosanne Kennedy, eds., *Feminist Legal Theory: Readings in Law and Gender* (Boulder, CO, 1991), 139.
17. Joan Wallach Scott, *Gender and the Politics of History* (New York, 1988), 177.
18. Bickford, *Dissonance of Democracy,* 173. Emphasis added.

PART ONE, INTRODUCTION

1. Ernest Barker, ed., *Politics of Aristotle* (New York, 1946), 35.
2. J. R. Tanner, *English Constitutional Conflicts of the Seventeenth Century* (Cambridge, England, 1962), 80.
3. Francis Bacon, "Of Plantations," 1625, in Jack Greene, ed., *Settlements to Society, 1607–1763: A Documentary History of Colonial America* (New York, 1975), 11.
4. Lois G. Carr and Lorena Walsh, "The Planter's Wife: The Experience of White Women in Seventeenth-Century Maryland," in Stanley Katz et al., eds., *Colonial America*, 4th ed. (New York, 1993), 77, 79.
5. John Winthrop, "A Model of Christian Charity," in Alan Heimert and Andrew Delbanco, eds., *The Puritans in America: A Narrative Anthology* (Cambridge, MA, 1985), 91.
6. David Konig, *Law and Society in Puritan Massachusetts* (Chapel Hill, NC, 1979), 18.
7. Elaine Crane, *Ebb Tide in New England: Women, Seaports, and Social Change, 1630–1800* (Boston, 1998), 103.

CHAPTER 1

1. For complete documentation, see Sandra VanBurkleo, " 'To Bee Rooted Out of Her Station': The Ordeal of Anne Hutchinson," in Michal Belknap, ed., *American Political Trials*, rev. ed. (Westport, CT, 1993), 1–24.
2. Christopher W. Marsh, *The Family of Love in English Society, 1550–1630* (New York, 1994).
3. Sermon of Reverend John Brinsely, quoted in Rosemary Skinner Keller, "New England Women: Ideology and Experience in First-Generation Puritanism (1630–1650)," in Rosemary Radford Ruether and Rosemary Skinner Keller, eds., *Women and Religion in America*, Vol. 2 (New York, 1983), 189.
4. "[Governor] Thomas Hutchinson on Ann Hibbins [sic]," in David Hall, ed., *Witchcraft in Seventeenth-Century New England* (Boston, 1991), 91.
5. Jane Kamensky, *Governing the Tongue: The Politics of Speech in Early New England* (New York, 1997), 83. Kamensky's account of the Hibbens trial is the best in print.
6. Kamensky, *Governing the Tongue*, 92; [Robert Keayne], "Proceedings of Excommunication against Mistress Ann Hibbens of Boston (1640)," in John Demos, ed., *Remarkable Providences*, rev. ed. (Boston, 1991), 262. See also Jane Kamensky, "Governing the Tongue: Speech and Society in Early New England," Ph.D. dissertation, Yale University (May 1993), 220.
7. Thomas Barnes, ed., *The Book of the General Lawes and Libertyes Concerning the Inhabitants of the Massachusets* (San Marino, CA, 1975, facsimile ed.), 35–36.
8. Kamensky, *Governing the Tongue*, 84.
9. Hall, *Witchcraft*, 91; Demos, *Remarkable Providences*, 262, 268–69, 271–72, 274–75, 279–80.
10. For "helpe and assistance," William Perkins, *Christian Oeconomie*, quoted in Ruether and Keller, *Women and Religion*, 156; Carol Pateman, *The Disorder of Women* (Stanford, CA, 1989).
11. John Winthrop, quoted in Kamensky, *Governing the Tongue*, 94.
12. Robert Bolton, quoted in Michael Walzer, *Revolution of the Saints: A Study in the Origins of Radical Politics* (Cambridge, MA, 1965), 193.
13. Thomas Shepard, "The Parable of the Ten Virgins," in Heimert and Delbanco, *Puritans in America*, 174.
14. Richard Sibbes, quoted in Lawrence Stone, *Causes of the English Revolution, 1529–1642* (New York, 1972), 99.
15. See J. H. Baker, *Introduction to English Legal History*, 3rd ed. (London, 1990), 530, 545–47.
16. Orlando Patterson, *Slavery and Social Death: A Comparative Study* (Cambridge, MA, 1982).

17. Baker, *Introduction*, 550.
18. Richard Allestree, quoted in Alice E. Natahews, "Religious Experience of Southern Women," in Ruether and Keller, *Women and Religion*, 206.
19. "An Antenuptial Contract, Massachusetts, 1653 [from Records and Files of the Quarterly Court of Essex County, vol. 5]," in Nancy Woloch, ed., *Early American Women: A Documentary History, 1600–1900* (Belmont, CA, 1992), 94–95.
20. Marylynn Salmon, "Women and Property in South Carolina: The Evidence from Marriage Settlements, 1730–1830," *William and Mary Quarterly*, 39 (1982): 684.
21. Bracton, quoted in Baker, *Introduction*, 551.
22. John Taylor, "A Juniper Lecture," London (1639), in Angeline Goreau, *The Whole Duty of a Woman: Female Writers in Seventeenth-Century England* (New York, 1985), 102.
23. Thomas G. Barnes, ed., *Book of the General Lawes and Libertyes Concerning the Inhabitants of the Massachusetts*, facsimile ed. (San Marino, CA, 1975), 6.
24. 15 Mass 167 (1818), quoted in Morton Horwitz, *The Transformation of American Law, 1780–1860* (Cambridge, MA, 1977), 57.
25. Laura Thatcher Ulrich, *Good Wives: Image and Reality in the Lives of Women in Northern New England, 1650–1750* (New York, 1980), 35–36, 249.
26. Cotton Mather, *The Widow of Nain*, quoted, with other material cited, in Alexander Keyssar, "Widowhood in Eighteenth-Century Massachusetts: A Problem in the History of the Family," *Perspectives in American History* 8 (1974): 94, 98–99; petition in Kim Lacy Rogers, "Relicts of the New World: Conditions of Widowhood in Seventeenth-Century New England," in Mary Kelley, ed., *Woman's Being, Woman's Place: Female Identity and Vocation in American History* (Boston, 1979), 26.
27. Roderick Phillips, *Putting Asunder: A History of Divorce in Western Society* (New York, 1988), 197.
28. Elaine Crane, "Paternalism and Tax Evasion in 18th-Century Rhode Island," in D. Kelly Weisberg, ed., *Women and the Law: The Social Historical Perspective*, Vol. 1 (Cambridge, MA, 1982), 36.
29. See generally Hendrik Hartog, *Man and Wife in America, A History* (Cambridge, MA, 2000).
30. Quoted in D. Kelly Weisberg, " 'Under Great Temptations Here': Women and Divorce in Puritan Massachusetts," in Weisberg, *Women and the Law*, Vol. 2, 123–24.
31. South Carolina legalized divorce between 1868 and 1895, then abolished it again until 1949; North Carolina permitted divorce in 1814, Maryland in 1790, Virginia in 1803, and Georgia in 1798; Phillips, *Putting Asunder*, 143.
32. Phillips, *Putting Asunder*, 243.
33. Law quoted in Alison Duncan Hirsch, " The Thrall Divorce Case: A Family Crisis in 18th-Century Connecticut," *Women and History* (Winter, 1982): 43; Phillips, *Putting Asunder*, 243. For regulation of friendship, see Edgar McManus, *Law and Liberty in Early New England* (Amherst, MA, 1993), 158. The classic account of divorce later in the period is Nancy Cott, "Divorce and Changing Status of Women in 18th Century Massachusetts," *William and Mary Quarterly* (1976): 613.
34. Samuel Pufendorf, *Elementorum Jurisprudentiae Universalis Libri Duo* (1672; reprint Oceana Publications 1964, ed. James Brown Scott), 275; John Winthrop, "Defence of an Order of Court," in Greene, ed., *Settlements to Society*, 109.
35. Cotton, quoted in Edmund Morgan, "The Puritans and Sex," in James K. Martin, ed., *Interpreting Colonial America, Selected Readings* (New York, 1978), 72; Susan Amussen quoting Dorothy Leigh, "Gender, Family, and the Social Order, 1560–1725," in Anthony Fletcher and John Stevenson, eds., *Order and Disorder in Early Modern England* (Cambridge, England, 1985), 201.
36. "Lawes Resolutions of Womens Rights: Or, The Lawes Provision for Women (1632)," in Mary Beth Norton, "The Constitutional Status of Women in 1787," *Law and Inequality* (1988): 10.

37. George Williams, *Radical Reformation* (Philadelphia, 1962), 506–07.
38. Christine Allen, "Women in Colonial French America," in Ruether and Keller, *Women and Religion*, 79–81, 117; for "free spaces," Sara Evans and Harry Boyte, *Free Democratic Spaces* (New York, 1986).
39. Wiesner, *Women and Gender in Early Modern Europe*, 243.
40. William Gouge, *Of Domesticall Duties*, quoted in Rosemary Skinner Keller, "New England Women: Ideology and Experience in First-Generation Puritanism," in Ruether and Keller, *Women and Religion*, 136.
41. John Robinson, *Works of John Robinson*, Vol. 1 (Boston, 1851), 236.
42. Walzer, *Revolution of the Saints*, 193; John Winthrop, "A Model of Christian Charity," in Heimert and Delbanco, *Puritans in America*, 90.
43. Sermons on state of matrimony, in Keller, "New England Women . . . ," in Ruether and Keller, *Women and Religion*, 151.
44. Samuel Willard, "A Compleat Body of Divinity" (1640–1707, pub. 1726), reprinted in Ruth Barnes Moynihan et al., eds., *Second to None: A Documentary History of American Women*, Vol. 1 (Lincoln NE, 1993), 58–59; William Perkins, quoted in Keller, "New England Women . . . ," in Ruether and Keller, *Women and Religion*, 156.
45. Samuel Richardson, *Pamela*, Vol. 2 (London: J. M. Dent & Sons, Everyman's Library, 1955, orig. pub. 1740), 467; misquoted in Richard Morris, *Studies in the History of American Law*, 2nd ed. (New York, 1964), 127 (". . . for women").
46. William Perkins, *Oeconomie*, quoted in Keller, "New England Women . . . ," in Ruether and Keller, *Women and Religion*, 136.
47. William Gouge, *Of Domesticall Duties* (1622), quoted in Keller, "New England Women . . . ," in Ruether and Keller, *Women and Religion*, 158.
48. Mary Beth Norton, *Founding Mothers and Fathers: Gendered Power and the Forming of American Society* (New York, 1996).
49. Montesquieu, *Oeuvres complètes*, 2 (Bibliothèque de la Pléiade, Paris, 1951), 565.
50. John Winthrop, "Speech on Liberty, July 3, 1645," in Greene, ed., *Settlements to Society*, 112.
51. Winthrop, "Speech on Liberty," 112.
52. Carol Karlsen, *The Devil in the Shape of a Woman: Witchcraft in Colonial New England* (New York, 1987), 238.
53. Johnson and Winthrop, quoted in McManus, *Law and Liberty*, 119–20, and Aileen Kraditor, ed., *Up From the Pedestal: Landmark Writings in the American Woman's Struggle for Equality* (Chicago, 1968), 30 (Winthrop's journal).
54. John Winthrop, "A Short Story," in David Hall, ed., *Antinomian Controversy: 1636–1638: A Documentary History* (Durham, NC, 1990), 244. Hooker and Cotton, quoted in David Leverenz, *The Language of Puritan Feeling: An Exploration in Literature, Psychology, and Social History* (New Brunswick, NJ, 1980), 82; and Cotton, "Singing of Psalms a Gospel-Ordinance, 1650," in Ruether and Keller, *Women and Religion*, 191–192; "A Sinner Cast Out," in Demos, *Remarkable Providences*, 265.
55. Eliza Fowler, "Female Spectator, London, 1744–46," in Goreau, *Whole Duty of a Woman*, 330–31.
56. McManus, *Law and Liberty in Early New England*, 158–59.
57. Amy Schrager Lang, *Prophetic Woman: Anne Hutchinson and the Problem of Dissent in the Literature of New England* (Berkeley, CA, 1987), 3.
58. Few procedural safeguards mattered more to the English than the privilege against self-incrimination; see Edgar McManus, *Law and Liberty*, 105.
59. Barry Levy, " 'Tender Plants': Quaker Farmers and Children in the Delaware Valley, 1681–1735," in Stanley Katz et al., eds., *Colonial America*, 4th ed. (New York, 1993), 157; Patricia Caldwell, *The Puritan Conversion Narrative: The Beginning of American Expression* (Cambridge, England, 1983), 59.

60. Margaret Fell, "Women's Meeting in Early Quakerism" [letter read at Newport, RI, women's meeting, 1675], in Ruether and Keller, *Women and Religion*, 283–84; and Fell, *Womens Speaking Justified, Proved and Allowed of by the Scriptures, All such as speak by the Spirit and Power of the Lord . . .*, (Amherst, MA: New England Yearly Meeting of Friends, 1980), 4.

61. Charles Cohen, *God's Caress: The Psychology of Puritan Religious Experience* (New York, 1986), 142–44; Mary Maples Dunn, "Saints and Sisters . . . ," *American Quarterly* (1978): 585–95.

62. Mary Beth Norton, "Gender, Crime, and Community in 17th-Century Maryland," in James Henretta et al., eds., *Transformation of Early American History* (New York, 1991), 133, 144–45, 147–48, 150. The four seventeenth-century Maryland juries contained 6, 9, 11, and 12 women. See also "The Case of Elizabeth Greene," in Moynihan, *Second to None*, Vol. 1, 69.

63. Ibid.

64. Ibid. For elaboration, see Norton, *Founding Mothers and Fathers*.

65. Diane Willen, "Women in the Public Sphere in Early Modern England: The Case of the Urban Working Poor," *Sixteenth Century Journal* 19 (Winter 1988): 574–75.

66. Lois Green Carr, "Diversification in the Chesapeake," in Carr, Philip D. Morgan, and Jean Russo, eds., *Colonial Chesapeake Society* (Chapel Hill, NC, 1988), 354.

67. John Lawson, "History of North Carolina" (1714), in Moynihan, *Second to None*, Vol. 1, 106.

68. Cornelia Dayton, "Turning Points and the Relevance of Colonial Legal History," *William and Mary Quarterly* (January, 1993): 16 (discussing Carol Karlsen).

69. Russell Menard, "British Migration," in Carr et al., *Colonial Chesapeake Society*, 131; Robert Beverley, "History and Present State of Virginia" (1705), in Greene, *Settlements to Society*, 284; Catherine Clinton and Michele Gillespie, eds., *The Devil's Lane: Sex and Race in the Early South* (New York, 1997), 19.

70. At common law, the terms *will* and *inheritance* are not synonymous. Technically, an inheritance applies only to property received outside of (or without) a will.

71. Lee, "Land and Labor," in Carr et al., *Colonial Chesapeake Society*, 338–41.

72. "Feme Sole Trader Acts," in Nancy Woloch, ed., *Early American Women: A Documentary History, 1600–1900* (Belmont, CA, 1992), 104–05; Crane, "Paternalism and Tax Evasion . . . ," 36.

73. Susan Staves, *Married Women's Separate Property in England, 1660–1833* (Cambridge, MA, 1990), 229; Eileen Spring, *Law, Land, and Family: Aristocratic Inheritance in England, 1300 to 1800* (Chapel Hill, 1993), 58.

74. Peter Charles Hoffer, *Law and People in Colonial America* (Baltimore, MD, 1992), 78.

75. "Came Mistress Margarett Brent," in Moynihan, *Second to None*, Vol. 1, 81.

76. "Women Merchants," in Moynihan, *Second to None*, 121–22.

77. Hoffer, *Law and People in Colonial America*, 91; Maryland statute (1664), in Moynihan, *Second to None*, Vol. 1, 74.

78. Willard, quoted in Edmund Morgan, "Puritans and Sex," in James Kirby Martin, ed., *Interpreting Colonial America* (New York, 1978), 72.

79. Morgan, "Puritans and Sex," in Martin, *Interpreting Colonial America*, 80.

80. Eli Faber, "Puritan Criminals: The Economic, Social, and Intellectual Background to Crime in Seventeenth-Century Massachusetts," *Perspectives in American History*, 11 (1977–78): 142–43.

81. Sir Matthew Hale, *History of the Pleas of the Crown* (Philadelphia, 1847, orig. pub. London, c. 1680), 627.

82. Gerrard Winstanley, *Law of Freedom and Other Writings*, ed. Christopher Hill (London, 1973), 388.

83. Alison Duncan Hirsch, "The Thrall Divorce Case," 62.

84. Norton, "Gender Crime, and Community," 141–42.

85. Barbara Lindemann, "'To Ravish and Carnally Know': Rape in Eighteenth-Century Massachusetts," *Signs*, 10 (1984): 66–67.

86. Morgan, "Puritans and Sex," in Martin, *Interpreting Colonial America*, 73–76; McManus, *Law and Liberty*, 31–32.

87. Cornelia Dayton, "Taking the Trade: Abortion and Gender Relations in an Eighteenth-Century New England Village," in Katz, *Colonial America*, 398–431, esp. 429.

88. Lois Green Carr, Russell Menard, and Lorena Walsh, eds., *Robert Cole's World: Agriculture and Society in Early Maryland* (Chapel Hill, NC, 1991), 139.

89. Jean Bodin, *Six Books of the Republic*, quoted in Merry Wiesner, *Women and Gender in Early Modern Europe* (New York, 1993), 243.

90. Anne Bradstreet, "The Prologue," c. 1660, in Heimert and Delbanco, *Puritans in America*, 132.

91. Carol Smart, "The Woman of Legal Discourse," *Social and Legal Studies* (March 1992), 29–44, esp. 37–39.

92. William Blackstone, *Commentaries on the Law of England*, Vol. 4 (1769, facsimile ed., Chicago, 1979, ed. Stanley Katz), 28–29.

93. Morgan, "Puritans and Sex," in Martin, *Interpreting Colonial America*, 76.

94. Toby Ditz, "Shipwrecked: or, Masculinity Imperiled: Mercantile Representations of Failure and the Gendered Self in Eighteenth-Century Philadelphia," *Journal of American History* (June 1994): 65; Morgan, "Puritans and Sex," in Martin, *Interpreting Colonial America*, 79.

95. Benjamin Colman, "Practical Discourses on the Parable of the Ten Virgins," in Heimert and Delbanco, *Puritans in America*, 373.

96. Quoted in George Dalzell, *Benefit of Clergy in America and Related Matters* (Winston-Salem, NC, 1955), 178.

97. Norton, "Gender, Crime, and Community in 17th-Century Maryland," 124–27, 142–43; on servants and bastardy, see Lois G. Carr and Lorena Walsh, "The Planters Wife: The Experience of White Women in Seventeenth-Century Maryland," in Katz, *Colonial America*, 72–73.

98. Thanks to Tom Green for this suggestion.

99. Norton, "Gender, Crime, and Community," in Henretta et al., *Transformation of Early American History*, 128–29, 134.

100. Deborah Rosen, "Mitigating Inequality: Women and Justice in Early New York," in Larry D. Eldridge, ed., *Women and Freedom in Early America* (New York, 1996); quotation from Rosen, "Changing Legal Culture in Colonial New York: Commercial Values, Ethnicity, and Gender in the Emerging Modern American Legal System," paper presented at Annual Meeting of Law and Society Association (June 1994). Quoted by permission of the author.

101. Larry Eldridge, *A Distant Heritage: The Growth of Free Speech in Colonial America* (New York, 1994), 44, 47.

102. Eldridge, *Distant Heritage*, 7–8, 36–37; Clara Ann Bowler, "Carted Whores and White Shrouded Apologies," *Virginia Magazine of History and Biography* (October 1977): 413.

103. Quoted in Frances Dolan, "Home-Rebels and House-Traitors: Murderous Wives in Early Modern England," *Yale Journal of Law and Humanities* (Winter 1992): 4; and Shelley Gavigan, "Petit Treason in Eighteenth Century England: Women's Inequality Before the Law," *Canadian Journal of Women and the Law* (Summer–Fall 1989): 337.

104. Jame Kamensky, *Governing the Tongue: The Politics of Speech in Early New England* (New York, 1997), 134.

105. Baker, *Introduction*, 587, n. 69, citing James Cockburn's work on the Assizes; for insanity, McManus, *Law and Liberty*, 105; William Perkins, "Discourse on the Damned Art of Witchcraft" (1592), in Ruether and Keller, *Women and Religion*, 154.

106. Peter C. Hoffer and N. E. H. Hull, *Murdering Mothers: Infanticide in England and New England, 1558–1803* (New York, 1984), 40–41.

107. Dayton, "Turning Points," 15.

108. Barnes, *Book of the General Lawes and Libertyes*, 5.

109. Deodat Lawson, "Christ's Fidelity: The Only Shield against Satan's Malignity," Scituate, Massachusetts (1693), in Greene, *Settlements to Society*, 202–03.

110. Cotton Mather, in McManus, *Law and Liberty*, 156–57.

111. Perkins (1590 and 1596) and the *Malleus Maleficarum* (1486), quoted in Keller, "New England Women," in Ruether and Keller, *Women and Religion,* 132–33.

112. Elizabeth Reis, *Damned Women* (Ithaca, NY, 1998).

113. McManus, *Law and Liberty*, 133, 155–57; Leverenz, *Language of Puritan Feeling*, 152–53; Kamensky, *Governing the Tongue*, 159.

114. William Monter, "Protestant Wives, Catholic Saints, and the Devil's Handmaid," in Renate Bridenthal et al., eds., *Becoming Visible: Women in European History*, 2nd ed. (Boston, 1987), 214–17; for "love sorcerers," Lavrin, "Women and Religion in Spanish America," in Ruether and Keller, *Women and Religion*, 76.

115. Hoffer, *Law and People in Colonial America*, 38.

116. Hall, *Witch-Hunting in Seventeenth-Century New England*, 32; McManus, *Law and Liberty*, 137; Karlsen, *Devil in the Shape of a Woman*, 47, 51.

117. McManus, *Law and Liberty*, 148.

118. Cotton Mather, quoted in Konig, *Law and Society in Colonial Massachusetts*, 148.

119. Paul Boyer and Stephen Nissenbaum, eds., *Salem-Village Witchcraft: A Documentary Record of Local Conflict in Colonial New England*, new ed. (Boston, MA, 1993), 156–58; Karlsen, *Devil in the Shape of a Woman*, 75, 104, 259; Konig, *Law and Society in Puritan Massachusetts*, 148–49; Hall, *Witch-Hunting in Seventeenth-Century New England*, 296–301, 313n.

120. Christina Larner, *Enemies of God* (Baltimore, 1981), 19, 194–95.

121. "America to the Printer," *Connecticut Journal, and the New-Haven Post-Boy*, June 28, 1775. My thanks to Marc Kruman for sharing this discovery.

CHAPTER 2

1. "The Salutatory Oration of Miss Priscilla Mason to the Young Ladies Academy of Philadelphia, May 15, 1793," in Mary Beth Norton and Carol Ruth Bekin, eds., *Women of America: A History* (Boston, 1979), 89–91.

2. Karlsen, *Devil in the Shape of a Woman*, 256.

3. "Declaration of Independence," in Samuel Eliot Morison, ed., *Sources and Documents Illustrating the American Revolution*, 2nd ed. (New York, 1965), 157.

4. Columbia College address, from *New York Magazine* (May 1795), quoted in Linda Kerber, "'History Can Do It No Justice': Women and the Reinterpretation of the American Revolution," in Ronald Hoffman and Peter J. Albert, eds., *Women in the Age of the American Revolution* (Charlottesville, VA, 1989), 37–38.

5. Jonathan Edwards, "A Faithful Narrative of the Surprising Work of God" (1737), in Greene, *Settlements to Society*, 321.

6. Laura Thatcher Ulrich, *A Midwife's Tale: The Life of Martha Ballard Based on Her Diary, 1785–1812* (New York, 1990).

7. Quoted in Susan Juster, *Disorderly Women: Sexual Politics and Evangelicalism in Revolutionary New England* (Ithaca, NY, 1994), 4, 40.

8. Martha Blauvelt and Rosemary Keller, "Great Awakening," in Ruether and Keller, *Women and Religion*, 318.

9. Richard Bushman, ed., *The Great Awakening: Documents on the Revival of Religion, 1740–1745* (New York, 1970), 103.

10. Quoted in Juster, *Disorderly Women*, 42.

11. Keller, "New England Women . . . ," in Ruether and Keller, *Women and Religion*, 144; Sarah Osborn, "To Fill a Larger Sphere," in Woloch, *Early American Women*, 155–57.

12. Quoted in Juster, *Disorderly Women*, 43, 86.

13. Juster, *Disorderly Women*, 126–27.

14. Joan R. Gunderson, *To Be Useful to the World: Women in Revolutionary America, 1740–1790* (New York, 1996), 180.

15. Blauvelt and Keller, "Great Awakening," in Ruether and Keller, *Women and Religion*, 366.
16. Gloria Main, "Gender, Work, and Wages in Colonial New England," *William and Mary Quarterly* (January 1994): 39–66.
17. Elaine Crane, *Ebb Tide in New England: Women, Seaports, and Social Change, 1630–1800* (Boston, 1998), 111–12.
18. Main, "Gender, Work, and Wages," 61–66.
19. Hoffer, *Law and People in Colonial America*, 53; Bernard Bailyn, *Voyagers to the West: A Passage in the Peopling of America on the Eve of the Revolution* (New York, 1987), 270.
20. Cadwallader Colden, "State of the Province of New York (1765)," in Greene, *Settlements to Society*, 299.
21. Elaine Crane, "Dealing with Dependence: Paternalism and Tax Evasion in 18th-Century Rhode Island," in Weisberg, *Women and the Law*, Vol. 1, 27–28.
22. Joan Hoff, *Law, Gender, and Injustice: A Legal History of U.S. Women* (New York, 1991), 86 (quoting Carole Shammas).
23. Hoff, *Law, Gender and Injustice*, 107; Anna Clark's discussion of the work of Susan Staves, "Humanity or Justice? Wifebeating and the Law in the 18th and 19th Centuries," in Carol Smart, ed., *Regulating Womanhood: Historical Essays on Marriage, Motherhood and Sexuality* (New York, 1992), 191.
24. *Britt v. Adams* (1780), in Carr et al., *Colonial Chesapeake Society*, 338.
25. Carr et al., *Colonial Chesapeake Society*, 12; Carr and Walsh, "The Planter's Wife," 93.
26. John Swanwick, quoted in Norton, *Women of America*, 72.
27. N. E. H. Hull, *Female Felons: Women and Serious Crime in Colonial Massachusetts* (Urbana, IL, 1987), 60–63; Philip Morgan, "Slave Life in Piedmont, Virginia," and Douglas Deal, "A Constricted World," in Carr et al., *Colonial Chesapeake Society*, 471, 285.
28. Daniel Scott Smith and Michael S. Hindus, "Pre-Marital Pregnancy in America, 1640–1971: An Overview and Interpretation," *Journal of Interdisciplinary History* 4 (Spring 1975): 548.
29. Carolyn Merchant, *Ecological Revolutions: Nature, Gender, and Science in New England* (Chapel Hill, NC, 1989), 233; Carole Shammas, "The Domestic Environment in Early Modern England and America," *Journal of Social History* 14 (Fall 1980): 17; "On Higher Learning for Women (1790–1801)," in Marlene Wortman, ed., *Women in American Law*, vol. 1 (New York, 1985), 79.
30. Joan Gundersen and Gwen Gampel, "Married Women's Legal Status in Eighteenth-Century New York and Virginia," *William and Mary Quarterly* 39 (1982): 133.
31. Nancy Cott, "Divorce and the Changing Status of Women in Eighteenth-Century Massachusetts," *William and Mary Quarterly* 33 (October 1976): 613.
32. Mary Beth Norton, "The Evolution of White Women's Experience in Early America," *American Historical Review* 89 (June 1984): 614; Hoff, *Law, Gender and Injustice*, 85; Anne Finch, "Miscellany Poems on Several Occasions . . . , London, 1713," in Goreau, *Whole Duty of a Woman*, 279–80.
33. Linda Kerber, *Women of the Republic* (Chapel Hill, NC, 1980), 228.
34. John Trumbull, quoted in Kerber, *Women of the Republic*, 185.
35. Gunderson, *To Be Useful to the World,* 175.
36. Mercy Otis Warren, "To the Honorable J. Winthrop . . . ," in Benjamin Franklin V, ed., *Plays and Poems of Mercy Otis Warren* (facsimile ed., Delmar NY, 1980), 210.
37. Samuel Adams to Betsy Adams, 1776, quoted in Norton, *Liberty's Daughters*, 171.
38. Crane, *Ebb Tide in New England*, 243.
39. Olympe de Gouges, "Declaration of the Rights of Woman and Citizen [1790]," in Eleanor Riemer and John Fout, eds., *European Women: A Documentary History, 1789–1945* (New York, 1980), 63.
40. Norton, *Liberty's Daughters*, 228.
41. Abigail Adams and Nabby Adams, quoted in Norton, *Liberty's Daughters*, 190.
42. Anonymous reviewer in *The Panoplist* (c. 1805), quoted in Rosemary Zagarri, *A Woman's Dilemma: Mercy Otis Warren and the American Revolution* (Wheeling, IL, 1995), 148.

43. Marc Kruman, *Between Authority and Liberty: State Constitution Making in Revolutionary America* (Chapel Hill, NC, 1997), esp. 90–94.

44. "Friend to the Ladies," in *True American*, October 18, 1802, reprinted in Moynihan, *Second to None,* Vol. 1, 203–04; Newark (New Jersey) *Sentinel*, October 18, 1797, quoted in Norton, *Liberty's Daughters*, 192.

45. The following derives from John Locke, *Two Treatises of Government*, ed. Peter Laslett (New York: New American Library, 1963), 308, 345–46, 350, 362, 364, and, more generally, Parts I, II, VI, VII.

46. Mary Beth Norton, "The Constitutional Status of Women in 1787," *Law and Inequality* 6 (May 1988): 11.

47. Mary Astell, *Some Reflections Upon Marriage*, 3rd ed. (London, 1706), 10–11.

48. John Filmer, *The Anarchy*, in Johann Sommerville, ed., *Patriarcha and Other Writings* (Cambridge, England, 1991), 138.

49. William Blackstone, *Commentaries on the Laws of England*, Vol. 1, 1765 (facsimile of first ed., Chicago, 1979), 430, 432–33.

50. *Dibble v. Hutton*, 1 Day's Reports (Connecticut) 221 (1804), 221–23.

51. Blackstone, *Commentaries*, Vol. 1, 430; *Dibble v. Hutton*, 228.

52. *Dibble v. Hutton*, 224.

53. *Dibble v. Hutton*, 237.

54. *Fitch v. Brainerd* (1805), quoted in Marylynn Salmon, *Women and the Law of Property in Early America* (Chapel Hill, NC, 1986), 128.

55. *James Martin v. Commonwealth [of Massachusetts] and William Bosson and Others, Tertenants*, 1 Massachusetts Reports 260 (1804–1805), 260–95.

56. George Haskins and Herbert Johnson, *Foundations of Power: John Marshall, 1801–15*, Oliver Wendell Holmes Devise History of the Supreme Court, Vol. 2 (New York, 1981), 552n.

57. *Kempe's Lessee v. Kennedy*, 5 Cranch 173 (1809), 176–77, 178, 186; Linda Kerber, "'May All Our Citizens Be Soldiers, and All Our Soldiers Citizens': The Ambiguities of Female Citizenship in the New Nation," in Joan Challinor et al., eds., *Arms at Rest: Peacemaking and Peacekeeping in American History* (Westport, CT, 1987), 1–22.

58. John Murrin, "1787: The Invention of American Federalism," in Peter Onuf et al., eds., *Essays on Liberty and Federalism: The Shaping of the U.S. Constitution* (College Station, TX, 1988), 36.

59. Phyllis Wheatley essay quoted in David Grimsted, "Anglo-American Racism and Phillis Wheatley's 'Sable Veil,' 'Length'ned Chain,' and 'Knitted Heart,'" in Hoffman and Albert, *Women in the Age of the American Revolution*, 443.

60. Judith Sargent Murray, "On the Equality of the Sexes," in Moynihan, *Second to None*, Vol. 1, 189.

PART TWO, INTRODUCTION

1. Editorial, Philadelphia *Public Ledger and Daily Transcript* [1848], reprinted in Elizabeth Cady Stanton et al., eds., *History of Woman Suffrage*, Vol. 1 (New York, 1881; Ayer reprint, 1985), 804, hereafter *HWS*.

2. Mildred Adams, "Rampant Women," in National American Woman Suffrage Association, *Victory: How Women Won It: A Centennial Symposium, 1840–1940* (New York 1940, introduction by Carrie Chapman Catt), 36.

3. Elizabeth Cady Stanton, Speech before the New York Legislature, January 1867, *HWS*, Vol. 2, 279.

4. Carl Degler, *At Odds: Women and the Family in America from the Revolution to the Present* (New York, 1980), 178, 196.

5. John Higham, *From Boundlessness to Consolidation: The Transformation of American Culture, 1848–1860* (Ann Arbor, MI, 1969).

6. Ann Douglas, *The Feminization of American Culture* (New York, 1977), 10; Donald Yacovone, "Abolitionists and the 'Language of Fraternal Love'," in Mark C. Carnes and Clyde Griffen, eds., *Meanings for Manhood: Constructions of Masculinity in Victorian America* (Chicago, 1990), 87.
7. Mary Ryan, "Gender and Public Access: Women's Politics in Nineteenth-Century America," in Craig Calhoun, ed., *Habermas and the Public Sphere* (Cambridge, MA, 1992), 286.
8. Linda Lumsden, *Rampant Women: Suffragists and the Right of Assembly* (Knoxville, TN, 1997), 8.
9. Elizabeth Oakes Smith, *Una*, June 1853, excerpted in *HWS*, Vol. 1, 253–54.

CHAPTER 3

1. The discussion to follow originates in *People ex rel. Barry v. Mercein*, 3 Hill [New York Supreme Court] 400 (1842), 400–27; *Mercein v. The People ex rel. Barry*, 25 Wendell [Court of Errors, New York] 66 (1840), 64–107. Paige's arguments (attributed to de Felice) closely follow Bartholome de Felice, *Leçons de Droit de la nature et des Gens* (Verdon and Lyon, 1769), Part 1, Lectures 29–32 ("On marriage" and "On the family"), esp. 150–200. For discussion of Hendrik Hartog's discovery of the unpublished opinion of 1844, see Stephen Presser and Jamil Zainaldin, eds., *Law and Jurisprudence in American History: Cases and Materials*, 3rd ed. (St. Paul, MN, 1995), 532–33.
2. *Ex Parte Barry*, 2 Howard 65 (1844).
3. Thomas M. Cooley, *A Treatise on the Constitutional Limitations . . .* (Boston, 1868), 340; *Charles McKim v. Anne McKim*, 12 Rhode Island 462 (1879), 462, 465–66.
4. Charles O'Conor, quoted in Peggy Rabkin, *Fathers to Daughters: The Legal Foundations of Female Emancipation* (Westport, CT, 1980), 95.
5. Joel Bishop, *New Commentaries on Marriage, Divorce, and Separation*, Vol. 1 (Chicago, 1891), 671.
6. Report of the Select Committee, New York Assembly, 1860, *HWS*, Vol. 1, 617.
7. Norma Basch, "From the Bonds of Empire to the Bonds of Matrimony," in David Konig, ed., *Devising Liberty: Preserving and Creating Freedom in the New American Republic* (Stanford, CA, 1995), 219.
8. *Miller v. Miller*, 78 Iowa 177 (1889), 183.
9. See Michael Grossberg, *A Judgment for Solomon* (New York, 1997).
10. "An Act annulling the marriage of James W. Dimmett and Catharine Dimmett," *Acts of the General Assembly of Maryland*, Ch. LXXVI, No. 1806 [unpaginated]. My thanks to Jim Schwartz for sharing this find.
11. Norma Basch, "Invisible Women: The Legal Fiction of Marital Unity in Nineteenth-Century America," *Feminist Studies* 5 (Summer 1979): 349.
12. Joel Bishop, *Commentaries on the Law of Marriage and Divorce and Evidence in Matrimonial Suits* (Boston, 1852), 220–21, 289n.
13. *Barber v. Barber*, 62 U. S. Reports [21 Howard] 582 (1858), 602–03.
14. For a discussion of these serious constitutional problems, see Hendrik Hartog, *Man and Wife in America, A History* (Cambridge, MA, 2000).
15. Bishop, *New Commentaries . . .* , Vol. 1 (1891), 295.
16. Bishop, *New Commentaries . . .* , Vol. 1 (1891), 618. Emphasis added.
17. Amy Dru Stanley, *From Bondage to Contract: Wage Labor, Marriage, and the Market in the Age of Slave Emancipation* (New York, 1998), 184.
18. Grossberg, *Governing the Hearth*, 289; Peter Bardaglio, *Reconstructing the Household: Families, Sex, and the Law in the Nineteenth-Century South* (Chapel Hill, NC, 1995), xvi.
19. Standard language in acts dissolving marriages in Pennsylvania in the 1810s; see, for example, Pennsylvania Assembly, Chapter LX or Chapter CLIV, 1814, 94, 193. Puzzlingly, talk about the *ex post facto* clause appeared despite the Supreme Court's early ruling in *Calder v. Bull*,

which restricted the clause to criminal matters. The author plans to write an article on this subject.

20. Joseph Story, separate concurring opinion, *Dartmouth v. Woodward*, 4 Wheaton 518 (1819), 696–97.

21. James Kent, *Commentaries on American Law*, 12th ed., Vol. 1 (Boston, 1873), 468–69.

22. Joseph Story, *Commentaries on the Conflict of Laws* (Boston, 1834; reprint Arno Press, 1972), 100–01.

23. Tapping Reeve, *The Law of Baron and Femme, of Parent and Child, Guardian and Ward, Master and Servant, and of the Power of the Courts of Chancery . . .* , 3rd ed. (1862, orig. pub. 1846, facsimile reprint, Source Book Press, 1970), 307, 315.

24. *Maguire v. Maguire*, 37 Kentucky Reports [7 Dana] 181 (1838), 183–85. In Europe, the idea was familiar. See, for example, the widely consulted James Dalrymple, Viscount of Stair, *Institutions of the Law of Scotland* (orig. ed., 1693; ed. David Walker; Yale University Press, 1981), as at 105.

25. *Maynard v. Hill*, 125 US Reports 191 (1887), 191–95, 204–16.

26. Bishop, *New Commentaries*, Vol. 1 (1891), 19.

27. Governor Elisha Ferry Veto Message, Papers of the Governors of Washington Territory, [1873], Folder "Legislative Divorce," Box 1K-1-5, Washington State Archive.

28. Bishop, *New Commentaries*, Vol. 1 (1891), 5–6.

29. Quoted in Amy Dru Stanley, *From Bondage to Contract: Wage Labor, Marriage, and the Market in the Age of Slave Emancipation* (New York, 1998), 183.

30. Joel Bishop, *Commentaries on the Law of Married Women Under the Statutes of the Several States and at Common Law and in Equity*, Vol. 1 (Philadelphia, 1871), 13, 26–27.

31. Practices described in detail in Bishop, *New Commentaries*, Vol. 1 (1891), 758–60.

32. *Shaw v. Shaw*, 17 Day's Reports (Conn. Supreme Court of Errors) 190 (1845), 190–96. In Bishop's view, and in the opinion of the Iowa Supreme Court (*Beebe v. Beebe*, 10 Iowa 133), a threat to health justified divorce; Bishop, *New Commentaries*, Vol. I (1891), 348. For Sir John Nicholl statement in *Smith v. Smith*, see ibid., 669.

33. *Shaw v. Shaw*, 17 Day's Reports 190 (1845), 190–96.

34. *Waldron v. Waldron*, 85 California 251 (1890); also in Kermit Hall et al., eds., *American Legal History: Cases and Materials* (New York, 1991), 281.

35. *Emily Peltier v. Charles Peltier*, 1 Harrington's Reports 19 (1842), 20–21, 25. My thanks to Debra Viles for bringing this opinion to my attention.

36. Bishop, *New Commentaries*, Vol. 1 (1891), 681.

37. Lushington, quoted in Bishop, *New Commentaries*, Vol. 1 (1891), 682.

38. *State v. Rhodes*, 61 North Carolina 453 (1868), 456–57, 459.

39. *Maria Wightman v. Joshua Coates*, 15 Mass. Reports 1 (1818), 3–6.

40. Bishop, *New Commentaries* Vol. 1 (1891), 510; Michael Grossberg, "Crossing Boundaries: Nineteenth-Century Domestic Relations Law and the Merger of Family and Legal History," *American Bar Foundation Research Journal* (1985): 810–11, which explores *Wells v. Padget* (1850).

41. Catharine Beecher, "On the Peculiar Responsibilities of American Women," in Nancy Cott, ed., *Root of Bitterness: Documents of the Social History of American Women* (Boston, 1986), 172.

42. Parsons, quoted in Dru Stanley, *From Bondage to Contract*, 182.

43. Resolutions [read by Rev. Antoinette Brown], Albany [NY] Convention, February 14–15, 1854, in *HWS*, Vol. 1, 593–95.

44. Reeve, *The Law of Baron and Femme*, Part 1, v. The discussion to follow derives largely from Part 1 ("Baron and Femme"), 49–343.

45. The discussion that follows derives largely from Reeve, *Law of Baron and Femme*, Part 1, 49–343.

46. Ibid.

47. Reeve, *Law of Baron and Femme*, 189, 229–32.

48. Reeve, *Law of Baron and Femme*, 150–51; Bishop, *Commentaries on the Law of Marriage and Divorce . . .* , (1852), 334.

49. Bishop, *New Commentaries*, Vol. 1 (1891), 512, 519. Earlier editions said much the same thing.

50. Bishop, *New Commentaries*, Vol. 1 (1891), 569.
51. Bishop, *New Commentaries*, Vol. 1 (1891), 571.
52. Said treatise writer James Schouler in 1870, "The rule of love has superseded the rule of force"; quoted in Reva Siegel, "'The Rule of Love': Wife Beating as Prerogative and Privacy," 105 *Yale Law Review* 8 (June 1996): 2143.
53. Reeve, *Law of Baron and Femme*, 141–42; Bishop, *New Commentaries*, Vol. 1 (1891), 674.
54. *Fulgham v. State*, 46 Alabama 143 (1871), 145. For *State v. Hussey* (1852) and *Commonwealth v. McAfee* (1871), see Siegel, "'The Rule of Love,'" 2130–31, 2134–35, 2153–54.
55. William Blackstone, *Commentaries on the Laws of England*, Vol. 1, ed. Stanley Katz (Chicago, 1979; facsimile of 1765–69 ed.), 125–26.
56. *Commonwealth v. Bangs*, 9 Mass. 387 (1812); Grossberg, *Governing the Hearth*, 161–62.
57. James Mohr, *Abortion in America: The Origins and Evolution of National Policy* (New York, 1978), 20–27; the quack, Russel Canfield, quoted in Janet Farrell Brodie, *Contraception and Abortion in 19th-Century America* (Ithaca, NY, 1994), 110.
58. "An act to authorize females to obtain divorces in court without cost," December 15, 1831, *Acts of the Tennessee Assembly*, 19th Legislature (1831), 35–36.
59. Elizabeth B. Clark, "The Sacred Rights of the Weak: Pain, Sympathy, and the Culture of Individual Rights in Antebellum America," *Journal of American History* (September 1995): 463–93.
60. Elizabeth Cady Stanton, *Address of Elizabeth Cady Stanton, on the Divorce Bill, Before the Judiciary Committee of the New York Senate, in the Assembly Chamber*, February 8, 1861 (Albany, NY, 1861), 4–5, 10–13 [Pamphlets in American History, W034].
61. Ibid., and Elizabeth B. Clark, "Matrimonial Bonds: Slavery and Divorce in Nineteenth-Century America," *Law and History Review* 8 (Spring 1990), 40.

CHAPTER 4

1. Paulina Wright Davis, Speech at First National Convention, Worcester, Massachusetts, October 2[3?], 1850, in Elizabeth Cady Stanton et al., *History of Woman Suffrage*, Vol. 1 (New York, 1881; Ayer reprint, 1985), 222–23 (hereafter *HWS*).
2. Dorothy Sterling, *Ahead of Her Time: Abby Kelley and the Politics of Antislavery* (New York, 1991), 62; Elizabeth Cady Stanton, Abby Kelley, and Lucretia Mott, recollections of the 1838 Philadelphia antislavery meeting, *HWS*, Vol. 1, 334, 336–37.
3. Abigail Kelley, *Connecticut Observer*, March 7, 1840; Stanton and Anthony, *HWS*, Vol. 1, 40.
4. Quoted in Sterling, *Ahead of Her Time*, 69–70.
5. Sterling, *Ahead of Her Time*, 373, 387.
6. Forest Sweet, "Local Colored Woman Known Far and Wide," Battle Creek [Mich.] *Enquirer*, July 10, 1910.
7. Sojourner Truth, *The Narrative of Sojourner Truth*, ed. Jeffrey Stewart (New York, 1991), 164.
8. Stowe's rendition, quoted in Victoria Ortiz, *Sojourner Truth* (New York, 1974), 167. Much of what we know about Truth was filtered through the sensibilities of white women, especially Stowe and Frances Gage; Nell Irvin Painter, *Sojourner Truth: A Life, A Symbol* (New York, 1996), Part III.
9. Truth, *Narrative of Sojourner Truth*, 133–34.
10. Sojourner Truth, quoted in Ortiz, *Sojourner Truth*, 183; Olive Gilbert, ed., *Narrative of Sojourner Truth* (New York, 1968), 243; and Carleton Mabee and Susan Mabee Newhouse, *Sojourner Truth: Slave, Prophet, Legend* (New York, 1995), 190–91.
11. Sojourner Truth, "Two Speeches at the American Equal Rights Association Convention, 1867," in Karlyn Kohrs Campbell, ed., *Man Cannot Speak for Her: Key Texts of the Early Feminists*, Vol. 2 (New York, 1989), 256.
12. Quoted in Mabee, *Sojourner Truth*, 224.

13. Elinor Rice Hays, *Those Extraordinary Blackwells* (New York, 1967), 118.
14. Antoinette Brown to Lucy Stone, Winter 1848, in Carol Lasser and Marlene Deahl Merrill, eds., *Friends and Sisters: Letters Between Lucy Stone and Antoinette Brown Blackwell, 1846–1893* (Urbana, IL 1987), 33–34.
15. Brown to Lucy Stone, June 1848, in Lasser and Merrill, *Friends and Sisters*, 42–43.
16. Proceedings of the Brick Church meeting, New York City, May 1853; John Marsh of the American Temperance Union; testimony of Brick Church delegates; speech at state temperance convention, New York, 1852; *HWS*, Vol. 1, 483, 502, 508–09.
17. Ibid.
18. "The Half World's Temperance Convention" [reported testimony of Antoinette Brown], *HWS*, Vol. 1, 507; for her own version, see *HWS*, Vol. 1, 153–58.
19. [Horace Greeley], New York *Tribune*, September 9, 1853, *HWS*, Vol. 1, 575.
20. [Elizabeth Cady Stanton], headnote to "New York *Tribune* September 3, 1853," *HWS*, Vol. 1, 511.
21. Horace Greeley [newspaper article excerpt, September 7, 1853], *HWS*, Vol. 1, 507.
22. Antoinette Brown Blackwell, *The Sexes Throughout Nature* (New York, 1875), 135; Brown Blackwell, "Relation of Woman's Work in the Household to the Work Outside," 1873, in Aileen Kraditor, ed., *Up From the Pedestal: Landmark Writings in the American Woman's Struggle for Equality* (Chicago, 1968), 151.
23. Brown Blackwell, "Relation of Woman's Work," 158–59; Brown Blackwell, *Sexes Throughout Nature*, 135.
24. Catharine Beecher, "An Address on Female Suffrage, Delivered in the Music Hall of Boston, December 1870," in Jeanne Boydston et al., eds., *The Limits of Sisterhood: The Beecher Sisters on Women's Rights and Woman's Sphere* (Chapel Hill, NC, 1988), 252; Beecher, "Essay on the Education of Female Teachers," 1835, quoted in Jane Rendall, *Origins of Modern Feminism: Women in Britain, France, and the United States, 1780–1860* (London, 1985), 128; Beecher, "Treatise on Domestic Economy for the Use of Young Ladies at Home or at School," 1841, in Boydston, *Limits of Sisterhood*, 133; Beecher, "An Appeal to American Women," 1869, in Boydston, *Limits of Sisterhood*, 249–50.
25. Ruth Plumbly, Westchester [PA] Convention, 1852, *HWS*, Vol. 1, 367.
26. Juan Luis Vives, *A Very Fruteful and Pleasant Booke Called the Instruction of a Christen Woman* (London, 1557), quoted in Peter Goodrich, "Law in the Courts of Love: Andreas Cappellanus and the Judgments of Love," *Stanford Law Review* 48 (February 1996): 652.
27. Seneca Falls *Democrat*, April 2, 1840, in Glenn Altschuler et al., *Revivalism, Social Conscience, and Community in the Burned-Over District: The Trial of Rhoda Bement* (Ithaca, NY, 1983), 59.
28. Anne Terrel, Bedford County, Virginia, "To the Ladies whose husbands are in the continental army," Dixon and Hunter *Virginia Gazette*, Williamsburg, VA, September 21, 1776.
29. Abigail Adams to John Adams, May 7, 1776; Abigail Adams to Mercy Otis Warren, April 27, 1776; and Abigail Adams to John Adams, July 31, 1777; in Lyman Butterfield, ed., *Adams Family Correspondence*, 4 vols. (Cambridge, MA, 1963), Vol. 1, 371, 375, 396–98; Vol. 2, 295. See also Abigail Adams to John Adams, July 5, 1780, Vol. 4, 328.
30. Caroline Gilman, ed., *Letters of Eliza Wilkinson* (Samuel Colman, ed., 1839; Arno Reprint, 1969), 17.
31. Mercy Otis Warren, "Conscious Dignity That Ought Rather To Be Cherish'd," in Moynihan, *Second to None*, Vol. 1, 170 (letter to niece); "The ladies going about for money exceeded everything . . . ," in Linda Kerber and Jane Sherron DeHart, eds., *Women's America*, 4th ed. (New York, 1995), 85; Harriet Martineau, quoted in Susan Faludi, "Speak for Yourself," in Wendy Martin, ed., *Beacon Book of Essays by Contemporary American Women* (Boston, 1996), 169.
32. Joan R. Gunderson, *To Be Useful to the World: Women in Revolutionary America* (New York, 1996), 80.

33. "Learned Ladies," *Ohio Repository*, July 11, 1822.
34. Benjamin Rush, "Thoughts Upon Female Education . . . ," Philadelphia, 1787, in Frederick Rudolph, ed., *Essays on Education in the Early Republic* (Cambridge, MA, 1965), 25–40; and a slightly different excerpt of the speech in Rosemary Ruether and Rosemary Keller, eds., *Women and Religion in America*, Vol. 2 (New York, 1983), 403. My thanks to Ann Fidler for reminding me of declamatory opportunities available to girls in common schools. For the Litchfield Declaration, 1839, see Linda Kerber, *Women of the Republic: Intellect and Ideology in Revolutionary America* (Chapel Hill, NC, 1980), 278.
35. Elizabeth Cady Stanton, Reminiscences of Paulina Wright Davis, *HWS*, Vol. 1, 284.
36. Catherine Brekus, *Strangers and Pilgrims: Female Preaching in America, 1740–1845* (Chapel Hill, NC, 1998), 300.
37. For the evaluation of Danforth, see Jane Rendall, *Origins of Modern Feminism: Women in Britain, France, and the United States, 1780–1860* (London, 1985), 85.
38. Alice Izard to Margaret Manigault, May 29, 1801, quoted in Moynihan, *Second to None*, Vol. 1, 202; [Elizabeth Cady Stanton, Introduction], *HWS*, Vol. 1, 122; Frances Gage narrative, *HWS*, Vol. 1, 121.
39. New York *Herald*, September 7, 1853, *HWS*, Vol. 1, 556.
40. Editors' essay on writers, *HWS*, Vol. 1, 42.
41. Elizabeth Cady Stanton to Susan B. Anthony, September 10, 1855, in Ellen Carol DuBois, ed., *The Elizabeth Cady Stanton–Susan B. Anthony Reader* (Boston, 1981), 58–59.
42. Peter Goodrich, "Gynaetopia: Feminine Genealogies of Common Law," *Journal of Law and Society* [Oxford, England], 20 (Autumn 1993): 299.
43. Mildred Adams, "Rampant Women," in National Woman Suffrage Association, *Victory: How Women Won It, 1840–1940* (New York, 1940), 37.
44. James A. Epstein, *Radical Expression: Political Language, Ritual, and Symbol in England, 1790–1850* (New York, 1994), 164–65. For "social revolution," see Introduction, *HWS*, Vol. 1, 16.
45. Elizabeth Oakes Smith, Speech at Syracuse [NY] Women's Rights Convention, 1852, *HWS*, Vol. 1, 524; Elizabeth Cady Stanton, *HWS*, Vol. 1, 18; letter from Esther Ann Lukens, October 2, 1851, *HWS*, Vol. 1, 311.
46. Richard D. Brown, *The Strength of a People: The Idea of an Informed Citizenry in America, 1650–1870* (Chapel Hill, NC, 1996), 164–65.
47. Jack Rakove, *Original Meanings: Politics and Ideas in the Making of the Constitution* (New York, 1996), 292.
48. Mary Grew, "Address," 10th Annual Women's Rights Convention, 1860, *HWS*, Vol. 1, 736.
49. Editorial, New York *Herald*, 1852, *HWS*, Vol. 1, 853–54.
50. "Harvard Resolutions," in Moynihan, *Second to None*, Vol. 1, 291–92.
51. Elizabeth Cady Stanton, Introduction, *HWS*, Vol. 1, 53.
52. Mariana Johnson, Presidential Address, Westchester Women's Rights Convention, June 2, 1852, *HWS*, Vol. 1, 352.
53. *HWS*, Vol. 1, 38, 82–85, 95, 206, 152–53, 160, 184, 218, 476; and Maria Weston Chapman, "Times that Try Men's Souls," 1837, *HWS*, Vol. 1, 82–83.
54. Margaret Fuller, *Woman in the Nineteenth Century*, ed. Bernard Rosenthal (New York, 1971), 93.
55. For writing, speaking, and press freedom, see, for example, *HWS*, Vol. 1, 49, 109, 246, 723; New York *Herald*, October 28, 1850, quoted in Andrea Moore Kerr, *Lucy Stone: Speaking Out for Equality* (New Brunswick, NJ, 1992), 60.
56. Maria Stewart, "Religion and the Pure Principles of Morality, the Sure Foundation on Which We Must Build," October 1831 [published in the *Liberator*], and "Farewell Address to her Friends in the City of Boston," December 21, 1833, in Marilyn Richardson, ed., *Maria W. Stewart: America's First Black Woman Political Writer: Essays and Speeches* (Bloomington, IN, 1987), 37–40, 68–69.

57. "Constitution of the Female Anti-Slavery Society of Salem," in Dorothy Sterling, ed., *We Are Your Sisters: Black Women in the Nineteenth Century* (New York, 1984), 113; Proceedings of the National Convention of the Colored Men of America, Washington, D.C., January 14, 1869, in Philip Foner and George Walker, eds., *Proceedings of the Black National and State Conventions, 1865–1900*, Vol. 1 (Philadelphia, 1986), n.p. My thanks to Bonnie Speck for bringing this passage to my attention.

58. Rendall, *Origins of Modern Feminism*, 261; Carroll Smith Rosenberg, "Beauty, the Beast and the Militant Woman: A Case Study in Sex Roles and Social Stress in Jacksonian America," *American Quarterly* (October 1971): 565–66, 568–73.

59. Celia Morris, *Fanny Wright: Rebel in America* (Urbana, IL, 1992), 242–73 ("The Woman Everybody Abuses"), esp. 249–50.

60. Discussion of Ernestine Rose speech, 1836, *HWS*, Vol. 1, 97.

61. Angelina Grimké resolution, May 10, 1837, and Grimké et al., "An Appeal to the Women of the Nominally Free States," Anti-Slavery Convention of American Women, May 9–12, 1837, in Dorothy Sterling, ed., *Turning the World Upside Down: The Anti-Slavery Convention of American Women . . .* (New York, 1987), 13, 31.

62. Angelina Grimké to Catharine Beecher, October 2, 1837, in Larry Geplair, ed., *The Public Years of Sarah and Angelina Grimké: Selected Writings, 1835–1839* (New York, 1989), 197.

63. In Glenna Matthews, *Rise of Public Woman* (New York, 1992), 119, 130; for "heretics" and other remarks at or about Syracuse, see *HWS*, Vol. 1, 543, 852. For Anthony, see Rochester convention proceedings, 1856, *HWS*, Vol. 1, 513.

64. Elizabeth Cady Stanton address [and Stanton letter, barred from meeting but read by Susan B. Anthony],1852, *HWS*, Vol. 1, 472–513; Stanton address, New York Woman's State Temperance Society, 1853, *HWS*, Vol. 1, 495–96. See also Stanton to S. B. Anthony, April 2, 1852, in DuBois, *The Elizabeth Cady Stanton–Susan B. Anthony Reader, 55.*

65. Jonathan Stearns, "Discourse on Female Influence," 1837, in Kraditor, *Up From the Pedestal,* 47–49.

66. Reverend Hubbard Winslow, *Discourse Delivered in the Bowdoin Street Church, July 9, 1837, "The Appropriate Sphere of Woman"* (Boston, 1837), 14–16 [Pamphlets in American History, W04].

67. "Pastoral Letter of the Congregational Ministers of Massachusetts" [from *Liberator*, August 1837], in Moynihan, *Second to None*, Vol. 1, 251–52.

68. Matilda Joslyn Gage, *Woman, Church and State*, 2nd ed. (1893, reprinted Ayer Co.: Salem, NH, 1985), 478–79.

69. See, for example, Aileen Kraditor, *Ways and Means in American Abolitionism: Garrison and His Critics on Strategy and Tactics, 1834–1850* (Chicago, 1989), esp. "The Woman Question," 39–77.

70. For "lovers" and speech demand, *HWS*, Vol. 1, 333, 142; for the apparent refusal of the Mayor of New York and "a large police force" to protect speech, ibid., 547. See also Mary Ryan, *Women in Public: Between Banners and Ballots* (Baltimore, 1990).

71. William Lloyd Garrison, World's Temperance Convention, 1853, *HWS*, Vol. 1, 160; Antoinette Brown's narration, 1853, ibid., 152–60.

72. Frederick Douglass, "Address before Bethel Literary Society," [post-Civil War, n.d.], in Philip Foner, ed., *Frederick Douglass on Women's Rights* (New York, 1992), 126–27.

73. Elizabeth Cady Stanton to Lucy Stone, November 24, 1856, *HWS*, Vol. 1, 860.

74. Frances Gage, *HWS*, Vol. 1, 119; Ernestine Rose address at Broadway Tabernacle, New York City, NY, September 6–7, 1853, *HWS*, Vol. 1, 572; Frances Gage, Address, Akron Convention, May 1851, *HWS*, Vol. 1, 113. See also Anneke's discussion of "freedom of speech" for women and America as the "only hope . . . for freedom of speech and action," *HWS*, Vol. 1, 572.

75. Syracuse [NY] *Standard*, September 13, 1852.

76. For exile and arson, see, for example, *HWS*, Vol. 1, 337, 405, 414. For speech as agent of re-

constitution and a positive duty, see *HWS*, 488, 312–13, 95, 459–60, 500, 180. See also Elizabeth Cady Stanton, "Reminiscences," *HWS*, Vol. 1, 459–60; Antoinette Brown Blackwell speech, 1860, *HWS*, Vol. 1, 723.

77. Ernestine Rose, National Convention in Philadelphia, October 1854, *HWS*, Vol. 1, 377; Ann Preston, Westchester Convention, 1852, *HWS*, Vol. 1, 364.

78. Frances Gage, speech at the 4th Women's Rights Convention, Cleveland, Ohio, 1853, *HWS*, Vol. 1, 123–24.

79. On the *Woman's Advocate*, *HWS*, Vol. 1, 388; Proceedings, National Convention in Philadelphia, October 1854, *HWS*, Vol. 1, 378–79.

80. Woman's Rights Convention, Salem, Ohio, April 1850, *HWS*, Vol. 1, 110; debate, 7th annual meeting, 1856, *HWS*, Vol. 1, 648–51; Susan B. Anthony speech, Loyal League National Convention, New York, May 1863, *HWS*, Vol. 2, 66.

81. Woman's Rights Convention, Salem, Ohio, April 1850, *HWS*, Vol. 1, 110, emphasis added; speech of Abby Price, Syracuse National Convention, 1852, *HWS*, Vol. 1, 532; Reverend Samuel Longfellow, Speech, 10th Annual Convention, New York City, 1860, *HWS*, Vol. 1, 711–15.

82. Fuller, *Woman in the Nineteenth Century*, 110–11.

83. Lucy Stone, *HWS*, Vol. 2, 242.

84. [The *Bulletin*], quoted in proceedings, National Convention in Philadelphia, October 18, 1854, *HWS*, Vol. 1, 375.

85. Editorial note, *HWS*, Vol. 1, 434.

86. Mary Livermore, *My Story of the War: The Civil War Memoirs of the Famous Nurse, Relief Organizer and Suffragette*, ed. Nina Silber (Hartford, CT, 1887; reprinted New York, 1995), 607–09.

87. Ibid.

88. Woman's Rights Convention, Seneca Falls, NY, 1848, *HWS*, Vol. 1, 70.

89. Stanton Runs for Congress, 1866, *HWS*, Vol. 2, 180; Wendell Phillips, on the power of Angelina Grimké's speech, *HWS*, Vol. 1, 401; for mixed-sex assemblies, Lucretia Mott, 1838, *HWS*, Vol. 1, 337; for "law" and "fact," Stanton quoting John Stuart Mill in headnote, *HWS*, Vol. 1, 225. See also *HWS*, Vol. 1, 331, 418.

90. Wendell Phillips, 10th annual convention, New York, 1860, *HWS*, Vol. 1, 702. Emphasis added.

CHAPTER 5

1. Dianne Avery and Alfred S. Konefsky, "The Daughters of Job: Property Rights and Women's Lives in Mid-Nineteenth-Century Massachusetts," *Law and History Review* (Fall 1992): 323–56 ("Kendall's" letter reprinted at 351–56). Avery and Konefsky were not able to confirm that Kendall actually existed; I therefore treat the name as a pseudonym.

2. Ibid.

3. Ibid.

4. Mariana Johnson speech, Westchester [PA] convention, 1852, in Elizabeth Cady Stanton et al., *History of Woman Suffrage*, Vol. 1 (New York, 1881; Ayer reprint 1985), 352 (hereafter *HWS*).

5. Aileen Kraditor, *The Ideas of the Woman Suffrage Movement, 1890–1920* (New York, 1981), 43–45. She dubbed another late-century approach the "expediency" position, denoting a line of argument that looked to social benefit rather than to abstract principles of justice, pursued on "whatever grounds might bring the most favorable response," 45.

6. Nancy Hewitt, "Feminist Friends: Agrarian Quakers and the Emergence of Woman's Rights in America," *Feminist Studies* (Spring 1986): 28; Paulina Wright Davis, Speech at First National Convention, Worcester, Massachusetts, October 2[3?], 1850, in *HWS*, Vol. 1, 222–23; Robert Abzug, *Cosmos Crumbling: American Reform and the Religious Imagination* (New York, 1994), 8.

7. Lucretia Mott speech, Philadelphia, 1849, *HWS*, Vol. 1, 367–73.

8. Ibid.; for "fundamental principles," Ann Preston speech, Westchester Convention, 1852, *HWS*, Vol. 1, 364; Angelina Grimké to Catharine Beecher, October 2, 1837, in Larry Ceplair, ed., *The Public Years of Sarah and Angelina Grimké: Selected Writings, 1835–1839* (New York, 1989), 197.

9. Mott speech, Philadelphia, 1849, *HWS*, Vol. 1, 367–73.

10. On class-based legislation and women as appendages of men, see "Theodore Parker—The Public Function of Woman," 1853, *HWS*, Vol. 1, 277; [J. Elizabeth Jones], "Address to the Women of Ohio," 1850, *HWS*, Vol. 1, 106–07; Paulina Wright Davis, "On the Education of Females," tract no. 3, *Women's Rights Commensurate With Her Abilities*, 1850.

11. Albany Convention, February 14–15, 1854, *HWS*, Vol. 1, 592.

12. Speeches of Mariana Johnson and Ruth Plumbly, Westchester Convention, 1852, *HWS*, Vol. 1, 352–53, 367.

13. Ann Preston, Westchester convention, 1852, *HWS*, Vol. 1, 364; [Rev. Henry Bellows], New York *Christian Inquirer*, 1851, *HWS*, Vol. 1, 245.

14. "Mr. Higginson's Speech," *HWS*, Vol. 1, 250 (Bills of Right were the "organic" law for both sexes); Fifth National Woman's Rights Convention, Cleveland, 1853, *HWS*, Vol. 1, 818; Henry Blackwell to Horace Greeley, [c. 1853], *HWS*, Vol. 1, 126; on harmonization, see, for example, "The Call," *HWS*, Vol. 1, 221; "President's Address," *HWS*, Vol. 1, 352–53. See also *HWS*, Vol. 1, 52, 94, 413.

15. Elizabeth Clark, "Matrimonial Bonds: Slavery and Divorce in Nineteenth-Century America," *Law and History Review* (Spring 1990): 45; Stanton, Introduction, *HWS*, Vol. 1, 15.

16. Davis, Speech at First National Convention, *HWS*, Vol. 1, 222–23.

17. Matilda Gage, *HWS*, Vol. 1, 789.

18. Clark, "Matrimonial Bonds," 26, 35, 40.

19. Elizabeth Cady Stanton, Speech before the New York legislature, January 1867, *HWS*, Vol. 2, 281.

20. Elizabeth Cady Stanton address, New York legislature, 1854 (printed as a pamphlet and "scattered like snowflakes" over the New York countryside), *HWS*, Vol. 1, 595.

21. Elizabeth Cady Stanton, Tenth National Woman's Rights Convention, Cooper's Institute, NY, May 1860, *HWS*, Vol. 1, 716–17.

22. Antoinette Brown Blackwell speech, Tenth National Woman's Rights Convention, Cooper's Institute, NY, May 1860, *HWS*, Vol. 1, 723–29; also in Karlyn Kohrs Campbell, comp., *Man Cannot Speak For Her: Key Texts of the Early Feminists*, Vol. 2 (New York, 1989), 202–14.

23. Ibid.

24. See Nancy Cott, *The Grounding of Modern Feminism* (New Haven, CT, 1987).

25. Call to Salem Convention, read by Mariana Johnson, April 1850, *HWS*, Vol. 1, 103–04; "From the Liberator—Rights of Women in Wisconsin," May 1856, *HWS*, Vol. 1, 315–17.

26. Seneca Falls Declaration of Sentiments, 1848, *HWS*, Vol. 1, 70, and surrounding commentary. See also Stanton's reference to "conscious possession" of rights as a species of property, headnote, "Women's Medical College of Pennsylvania," 1850, *HWS*, Vol. 1, 391.

27. William Sampson quoted in Peggy Rabkin, *Fathers to Daughters: The Legal Foundations of Female Emancipation* (Westport, CT, 1980), 44.

28. Stanton on Gage, *HWS*, Vol. 1, 466; for "arsenal," *HWS*, Vol. 1, 7. Related material is abundant. But see, for example, Matilda Gage, "Woman, Church, and State," *HWS*, Vol. 1, 753–99; "Salem Convention," 1850, *HWS*, Vol. 1, 104; Lucretia Mott remarks about St. Paul, Rochester Convention, August 2, 1848, *HWS*, Vol. 1, 79; excerpt from David Walker treatise, *HWS*, Vol. 1, 109; Garrison on women and the Bible, Fifth National Convention, Philadelphia, 1853, *HWS*, Vol. 1, ibid., 382; 1853 discussion of church-state collaboration, *HWS*, Vol. 1, 128. For women's use of spiritualism as an antidote to "silence," see Ann Braude, *Radical Spirits: Spiritualism and Women's Rights in Nineteenth-Century America* (Boston, 1989).

29. Lucy Stone speech, Broadway Tabernacle convention, 1856, *HWS*, Vol. 1, 652.

30. Elizabeth Cady Stanton to Susan B. Anthony, March 1, 1853, in Ellen DuBois, ed., *The Elizabeth Cady Stanton–Susan B. Anthony Reader: Correspondence, Writings, Speeches*, rev. ed. (Boston, 1981), 55–56; Elizabeth Cady Stanton, Speech before the New York legislature, 1854, *HWS*, Vol. 1, 598.

31. *Revolution*, October 27, 1870; Lucy Stone to Susan B. Anthony, 1856, cited in Karen Sánchez-Eppler, *Touching Liberty: Abolition, Feminism and the Politics of the Body* (Berkeley, CA, 1993), 23; Susan B. Anthony, "Social Purity," 1875, in Aileen Kraditor, *Up From the Pedestal: Landmark Writings in the American Woman's Struggle for Equality* (Chicago, 1968), 166 [also in *HWS*, Vol. 1, 598–99].

32. For Owen and the Blackwell-Stone agreements, see *HWS*, Vol. 1, 294–95, 260–61; also in Kraditor, *Up From the Pedestal*, 148–50. Wedding protest of Lucy Stone and Henry Blackwell, *HWS*, Vol. 1, 261–62.

33. Paper of Judge William Hay [presented by Susan B. Anthony], March 3, 1854, New York House Committee, *HWS*, Vol. 1, 607.

34. Elizabeth Cady Stanton, Introduction, *HWS*, Vol. 1, 15.

35. Minority Report of C. L. Sholes, Committee on Re-Enactment of Laws, Wisconsin, reprinted from *Liberator* in *HWS*, Vol. 1, 316; for taxation, see, for example, Resolutions [Ohio and New York women's rights convention], Appendix to Chapter 8 in *HWS*, Vol. 1, 819–21.

36. Elizabeth Cady Stanton, Speech, Seneca Falls Convention, 1848, in *HWS*, Vol. 1, 238–39.

37. Seneca Falls Declaration, 1848, in ibid.

38. Ibid.

39. Ibid.

40. Ibid.

41. Resolutions of the Syracuse convention, 1852, *HWS*, Vol. 1, 537; Ernestine Rose, 10th annual conference, New York City, 1860, *HWS*, Vol. 1, 702.

42. Elizabeth Oakes Smith speech, Syracuse convention, 1852, *HWS*, Vol. 1, 522–23.

43. Elizabeth Blackwell to Mrs. Emily Collins, August 12, 1848, *HWS*, Vol. 1, 90–91; Stanton, Introduction, *HWS*, Vol. 1, 13–24; Stanton speech before New York legislature, 1854, *HWS*, Vol. 1, 596; Sarah Grimké, "Two Essays," 1837–38, in Kraditor, *Up From the Pedestal*, 56; Charles Burleigh, Tabernacle convention, September 1853, *HWS*, Vol. 1, 559.

44. William Lloyd Garrison, Speech at New York Women's Rights Convention, 1853, *HWS*, Vol. 1, 137.

45. Asa Mahan, Speech at New York Women's Rights Convention, 1853, *HWS*, Vol. 1, 133.

46. Stanton, Speech before New York legislature, January 1867, *HWS*, Vol. 2, 273.

47. Jack Greene, *Imperatives, Behaviors, and Identities: Essays in Early American Cultural History* (Charlottesville, VA, 1992), 265–66.

48. Nancy Fraser and Linda Gordon, *Social Politics* 1 (Spring 1994): 4–31, esp. 9.

49. Judge William Hay to Susan B. Anthony, March 20, 1856, *HWS*, Vol. 1, 631; *Sturgineger et al. v. Hannah et al.*, 2 Nott and McCord's Law and Equity Reports (South Carolina 1819), 148–49, emphasis added; discussed in Marylynn Salmon, "'Life, Liberty, and Dower': The Legal Status of Women After the American Revolution," in Carol Berkin and Clara Lovett, eds., *Women, War, and Revolution* (New York, 1980), 95.

50. Minority Report of C. L. Sholes, Committee on Re-Enactment of Laws, Wisconsin, reprinted from *Liberator* in *HWS*, Vol. 1, 316.

51. Biographical sketch of Lucretia Mott, *HWS*, Vol. 1, 422.

52. On clear sight, Cleveland convention proceedings, 1853, *HWS*, Vol. 1, 128; on "triple bondage," Stanton to Lucy Stone, November 24, 1856, *HWS*, Vol. 1, 1860; Seneca Falls resolution, 1848, *HWS*, Vol. 1, 73; Lucretia Mott and William Lloyd Garrison, Philadelphia convention, 1854, *HWS*, Vol. 1, 381–82.

53. Nancy Isenberg, *Sex and Citizenship in Antebellum America* (Chapel Hill, NC, 1998), 77.

54. Introduction, *HWS*, Vol. 1, 28; Elizabeth Cady Stanton, letter to the editor, *The Critic*, March 28, 1896, 218–19.

55. Elizabeth Cady Stanton, "The Matriarchate, or Mother-Age," *Transactions of the National Council of Women of the United States* (Philadelphia, 1891), 218.

56. Matilda Gage, *HWS*, Vol. 1, 796; Lucretia Mott, Women's Rights Convention, 1854, Philadelphia, *HWS*, Vol. 1, 380. On Mott's excommunication and views of conscience, see *HWS*, Vol. 1, 422, 429. See also Matilda Gage, *Woman Church, and State* (New York, 1893; Ayers reprint, 1985); Gage, essay on church and state, *HWS*, Vol. 1, 765.

57. Antoinette Brown speech, Syracuse Women's Rights Convention, 1852, *HWS*, Vol. 1, 524.

58. Ernestine Rose, Cleveland convention, 1853, *HWS*, Vol. 1, 144; J. Elizabeth Jones speech, Syracuse Women's Rights Convention, 1852, *HWS*, Vol. 1, 530.

59. For "blow," George Geddes to Matilda Gage, November 25, 1880, *HWS*, Vol. 1, 65; for "old Blackstone code," biographical sketch of Parker Pillsbury, *HWS*, Vol. 1, 429; for "whole theory," Mariana Johnson, "Memorial," Salem convention, OH, 1850, *HWS*, Vol. 1, 105; for "sophistries," headnote, *HWS*, Vol. 1, 498; for a typical discussion of legal harmonics, Reminiscences of Clarina Nichols, *HWS*, Vol. 1, 193.

60. Headnote, *HWS*, Vol. 1, 103. See also "The World's Anti-Slavery Convention, London, June 12, 1840," *HWS*, Vol. 1, 52; on clergy as enemies, headnote, *HWS*, Vol. 1, 152; speech urging women to resist repeated references to biblical "truth," *HWS*, Vol. 1, 142.

61. In the 1850s, Clarina Nichols noted that there were "too many old lawyers" opposing change in Kansas; *HWS*, Vol. 1, 194.

62. Abigail Kelley, Cleveland convention, 1853, *HWS*, Vol. 1, 134; Ernestine Rose, Cleveland (OH) convention, 1855, *HWS*, Vol. 1, 133; Rose, Second Worcester (MA) convention, 1851, *HWS*, Vol. 1, 239; Wendell Phillips, Cooper Institute, New York, 1860, *HWS*, Vol. 1, 706. See also Lucretia Mott speech, Women's Rights Convention, Cleveland [OH], 1853, *HWS*, Vol. 1, 381. On "false education," see *HWS*, Vol. 1, 482; for "shackles," see Stanton, Rochester [NY] temperance convention, 1852, *HWS*, Vol. 1, 482.

63. Matilda Gage, Broadway Tabernacle convention, 1853, *HWS*, Vol. 1, 563.

64. Resolutions of Massilon [OH] Convention, 1852, *HWS*, Vol. 1, 817; Elizabeth Cady Stanton, "Seneca Falls Convention," *HWS*, Vol. 1, 73; Paulina Wright Davis, *Una*, [June 1853], quoted in Frederick Douglass, "Some Thoughts on Human Rights," *Frederick Douglass' Paper*, June 10, 1853.

65. For "mould," see President Mary Vaughan address, Albany, January 1852, *HWS*, Vol. 1, 477; on women's false consciousness and two-step process, see Stanton, "Reminiscences," *HWS*, Vol. 1, 460–61, 464.

66. Amelia Jenks Bloomer, in Ruth B. Moynihan et al., eds., *Second to None: A Documentary History of American Women*, Vol. 1 (Lincoln, NE, 1993), 253–54.

67. On equal "pay" or "wages," *HWS*, Vol, 1, 79, 385; for Mott, Seneca Falls convention proceedings, 1848, *HWS*, Vol. 1, 79; Susan B. Anthony, "Social Purity," 1875, in Kraditor, *Up From the Pedestal*, 164; Frederick Douglass, "Address before the Bethel Literary Society" (n.d.), in Philip Foner, ed., *Frederick Douglass on Women's Rights* (New York, 1992), 127; for resolutions demanding economic and personal security, *HWS*, Vol. 1, Appendix.

68. George Francis Train, speech on suffrage in Kansas, 1867, *HWS*, Vol. 2, 245.

69. John Stuart Mill, *The Subjection of Women*, ed. Sue Mansfield (Arlington Heights, IL, 1980), 48.

70. Betsey Chamberlain, "A New Society," *The Lowell Offering*, ed. Benita Eisler (New York, 1977), 209; Barbara Leigh Smith Bodichon, *Women and Work*, ed. Catharine M. Sedgwick (New York, 1859), 3 [Pamphlets in American History, W043]; Caroline Dall speech at New England Convention, 1859, *HWS*, Vol. 1, 269.

71. Clarina Howard Nichols, speech at Syracuse, NY, 1852, *HWS*, Vol. 1, 525; Stanton, speech before New York legislature, 1854, *HWS*, Vol. 1, 601.

72. See, for example, *HWS*, Vol. 1, 347.

73. On women's bodies, babies, claustrophobia, locomotion, and Grimké, see *HWS*, Vol. 1, 176, 771–72, 292, 89, 405; for "buttons," see *HWS*, Vol. 1, 178. Gerritt Smith used the term *locomotion*; see *HWS*, Vol. 1, 572.
74. Elizabeth Cady Stanton, *HWS*, Vol. 1, 470.
75. "How a Young Lady Goes To Bed," Detroit *Free Press*, June 3, 1867. Emphasis added. My thanks to Beth Onusko Savalox for sharing this find.
76. Sarah Moore Grimké, "Dress of Women," 1838, in Kraditor, *Up From the Pedestal*, 123.
77. Elizabeth D. Leonard, *Yankee Women: Gender Battles in the Civil War* (New York, 1994), 109–10 (including Walker quotations).
78. For bloomer costume, see *HWS*, Vol. 1, 470; Gerrit Smith to Elizabeth Cady Stanton, December 1855, reprinted in Kraditor, *Up From the Pedestal*, 125–29; Stanton, *HWS*, Vol. 2, 541.
79. Elizabeth Cady Stanton, *Revolution*, October 21, 1869; also in *HWS*, Vol. 2, 334.
80. Amelia Bloomer, Rochester [NY] convention, *HWS*, Vol. 1, 484.
81. Sara Grimké, *Letters on the Equality of the Sexes and the Condition of Women* (Boston, 1838), 13, 75.
82. Susan B. Anthony, "Social Purity," 1875, in Kraditor, *Up From the Pedestal*, 167.
83. See, for example, Elisabeth Griffith's discussion of Stanton's vision of the self-sovereign woman, *In Her Own Right: The Life of Elizabeth Cady Stanton* (New York, 1984), chap. 11 ("Self Sovereign . . .").
84. Gerrit Smith to Stanton and Stanton to Smith, 1855, in *HWS*, Vol. 1, 836, 840; Lucy Stone and Ernestine Rose, Broadway Tabernacle convention, 1853: *HWS*, Vol. 1, 576, 579.
85. Sara Grimké, "Marriage," 1855, Weld-Grimké Papers, William Clements Library, University of Michigan, 18–19, 21.
86. Lydia Maria Child, *Letters from New York* (New York, 1843), 232, 234.
87. Benjamin Drew, ed., *A Northside View of Slavery: The Refugee, or the Narratives of Fugitive Slaves in Canada . . .* (Boston, 1856), 41–43.
88. Linda Brent [Harriet Jacobs], *Incidents in the Life of a Slave Girl*, ed. Walter Teller (New York, 1973), 56.
89. Stanton, Introduction, *HWS*, Vol. 1, 28; for Rebecca Sanford, *HWS*, Vol. 1, 77. For other rights mentioned, see, for example, *HWS*, Vol. 1, 181, 210, 220, 73, 89, 242, 418, 85, 338, 370.
90. Ibid.; Frederick Douglass, "Some Thoughts on Women's Rights," *Frederick Douglass' Paper*, June 10, 1853; Mary C. Vaughan temperance and women's rights speech, *HWS*, Vol. 1, 476.
91. "An Act to Abolish Imprisonment for Debt Except in Cases of Fraud," *General Assembly of Tennessee*, Public Acts, 19th Assembly, 1831, Chap 40, 56; Angelina Grimké, excerpt from "An Appeal to the Women of the Nominally Free States . . . ," in Nancy Cott, ed., *Root of Bitterness: Documents of the Social History of American Women* (Boston, 1986), 194.
92. Fourth resolution, Broadway Tabernacle [NY] convention, 1856, *HWS*, Vol. 1, 633; Harriet Martineau letter, second Worcester [MA] convention, 1851, *HWS*, Vol. 1, 230–31.
93. Carrie Burnham Kilgore, *Address of Carrie Burnham Kilgore Before the Legislature of Pennsylvania . . . March 23d, 1881* (Philadelphia, 1881), 6 [Pamphlets in American History, W089].
94. Lucretia Mott speech, Syracuse Convention, 1852, *HWS*, Vol. 1, 528.
95. Lucy Stone, Speech at Women's Rights Convention, Cincinnati, Ohio (1855), in Kraditor, *Up From the Pedestal*, 72.
96. Elizabeth Clark, "Religion and Rights Consciousness in the Antebellum Woman's Rights Movement," in Martha Fineman et al., eds., *At the Boundaries of Law: Feminism and Legal Theory* (New York, 1991), 188–208, esp. 189. On the irrationality of seeking ballots, see also *HWS*, Vol. 1, 73; on the importance of votes, see *HWS*, Vol. 1, 262.
97. Introduction, *HWS*, Vol. 1, 13–24, and passim; Stanton to Gerrit Smith, December 21, 1855, in Kraditor, *Up From the Pedestal*, 129–30.
98. Stanton to Smith, December 21, 1855, in Kraditor, *Up From the Pedestal*, 131.
99. Elizabeth Oakes Smith Address, Syracuse Convention, 1852, *HWS*, Vol. 1, 524.

CHAPTER 6

1. Mary Livermore, *My Story of the War: A Woman's Narrative of Four Years Personal Experience as Nurse in the Union Army* . . . (Hartford, CT, 1890), 550–51.
2. "Act authorizing permanent provision for resident females, in Kentucky stocks, and guardians to invest the money of their wards in Bank stocks," *Acts of Kentucky General Assembly*, regular session (1838), chap. 955, 338–40.
3. See, for example, Nancy F. Cott, "Marriage and Women's Citizenship in the United States," *American Historical Review* (December 1998), 1440. Rogers Smith disagrees; in *Civic Ideals: Conflicting Visions of Citizenship in U.S. History* (New Haven, CT, 1997), he plumps for Martin.
4. *Ann Shanks et al. v. Abraham Dupont et al.*, 28 U.S. Reports [2 Peters] 242 (1830), 246–47. Emphasis added. During these years, Story was busily working to restore "scientific" rules of practice in many areas of the law, such as in admiralty law.
5. *American Law Review* 6 (1871): 73.
6. "An Act to Define and Protect the Rights of Married Women," *Laws of Michigan*, 1844.
7. "General Provisions Concerning Husband and Wife" and "Of Wills of Real and Personal Estate," *Revised Statutes of Michigan*, 1846; Constitution of Michigan, Article 16, Section 5, 1850; "An Act Relative to the Rights of Married Women," *Laws of Michigan*, No. 168, February 13, 1855. For quoted material and elaboration, see Debra Viles, "Disabilities of Marriage: Gender and Law in Antebellum Michigan," M.A. essay, Wayne State University, 1995.
8. Carole Shammas, "Re-Assessing the Married Women's Property Acts," *Journal of Women's History* (Spring 1994), 21.
9. For statistics and discussion of "working girls," see Julie A. Matthaei, *An Economic History of Women in America: Women's Work, the Sexual Division of Labor, and the Development of Capitalism* (New York, 1982), 141–44.
10. Joan Hoff, *Law, Gender and Injustice: A Legal History of U. S. Women* (New York, 1991), 112–14, 129 [charts], 130–31.
11. Letter from Miriam H. Fish of Lasalle County, Illinois, to Susan B. Anthony, May 8, 1863, *HWS*, Vol. 2, 884–85.
12. Marylynn Salmon, " 'Life, Liberty, and Dower': The Legal Status of Women after the American Revolution," in Carol Berkin et al., eds., *Women, War, and Revolution* (New York, 1980), 100.
13. Mrs. Elizabeth Packard (1866), quoted in Martha Minow, " 'Forming Underneath Everything That Grows': Toward a History of Family Law," *Wisconsin Law Review* (1985): 819. Emphasis added.
14. Ray August, "The Spread of Community Property Law to the Far West," *Western Legal History* (Winter–Spring 1990): 35.
15. "An Act to adapt the Common Law of England, to repeal certain Mexican Laws, and to regulate the Ma[r]ital Rights of parties," *Republic of Texas Laws*, 1839, 1st sess.: 4, 5.
16. Debates of the Texas Constitutional Convention, 1846; and delegate John Hemphill, quoted in August, "Spread of Community Property Law," 50–51; Delegate Love, quoted in James Paulsen, "Community Property and the Early American Women's Rights Movement: The Texas Connection," *Idaho Law Review* 32 (1996): 657.
17. "Act to Provide for Registration of Separate Property of Married Women," *First Legislature of Texas, General and Special Laws*, Regular Session: 153–54; "Act to authorize the several Clerks of the County Courts . . . to take the separate acknowledgment of Married Women to Deeds executed by them," *Third Legislature of Texas, General Laws*, 1849: 11.
18. August, "Spread of Community Property Law," 54–56. Emphasis added.
19. Mari Matsuda, "The West and the Legal Status of Women: Explanations of Frontier Feminism," *Journal of the West* 24 (January 1985): 50.
20. *Brown v. Worden*, 39 Wisconsin 432 (1876), 434.

21. Richard H. Chused, "The Oregon Donation Act of 1850 and Nineteenth Century Federal Married Women's Property Law," *Law and History Review* (Spring 1984): 45.

22. Samuel Thurston, quoted in Chused, "Oregon Donation Act," 69–70. Emphasis added. Thomas Herttell, quoted in Peggy Rabkin, *Fathers to Daughters: The Legal Foundations of Female Emancipation* (Westport, CT, 1980), 87. For Mary Ferrin and the situation in Ohio, see Linda Speth, "The Married Women's Property Acts, 1839–1865," in D. Kelly Weisberg, ed., *Women and the Law: The Social Historical Perspective*, Vol. 2 (Cambridge, MA, 1982), 82–83.

23. Elizabeth Cady Stanton, *Eighty Years and More: Reminiscences of Elizabeth Cady Stanton* (New York, 1898), 150.

24. David Dudley Field, quoted in Rabkin, *Fathers to Daughters*, 58.

25. Mary Ryan, *Cradle of the Middle Class: The Family in Oneida County, New York, 1790–1865* (New York, 1981).

26. Richard Chused, "Married Women's Property Law: 1800–1850," *Georgetown Law Journal* 71 (1983): 1361.

27. Stanton, Introduction, *HWS*, Vol. 1, 16.

28. John Stuart Mill, *The Subjection of Women* (1869, Sue Mansfield, ed., reprinted Arlington Heights, IL, 1980), 47, 19.

29. My thanks to James Paulsen for examples and ideas.

30. Reva B. Siegel, "The Modernization of Marital Status Law: Adjudicating Wives' Rights to Earnings, 1860–1930," *Georgetown Law Journal* (September 1994): 2151.

31. "An Act concerning the rights and liabilities of husband and wife," chap. 90, March 20, 1860, *Laws of New York*, 83rd Session, 1860, 157–59; Andrew Colvin to Susan B. Anthony, 1862, *HWS*, 749.

32. "An Act to amend the act entitled "An Act concerning the rights and liabilities of husband and wife," chap. 172, April 10, 1862, *Laws of New York*, 85th Sess., 1862, 343–44; "An Act to amend section nine, title three . . . ," chap. 470, *Laws of New York*, 97th Legislature, 1874, 612.

33. Dr. Mary Putnam Jacobi, Mrs. Henry Sanders, Miss Adele Fielde, Mrs. C. A. Runkle, and Mrs. Robert Abbe, *A Dialogue—Laws of the State of New York Affecting Women* (n.p., c. 1884) [Pamphlets in American History, W063], 7–8.

34. Hendrik Hartog explores the Brooks case in Chapter 7, *Man and Wife in America, A History* (Cambridge, MA, 2000), which he graciously shared in advance of publication.

35. *Frecking v. Rolland*, 53 N.Y. 423 (1873), 425. For *Cashman v. Henry* (1878) and discussion of the May 18, 1884, act, see Siegel, "Modernization of Marital Status Law," 2152–53.

36. *Brooks v. Schwein*, 54 N.Y. 343 (1873); *Birkbeck v. Ackroyd*, 74 N.Y. 356 (1878); Siegel, "Modernization of Marital Status Law," 2154–55.

37. *Lashaw v. Croissant*, 34 N.Y.S. 667, 669; "Act to amend an act entitled 'An Act for the more effectual protection of the property of married women,'" *Laws of New York*, 1884, chap. 200. For emasculation of statutes, see Norma Basch, *In the Eyes of the Law* (Ithaca, NY, 1982). For Judge Vann and *Winter v. Winter* (1908), see Rabkin, *Fathers to Daughters*, 149–51.

38. "An Act to protect Married Women in their separate property," *Acts of Illinois*, 22nd General Assembly, 1st session, 1861: 143; *Jesse Thomas v. City of Chicago*, 55 Illinois 403 (1870), 403, 406; *John Wilson v. John Loomis et al.*, 55 Illinois 352 (1870), 352–53.

39. Linda Kerber, "Separate Spheres, Female Worlds, Woman's Place: The Rhetoric of Women's History," *Journal of American History* (June 1988): 21.

40. Julie Matthaei, *An Economic History of Women in America* (New York, 1982), 105.

41. Wendy Gamber, "'Reduced to Science': Gender, Technology, and Power in the American Dressmaking Trade, 1860–1910," *Technology and Culture* (July 1995): 481.

42. Thorstein Veblen, "Economic Theory of Women's Dress," *Popular Science Monthly* 46 (December 1894): 205.

43. Bethany Ruth Berger, "After Pocahontas: Indian Women and the Law, 1830 to 1934," *American Indian Law Review* (1997): 1–62.

44. Mary H. Blewett, "The Sexual Division of Labor and the Artisan Tradition in Early Industrial Capitalism: The Case of New England Shoemaking, 1780–1860," in Carol Groneman and Mary Beth Norton, eds., *"To Toil the Livelong Day": America's Women at Work, 1780–1980* (Ithaca, NY, 1987), 37.

45. *Denver & Rio Grande RR v. Lorentzen*, 79 C.C.A. Colo. (1897), discussed in Welke, "Unreasonable Women," 387.

46. Thomas R. Dew, "Dissertation on the Characteristic Differences between the Sexes," 1835, in Aileen Kraditor, ed., *Up From the Pedestal: Landmark Writings in the American Woman's Struggle for Equality* (Chicago, 1968), 46–47.

47. Norma Basch, "Invisible Women: The Legal Fiction of Marital Unity in Nineteenth-Century America," *Feminist Studies* (Summer 1979): 360.

48. James Curry, in John Blassingame, ed., *Slave Testimony* (Baton Rouge, LA, 1977), 132–33.

49. Susan B. Anthony, "Homes of Single Women," October 1877, in Ellen Carol DuBois, ed., *The Elizabeth Cady Stanton–Susan B. Anthony Reader* (Boston, 1992), 148.

50. Virginia Merwin, "The Relation of Women to Work in the Southern States, read before the Association for the Advancement of Women at its Annual Congress . . . 1880" (Boston, 1881) [Pamphlets in American History, W055], 4.

51. Matthaei, *Economic History of Women in America*, 137.

52. Reva Siegel, "Home as Work: The First Woman's Rights Claims Concerning Wives' Household Labor, 1850–1880," *Yale Law Journal* 103 (March 1994): 1111.

53. "William Thompson and *Appeal of One Half the Human Race*," in Elizabeth K. Helsinger et al., eds., *The Woman Question: Society and Literature in Britain and America, 1837–1883*, Vol. 1, "Defining Voices" (Chicago, 1983), 27.

54. Christopher Tiedeman on the Limitations of Police Power, 1886, in Kermit Hall, ed., *Major Problems in American Constitutional History*, Vol. 2 (Lexington, MA, 1992), 85. Emphasis added.

55. Helen P. Jenkins, "Do Mothers Earn Their Own Support?" *New Northwest* (July 5, 1872), 2, quoted in Siegel, "Home as Work," 1157.

CHAPTER 7

1. "Act to amend the laws relating to elections," April 27, 1870, chap. 388, *Laws of New York* (1870), 922.

2. Richard Brown, *The Strength of a People: The Idea of an Informed Citizenry in America, 1650–1870* (Chapel Hill, NC, 1996), 183; Linda Kerber, "Separate Spheres, Female Worlds, Woman's Place: The Rhetoric of Women's History," *Journal of American History* (June 1988): 22.

3. *Dred Scott v. Sandford*, 60 U.S. 393 (1857), 422.

4. Preamble, American Equal Rights Association Constitution, approved May 10, 1866, New York City, in Elizabeth Cady Stanton et al., *History of Woman Suffrage*, Vol. 2 (New York, 1881; Ayer reprint, 1985), 173 (hereafter *HWS*).

5. Clarina Howard Nichols, Kansas constitutional convention, 1859, *HWS*, Vol. 1, 194.

6. "An Act in relation to the powers and jurisdictions of Surrogates' Courts," *Laws of New York*, Chap. 782 (1867), 1926; "An Act relating to powers of attorney by married women," *Laws of New York*, chap. 300 (1878), 390.

7. *Laws of New York*, 1864–1877, esp. "Act to incorporate the Working Women's Protective Union," chap. 585, 1868, 1205, and "Act to Incorporate the Working Women's National Association," chap. 250, 1869, 462.

8. Anna G. Spencer, "Women's Sphere in Social Culture" (1912), in Aileen Kraditor, ed., *Up From the Pedestal: Landmark Writings in the American Woman's Struggle for Equality* (Chicago, 1968), 102.

9. John M. Brumgardt, ed., *Civil War Nurse: The Diary and Letters of Hannah Ropes* (Knoxville, TN, 1980), 116–117. I am indebted to Tiffany Dziurman for conversations about civil war nursing.

10. Lauren Cook Burgess, ed., *An Uncommon Soldier: The Civil War Letters of Sarah Rosetta Wakerman, alias Private Lyons Wakerman, 153rd Regiment, New York State Volunteers, 1862–1864* (New York, 1994), 36.

11. Elizabeth D. Leonard, *Yankee Women: Gender Battles in the Civil War* (New York, 1994), 139.

12. Chicago *Tribune*, September 10, 1864. My thanks to David Collins for sharing this find.

13. Mary E. Shelton, quoted in Leonard, *Yankee Women*, 83–84.

14. Louisa County [VA] correspondent to the Richmond *Enquirer*, April 18, 1861, quoted in Elizabeth Varon, *We Mean To Be Counted: White Women and Politics in Antebellum Virginia* (Chapel Hill, NC, 1998), 163; Mary Livermore, *My Story of the War . . . .* (Hartford, CT, 1890), 144–46, 149.

15. Mary Livermore, *The Story of My Life. . . .* (Arno Press reprint ed., New York, 1974; orig. 1897), 485; for widows, see Amy E. Holmes, "Widows and the Civil War Pension System," in Maris A. Vinovskis, ed., *Toward a Social History of the American Civil War: Exploratory Essays* (New York, 1990), 174–76.

16. Livermore, *The Story of My Life,* 491–92.

17. Lucy Skipwith, letter from Hopewell, August 1863, in Ruth Moynihan, ed., *Second to None: A Documentary History of American Women*, Vol. 1 (Lincoln, NE, 1993), 399.

18. Susie King Taylor, *Reminiscences . . . ,* 1902, quoted in Catherine Clinton, *Tara Revisited: Women, War, and the Plantation Legend* (New York, 1995), 103–04; Harriet Tubman to [friends], June 30, 1862, *Commonwealth* (Boston), July 17, 1863.

19. Frances Harper, "Bury Me In A Free Land," in C. Peter Ripley et al., eds., *Witness for Freedom: African American Voices on Race, Slavery, and Emancipation* (Chapel Hill, NC, 1993), 102–03.

20. Freedman's Bureau agent, King Williams County, Virginia, 1866, quoted in Catherine Clinton, "Bloody Terrain: Freedwomen, Sexuality, and Violence during Reconstruction," in Clinton, *Half Sisters of History: Southern Women and the American Past* (Durham, NC, 1994), 141; Sojourner Truth, "When Woman Gets Her Rights, Man Will Be Right" [speech at the 1867 American Equal Rights Association convention], in Beverly Guy-Sheftall, ed., *Words of Fire: An Anthology of African-American Feminist Thought* (New York, 1995), 37, emphasis added.

21. Catherine Clinton, "Reconstructing Freedwomen," in Clinton and Nina Silber, eds., *Divided Houses: Gender and the Civil War* (New York, 1992), 318.

22. George Band quoted in Clinton, "Reconstructing Freedwomen," 317.

23. Ira Berlin et al., eds., *Freedom: A Documentary History of Emancipation, 1861–1867*, Ser. 2 (Cambridge, MA, 1982), 807–08. For a slightly different version and name (Rhoda), see Clinton, "Bloody Terrain," 147.

24. A. S. Hitchcock, "Young women particularly flock back and forth . . . ," August 25, 1864, and General Order No. 130, September 6, 1864, in Linda Kerber et al., eds., *Women's America*, 4th ed. (New York, 1995), 220.

25. Laura Edwards, " 'The Marriage Covenant is at the Foundation of all Our Rights': The Politics of Slave Marriages in North Carolina after Emancipation," *Law and History Review* 14 (Spring 1996): 85, 97.

26. "Bayou Boeuf " observer, quoted in Deborah Gray White, "Sex Roles and Status in the Antebellum Plantation South," in Clinton, *Half Sisters*, 59.

27. Dink Watkins, quoted in Edwards, "Marriage Covenant," 112; and Suzanne Lebsock, *The Free Women of Petersburg*, 23.

28. B. A. Bodkin, ed., *Lay My Burden Down: A Folk History of Slavery* (Chicago, 1945), 124; on group marriages, see Joel Williamson, *After Slavery: The Negro in South Carolina during*

Reconstruction (Chapel Hill, NC, 1965), 307; the Tennessee freedman in E. Franklin Frazier, *The Negro Family in the United States* (Chicago, 1939), 114; Bishop D. A. Payne, "To the National Convention of Colored Citizens of the United States, at Washington, Assembled," 1869, in Philip Foner and George Walker, eds., *Proceedings of the Black National and State Conventions, 1865–1900*, Vol. I (Philadelphia, 1986–), n.p.; Susan Dabney Smedes, *A Southern Planter* (Baltimore, 1887), 179. Tiffany Dziurman and Bonnie Speck generously brought some of this material to my attention.

29. Clinton, "Bloody Terrain," 145; for Chilton's case, see Barbara Welke, "When All the Women Were White, and All the Blacks Were Men: Gender, Race, and the Road to *Plessy*, 1855–1914," *Law and History Review* 13 (Fall 1995): 308; New Orleans *Picayune*, August 5, 1860.

30. Linda Speth, "The Married Women's Property Acts, 1839–1865," in D. Kelly Weisberg, ed., *Women and the Law: The Social Historical Perspective*, Vol. 2. (Cambridge, MA, 1982), 84.

31. "An act to enable husband and wife, or either of them, to be a witness for or against the other, or on behalf of any party . . . ," *Laws of New York*, chap. 887 (1867), 2221; "An act to legalize the adoption of minor children by adult persons," *Laws of New York*, chap. 830 (1873), 1243–44; "An act to provide redress for words imputing unchastity to a female," *Laws of New York*, chap. 219 (1871), 448.

32. "An act in relation to persons who abandon or threaten to abandon their families in the county of Kings," *Laws of New York*, chap. 395 (1971), 784.

33. Columbia University trustee, 1870, quoted in Joan Hoff, *Law, Gender and Injustice* (New York, 1991), 163; Kerber, "Separate Spheres," 28.

34. *HWS*, Vol. 2, 53, 892.

35. *HWS*, Vol. 1, 747.

36. *HWS*, Vol. 2, 882.

37. [Stanton], headnote, *HWS*, Vol. 1, 752; [Stanton], "Betrayal of New York Legislature," *HWS*, Vol. 1, 748.

38. Belle Boyd, *Belle Boyd in Camp and Prison*, eds. Drew Gilpin Faust and Sharon Kennedy-Nolle (reprint ed., Baton Rouge, LA, 1998; orig., 1865), 266.

39. Varon, *We Mean To Be Counted*, 174–175.

40. Helen Ekin Starrett [Kansas] commentary, 1867, *HWS*, Vol. 2, 255; Horace Greeley Report, New York Committee of the Whole, 1867, *HWS*, Vol. 2, 285; Elizabeth Cady Stanton, Response to Greeley Report, 1867, *HWS*, Vol. 2, 306–07; George William Curtis speech against the Greeley report, NY Convention, 1867, *HWS*, Vol. 2, 293.

41. Senator John Brooks Henderson, *Congressional Globe*, 39th Congr., 1st Sess., February 21, 1866, 952; Clara Barton letter, read at the Second Washington Conference, January 1870, Lincoln Hall, *HWS*, Vol. 2, 418.

42. Henry Brown Blackwell, "What the South Can Do" (1867), in Kraditor, *Up From the Pedestal*, 255.

43. *HWS*, Vol. 2, 93, 96, 101.

44. Senator George H. Williams speech against woman suffrage, *Congressional Globe*, December 11, 1866, 55–56.

45. J. R. Pole, *The Pursuit of Equality in American History*, 2nd ed. (New York, 1993), 388; *Congressional Record*, December 11, 1866.

46. Senator Buckalew and Doolittle, December 12, 1866, quoted in *HWS*, Vol. 2, 148, 151, emphasis added; *Congressional Record*, February 27, 1866.

47. Albany [New York] *Evening Journal*, January 24, 1867, in *HWS*, Vol. 2, 282; Lucy Stone to Elizabeth Cady Stanton, April 1867, *HWS*, Vol. 2, 235.

48. *Congressional Record*, Senate, 43rd Cong., 2nd Sess., January 11, 1875, 365.

49. *HWS*, Vol. 2, 101; Stanton, *HWS*, Vol. 2, 267–68. Emphasis added.

50. Constitution of the American Equal Rights Association, May 1866, New York, and Anniver-

sary Report, American Equal Rights Association Convention, Steinway Hall [New York], 1869, *HWS*, Vol. 2, 173, 378.

51. Quoted in Joan Hoff, *Law, Gender and Injustice: A Legal History of U.S. Women* (New York, 1991), 145; *Revolution*, 1869, in *HWS*, Vol. 2, 340.

52. Elizabeth Cady Stanton, headnote, *HWS*, Vol. 2, 320; Susan B. Anthony to Lydia Mott, 1862, *HWS*, Vol. 1, 748–49.

53. Elizabeth Cady Stanton, Woman's Suffrage Convention, Washington, D.C., January 1869, *HWS*, Vol. 2, 350; Matilda Joslyn Gage, NWSA Convention, 1873, *HWS*, Vol. 2, 528.

54. *Congressional Record*, May 23, 1866; Elizabeth Cady Stanton, Introduction, *HWS*, Vol. 1, 15.

55. Susan B. Anthony and Elizabeth Cady Stanton, Petition to Congress, 1865, *HWS*, Vol. 2, 91.

56. "Petitions and Memorials," *Congressional Record*, Senate, 44th Cong., 2nd Sess., January 30, 1877, 1095.

57. Frederick Douglass, *The New National Era*, September 21, 1871.

58. Elizabeth Cady Stanton, "Home Life," c. 1875, in Ellen Du Bois, ed., *The Elizabeth Cady Stanton–Susan B. Anthony Reader* (Boston, 1992), 132; Susan B. Anthony to Isabella Hooker, June 1871, quoted in Kathleen Barry, *Susan B. Anthony: A Biography of a Singular Feminist* (New York, 1988), 237.

59. Victoria Woodhull, House Judiciary Committee, January 11, 1871, *HWS*, Vol. 2, 445.

60. Speech of A. G. Riddle, House Judiciary Committee, January 11, 1871, *HWS*, Vol. 2, 457.

61. Quoted in Ellen Carol DuBois, *Woman Suffrage and Woman's Rights* (New York, 1998), 122.

62. 16 Statutes at Large 144 (1870).

63. *Revolution*, March 15, 1869.

64. New York *World*, November 21, 1866, reproduced in Elizabeth Frost and Kathryn Cullen-DuPont, eds., *Women's Suffrage in America: An Eyewitness History* (New York, 1992), 185.

65. Anna Julia Cooper, "The Status of Woman in America," in *A Voice From the South* (1892), excerpted in Beverly Guy-Sheftall, ed., *Words of Fire: An Anthology of African-American Feminist Thought* (New York, 1995), 45.

66. Stephen Foster, American Equal Rights Association Convention, 1866, *HWS*, Vol. 2, 175; George Francis Train, 1867, quoted in Ellen Carol DuBois, *Feminism and Suffrage: The Emergence of an Independent Women's Movement in America, 1848–1869* (Ithaca, NY, 1978), 94; Lucy Stone to Susan B. Anthony, May 9, 1867, in *HWS*, Vol. 2, 238.

67. Proceedings of 1874 NWSA convention, Washington, D.C., *HWS*, Vol. 2, 541–42.

68. Editorial, New York *Herald* (1852), in Kraditor, *Up From the Pedestal*, 190–191; Karen Sanchez-Eppler, *Touching Liberty: Abolition, Feminism, and the Politics of the Body* (Berkeley, CA, 1993), 18.

69. Mr. A. G. Riddle, Judiciary Committee of the House, January 11, 1871, *HWS*, Vol. 2, 457.

70. *Livestock Dealers and Butchers Association v. Crescent City Livestock Landing and Slaughterhouse Company*, 15 Fed. Cases 649 (1870), 650, 652–54.

71. *Sara Spencer v. Board of Registration* and *Sarah Webster v. Superintendents of Election*, 1 MacArthur 169 (8 DC S Ct.).

72. Francis Miller and Belva Lockwood speeches, 1873 meeting of NWSA, Washington, D.C., *HWS*, Vol. 2 (1881), 523.

73. *Slaughterhouse Cases*, 83 U.S. Reports 36 (1873): 71–72.

74. Louisa S. Ruffine, "Civil Rights and Suffrage: Myra Bradwell's Struggle for Equal Citizenship for Women," *Hasting's Women's Law Journal* (Summer 1993); Nancy T. Gilliam, "A Professional Pioneer: Myra Bradwell's Fight to Practice Law," *Law and History Review* (1987).

75. Barbara Babcock et al., eds., *Sex Discrimination and the Law* (Boston, 1975), 8.

76. *In Re Bradwell*, 55 Illinois 535 (1869), 535–36; *Bradwell v. The State*, 83 U.S. Reports 130 (1873), 140–42; emphasis added in Bradley opinion. For Matthew Carpenter's brief, see *HWS*, Vol. 2, 620.

77. Ibid.

78. Ibid.

79. Susan B. Anthony to Elizabeth Cady Stanton, November 5, 1872, quoted in Barry, *Susan B. Anthony*, 249–50.

80. Marlene Deahl Merrill, ed., *Growing Up in Boston's Gilded Age: The Diary of Alice Stone Blackwell, 1872–1874* (New Haven, CT, 1990), 216.

81. Susan B. Anthony, "Constitutional Argument," *HWS*, Vol. 2, 977–87; reprinted in Kraditor, *Up From the Pedestal*, 244–46.

82. Anthony, "Constitutional Argument" and trial proceedings, *HWS*, Vol. 2, 977–87; Resolutions of the NWSA meeting, January 1874, *HWS*, Vol. 2, 538n; Petition of Susan B. Anthony, *Congressional Record*, Senate, 43rd Cong., January 22, 1874, 830–31.

83. *Bradwell v. The State*, 83 U.S. 130 (1873), 133.

84. *Minor v. Happersett*, 88 U.S. 162 (1874), 163–78.

85. Ibid.

86. Ibid.

87. Ibid.

88. *Congressional Record*, House of Representatives, 1st Sess., March 31, 1876, 2121.

89. *Ex parte Yarbrough*, 110 U.S. 651 (1884); see also W. William Hodes, "Women and the Constitution: Some Legal History and a New Approach to the Nineteenth Amendment," *Rutgers Law Review* 25 (1970): 52, arguing that federal subjugation of women began with *Minor*.

90. "Removal of Woman's Legal Disabilities," House of Representatives, 44th Cong., 2nd Sess., 1877, 661.

91. *Lelia J. Robinson's Case*, 131 Mass. 376 (1881), 376–377, 379, 380–83.

92. Ibid.

93. *In the Matter of the Motion to admit Miss Lavinia Goodell to the Bar of this Court*, 39 Wisc. 232 (1875), 240–41, 244–46, emphasis added.

94. Diary of Louisa May Alcott, February 14, 1868, quoted in Lee Virginia Chambers-Schiller, *Liberty a Better Husband: Single Women in America—The Generations of 1780–1840* (New Haven, CT, 1984), xi.

95. Act to Punish and Prevent the Practice of Polygamy in the Territories of the United States . . . , July 1, 1862, Chap. 126, 12 Stat. at Large 501. I am immensely grateful to Sally Gordon for helping me to think through these paragraphs.

96. Sarah Barringer Gordon, " 'The Liberty of Self-Degradation': Polygamy, Woman Suffrage, and Consent in Nineteenth-Century America," *Journal of American History* (December 1996): 816, 823.

97. An Act to Amend Section 5352 of the Revised Statutes . . . in Reference to Bigamy, and for Other Purposes, Chap. 47, Sect. 8, 22 Stat. at Large 30 (1882), 31–32.

98. *Reynolds v. United States*, 98 U.S. 145 (1878): 145–68.

99. *Murphy v. Ramsey*, 114 U.S. 15 (1885): 45.

100. *Davis v. Beason*, 133 U.S. 333 (1889): 341–42.

101. T. W. Curtis, *The Mormon Problem* (1885), quoted in Carol Weisbrod and Pamela Sheingorn, "*Reynolds v. United States:* Nineteenth-Century Forms of Marriage and the Status of Women," *Connecticut Law Review* 10 (Summer 1978): 829.

102. Sarah Barringer Gordon, " 'Monogamy is Woman's Doctrine, as Polygamy is Man's': Anti-Polygamy and the Critique of Marriage in Nineteenth-Century America," 10, paper presented at Law and Society Association meeting, 1995.

103. Victoria Bynum, "Reshaping the Bonds of Womanhood: Divorce in Reconstruction North Carolina," in Catherine Clinton and Nina Silber, eds., *Divided Houses: Gender and the Civil War* (New York, 1992), 321, 324, 330–31, 333.

104. See Burton Historical Collection, Detroit [MI] Public Library, Papers of the Detroit House of Corrections.

105. "An Act to incorporate 'The Society for the Aid of Friendless Women and Children,' " *Laws of New York*, chap. 472 (1870), 1054; "An Act to incorporate 'The Ladies' Helping Hand As-

sociation of the City of New York,'" *Laws of New York*, chap. 668 (1870), 1532.

106. Michael Grossberg, *Governing the Hearth: Law and Family in Nineteenth-Century America* (Chapel Hill, NC, 1985), 172.

107. Leslie Reagan, *When Abortion Was a Crime: Women, Medicine, and Law in the United States, 1867–1973* (Berkeley, CA, 1997), 18; Janet Farrell Brodie, *Contraception and Abortion in Nineteenth-Century America* (Ithaca, NY, 1994), 255.

108. "An Act for the suppression of the trade in and circulation of obscene literature . . . ," *Laws of New York*, April 28, 1868, Chap. 430, 856; "An Act relating to the procurement of abortions and other like offenses," *Laws of New York*, May 6, 1869, Chap. 631, 1502; "An Act for the better prevention of the procurement of abortions and other like offenses," *Laws of New York*, April 6, 1872, Chap. 181, 509; An Act to Amend . . . 'An Act for the better prevention . . .'," *Laws of New York*, May 15, 1875, Chap. 352, 837; "An Act to amend chapter 181 of the laws . . . ," *Laws of New York*, May 13, 1880, Chap. 283, 419; "An Act to declare women eligible to serve as school trustees," *Laws of New York*, February 12, 1880, Chap. 9, 10.

109. Mary Hallock Foote, 1878, in Brodie, *Contraception and Abortion in 19th-Century America*, 206.

110. "Act for the Suppression of Trade in, and Circulation of, Obscene Literature and Articles of Immoral Use," 42nd Cong., 3rd Sess. Chap. 258, 17 Stat. at Large, 598–600.

111. [AMA Secretaries S. M. Bemiss and S. G. Hubbard, and President Henry Miller], "Memorial," c. 1860 (dated from internal evidence), Governors' Papers, Elisha Ferry Administration, Box 1K-1-1, "Abortion" folder, Washington State Archives, Olympia, WA.

112. Quoted in Reagan, *When Abortion Was A Crime*, 94.

113. Barbara Welke, "Unreasonable Women: Gender and the Law of Accidental Injury, 1870–1920," *Law and Social Inquiry* (Spring 1994): 380.

114. Livermore, *Story of My Life*, 481.

115. *HWS*, Vol. 2, 350.

116. A[mory] D[wight] Mayo, *The Woman's Movement in the South* (1891) [Pamphlets in American History, W031], 249.

117. Charles Burleigh, Equal Rights Association Meeting, New York, 1867, *HWS*, Vol. 2, 196.

118. Orestes A. Brownson, "The Woman Question" (1869, 1873), in Kraditor, *Up From the Pedestal*, 192–94.

119. Sherman-Dehlgren petition, NWSA convention proceedings, 1882, *HWS*, Vol. 2, 494–95.

120. *Woodhull and Claflin's Weekly*, September 10, 1870, quoted in Elizabeth Clark, "Matrimonial Bonds: Slavery and Divorce in Nineteenth-Century America," *Law and History Review* (Spring 1990): 35; Gerrit Smith to Susan B. Anthony, January 5, 1874, *HWS*, Vol. 2, 539.

121. AERA meeting, *HWS*, Vol. 2, 385; Stanton introduction, *HWS*, Vol. 1, 14 (written in 1881); Clarina Nichols, *HWS*, Vol. 2, 173.

122. [Stanton], headnote, *HWS*, Vol. 2, 319.

123. Frederick Douglass, "Resolution Adopted at First Annual Meeting, American Equal Rights Association, New York City, May 9–10, 1867," in Philip S. Foner, ed., *Frederick Douglass on Women's Rights* (New York, 1992), 83.

124. Declaration of Rights for Women, Independence Hall, Philadelphia, July 4, 1876, *HWS*, Vol. 3, 31.

125. Paulina Wright Davis opening speech, 20th anniversary convention, Apollo Hall, New York City, October 19–20, 1870, *HWS*, Vol. 2, 428–29.

126. *Code of Georgia Annotated*, Section 53–501, 1981; Husband as Head of Family, *Acts of Georgia*, 1855–56, 229.

127. Senator Doolittle, Senate discussion of Washington D.C. suffrage, December 12, 1866, *HWS*, Vol. 2, 151.

128. Hoff, *Law, Gender and Injustice*, 60; Susan B. Anthony, "Social Purity," 1875, in Kraditor, *Up from the Pedestal*, 164–65.

129. Speech [Mr. Bingham], Syracuse [NY] Convention, 1852, *HWS*, Vol. 1, 527.
130. Mariana Johnson, "The President's Address," June 2, 1852, in *HWS*, Vol. 1, 352; *Congressional Record*, 44th Congr., Senate, 2nd Sess., January 20, 1877, 762; Frederick Douglass, "The Woman's Cause," *Woman's Journal*, June 2, 1888.
131. *Dred Scott v. Sandford*, 60 U.S. 393 (1857), 417; Horace Greeley, New York *Tribune*, July 26, 1867.
132. Virginia Minor and Francis Minor, brief submitted in *Minor v. Happersett*, in *HWS*, Vol. 2, 732.

PART THREE, INTRODUCTION

1. Alice Duer Miller, "An Unauthorized Interview Between the Suffragists and the Statue of Liberty," from *Women Are People!* (1917) in Bettina Friedl, ed., *On To Victory: Propaganda Plays of the Woman Suffrage Movement* (Boston, 1987), 371.
2. Elizabeth Cady Stanton, "The Solitude of Self," 1892, in Ellen Carol DuBois, ed., *The Elizabeth Cady Stanton–Susan B. Anthony Reader*, rev. ed. (Boston, 1981), 247–48, 251–53.
3. Elizabeth Cady Stanton, "Kansas State Referendum Campaign Speech at Lawrence, Kansas, 1867," in Karlyn Kohrs Campbell, ed., *Man Cannot Speak for Her*, Vol 2, "Key Texts of the Early Feminists" (New York, 1989), 274.
4. Mary Church Terrell, "The Progress of Colored Women," 1898, in Beverly Guy-Sheftall, ed., *Words of Fire: An Anthology of African-American Feminist Thought* (New York, 1995), 64–65.
5. Jane Edna Hunter, quoted in Stephanie J. Shaw, "Black Club Women and the Creation of the National Association of Colored Women," in Darlene Clark Hine et al., eds., *"We Specialize in the Wholly Impossible": A Reader in Black Women's History* (Brooklyn, NY, 1995), 438.
6. Jane Addams, "A Modern Lear" (1894) and "A Function of the Social Settlement" (1899), in Christopher Lasch, ed., *The Social Thought of Jane Addams* (Indianapolis, IN, 1965), 116, 185.
7. The phrase derives from Robyn Muncy, *Creating a Female Dominion in American Reform, 1890–1935* (New York, 1991).
8. Noralee Frankel and Nancy Dye, eds., *Gender, Class, Race, and Reform in the Progressive Era* (Lexington, KY, 1991), 2–3.
9. Mark Sullivan, *Our Times: The United States, 1900–1925, Turn of the Century* (New York, 1926), 388–90.
10. Sara Hunter Graham, *Woman Suffrage and the New Democracy* (New Haven, CT, 1996), xviii.
11. For the useful term *left feminism,* see Ellen Carol DuBois, *Harriot Stanton Blatch and the Winning of Woman Suffrage* (New Haven, CT, 1997), 277. The term encompasses all feminists who recognize "the systematic oppression of women," appreciate "other structures of power underlying American society," and believe that the "realization of genuine equality for women, all women, requires a radical challenge of American society."
12. Morton G. White, *Social Thought in America: The Revolt Against Formalism* (New York, 1949).
13. Evelyn A. Kirkley, "'This Work Is God's Cause': Religion in the Southern Woman Suffrage Movement," *Church History* (December 1990): 521.
14. Woodrow Wilson, speech before the U.S. Senate, September 30, 1918, in Eleanor Flexner, *Century of Struggle: The Woman's Rights Movement in the United States*, rev. ed. (Cambridge, MA, 1975), 322.
15. For the phrase, see Justice Stone's footnote four in *U.S. v. Carolene Products*, 304 U.S. 144 (1938).
16. The phrase appears in Betty Friedan, *The Feminine Mystique* (New York, 1963), chap. 1, "The Problem that Has No Name" (later described as "a strange stirring, a sense of dissatisfaction" among middle-class married women).
17. Anna Quindlen, "And Now, Babe Feminism," *New York Times*, January 19, 1994, A-19.
18. For backlash, see Susan Faludi, *Backlash* (New York, 1991). See also "Wimmin Are from Mars, Women Are from Venus," *Economist*, June 31, 1997: 88–89.

CHAPTER 8

1. Declaration of Rights for Women, Independence Hall, Philadelphia, July 4, 1876, in Elizabeth Cady Stanton et al., *History of Woman Suffrage*, Vol. 3 (New York, 1881; Ayer reprint, 1885), 31 (hereafter *HWS*).

2. Madeleine Vinton Dahlgren, "Arguments before the Committee on Privileges and Election of the United States Senate . . . ," January 11 and 12, 1878, quoted in Sarah Barringer Gordon, " 'The Liberty of Self-Degradation': Polygamy, Woman Suffrage, and Consent in Nineteenth-Century America," *Journal of American History* (December 1996): 840.

3. Susan B. Anthony, "Women's Half-Century of Evolution," *North American Review* (December 1902): 808–09.

4. Alice Duer Miller, *Are Women People? A Book of Rhymes for Suffrage Times* (New York, 1915), Introduction.

5. "An Act to Establish a System of Common Schools in the State of Kentucky," February 16, 1838, *Acts of the General Assembly of Kentucky*, 1837–38, Sec. 36–38, 282; Theophilus Parsons, "The Essex Result, Newburyport, Massachusetts, 1778," in Charles S. Hyneman and Donald S. Lutz, eds., *American Political Writing during the Founding Era, 1760–1805* (Indianapolis, IN, 1983), 497.

6. Excerpt from Thorstein Veblen, *Theory of the Leisure Class* (1899), in Miriam Schneir, ed., *Feminism: The Essential Historical Writings* (New York, 1992), 223–224; Elizabeth Cady Stanton [headnote], *HWS*, Vol. 2, 314.

7. Elizabeth Barr, narrative of the Populist campaigns of 1890, quoted in Meridel Le Sueur, *North Star Country* (Lincoln, NE, 1984, orig. pub. 1945), 218–19.

8. Quoted in Joanna L. Grossberg, "Women's Jury Service: Right of Citizenship or Privilege of Difference?" *Stanford Law Review* 46 (May 1994): 1134, 106n.

9. Constitution of the State of Wyoming, 1889, Article No. VI, Sections 1 and 2.

10. Marjorie Spruill Wheeler, ed., *Votes for Women! The Woman Suffrage Movement in Tennessee, the South, and the Nation* (Knoxville, TN, 1995), 17–19.

11. Aileen Kraditor, *Ideas of the Woman Suffrage Movement, 1890–1920* (New York, 1981), 4–5.

12. Mary Johnston, "Address . . . ," December 1912, in Wheeler, *Votes for Women*, 160.

13. "An Act to Establish the Territorial Government of Washington," Ch. XC, March 2, 1853, in William Swindler, *Sources and Documents of the U.S. Constitutions*, Vol. 10 (Dobbs Ferry, NY, 1979), 231.

14. Mary Olney Brown, Account of Attempts to Vote in Washington Territory, *HWS*, Vol. 3, 780–81. The author is writing a book about Washington's electoral crisis (1879–1913).

15. Ibid., 786.

16. *Mary Phelps v. S. S. City of Panama*, 1 Wash. Terr. 518 (July 1877), 532–533.

17. "An Act Relating to and Defining the Property Rights of Husband and Wife," *Laws of Washington Territory*, 1879–80, 77–81.

18. "An Act to Establish and Protect the Rights of Married Women," *Laws of Washington Territory*, 1879–80, 151.

19. *Richard Holyoke v. D. B. Jackson*, 3 Wash. Terr. Rpts. 235 (July 1882), 238–39, 241.

20. "An Act to Amend Chapter CXIII of the Code of Washington, Entitled, 'To Declare Certain Persons Habitual Drunkards . . . ,' " "An Act to Amend Section 3050, Chapter 238 of the Code of Washington," "An Act to Amend Section 2080, of Chapter CLII of the Code of Washington Territory, Relating to Grand and Petit Jurors," *Laws of Washington Territory*, 1883–84, 32–33, 33–34, 39.

21. *Lovica Hamilton v. Leopold Hirsch and James Hayden*, 2 Wash. Terr. Rpts. 223 (July 1884), 227.

22. *Rosencrantz v. Territory of Washington*, 2 Wash. Terr. Rpts. 267 (July 1884), 271–72.

23. Ibid.

24. Ibid., 274–75.

25. Ibid., emphasis added.
26. *George Schilling v. Territory of Washington, Annie Walker v. Territory of Washington, Charles Hayes, et al. v. Territory of Washington,* 2 Wash. Terr. Rpts. 283, 286 (July 1884).
27. "An Act to Amend Sections 3079 and 3084 of Chapter 242 . . . Relating to Elections," *Laws of Washington Territory,* 1885–86 [February 3, 1886], 128–29; "An Act to amend Section 3050 of Chapter 238 of the Code of Washington Territory . . . ," *Laws of Washington Territory,* 1885–86, 113–114; "An Act Prescribing the Qualifications of Electors in the Territory of Washington," *Laws of Washington Territory,* 1887–88, chap. 51, 94.
30. *Harland v. Territory of Washington,* 3 Wash. Terr. Rpts. 131 (1887), 132–33, 136–52, Justice Langford concurring in a separate opinion; Greene's dissent at 162. For Maggie Farr, see *William M. White v. Territory of Washington,* 3 Wash. Terr. Rpts. 397 (Jan. 1888), 402.
31. *Nevada Bloomer v. John Todd, J. E. Gandy, and H. A. Clarke,* 3 Wash. Terr. Rpts. 599 (August 1888), 600, 602.
32. Ibid., 603–09.
33. Ibid., 612–23.
34. May Sylvester, "Some Reasons Why Women Should Not Be Deprived of the Ballot," *Washington Standard* [Olympia, WA], February 25, 1887.
35. Susan B. Anthony, "Washington," *HWS,* Vol. 4, 969. For constitutional amendment election returns, see 970.
36. G. Stanley Hall, 1894, quoted in Cynthia Eagle Russett, *Sexual Science: The Victorian Construction of Womanhood* (Cambridge, MA, 1989), 120.
37. John Bascom, "Woman Suffrage. Meeting of the Wisconsin Advocates of the Movement" (1887?) [Pamphlets in American History, W070], 3, 5.
38. Senator [John Tyler] Morgan, Debate in Congress, December 20, 1881, *HWS,* Vol. 3, 211.
39. [Henry Billings] Brown, "Woman Suffrage. A Paper read by Ex-Justice Brown of the Supreme Court of the United States before the Ladies' Congressional Club of Washington, D.C.," April 1910, later circulated as a pamphlet [Pamphlets in American History, W090], 3.
40. Ibid., 4.
41. Ibid., 4, 6–11, 14–15. Emphasis added.
42. Emily P. Bissell, *A Talk to Women on the Suffrage Question* (1909) [Pamphlets in American History, W083], 2–7.
43. Ibid.
44. Ibid.
45. May Collins, *A Plea for the New Woman* (New York, 1896), 4.
46. Jane Addams, "On Woman Suffrage," 1906 and 1915, in Aileen S. Kraditor, ed., *Up From the Pedestal: Landmark Writings in the American Woman's Struggle for Equality* (Chicago, 1968), 284.
47. Susan Wixon, *Woman: Four Centuries of Progress* (New York, 1896) [Pamphlets in American History, W03], 33–34.
48. "Addresses of the Advocates of Woman's Suffrage before the Constitutional Convention Committee, June 7, 1894," Albany, NY, 1894 [Pamphlets in American History, W068], 10, 25.
49. Mrs. O. H. P. Belmont and Elsa Maxwell (music and lyrics by Maxwell), *Melinda and Her Sisters,* 1916, in Bettina Friedl, ed., *On to Victory: Propaganda Plays of the Woman Suffrage Movement* (Boston, 1987), 360.
50. "Addresses of the Advocates of Woman's Suffrage . . . June 7, 1894," 25–26.
51. Elizabeth Boynton Harbert, quoted in Steven Buechler, "Elizabeth Boynton Harbert and the Woman Suffrage Movement," *Signs* (Autumn 1987): 84–94.
52. "Addresses of the Advocates of Woman's Suffrage . . . June 7, 1894," 28.
53. "Addresses of the Advocates of Woman's Suffrage . . . June 7, 1894," 28–29.
54. Brown, Account, *HWS,* Vol. 3, 782.
55. Miller, "Our Own Twelve Anti-Suffragist Reasons," in *Are Women People?* 43.

56. "Addresses of the Advocates of Woman's Suffrage . . . June 7, 1894," 5; Adella Hunt Logan, lyrics originally published in *Women's Journal* (1912 conference of National Medical Association, Tuskegee, AL), in Wheeler, *Votes for Women*, 92; NAWSA convention of 1893, Third Resolution, *HWS*, Vol. 4, 216n.
57. Carry A. Nation, *The Use and Need of the Life of Carry A. Nation,* (Topeka, KS, 1905), 209–210.
58. In Ellen C. DuBois, "Harriot Stanton Blatch and the Transformation of Class Relations among Woman Suffragists," in Noralee Frankel and Nancy Dye, eds., *Gender, Class, Race, and Reform in the Progressive Era* (Lexington, KY, 1991), 164, 169.
59. Kraditor, *Ideas of the Woman Suffrage Movement,* 44–46 and passim.
60. Henry A. Wise Wood, 1919, quoted in Wheeler, *Votes for Women*, 132.
61. "Addresses of the Advocates of Woman's Suffrage . . . June 7, 1894," 46; Frances Willard, "How to Win: A Book for Girls," 1888, in Kraditor, *Up From The Pedestal*, 317–18. Emphasis added in Mary Gannette speech.
62. Emma Goldman, in Wheeler, *Votes for Women*, 135–136.
63. Susan Wixon, *Woman: Four Centuries of Progress* (New York, 1893), 31.
64. Evelyn Brooks Higginbotham, "Clubwomen and Electoral Politics in the 1920's," in Ann D. Gordon et al., eds., *African American Women and the Vote, 1837–1965* (Amherst, MA, 1997), 143.
65. Michael Lewis Goldberg, *An Army of Women: Gender and Politics in Gilded Age Kansas* (Baltimore, 1997), 176–77.
66. Quoted in Wheeler, *Votes for Women*, 156.
67. Gertrude Foster Brown, "A Decisive Victory Won," in National Woman Suffrage Association, *Victory: How Woman Won It: 1840–1940* (New York, 1940), 110.
68. Broadside, "MEN OF THE SOUTH," in Wheeler, *Votes for Women*, 305.
69. Jane Addams, *Why Women Should Vote* (New York, 1912), reprinted from *Ladies Home Journal* [Pamphlets in American History, W071]. Emphasis added.
70. For the notorious "Russian" banner, see Doris Stevens, *Jailed for Freedom* (New York, 1920), 92.
71. Harriot Stanton Blatch, in Blatch and Alma Lutz, *Challenging Years: The Memoirs of Harriot Stanton Blatch* (New York, 1940), 280–81; for Shippen, see Wheeler, *Votes for Women*, 178.
72. Gilson Gardner, Washington correspondent for Scripps newspapers, Spring 1917, in Blatch and Lutz, *Challenging Years*, 279.
73. Woodrow Wilson to Carrie Chapman Catt, May 8, 1917, reprinted in Elizabeth Frost and Kathryn Cullen-Dupont, *Women's Suffrage in America: An Eyewitness History* (New York, 1992), 321; Kate Burch Warner speech, in Wheeler, *Votes for Women*, 195.
74. Inez Haynes Irwin, *Up Hill With Banners Flying: The Story of the Woman's Party* (New York, 1921), 302–06.
75. Mary Putnam-Jacobi, " 'Common Sense' Applied to Woman Suffrage . . . ," 1894, in Dawn Keetley and John Pettegrew, *Public Women, Public Words: A Documentary History of American Feminism*, Vol. 1 (Madison, WI, 1997), 270–71.
76. Minneapolis [MN] *Sunday Tribune*, May 3, 1914, 1, 11.
77. Estelle Freedman, "Separatism as Strategy: Female Institution Building and American Feminism, 1870–1930," *Feminist Studies* (Fall 1979): 524.
78. *Congressional Record*, 49th Cong., 2nd Sess., January 25, 1887, 986.
79. Mrs. James Bennett, "An Appeal for Woman Suffrage made by Mrs. James Bennett in the Legislative Hall, Frankfort, Kentucky, January, 1884" [Pamphlets in American History, W069], 3. Emphasis added.
80. Virginia broadside [1910s], in Wheeler, *Votes for Women*, 283.
81. Rosalie Jonas, "Brother Baptis' on Woman Suffrage," *Crisis*, September 1912, 247.

82. Belle Kearney, "The South and Woman Suffrage," *Woman's Journal*, April 4, 1903.
83. Marjorie Spruill Wheeler, "The Woman Suffrage Movement in the Inhospitable South," in Wheeler, ed., *Votes for Women*, 39.
84. [North Carolina] Chief Justice Walter Clark, "Ballots for Both," Equal Suffrage League of Greenville, NC, December 9, 1916 [Pamphlets in American History, WO48], 1.
85. Tennessee broadside reprinted in Wheeler, *Votes for Women*, 113.
86. Anne Dallas Dudley address, "Dixie Night" session of NAWSA convention, Atlantic City, September 8, 1916, in Wheeler, ed., *Votes for Women*, 163–65.
87. Harry Burn speech before the Tennessee legislature, in Wheeler, *Votes for Women*, 266.
88. Linda Kerber, "Separate Spheres, Female Worlds, Woman's Place: The Rhetoric of Women's History," *Journal of American History* 75 (June 1988): 24.
89. Carrie Chapman Catt, President's Address, NAWSA convention, Washington D.C., 1902, in Kraditor, *Up From the Pedestal*, 210–11; Mary Johnston, "Address . . . ," Richmond, VA, December 1912, reprinted in Wheeler, *Votes for Women*, 161; Hon. John M. Baer, *Woman Suffrage: Remarks of Hon. John M. Baer*, Washington, D.C. (1918) [Pamphlets in American History, W080], 4–5; Chief Justice Walter Clark, *Ballots for Both* (Greenville NC, 1916) [Pamphlets in American History WO48], 8.
90. *Fairchild v. Hughes* and *Leser v. Garnett*, 258 U.S. 127, 130 (1922), 129.
91. Abraham L. Kellogg [Speech], *Revised Record of the Constitutional Convention of the State of New York* (Albany 1900), Vol. 2, 433–36.
92. *People v. Barnett*, 319 Illinois Reports 403 (1926), 407–08, 410.
93. *Commonwealth v. Welosky*, 276 Mass. Reports 398 (1931), 401–402, 407, 414–15.
94. My thanks to Richard Hamm for reminding me of NWP's activity, about which he is writing a book.
95. Matilda Fenberg, *Women Jurors and Jury Service in Illinois* (Chicago, 1940), 5–6 [Pamphlets in American History, W062].
96. Walla Walla County and Columbia County District Court Journals, 1910–1913, Eastern Branch, Washington State Archive, Cheney, Washington.
97. Senator David Trask, quoted in Judith Dean Gething Hughes, *Women and Children First: The Life and Times of Elsie Wilcox of Kaua'i* (Honolulu, 1996), 134.
98. *State v. John Emery, et al.*, 224 NC Rpts. 581 (1944), 587.
99. *Ballard v. United States*, 329 U.S. 187 (1946), 194.
100. Joseph Tussman and Jacob TenBroek, "The Equal Protection of the Laws," *California Law Review* (1949): 342–46.
101. *Hoyt v. Florida*, 368 U.S. 57 (1961), 58–59, 62; *Fay v. New York*, 332 U.S. 261 (1947). Briefs quoted in Linda Kerber, *"No Constitutional Right to Be Ladies": Women and the Obligations of Citizenship* (New York, 1998), 173–75.
102. Ibid.
103. Ruth Bader Ginsburg, "Remarks on Women Becoming Part of the Constitution," *Law and Inequality* (May 1988): 20.
104. *State v. Hall*, 187 So. 2d (Miss.) 861; *Leighton v. Goodman*, 311 F. Supp. 1181 (SDNY 1970), 1183.
105. *Maria DeKosenko v. Arthur Brandt et al.*, 313 New York Supplement, 2d Series 827 (July 1970), 830.
106. For details, see Nancy Cott, "Marriage and Women's Citizenship in the United States, 1830–1934," *American Historical Review* (December 1998): 1440–74, esp. 1461–62.
107. "Act Relative to the Naturalization and Citizenship of Married Women," 42 Stat. at Large 1021, Chap. 411, 1022; *Mackenzie v. Hare et al., Board of Election of San Francisco*, 239 U.S. 299 (1915), 311–12. For Mackenzie's words, see Kerber, *"No Constitutional Rights to Be Ladies,"* 42.
108. J. Stanley Lemons, *The Woman Citizen: Social Feminism in the 1920's* (Urbana, IL, 1973), 66.

109. Debate in Congress between Lawrence of Ohio and Wood of New York, December 16, 1869, *HWS*, Vol. 2, 326.
110. Advisory Opinion, 119 Maine 603 (1921), 608.
111. *United States v. Hinson*, 3 Fed. Cases 2d 200 (1925).
112. *Breedlove v. Suttles*, 302 U.S. 277 (1937), 282.
113. *In Re Wickes' Estate* in Kevin C. Paul, "Private/Property: A Discourse on Gender Inequality in American Law," *Law and Inequality* (July 1989): 409.
114. *Wilkerson v. Lee*, 236 Alabama 104 (1938), 107.
115. Name-change cases, statutes, and quotation in Kevin Paul, "Private/Property," 406–08, 410.
116. Carrie Chapman Catt speech (1920), quoted in Eleanor Flexner, *Century of Struggle*, rev. ed. (Cambridge, MA, 1975), 340–41.
117. Emily Newell Blair, "Discouraged Feminists," 1931, in Kraditor, *Up From the Pedestal*, 342–43; Eleanor Roosevelt, "Women in Politics," *Good Housekeeping*, April 1940, 45.
118. Ann Gordon, in Wheeler, *Votes for Women*, 4.
119. Jessie Ashley, "Relation of Suffragism to Working-Class Women," 1911, in Kraditor, *Up From the Pedestal*, 280.
120. Adella Hunt Logan, *Crisis*, September 1912; W. E. B. DuBois, *Crisis*, July 1912.
121. Doxology quoted in Sara Hunter Graham, *Woman Suffrage and the New Democracy* (New Haven, CT, 1996), 145.
122. Dorothy Height, quoted in Charlayne Hunter, "Many Blacks Wary of 'Women's Liberation' Movement," *New York Times*, November 17, 1970, 15.

CHAPTER 9

1. Quoted in Henry Mussey, ed., "The Economic Position of Women," *Proceedings of the Academy of Political Science in the City of New York* (October 1910), 10.
2. Josephine C. Goldmark, *Impatient Crusader: Florence Kelley's Life Story* (Champaign-Urbana, IL, 1953), 16.
3. Florence Kelley, *Autobiography of Florence Kelley,* ed. Kathryn Kish Sklar (Chicago, 1986), 78.
4. Jane Addams, *My Friend, Julia Lathrop* (New York, 1935), 116.
5. Florence Kelley, "The Need of Theoretical Preparation for Philanthropic Work," reprint in Kelley, *Autobiography . . .* , 95.
6. Kelley, *Autobiography*, 92–93, 95–97, 100–01, 104.
7. Frances Perkins, "My Recollections of Florence Kelley," *Social Service Review* (March 1954), 18.
8. Louise Wade, "Florence Kelley," *Notable American Women*, Vol. 2 (Cambridge, MA, 1971), 318; Joan Zimmerman, "The Jurisprudence of Equality: The Women's Minimum Wage, the First Equal Rights Amendment, and *Adkins v. Children's Hospital*, 1905–1923," *Journal of American History* (June 1991): 195–98.
9. Ibid.
10. Ibid.
11. Florence Kelley, "Married Women in Industry," in Mussey, *Proceedings of the Academy of Political Science*, 90–91, 93–94.
12. Vivien Hart, *Bound By Our Constitution: Women, Workers, and the Minimum Wage* (Princeton, NJ, 1994), 98.
13. Minow and Boris quoted in Noralee Frankel and Nancy Dye, eds., *Gender, Class, Race, and Reform in the Progressive Era* (Lexington, KY, 1991), 82.
14. For the phrase, see, for example, Theda Skocpol, *Protecting Soldiers and Mothers: The Political Origins of Social Policy in the United States* (Cambridge, MA, 1992), 311.

15. *Congressional Record*, July 3, 1926, 12, 919; Perkins, "My Recollections of Florence Kelley," 18.
16. Florence Kelley, *Twenty Questions About the Federal Amendment Proposed by the National Woman's Party* (New York, 1922), 6–7.
17. Kelley in Zimmerman, "Jurisprudence of Equality," 202, 225.
18. Alice Hamilton and Doris Stevens, "The Blanket Amendment—A Debate," *Forum* (August 1924), excerpted in Woloch, *Muller v. Oregon: A Brief History with Documents* (New York 1996), 178–180, 182–185.
19. Ibid.
20. Gail Laughlin, Hearing before the Select Committee on Woman Suffrage . . . February 18, 1902, on the joint resolution (S. R. 53) proposing an amendment to the Constitution of the United States, extending the right of suffrage to women, National American Woman Suffrage Association Collection, 1848–1921, DLC (http://www.lcweb2.loc.gov).
21. Adeline Harrington, compiler, *Abstract of Colorado State Laws Affecting the Rights and Property of Women* (Denver, CO, 190?), 3–6, 8–15 [Pamphlets in American History, W066].
22. Doris Stevens, "A Debate in the Forum," 1924, in Woloch, *Muller v. Oregon*, 179.
23. Florence Kelley, quoted in Nancy F. Cott, *The Grounding of Modern Feminism* (New Haven, CT, 1987), 138.
24. Carina C. Warrington, comp., *What Has Been Done in Conformity with the Program of the National League of Women Voters to Remove Legal Discriminations against Women . . .* (1923), 27–28. The 1921 Wisconsin statute is reprinted at 28 [Pamphlets in American History, W061].
25. Martha Minow and Eileen Boris compared in Noralee Frankel and Nancy S. Dye, eds., *Gender, Class, Race, and Reform in the Progressive Era* (Lexington, KY, 1991), 82.
26. Ernst Freund, "The Constitutional Aspect of the Protection of Women in Industry," *Proceedings of the Academy of Political Science in the City of New York* (New York, 1910), 169.
27. Hester Johnson, "On to Victory: A Comedy in Two Acts," in Bèttina Friedl, ed., *On to Victory: Propaganda Plays of the Woman Suffrage Movement* (Boston, 1987), 310.
28. Ulla Wikander, "Some 'Kept the Flag of Feminist Demands Waving': Debates at International Congresses on Protecting Women Workers," in Wikander et al., eds., *Protecting Women: Labor Legislation in Europe, the United States, and Australia, 1880–1920* (Urbana, IL, 1995), 54–56.
29. Edward M. Steel, ed., *The Speeches and Writings of Mother Jones* (Pittsburg, PA, 1988), 95, 197. For excerpts from Emma Goldman, *Marriage and Love*, 1910, and Charlotte Perkins Gilman, *Women and Economics*, 1898, see Miriam Schneir, ed., *Feminism: The Essential Historical Writings* (New York, 1992), 241, 322.
30. Peggy Pascoe, "Gender Systems in Conflict: The Marriages of Mission-Educated Chinese American Women, 1874–1939," in Ellen DuBois and Vicki Ruiz, eds., *Unequal Sisters: A Multi-Cultural Reader in U.S. Women's History* (New York, 1990), 135.
31. Mamie Garvin Fields, "Listening to Mary Church Terrell," [1920s], in DuBois and Ruiz, *Unequal Sisters*, 170.
32. *In Re Jacobs*, 98 New York 98 (1885), 113.
33. For affirmance of a conviction under the act, see *People of the State of New York v. Balofsky*, 167 App. Div. 913 (2d Dept. 1915), appeal dismissed, 216 N.Y. 666 (1915).
34. Mary Kingsbury Simkhovitch, New York constitutional amendment hearings, 1915, quoted in Eileen Boris, "Reconstructing the 'Family': Women, Progressive Reform, and the Problem of Social Control," in Frankel and Dye, *Gender, Class, Race and Reform in the Progressive Era*, 75; Simkhovitch, "A New Social Adjustment," in Mussey, *Proceedings*, 88–89.
35. Strasser quoted in Candice Dalrymple, *Sexual Distinctions in the Law: Early Maximum Hour Decisions of the United States Supreme Court, 1905–1917* (New York, 1987), 31.
36. Samuel Gompers, quoted in Kermit Hall, ed., *Major Problems in American Constitutional History*, Vol. 2 (Lexington, MA, 1992), 100–01.

37. Alice Kessler Harris in Frankel and Dye, *Gender, Class, Race and Reform in the Progressive Era*, 95.

38. Alice Henry, "Women in the Trade-Union Movement in the United States," in Mussey, *Proceedings*, 128; Mollie Ray Carroll, *Women and the Labor Movement in America* (Washington, D.C., 1923) [Pamphlets in American History, W058], 11–13.

39. Helen Sumner, "The Historical Development of Women's Work in the United States," in Mussey, *Proceedings*, 25; and Sumner, "Senate Report . . . ," excerpted in Schneir, *Feminism*, 255–256.

40. *State of Washington v. Somerville*, 67 Wash. Rpts. 638 (1912), 644–45.

41. *Ritchie v. People*, 155 Illinois 98 (1895), 102, 107–109, 111–12.

42. *Holden v. Hardy*, 169 U.S. 366 (1898); Utah Smelter Acts, 1896, reprinted in Kermit Hall et al., eds., *American Legal History: Cases and Materials* (New York, 1991), 358.

43. *Bosley v. McLaughlin, Labor Commissioner of the State of California*, and *Same v. Same*, 236 U.S. 385 (1914), 389.

44. *People v. Williams*, 189 New York 131 (1907), 135–36; Melvin Urofsky, "The Courts and the Limits of Liberty to Contract," reprinted in Hall, *Major Problems in American Constitutional History*, Vol. 2, 140.

45. *Lochner v. New York*, 198 U.S. 4 (1905), 61–62.

46. Ibid., 70, 75–76.

47. Ibid.

48. Louis Brandeis and Josephine Goldmark, *Women in Industry* (Arno reprint, New York, 1969), 19, 38, 41, 49–50.

49. *Muller v. Oregon*, 208 U.S. 412 (1908), 420–22.

50. William Chafe, *The American Woman: Her Changing Social, Economic, and Political Roles, 1920–1970* (New York, 1972), 80.

51. Florence Kelley, *Women in Industry: The Eight Hours Day and Rest at Night . . .* (Women in Industry, Series No. 13, May 1916) [Pamphlets in American History, W045].

52. Felix Frankfurter, quoted in Kathryn Kish Sklar, "Why Were Most Women Opposed to ERA in the 1920's?" in Joan Hoff-Wilson, ed., *Rights of Passage: The Past and Future of the ERA* (Bloomington, IN, 1986), 27.

53. *Bunting v. Oregon*, 243 U.S. 426 (1917), 437–38; Felix Frankfurter, "Hours of Labor and Realism in Constitutional Law," *Harvard Law Review*, Vol. 29 (1916): 367.

54. *Quong Wing v. Kirkendall*, 223 U.S. 59 (1912), 63.

55. Susan Becker, *The Origins of the Equal Rights Amendment* (Westport, CT, 1981), 15; Ida Tarbell, quoted and discussed by Charlotte Perkins Gilman, 1912, in Kraditor, *Up From the Pedestal*, 326.

56. Kelley and ERA drafts in Zimmerman, "Jurisprudence of Equality," 211, 213, 215, 217, 223; Alice Paul, quoted in Becker, *Origins of ERA*, 19; 1923 *New York Times* article in Hoff-Wilson, *Rights of Passage*, 33.

57. Ibid.

58. "A Debate in Life and Labor: Marguerite Mooers Marshall versus Rose Schneiderman, 1920," in Nancy Woloch, *Muller v. Oregon,* 166–70.

59. *Adkins v. Children's Hospital* (decided with *Adkins v. Lyons*), 261 U.S. 525 (1923), 532–35, 538, 542. See also Brief for Appellees, *Adkins v. Children's Hospital* and *Adkins v. Lyons*, in Philip B. Kurland et al., eds., *Landmark Briefs and Arguments of the Supreme Court of the United States: Constitutional Law*, Vol. 21 (Arlington, VA, 1975), 6–13.

60. Ibid.

61. *Adkins v. Children's Hospital*, 261 U.S. 525 (1923), 540–42, 553, 555, 558.

62. Ibid.

63. Anti-*Adkins* cartoon reproduced in "Looking Back on *Muller v. Oregon*," *American Bar Association Journal* (April 1983): 472.

64. *Adkins v. Children's Hospital*, 261 U.S. 525 (1923), 567, 569–70.
65. Emily Newell Blair, "Discouraged Feminists," 1931, in Aileen Kraditor, ed., *Up From the Pedestal: Landmark Writings in the American Woman's Struggle for Equality* Chicago, 1968), 340.
66. Cathryn H. House [Miami, Ohio] and Lois Lundell Higgins, quoted in "The Changing Role of Women in Law Enforcement," *The Police Chief* (October 1993): 139, 141.
67. "Admission of Women to the Bar," *Chicago Law Times* (1885): 83.
68. Clara Shortridge Foltz story in Mortimer D. Schwartz et al., "Clara Shortridge Foltz: Pioneer in the Law," in D. Kelly Weisberg, ed., *Women and the Law: The Social Historical Perspective*, Vol. 2 (Cambridge, MA, 1982); Ruth Bader Ginsburg, "Speech: American University Commencement Address, May 10, 1981," *American University Law Review* (Summer 1981): 893 (quoting *Nation* magazine).
69. Joan Wallach Scott, "The Woman Worker," in Genevieve Fraisse and Michelle Perrot, eds., *A History of Women in the West: Emerging Feminism from Revolution to World War* (Cambridge, MA, 1993), 416–17.
70. *Radice v. New York*, 264 U.S. 292 (1923), 294.
71. *Muller v. Oregon*, 208 U.S. 412 (1908), 423; *Adkins v. Children's Hospital*, 261 U.S. 525 (1923), 553.
72. *Wenham v. State*, 65 Nebraska 394 (1902), 405. The U.S. Supreme Court cited *Wenham* in both *Muller* and *Ritchie*; Roscoe Pound, who sat on the Nebraska bench in 1902, concurred.
73. *West Coast Hotel Company v. Parrish*, 300 U.S. 379 (1937), 391, 397–99, 411–12.
74. Eleanor Roosevelt, quoted in Eileen Boris, "The Quest for Labor Standards in the Era of Eleanor Roosevelt: The Case of Industrial Homework," *Wisconsin Women's Law Journal* (Spring 1986): 58–59.
75. Alan Brinkley, *The End of Reform: New Deal Liberalism in Recession and War* (New York, 1995).
76. *Morehead v. New York ex rel Tipaldo*, 298 U.S. 587 (1936), 616.
77. *U.S. v. Darby*, 312 U.S. 100 (1941), 125.
78. See Nancy Cott, *Grounding of Modern Feminism*, 274–75.
79. Helen Elizabeth Brown, *Unequal Justice Under Law: Women and the Constitution* (Washington, D.C. 1942), 3. Published by the National Woman's Party.
80. Ibid.
81. *Goesaert v. Cleary*, 335 U.S. 464 (1948), 465–68.
82. Edith Valet Cook, *The Married Woman and Her Job* (Washington, D.C., 1936), 23–25.
83. "Genevieve the Riveter," in Ruth Barnes Moynihan et al., eds., *Second to None: A Documentary History of American Women*, Vol. 2 (Lincoln, NE, 1993), 211.
84. Ruth Milkman, *Gender At Work: The Dynamics of Job Segregation by Sex During World War II* (Urbana, IL, 1987), 137–39.
85. Report of the Committee on Industrial Home Work, from Proceedings of 1936 Conference on Labor Legislation, and Eleanor Roosevelt, quoted in Eileen Boris, "The Quest for Labor Standards," 53, 68–69.
86. Ferdinand Lundberg and M. F. Farnham, *Modern Woman: The Lost Sex* (New York, 1947), 236.
87. Alice Kessler-Harris, *Out To Work: A History of Wage-Earning Women in the United States* (New York, 1982); Evelyn Nakano Glenn, "The Dialectics of Wage Work: Japanese American Women and Domestic Service, 1905–1940," in DuBois and Ruiz, eds., *Unequal Sisters*, 345–72; Evelyn Nakano Glenn, "Cleaning Up/Kept Down . . . ," *Stanford Law Review* (1991): 1340.
88. Phyllis Palmer, "Housewife and Household Worker: Employer-Employee Relationships in the Home, 1928–1941," and Dolethia Otis, September 1982, interview in Elizabeth Clark-Lewis, "'This Work Had an End': African-American Domestic Workers in Washington, D.C., 1910–1940," both in Carol Groneman and Mary Beth Norton, eds., *"To Toil the Livelong Day":*

America's Women at Work, 1780–1980 (Ithaca, NY, 1987), 179. See also Serena Elizabeth Ashford to Franklin Roosevelt, March 9, 1934, reprinted in Rosalyn Baxandall et al., eds., *America's Working Women* (New York, 1976), 248. For clerical figures, see Linda Gordon, *Woman's Body, Woman's Rights*, rev. ed. (New York, 1990), 200.

89. Caterpillar Tractor Company brochure, *At Last We Wives Can Have Vacations*, 1936, quoted in Corlann Gee Bush, "'He Isn't Half So Cranky As He Used To Be': Agricultural Mechanization . . . ," in Groneman and Norton, *"To Toil the Livelong Day,"* 213.

90. Anna Garlin Spencer, "Women's Share in Social Culture" (1912), in Aileen Kraditor, ed., *Up From the Pedestal: Landmark Writings in the American Woman's Struggle for Equality* (Chicago, 1968), 98, 100.

91. "How To Keep a Good Figure," Detroit *News*, September 9, 1923. My thanks to Nick Ligorakis for sharing this article.

92. "Uncomplaining Labor," *Washington Standard* [Olympia, WA], May 28, 1886.

93. Edith M. Stern, "Women are Household Slaves," *American Mercury* (January 1949), 71–76.

CHAPTER 10

1. *John H. De May and Alfred B. Scattergood v. Alvira Roberts*, 46 Mich. Reports 160 (1881), 160–166. Conversations with Edward Wise greatly enriched the *De May* discussion.

2. Ibid.

3. Ibid.

4. Beverly Blair Cook, "The Burger Court and Women's Rights, 1971–1977," in Winifred Hepperle et al., eds., *Women in the Courts* (Williamsburg, VA, 1978), 52.

5. *State of Kansas v. Josie Dunkerton*, 103 Kansas Reports 748 (1918), 749.

6. *In Re Josie Dunkerton*, 104 Kansas Reports 481 (1919), 481–84.

7. *State of Kansas v. Mrs. L. O. Heitman*, 105 Kansas Reports 139 (1919), 140–41.

8. *State v. Heitman*, 105 Kansas Reports 139 (1919), 141–43.

9. Susan Hammon Barney, quoted in Estelle Friedman, "Nineteenth-Century Women's Prison Reform and its Legacy," in D. Kelly Weisberg, ed., *Women and the Law: The Social Historical Perspective*, Vol. 2 (Cambridge, MA, 1982). I am grateful for exchanges with Yvonne Pitts about Emma Hall and the Detroit House of Shelter.

10. Jesse Hodder, "The Treatment of Delinquent Women," American Prison Association, *Proceedings* (1922): 16.

11. Jacob Riis, *How the Other Half Lives*, ed. David Leviatin (repr. Boston, 1996; orig., 1890), 214.

12. David Langum, *Crossing Over the Line: Legislative Morality and the Mann Act* (Chicago, 1994), 27–28, 244–45.

13. Frances Willard, "A White Life for Two, 1890," in Karlyn Kohrs Campbell, ed., *Man Cannot Speak for Her*, Vol 2, "Key Texts of the Early Feminists" (New York, 1989), 328, 330.

14. William Blackstone, *Commentaries on the Law of England*, Vol. 4, ed. Thomas Green (Chicago 1979, facsimile ed.), 210.

15. Susan Estrich, "Rape," *Yale Law Journal* (May 1986): 1092–93.

16. Ralph Slovenko, "A Panoramic Overview: Sexual Behavior and the Law," in Slovenko, ed., *Sexual Behavior and the Law* (Springfield, IL, 1965), 51.

17. Quoted in Elizabeth Schneider and Susan Jordan, "Representation of Women Who Defend Themselves in Response to Physical or Sexual Assault," *Women's Rights Law Reporter* (Spring 1978): 150, 154.

18. Susan Brownmiller, *Against Our Will: Men, Women and Rape* (New York, 1975), 364.

19. "Rape Views Spur Drive to Recall Wisconsin Judge," *Washington Post*, June 11, 1977, A-4.

20. *In re Freche*, 109 Federal Reporter (1901), 620–21. The case involved a New Jersey bankrupt's attempt to avoid paying damages to a man named Charles Combs.

21. Anne M. Coughlin, "Sex and Self-Government," *McGeorge Law Review* (Fall 1997): 26. On "to the uttermost" (or "utmost"), see Rollin M. Perkins and Ronald N. Boyce, *Criminal Law*, 3rd ed. (Mineola, NY), 210. I am grateful to Edward Wise for conversations on these points.

22. Sir Matthew Hale, *History of the Pleas of the Crown* (Philadelphia, 1847, orig. pub. London, c. 1680), 628.

23. *Tinker v. Caldwell*, 193 U.S. 472 (1903), 481.

24. Kathleen Norris quotation and Sullivan commentary, in Mark Sullivan, *Our Times: The United States, 1900–1925* (New York, 1928), 388–90.

25. Linda Gordon, *Woman's Body, Woman's Right: Birth Control in America*, rev. ed. (New York, 1990), 62.

26. Quoted in Leslie Reagan, *When Abortion Was a Crime: Women, Medicine, and Law in the United States, 1867–1973* (Berkeley, CA, 1997), 26, 28, 32.

27. Gordon, *Woman's Body, Woman's Rights*, 183–84, 190. Says Gordon, "Freud was inclined to view repression as the inevitable cost of human progress . . . ," but "American sex radicals transformed Freud's ideas into support for a campaign against sexual repression"; at 194.

28. Edward Carpenter, quoted in Gordon, *Woman's Body, Woman's Right*, 184.

29. Gordon, *Woman's Body, Woman's Right*, 189; and quoting Robert Lynd et al., *Middletown*, on p. 198.

30. New York statute and *People v. Sanger* excerpted in Kermit Hall et al., eds., *American Legal History: Cases and Materials* (New York, 1991), 283–84.

31. Crystal Eastman, "Now We Can Begin, 1920," in Karlyn Kohrs Campbell, ed., *Man Cannot Speak for Her*, Vol 2, "Key Texts of the Early Feminists" (New York, 1989), 538–39.

32. Gordon, *Woman's Body, Woman's Right*, 203–04.

33. Placard photograph in Constance M. Chen, *"The Sex Side of Life": Mary Ware Dennett's Pioneering Battle for Birth Control and Sex Education* (New York, 1996), 263.

34. Margaret Sanger, *Margaret Sanger, An Autobiography* (New York, 1971; orig. 1938), 98.

35. Sanger, in Gordon, *Woman's Body, Woman's Right*, 310.

36. Ibid., 265.

37. Reagan, *When Abortion Was a Crime*, 134.

38. Elaine Tyler May, *Homeward Bound: American Families in the Cold War Era* (New York, 1988), 207.

39. Quoted in Rickie Solinger, *Wake Up Little Susie: Single Pregnancy and Race before Roe v. Wade* (New York, 1992), 23.

40. Solinger, *Wake Up Little Susie*, 22, 122.

41. Medical director of the British Control Federation of America, 1941, quoted in Gordon, *Woman's Body, Woman's Right*, 340.

42. Reagan, *When Abortion Was a Crime*, 190–91.

43. Ibid., 213–14.

44. Solinger, *Wake Up Little Susie*, 27.

45. Ibid., 207–09.

46. Ibid., 216–17, 225. See also Population Policy Panel of the Hugh Moore Fund, *The Population Bomb* (New York, 1965), 3. Four years later, Paul Ehrlich's *The Population Bomb* (San Francisco, 1969) had the same title.

47. Joseph Story, *Commentaries on the Constitution of the United States*, Vol. 2, quoted in Alan F. Westin, *Privacy and Freedom* (New York, 1968), 331.

48. *Newell v. Whitcher*, 53 Vermont Rpts. 589 (1880), 591.

49. Thomas M. Cooley, *A Treatise on the Law of Torts*, 1st ed. (Chicago, 1879), 29 (in Chap. 2, "Classification of Legal Rights").

50. *Poe v. Ullman*, 367 U.S. 497 (1961), 539–51.

51. Quoted in Judith A. Baer, *Women in American Law: The Struggle toward Equality from the New Deal to the Present*, 2nd ed. (New York, 1996), 57.

52. *Olmstead v. United States*, 277 U.S. 438 (1928), 479.

53. *Griswold v. Connecticut*, 381 U.S. 479 (1965), 480.

54. Ibid., 482, 484–86.

55. Robert H. Bork, "Neutral Principles and Some First Amendment Problems," *Indiana Law Journal* (1971): 1, 8–9.

56. Louis Brandeis dissent, *Olmstead v. United States*, 277 U.S. 438 (1928), 474–75.

57. *Griswold v. Connecticut*, 381 U.S. 479 (1965), 486.

CHAPTER 11

1. In the 1980s, the largest employer of women was the federal government.

2. *Equal Employment Opportunity Commission v. Sears, Roebuck & Company*, 504 F. Supp. 241 (1980), 241.

3. *E.E.O.C. v. Sears, Roebuck & Co.*, 628 F. Supp. 1264 (N.D. Ill. 1986), 1288–90.

4. Ibid., 1289.

5. Ibid., 1290, 1313. For the manual, see Ruth Milkman, "Women's History and the Sears Case," *Feminist Studies* (Summer 1986): 382.

6. "Despite Doubts, U.S. Presses to Resolve Sears Bias Case," Washington *Post*, July 9, 1985, A1, A6; *E.E.O.C. v. Sears, Roebuck & Co.*, 628 F. Supp. 1264 (N.D. Ill. 1986), 1314.

7. Ibid., 1306–09.

8. Ibid., 1315; Alice Kessler-Harris, "Response: Academic Freedom and Expert Witnessing . . . ," *Texas Law Review* (December 1998): 434; Kessler-Harris, quoted in Milkman, "Women's History and the Sears Case," 394.

9. *E.E.O.C. v. Sears, Roebuck & Co.*, 628 F. Supp. 1264 (N.D. Ill. 1986), 1308. Rosenberg, quoted in Thomas Haskell and Sanford Levinson, "Symposium on Academic Freedom: Academic Freedom and Expert Witnessing . . . ," *Texas Law Review* (June 1988): 1650.

10. *E.E.O.C. v. Sears, Roebuck & Co.*, 839 F. 2d (7th Cir. 1988), 365–66.

11. Statement of Mrs. William J. Carson, Philadelphia, Senate Hearings of 1931, in Aileen Kraditor, ed., *Up From the Pedestal: Landmark Writings in the American Woman's Struggle for Equality* (Chicago, 1968), 301.

12. *Harper v. Virginia State Board of Elections*, 383 U.S. 663 (1966).

13. Kristi Anderson, *After Suffrage: Women in Partisan and Electoral Politics before the New Deal* (Chicago, 1996), 72–73.

14. "Women Smash Yet Another Barrier," *New York Times*, August 15, 1998, A 10. My thanks to David Weinberg for his assistance.

15. Kenneth Karst, *Law's Promise, Law's Expression: Visions of Power in the Politics of Race, Gender, and Religion* (New Haven, CT, 1993), 136.

16. Linda Kerber, " 'A Constitutional Right to be Treated Like . . . Ladies': Women, Civic Obligation and Military Service," *University of Chicago Law School Roundtable* (1993): 116–17, 121.

17. *U.S. v. St. Clair*, 291 F. Supp. 122 (SDNY 1968), 124–25.

18. Miriam Goldman Cedarbaum, "Essay: Women on the Federal Bench," *Boston University Law Review* (January 1993): 42.

19. Sandra Day O'Connor, "Madison Lecture: Portia's Progress," *New York University Law Review* (December 1991): 1549.

20. Gail Collins, "Why the Women Are Fading Away," *New York Times Magazine*, October 25, 1998, 54.

21. Jean Bethke Elshtain, "Woman Suffrage and the Gender Gap," in Marjorie Spruill Wheeler, ed., *Votes for Women! The Woman Suffrage Movement* . . . (Knoxville, TN, 1995), 137.

22. Collins, "Why the Women Are Fading Away," 55.

23. Sylvia Law, " The Reality of Biological Differences for Gender Equality," in Kermit Hall, ed., *Major Problems in American Constitutional History*, Vol. 2 (Lexington, MA, 1992), 450–51.

24. Documents collected in Joan Hoff-Wilson, ed., *Rights of Passage: The Past and Future of the ERA* (Bloomington, IN, 1986), Appendix, 121–23.

25. Ibid.

26. Ibid., 123–24.

27. Ibid.

28. Michael Walzer writing in *Dissent*, quoted in Cynthia Harrison, *On Account of Sex: The Politics of Women's Issues* (Berkeley, CA, 1988), 70; and Harrison, 80–81.

29. Katharine St. George, quoted in Harrison, *On Account of Sex*, 96.

30. 29 U.S.C. Section 206 (d) (1) (1970).

31. Harrison, *On Account of Sex*, 104.

32. Ibid., 126–27; Pauli Murray and Mary O. Eastwood, "Jane Crow and the Law: Sex Discrimination and Title VII," *George Washington Law Review* (December 1965): 239.

33. Harrison, *On Account of Sex*, 133–34, 137.

34. In Melvin Urofsky, *A Conflict of Rights: The Supreme Court and Affirmative Action* (New York, 1991), 16–17.

35. Murray and Eastwood, "Jane Crow and the Law," 243n.

36. Harrison, *On Account of Sex*, 178; *Playboy* bunnies in Suzanne Rice, "The 'Discovery' and Evolution of Sexual Harassment as an Educational Issue," *Initiatives*, 57, Vol. 2 (Journal of the National Association for Women in Education, 1996): 3.

37. Jo Freeman, "How Sex Got into Title VII: Persistent Opportunism as a Maker of Public Policy," copyright 1991, published by H-Women@h-net.msu.edu, March 9, 1998, 10–12.

38. P. L. 88–352, Title VII, 78 Stat. at Large 253 (1964).

39. Quoted in Joan Hoff, *Law, Gender, and Injustice: A Legal History of U.S. Women* (New York, 1991), 235.

40. Richard Graham quoted in Harrison, *On Account of Sex*, 190.

41. Mary Bunting, "The Radcliffe Institute for Independent Study" (1961), in Kraditor, *Up From the Pedestal*, 357, 362.

42. Excerpt from Pauli Murray, *Song In a Weary Throat* (1987), and "NOW Statement of Purpose" (1966), in Moynihan et al., *Second to None*, Vol. 2, 277–78, 279–81.

43. Ibid.

44. Eleanor Holmes Norton, "A Strategy for Change" [Hearings on Women's Rights, New York City Commission on Human Rights], in Miriam Schneir, ed., *Feminism in Our Time: The Essential Writings, World War II to the Present* (New York, 1994), 376.

45. Susan Faludi, "Speak for Yourself," in *Beacon Book of Essays by Contemporary American Women* (Boston, 1996), 169–70.

46. For NCNP story, see Sara Evans, *Personal Politics: The Roots of Women's Liberation in the Civil Rights Movement and the New Left* (New York, 1979), 196–99; for Black Nationalist statement, see "The Combahee River Collective," in Beverly Guy-Sheftall, ed., *Words of Fire: An Anthology of African-American Feminist Thought* (New York, 1995), 237.

47. Barbara Brown, Thomas Emerson, Gail Falk, and Ann Freedman, "The Equal Rights Amendment: A Constitutional Basis for Equal Rights for Women," *Yale Law Journal* (April 1971): 874, 890–92.

48. Quoted in Jane Mansbridge, *Why We Lost the ERA* (Chicago, 1986), 64.

49. Quoted in Mary Frances Berry, *Why ERA Failed: Politics, Women's Rights, and the Amending Process of the Constitution* (Bloomington, IN, 1986), 63–64.

50. Joan Hoff-Wilson, *Rights of Passage: The Past and Future of ERA* (Bloomington, IN, 1986), 124–125.

51. "Equal Pay for Equal Work Is No. 1 Goal of Women," *New York Times*, September 5, 1997, A 13.

52. Martha W. Barnett, "Women Practicing Law: Changes in Attitudes, Changes in Platitudes," *Florida Law Review* (1990): 212–218.

53. Johnson speech, quoted in Urofsky, *A Conflict of Rights*, 17.

54. Judith Baer, *Women in American Law: The Struggle Toward Equality from the New Deal to the Present* (New York, 1991), 29.
55. Ruth Bader Ginsburg, "Remarks on Women Becoming Part of the Constitution," *Law and Inequality* (May 1988): 19.
56. 485 P. 2nd 529 (Supreme Court of California, 1971), 541.
57. Ann Corinne Hill, "Protection of Women Workers and the Courts: A Legal Case History," *Feminist Studies* (Summer 1979): 261.
58. Vivien Hart, *Bound by Our Constitution: Women, Workers, and the Minimum Wage* (Princeton, NJ, 1994), xi.
59. "American Women: Report of the President's Commission on the Status of Women" (1965), in Kraditor, *Up From the Pedestal*, 305.
60. *Reed v. Reed*, 404 U.S. 71 (1971), 75–76.
61. J. Ralph Lindgren and Nadine Taub, *The Law of Sex Discrimination* (St. Paul, MN, 1988), 48.
62. *Frontiero v. Richardson*, 411 U.S. 677 (1973), 677.
63. Ibid., 685–686, 688.
64. Deborah Blake et al., "Centennial Panel: Two Decades of Intermediate Scrutiny: Evaluating Equal Protection for Women," *American University Journal of Gender and the Law* (Fall 1997): 5–6.
65. *Frontiero v. Richardson*, 411 U.S. 677 (1973), 691–92.
66. *Weinberger v. Weisenfeld*, 420 U.S. 636 (1975), 645.
67. *Stanton v. Stanton*, 421 U.S. 7 (1975), 13–17.
68. *Craig v. Boren*, 429 U.S. 190 (1976).
69. *Michael M. v. Superior Court of Sonoma County*, 450 U.S. 464 (1981), 464.
70. For a discussion, see Nadine Taub, "Sandra Day O'Connor and Women's Rights," *Women's Rights Law Reporter*, Vol. 13 (1991): 116.
71. *Weeks v. Southern Bell Telephone and Telegraph Co.*, 408 F. 2d 228 (5th Cir. 1969), 235–36.
72. 29 C.F.R. 1604.1 (b), August 19, 1969; *Rosenfeld v. Southern Pacific*, 444 F. 2d 1219 (9th Cir. 1971), 1223, 1225.
73. *Phillips v. Martin-Marietta*, 400 U.S. 542 (1971); *Hishon v. King and Spalding*, 467 U.S. 69 (1984).
74. Baer, *Women in American Law*, chap. 2.
75. *Kahn v. Shevin*, 416 U.S. 351 (1974), 352–53, 362.
76. *Cleveland Board of Education v. LaFleur*, 414 U.S. 632 (1973), 639–40.
77. *Geduldig v. Aiello*, 417 U.S. 484 (1974); *General Electric Co. v. Gilbert*, 429 U.S. 125 (1976).
78. *Nashville Gas Company v. Satty*, 434 U.S. 136 (1977), 142.
79. *Price Waterhouse v. Hopkins*, 490 U.S. 228 (1989). For Ann Hopkins' testimony, see Leslie Goldstein, ed., *Contemporary Cases in Women's Rights* (Madison, WI, 1994), 211.
80. Goldstein, *Contemporary Cases*, 208.
81. Urofsky, *Conflict of Rights*, 53.
82. *Johnson v. Santa Clara* majority opinion reprinted in ibid., 189–209.
83. Terry Arendell, "Women and the Economics of Divorce in the Contemporary United States," *Signs* (Autumn 1987): 122.
84. Glenda Riley, *Divorce: An American Tradition* (New York, 1991), 156.
85. Susan Moller Okin, *Justice, Gender, and the Family* (New York, 1989), 161.
86. Johnie Tillmon, "Welfare Is a Women's Issue," *Liberation News Service* (No. 415), February 26, 1972.
87. *DeGraffenreid v. General Motors*, 413 F Supp 142 (1976); *Moore v. Hughes Helicopters, Inc.*, 708 F2d 475 (9th Cir 1983), 480.
88. *Adarand Constructors, Inc. v. Pena*, 515 U.S. 200 (1995).
89. Emily Newell Blair, "Discouraged Feminists," 1931, in Kraditor, *Up From the Pedestal*, 343; "Looney Tunes" in Joan Hoff, *Law, Gender and Injustice*, 254.

90. Bonnie Watkins and Nina Rothchild, eds., *In the Company of Women: Voices from the Women's Movement* (St. Paul, MN, 1996), 110.
91. Hoff, *Law, Gender and Injustice,* 288.
92. Quoted in Woloch, *Muller v. Oregon,* 67.
93. "Survey of Women and Work," *The Economist,* July 1998, 3, 15–16.
94. Baer, *Women in American Law,* 221–24.
95. Paula Ries and D. H. Thurgood, *Summary Report 1991: Doctorate Recipients from United States Universities* (Washington, DC 1993), 5; and Organization of American Historians *Newsletter,* November 1993, 15.
96. Baer, *Women in American Law,* 224.
97. *Vorchheimer v. School District of Philadelphia,* 532 F.2d 880 (1976), 882.
98. *Newberg v. Board of Public Education,* 22 Pa. D&C. 3d 682 (1983), 709.
99. Quoted in Baer, *Women in American Law,* 237–39.
100. *United States* v. *Virginia,* 518 U.S. 515 (1996).
101. "For Women, 25 Years of Title IX . . . ," C18.
102. *NYC Club Association v. New York City,* 108 SCt 2225 (1988), discussed in Hoff, *Law, Gender and Injustice,* 255.
103. *Eisenstadt v. Baird,* 405 U.S. 438 (1972), 453.
104. Laura Kaplan, *The Story of Jane: The Legendary Underground Feminist Abortion Service* (Chicago, 1995), 24, 28.
105. *Roe v. Wade,* 410 U.S. 113 (1973), 116, 120, 129.
106. Ibid., 162, 160, 159.
107. Ibid., 174.
108. Ibid.; Ginsburg, quoted in David Garrow, *Liberty and Sexuality: The Right to Privacy and the Making of Roe v. Wade* (New York, 1994), 613.
109. John Hart Ely, "Was *Roe v. Wade* a Mistake?" in Kermit Hall, ed., *Major Problems in American Constitutional History,* Vol. 2 (Lexington, MA, 1992), 440, 445.
110. Orrin Hatch, Hearings before Subcommittee on the Constitution of the Committee on the Judiciary, U.S. Senate, September 1981, in Neal Devins et al., eds., *Federal Abortion Politics: A Documentary History,* Vol. 1, Part 2 (New York, 1995), 357.
111. Rayman Solomon, "The Politics of Appointment and the Federal Courts' Role in Regulating America: U.S. Courts of Appeals Judgeships from T.R. to F.D.R.," *American Bar Foundation Research Journal,* No. 2 (1984): 285.
112. *Planned Parenthood of Central Missouri v. Danforth, Attorney General of Missouri,* 428 U.S. 52 (1976), 52–53.
113. *Maher v. Roe,* 432 U.S. 464 (1977), 464.
114. *Webster v. Reproductive Health Services,* 492 U.S. 490 (1989), 559–60.
115. Bruce Fein, "A Court That Obeys the Law," *National Review* (September 29, 1989), 51.
116. *Planned Parenthood of Southeastern Pennsylvania v. Robert P. Casey,* 112 S.Ct. 2791 (1992), 2796.
117. Ibid., 2815.
118. Partial Birth Abortion Ban Act of 1997, Chapter 74, Sec. 1531; www.thomas.loc.govt, p. 2 of 3.
119. "House Approves Bill to Overturn Veto on Abortion," *New York Times,* September 20, 1996, A1, A11. "Wisconsin Abortion Clinics Shut Down . . . ," *New York Times,* May 15, 1998, A16.
120. "Wisconsin Abortion Clinics Shut Down," A16.
121. *Planned Parenthood of Wisconsin v. Doyle,* 9 F. Supp. 2d 1033 (1998); *Planned Parenthood of Wisconsin v. Doyle,* 162 F. 3d 463 (7th Cir. 1998), 466, 477; *Hope Clinic v. Ryan,* 195 F. 3d 857 (7th Cir. 1999); *Stenberg v. Carhart,* U.S. Supreme Court Docket No. 99-830.
122. 90 Stat. at Large 1418 (1976), 1434.
123. Senator Stennis speech in the Senate, August 25, 1976, reprinted in Devins et al., *Federal Abortion Politics,* Vol. 1, Part 1, 57.

124. *Patricia Harris v. Cora McRae*, 448 U.S. 297 (1980): 338, 342.

125. George Bush, Letter to Members of the Senate Appropriations Committee on Federal Funding of Abortion, October 17, 1989, in Devins et al., *Federal Abortion Politics*, Vol. 1, Part 1, 84.

126. *Rust v. Sullivan*, 111 U.S. 1759 (1991), 1767.

127. "Introduction," in Devins et al., *Federal Abortion Politics*, Vol. 2, Part 1, xxx.

128. Ronald Dworkin, "Feminism and Abortion," *New York Review of Books*, June 10, 1993: 27.

129. "Right to Abortion Quietly Advances in State Courts," *New York Times*, December 6, 1998, A1, A25.

130. Pat Buchanan, "The Election Is About Who We Are: Taking Back Our Country," in *Vital Speeches of the Day*, Vol. 58, September 1992: 712–13.

131. "Women's Issues and Wariness in Congress," *New York Times*, May 26, 1997, A7.

132. *In re A.C.*, 533 A. 2d 611 (D.C. Cir. 1987); *In re A.C.*, 573 A. 2d 1235 (D.C. Cir. 1990).

133. *Paul Schenck et al. v. Pro-Choice Network of Western New York*, 117 S.Ct. 855 (1997), 855; *Jayne Bray v. Alexandria Women's Health Clinic*, 113 S.Ct. 753 (1993), 753, 802.

134. 141 Congressional Record, S1290–91 (1995).

135. Reuthers News Service, "Bomb Kills One at Alabama Abortion Clinic," January 30, 1998 (www.infoseek.com).

136. Vicki Schultz, "Telling Stories About Women and Work: Judicial Interpretations of Sex Segregation in the Workplace in Title VII Cases Raising the Lack of Interest Argument," in Katherine T. Bartlett and Roseanne Kennedy, *Feminist Legal Theory: Readings in Law and Gender* (Boulder, CO, 1991), 139.

137. Research by Cynthia Cockburn, discussed in Schultz, "Telling Stories . . . ," 139.

138. "High Court Ruling Says Harassment Includes Same Sex," *New York Times*, March 5, 1998, A1. Joseph Oncale, an oil rig worker, sued under Title VII for alleged harassment by his employer and three members of an all-male crew.

139. Catharine MacKinnon, *Sexual Harassment of Working Women* (New Haven, CT, 1979), 10.

140. *Meritor Savings Bank v. Vinson*, 477 U.S. 57 (1986); *Harris v. Forklift Systems, Inc.*, 510 U.S. 17 (1993); *Bohen v. City of East Chicago*, 799 F. 2d 1180 (7th Cir. 1986); *Ellison v. Brady*, 924 F.2d 872 (9th Cir. 1991), 878–79.

141. "Shockingly Abnormal," *The Economist*, April 13, 1996, 26.

142. For "honey" and "dear," see *Beardsley v. Webb*, 30 F. 3d 524 (4th Cir. 1994), 528–29.

143. *Burlington Industries, Inc. v. Ellerth*, 118 S. Ct. 2257 (1998); *Faragher v. City of Boca Raton*, 118 S. Ct. 2275 (1998).

144. "Military Women Say Complaints of Sex Harassment Go Unheeded," *New York Times*, March 10, 1994, A1, A11.

145. Jeffrey Sarles, "The Case of the Missing Woman: Sexual Harassment and Judicial Review of Arbitration Awards," *Harvard Women's Law Journal* (Spring 1994): 17.

146. Leslie Heywood, "Female Harassment Is Still Widespread in Sport," *New York Times*, November 8, 1998, Y-39 [discussion of book].

147. Linda Hirshman, "Making Safety A Civil Right," *Ms.*, September–October 1994, 45.

148. Quoted in Diana E. H. Russell, "Wife Rape and the Law," in Mary Odem and Jody Clay-Warner, *Confronting Rape and Sexual Assault* (Wilmington, DE, 1998), 73; for the Maine law, see Kevin Paul, "Private/Property: A Discourse on Gender Inequality in Law," *Law and Inequality* (1989): 414.

149. This insight belongs to Edward M. Wise.

150. See Boston *Globe*, March 7, 1993. My thanks for this citation to Edward Greer, Southern New England School of Law, "The Old Test Oaths and the New: A Study in American 'Otherness,'" unpublished paper presented at Law and Society Association, 1995.

151. Quoted in Diana Scully and Joseph Marolla, "'Riding the Bull at Gilley's': Convicted Rapists Describe the Rewards of Rape," in Odem and Clay-Warner, *Confronting Rape and Sexual Assault*, 118–21, 124.

152. Deborah Rhode, *Speaking of Sex: The Denial of Gender Inequality* (Cambridge, MA, 1997), 119.

153. U.S. Department of Justice, Bureau of Justice Statistics, Female Victims of Violent Crime, January 1991, reprinted in Joshua Dressler, *Criminal Law* (St. Paul, MN, 1994), 320–22.

154. Susan Brownmiller, *Against Our Will: Men, Women and Rape* (New York, 1975), 362.

155. Andi Rosenthal, "Rape Sonnets," in Odem and Clay-Warner, *Confronting Rape and Sexual Assault*, 22.

156. Richard A. Posner, *Sex and Reason* (Cambridge, MA, 1992), 177.

157. Anthony Giddens, *The Transformation of Intimacy: Sexuality, Love and Eroticism in Modern Societies* (Stanford, CA, 1992), 2–3.

158. *American Booksellers Ass'n v. Hudnut*, 771 F.2d 323 (7th Cir. 1985); aff'd mem. 475 U. S. 1001 (1986).

159. Andrea Dworkin, *Pornography: Men Possessing Women* (New York, 1989 ed.), 205.

160. Lynn S. Chancer, "Review Essay: Feminist Offensives . . . ," *Stanford Law Review* (February 1996): 739–60.

161. Dworkin, *Pornography*, 199–200.

162. *United States v. Betty*, 208 U.S. 393 (1908), 401.

163. Brownmiller, *Against Our Will*, 392.

164. Barbara Meil Hobson, *Uneasy Virtue: The Politics of Prostitution and the American Reform Tradition* (Chicago, 1990), 212.

165. Alice Kessler-Harris, *Out To Work: A History of Wage-Earning Women in the United States* (New York, 1982), 319.

166. Quoted in Rhode, *Speaking of Sex*, 119–20.

167. Harrison, *On Account of Sex*, 212.

168. "Phyllis Schlafly Opposes the ERA," in Kermit Hall, ed., *Major Problems in American Constitutional History*, Vol. 2 (Lexington, MA, 1992), 413, 416; and *ERA = Gay = AIDS Connection*, pub. by Eagle Forum (1983), in Elaine Donnelly Collection, Bentley Historical Library, Ann Arbor, MI. I am grateful to Beth Onusko Savalox for sharing this material.

169. Quoted in Berry, *Why ERA Failed*, 65.

170. "The Reverend Jerry Falwell on the ERA, 1980," in Hall, *Main Problems*, Vol. 2, 422–23.

171. Donald G. Mathews and Jane Sherron DeHart, *Sex, Gender, and the Politics of ERA* (New York, 1990), 168.

172. Ruth Bader Ginsburg, "Sexual Equality Under the Fourteenth and Equal Rights Amendments," *Washington University Law Quarterly* (1979): 161.

173. Quoted in Kerber, " 'A Constitutional Right to be Treated Like . . . Ladies," 118–19.

174. Berry, *Why ERA Failed*, 73–75.

175. Quoted in ibid., 82.

176. "Marlow W. Cook Supports the ERA," in Hall, *Main Problems*, Vol. 2, 418.

177. Ginsburg, "Sexual Equality. . . ," 198–99.

178. Eleanor Roosevelt, "Women in Politics," *Good Housekeeping*, April 1940, 45.

179. *New York Times Magazine*, April 19, 1998, 94.

180. "Mars and Venus" [interview with John Gray], *Currency* (April 1998), 56.

CHAPTER 12, AFTERWORD

1. Mary Beard to Harriot Stanton Blatch, September 7, 1934, in Nancy Cott, ed., *A Woman Making History: Mary Ritter Beard Through Her Letters* (New Haven, CT, 1991), 118.

2. Joan Hoff, *Law, Gender and Injustice: A Legal History of U.S. Women* (New York, 1991), 229.

3. Susan Bickford, *The Dissonance of Democracy: Listening, Conflict, and Citizenship* (Ithaca, NY, 1996), 11.

4. "U.S. Colleges Begin to Ask, Where Have the Men Gone?" *New York Times*, December 6, 1998, A1.
5. Barbara Johnston, *Hagar* (New York, 1913), 367–69.
6. Nancy Cott, "Marriage and Women's Citizenship in the United States, 1830–1934," *American Historical Review* (December 1998): 1442.
7. Carrie S. Burnham, "Suffrage—The Citizen's Birthright, An Address delivered before the Constitutional Convention of Pennsylvania, January 16, 1873 . . ." (Philadelphia, 1873) [Pamphlets in American History, W087], 11; Announcement of the Annual Convention of NWSA, 1874, in Elizabeth Cady Stauton et al., *History of Woman Suffrage*, (New York, 1881; reprint Ayer, 1985), Vol. 2, 545
8. Susan B. Anthony, Declaration of Rights, 1876.
9. Josephine S. Griffing, NWSA Meeting, May 11, 1871, New York Apollo Hall, *HWS*, Vol. 2, 485.
10. "Sexual Politics, The Real Thing," *New York Times*, December 2, 1992.
11. Andrew Greeley, *The Catholic Myth* (New York, 1990), 100.
12. Mary Johnston, from 1910–11 suffrage speeches, quoted in Marjorie Spruill Wheeler, *New Women of the New South* (New York, 1993), 96.
13. Aileen Kraditor, ed., *Up From the Pedestal: Landmark Writings in the American Woman's Struggle for Equality* (Chicago, 1968), 22–23.
14. Linda Kerber, *"No Constitutional Right To Be Ladies": Women and the Obligations of Citizenship* (New York, 1998), 309.
15. Tamar Lewin, "Wage Difference Between Women and Men Widens," *New York Times*, September 15, 1997, 1A.
16. Adeline Champney, *The Woman Question* (New York, 1902) [Pamphlets in American History, WO18], 29.
17. Catharine A. MacKinnon, "Feminism, Method, and the State: An Agenda for Theory," *Signs* 7 (Spring 1982): 529.
18. Olga Knopf, *The Art of Being a Woman* (Boston, 1932), 291.
19. Cynthia Grant Bowman, "Street Harassment and the Informal Ghettoization of Women," *Harvard Law Review* (January 1993): 517.
20. Rose Schneiderman, Senate Hearings (1931), in Kraditor, *Up From the Pedestal*, 298–99.
21. Barbara Johnston, *Hagar* (New York, 1913), 292–93.

Bibliographic Essay

No well-bounded literature yet encompasses the subject of women's rights and American constitutional culture. Readers must begin with general texts in constitutional, legal, and women's history and then draw on an eclectic array of sources, many of them created for different purposes. Because of the far-flung character of relevant scholarship, what follows is an advisory and, inevitably, personal discussion of some of the writing that I found helpful. I have not tried to list everything of merit; indeed, I excluded many sources already cited in the notes and, with some exceptions, general accounts of social or political development, despite references to such developments in the text. Many works listed here have good bibliographies; students should consult them for additional reading. See also Kermit Hall, comp., *A Comprehensive Bibliography of American Constitutional and Legal History*, 5 vols. (1984), a dated but still valuable resource.

THE HISTORY OF CONSTITUTIONAL AND LEGAL RIGHTS

Several texts in American constitutional and legal history supply basic narratives. Kermit Hall, *The Magic Mirror* (New York, 1989) elegantly merges constitutional and legal history and includes woman-friendly sections as well as a fine bibliographic essay. Michael Les Benedict, *The Blessings of Liberty* (Lexington, MA, 1996) offers a brief account of the constitutional past; Melvin Urofsky, *A March of Liberty* (New York, 1988) provides more detail from a liberal-nationalist perspective; and the more conservative Alfred Kelly et al., *The American Constitution*, 7th ed. (New York, 1991), has extensive case and bibliographic detail. Such texts typically devote only a few pages to the "woman question." Lawrence Friedman's encyclopedic *History of American Law*, 2nd ed. (New York, 1985), a useful "law and society" account of the development of the legal system, is not especially sensitive to gender distinctions. The best general history of the criminal justice system is Lawrence Friedman, *Crime and Punishment in American History* (New York, 1993), which treats women's experiences. Document and essay collections include Kermit Hall et al., eds., *American Legal History: Cases and Materials* (New York, 1991); Hall, ed., *Major Problems in American Constitutional History*, Vols. 1 and 2 (Lexington, MA, 1992); and Michael Les Benedict, *Sources in American Constitutional History* (Lexington, MA, 1996). Stephen Presser and Jamil Zainaldin, eds., *Law and Jurisprudence in American History*, 3rd ed. (St. Paul, MN, 1995) reprints several feminist texts, but does not explore gender's imprint throughout the legal system. The fourth edition promises to be much better. Lawrence Friedman and Harry Scheiber, eds., *American Law and the Constitutional Order: Historical Perspectives*, enlarged ed. (Cambridge, MA, 1988) provides key essays. A sound reference work is Kermit Hall, ed., *Oxford Companion to the Supreme Court of the United States* (New York, 1992).

Scholarly writing about citizenship has burgeoned. Basic studies include James Kettner, *Development of American Citizenship, 1608–1870* (Chapel Hill, NC, 1978), which examines volitional citizenship, and political scientist Judith Shklar's thoughtful *American Citizenship: The Quest for Inclusion* (Cambridge, MA, 1991). Richard D. Brown's *The Strength of a People: The Idea of an Informed Citizenry in America, 1650–1870* (Chapel Hill, NC, 1996); Robert Wiebe, *Self-Rule: A Cultural History of American Democracy* (Chicago, 1995); and Eric Foner, *The Story of American Freedom* (New York, 1998), though differing substantially in approach and argument, all give space to gender inequality. Key essays include Blanche Crozier, "Constitutionality of Discrimination Based on Sex," *Boston University Law Review* (1935): 723–755, and Rogers Smith, "'One United People': Second-Class Female Citizenship and the American Quest for Community," *Yale Journal of Law and the Humanities* (1989): 229–293, which contends that Americans drew on multiple political discourses to subjugate women. For elaboration, see Rogers Smith, *Civic Ideals: Conflicting Visions of Citizenship in U.S. History* (New Haven, CT, 1997). See also Kenneth Karst, *Belonging to America: Equal Citizenship and the Constitution* (New Haven, CT, 1989) and his more speculative *Law's Promise, Law's Expression: Visions of Power in the Politics of Race, Gender, and Religion* (New Haven, CT, 1993); J. R. Pole, *The Pursuit of Equality in American History*, 2nd ed. (Berkeley, CA, 1993), which includes new material about women; Stanley Katz, "The Strange Birth and Unlikely History of Constitutional Equality," *Journal of American History* (1988): 747–762, hereafter *JAH*, urging scholars to move beyond formal study of the equality norm into its social manifestations; the symposium in *JAH* (1997) featuring Linda Kerber, "The Meanings of Citizenship," and related commentary about the Golden Age of participatory democracy; and Gisela Bock and Susan James, eds., *Beyond Equality and Difference: Citizenship, Feminist Politics and Female Subjectivity* (New York, 1992), especially Susan James, "The Good-Enough Citizen: Female Citizenship and Independence." Nancy Cott, "Marriage and Women's Citizenship in the United States, 1830–1934," *American Historical Review* (1998): 1440–74, hereafter *AHR*, explores linkages between coverture and citizenship; Candice Lewis Bredbenner, *A Nationality of Her Own: Women, Marriage, and the Law of Citizenship* (Berkeley, CA, 1998) offers a different treatment. See also Virginia Sapiro, "Women, Citizenship, and Nationality: Immigration and Naturalization Policies in the United States," *Politics and Society* (1984): 1–26. For indigenous women's struggle to preserve their precontact status, see Bethany Ruth Berger, "After Pocahontas: Indian Women and the Law, 1830–1934," *American Indian Law Review* (1997): 1–62, one of a handful of studies on the subject.

Topical works provide detail. In constitutional history, see the New American Nation series—e.g., for the nineteenth century, Harold Hyman and William Wiecek, *Equal Justice Under Law* (New York, 1982), and for the twentieth, Paul Murphy, *The Constitution in Crisis Times, 1918–1969* (New York, 1972). On the Marshall-Taney era, see R. Kent Newmyer's *The Supreme Court Under Marshall and Taney* (Arlington Heights, IL, 1986). Morton Horwitz explores relations between economy, law, and political ideology in *The Transformation of American Law*, Vols. 1 and 2 (New York, 1977 and 1992), which should be read with J. Willard Hurst—e.g., *Law and the Conditions of Freedom in the Nineteenth-Century United States* (Madison, WI, 1957)—and Peter Karsten's *Heart versus Head: Judge-Made Law in Nineteenth-Century America* (Chapel Hill, NC, 1997). For leading judges, see G. Edward White, *The American Judicial Tradition: Profiles of Leading American Judges*, expanded ed. (New York, 1988). On speech freedom, see Paul Murphy, *The Meaning of Freedom of Speech* (Westport, CT, 1972), and Harry Kalven, *A Worthy Tradition: Freedom of Speech in America* (New York, 1988). For the post–Civil War amendments, see David Kyvig, *Explicit and Authentic Acts: Amending the Consti-*

tution, 1776–1995 (Lawrence, KS, 1996). On slavery, see Paul Finkelman, *Slavery and the Founders: Race and Liberty in the Age of Jefferson* (Armonk, NY, 1996); Robert Cover, *Justice Accused: Antislavery and the Judicial Process* (New Haven, CT, 1975); Mark Tushnet, *The American Law of Slavery* (Princeton, NJ, 1981); and William Wiecek's important book, *The Sources of Anti-Slavery Constitutionalism, 1760–1848* (Ithaca, NY, 1977). For *Dred Scott* and its antecedents, Don Fehrenbacher's *The Dred Scott Case* (New York, 1978) is indispensable; for racial "science" and the "separate but equal" decision in *Plessy v. Ferguson*, see Charles Lofgren, *The Plessy Case* (New York, 1987). The best account of the Fourteenth Amendment's adoption is William Nelson, *The Fourteenth Amendment: From Political Principle to Judicial Doctrine* (Cambridge, MA, 1988). On early labor relations, see Robert Steinfeld, *The Invention of Free Labor: The Employment Relation in English and American Law and Culture, 1350–1870* (Chapel Hill, NC, 1991), and David Montgomery, *Citizen Worker: The Experience of Workers in the United States with Democracy and the Free Market during the Nineteenth Century* (New York, 1993). On equity, see Peter Hoffer, *The Law's Conscience: Equitable Constitutionalism in America* (Chapel Hill, NC, 1990); on the South, see Kermit Hall and James Ely, eds., *An Uncertain Tradition: Constitutionalism and the History of the South* (Athens, GA, 1988), and David Bodenhamer and James Ely, *Ambivalent Legacy: A Legal History of the South* (Jackson, MS, 1984).

THE HISTORY OF WOMEN

The best general history of American women is Sara Evans's engaging *Born for Liberty* (New York, 1989). Nancy Cott's *The Grounding of American Feminism* (New Haven, CT, 1987) analyzes the shifting configurations of post–World War I feminism. See also two classic studies—William Chafe, *The American Woman* (New York, 1972), and Eleanor Flexner, *A Century of Struggle* (New York, 1974)—and Glenna Matthews, *The Rise of Public Woman: Woman's Power and Woman's Place in the United States, 1630–1970* (New York, 1992). Twayne Publishers commissioned a series organized by decade; see, for example, Dorothy Brown, *American Women in the 1920's: Setting a Course* (Boston, 1987). Many of the essays in Linda Kerber et al., eds., *U. S. History as Women's History* (Chapel Hill, NC, 1995) are relevant to legal history. Nancy Hewitt et al., eds., *Visible Women: New Essays on American Activism* (Urbana, IL, 1993) includes Sara Evans's fine essay about women's historians' uneasy relationship with the state. For black women, see Darlene Clark Hine and Kathleen Thompson, *A Shining Thread of Hope: The History of Black Women in America* (New York, 1998); Paula Giddings, *When and Where I Enter: The Impact of Black Women On Race and Sex in America* (New York, 1984); and Jacqueline Jones, *Labor of Love, Labor of Sorrow: Black Women, Work, and Family from Slavery to the Present* (New York, 1985). Reference works include Edward James and Janet Wilson James, eds., *Notable American Women: A Biographical Dictionary*, Vols. 1–4 (Cambridge, MA, 1971, 1980); Darlene Clark Hine et al., eds., *Black Women in America: An Historical Encyclopedia*, Vols. 1 and 2 (Bloomington, IN, 1993); and Darlene Clark Hine, ed., *Black Women in United States History* (Brooklyn, NY, 1990). For a seminal statement about gender analysis, see Joan Scott, "Gender: A Useful Category of Historical Analysis," *AHR* (1986): 1053–75.

Women's movements in the Atlantic basin often cross-pollinated. For European women's early history, see Olwen Hufton's magnificent *The Prospect Before Her: A His-*

tory of Women in Western Europe, 1500–1800 (New York, 1996) or the explicitly comparative but quirky five-volume series edited by Françoise Thébaud, *A History of Women in the West* (Cambridge, MA, 1994), which includes some American history and extends into modern times. For comparisons of movements, see Christine Bolt, *The Women's Movements in the United States and Britain from the 1790's to the 1920's* (Amherst, MA, 1993), which is particularly strong on suffragism; Mary Fainsod Katzenstein and Carol McClurg Mueller, eds., *The Women's Movements of the United States and Western Europe* (Philadelphia, 1987), comparing public policy in seven countries; Richard Evans, *The Feminists: Women's Emancipation Movements in Europe, America, and Australasia, 1840–1920* (London, England, 1984); and Jane Rendall, *The Origins of Modern Feminism: Women in Britain, France, and the United States, 1780–1860* (Basingstoke, England, 1985). Elizabeth Helsinger et al., eds., *The Woman Question: Society and Literature in Britain and America, 1837–1883*, 3 vols. (Chicago, 1983), documents women's attempts to be heard. Eleanor Riemer and John Fout, eds., *European Women: A Documentary History, 1789–1945* (New York, 1980) supplies basic texts.

Topical surveys provide additional information. On education, see John Mack Faragher and Florence Howe, eds., *Women and Higher Education in American History* (New York, 1988); and on domesticity, see Glenna Matthews, *"Just a Housewife": The Rise and Fall of Domesticity in America* (New York, 1987). For work and the economy, see Julie Matthaei, *An Economic History of Women in America: Women's Work, the Sexual Division of Labor, and the Development of Capitalism* (New York, 1982), to be read with Alice Kessler-Harris, *Out to Work: A History of Wage-Earning Women in the United States* (New York, 1982); Teresa Amott and Julie Matthaei, eds., *Race, Gender, and Work: A Multicultural Economic History of Women in the United States* (Boston, 1991); and Claudia Goldin, *Understanding the Gender Gap: An Economic History of American Women* (New York, 1990), which sheds light on the "marriage bar." For working women's voices, see Carol Groneman and Mary Beth Norton, eds., *"To Toil the Livelong Day": America's Women at Work, 1780–1980* (Ithaca, NY, 1987). On the creation of gender difference, see Thomas Walter Laqueur, *Making Sex: Body and Gender from the Greeks to Freud* (Cambridge, MA, 1990). On masculinity in culture, see Mark Carnes et al., eds., *Meanings for Manhood: Constructions of Masculinity in Victorian America* (Chicago, 1990), a fascinating essay collection, as well as J. A. Mangen et al., eds., *Manliness and Morality: Middle-Class Masculinity in Britain and America, 1800–1940* (Manchester, England, 1987). On lesbian and gay experiences, see Diane H. Miller, *Freedom to Differ: The Shaping of the Gay and Lesbian Struggle for Civil Rights* (New York, 1998) and especially D'Emilio and Estelle Freedman, *Intimate Matters: A History of Sexuality in America* (New York, 1988). On divorce, see Roderick Phillips, *Putting Asunder: A History of Divorce in Western Society* (New York, 1988), a comparative account; Lawrence Stone, *The Road to Divorce: England, 1530–1987* (New York, 1990), for the Anglo-American story; and Glenda Riley, *Divorce: An American Tradition* (New York, 1991). Norma Basch's *Framing American Divorce: From the Revolutionary Generation to the Victorians* (Berkeley, CA, 1999), which appeared just as this book went to the publisher, situates nineteenth-century divorce law and experiences *of* divorce in culture. On marriage and families, see Michael Gordon, eds., *The American Family in Socio-Historical Perspective* (New York, 1973), an essay collection; Carl Degler, *At Odds: Women and the Family in America from the Revolution to the Present* (New York, 1980); Herbert Gutman, *The Black Family in Slavery and Freedom* (New York, 1976); Jacques Donzelot, *The Policing of Families* (New York, 1979); Tamara Hareven, ed., *Family and*

Kin in Urban Communities, 1700–1930 (New York, 1977); Steven Mintz and Susan Kellogg, *Domestic Revolutions: A Social History of American Family Life* (New York, 1988); and Susan Groag Bell and Karen M. Offen, eds., *Women, the Family, and Freedom: The Debate in Documents*, Vols. 1 and 2 (Stanford, CA, 1983), a comparative collection.

In recent years, anthologies and document collections have multiplied. But see Ruth Barnes Moynihan et al., eds., *Second to None: A Documentary History of American Women*, Vols. 1 and 2 (Lincoln, NE, 1993), an invaluable collection of primary sources; Linda Kerber and Jane Sherron DeHart, eds., *Women's America*, 4th ed. (New York, 1995), a premier anthology; Miriam Schneir, ed., *Feminism: The Essential Historical Writings* (New York, reprint 1994) and a sequel, *Feminism in Our Time: The Essential Writings, World War II to the Present* (New York, 1994); and Karlyn Kohrs Campbell, ed., *Man Cannot Speak for Her*, esp. Vol. 2, "Key Texts of the Early Feminists" (Westport, CT, 1989). Dawn Keetley and John Pettegrew, eds., *Public Women, Public Words: A Documentary History of American Feminism* (Madison, WI, 1997), Vol. 1, is particularly rich on early rights consciousness and the "first wave"; a second volume is forthcoming. Useful older collections include Aileen Kraditor, ed., *Up From the Pedestal: Landmark Writings in the American Woman's Struggle for Equality* (Chicago, 1968); Gerda Lerner, *The Female Experience* (Indianapolis, IN, 1977); Nancy Cott, ed., *Root of Bitterness: Documents of the Social History of American Women* (Boston, 1986); and Mary Beth Norton and Carol Ruth Berkin, eds., *Women of America: A History* (Boston, 1979), esp. the Norton and Marylynn Salmon essays. For women of color, see Ellen Carol DuBois and Vicki Ruiz, eds., *Unequal Sisters: A Multi-Cultural Reader in U.S. Women's History* (New York, 1990); Beverly Guy-Sheftall, ed., *Words of Fire: An Anthology of African-American Feminist Thought* (New York, 1995); and Barbara Smith, ed., *Home Girls: A Black Feminist Anthology* (New York, 1983). Linda Kerber, *Toward An Intellectual History of Women: Essays by Linda Kerber* (Chapel Hill, NC, 1997), reprints articles relevant to both legal and women's history. Rosemary Radford Ruether and Rosemary Skiller Keller, eds., *In Our Own Voices: Four Centuries of American Women's Religious Writing* (New York, 1995) offers writing by and about religious women. See also Michael Kimmel and Thomas Mosmiller's *Against the Tide: Pro-Feminist Men in the United States, 1776–1990: A Documentary History* (Boston, 1992), especially for the nineteenth century. Karlyn Kohrs Campbell, ed., *Women Public Speakers in the United States, 1800–1925* (Westport, CT, 1993) celebrates female oratory. The Library of Congress has published on-line, as part of its *American Memory* collection, "Votes for Women: Selections from the NAWSA Collection, 1848–1921" (http://www.lcweb2.gov), which includes proceedings of the trial of Susan B. Anthony.

BEYOND HISTORY'S BORDERS

Many scholars work at the intersection of law and history. The starting point for study of women's relationship to the state is Linda Kerber, *No Constitutional Right to Be Ladies: Women and the Obligations of Citizenship* (New York, 1998), which links inequality to exclusion from civic obligations. Deborah Rhode, *Justice and Gender* (Cambridge, MA, 1989) traces the path of modern law. For a provocative study of the layered character of "law," the lawlike features of custom, and the power of rights consciousness in forging change, see Hendrik Hartog, "Pigs and Positivism," *Wisconsin Law Review* (1985): 899–935, and Hartog, "The Constitution of Aspiration and 'The Rights That Belong to

Us All,' " *JAH* (1987): 1014. Joan Hoff's *Law, Gender, and Injustice: A Legal History of U.S. Women* (New York, 1991), the only comprehensive account of the imprint of sex on American law, argues basically that women got rights only when men no longer wanted them. Many anthologies collect feminist commentary on law. See, for example, D. Kelly Weisberg, ed., *Women and the Law: The Social-Historical Perspective*, 2 vols. (Cambridge, MA, 1982); D. Kelly Weisberg, ed., *Feminist Legal Theory: Foundations* (Philadelphia, 1993); Martha Albertson Fineman et al., eds., *At the Boundaries of Law: Feminism and Legal Theory* (New York, 1991), which contains several fine pieces; Patricia Smith, ed., *Feminist Jurisprudence* (New York, 1993); Katharine Bartlett and Rosanne Kennedy, eds., *Feminist Legal Theory: Readings in Law and Gender* (Boulder, CO, 1991); and Frances Olsen, ed., *Feminist Legal Theory*, Vols. 1 and 2 (New York, 1995), containing both theoretical and applied material. Sociologist Carol Smart examines shifting treatment of bodies and "badness" in *Feminism and the Power of Law* (New York, 1989) and in "The Woman of Legal Discourse," *Social and Legal Studies* (1992): 29–44. See also Winston Langley and Vivian Fox, eds., *Women's Rights in the United States: A Documentary History* (Westport, CT, 1994) and Marlene Wortman's *Women in American Law*, Vols. 1 and 2 (New York, 1985). Kermit Hall, *Women, the Law, and the Constitution: Major Historical Interpretations* (New York, 1987) is part of a multivolume compendium of articles in constitutional history.

Nothing takes the place of work in governmental records—particularly territorial and state records, which often are untouched by human hands. Casebooks, however, efficiently collect material about both the path of the law (particularly at the federal level) and feminist jurisprudence. Reprinted cases should be checked against originals because of heavy editing and occasional silent "corrections" of old texts for ease of reading, and because they are concerned mainly with helping lawyers win cases, casebooks can be insensitive to context and outmoded legal rules. But with these caveats in mind, see Barbara Babcock et al., eds., *Sex Discrimination and the Law: Causes and Remedies* (Boston, 1975, and supplement); Mary Jo Frug, *Woman and the Law* (Westbury, NY, 1992); J. Ralph Lindgren and Nadine Taub, *The Law of Sex Discrimination* (St. Paul, MN, 1988); political scientist Leslie Friedman Goldstein's twin collections, *The Constitutional Rights of Women*, new ed. (Madison, WI, 1988) and *Contemporary Cases in Women's Rights* (Madison, WI, 1994); William Eskridge and Nan Hunter, *Sexuality, Gender, and the Law* (Westbury, NY, 1997); and Mary Becker et al., eds., *Feminist Jurisprudence: Taking Women Seriously, Cases and Materials* (St. Paul, MN, 1994). On the First Amendment and privacy, see Laurence Tribe, *American Constitutional Law*, 2nd ed. (Mineola, NY, 1988); for intersecting race discrimination cases, see Derrick Bell, *Race, Racism and American Law*, 2nd ed. (Boston, 1980).

Other disciplines provide help in reconceptualizing male-female interactions in culture and over time. Psychologists, for example, contribute to the debate over "difference" and "sameness"; see Carol Gilligan's classic *In a Different Voice: Psychological Theory and Women's Development* (Cambridge, MA, 1982) and an update of an old classic, Mary Field Belenky et al., *Women's Ways of Knowing: The Development of Self, Voice, and Mind*, 10th ed. (New York, 1997). Ranya Reiter, *Toward an Anthropology of Women* marries anthropology to feminism. Susan Bickford's *The Dissonance of Democracy: Listening, Conflict, and Citizenship* (Ithaca, NY, 1996) explores the role of speaking and listening in democracies. On John Locke and other political thinkers, see Gordon Schochet, *Patriarchalism in Political Thought* (New York, 1975), which should be read with two Carole Pateman works, *The Sexual Contract* (Stanford, CA, 1988) and *The Disorder of*

Women: Democracy, Feminism, and Political Theory (Stanford, CA, 1989). Dan Danielsen and Karen Engle, eds., *After Identity: A Reader in Law and Culture* (New York, 1995) and Linda Nicholson, ed., *Feminism/Postmodernism* (New York, 1990) are gateways into "cultural studies"; for sociological analysis, see Carol Smart, *Regulating Womanhood: Historical Essays on Marriage, Motherhood and Sexuality* (New York, 1992). Jürgen Habermas, *The Structural Transformation of the Public Sphere: An Inquiry into a Category of Bourgeois Society* (Cambridge, MA, 1989) makes it possible to think creatively about a republican forum, but neglects sex differences. For criticism, see Mary Lyndon Shanley and Uma Narayan, eds., *Reconstructing Political Theory: Feminist Perspectives* (University Park, PA, 1995) and Johanna Meehan, ed., *Feminists Read Habermas: Gendering the Subject of Discourse* (New York, 1995). For tensions between Lockean individualism and institutional practices that constrain liberty, see Uday Singh Mehta, *The Anxiety of Freedom: Imagination and Individuality in Locke's Political Thought* (Ithaca, NY, 1992). Jean Bethke Elshtain, *Public Man, Private Woman: Women in Social and Political Thought* (Princeton, NJ, 1981) and Elshtain, *Meditations on Modern Political Thought: Masculine/Feminine Themes from Aristotle to Arendt* (New York, 1986) are basic texts in feminist political philosophy. Lawyer-philosopher Martha Nussbaum's *Sex and Social Justice* (New York, 1999), which proposes remaking liberalism in light of feminism, is a mesmerizing tour de force.

Feminist theory, whether "pure" or applied, provides additional angles of vision. The literature is enormous. But see, for example, Joan Kelly, *Women, History, and Theory: The Essays of Joan Kelly* (Chicago, 1984), and Gerda Lerner's *The Creation of Patriarchy* (New York, 1986) and *Creation of Feminist Consciousness: From the Middle Ages to 1870* (New York, 1993). Successive generations have confronted the challenges set out in Mary Beard's *Woman as Force in History: A Study in Traditions and Realities* (New York, 1946, reprint 1976). For "free spaces," see Sara Evans and Harry Boyte, *Free Spaces: The Sources of Democratic Change in America* (Chicago, reprint 1992); on the importance of "voice"—both for individuals and in women's studies—see Sara Evans, "Afterword," in Nancy Hewitt et al., *Talking Gender* (Chapel Hill, NC, 1996), 190–97, and Robin Lakoff, *Language and Woman's Place* (New York, 1976). Judith Butler and Joan Wallach Scott, eds., *Feminists Theorize the Political* (New York, 1992) includes intriguing essays about woman as a "subject before the law." Several chapters in John Wallach Scott's *Gender and the Politics of History* (New York, 1988) seek to reconcile "difference" and equality. Linda Nicholson, *Gender and History: The Limits of Social Theory in the Age of the Family* (New York, 1986) urges scholars to historicize feminist (as well as liberal and Marxist) theories of public and private power. Catharine MacKinnon's pivotal works "theorize the legal"; see, for example, *Feminism Unmodified: Discourses on Life and Law* (Cambridge, MA, 1987), which ties the debasement of women's bodies to persistent inequality, and *Toward a Feminist Theory of the State* (Cambridge, MA, 1989), an attempt to reconstitute the state. Essays collected in Dorothy Helly and Susan Reverby, eds., *Gendered Domains: Rethinking Public and Private in Women's History* (Ithaca, NY, 1992) explore the fuzzy line between "public" and "private" realms.

PART ONE: ANGLO-AMERICAN BEGINNINGS

Surveys of colonial history are numerous. For a controversial synthesis of the "new" social history, see Jack P. Greene, *Pursuits of Happiness: The Social Development of Early*

Modern British Colonies and the Formation of American Culture (Chapel Hill, NC, 1988). On market development, see John McCusker and Russell Menard, *The Economy of British America, 1607–1789* (Chapel Hill, NC, 1985). For solid article and document collections, see Greene and J. R. Pole, eds., *Colonial British America: Essays . . .* (Baltimore, 1984), and Jack P. Greene, ed., *Settlements to Society, 1607–1763: A Documentary History of Colonial America* (New York, 1975). Surveys of colonial legal development include Peter Hoffer, *Law and People in Colonial America*, rev. ed. (Baltimore, 1998); Stephen Botein, *Early American Law and Society: Essays and Materials . . .* (Chicago, 1980); Edgar McManus, *Law and Liberty in Early New England: Criminal Justice and Due Process, 1620–1692* (Amherst, MA, 1993); and Jack P. Greene, *Peripheries and Center: Constitutional Development in the Extended Polities of the British Empire and the United States, 1607–1788* (Athens, GA, 1986). John Murrin, "The Legal Transformation: The Bench and Bar of Eighteenth-Century Massachusetts," in Stanley Katz et al., eds., *Colonial America*, 3rd ed. (New York, 1983), coined the term *Anglicization*. For women's history, see Carol Berkin, *First Generations: Women in Colonial America* (New York, 1996); Sylvia Frey and Marion Norton, eds., *New World, New Roles: A Documentary History of Women in Pre-Industrial America* (Westport, CT, 1986); and Nancy Woloch, ed., *Early American Women: A Documentary History, 1600–1900* (New York, 1997). Mary Beth Norton explores the changing contours of women's lives in "The Evolution of White Women's Experience in Early America," *AHR* (1984): 593–619.

Colonial history cannot be divorced from British history. For background and useful topical studies, see J. H. Baker, *An Introduction to English Legal History*, 3rd ed. (London, England, 1990); John Brewer and John Styles, eds., *An Ungovernable People: The English and Their Law in the Seventeenth and Eighteenth Centuries* (New Brunswick, NJ, 1980); Susan Amussen, *An Ordered Society: Gender and Class in Early Modern England* (New York, 1988); Merry E. Weisner, *Women and Gender in Early Modern Europe* (Cambridge, England, 1993); and Mary Prior, ed., *Women in English Society, 1500–1800* (New York, 1985), which includes Patricia Crawford's fine essay about "women writing." See also Susan Staves, *Married Women's Separate Property in England, 1660–1833* (Cambridge, MA, 1990); Lawrence Stone, *The Family, Sex, and Marriage in England, 1500–1800* (New York, 1977); Eileen Spring, *Law, Land, and Family: Aristocratic Inheritance in England, 1300 to 1800* (Chapel Hill, NC, 1993), a study of the vanishing heiress-at-law; Anna Clark, *Women's Silence, Men's Violence: Sexual Assault in England, 1770–1845* (New York, 1987), useful for the late colonial years; and Frances Dolan, *Dangerous Familiars: Representations of Domestic Crime in England, 1550–1700* (Ithaca, NY, 1994). On "scribblers," see Moira Ferguson, ed., *First Feminists: British Women Writers, 1578–1799* (Bloomington, IN, 1985). James A. Epstein's *Radical Expression: Political Language, Ritual, and Symbol in England, 1790–1850* (New York, 1994) underscores the power of popular constitutionalism and radical speech within English dissenting communities.

Several studies of colonial women and the law cast doubt on the utility of the traditional "from Puritan to Yankee" template. See, for example, Carole Shammas et al., eds., *Inheritance in America from Colonial Times to the Present* (New Brunswick, NJ, 1987), and especially Cornelia Hughes Dayton's *Women before the Bar: Gender, Law, and Society in Connecticut, 1639–1789* (Chapel Hill, NC, 1995), a pioneering account of women's changing status in the face of economic and social revolution. Dayton comports nicely with Mary Beth Norton's *Founding Mothers and Fathers: Gendered Power and the Forming of American Society* (New York, 1996), a study of gender relations in the early Chesapeake and in New England. Both of these works, in turn, provide context for Carole Shammas, "Anglo-American Household Government in Comparative Perspective," *William and Mary Quarterly* (1995): 104–44, hereafter *WMQ*. See also Marylynn Salmon's indispensable *Women and the Law of Property in Early America* (Chapel Hill, NC, 1986), and Larry Eldridge, ed., *Women and Freedom in Early America* (New York, 1997), which carries several strong entries. The idea of a "golden age" for first-generation colonists derives from Richard Morris, *Studies in the History of American Law* (Philadelphia, 1959). We know remarkably little about American Indian women's legal-political consciousness, but see Theda Perdue, *Cherokee Women: Gender and Culture Change, 1700–1835* (Lincoln, NE, 1998), which examines Cherokee women's experiences of work, marriage, and power; Anthony Wallace, *Death and Rebirth of the Seneca* (New York, 1970), which describes change in a matrilocal culture; and Laura F. Klein and Lillian Ackerman, eds., *Women and Power in Native North America* (Norman, OK, 1995).

The New England Way has long preoccupied colonial historians, and while it now shares the stage with studies of the Middle Colonies and the Chesapeake, Puritanism's importance can scarcely be doubted. See David Konig, *Law and Society in Puritan Massachusetts* (Chapel Hill, NC, 1979), and David Allen, *In English Ways* (New York, 1982), for divergent analyses of early institutional and legal-cultural developments, the collapse of a Puritan moral order, and the resort to law courts. Edmund Morgan, *The Puritan Family: Religion and Domestic Relations in Seventeenth-Century New England*, rev. ed. (New York, 1966) remains the most accessible and compelling account of the Puritan family. Two pioneering explorations of women's lives—Nancy Cott's *The Bonds of Womanhood: "Woman's Sphere" in New England, 1780–1835* (New Haven, CT, 1977), and Laurel Thatcher Ulrich's *Good Wives: Image and Reality in the Lives of Women in Northern New England, 1650–1750* (New York, 1982)—form the starting point. But see also Lyle Koehler's provocative *A Search for Power: The "Weaker Sex" in Seventeenth-Century New England* (Chicago, 1980); Helena Wall, *Fierce Communion: Family and Community in Early America* (Cambridge, MA, 1990); Barbara Laslett, "The Family as a Public and Private Institution: An Historical Perspective," *Journal of Marriage and the Family* (1973): 480–92; and Toby Ditz, *Property and Kinship: Inheritance in Early Connecticut, 1730–1820* (Princeton, NJ, 1986). Elaine Forman Crane, *Ebb Tide in New England: Women, Seaports, and Social Change, 1630–1800* (Boston, 1998) describes changing lives in commercial centers.

The Middle Colonies and plantation South present quite different faces. For the most telling work, see Julia Cherry Spruill's classic *Women's Life and Work in the Southern Colonies* (Chapel Hill, NC, 1938, reprint New York, 1972); Joan Jensen, *Loosening the Bonds: Mid-Atlantic Farm Women, 1750–1850* (New Haven, CT, 1986); Lois Green Carr and Lorena Walsh's important essay, "The Planter's Wife: The Experience of White Women in Seventeenth-Century Maryland," *WMQ* (1977): 542–71; Kathleen Brown, *Good Wives, Nasty Wenches, and Anxious Patriarchs: Gender, Race, and Power in Colonial Virginia* (Chapel Hill, NC, 1996), which shows how gender and race ascriptions interacted to yield new systems of governance; Deborah Gray White's brilliant *Ar'n't I a Woman?: Female Slaves in the Plantation South* (New York, 1985); and Joan Gunderson and Gwen Victor Gampel, "Married Women's Legal Status in Eighteenth-Century New York and Virginia," *WMQ* (1982): 114–34. For political economy, regional culture, and criminal procedure, see Thad Tate and David Ammerman, eds., *The Chesapeake in the Seventeenth Century* (Chapel Hill, NC, 1979); James Lemon, *The Best Poor Man's Country: A Geographical Study of Early Southeastern Pennsylvania* (Baltimore 1972); Lois

Green Carr et al., eds., *Colonial Chesapeake Society* (Chapel Hill, NC, 1988); and Douglas Greenberg, *Crime and Law Enforcement in the Colony of New York, 1691–1776* (Ithaca, NY, 1976). On New York, see David Narrett, *Inheritance and Family in Colonial New York City* (Ithaca, NY, 1992), and Linda Briggs Biemer, *Women and Property in Colonial New York: The Transition from Dutch to English Law, 1643–1727* (Ann Arbor, MI, 1983).

Women's prospects after marriage occupy a large literature. On widowhood, for example, see Alexander Keyssar, "Widowhood in Eighteenth-Century Massachusetts: A Problem in the History of the Family," *Perspectives in American History* (1974): 83–119; William Ricketson, "To Be Young, Poor, and Alone: The Experience of Widowhood in the Massachusetts Bay Colony, 1675–1676," *New England Quarterly* (1991): 113–27; and Kim Lacy Rogers, "Relicts of the New World: Conditions of Widowhood in Seventeenth-Century New England," in Mary Kelley, ed., *Woman's Being, Woman's Place: Female Identity and Vocation in American History* (Boston, 1979). For the Middle Colonies, see Lisa Wilson, *Life After Death: Widows in Pennsylvania, 1750–1850* (Philadelphia, 1992), and Christine H. Tompsett, "A Note on the Economic Status of Widows in Colonial New York," *New York History* (1974): 319–32. On divorce, see Nancy Cott's now-classic "Divorce and the Changing Status of Women in Eighteenth-Century Massachusetts," *WMQ* (1976): 586–614, and Alison Duncan Hirsch, "The Thrall Divorce Case: A Family Crisis in Eighteenth-Century Connecticut," *Women and History* (1982): 43–75; and Merril D. Smith, *Breaking the Bonds: Marital Discord in Pennsylvania, 1730–1830* (New York, 1991).

Labor figured large in colonists' lives. For the coming of market economies, see James Henretta, *The Origins of American Capitalism: Collected Essays* (Boston, 1991); Allan Kulikoff, *The Agrarian Origins of American Capitalism* (Charlottesville, VA, 1992); William Chester Jordan, *Women and Credit in Pre-Industrial and Developing Societies* (Philadelphia, 1993); and, for late colonial economies, Alice Hanson Jones, *Wealth of a Nation to Be: The American Colonies on the Eve of the American Revolution* (New York, 1980). On the shift from cottage to shop work, see Daniel Vickers, *Farmers and Fishermen: Two Centuries of Work in Essex County, Massachusetts, 1630–1850* (Chapel Hill, NC, 1994), which mostly neglects women. Local and regional studies add complexity. See, for example, Christine Heyrman, *Commerce and Culture: The Maritime Communities of Colonial Massachusetts, 1690–1750* (New York, 1984); James Lemon, "Household Consumption in Eighteenth-Century America and Its Relationship to Production and Trade . . . [in] Southeastern Pennsylvania," *Agricultural History* (1967): 59–70; Gloria Main, "Gender, Work, and Wages in Colonial New England, *WMQ* (1994): 39–66; Patricia A. Cleary, "'She Will Be in the Shop': Women's Sphere of Trade in Eighteenth-Century Philadelphia and New York," *Pennsylvania Magazine of History and Biography* (1995): 181–202; Joan Jensen, "Butter Making and Economic Development in Mid-Atlantic America from 1750 to 1850," *Signs* (1988): 813–29; Christopher Clark, "The Household Economy, Market Exchange, and the Rise of Capitalism in the Connecticut Valley, 1800–1860," *Journal of Social History* (1979–80): 169–89; Jean Jordan, "Women Merchants in Colonial New York," *New York History* (1977): 412–39; and Deborah Rosen, *Courts and Commerce: Gender, Law and the Market Economy in Colonial New York* (Columbus, OH, 1997). On leisure, see Richard Bushman, *The Refinement of America: Persons, Houses, Cities* (New York, 1992).

Beyond heresy and witchcraft trials, writing about women's courtroom experiences is sparse. But see Norton, *Founding Mothers and Fathers*, for trials of Hibbens, Hutchinson, and many others. See also relevant chapters in Dayton, *Women Before the Bar*; Jane Kamensky, *Governing the Tongue: The Politics of Speech in Early New England* (New York, 1997), particularly for Hibbens and Hutchinson; Elaine Huber, *Women and the Authority of Inspiration: A Re-Examination of Two Prophetic Movements from a Contemporary Feminist Perspective* (Lanham, MD, 1985); the documents collected in David Hall, ed., *The Antinomian Controversy, 1636–1638* (Durham, NC, 1990); and for trials in church courts after the Great Awakening, Susan Juster, *Disorderly Women: Sexual Politics and Evangelicalism in Revolutionary New England* (Ithaca, NY, 1994). Elizabeth Reis, *Damned Women: Sinners and Witches in Puritan New England* (Ithaca, NY, 1997) shows how theology contributed to witchhunts. For the Salem debacle, see Peter Hoffer, *The Salem Witchcraft Trials: A Legal History* (Lawrence, KS, 1997) and Carol Karlsen, *The Devil in the Shape of a Woman: Witchcraft in Colonial New England* (New York, 1989). See also N. E. H. Hull, *Female Felons: Women and Serious Crime in Colonial Massachusetts* (Urbana, IL, 1987), which downplays discrimination.

Similarly, we know little about women's physical security on either side of the Atlantic. Parts of the story are told in Paul Finkelman, "Crimes of Love, Misdemeanors of Passion: The Regulation of Race and Sex in the Colonial South," in Catharine Clinton et al., eds., *The Devil's Lane: Sex and Race in the Early South* (New York, 1997): 124–35; David Flaherty, *Privacy in Colonial America* (Charlottesville, VA, 1970); Marybeth Hamilton Arnold, " 'The Life of a Citizen in the Hands of a Woman': Sexual Assault in New York City, 1790 to 1820," in Kathy Peiss and Christina Simmons, eds., *Passion and Power: Sexuality in History* (Philadelphia, 1989); Cornelia Hughes, "Taking the Trade: Abortion and Gender Relations in an Eighteenth Century New England Village," *WMQ* (1991): 19–49; Robert Wells, "Illegitimacy and Bridal Pregnancy in Colonial America," in Peter Laslett, ed., *Bastardy in Comparative History* (London, 1976); Daniel Scott Smith and Michael Hindus, "Premarital Pregnancy in America, 1640–1971: An Overview and Interpretation," *Journal of Interdisciplinary History* (1975): 537–70; Peter Hoffer and N. E. H. Hull, *Murdering Mothers* (New York, 1981), a study of infanticide; and Barbara Lindemann, " 'To Ravish and Carnally Know': Rape in Eighteenth-Century Massachusetts," *Signs* (1984–85): 63–82.

Women's religious practices and oratory are slightly better documented. See especially Catherine Brekus, *Strangers and Pilgrims: Female Preaching in America, 1740–1845* (Chapel Hill, NC, 1998); the essays in David Hall et al., eds., *Saints and Revolutionaries: Essays on Early American History* (New York, 1984); Richard Shiels, "The Feminization of American Congregationalism, 1730–1835," *American Quarterly* (1981): 46–82; Mary Dunn's classic article, "Holy Maydens, Holy Wyfes: Congregational and Quaker Women in the Early Colonial Period," *American Quarterly* (1978): 582–601; Richard Greaves, ed., *Triumph over Silence: Women in Protestant History* (Westport, CT, 1985), which contains valuable information about New England; Sheryl Kujawa, "The Great Awakening of Sarah Osborn and the Female Society of the First Congregational Church . . . ," *Newport History* (1994): 133–53; and Konig, *Law and Society in Puritan Massachusetts*. Amanda Porterfield, *Female Piety in Puritan New England* (New York, 1992) shows how piety affected both Puritanism and women's political power. Susan Juster's *Disorderly Women* explores both the Awakening's potential for female liberation and its repressive aftermath. For women's speech, see Robert St. George, " 'Heated' Speech and Literacy in Seventeenth Century New England," in David Hall et al., eds., *Seventeenth-Century New England* (Boston, 1984), and Mary Beth Norton, "Gender and Defamation in Seventeenth-Century Maryland," *WMQ* (1987): 3–39. Two remarkable volumes that appeared after this book was written—Marilyn Westerkamp's *Women and Religion in Early America, 1600–1850* (New York, 1999), and Rebecca Larson, *Daughters of Light: Quaker Women Preaching and Prophesying in the Colonies and Abroad, 1700–1775* (New York, 1999)—situate Protestant women firmly in the circle of religious educators and preachers.

Extensive information about the revolutionary experience can be found in Gordon Wood, *The Radicalism of the American Revolution* (New York, 1993), which mostly eschews gender analysis; John Phillip Reid's multivolume *Constitutional History of the American Revolution* (Madison, WI, 1986–1993), and the one-volume abridged version; Gordon Wood, *Creation of the American Republic* (Chapel Hill, NC, 1969); Jack Rakove, *Original Meanings* (New York, 1996); and, for state constitution making, Marc Kruman, *Between Authority and Liberty* (Chapel Hill, NC, 1998), which describes the formalization of sex-specific suffrage practices. Study of women's revolutionary experiences begins with Ronald Hoffman and Peter Albert's wide-ranging collection, *Women in the Age of the American Revolution* (Charlottesville, VA, 1989). See also Joan Gunderson's analysis of women's history during the early and middle decades of revolution, *"To Be Useful to the World": Women in Revolutionary America, 1740–1770* (New York, 1996), especially for nonwhite and lower-class women. For the French analogue and wars generally, see Carol Berkin, ed., *Women, War, and Revolution* (New York, 1980); Olwen Hufton, *Women and the Limits of Citizenship in the French Revolution* (Toronto, 1992); Candice Proctor, *Women, Equality, and the French Revolution* (Westport, CT, 1990); Lynn Hunt, *The Family Romance of the French Revolution* (Berkeley, CA, 1992); and Joan Landes, *Women and the Public Sphere in the Age of the French Revolution* (Ithaca, NY, 1988).

Writing about white women as revolutionary agents has expanded. The point of departure is Linda Kerber's *Women of the Republic: Intellect and Ideology in Revolutionary America* (Chapel Hill, NC, 1980), with its discussion of Republican Motherhood; Mary Beth Norton's equally important *Liberty's Daughters: The Revolutionary Experience of American Women, 1750–1800* (Boston, 1980); Kerber's classic "The Republican Mother: Women and the Enlightenment, An American Perspective," *American Quarterly* (1976): 187–205; Jan Lewis, "The Republican Wife: Virtue and Seduction in the Early Republic," *WMQ* (1987): 689–721; Ruth Bloch's bedrock study, "The Gendered Meanings of Virtue in Revolutionary America," *Signs* (1987–88): 37–58; Harriet Applewhite et al., eds, *Women and Politics in the Age of the Democratic Revolution* (Ann Arbor, MI, 1990); and Joy Day Buel and Richard Buel, *The Way of Duty: A Woman and her Family in Revolutionary America* (New York, 1984). On black women, see Jacqueline Jones, "Race, Sex, and Self-Evident Truths: The Status of Slave Women during the Era of the American Revolution," in Catherine Clinton, ed., *Half Sisters of History: Southern Women and the American Past* (Durham, NC, 1994): 18–35. For retrenchment, see Linda Kerber's study of the *Martin* case, "The Paradox of Women's Citizenship in the Early Republic: The Case of *Martin vs. Massachusetts*, 1805," *AHR* (1992): 349–78, reprinted in Kerber, *Toward an Intellectual History of Women* (Chapel Hill, NC, 1997). See also Joan Hoff, "The Illusion of Change: Women and the American Revolution," in Jean Friedman et al., eds., *Our American Sisters: Women in American Life and Thought*, 4th ed. (Lexington, MA, 1987); and Carroll Smith-Rosenberg, "Dis-Covering the Subject of the 'Great Constitutional Discussion,' 1786–1789," *JAH* (1992): 841–73. On killing the father-king, see Jay Fliegelman, *Prodigals and Pilgrims: The American Revolution Against Patriarchal Authority, 1750–1800* (New York, 1982); for divorce as an expression of the same impulse, see Norma Basch, "From the Bonds of Empire to the Bonds of Matrimony," in

David Konig, ed., *Devising Liberty: Preserving and Creating Freedom in the New American Republic* (Stanford, CA, 1995). For the lives of two important women, see Rosemary Zagarri, *A Woman's Dilemma: Mercy Otis Warren and the American Revolution* (Wheeling, IL, 1995), and Sharon Harris, ed., *Selected Writings of Judith Sargent Murray* (New York, 1995).

PART TWO: REPUBLICAN SPEECH COMMUNITIES AND COEQUALITY

Studies of first-wave agitation begin with Elizabeth Cady Stanton et al., eds., *History of Woman Suffrage*, 6 vols. (Rochester, NY, 1881–1922, Ayers reprint, 1985). Undertaken in part to document woman's rise to power, these volumes range well beyond suffragism, particularly the first two volumes, where the title is a misnomer. Yet *HWS* is neither infallible nor sufficient. Transcriptions can be inaccurate or partial, women's accounts of developments in states and territories require corroboration, and the editors' selections reflect their own sense of the importance of people and events. The harshly abridged *A Concise History of Woman Suffrage: Selections from the Classic Work . . .* , edited by Mary Jo and Paul Buhle (Urbana, IL, 1978), does not capture the richness of the original work. The microfilm edition of *Papers of Elizabeth Cady Stanton and Susan B. Anthony*, eds. Patricia G. Holland and Ann D. Gordon (Wilmington, DE, 1991) has a separate printed index and contains the full run of the *Revolution* newspaper. See also the print edition as it emerges; Ann Gordon, ed., *The Selected Papers of Elizabeth Cady Stanton and Susan B. Anthony*, Vol. 1, "In the School of Anti-Slavery, 1840–1866" (New Brunswick, NJ, 1997). Many women's newspapers (e.g., *Lily*, the *Woman's Journal*, and *Revolution*), organizational papers (e.g., NAWSA, WCTU, NWP), and pamphlets can be read in microform (e.g., the Pamphlets in American History collection).

The Victorian era was long and complex. For general information, see Daniel Walker Howe, ed., *Victorian America* (Philadelphia, 1976). See also Ann Douglas's important study of sentimentalism, *The Feminization of American Culture* (New York, 1977, reprint, 1988), and Barbara Welter's classic account of the crystallization of male-female realms, "The Cult of True Womanhood: 1820–1860," *American Quarterly* (1966): 151–75. On first-wave agitation, see Jean Matthews, *Woman's Struggle for Equality: The First Phase, 1828–1876* (Chicago, 1997) and Catherine Clinton, *The Other Civil War: American Women in the Nineteenth Century* (New York, 1984); Ellen Carol DuBois's classic *Feminism and Suffrage: The Emergence of an Independent Woman's Movement in America, 1848–1869* (Ithaca, NY, 1978); Sylvia Hoffert, *When Hens Crow: The Woman's Rights Movement in Antebellum America* (Bloomington, IN, 1995), an analysis of the movement's ideology; and, for black-white relations, Barbara Hilkert Andolsen, *"Daughters of Jefferson, Daughters of Bootblacks': Racism and American Feminism* (Macon, GA, 1986). See also Nancy Isenberg's important study, *Sex and Citizenship in Antebellum America* (Chapel Hill, NC, 1998), which emphasizes organized churches more than I do; and William Leach, *True Love and Perfect Union: The Feminist Reform of Sex and Society* (New York, 1980), an exploration of relations between feminist thought and cultural change. On black women, see Deborah Gray White, "Female Slaves: Sex Role and Status in the Antebellum Plantation South," in Catherine Clinton, ed., *Half Sisters of History: Southern Women and the American Past* (Durham, NC, 1994), and Dorothy Sterling, ed., *We Are Your Sisters: Black Women in the Nineteenth Century* (New York, 1984).

On southern women, see Joanne Hawks et al., eds., *Sex, Race, and the Role of Women in the South* (Jackson, MS, 1983).

Historians of women have long been sensitive to matters of conscience and voice. For experimental religion and its ties to reformism, see Wendy Chmielewski et al., eds., *Women in Spiritual and Communitarian Societies in the United States* (Syracuse, NY, 1993); Nancy Hewitt's invaluable *Women's Activism and Social Change: Rochester, NY, 1822–1872* (Ithaca, NY, 1984), which underscores the power of religious commitment; Elizabeth B. Clark's equally indispensable "Religion, Rights, and Difference in the Early Woman's Rights Movement," *Wisconsin Women's Rights Journal* (1987): 29–57, abridged as "Religion and Rights Consciousness in the Antebellum Woman's Rights Movement," in Fineman and Thomadsen, eds., *At the Boundaries of the Law* (New York, 1991); and Clark, "Matrimonial Bonds: Slavery and Divorce in Nineteenth-Century America," *Law and History Review* (1990): 25–54. On women's writing, speaking, and assemblies, see Ann Russo and Cheris Kramarae, *The Radical Women's Press of the 1850's* (New York, 1991); Martha Solomon, ed., *A Voice of Their Own: The Woman Suffrage Press, 1840–1910* (Tuscaloosa, AL, 1991); Lana Rakow et al., eds., *The Revolution in Words: Righting Women, 1868–1871* (New York, 1990), which explores the Stanton-Anthony paper; Donald Scott's valuable "The Popular Lecture and the Creation of a Public in Mid-Nineteenth-Century America," *JAH* (1980): 791–809; Linda Lumsden, *Rampant Women: Suffragists and the Right of Assembly* (Knoxville, TN, 1997); Cathy Davidson, *Revolution and the Word: The Rise of the Novel in America* (New York, 1986); Margaret Beetham, *A Magazine of Her Own? Domesticity and Desire in the Woman's Magazines, 1800–1914* (New York, 1996); Carla L. Peterson, *Doers of the Word: African-American Speakers and Writers in the North, 1830–1880* (New York, 1995), which explores male and female speech; and, for a powerful black voice, Melba Boyd, *Discarded Legacy: Politics and Poetics in the Life of Frances Ellen Watkins Harper, 1825–1911* (Detroit, MI, 1994). Kenneth Cmiel's provocative *Democratic Eloquence: The Fight over Popular Speech in Nineteenth-Century America* (New York, 1990) is more interested in the content of speech than in access to the forum. On publishing, see Mary Kelley, *Private Woman, Public Stage: Literary Domesticity in Nineteenth-Century America* (New York, 1984), and Susan Coultrap-McQuin, *Doing Literary Business: American Women Writers* (Chapel Hill, NC, 1990). For the emergence of a female pastorate in the Atlantic basin, see Deborah Valenze, *Prophetic Sons and Daughters: Female Preaching and Popular Religion in Industrial England* (Princeton, NJ, 1985); Christine Krueger, *The Reader's Repentance: Women Preachers, Women Writers, and Nineteenth-Century Social Discourse* (Chicago, 1993); and Brekus, *Strangers and Pilgrims* (Chapel Hill, NC, 1998), which identifies the 1830s as the decade of greatest resistance to women's public oratory. Caroll Smith-Rosenberg, "The Female World of Love and Ritual: Relations between Women in Nineteenth-Century America," *Signs* (1975): 1–30, is immensely important for understanding the formation of antebellum speech communities. Elizabeth Clark, " 'The Sacred Rights of the Weak': Pain, Sympathy, and the Culture of Individual Rights in Antebellum America," *JAH* (September 1995): 463–93, limns relationships between rights consciousness and an emerging culture of sympathy. Ann Braude, *Radical Spirits: Spiritualism and Women's Rights in Nineteenth-Century America* (Boston, 1989), shows how religious and extra-sensory experimentation advanced female emancipation. On revivalism, see Whitney Cross's classic *The Burned-Over District* (Ithaca, NY, 1950); Paul Johnson, *A Shopkeeper's Millennium: Society and Revivals in Rochester, New York, 1815–1837* (New York, 1978); Robert Abzug's fascinating study of linkages between religion and reform,

Cosmos Crumbling: American Reform and the Religious Imagination (New York, 1994); and William McLoughlin's seminal *Revivals, Awakenings, and Reform: An Essay on Religion and Social Change* (Chicago, 1978).

Nineteenth-century views of women's bodies and reproductive capabilities dramatically affected liberty prospects. For a prize-winning account of a midwife's experiences, see Laurel Thatcher Ulrich, *A Midwife's Tale: The Life of Martha Ballard, Based on Her Diary, 1785–1812* (New York, 1990). See also Karen Sanchez-Eppler, *Touching Liberty: Abolitionism, Feminism, and the Politics of the Body* (Berkeley, CA, 1993); Judith Walzer Leavitt, *Brought to Bed: Childbearing in America, 1750–1850* (New York, 1986); G. J. Barker-Benfield's sensationalist account of Victorian medicine's view of women, *The Horrors of the Half-Known Life: Male Attitudes Toward Women and Sexuality in Nineteenth-Century America* (New York, 1976), which should be read with James Mohr, *Medicine and the Law: Medical Jurisprudence in Nineteenth-Century America* (New York, 1993); and Alan Westin, *Privacy and Freedom* (New York, 1967), which describes state developments. For abridgments of personal security when husbands or the state incarcerated women, see Ellen Dwyer, "The Weaker Vessel: Legal Versus Social Reality in Mental Commitments in 19th-Century New York," in D. Kelly Weisberg, ed., *Women and the Law: The Social-Historical Perspective*, Vol. 1 (Cambridge, MA, 1982): 85–106; Barbara Sapinsley, *The Private War of Mrs. Packard* (New York, 1991), to be read with Hendrik Hartog's brilliant "Mrs. Packard on Dependency," *Yale Journal of Law and the Humanities* (1988): 79–104; and Francis Allen, *The Decline of the Rehabilitative Ideal: Penal Policy and Social Purpose* (New Haven, CT, 1981).

Capitalism both constrained and emancipated Victorian women. Gerda Lerner's "The Lady and the Mill Girl: Changes in the Status of Women in the Age of Jackson," *Mid-Continent American Studies Journal* (1969): 5–15, is still a foundation study. For accounts of change over time, see Christine Stansell's *City of Women: Sex and Class in New York, 1789–1860* (Urbana, IL, 1982), which shows how New York working-class men and women negotiated access to civic spaces after the Revolution and "invented" gender; and Suzanne Lebsock, *The Free Women of Petersburg: Status and Culture in a Southern Town, 1784–1860* (New York, 1984), which explores connections between property and power. See also Jeanne Boydston, *Home and Work: Housework, Wages, and the Ideology of Labor in the Early Republic* (New York, 1990); Nancy Grey Osterud, *Bonds of Community: The Lives of Farm Women in Nineteenth-Century New York* (New York, 1991); Anne Firor Scott, *The Southern Lady: From Pedestal to Politics, 1830–1930* (Chicago, 1970); Thomas Dublin, *Transforming Women's Work: New England Lives in the Industrial Revolution* (Ithaca, NY, 1994); and Teresa Anne Murphy, *Ten Hours' Labor: Religion, Reform, and Gender in Early New England* (Ithaca, NY, 1992), which shows how working-class women carved out a niche in the labor market. Benita Eisler, ed., *The Lowell Offering* (New York, 1977) collects the writings of New England women employed in textile mills. Writing about women's paid and unpaid labor takes on fresh significance when read with Christopher Tomlins, "Subordination, Authority, Law: Subjects in Labor History," *International Labor and Working-Class History* (Spring 1995), which explores boundaries between markets and households and sheds light on the power of families in public life; for a suggestive account of the eclipse of nineteenth-century political discourses by "law talk," see Tomlins, *Law, Labor, and Ideology in the Early American Republic* (Baltimore, 1992).

Biographies bring circumscription to life and show how well-known women came to public attention. In the Victorian era, the list is long. But see, for example, Nell Irvin Painter, *Sojourner Truth: A Life, A Symbol* (New York, 1996); Kathleen Barry, *Susan B. Anthony: A Biography* (New York, 1988); Elisabeth Griffith, *In Her Own Right: The Life of Elizabeth Cady Stanton* (New York, 1984); Ellen Carol DuBois, ed., *Elizabeth Cady Stanton, Susan B. Anthony, Correspondence, Writings, Speeches* (New York, 1981); Margaret Hope Bacon, *Valiant Friend: The Life of Lucretia Mott* (New York, 1980); Gerda Lerner, *The Grimké Sisters from South Carolina: Pioneers for Woman's Rights and Abolition* (New York, 1971); Larry Ceplair, ed., *The Public Years of Sarah and Angelina Grimké: Selected Writings, 1835–1839* (New York, 1989); Katharine Lumpkin, *The Emancipation of Angelina Grimké* (Chapel Hill, NC, 1974); Dorothy Sterling, *Ahead of Her Time: Abby Kelley and the Politics of Antislavery* (New York, 1991); Elizabeth Cazden, *Antoinette Brown Blackwell: A Biography* (Old Westbury, NY, 1983); Paula Blanchard, *Margaret Fuller: From Transcendentalism to Revolution* (Reading, MA, 1978, reprint 1987); Katherine Kish Sklar, *Catharine Beecher: A Study in American Domesticity* (New Haven, CT, 1973); Jeanne Boydston et al., eds., *The Limits of Sisterhood: The Beecher Sisters on Women's Rights and Woman's Sphere* (Chapel Hill, NC, 1988); Celia Morris, *Fanny Wright: Rebel in America* (Urbana, IL, 1984); Marilyn Richardson, ed., *Maria W. Stewart, America's First Black Woman Political Writer* (Bloomington, IN, 1987); Joan Hedrick, *Harriet Beecher Stowe: A Life* (New York, 1994), which explores freedom of speech and reformers' use of words; Andrea Moore Kerr, *Lucy Stone: Speaking Out For Equality* (New Brunswick, NJ, 1992); Lois Beachy Underhill, *The Woman Who Ran for President: The Many Lives of Victoria Woodhull* (New York, 1996); and Jill Norgren, "Before It Was Merely Difficult: Belva Lockwood's Life in Law and Politics," *Journal of Supreme Court History* (1999), part of a book in progress.

Associated reformism and partisanship provided opportunities for self-expression. Again, the literature is rich. See, for example, William Leach, *True Love and Perfect Union: The Feminist Reform of Sex and Society* (New York, 1980), an analysis of feminism's drift toward the social sciences; and, for the abolitionist connection, Aileen S. Kraditor, *Means and Ends in American Abolitionism: Garrison and His Critics on Strategy and Tactics, 1834–1850* (Chicago, 1967, reprint 1989), chap. 3, "The Woman Question." Many studies flow from the idea that abolitionism was *the* main fount of women's rights agitation; see Wendy Hamand Venet, *Neither Ballots nor Bullets: Women Abolitionists and the Civil War* (Charlottesville, VA, 1991), or Jean Fagan Yellin, *Women and Sisters: The Antislavery Feminists in American Culture* (New Haven, CT, 1989). For temperance agitation, see Barbara Epstein, *The Politics of Domesticity: Women, Evangelism, and Temperance in 19th Century America* (Middletown, CT, 1981). For changes in men's lives, see David Leverenz, *Manhood and the American Renaissance* (Ithaca, NY, 1989), and Carnes, *Meanings for Manhood.* Beyond accounts of early suffrage campaigns, a few scholars offer fresh views of women's political involvement. See, for example, Mary Ryan, *Women in Public: Between Banners and Ballots, 1825–1880* (Baltimore, 1990), which traces women's attempts to occupy public spaces and Americans' replacement of real women with symbolic ones; Norma Basch, "Equity vs. Equality: Emerging Concepts of Women's Political Status in the Age of Jackson," *Journal of the Early Republic* (1983): 297–318; and especially Elizabeth Varon's pathbreaking *"We Mean to be Counted": White Women and Politics in Antebellum Virginia* (Chapel Hill, NC, 1998), which will force scholars to rethink what they mean by "political." On the New Jersey woman suffrage experiment, see Judith Apter Klinghoffer and Lois Elkis, "'The Petticoat Electors': Woman's Suffrage in New Jersey, 1776–1807," *Journal of the Early Republic* (1992): 159–93.

Studies of "westering" women often contain information relevant to legal history. For overviews, see Sandra Myres, *Westering Women and the Frontier Experience, 1800–1915* (Albuquerque, NM, 1982), and Julie Roy Jeffrey, *Frontier Women* (New York, 1979; rev.

ed. 1998). Glenda Riley, *The Female Frontier: A Comparative View of Women on the Prairie and the Plains* (Lawrence, KS, 1988) contains four chapters on late-century female employment and civic work at the frontier. See also Elizabeth Jameson and Susan Armitage, eds., *Writing the Range: Race, Class, and Culture in the Women's West* (Norman, OK, 1997), especially Peggy Pascoe's essay, "Race, Gender, and Interracial Relations: The Case of Interracial Marriage," and Wendy Wall's intriguing "Gender and the 'Citizen Indian.'" Among the essays in Susan Armitage and Elizabeth Jameson's *The Women's West* (Norman, OK, 1987) is Sherry Smith's account of white army officers' views of Indian marriages and "squaws." Regional studies include such works as Sandra Haarsager, *Organized Womanhood: Cultural Politics in the Pacific Northwest, 1840–1920* (Norman, OK 1997); Arlene Scadron, ed., *On Their Own: Widows and Widowhood in the American Southwest, 1848–1939* (Urbana, IL, 1988); and Paula Petrick, *No Step Backward: Women and Family on the Rocky Mountain Mining Frontier, Helena, Montana, 1865–1900* (Helena, MT, 1987), which shows how Montana women secured a public voice. Glenda Riley, *Building and Breaking Families in the American West* (Albuquerque, NM, 1996) attributes rising divorce rates in the West to cultural stress.

When legal historians think of women and Victorian law reform, married women's property acts spring to mind. Norma Basch, *In the Eyes of the Law: Women, Marriage, and Property in Nineteenth-Century New York* (Ithaca, NY, 1982), provides an account of change in a widely emulated state. See also Lebsock's important *Free Women of Petersburg*, cited earlier; Elizabeth Bowles Warbasse, *The Changing Legal Rights of Married Women, 1800–1861* (New York, 1987); Carole Shammas's instructive "Re-Assessing the Married Women's Property Acts," *Journal of Women's History* (Spring 1994): 9–30; Peggy Rabkin, *Fathers to Daughters: The Legal Foundations of Female Emancipation* (Westport, CT, 1980); and Richard Chused, "Married Women's Property Law: 1800–1850," *Georgetown Law Journal* (1983): 1359–1425. Reva Siegel explores interconnected legal threads and shows how judges produced gender inequalities; on economic topics, see "The Modernization of Marital Status Law: Adjudicating Wives' Rights to Earnings, 1860–1930," *Georgetown Law Journal* (1994): 2127–2211; and "Home as Work: The First Woman's Rights Claims concerning Wives' Household Labor, 1850–1880," *Yale Law Journal* (1994): 1073–1217.

Yet Americans felt the weight of law well beyond the marketplace. At the heart of Victorian society lay the "private" family, which interacted with law and served public interests; see Mary Ryan, *Cradle of the Middle Class: The Family in Oneida County, New York, 1790–1865* (Cambridge, England, 1981). Study commences with Michael Grossberg, *Governing the Hearth: Law and the Family in Nineteenth-Century America* (Chapel Hill, NC, 1985), the source of the term *judicial patriarchy,* and his *A Judgment for Solomon* (New York, 1996), which explores a notorious custody case and pairs nicely with Laura Hanft Korobkin, *Criminal Conversations: Sentimentality and Nineteenth-Century Legal Stories of Adultery* (New York, 1998). Hendrik Hartog's *Man and Wife in America, A History* (Cambridge, MA, 2000) which appeared as this book went into production, promises to change how we think about marriage before modern times. See also Mary Ann Mason, *From Father's Property to Children's Rights: The History of Child Custody in the United States* (New York, 1994), which should be read with Grossberg and Hartog. On southern "state patriarchy," see Peter Bardaglio, *Reconstructing the Household: Families, Sex, and the Law in the 19th Century South* (Chapel Hill, NC, 1995), which complements both Victoria Bynum's *Unruly Women: The Politics of Social and Sexual Control in the Old South* (Chapel Hill, NC, 1992), esp. chap. 4 ("The State as Patriarch"), and Amy Dru Stanley's post–Civil War study, *From Bondage to Contract: Wage Labor, Marriage, and the Market in the Age of Slave Emancipation* (New York, 1998). On domestic violence, see Reva Siegel, "'The Rule of Love': Wife Beating as Prerogative and Privacy," *Yale Law Journal* (1996): 2117–2207; and Elizabeth Pleck, *Domestic Tyranny: The Making of Social Policy Against Family Violence from Colonial Times to the Present* (New York, 1987). On custody and divorce, see Hendrik Hartog's important article, "Marital Exits and Marital Expectations in Nineteenth Century America," *Georgetown Law Journal* (1991): 95–129; Jamil Zainaldin, "The Emergence of a Modern American Family Law: Child Custody, Adoption, and the Courts, 1796–1851," *Northwestern University Law Review* (1979): 1038–89; Robert Griswold, "The Evolution of the Doctrine of Mental Cruelty in Victorian American Divorce, 1790–1900," *Journal of Social History* (1986): 127–48; Griswold, *Family and Divorce in California, 1850–1890* (Albany, NY, 1982); Norma Basch, "Relief in the Premises: Divorce as a Woman's Remedy in New York and Indiana, 1815–1870," *Law and History Review* (1990): 1–24; Richard Chused's study of Maryland development, *Private Acts in Public Places: A Social History of Divorce . . .* (Philadelphia, 1994); and Glenda Riley, *Divorce: An American Tradition* (New York, 1991).

The Civil War altered women's circumstances. Two books suggest the need to rethink basic analytical categories. Rebecca Edwards, *Angels in the Machinery: Gender in American Party Politics from the Civil War to the Progressive* Era (New York, 1997), in demonstrating female involvement in partisan affairs, works toward a new definition of politics; Laura Edwards, *Gendered Strife and Confusion: The Political Culture of Reconstruction* (Urbana, IL, 1997) ties the quest for full citizenship to postwar systems of racial and sex segregation and to family life and shows how law reinforced cultural decisions. For interesting readings on the war years, see Ellen Carol DuBois, "Outgrowing the Compact of the Fathers: Equal Rights, Woman Suffrage, and the United States Constitution, 1820–1878," *JAH* (1987): 836–62, and Norma Basch, "Reconstructing Female Citizenship," in Donald Nieman, ed., *The Constitution, Law, and American Life: Critical Aspects of the Nineteenth Century Experience* (Athens, GA, 1992). On late antebellum and wartime experiences, see Joan Cashin, "Women and the Search for Manly Independence," and Deborah G. White, "Female Slaves: Sex Roles and Status in the Antebellum Plantation South," both in J. William Harris, ed., *Society and Culture in the Slave South* (New York, 1992); Mary Elizabeth Massey's old classic, *Women in the Civil War* (Lincoln, NE, 1966); Catherine Clinton, *Divided Houses: Gender and the Civil War* (New York, 1992); Drew Gilpin Faust, *Mothers of Invention: Women of the Slaveholding South in the American Civil War* (Chapel Hill, NC, 1996), for the confederate side; Elizabeth Leonard, *Yankee Women: Gender Battles in the Civil War* (New York, 1994); and Catherine Clinton, *Tara Revisited: Women, War, and the Plantation Legend* (New York, 1995). On postbellum fears of black men's liaisons with white women, see Martha Hodes, "The Sexualization of Reconstruction Politics: White Women and Black Men in the South after the Civil War," in John Fout and Maura Shaw Tantillo, eds., *American Sexual Politics: Sex, Gender, and Race since the Civil War* (Chicago, 1993): 59–74; and Hodes's more extensive *White Women, Black Men: Illicit Sex in the Nineteenth-Century South* (New Haven, CT, 1997). Tera Hunter examines black women's work and resistance strategies in *To 'Joy My Freedom: Southern Black Women's Lives and Labors after the Civil War* (Cambridge, MA, 1997). Mary Farmer explores Freedmen's Bureau perceptions of gender difference among blacks; see, for example, "'Because They Are Women': Gender and the Virginia Freedmen's Bureau's 'War on Dependency'," in Paul Cimbala, et al., eds., *The Freedmen's Bureau and Reconstruction: Reconsiderations* (New York, 1999). See also Suzanne Lebsock, "Radical Reconstruction and the Property Rights of Southern Women," and Catherine Clinton, "Bloody Terrain: Freedwomen, Sexuality, and Violence during Reconstruction," in Clinton, ed., *Half Sisters of History* (Durham, NC, 1994). Philip Foner collects Frederick Douglass' women's rights essays in *Frederick Douglass on Women's Rights* (New York, 1992).

PART THREE: DEMOCRATIC SUFFRAGE
COMMUNITIES AND EQUALITY

The classic account of postbellum public life is Morton Keller, *Affairs of State* (Cambridge, MA, 1977), which proposes several reasons for constitutional and political backsliding. John Johnson, *American Legal Culture, 1908–1940* (Westport, CT, 1981) offers a window into shifting legal-professional values. On social thought, see Mike Hawkins, *Social Darwinism in European and American Thought, 1860–1945* (New York, 1997); for Progressivism, see Arthur Link and Richard McCormick's tiny classic, *Progressivism* (Arlington Heights, IL, 1983); on lawyers and industrialization, see Gerald Gawalt, ed., *The New High Priests* (Westport, CT, 1984). On state paternalism, see William Nelson, *The Roots of American Bureaucracy, 1830–1900* (Cambridge, MA, 1982), and Morton Keller's studies, *Regulating a New Society* (Cambridge, MA, 1994) and *Regulating a New Economy* (Cambridge, MA, 1990). Two indispensable books examine Progressivism in its Atlantic context: Daniel T. Rodgers's *Atlantic Crossings: Social Politics in a Progressive Age* (Cambridge, MA, 1998), and James Kloppenberg, *Uncertain Victory: Social Democracy and Progressivism in European and American Thought, 1870–1920* (New York, 1986).

Women's experiences with the modern state occupy a growing literature. Paula Baker's essential article, "The Domestication of Politics: Women and American Political Society, 1780–1920," *AHR* (1984): 620–47, analyzes state absorption of responsibilities previously associated with women and families. For a slightly different take on renegotiations of public and private work, see Baker, *The Moral Frameworks of Public Life: Gender, Politics, and the State in Rural New York, 1870–1930* (New York, 1991). On Progressives' razing of boundaries between home and polity, see Noralee Frankel and Nancy S. Dye, eds., *Gender, Class, Race and Reform in the Progressive Era* (Lexington, KY, 1991). On cultural ascriptions, see Carroll Smith-Rosenberg, *Disorderly Conduct: Visions of Gender in Victorian America* (New York, 1985). Peggy Pascoe's *Relations of Rescue: The Search for Female Moral Authority in the American West, 1874–1939* (New York, 1990) examines western "purity" crusades; see also Robyn Muncy, *Creating a Female Dominion in American Reform, 1890–1935* (New York, 1991). On Florence Kelley, see Kathryn Kish Sklar, ed., *Notes of Sixty Years: The Autobiography of Florence Kelley* (Chicago, 1986); Josephine Goldmark, *Impatient Crusader* (1953); and Sklar, *Florence Kelley and the Nation's Work: The Rise of Women's Political Culture, 1830–1900* (New Haven, CT, 1995). For an attempt to break Victorian shackles, see Mary Hill, *Charlotte Perkins Gilman: The Making of a Radical Feminist, 1860–1896* (Philadelphia, 1980). On Jane Addams and Hull House, see Allen Davis, *American Heroine: The Life and Legend of Jane Addams* (New York, 1973); Eleanor Stebner, *The Women of Hull House* (Albany, NY, 1997); and Christopher Lasch, ed., *The Social Thought of Jane Addams* (Indianapolis, IN, 1965).

The Gilded Age and Progressive Era bubbled with group mobilization. Mari Jo Buhle, *Women and American Socialism, 1870–1920* (Urbana, IL, 1983) limns the development of a radical thread in the political fabric. For organized might in the West, see Michael Lewis Goldberg, *An Army of Women: Gender and Politics in Gilded Age Kansas* (Baltimore, 1997). On the WCTU and temperance, see Ian Tyrrell, *Woman's World, Woman's Empire* (Chapel Hill, NC, 1991), and Ruth Bordin, *Women and Temperance: The Quest for Power and Liberty, 1873–1900* (Philadelphia, 1981). On social workers, see Roy Lubove, *The Professional Altruist: The Emergence of Social Work as a Career, 1880–1930* (Cambridge, MA, 1965); on club women, see Karen Blair, *The Clubwoman as Feminist: True Womanhood Redefined, 1868–1914* (New York, 1980), and Theodora Penny Martin, *The Sound of Our Own Voices: Women's Study Clubs, 1860–1910* (Boston, 1987), which is sensitive to problems of vocality and silence. For associations, education, and the professions, see Anne Firor Scott's splendid *Natural Allies: Women's Associations in American History* (Urbana, IL, 1991); Lynn Gordon, *Gender and Higher Education in the Progressive Era* (New Haven, CT, 1990); Ellen Fitzpatrick's *Endless Crusade: Women Social Scientists and Progressive Reform* (New York, 1990); and Penina Megdal Glazer and Miriam Slater, *Unequal Colleagues: The Entrance of Women into the Professions, 1890–1940* (New Brunswick, NJ, 1987). For workplace segregation and wage inequities, see Joanne Meyerowitz, *Women Adrift: Independent Wage Earners in Chicago, 1880–1930* (Chicago, 1988); Sharon Hartman Strom, *Beyond the Typewriter: Gender, Class, and the Origins of Modern American Office Work, 1900–1930* (Urbana, IL, 1992); Alice Kessler-Harris, *A Woman's Wage: Historical Meanings and Social Consequences* (Lexington, KY, 1990); and Eileen Boris, ed., *Major Problems in the History of American Workers: Documents and Essays* (Lexington, MA, 1991). Articles about woman lawyers abound, particularly in law journals. But see Jane Friedman, *America's First Woman Lawyer: The Biography of Myra Bradwell* (Buffalo, NY, 1993), which lacks historical grounding but contains useful material; D. Kelly Weisberg, "Barred from the Bar: Women and Legal Education in the United States, 1870–1890," *Journal of Legal Education* (1977): 485–507; and Nancy Gilliam, "A Professional Pioneer: Myra Bradwell's Fight to Practice Law," *Law and History Review* (1987): 105–33. On black leaders, see Stephanie Shaw, *What a Woman Ought to Be and to Do: Black Professional Women Workers During the Jim Crow Era* (Chicago, 1996) and Cynthia Neverdon-Morton, *Afro-American Women of the South and the Advancement of the Race, 1895–1925* (Knoxville, TN, 1989). On feminism among Baptists, see Evelyn Brooks Higginbotham, *Righteous Discontent: The Women's Movement in the Black Baptist Church, 1880–1920* (Cambridge, MA, 1993). For two leading figures, see Beverly Washington Jones, *Quest for Equality: The Life and Writings of Mary Eliza Church Terrell, 1863–1954* (New York, 1990); and Miriam DeCosta-Willis, ed., *The Memphis Diary of Ida B. Wells* (Boston, 1995).

New ways of regulating sexuality and restraining "bad" women solidified by the turn of the century. On "promiscuity," see Hal Sears, *The Sex Radicals: Free Love in High Victorian America* (Lawrence, KS, 1977). For fears about juvenile sex, see Steven Schlossman and Stephanie Wallach, "The Crime of Precocious Sexuality: Female Juvenile Delinquency in the Progressive Era," *Harvard Educational Review* (1978): 65–94; for the policing of teenage girls, see Mary Odem, *Delinquent Daughters: Protecting and Policing Adolescent Female Sexuality in the United States, 1885–1920* (Chapel Hill, NC, 1995). Economic legislation also affected how women's bodies would be used; see, for example, Vivian Hart, *Bound by our Constitution: Women, Workers, and the Minimum Wage* (Princeton, NJ, 1994); Nancy Woloch's useful *Muller v. Oregon: A Brief History with*

Documents (Boston, 1996); Candice Dalrymple, *Sexual Distinctions in the Law: Early Maximum Hour Decisions of the United States Supreme Court, 1905–1917* (New York, 1987), which capably describes the High Court's "protective" rulings; and Nancy Erickson, *"Muller v. Oregon* Reconsidered: The Origins of a Sex-Based Doctrine of Liberty of Contract," *Labor History* (1989): 228–50. On prison reform, see especially Estelle Freedman, *Their Sisters' Keepers: Women's Prison Reform in America, 1830–1930* (Ann Arbor, MI, 1981), but also Anne Butler, *Gendered Justice in the American West: Women Prisoners in Men's Penitentiaries* (Urbana, IL, 1997), which describes the violence to which female prisoners were subjected in mixed-sex facilities in the West.

Prostitution, demands for birth control, and abortion all symbolized female sexuality run amok. For an overview of prostitution in America, see Barbara Meil Hobson, *Uneasy Virtue: The Politics of Prostitution and the American Reform Tradition* (Chicago, 1987). See also Karen Halttunen, *Confidence Men and Painted Ladies: A Study of Middle-Class Culture in America, 1830–1870* (New Haven, CT, 1982); David Pivar, *Purity Crusade: Sexual Morality and Social Control, 1868–1900* (Westport, CT, 1973); Mark Thomas Connelly, *The Response to Prostitution in the Progressive Era* (Chapel Hill, NC, 1980); and Ruth Rosen, *The Lost Sisterhood: Prostitution in America, 1900–1918* (Baltimore, 1982). Ann Snitow et al., eds., *Powers of Desire: The Politics of Sexuality* (New York, 1983) contains relevant essays. On "white slavery," see David Langum, *Crossing Over the Line: Legislating Morality and the Mann Act* (Chicago, 1994). On abortion, the old classic is James Mohr, *Abortion in America* (New York, 1978), which should be read with Leslie Reagan, *When Abortion Was a Crime: Women, Medicine, and Law in the United States, 1867–1973* (Berkeley, CA, 1997); Janet Farrell Brodie, *Contraception and Abortion in 19th-Century America* (Ithaca, NY, 1994); and Linda Gordon, *Woman's Body, Woman's Right, A Social History of Birth Control in America* (New York, 1974). There is yet no definitive biography of Comstock; see Anna Louise Bates, *Weeder in the Garden of the Lord: Anthony Comstock's Life and Career* (Lanham, MD, 1995), and Heywood Broun, *Anthony Comstock: Roundsman of the Lord* (New York, 1927). To some extent, anti-birth control and anti-abortion agitation reflected shifts within Protestantism; see George Marsden, *Fundamentalism and American Culture: The Shaping of Twentieth-Century Evangelicalism, 1870–1925* (New York, 1980) and Martin Marty, *Righteous Empire: The Protestant Experience in America* (New York, 1970). On medical views, see Cynthia Eagle Russett, *Sexual Science: The Victorian Construction of Womanhood* (Cambridge, MA, 1989).

Americans worried incessantly about irregular or failed marriages. On divorce, see William O'Neill, *Divorce in the Progressive Era* (New Haven, CT, 1967). Mormonism and plural marriages elicited great anxiety. See Sarah Barringer Gordon's indispensable " 'The Liberty of Self-Degradation': Polygamy, Woman Suffrage, and Consent in 19th-Century America," *JAH* (1996): 815–47; Gordon, " 'Our National Hearthstone': Anti-polygamy Fiction and the Sentimental Campaign against Moral Diversity in Antebellum America," *Yale Journal of Law and the Humanities* (1996): 295–350; and, for fuller analysis, Gordon's *Antipolygamy: Law, Religion, and Marriage in Nineteenth-Century America* (Chapel Hill, NC, forthcoming 2001). See also Maureen Ursenbach Beecher et al., eds., *Sisters in Spirit: Mormon Women in Historical and Cultural Perspective* (Urbana, IL, 1987); and Carol Weisbrod and Pamela Sheingorn, *"Reynolds v. United States*: Nineteenth-Century Forms of Marriage and the Status of Women," *Connecticut Law Review* (1978): 828–58.

Suffragism became an irresistible force after 1900. Contemporary accounts provide a starting point—among them, Carrie Chapman Catt and Nettie Rogers Shuler, *Woman Suffrage and Politics: The Inner Story of the Suffrage Movement* (1923; reprint Seattle, WA, 1970); Abigail Scott Duniway, *Path Breaking: An Autobiographical History of the Equal Suffrage Movement in Pacific Coast States* (1914, reprint, New York, 1971); Inez Haynes Irwin, *Up Hill With Banners Flying: The Story of the Woman's Party* (New York, 1921; reprint, Penobscot, ME, 1964); Doris Stevens, *Jailed for Freedom* (New York, 1920); and NAWSA's telling volume, *VICTORY: How Women Won It: A Centennial Symposium, 1840–1940* (New York, 1940). Anne Firor Scott and Andrew M. Scott, eds., *One Half the People: The Fight for Woman Suffrage* (Philadelphia, 1975), offers basic documents. Aileen Kraditor's *Ideas of the Woman Suffrage Movement, 1890–1920* (New York, 1965; reprint, 1981), describes suffragists as proponents either of "justice" or "expediency"; in *Harriot Stanton Blatch and the Winning of Woman Suffrage* (New Haven, CT), Ellen Carol DuBois uses the life of Elizabeth Cady Stanton's daughter to challenge old categories and explore "left feminism." See also DuBois's collected essays, *Woman Suffrage and Women's Rights* (New York, 1998), arguing that the struggle for ballots, precisely because it bypassed the family, emancipated women. For a more pessimistic view, see Suzanne Marilley, *Woman Suffrage and the Origins of Liberal Feminism in the United States, 1820–1920* (Cambridge, MA, 1996), which treats the first wave largely as a seedbed for liberal feminism. On Carrie Chapman Catt, see Jacqueline Van Voris, *Carrie Chapman Catt* (New York, 1987). On the NWP, see Nancy Cott, "Feminist Politics in the 1920s: The National Woman's Party," *JAH* (1984): 43–68; Christine Lunardini, *From Equal Suffrage to Equal Rights: Alice Paul and the National Woman's Party, 1910–1928* (New York, 1986); and Linda Ford's uncritical *Iron-Jawed Angels: The Suffrage Militancy of the National Woman's Party, 1912–1920* (Lanham, MD: reprint, 1991). On the antisaloon connection, see Ross Evans Paulson, *Women's Suffrage and Prohibition: A Comparative Study of Equality and Social Control* (Glenview, IL, 1973). For the Triangle fire, see John McClymer, *The Triangle Strike and Fire* (Fort Worth, TX, 1998).

The West and South were not the East. See Beverly Beeton, *Women Vote in the West: The Woman Suffrage Movement, 1869–1896* (New York, 1980); Genevieve McBride, *On Wisconsin Women: Working for Their Rights from Settlement to Suffrage* (Madison, WI, 1993); Ruth Barnes Moynihan, *Rebel for Rights: Abigail Scott Duniway* (New Haven, CT, 1983), a biography of Oregon's leading suffragist; Elna Green, *Southern Strategies: Southern Women and the Woman Suffrage Question* (Chapel Hill, NC, 1997); Marjorie Spruill Wheeler, *Votes for Women: The Woman Suffrage Movement in Tennessee, the South, and the Nation* (Knoxville, TN, 1995); Wheeler, *New Women of the New South* (New York, 1993), which describes the southern suffragists' uphill struggle; Wheeler, *One Woman, One Vote: Rediscovering the Woman Suffrage Movement* (Troutdale, OR, 1995); and, for religion in southern suffragism, see Evelyn Kirkley, " 'This Work is God's Cause': Religion in the Southern Woman Suffrage movement, 1880–1920," *Church History* (1990): 507–22. On blacks, see Ann Gordon et al., *African American Women and the Vote, 1837–1965* (Amherst, MA, 1997), and Rosalyn Terborg-Penn, *African American Women in the Struggle for the Vote, 1850–1920* (Bloomington, IN, 1998).

Much recent writing about political freedom has been interdisciplinary. See, for example, Steven Buechler, *The Transformation of the Woman Suffrage Movement: The Case of Illinois, 1850–1920* (New Brunswick, NJ, 1986), which employs sociological theory; Sara Hunter Graham, *Woman Suffrage and the New Democracy* (New Haven, CT, 1996), presenting NAWSA as one of the harbingers of modern party politics; and Lee Ann Banaszak, *Why Movements Succeed or Fail: Opportunity, Culture, and the Struggle for Woman Suffrage* (Princeton, NJ, 1996), a political scientist's comparative attempt to understand why reform movements succeed at certain moments. On the impact of enfranchisement, see Joel Goldstein, *The Effects of the Adoption of Woman Suffrage: Sex Differences in Voting Behavior—Illinois, 1914–1921* (New York, 1984), and Sarah Alpern and Dale Baum, "Female Ballots: The Impact of the Nineteenth Amendment," *Journal of Interdisciplinary History* (1985): 43–67. On jury service and other ancillary rights, see especially Kerber, *No Constitutional Right To Be Ladies*; Joanna Grossman, "Women's Jury Service: Right of Citizenship or Privilege of Difference?" *Stanford Law Review* (1994): 1115–60; and Andrew Deiss, "A Brief History of the Criminal Jury in the United States," *University of Chicago Law Review* (1994): 867–928. For the military service obligation, see Robert Westbrook, " 'I Want a Girl Just Like the Girl That Married Harry James': Women and the Problem of Political Obligation in World War II," *American Quarterly* (1990): 587–614; and Kenneth Karst, "The Pursuit of Manhood and the Desegregation of the Armed Forces," *UCLA Law Review* (1991): 499–581. On antisuffragism, see Suzanne Lebsock's important "Woman Suffrage and White Supremacy: A Virginia Case Study," in Hewitt, *Visible Women*; Angela Howard et al., eds., *Antifeminism in America: A Collection of Readings from the Literature of the Opponents to U.S. Feminism, 1848 to the Present* (New York, 1997), a three-volume collection of antifeminist texts; and Susan Marshall, *Splintered Sisterhood: Gender and Class in the Campaign against Woman Suffrage* (Madison, WI, 1997).

    With enfranchisement came renewed pressure for economic and domestic freedom. For a general account of the Roaring Twenties, see Burt Noggle, *Into the 1920s: The United States from Armistice to Normalcy* (Urbana, IL, 1974); on culture and sexual habits, see Paula Fass, *The Damned and the Beautiful: American Youth in the 1920s* (New York, 1977). For expanded state intrusiveness during and after World War I, see Paul Murphy, *World War I and the Origins of Civil Liberties in the United States* (New York, 1979). Divisions within organized feminism led to a scattering of women's reform efforts. See, for example, Jacqueline Dowd Hall, *Revolt Against Chivalry: Jessie Daniel Ames and the Women's Campaign Against Lynching* (New York, 1979), for southern women's defiance of gender and race norms; J. Stanley Lemons, *The Woman Citizen: Social Feminism in the 1920s* (Urbana, IL, 1973); and Kristi Anderson, *After Suffrage: Women in Partisan and Electoral Politics before the New Deal* (Chicago, 1996). On the importance of women in repealing the Eighteenth Amendment, see Kenneth Rose, *American Women and the Repeal of Prohibition* (New York, 1996). Female reformers persisted in their quest to realize a maternalist state—which, in turn, has yielded an important new literature. See Wendy Sarvasy, "Beyond the Difference versus Equality Policy Debate: Postsuffrage Feminism, Citizenship, and the Quest for a Feminist Welfare State," *Signs* (1992): 329–62; Seth Koven and Sonja Michel, *Mothers of a New World and the Origins of Welfare States* (New York, 1993), especially on state maternalism; Gwendolyn Mink, *The Wages of Motherhood: Inequality in the Welfare State, 1917–1942* (Ithaca, NY, 1995); Eileen Boris, *Home to Work: Motherhood and the Politics of Industrial Homework in the United States* (New York, 1994); Linda Gordon, ed., *Women, the State, and Welfare* (Madison, WI, 1990); and Theda Skocpol's blockbuster, *Protecting Soldiers and Mothers: The Political Origins of Social Policy in the United States* (Cambridge, MA, 1992). On Mothers' Pensions, see Joanne Goodwin, *Gender and the Politics of Welfare Reform: Mothers' Pensions in Chicago, 1911–1929* (Chicago, 1977). Sonja Michel's *Children's Interests/ Mothers' Rights: The Shaping of America's Child Care Policy* (New Haven, CT, 1999), which appeared after this book was written, fills a yawning gap in the literature.

The Great Depression and New Deal profoundly marked an entire generation. For a brief account of national initiatives, see Paul Conkin, *The New Deal* (Arlington Hts., IL, 1992). William Wiecek's brilliant *The Lost World of Classical Legal Thought: Law and Ideology in America, 1886–1937* (New York, 1998) traces persistent legal classicism (and the fear of equality-minded change) into the New Deal. On corporate benefits from public programs, see Christopher Tomlins, *The State and the Unions: Labor Relations, Law and the Organized Labor Movement, 1880–1960* (New York, 1985); see also Alan Brinkley, *The End of Reform: New Deal Liberalism in Recession and War* (New York, 1995), and, for the origins of modern legal liberalism, Peter Irons, *The New Deal Lawyers* (1982). For an analysis of New Dealers' construction of gender norms, see Suzanne Mettler, *Dividing Citizens: Gender and Federalism in the New Deal Public Policy* (New York, 1990). On women's lives during the depression, see Susan Ware's books, *Holding Their Own: American Women in the 1930s* (Boston, 1982) and *Beyond Suffrage: Women in the New Deal* (Cambridge, MA, 1981). For an indispensable account of the post-1920s legal struggle, particularly in economic matters, see Judith Baer, *Women in American Law* (New York, 1996). On Eleanor Roosevelt, see Blanche Wiesen Cook, *Eleanor Roosevelt*, Vols. 1 and 2 (New York, 1992, 1999). On other movers and shakers, see Susan Ware, *Partner and I: Molly Dewson, Feminism, and New Deal Politics* (New Haven, CT, 1987); George Martin, *Madam Secretary, Frances Perkins* (Boston, 1976); and John Chalberg, *Emma Goldman* (New York, 1991). Several of the essays collected in Ava Baron, ed., *Work Engendered: Toward a New History of American Labor* (Ithaca, NY, 1991) explore gender's operation in the workplace. For the World War II story, see Ruth Milkman, *Gender at Work: The Dynamics of Job Segregation by Sex during World War II* (Urbana, IL, 1987). On intersections among race, gender, and ethnicity, see Melvin Dubofsky and Stephen Burwood, eds., *Women and Minorities during the Great Depression* (New York, 1990); for testimony, see Bernard Sternsher and Judith Sealander, eds., *Women of Valor: The Struggle Against the Great Depression As Told in Their Own Life Stories* (Chicago, 1990); and for the modern female-headed household, see Linda Gordon, *Pitied but Not Entitled: Single Mothers and the History of Welfare* (Cambridge, MA, 1994). Studies of taxation and gender are scarce, but see Edward McCaffery, *Taxing Women* (Chicago, 1997), and Carolyn Jones, "Split Income and Separate Spheres: Tax Law and Gender Roles in the 1940s," *Law and History Review* (1980): 259–310. On the comparable-worth question, see Sara Evans and Barbara Nelson, *Wage Justice: Comparable Worth and the Paradox of Technocratic Reform* (Chicago, 1989).

The second wave continues to attract leading scholars. William Chafe broke new ground with *The American Woman: Her Changing Social, Economic, and Political Roles, 1920–1970* (New York, 1972). In addition to works listed earlier, see Jo Freeman, *The Politics of Women's Liberation* (New York, 1975), and Sara Evans, *Personal Politics: The Roots of Women's Liberation in the Civil Rights Movement and the New Left* (New York, 1979), which showed how radical feminism emerged from the black movement. Flora Davis's mountainous *Moving the Mountain: The Women's Movement in America Since 1960* (New York, 1991) is a treasure trove. For a brief study of political mobilization, see Susan Hartmann, *From Margin to Mainstream: American Women and Politics Since 1960* (Philadelphia, 1989). A French scholar, Ginette Castro, provides one of the best accounts of the second wave in *American Feminism: A Contemporary History* (New York, 1990). On radicalism, see Alice Echols, *Daring to Be Bad: Radical Feminism in America, 1967–1975* (Minneapolis, MN, 1989); for women's testimony, see Bonnie Watkins and Nina Rothchild, eds., *In the Company of Women: Voices from the Women's Movement* (St. Paul, MN, 1996). On female leadership in the civil rights movement, see

Vicky Crawford et al., eds., *Women in the Civil Rights Movement: Trailblazers and Torchbearers* (Bloomington, IN, 1993) and David Garrow, ed., *The Montgomery Bus Boycott and the Women Who Started It* (Knoxville, TN, 1987).

Legal-cultural developments since the Great Depression resist summation. For elements of the story, see Michal Belknap, *Cold War Political Justice: The Smith Act, the Communist Party, and American Civil Liberties* (Westport, CT, 1977); Jerold Auerbach, *Unequal Justice: Lawyers and Social Change in America* (New York, 1976), which criticizes lawyers' antiegalitarian practices; Mark Tushnet, ed., *The Warren Court in Historical and Political Perspective* (Charlottesville, VA, 1993); and Morton Horwitz's sketchy *The Warren Court and the Pursuit of Justice* (New York, 1998). No adequate general account yet exists of the course of federal judicial policy after the Warren years, much less of the judiciary's treatment of women. Nor have modern domestic relations attracted constitutional historians, despite obvious linkages to citizenship and legal rights. For a capable summary of recent federal judicial decisions, see Susan Gluck Mezey, *In Pursuit of Equality: Women, Public Policy, and the Federal Courts* (New York, 1992). Scholars working beyond the history of law have mapped out areas ripe for legal-historical spadework. See, for example, Elaine Tyler May, *Great Expectations: Marriage and Divorce in Post-Victorian America* (Chicago, 1980); May, *Homeward Bound: American Families in the Cold War Era* (New York, 1988);and Martha Albertson Fineman, *The Illusion of Equality: The Rhetoric and Reality of Divorce Reform* (Chicago, 1991). For a communitarian perspective, see Milton Regan, Jr., *Family Law and the Pursuit of Intimacy* (New York, 1993), to be read with Patricia Boling, *Privacy and the Politics of Intimate Life* (Ithaca, NY, 1996). Political scientist Susan Moller Okin's *Justice, Gender, and the Family* (New York, 1989) analyzes how prevailing divisions of labor in households stand in the way of equality and what she calls "humanist justice." Lesbians' experiences of law have been largely ignored. In addition to studies listed earlier, see Vincent Samar, *The Right to Privacy: Gays, Lesbians, and the Constitution* (Philadelphia, 1991), which devotes more space to privacy per se than to the plight of gays and lesbians; for a legal analysis, see also Editors of the Harvard Law Review, *Sexual Orientation and the Law* (Cambridge, MA, 1990).

Similarly, the ERA has attracted few constitutional historians. On the early ERA, the basic text is Susan Becker, *The Origins of the Equal Rights Amendment: American Feminism between the Wars* (Westport, CT, 1981). Cynthia Harrison's *On Account of Sex: The Politics of Women's Issues, 1945–1968* (Berkeley, CA, 1988) is an invaluable treatment of the post–World War II career and defeat of ERA. For an influential evaluation of Title VII, see Pauli Murray and Mary Eastwood, "Jane Crow and the Law: Sex Discrimination and Title VII," *George Washington Law Review* (1965): 232–56; on polarization, see Joan Zimmerman, "The Jurisprudence of Equality: The Women's Minimum Wage, the First Equal Rights Amendment, and *Adkins v. Children's Hospital*, 1905–1923," *JAH* (June 1991): 188–205; and, for a groundbreaking defense of ERA, see Barbara Brown et al., "The Equal Rights Amendment: A Constitutional Basis for Equal Rights for Women," *Yale Law Journal* (1971): 871–985. Donald Mathews and Jane Sherron De Hart, *Sex, Gender, and the Politics of ERA: A State and the Nation* (New York, 1990) examine ERA's defeat in North Carolina; for additional analyses, see Mary Frances Berry, *Why ERA Failed* (Bloomington, IN, 1986), and Jane Mansbridge, *Why We Lost the ERA* (Chicago, 1986). For a sitting Supreme Court justice's early thoughts, see Ruth Bader Ginsburg, "Sexual Equality Under the Fourteenth and Equal Rights Amendments," *Washington University Law Quarterly* (1979): 161–206.

Workplace inequities persist into the 1990s; so does widespread ambivalence about absolute economic equality. Nancy Walker, ed., *Women's Magazines, 1940–1960* (Boston, 1998) reprints magazine articles about "equal rights," careerism, and other topics. Evelyn Nakano Glenn describes race-sex discrimination in "Cleaning Up/Kept Down: A Historical Perspective on Racial Inequality in 'Women's Work,'" *Stanford Law Review* (1991): 1333–56. On affirmative action, see Michel Rosenfeld, *Affirmative Action and Justice: A Philosophical and Constitutional Inquiry* (New Haven, CT, 1991), an interdisciplinary defense of the practice, and Mel Urofsky's study of the *Johnson v. Santa Clara County* case, *Affirmative Action on Trial: Sex Discrimination in Johnson v. Santa Clara* (Lawrence, KS, 1997). On the *Sears* case, see chap. 8 in Joan Scott, *Gender and the Politics of History*, and Ruth Milkman, "Women's History and the Sears Case," *Feminist Studies* (1986): 375–400. Joan Williams, "Deconstructing Gender . . . ," in Bartlett and Kennedy, *Feminist Legal Theory*, 102–06, examines judicial bias.

For many feminists, pornography and "rape culture" symbolize the sex's physical insecurity. For a classic text, see Susan Griffin, *Pornography and Silence: Culture's Revenge Against Nature* (New York, 1981); for a survey of modern law as it affects women's bodies, see Rosemary Tong, *Women, Sex, and the Law* (Savage, MD, 1984). On the side of regulation of pornography, see Laura Lederer and Richard Delgado, eds., *The Price We Pay: The Case Against Racist Speech, Hate Propaganda, and Pornography* (New York, 1995); Laura Lederer, *Take Back the Night: Women on Pornography* (New York, 1980); Diana E. H. Russell, ed., *Making Violence Sexy: Feminist Views on Pornography* (New York, 1993); Catherine Itzin's mammoth *Pornography: Women, Violence, and Civil Liberties, A Radical New View* (New York, 1992); and Catharine MacKinnon's *Only Words* (Cambridge, MA, 1993), reframing the debate as a problem in equality. On the "free speech" side, see Nadine Strossen, *Free Speech, Sex, and the Fight for Women's Rights* (New York, 1995); and for women's right to provide pornographic images, see Wendy McElroy, *A Woman's Right to Pornography* (New York, 1995). Susan Dwyer, *The Problem of Pornography* (Belmont, CA, 1995); Susan Easton, *The Problem of Pornography: Regulation and the Right to Free Speech* (New York, 1994); and Lynn Chancer's important "Review Essay: Feminist Offensives . . . ," *Stanford Law Review* (1996): 739–60, all try to reconcile oil-and-water arguments. For a grim collection of images, see Diana Russell's privately published *Against Pornography: The Evidence of Harm* (Berkeley, CA, 1993); see also Andrea Dworkin's unsparing *Pornography: Men Possessing Women* (New York, 1979; reprint, 1989). Catharine MacKinnon and Andrea Dworkin, eds., *In Harm's Way: The Pornography Civil Rights Hearings* (Cambridge, MA, 1997) reproduces the testimony of victims of pornographers.

Modern Americans have been preoccupied with falling birthrates, extramarital sex, and homosexuality. For an account of "voluntary motherhood" crusades and their aftermath, see Linda Gordon, *Woman's Body, Woman's Right: A Social History of Birth Control in America* (New York, 1976). See also James Reed, *The Birth Control Movement and American Society: From Private Vice to Public Virtue* (Princeton, NJ, 1983), and Richard Wertz and Dorothy Wertz, *Lying-In: A History of Childbirth in America*, rev. ed. (New Haven, CT, 1989). On Margaret Sanger and planned parenthood, see David Kennedy, *Birth Control in America: The Career of Margaret Sanger* (New Haven, CT, 1970); Sanger's version of the story in *Margaret Sanger, An Autobiography* (New York, 1938; reprint, 1971); and Ellen Chesler's encyclopedic *Woman of Valor: Margaret Sanger and the Birth Control Movement in America* (New York, 1992). On Mary Ware Dennett, see Constance Chen, *"The Sex Side of Life": Mary Ware Dennett's Pioneering Battle for*

Birth Control and Sex Education (New York, 1996). Carole McCann, *Birth Control Politics in the United States, 1916–1945* (Ithaca, NY, 1994), links eugenicism to the birth control movement. On domestic violence, see Martha Albertson Fineman and Roxanne Mykitiuk, eds., *The Public Nature of Private Violence: The Discovery of Domestic Abuse* (New York, 1994), especially Kimberley Crenshaw's piece about violence against women of color and Elizabeth Schneider's exploration of the "violence of privacy." See also Linda Gordon, *Heroes of Their Own Lives: The Politics and History of Family Violence* (New York, 1988), and sociologists Pauline Bart and Eileen Moral's edited volume, *Violence Against Women: The Bloody Footprints* (Newbury Park, CA, 1993).

Abortion rights and "fetal rights" provoke both disagreement and violence. Rickie Solinger provides three crucial studies—*Wake Up Little Susie: Single Pregnancy and Race before Roe v. Wade* (New York, 1992); *Abortion Wars: A Half Century of Struggle, 1950–2000* (Berkeley, CA, 1998), an essay collection; and *The Abortionist: A Woman Against the Law* (Berkeley, CA, 1996), which describes one woman's pre-*Roe v. Wade* abortion practice. See also Laura Kaplan, *The Story of Jane: The Legendary Underground Feminist Abortion Service* (Chicago, 1995). Ellen Messer and Kathryn May, eds., *Back Rooms: Voices from the Illegal Abortion Era* (Buffalo, NY, 1994) collects women's stories. David Garrow's exhaustive *Liberty and Sexuality: The Right to Privacy and the Making of Roe v. Wade* (New York, 1994) describes *Griswold v. Connecticut* and other decisions in advance of *Roe*. For audiotapes and transcripts of eight Supreme Court arguments, see Stephanie Guitton and Peter Irons, eds., *"May It Please the Court": Arguments on Abortion* (New York, 1995). Leon Friedman, *The Supreme Court Confronts Abortion* (New York, 1993) reprints the briefs and judicial record in *Planned Parenthood v. Casey*. For early warnings, see Andrew Merton, *Enemies of Choice: The Right-to-Life Movement and Its Threat to Abortion* (Boston, 1981). In *Wrath of Angels: The American Abortion War* (New York, 1998), James Risen and Judy Thomas cast the antiabortion crusade as the first significant social movement since the 1960s. For a different treatment of fundamentalism, see Margaret Lamberts Bendroth, *Fundamentalism and Gender, 1875 to the Present* (New Haven, CT, 1993). On an especially nasty episode, see Dallas Blanchard and Terry Prewitt, *Religious Violence and Abortion: The Gideon Project* (Gainesville, FL, 1993). On fetal rights, see Suzanne Uttaro Samuels, *Fetal Rights, Women's Rights: Gender Equality in the Workplace* (Madison, WI, 1995), which explores the *Johnson Controls* ruling, and Cynthia Daniels, *At Women's Expense: State Power and the Politics of Fetal Rights* (Cambridge, MA, 1993).

Many scholars have tried to reconcile competing views. See, for example, Joan Callahan, ed., *Reproduction, Ethics, and the Law: Feminist Perspectives* (Bloomington, IN, 1995), an assessment of differences among feminists; Eileen McDonagh, *Breaking the Abortion Deadlock: From Choice to Consent* (New York, 1996), an attempt to surmount the terms of the debate by characterizing women as hosts capable of withholding consent to impregnation; and Laurence Tribe, *Abortion: The Clash of Absolutes* (New York, 1992). In *Life's Dominion: An Argument about Abortion, Euthanasia, and Individual Freedom* (New York, 1993), Ronald Dworkin explores the moral complexities of arguments about the preservation of life. See also Elizabeth Mensch and Alan Freeman, *The Politics of Virtue: Is Abortion Debatable?* (Durham, NC, 1993), and, for a comparative view from conservative ground, Mary Ann Glendon, *Abortion and Divorce in Western Law: American Failures, European Challenges* (Cambridge, MA, 1987). In *Re-Thinking Abortion: Equal Choice, the Constitution, and Reproductive Politics* (Princeton, NJ, 1996), Mark Graber uses economic theory to argue against the recriminalization of abortion. Rosalind

Pollack Petchesky, *Abortion and Woman's Choice: The State, Sexuality, and Reproductive Freedom* (Boston, 1984) analyzes connections between women's social situation and abortion views; Phillipa Strum, *Privacy: The Debate in the United States Since 1945* (Orlando, FL, 1998), situates abortion and contraception in the context of a constitutional right to privacy.

Rape and harassment continue to perplex both policy makers and the citizenry. For a pivotal call to action, see Susan Brownmiller, *Against Our Will: Men, Women, and Rape* (New York, 1975); for equally consequential briefs, see Catharine MacKinnon, *Sexual Harassment of Working Women* (New Haven, CT, 1979), and Susan Estrich, *Real Rape* (Cambridge, MA, 1987). On the Hill-Thomas sexual harassment hearings, see Toni Morrison, ed., *Race-ing Justice, En-gendering Power: Essays on Anita Hill, Clarence Thomas, and the Construction of Reality* (New York, 1992). Charlotte Pierce-Baker, ed., *Surviving the Silence: Black Women's Stories of Rape* (New York, 1998) offers women's and men's stories of rape; Celia Morris, *Bearing Witness: Sexual Harassment and Beyond* (Boston, 1994) provides yet more stories. For an evaluation of law reform, see Ronald Berger et al., "The Dimensions of Rape Reform Legislation," *Law and Society Review* (1988): 329–57. For warnings about the law's tendency to think only of women's bodies, see Zillah Eisenstein, *The Female Body and the Law* (Berkeley, CA, 1988). On routine hassling of women, see Cynthia Grant Bowman, "Street Harassment and the Informal Ghettoization of Women," *Harvard Law Review* (January 1993): 517–80. On restoring personal security, see Emilie Buchwald et al., eds., *Transforming a Rape Culture* (Minneapolis, MN, 1993).

Over the past decade and despite the counteroffensives described in Susan Faludi, *Backlash* (New York, 1991), writing and theorizing about women's condition has flourished. Partisan women and political scientists hammer away at the glass ceiling in political life. For women's prospects in modern parties, see Susan J. Carroll's painstaking *Women as Candidates in American Politics* (Bloomington, IN, 1985), and R. Darcy et al., eds., *Women, Elections, and Representation*, 2nd ed. (Lincoln, NE, 1994). Black feminists have developed a rich and compelling literature. See, for example, Patricia Hill Collins, *Black Feminist Thought: Knowledge, Consciousness, and the Politics of Empowerment* (New York, 1990); for a fine selection of theoretical and political readings, see Linda S. Kauffman, ed., *American Feminist Thought at Century's End: A Reader* (Cambridge, MA, 1993). For a useful, fine-grained study of the ways in which both race and gender affect professional life, see Natalie Sokoloff, *Black Women and White Women in the Professions* (New York, 1992). Linda Nicholson edited a valuable collection of texts emblematic of second-wave feminist thought, *The Second Wave: A Reader in Feminist Theory* (New York, 1997).

Much the same may be said of feminist jurisprudence, where scholars increasingly address bedrock issues—the merits, for example, of the constitutional order, the criminal justice system, rights regimes, federal constitutional practice, and liberal legalism. For a critique of prevailing modes of legal reasoning, see Lucinda Finley, "Breaking Women's Silence in Law: The Dilemma of the Gendered Nature of Legal Reasoning," *Notre Dame Law Review* 64 (1989): 886–910. Kathryn Abrams in "Sex Wars Redux: Agency and Coercion in Feminist Legal Theory," *Columbia Law Review* (1995): 304–76, explores challenges to "dominance feminism," by which she means Catharine MacKinnon's views. For criticism of the "reasonable man" standard in criminal law, see Barbara Gutek and Maureen O'Connor, "The Empirical Basis for the Reasonable Woman Standard," *Journal of Social Issues* (1995): 151–66. For an important critique of rights regimes, see Elizabeth

Kingdom, *What's Wrong with Rights? Problems for Feminist Politics of Law* (Edinburgh, Scotland, 1991). Deborah Rhode trains an unflinching eye on persistent discrimination in *Speaking of Sex: The Denial of Gender Inequality* (Cambridge, MA, 1997). See also the essays in Deborah Rhode, ed., *Theoretical Perspectives on Sexual Difference* (New Haven, CT, 1990), which investigate the imprint of gender in and beyond the law. On the inadequacy of the criminal justice system, see Barbara Raffel Price and Natalie Sokoloff, eds., *The Criminal Justice System and Women* (New York, 1982). Black scholars continue to denounce racism. For early statements, see Angela Davis, *Women, Race, and Class* (New York, 1981) and bell hooks, *Ain't I a Woman: Black Women and Feminism* (Boston, 1981); for recent work, see Patricia Williams, *The Alchemy of Race and Rights* (Cambridge, MA, 1991), and especially Kimberly Crenshaw, "A Black Feminist Critique of Anti-Discrimination Law and Politics," in David Kairys, ed., *The Politics of Law*, rev. ed. (New York, 1990), 195–218. For a useful summary of this complex literature, see Carol Weisbrod, "Practical Polyphony: Theories of the State and Feminist Jurisprudence," *Georgia Law Review* (1990): 985–1018.

Index of Cases

Adarand Constructors, Inc., v. Pena, 515 U.S. 200 (1995), 282

Adkins v. Children's Hospital, 261 U.S. 525 (1923), 227–28, 231–33, 279

Adkins v. Lyons, 261 U.S. 525 (1923), 227–28

Annie Walker v. Territory of Washington, 2 Washington Territory 283 (1884), 186

Akron v. Akron Center for Reproductive Health, 462 U.S. 416 (1983), 288–89

Allgeyer v. Louisiana, 165 U.S. 578 (1897), 222

American Booksellers Association v. Hudnut, 771 F. Supp. 2d (1985), 299

Ann Shanks v. Abraham Dupont, 28 U.S. 242 (1830), 55, 126

Ballard v. United States, 329 U.S. 187 (1946), 203

Barber v. Barber, 62 U.S. 582 (1858), 68

Beardsley v. Webb, 30 F. Supp. 3d 524 (1994), 295

Birkbeck v. Ackroyd, 74 New York 356 (1878), 134

Bohen v. City of East Chicago, 799 F. Supp. 2d 1180 (7ᵗʰ Cir. 1986), 295

Bosley v. McLaughlin, 236 U.S. 385 (1914), 222, 225

Bradwell v. State of Illinois, 83 U.S. 130 (1873), 157–60, 187, 189, 221

Bray v. Lee, 337 F. Supp. 934 (1970), 284

Breedlove v. Suttles, 302 U.S. 277 (1937), 207

Brooks v. Schwein, 54 New York 343 (1873), 133–34

Brown v. Board of Education, 347 U.S. 483 (1954), 272

Brown v. Worden, 39 Wisconsin 432 (1876), 130

Bunting v. Oregon, 243 U.S. 426 (1917), 225, 229

Burlington Industries v. Ellerth, 524 U.S. 742 (1998), 295

Califano v. Goldfarb, 430 U.S. 199 (1977), 275

Califano v. Webster, 430 U.S. 313 (1977), 278

Califano v. Westcott, 443 U.S. 76 (1979), 276

Charles Hayes v. Territory of Washington, 2 Washington Territory 286 (1884), 186

Charles McKim v. Anne McKim, 12 Rhode Island 462 (1890), 66

Chrysler Motors Corporation v. International Union, 2 F. Supp. 3d 760 (1993), 296

Cleveland Board of Education v. LaFleur, 414 U.S. 632 (1973), 278

Coleman v. Miller, 307 U.S. 433 (1939), 303

Commonwealth v. Bangs, 9 Massachusetts 387 (1812), 78

Commonwealth v. Welosky, 276 Massachusetts 398 (1931), 202, 206

Craig v. Boren, 429 U.S. 190 (1976), 276

Dartmouth College v. Woodward, 17 U.S. 518 (1819), 69

Davis v. Beason, 133 U.S. 333 (1889), 165

DeGraffenreid v. General Motors, 413 F. Supp. 142 (1976), 282

DeMay v. Roberts, 46 Michigan 160 (1881), 239–40, 252

Denver v. Rio Grande RR v. Lorentzen, 79 C.C.A. Colorado (1897), 136

Diaz v. Pan American Airways, 311 F. Supp. 559 (1970), and 442 F. 2d 385, (5ᵗʰ Cir. 1971), 278

Dibble v. Hutton, 1 Day's Reports (Conn.) 221 (1804), 51–53

Dillon v. Gloss, 256 U.S. 368 (1921), 302

Dothard v. Rawlinson, 433 U.S. 321 (1977), 279

Dred Scott v. Sandford, 60 U.S. 393 (1857), 139, 142, 149, 172, 188

Duren v. Missouri, 439 U.S. 357 (1979), 260

Eisenstadt v. Baird, 405 U.S. 438 (1972), 286–87

EEOC v. Sears, Roebuck & Co., 504 F. Supp. 241 (1980), 628 F. Supp. 1264 (1986), and 839 F. Supp. 2d 365 (7ᵗʰ Cir. 1988), 256–59, 280

Ellison v. Brady, 924 Fed. Supp. 2d 872 (1991), 295

Emily Peltier v. Charles Peltier, 1 Harrington's Reports (Mich.) 19 (1842), 72–73

Ex parte Barry, 43 U.S. 65 (1844), 63–65, 67, 133

Ex parte Yarbrough, 110 U.S. 651 (1884), 162

Fairchild v. Hughes, 258 U.S. 127 (1922), 201
Faragher v. City of Boca Raton, 524 U.S. 775 (1998), 295
Fay v. New York, 332 U.S. 261 (1947), 203–4
Fitch v. Brainerd, 2 Day's Reports (Conn.) 184 (1805), 53
Frecking v. Rolland, 53 New York 423 (1873), 134
Frontiero v. Richardson, 411 U.S. 677 (1973), 274–75
Fulgham v. State, 46 Alabama 143 (1871), 77–78
Fullilove v. Klutznick, 448 U.S. 448 (1980), 280

Geduldig v. Aiello, 417 U.S. 484 (1974), 279
Gemsco v. Walling, 324 U.S. 244 (1945), 236
General Electric Company v. Gilbert, 429 U.S. 125 (1976), 279
George Schilling v. Territory of Washington, 2 Washington Territory 283 (1884), 186
Goesaert v. Cleary, 335 U.S. 464 (1948), 235, 264, 273, 277
Griswold v. Connecticut, 381 U.S. 479 (1965), 253–55, 286–88, 297
Grove City College v. Bell, 465 U.S. 555 (1984), 284

H. L. v. Matheson, 450 U.S. 398 (1981), 288
Harper v. Virginia State Board of Election, 383 U.S. 663 (1966), 259
Harris v. Forklift Systems, 510 U.S. 17 (1993), 295
Heckler v. Matthews, 465 U.S. 728 (1984), 278
Hishon v. King and Spalding, 467 U.S. 69 (1984), 278
Holden v. Hardy, 169 U.S. 366 (1898), 222, 232
Hope Clinic v. Ryan, 195 F. Supp. 3d 857 (7th Cir. 1999), 290
Hoyt v. Florida, 368 U.S. 57 (1961), 204, 260–61

Idaho v. Freeman, 507 F. Supp. 706 (1981), 303
In re A.C. [Angela Carder], 533 A. 2d 611 (D.C. Cir. 1987), 293
In re A.C. [Angela Carder], 573 A. 2d 1235 (D.C. Cir. 1990), 293
In re Bradwell, 55 Illinois 535 (1869), 157–60
In re Graves, 325 Missouri 888 (1930), 206–7
In re Jacobs, 98 New York 98 (1885), 219
In re Josie Dunkerton, 104 Kansas 481 (1919), 241–42

In re Lavinia Goodell, 39 Wisconsin 232 (1875), 163
In re Wickes' Estate, 128 California 270 (1900), 207

James Martin v. Commonwealth of Massachusetts, 1 Massachusetts 260 (1805), 53–55, 111, 126
Jayne Bray v. Alexandria Women's Health Clinic, 506 U.S. 263 (1993), 293
Jeffrey Harland v. Territory of Washington, 3 Washington Territory 131 (1887), 186–87
Jesse Thomas v. City of Chicago, 55 Illinois 403 (1870), 134
Johnson v. Transportation Agency, Santa Clara County, 480 U.S. 616 (1987), 280
John Wilson v. Loomis, 55 Illinois 352 (1870), 134

Kahn v. Shevin, 416 U.S. 351 (1974), 278
Katz v. United States, 389 U.S. 347 (1967), 255
Kempe's Lessee v. Kennedy, 9 U.S. 173 (1809), 54–55
Kirchberg v. Feenstra, 450 U.S. 455 (1981), 276
Kirstein v. University of Virginia, 309 F. Supp. 184 (1970), 284

Lashaw v. Croissant, 34 N.Y.S. 667 (1895), 134
Late Corporation of the Church of . . . Latter-Day Saints v. United States, 136 U.S. 1 (1890), 165
Leighton v. Goodman, 311 F. Supp. 1181 (SDNY 1970), 205, 260
Lelia Robinson's Case, 131 Massachusetts 376 (1881), 162
Leser v. Garnett, 258 U.S. 130 (1922), 201, 206
Livestock Dealers and Butchers Association v. Crescent City Livestock, 15 F. Supp. 649 (1870), 156–57
Lochner v. New York, 198 U.S. 4 (1905), 223, 225
Lovica Hamilton v. Leopold Hirsch and James Hayden, 2 Washington Territory 223 (1884), 185

Mackenzie v. Hare, 239 U.S. 299 (1915), 205
Maguire v. Maguire, 37 Kentucky 181 (1838), 70
Maher v. Roe, 432 U.S. 464 (1977), 288
Marcoux v. State of Maine, 797 F. Supp. 2d 1100 (1986), 265

Maria DeKosenko v. Arthur Brandt, 313 NY Supp. 2d 827 (1970), 205

Maria Wightman v. Joshua Coates, 15 Massachusetts 1 (1818), 73

Mary Phelps v. S. S. City of Panama, 1 Washington Territory 518 (July 1877), 184

Mayburry v. Brien, 40 U.S. 21 (1841), 128

Maynard v. Hill, 125 U.S. (1887), 70, 164–65

Mercein v. People ex rel. Barry, 25 Wendell (Court of Errors, NY) 66 (1840), 63–65, 67, 133

Meritor Savings Bank v. Vinson, 477 U.S. 57 (1986), 295

Michael M. v. Superior Court of Sonoma County, 450 U.S. 464 (1981), 276

Miller v. Wilson, 236 U.S. 373 (1915), 222, 225

Miller v. Miller, 78 Iowa 177 (1889), 67

Minor v. Happersett, 88 U.S. 162 (1874), 160–62, 173, 187, 201

Mississippi University for Women v. Hogan, 458 U.S. 718 (1982), 276

Moore v. Hughes Helicopters, Inc., 708 F. Supp. 2d 475 (9th Cir. 1983), 282

Morehead v. New York ex rel Tipaldo, 298 U.S. 587 (1936), 233

Muller v. Oregon, 208 U.S. 412 (1908), 213, 223, 228–29, 231, 266, 284

Murphy v. Ramsey, 114 U.S. 15 (1885), 165

Nashville Gas Company v. Satty, 434 U.S. 136 (1977), 279

Neal v. Delaware, 103 U.S. 370 (1881), 202

Nevada Bloomer v. John Todd, et al., 3 Washington Territory 599 (1888), 187, 202

Newberg v. Board of Public Education, 22 Pa. D&C 3d 682 (1983), 284

Newell v. Whitcher, 53 Vermont 589 (1880), 252–53

New York City Club Association v. New York City, 108 NY SCt 2225 (1988), 285

Olmstead v. United States, 277 U.S. 438 (1928), 253

Oncale v. Sundowner Offshore Service, Inc., 523 U.S. 75 (1998), 294–95

Orr v. Orr, 440 U.S. 268 (1979), 276

Patricia Harris v. Cora McRae, 448 U.S. 297 (1980), 291

Paul Schenck v. Pro-Choice Network of Western New York, 519 U.S. 357 (1997), 293

People ex rel. Barry v. Mercein, 3 Hill (NY Supr Court) 400 (1842), 63–65, 67, 133

People v. Balofsky, 167 App Div (2d Dept 1915) 913, appeal dismissed, 216 N.Y. 666 (1915), 350n

People v. Barnett, 319 Illinois 403 (1926), 202

People v. Sanger, 118 N.E. (N.Y. 1918) 637, appeal dismissed, 251 U.S. 537 (1919), 248

People v. Williams, 189 New York 131 (1907), 222

Personnel Administrator of Massachusetts v. Feeney, 442 U.S. 256 (1979), 276

Phillips v. Martin-Marietta, 400 U.S. 542 (1971), 277

Planned Parenthood of Central Missouri v. Danforth, 428 U.S. 52 (1976), 288

Planned Parenthood of S. E. Pennsylvania v. Robert J. Casey, 505 U.S. 833 (1992), 289–90

Planned Parenthood of Wisconsin v. Doyle, 9 F. Supp. 2d 1033 (1998), 290

Planned Parenthood of Wisconsin v. Doyle, 162 F. Supp. 3d 463 (7th Cir. 1998), 290

Plessy v. Ferguson, 163 U.S. 537 (1896), 188–89

Poe v. Ullman, 367 U.S. 497 (1961), 253

Poelker, Mayor of St. Louis v. Doe, 432 U.S. 519 (1977), 288

Prewitt v. Wilson, 242 Kentucky 231 (1931–32), 206

Price Waterhouse v. Hopkins, 490 U.S. 228 (1989), 279–80

Quong Wing v. Kirkendall, 223 U.S. 59 (1912), 225

Radice v. New York, 264 U.S. 292 (1923), 231

Reed v. Reed, 404 U.S. 71 (1971), 274, 284

Regents of the University of California v. Bakke, 438 U.S. 265 (1978), 280

Reynolds v. United States, 98 U.S. 145 (1879), 164

Richard Holyoke v. D. B. Jackson, 3 Washington Territory 235 (1882), 185

Ritchie and Company v. Wayman, 244 Illinois 509 (1910), 225

Ritchie v. People of Illinois, 155 Illinois 98 (1895), 221–22, 225

Roberts v. U. S. Jaycees, 468 U.S. 609 (1984), 285

Roe v. Wade and *Doe v. Bolton*, 410 U.S. 113 (1973), 179, 287–91

Rosencrantz v. Territory of Washington, 2 Washington Territory 267 (1884), 186–87

Rosenfeld v. Southern Pacific, 444 F. Supp. 2d 1219 (9th Cir. 1971), 277

Rust v. Sullivan, 111 U.S. 1759 (1991), 291

Sail'er Inn, Inc. v. Kirby, P. 2d (Calif. 1971) 529, 273

Sara Spencer v. Board of Registration, 1 McArthur (8 D.C.S.C.) 169 (1873), 157, 161

Shaw v. Shaw, 17 Day's Reports (Conn.) 190 (1845), 72, 77

Slaughterhouse Cases, 83 U.S. 36 (1873), 157–58, 160

Stanton v. Stanton, 421 U.S. 7 (1975), 276

State ex rel Klein v. Hillenbrand, 101 Ohio 370 (1920), 206

State v. Bunting, 71 Oregon 259 (1914) 225

State v. Hall, 187 So. 2d (Miss.) 861, appeal dismissed, 385 U.S. 98 (1966), 205

State v. Henrietta Somerville, 67 Washington 638 (1912), 221

State v. John Emery, 224 North Carolina 581 (1944), 203

State v. Josie Dunkerton, 103 Kansas 748 (1918), 241–42

State v. Mrs. L. O. Heitman, 105 Kansas 139 (1919), 241

State v. Rhodes, 61 North Carolina 453 (1868), 73

Steelworkers v. Weber, 440 U.S. 954 (1979), 280

Stelle v. Carroll , 37 U.S. 201 (1838), 128

Stenberg v. Carhart, U.S. Supreme Court Docket No. 99–830 (2000), 290

Stettler v. O'Hara, 69 Oregon 519 (1914), 225

Sturgineger v. Hannah, 2 Nott & McC. (S.C.) 147 (1819), 115

Taylor v. Louisiana, 419 U.S. 522 (1975), 260

Tinker v. Caldwell, 193 U.S. 472 (1903), 245

U.A.W. v. Johnson Controls, 499 U.S. 187 (1991), 279

U.S. v. Betty, 208 U.S. 393 (1908), 300

U.S. v. Darby, 312 U.S. 100 (1941), 233, 235

U.S. v. Hinson, 2 F. Supp. 200 (1925), 206

U.S. v. St. Clair, 291 F. Supp. 122 (SDNY 1968), 261

U.S. v. Virginia, 518 U.S. 515 (1996), 285

Vorchheimer v. School District of Philadelphia, 532 F. Supp. 2d 880 (1976), 284

Waldron v. Waldron, 85 California 251 (1890), 72

Webster v. Reproductive Health Services, 492 U.S. 490 (1989), 289

Weeks v. Southern Bell Telephone and Telegraph, 408 F. Supp. 2d 228 (1969), 277

Weinberger v. Weisenfeld, 420 U.S. 636 (1975), 275

Wenham v. State, 65 Nebraska 394 (1902), 232

West Coast Hotel Co. v. Parrish, 300 U.S. 379 (1937), 232

White v. Territory of Washington, 3 Washington Territory 397 (1888), 187

Wilkerson v. Lee, 236 Alabama 104 (1938), 207

Index

Abolitionism, 60, 82, 84–85, 96, 117, 152, 171, 188
Abortion: in early America, 21, 26–27; in nineteenth century, 78–79, 166–68; in modern era, 246–52, 286–94, 301; and racism, 251–52; and self-rule, 294; and violence, 293–94. *See also* Reproductive freedom
Abortion Counseling Service of Women's Liberation ("Jane"), 286
Action, freedom [right] of, 122–23, 126, 132, 228
Adams, Abigail, and John Adams, ix, 47, 89, 172
Adams, Mildred, 92
Adams, Samuel, and Betsy Adams, 47
Addams, Jane, 176, 191, 195, 211
Adultery: in early America, 15, 29–30, 45, 77; and modern rape law, 245
Affirmative action, 256–60, 267–68, 272, 279, 280, 302. *See also* Economic rights
AFL-CIO, 272. *See also* American Federation of Labor; Congress of Industrial Organizations
Aid to Families with Dependent Children [Aid to Dependent Children], 250, 281
Alabama: and married women's property acts, 129; and jury service, 204–5; and marital residence, 207; and naming, 209
Alaska, and abortion, 287
Alcott, Louisa May, 163
Allen, Judge Florence Ellinwood, 233
Amalgamated Clothing Workers of America, 220, 233
American Association for Organizing Family Social Work, 227
American Association of University Women, 215, 227, 265
American Bar Association, 272
American Birth Control League, 249–50
American Civil Liberties Union, 204, 227, 266, 288
American Constitutional League, 201
American Equal Rights Association, 84, 143, 150–51, 154, 171
American Federation of Labor, 208, 220, 227. *See also* AFL-CIO
American Law Institute Model Penal Code, and abortion, 287
American Medical Association, 166–68

American Woman Suffrage Association, 88, 151, 176
Anthony, Susan B., 82, 92, 94, 96, 100, 106, 110–11, 114, 128, 137, 140, 147, 152, 155, 159–60, 171–72, 181, 183, 187, 311
Anthony, Daniel, 227
Anti-Slavery Convention of American Women, 96
Antifeminism, 95–96, 178–80, 227, 301–4.
Antinomianism, 5–16, 19, 33, 105
Antioch College, 176
Antisuffragism, 169, 172, 178–79, 181, 188–90, 193, 197–200
Arizona: and married women's property, 18–19; and suffrage, 200; and office holding, 262
Arkansas: and married women's property, 126
Arnold, Sarah Louise, 210
Arrington, Richard, 294
Ashford, Serena Elizabeth, 237
Ashley, Jessie, 208
Assembly, right of, 92–93
Association, right of, 19, 93, 283, 285
Astell, Mary, 50, 90, 92
Athletics, and sex discrimination, 284–85, 296–97
Atlanta Washerwoman's Association, 208
Attainder, bills of, 161
Attorneyship, 40–42, 89, 123, 140–41, 146, 155–58, 162–63, 230. *See also* Law, practice of
Austin, Warren, 264

Backus, Isaac, 39
Baer, John, 201
Bailey, Ann, 89
Bailey, Carolen, x
Band, George, 144
Baptists, 38–40
Barney, Susan Hammon, 242
Baron: defined, 10–11, 28. *See also* Coverture; domestic government
Barr, Elizabeth, 182
Bartending, 235, 273, 276
Barton, Clara, 148
Bascom, John, 188
Bastardy, 21, 30
Bayh, Birch, 271

Beard, Mary, 306, 309
Beauvoir, Simone de, 268
Beecher, Catharine, 74, 88, 91, 95–96, 170
Bellows, Henry, 106
Belmont, Mrs. O. H. P., 226
Benefit of clergy, and of the belly, 30–31
Bill of Rights. *See specific provisions*
Bingham, Anne Willing, 47
Bingham, John, 148, 161
Birth Control League, 251
Birth control movement, 248–49. *See also* Abortion; contraception
Bishop, Joel, and *Commentaries*, 66–68, 70–71, 73–74, 77, 108, 111
Bissell, Emily, 189–90
Black women: in early America, 24–25, 46; in nineteenth century, 83–85; in modern America, 208, 250–52, 262, 280–81, 302, 309; and black feminism, 270, 301–2. *See also* Racism
Blackmun, Justice Harry, 275, 287, 289
Blackstone, William, and *Commentaries*, 28, 50, 52, 74, 78, 116, 255; definition of rape, 244
Blackwell, Alice Stone, 159
Blackwell, Antoinette Brown, 85–88, 91, 98, 108–9, 113, 116, 119, 156, 302, 314
Blackwell, Dr. Elizabeth, 106
Blackwell, Henry Brown, 87, 94, 110–11, 148–49
Blackwell, Samuel Charles, 87
Blair, Emily Newell, 208, 230, 282
Blanch, Harriot Stanton, 178, 194, 196, 306
Bloomer, Amelia Jenks, 117–18
Bloomers, 88, 117–20, 142. *See also* Clothing
Bodeker, Anna Whitehead, 147
Bodichon, Barbara, 118
Bolton, Robert, 9
Bona Fide Occupational Qualification (BFOQ), 267–68, 278–79
Bork, Judge Robert, 254
Bossard, James, 248
Bourgeois, Margeurite, 16
Boyd, Belle, 147
Bradley, Joseph, 156, 158
Bradstreet, Anne, 27
Bradwell, Myra, 157–59
Brandeis, Louis, and "Brandeis brief," 201, 213, 223–28, 253
Brawling, 11–12, 31
Breach of promise of marriage, 73–74
Brennan, Justice William, 274–75, 280
Brent, Margarett, 24
Brewer, Justice David, 223
Brinsley, John, 8
Brower, Wendy Robinson, 282

Brown, Antoinette. *See* Blackwell, Antoinette Brown
Brown, Barbara, 271
Brown, Gertrude Foster, 195
Brown, Helen Elizabeth, 234
Brown, Justice Henry Billings, 188–90
Brown, Mary Olney, 184–85, 193
Brown, Mercy, 32
Brownmiller, Susan, 299–300
Brownson, Orestes, 169
Buchanan, Pat, 292
Bundling, 44
Bunting, Mary, ix, 306
Burger, Chief Justice Warren, 273–74, 280
Burleigh, Charles, 113, 169
Burn, Harry, 200
Burnham, Carrie. *See* Kilgore, Carrie Burnham
Burns, Lucy, 196
Bush, President George, 277, 279, 288

Cable Act, 206
California: and married women's property, 129–30; and suffrage, 200; and jury service, 205; and marital residence, 207; and no-fault divorce, 281
Cambridge Platform, 27
Capitalism: in early America, 2–3, 37, 41–45, 60–61; in the nineteenth century, 125–38; in modern America, 176, 211, 219, 312. *See also* Economic rights; labor; protectionism; wage labor
Carder, Angela, 293
Carpenter, Matthew, 158, 160
Carroll, Mollie Ray, 221
Carter, President James Earl, 261–62
Cartter, Judge David, 157
Cary, Mary Shadd, 155
Catholicism. *See* Roman Catholicism
Catt, Carrie Chapman, 183, 201, 210, 228
Cedarbaum, Judge Miriam Goldman, 261
Celler, Emanuel, 267
Chamberlain, Betsy, 118
Champney, Adeline, 314
Chancery courts. *See* Equity.
Channing, William Henry, 86
Chapman, Maria Weston, 94
Charity Organization Society, 227
Chase, Margaret, 267
Child care, 236, 261, 263, 269, 272, 277–79
Child labor, 211–13, 233–38. *See also* Protectionism
Child, Lydia Maria, 120
Child molestation, 12, 26
Children's Bureau, 212, 251
Childs, Roda [Rhoda] Ann, 144
Child support, 276

Chilton, Mary Jane, 145
Chinese, 219, 225, 229
Christianity: in early America, 1–2, 5–9, 13–20, 33–35, 39–40,48; in nineteenth century, 97, 104–7, 115–17, 169, 178; in modern era, 190, 259–62. *See also specific religions or revivals*
Church and state, separation of, 115–19
Citizen's Advisory Committee on the Status of Women, 267
Civil disobedience, 153–55, 159–60
Civil law. *See* Continental law
Civil Rights Act: of 1866, 285; of 1870, 154, 156; of 1875, 155; of 1957, 205; of 1964, and Title VII, 256, 260, 265, 267–68, 282, 286, 295; of 1991, 279
Civil rights movement, 179, 209, 270, 273
Civil Rights Restoration Act [1988], 284
Clark, Justice Walter, 199, 201
Clarke, Ida Clyde, 234
Class legislation, 132, 139, 149, 178–80, 190, 192, 202–3, 212, 217, 259–308
Clergy, 95–98, 169. *See also* Christianity; *specific individuals*
Cleveland, President Grover, 186
Clinton, Hillary Rodham, 292
Clinton, President William J., 290–91, 294
Clothing, 119–20, 124, 141–42, 168, 177; and black women, 84; and rape, 245–46
Club movement, 176, 195
Colden, Cadwallader, 42
Collins, Gail, 262
Collins, May, 190
Colorado: and tort, 136; and suffrage, 183; and list of citizenship rights, 215
Columbia College, 37
Columbia Law School, 146, 230
Combahee River Collective, 270
Common law, 73, 110, 115–16. *See also specific doctrines or rights*
Community property. *See* Continental law
Comstock Act, and Anthony Comstock, 167–68, 247–48
Confiscation statutes, 53–55
Congress of Industrial Organizations [CIO], 233. *See also* AFL-CIO
Congressional Union. *See* National Woman's Party
Conjugal [sex] rights, 72, 76–77, 119, 245–46
Connecticut: and early law, 13–15, 26–28, 51–53, 71, 78; and witchcraft, 34; and married women's property, 129, 140; and suffrage, 201; and contraception, 253
Conscience, liberty of, 19
Conspiracy, and abortion, 293

Constitution, federal, 111–12, 122, 159–60. *See also specific provisions*
Constitutional history, xv-xvi
Constitutional review, standards of, 203, 235–36, 260, 273, 276–78, 280–82, 305
Constitutions, state, 47–48, 129–30, 159. *See also specific states*
Continental law, 45, 64, 70–71, 116, 118, 126, 128–30, 184–85.
Contraception: in early America, 26–27, 78; in nineteenth century, 166–68; in modern America, 246–53, 286; oral, 251–52
Contract, liberty of, and Fourteenth Amendment, 107, 213–14, 222, 228, 232–33
Contract, right of: in early America, 11, 42, 68, 76; between spouses, 52, 64, 67–68; in nineteenth century, 107, 114, 127, 136–38. *See also* Economic rights
Cook, Edith Valet, 235
Cooley, Justice Thomas, 66, 253
Cooper, Anna Julia, 155
Correction, right of: in early America, 12, 17; in nineteenth century, 77; in modern era, 243
Cotton, John, 5–9, 15, 19, 21
Council of Jewish Women, 227
Coverture, law of, 10, 15–16, 26, 54–55, 75, 103–104, 109–11, 119, 126–27, 133–34, 145, 153, 156, 216–18, 224–26, 273, 276, 304; and suffragism, 181–209. *See also* Domestic government; marriage
Cowen, Judge Ezek, 63–67
Craigie, Mary, 191
Crane, William, 48
Craven, Reverend Dr., 98
Crime: in early America, 28–31, 37–38, 76; in modern period, 240–41
Criminal conversation. *See* Conjugal rights; rape
Crisp, Jane, 21
Cross dressing, 19–20, 141, 147, 246
Cruelty, as grounds for divorce, 60, 72–73, 166
Cultural feminism, 179
Curry, James, 137
Curtis, George William, 147
Custody: in early America, 45, 63–64, 66; of women's bodies, 76–77; among slaves, 84–85; in nineteenth century, 127–28, 130, 132–33, 143; in modern era, 185–86, 216, 281
Custom, and customary constitutions, xvi, 115–17, 119, 137, 149, 179

Dahlgren, Madeline Vinton, 181
Dakota Territory: and married women's property, 130; and partial suffrage, 183

Dall, Caroline, 118
Dana, Francis, 54
Dana, Richard Henry, 104
Danforth, Clarissa, 91
Date rape, 297–98
Davis, Angela, 270
Davis, Daniel, 53
Davis, Estele R., 195
Davis, Paulina Wright, 81, 88, 91, 104–5, 107, 117, 152, 171, 192
Declaration of Independence, 37, 99, 106, 111–12, 114, 159
Declaration of Rights for Women [1876], 171, 311
Declaratory act, and suffrage, 151–53, 157
Dehlgren, Mrs. Admiral, 170
Delaware: and divorce, 14; and political rights, 20, 48; and bar admission, 162
Democratic Party, 148, 208
Dennett, Mary Ware, 248
Department of Defense, 260–61
Deportment, 47, 89, 147, 191–92, 195–98; of blacks, 144–45. See also Speech
Detroit House of Corrections, 166, 242
Deutsch, Helene, 244
Dew, Thomas, 136
Dewson, Mary, 228
Difference feminism, xiii, 105, 109, 190–92, 214–18, 256–308
Discrimination, employment, 234–36. See also Economic rights
Division of labor by sex: in early America, 21–22, 41–42; and black women, 22; in nineteenth century, 135–38; in modern era, 177, 190, 230–31, 263, 294
Divorce: in early America, 13–15, 45; customary [conventional], 64–68; and kingship, 60, 66–67; and contract clause, 69–71, 79; in nineteenth century, 52, 65–79, 70, 72, 74, 79–80, 108, 119, 163, 165–66; and federal government, 67; and race, 166; in modern era, 281, 302; no-fault, 276
Domestic government, xi; in early America, 5–9, 9–15, 18, 28, 36, 44–45, 48–56; in nineteenth century, 61, 66–67, 74, 79, 81, 106, 132–36, 144–45, 149–50, 158–59, 169–70; and blacks, 67–68, 144–45; and Mormonism, 164–65; and sovereignty, 180, 183–88, 191, 193, 197–98, 270–81, 313; in modern era, 204–6, 213, 219, 273, 276, 291–92, 303–4; and culture, 313. See also Head of household
Domestic relations law. See Domestic government
Domestic services, men's right to, 76–77, 119, 132
Domestic violence: in early America, 27; in nineteenth century, 71, 77; and black

women, 120–22; and modern era, 243, 255, 294–300, 305
Domesticity: in early America, 31–33, 39–51, 56–57, 73–80; in nineteenth century, 88–92, 97 103–22, 135–38, 145, 163, 179; and modern era, 189–92, 230–31, 236–38, 253, 256–59, 269, 277–83, 291–92, 303, 313; and suffragism, 191–95
Doolittle, James Rood, 172
Dorn, Edwin, 296
Douglas, Justice William, 253–55
Douglass, Frederick, 98, 118, 122, 148, 152, 171–72
Dower, right of: in early America, 12–13, 23–24, 42; in nineteenth century, 51–54, 75, 109, 119, 128, 184–85; in modern era, 217. See also Widows
Dressmaking, 135
DuBois, William E. B., 209
Dudley, Anne Dallas, 199
Due process of law, 27, 223, 278, 289. See also Fourteenth Amendment
Duniway, Abigail Scott, 185
Duress, and rape law, 245
Dworkin, Andrea, 299
Dworkin, Ronald, 292, 294
Dyer, Mary, 7, 21

Eagle Forum, 261, 301
Earnings legislation, 127–28, 132, 134, 184
Eastman, Crystal, 248, 313
Economic protection. See Protectionism
Economic rights: in early America, 40–43, 51, 61, 75; in nineteenth century, 103, 114–15, 117–19, 125–38, 141–43, 145, 148, 156, 177; in modern era, x, 201, 210–38, 256–59, 262–83, 300–306, 313–14; linked to political rights, 137, 162–63, 181
Edelsberg, Herman, 28
Education Amendments Act, and Title IX, 275, 284, 296
Education: in early America, 19, 46–47; in nineteenth century, 85–86, 88, 90–91, 115–16, 118–19; and professions, 93–94, 140–42, 155–56, 176–77, 230, 283; and suffragism, 195; and equality, 276, 283–85, 306, 308
Edwards, Jonathan, 37, 40
Eighteenth Amendment, 178, 201, 302
Elizabeth [preacher], 91
Elliot-Larsen Civil Rights Act [MI], 305
Ely, John Hart, 288
Emerson, Thomas, 271
Employment discrimination. See Economic rights
Enforcement Act [1870], and civil disobedience, 154

Engels, Fredrich, and *Condition of the Working Class in England*, 210, 212
English Quaker Act, 20
Equal Economic Opportunity Commission [EEOC], 256–59, 267–68, 277–80. *See also* Civil Rights Act of 1964, Title VII
Equal Employment Opportunity Act, 275
Equal Nationality Treaty, 226
Equal Pay Act, 265
Equal protection of law, x, xiv, 27, 122, 149, 161–62, 178–79, 182, 203–5, 210–38, 240–42; and disparate impact/treatment theory, 256–59. *See also* Equal Rights Amendment; Fourteenth Amendment; *specific cases*
Equal Rights Amendment, x, xiv, 178–79, 210–38, 253, 259–309; text of, 271; and recission, 302–3
Equal rights amendments, state, 217, 292
Equal Rights Treaty, 226
Equity: in early America, 11–12, 51–52; and divorce, 72; and charging doctrine, 132–34. *See also* Marriage settlements; married women's property acts
Ethical gains doctrine, and Florence Kelley, 212–13, 224, 229
Eugenics, and birth control, 248
Ex post facto clause, and legislative divorce, 69
Executors, 42, 274
Expediency, and woman suffrage, 148–49, 154–55, 194
Extra-marital sex, 25, 43–44, 276–77. *See also* Pregnancy

Factory laws. *See* Protectionism; wage and hour legislation
Fair Labor Standards Act, 233–34, 236, 265
Fairfield, Daniel, 26
Falk, Gail, 271
Faludi, Susan, 270
Falwell, Jerry, 301
Familism [Family of Love], 7
Family, family government, family law. *See* Domestic government
Family wage, 135–36, 213, 220, 282
Farmer's Alliances, 182
Faulkner, Shannon, and the Citadel, 285
Federal government, expanded role of, 151–56, 178; and law of domestic relations, 170
Fein, Bruce, 289
Fell, Margaret, and *Women's Speaking Justified* (1666), 20
Female Anti-Slavery Society of Salem [MA], 95
Female traders, 23, 40, 76
Feme covert, and *Feme sole*: defined, 10. *See also* Coverture

Feminism, ix, 177, 179, 234, 273. *See also* Suffragism; *varieties of feminism*
Fenberg, Matilda, 203
Fenton, William, 223
Ferguson, Miriam, 262
Ferrin, Mary Upton, 131
Ferry, Elisha, 71
Fess, Simeon, 214
Feudalism, 37, 48–51, 66, 107–8, 132, 164. *See also* Head of household; kingship
Field, David Dudley, 132
Field, Justice Stephen, 70–71, 165
Fields, Mamie Garvin, 219
Fifteenth Amendment, 139, 148–50, 152, 161, 200; and jury service, 202; and relation to Nineteenth, 206
Fifth Amendment, 261, 275
Filmer, John, and *Patriarcha*, 18, 48–51
Finch, Ann, 45–46
Finney, Charles, 85–86
First Amendment, 164, 173, 252, 291, 299. *See also* Speech
First-wave women's movement: objectives of, 59–60, 81, 115, 117–19; compared to second wave, 306–7
Fish, Miriam, 128
Fish, Joseph, 39
Florida: and married women's property, 126; and jury service, 204; and crime, 206
Foltz, Clara Shortridge, 230
Ford Motor Company, 235
Fornication, and rape law, 245
Foster, Stephen, 82, 155
Fourteenth Amendment, x, 139, 148–50, 152, 156–58, 160–61, 205, 223, 226, 235, 241–42, 259–308. *See also* Contract, liberty of; due process; economic rights; equal protection; Equal Rights Amendment; privileges and immunities
Fourth Amendment, and privacy, 253–54
Fowler, Eliza, 19
Frankfurter, Justice Felix, 213, 225, 228, 235–36
Freedman, Ann, 271
Freedman's Bureau, 143–44, 154
French Revolution, xii, 47
Freudian analysis, 177, 236, 244, 247, 253
Freund, Ernst, 218
Friedan, Betty, 179, 249, 253, 268–69, 286
Fuller, Margaret, 94, 100
Fyfe, Mrs. Hannah Beye, 202

Gage, Frances, 98–99
Gage, Matilda Joslyn, 98, 107, 110, 115–17, 147, 151, 161, 311
Gale, Zona, 218
Gallagher, Ursula, 251

Gannett, Mary Lewis, 194
Garcia, Inez, 244
Gardner, Nadine, 154
Garrison, William Lloyd, 82, 98, 109, 114–15, 148
Gay rights, 261, 301
General Federation of Women's Clubs, 218, 227
George, Julian, and suffrage amendment, 152–53
Georgia: and head of household, 171–72; and poll taxes, 207
Giddens, Anthony, 298
Gilman, Charlotte Perkins, 218
Ginsburg, Justice Ruth Bader, 204, 230, 261, 272, 274, 288, 302, 304, 314
Girls' Friendly Society, 227
Goldman, Emma, 170, 194, 219, 248
Goldmark, Josephine, 213, 223, 225, 228
Gompers, Samuel, 213, 220
Goodhue, Sarah Whipple, 38
Gouge, William, 17–18
Gouges, Olympe de, 47
Grange, 182
Gray, Hannah, 29
Great Awakening, 36–39, 56
Greeley, Andrew, 312
Greeley, Horace, 87, 147, 172
Greene, Elizabeth, 21
Greene, Judge Roger Sherman, 184–85
Greenleaf, Simon, 103, 309
Grew, Mary, 93
Griffing, Josephine, 311
Griffiths, Martha, 267, 271
Grimké, Angelina and Sarah, 82, 96, 103, 105, 119–20, 122
Grosvenor, Sarah, and Amasa Sessions, 27
Guarantee clause, 152, 161

Habeas corpus, 63–64. See also Custody
Hale, Sir Matthew, 25, 245
Hale, Robert, 149
Hamilton, Alice, 214–18
Hamlin, Hannibal, 149–50
Hammon, Mary, 26
Harbert, Elizabeth Boynton, 192
Hardy, Matthew, 24
Harlan, Justice John Marshall, 202, 223, 253
Harper, Frances, 143
Harrington, Adeline, 216
Harvard University, and Law School, 93, 230
Hatch, Orrin, 288
Hawaii: and jury service, 203; and abortion, 287
Hay, Judge William, 111, 114
Hayden, Carl, 264

Head of household, xiii, 36, 61, 65, 73, 120; in early America, 16, 31–32, 56–58; division of sovereignty, 18, 98, 106, 140, 169–70, 177, 183, 188, 190–91, 193, 197–98, 216, 270, 272–73, 276, 281, 303, 309; unitary character of, 99, 135–36; in nineteenth century, 124, 129–30, 133, 146, 158–59; female, 137; and Civil War, 141–42; and black men, 148; and suffrage, 149; and Mormonism, 164–65; in modern era, 171–72, 291–92, 309; and jury service, 185–88. See also Domestic government
Health and welfare legislation, 217–19, 223, 241–42
Height, Dorothy, 209
Hemphill, Judge John, 129–30, 132
Henderson, John Brooks, 148
Henry, Alice, 220
Heresy, 95–96
Hertell, Judge Thomas, 131
Heywood, Leslie, 296
Hibbens, Ann, and William Hibbens, 5, 8–9, 15–16, 20, 31, 33
Higgins, Lois Lundell, 230
Higginson, Thomas, 100
Hill, Anita, 279, 296
Hitchcock, A. S., 144
Hodder, Jessie, 242
Hodgers, Jennie [a.k.a. Albert D.J. Cashier], 141
Hog, Mistress, and sedition, 31
Holmes, Justice Oliver Wendell, Jr., 222–23, 226, 228–29
Home work: in early America, 2, 40; in the nineteenth century, 118, 128, 137–38; in modern era, 210–14, 218, 235–36. See also Wage labor.
Homemaking. See Domesticity
Homes, for delinquent women, 166, 250–51
Homestead exemptions, 127
Homesteading, 130–31
Hood, Cornelia, 193
Hooker, Isabella Beecher, 140, 152–53
Hooker, Thomas, 19
Hooper, Relief, 38
Hopkins, Governor Edward, 19
House Committee on Armed Services, 261
Howard, Senator Jacob, 152
Howell, Mary, 91
Hoyt, Justice [Governor] John P., 185–86
Hugh Moore Fund, 252
Hughes, Chief Justice Charles Evans, 232
Hull, Jane Dee, 262
Hull House, 176, 211
Human rights, 86, 124, 150–51, 178. See also specific rights

Humphreys, James, 132
Hunger strikes, 196
Hunt, Dr. Harriot, 93, 113
Hunt, Judge Ward, 160
Hunter, Jane Edna, 176
Hutchinson, Anne, and William Hutchinson, 5–8, 16, 20, 26, 31, 33, 314
Hyde Amendment, 290–92

Idaho, and married women's property, 129
Illinois: and divorce, 71; and abortion, 78; and married women's property, 134, 140; and bar admission, 141, 159; and suffrage, 200; and jury service, 202–3; and naming, 209; and industrial reform, 211
Incest, and abortion, 246
Income tax, federal, 201, 308
Indiana: and married women's property, 129; and jury service, 202–3
Indians, American, 33, 40, 46, 135–36, 219
Industrial regulation, 136, 211, 213, 222–25, 268, 277. See also Protectionism
Infanticide, 13, 21, 29–30, 32
Inglis, William, 64
Inheritance: in early America, 13, 22–24, 42–43; and revolution, 51–53; in nineteenth century, 75, 126–28, 130, 132–36
Insanity, 19, 32–33, 120, 129, 309
International Association of Policewomen, 230
International Cigar Makers, 220
Internationalism, in reform culture, 177, 194–95, 200–201, 218–19
International Ladies' Garment Workers Union, 220, 233
International Women's Congresses, 218–19
Involuntary servitude. See Thirteenth Amendment
Iowa: and married women's property, 129; and bar admission, 141; and juries, 202–3; and naming, 209
Irwin, Inez Haynes, 197
Izard, Alice, 91

Jacobs, Harriet, 122
Jarrett, Dr. Elizabeth, 168
Jefferson, President Thomas, 47
Jenkins, Helen, 138
John Birch Society, 301
Johnson, Edward, 19
Johnson, President Lyndon, 252, 267, 272
Johnson, Mariana, 94, 104, 109, 116, 172
Johnston, Barbara, and Hagar, 308–9, 315
Johnston, Mary, 183, 195, 201, 313
Joint Commission on Accreditation of Hospitals, 251
Jonas, Rosalie, 199

Jones, Elizabeth, 116
Jones, Margaret, and John Butterfield, 31
Jones, Mary Harris ("Mother Jones"), 219
Jones, Minnie, 235
Jones, Chief Justice Walter, 187
Judaism, 259–62
Judicial appointments, 233, 261
Judicial bypass, in abortion, 288–89
Jury service: in early America, 21, 75; and black women, 143; in modern era, 160, 172, 198, 185–206, 260–62; in Wyoming, 182; and head of household, 182, 185; in Washington Territory, 185–88; and black men, 202; and exemption, 201–6
Juvenile delinquency, 252

Kansas: and married women's property, 130; and suffrage, 139, 147, 150, 182, 200; and prisons, 240–41
Kearney, Belle, 199
Keating-Owen Child Labor Act, 213
Kefauver, Estes, 264
Kelley, Abigail, 81–82, 100, 116–17, 309
Kelley, Florence, 194, 210–14, 219–26, 229, 234–35, 302, 312
Kellogg, Abraham, 201
Kendall, Keziah [pseud.], 103–4, 123, 309
Kennedy, Justice Anthony, 289
Kennedy, President John F., 253, 265, 267
Kent, James, and Commentaries, 69, 72, 74
Kentucky: and married women's property, 126; and suffrage, 183; and naming, 209; and spousal rape, 297
Kepley, Ada, 140
Kessler-Harris, Alice, 257
Kilgore, Carrie Burnham, 123, 311
Kilgore, Harley, 264
Kingship, 16, 31, 48–51. See also Domestic government; feudalism
Kitchens, public, 218–19
Knopf, Olga, 314
Ku Klux Klan, 144, 293

Labor: in early America, 12, 21–22, 41–44; in nineteenth century, 76–77, 118, 128, 141–42, 145; parental rights to children's, 127; husband's right to women's, 134, 156; of enslaved women, 137; and association with servility, 137, 145; among emancipated blacks, 143–45; in modern era, 210, 218–21; agricultural, 236–38. See also Capitalism; economic rights; protectionism; wage labor.
Labor, Department of, 236
Ladies' Christian Union, 140
Ladies' Congressional Club of Washington, D.C., 188

Ladies' Helping Hand Association of New
  York City, 166
Laissez-faire theory, xiv, 136, 176–77, 214,
  217, 223, 231, 234, 270, 279, 302
Lathrop, Julia, 212
Laughlin, Gail, 215
Law enforcement, x, 230
Law, practice of, 155–59, 162–63, 230,
  233–35, 261, 272; and suffrage, 160–62
Lawson, John, 22
League of Women Voters, 215, 217, 220–21,
  227, 235, 259
Lease, Mary, 195
Lee, Rex, 288–89
Lee, Jarena, 91
Left feminism. See Radicalism
Legislatures, sex-segregated, 172
Lenhoff, Donna, 275
Lesbianism, 26, 163, 262, 301–4, 312. See
  also Gay rights
Letter writing, 89, 142
Lewin, Tamar, 313–14
Liberal feminism, 259–308.
Lincoln, President Abraham, 83, 125
Livermore, Mary, 101, 125, 141–42, 152,
  168–69, 270, 309
Livingstone, Edward, 132
Locke, John, xi, 48–51, 56, 183
Lockwood, Belva, 157, 162, 206
Locomotion, right of: in early America, 10, 12;
  in nineteenth century, 119, 148, 172; for
  black women, 144
Logan, Adella Hunt, 193, 209
Lorentzen, Anna Marie, 136
Louisiana: and married women's property,
  129; and partial suffrage, 183
Lowell factories [MA], 40, 118
Loyal League, 146
Loyalism, and married women, 53–55,
  126–27
Lukens, Esther Ann, 93
Lynching, 143

Mackinnon, Catharine, 294, 299, 314
Madison, James, 56
Magna C[h]arta, 106
Mahan, Asa, 114
Maine: and domestic violence, 71, 119, 297;
  and married women's property, 129; and
  office holding, 206
Managerial rights, and property, 11, 130–34.
  See also Married women's property acts;
  property rights
Mann Act, and James Mann, 214, 243
Manning, Barbara, 218
Mansfield, Arabella, 140–41
Mansfield, Judge Walter, 205

Marital unity doctrine, 10, 103, 171–72. See
  also Coverture
Marriage, and marital contract, 48–51, 68–71,
  79, 108, 110–11, 130–34, 144–45, 216, 269,
  276; in early America, 9–18, 28, 43, 111;
  property rights in, 67–69; and the public
  interest, 70–71; compared to slavery, 74; as
  private agreement, 80; among freed blacks,
  144–45; and Mormonism, 164–65; and radicalism, 219; and privacy, 255. See also
  Domestic government
Marriage settlements: in early America, 10–11;
  in nineteenth century, 127, 134; registration
  of estates, 130. See also Equity; trusts
Married women's property acts, 119, 125–38,
  183–88, 308–9. See also Economic rights
Marshall, Chief Justice John, 55
Marshall, Marguerite Mooers, 227
Marshall, Justice Thurgood, 291
Martineau, Harriet, 90, 123
Maryland: and early law, 11, 21, 13–14, 66,
  71; and suffrage, 48; and married women's
  property, 129; and ratification of amendments, 201
Mason, Priscilla, 36
Massachusetts: and early law, 8, 14–15, 19,
  25, 28–30, 37–38; and political rights, 21,
  61; and witchcraft, 33–35; and nationality,
  53–54; and married women's property, 129;
  and bar admission, 162; and office holding,
  206; and wage and hour legislation, 222–24
Maternalism, 280–81, 303; and modern welfare state, 177
Maternity: in early America, 27–28; in nineteenth century, 135–36, 158–59, 180; regulation of in the public interest, 163–68, 214,
  223–25, 250–52, 288; as ground for disfranchisement, 189; in modern era, 190–91, 217,
  220–25, 228–29, 236, 239–40, 247–48,
  263–64, 266–69, 277–81, 286–94, 291–92;
  and labor unions, 220; as public work,
  247–48. See also Coverture; Republican
  Motherhood
Maternity leave, 236
Mather, Cotton, 13, 33–34
Matrons' juries: in early America, 21; in nine-
  teenth century, 75. See also Jury service
Matthews, Judge Burnita Shelton, 233
Maxwell, Elsa, 191–92
May, Samuel, 82–83
Mayo, Amory Dwight, 169
McKenna, Justice Joseph, 205, 225
Medicaid funding, abortion, 288, 290, 292
Medicine, professional, 237. See also Education
Mental cruelty. See Cruelty.
Merwin, Virginia, 137
Michelman, Kate, 290

Michigan: and divorce, 72; and homestead exemptions, 127; and married women's property, 127–28; and suffrage, 154, 183; and jury service, 202–3; and privacy, 239–40
Michigan Bridget, 141
Midwives, 11, 167–68, 251
Military academies, 260
Military Selective Service Act of 1967, 261
Military service: in Civil War, 139, 141, 148; among black women, 142; in modern era, 189, 260–61, 271–76; and ERA, 303, 305
Mill, John Stuart, 118, 132
Miller, Justice Samuel, 157–58
Miller, Alice Duer, 175, 181, 193
Mini-Comstock acts, 167–68, 247–48, 253. *See also* Comstock Act
Minnesota Working Women, 282
Minnesota: and married women's property, 131; and suffrage, 182–83, 197–98
Minor, Virginia, and Francis Minor, 160–61
Miscegenation, 24
Miss America Pageant, and scholarships, 283
Mississippi: and married women's property, 126, 128–29; and jury service, 205
Missouri: and ratification of amendments, 201; and sex-specific ballots, 207; and spousal rape, 297
Mitsubishi Motor Manufacturing of America, 295
Montesquieu, Baron de, 18, 46
Moravians, 18, 260
Morgan, John Tyler, 188
Mormonism, 163–65, 208, 242–43
Morrill Act, 164
Motherhood. *See* Maternity; Republican Motherhood
Mothers' pensions, 214, 236
Mott, Lucretia, 82, 91, 94, 100, 104–5, 115, 116, 123, 161
Murray, Pauli, 266, 268, 274
Murray, Judith Sargent, 57, 90
Murrell, Ethel Ernest, 264

Naming: and property rights in women's labor, 10; in nineteenth century, 120, 123; in modern era, 209
Nation, Carry, 194
National Abortion [and Reproductive Rights] Action League, 286, 290
National American Woman Suffrage Association, 176–77, 183, 193, 215, 219, 268
National Association for the Advancement of Colored People, 213
National Association of Colored Citizens, 145
National Association of Colored Women, 176
National Association for Labor Legislation, 227

National Campaign Fund, 269
National Child Labor Committee, 213
National Committee on Household Employment, 236
National Conference for New Politics, 270
National Congress of Mothers, 227
National Consumer's League, 211, 213, 215–16, 218, 225, 227, 282
National Council of Catholic Women, 227
National Council of Negro Women, 209
National Equal Rights Party, 206
National Federation of Business and Professional Women's Clubs, 227, 265
National Federation of Federal Employees, 227
National Industrial Recovery Act, 233
National Labor Relations Act, 233
National League of Girls' Clubs, 227
National Medical Association, 193
National Organization for Women, xiv, 179, 256, 268, 271, 285, 302
National Welfare Rights Organization, 281
National Woman Suffrage Association, 150–51, 153–54, 157, 176, 311
National Woman's Party, xiii–xiv, 177, 183, 196–97, 200, 202, 210–19, 226, 228, 263–65, 302
National Woman's Trade Union League, 218
National Women's Political Caucus, 269
Nationality, 53–55, 126–27, 206
Natural relations, 17, 50–51. *See also* Domestic government
Natural rights [natural law], 48–51, 99, 108–9, 107, 112, 117, 150–54, 163, 188–89; and suffrage, 201–2
Nebraska: and suffrage, 184; and wage and hour legislation, 223, 232
Nevada: and married women's property, 129; and jury service, 202–3
New Deal, 179, 231, 234, 236–38, 249, 259
New Departure, 61, 150–55
New England Anti-Resistant Society, 82
New France, 16
New Hampshire: and political rights, 21, 47–48; and early crime, 31; and witchcraft, 34; and legislative divorce, 69; and married women's property, 129; and office holding, 206, 262
New Haven Colony, and rape, 26
New Jersey: and equity, 11; and divorce, 14; and political rights, 21, 47–48, 54, 183; and marital residence, 207; and office holding, 262
New Mexico: and married women's property, 129; and abortion, 292; and spousal rape, 297
New Spain, 16

New York: and early law, 11, 14–15, 21, 23, 31, 34, 45; and political rights, 21, 47–48, 147, 191–92, 200; and abortion, 79, 287; and married women's property, 129, 132–33, 140, 145–46; and black suffrage, 139; and protective societies, 140; and education, 140–41; and maternity, 167; and divorce, 281
New York Child Labor Committee, 212
New York Committee for the Suppression of Vice, 167
New York Magdalene Society, 95
New York Political Equality League, 191–93
New York State Association Opposed to Woman Suffrage, 189
Newspapers, 94–95, 99–100, 146, 195
Nichols, Clarina Howard, 119, 139, 170
Night work, regulation of, 221, 227, 231. See also Protectionism
Nineteenth Amendment, xiii, 106, 109, 162, 178, 200–202, 209, 217, 226–29, 231, 304; and Civil War antecedents, 152–53; and jury service, 205; relationship to the Fifteenth, 206. See also Suffrage
Nordberg, Judge John, 256–59
Norris, Kathleen, 245–46
North Carolina: and suffrage, 48; and divorce, 165–66; and racism in suffragism, 199; and office holding, 206; and spousal rape, 297
North Dakota, and suffrage, 183
Norton, Eleanor Holmes, 269
Nursing, 141, 146, 277

Obedience, as women's duty, 16–18, 74
Oberlin College, 82, 85–86, 176
Obligations: of wives, 66, 245–46; of husbands, 76–77; of citizens, 139–40, 149, 156, 186, 189; of female citizens after enfranchisement, 201–9, 216, 260–62, 304, 313. See also specific obligations
Occupation, right to, 157–58
Office holding. See Political rights; specific jurisdictions
Ohio: and homestead exemptions, 127; and married women's property, 129, 131; and ratification of amendments, 201; and jury service, 202–3; and age discrimination, 206
Ohio Woman's Temperance Society, 91
Oklahoma, and spousal rape, 297
Oregon: and married women's property, 130; and suffrage, 200; and protectionism, 223
Oregon Donation Act, 70, 130
Osborn, Sarah, 39
Otis, James, 147
Owen, Robert Dale, 110–11
O'Connell, Cardinal, 249

O'Connor, Justice Sandra Day, 261–62, 276, 289
O'Conor, Charles, 66

Packard, Elizabeth Parsons, 120, 129, 309
Paige, Senator Alonzo, 64
Paraphernalia, 10, 75
Parent Teachers' Association, 227
Parker, Isaac, 73
Parliament: and divorce, 14; and division of sovereign authority, 56
Parsons, Theophilus, 74, 182
Parsons, Mary, 34
Partial-birth abortion, 290
Partial suffrage. See Suffrage; specific jurisdictions
Patterson, James, 149
Paul, Alice, 177, 196, 226–27, 264, 271
Pauline Doctrine, 19, 85
Payne, Bishop D. A., 145
Peckham, Justice Rufus, 223
Penal policy, 240–42, 265
Pennsylvania: and divorce, 14–15; and political rights, 20–21, 48; and female traders, 23; and inheritance, 24; and early crime, 29; and benefit of clergy, 30; and legislative divorce, 69; and jury service, 202–3; and protectionism, 223
Pension plans, 278
Perfectionism, 86, 105–7, 109. See also Christianity
Perkins, Frances, 211, 213, 233
Perkins, William, 17, 32, 33
Personal security, 76; in colonies, 11–12, 24–28, 76; in nineteenth century, 119–22, 163–68; in modern era, 143–44, 179, 239–55, 259–308, 263, 287–88; and governmental obligation to ensure, 292; and sovereignty, 294, 305
Peterson, Esther, 265
Petition, right of, 99, 112, 122
Philadelphia Baptists Association, 39
Phillips, Wendell, 102, 117
Physical security. See Personal security
Picketing: by NWP, 196; anti-abortion, 293
Pierce School, 91
Pisan, Christine de, and Boke of the Citye of Ladys, 92
Planned Parenthood Federation of America, 251
Planned Parenthood League of Connecticut, 254
Planned Parenthood of Wisconsin, 290
Plumbly, Ruth, 88, 106
Plymouth Colony, and witchcraft, 34
Policing. See Law enforcement; penal policy

Political parties, 209–10, 259–62, 269–70. *See also specific parties*
Political rights: in early America, 20, 53–55; in nineteenth century, 122–27, 177–209; in modern era, 152–61, 168–69, 177–209, 259–62; and bar admission, 162–63; ancillary, 178, 261; and economic rights, 181. *See also* Jury service; nationality; Nineteenth Amendment; suffrage; *specific jurisdictions*
Poll taxes, and sex discrimination, 259
Polygamy. *See* Mormonism
Populism, 182, 195
Pornography, 298–300
Posner, Judge Richard, 290, 298
Pound, Roscoe, 226
Poverty: and widowhood, 13; in early nation, 135–36; and pregnancy, 251–53; and abortion, 291
Powell, Justice Lewis, 275
Power of attorney. *See* Attorneyship
Pre-marital agreements. *See* Equity; marriage settlements
Preaching, 39, 81, 85, 89, 91
Pregnancy: in early America, 24–26, 44; in nineteenth century, 119–20, 156, 167; in modern era, 239–40, 246–52, 263, 266–67, 277–79, 280–94; and teenagers, 247, 250–51. *See also* Maternity
Pregnancy Discrimination Act, 279
President's Commission on the Status of Women, 253, 265–66, 274–75
Press, liberty of, 93, 195
Preston, Ann, 106
Prisons, 241–42, 265
Privacy: in colonial America, 26–27; and domestic violence cases, 78; in nineteenth century, 119; among blacks, 144–45; in modern era, 177, 179, 239–40, 254–55, 278, 286; constitutional right compared to legal right, 240, 252–54; and sexual revolution, 278, 286; and reproductive freedom, 287–89, 293, 301; and sovereignty, 292
Private clubs, and female memberships, 285
Privilege, grants of, and rights, 151–52, 201
Privileges and immunities clause, 156–57, 160–62, 241–42. *See also* Fourteenth Amendment
Procedural rights: and gender, 20; in early America, 27–32; and witchcraft, 33–35; and equal protection, 80; in nineteenth century, 122, 172; in modern era, 242
Progressivism, and Progressive Party, 176–78, 190, 210–14, 220, 240–41
Property rights, 10–11, 52–53, 75, 109, 107, 114, 118–19, 125–38, 201. *See also* Economic rights; married women's property acts

Prostitution, 95, 166, 216, 242–43
Protectionism, physical, 239–55
Protectionism, economic, 136–40, 158–59, 176–78, 210–38, 259–308; among blacks, 136; and labor unions, 220–21; and persistence in law, 312
Protestantism, 13–14, 81, 104, 260. *See also specific religions and revivals*
Public interest doctrine, and maternity, 210, 212, 214, 224–25, 228, 241–42, 288, 292–93, 304
Publication. *See* Letter writing; press, freedom of
Pufendorf, Samuel, 15
Puritanism, 1–2, 5–9, 17, 20, 21; and witchcraft, 33–35. *See also* Christianity
Putnam-Jacobi, Mary, 197

Quakerism, 7, 16–17, 20, 35, 82–83, 96, 104, 116, 188, 213
Quayle, Daniel, 312
Quickening doctrine, 78–79, 287. *See also* Abortion
Quindlen, Anna, 180

Racism: and divisions of labor, 22; and domestic violence cases, 77–78; in women's rights movements, 84, 147–50, 154–55, 198–99, 202, 208–9, 219; and birth control, 248–49; and office holding, 262; in public policy, 267, 280–81. *See also* Black women; slavery
Radcliffe Institute for Independent Study, 268
Radicalism: in early nation, 47, 104; in Europe, 92; and threat of revolution, 113–114; in suffragism, 170, 177, 191–92, 194; in modern feminism, 178–79, 270
Rape: in early America, 12, 24–26; defined, 25, 244; in nineteenth century, 77, 119–20, 143–44; in modern era, 244–45, 292–300; spousal, 245, 297; and abortion, 246; statutory, 276; and crisis centers, 294
Rawalt, Margeurite, 266
Read, Ruth, 29
Reagan, President Ronald, 257, 261, 262, 277, 282, 284, 288, 291
Reed, Esther de Berdt, 90
Reeve, Tapping, 70, 74–76
Rehnquist, Chief Justice William, 275–76, 279, 289, 293, 287–88
Religion. *See* Christianity; *specific religions*
Representation: virtual, xv, 37, 147, 158–59, 188, 191, 200–201, 309; direct, 188, 171–72, 200–201

Reproduction. *See* Maternity; pregnancy
Reproductive rights, 179, 223, 247, 286–94.
    See also Abortion; contraception
Republican Party, 264
Republican Motherhood, xi-xii, 3, 46–48, 56,
    88, 90–91, 142, 163–64, 170, 190
Republican Party: in Civil War, xii, 142,
    147–54; in nineteenth century, 82, 84, 125,
    182; in modern America, 195, 264, 292, 303
Republicanism: in early America, 37, 46–47,
    51; and revolutionary settlement, 56–57; and
    dependence, 65; in nineteenth century, 86,
    105–7, 111–13; and constitutionalism,
    106–7, 111, 309–10; and suffrage, 161; and
    Mormonism, 164
Reverse discrimination, 280
Revivalism, 92, 182. *See also* Christianity;
    Great Awakening; Second Great Awaken-
    ing.
Rhode Island: and divorce, 14; and suffrage,
    21; and traders, 23; and rape, 26; and witch-
    craft, 34; and bar admission, 162
Richards, Ann, 262
Richardson, Samuel, 17
Riddle, Albert G., 154–57
Right to Life Committee, 290, 293–94
Rights. *See specific rights and liberties*
Riis, Jacob, 243
Robertson, Judge George, 70
Robinson, Lelia J., 162
Roman Catholicism: and corporal punishment,
    12; and early views of marriage and divorce,
    13–15; and women's autonomy, 16; and
    birth control, 249; and feminism, 260
Roosevelt, Eleanor, 208, 232, 235, 253, 265,
    304
Roosevelt, President Franklin Delano, 211,
    233–34
Roosevelt, President Theodore, 220
Ropes, Hannah, 141
Rose, Ernestine, 96, 99, 106, 111, 116–17,
    131, 169
Rosenberg, Rosalind, 258
Rosenthal, Andi, 299
Ross, Nellie Taloe, 262
Rush, Benjamin, 90–91
Ryan, Representative William, 252

Salem witchcraft trials, 34–35. *See also* Witch-
    craft
Sameness feminism, xiii, 109, 190–91,
    214–18, 256–308
Sampson, William, 110
Sandford, Alice, and benefit of clergy, 30
Sanford, Rebecca, 122
Sanger, Margaret, 248–49, 251
Sargent, Senator Aaron, 154

Scalia, Justice Antonin, 293
Schlafly, Phyllis, 261, 301, 303, 314
Schneiderman, Rose, 227, 314
Schriffen, Lisa, 312
Schroeder, Patricia, 262, 292
Scolding, 11–12, 19, 31–32
Second Great Awakening, xii, 60, 91–94, 98,
    182
Second-wave women's movement, 178, 210,
    256–308, 301. *See also* Feminism
Sedgwick, Catharine, 118
Sedgwick, Theodore, 54
Sedition, 31–32
Seduction, 74, 77; and rape, 245, 301
See, Isaac, 98
Selden, Judge Henry, 159–160
Self-sovereignty [self-ownership], 99, 117,
    120, 124. *See also specific liberties*
Seneca Falls Convention, and *Declaration of
    Rights and Sentiments*, ix, 81, 101, 104,
    109, 112–17, 124
Separate estates. *See* Marriage settlements
Separate spheres, 43–46, 49–51, 73, 88, 105–6,
    118–20, 132, 135–36, 158, 163, 189,
    192–94, 177–78, 197–98, 210, 226, 230–31,
    237. *See also* Division of labor by sex
Seward, Mrs. James, 120–21
Sex-plus claims, and Title VII, 281–82
Sexual harassment, 119, 261, 272, 279–80; of
    prisoners, 241–42; in the workplace,
    294–95; of athletes, 296
Sexual [or social] purity, 152, 163, 167–68,
    242–44, 248
Shaw, Dr. Anna Howard, 183
Shepard, Thomas, 7, 9
Sheppard-Towner Maternity and Infancy Act,
    213
Sherman, Mrs. General, 170
Shoemaking, 136
Simkhovitch, Mary Kingsbury, 219
Simonson, Judge Archie E., 245
Sims, Edwin, 243
Sixteenth Amendment [woman suffrage],
    152–53
Sixth Amendment, 260
Slander, 145–46
Slavery, 3, 43, 120–22; and southern women's
    involvement in, 22; and children, 24; and
    rape, 24; and petit treason, 32; and law of
    marriage, 68, 74, 108; and domestic vio-
    lence, 77; and coverture, 103–4, 311; and
    physical security, 119–21; and duty to avoid,
    122–23; and work, 136–37. *See also* Racism
Smith, Elizabeth Oakes, 61, 92, 113, 124
Smith, Gerrit, 119, 124, 148, 170
Smith, Howard, 267
Smith, James McCune, 86

Social compacts, 48–51, 117, 150
Social Darwinism, 87, 176
Social feminism, 104, 232–33
Socialism, 211–13, 218–19
Social Security Act, 236, 275
Social theory, 190, 217; and Progressive reform, 194–95; and judicial reliance on, 223–25, 258, 289
Society for the Aid of Friendless Women and Children, 166
Sociological jurisprudence, 229, 233
Souter, Justice David, 289
South: and Civil War, 141; women's rights in, 147; and suffrage, 197. *See also specific states and rights*
South Carolina: and equity, 11, 51; and divorce, 14, 67, 281; and political rights, 20, 48; and economic rights, 22; and separate estates, 128; and spousal rape, 297
South Dakota: and suffrage, 183; and spousal rape, 297
Sovereignty, 179, 183–84, 188, 193, 197–98; and headship in early America, 16–18; in families, 36, 48–51, 56, 61, 63, 66–67, 120; and speech, 94; and citizenship, 146, 152–54, 171–72; divisions of, 276; and abortion, 294. *See also* Head of household
Speech communities: defined, xi; in early America and Europe, 39, 60–61, 92; in the early nation, 81–102; in Civil War, 168–69; in modern era, 195, 268, 308–9
Speech, liberty of: in democracy, xvii, 311–12; and dissent, 5–10, 27–28, 32–34; in early America, 15, 19; and criminality, 28; and revolution, 36–37; and Baptists, 39–40; in the nineteenth century, xiii, 81–102, 100, 122–26; and black women, 95, 142; as women's obligation, 99–100; during Civil War, 146, 149–51, 169–72; and trial of Anthony, 160; and modern suffragism, xiii, 195–99; and picketing, 196–97; in modern feminism, 269; and abortion policy, 291–94; and pornography, 299–300
Spencer, Anna Garlin, 237
Spenserian sociology, 158
Spiritual equality, 2, 16–18, 84, 91, 259–62. *See also* Christianity; religion
Spying, in wartime, 141, 147
St. George, Katharine, 265
St. Paul. *See* Pauline Doctrine
Stanton, Elizabeth Cady, 59, 65, 79–80, 81–82, 87, 91–92, 94, 96, 102, 106–13, 115–17, 119–20, 122–24, 131–32, 147, 150–53, 159, 161, 169–70, 176, 182–83, 216, 255, 305, 311
Stark, Justice George, 205
Starrett, Helen Elim, 147

State Industrial Farm for Women [Kansas], 240–41
States, and citizenship rights, 47–48, 151–57. *See also specific rights*
Status disabilities, 10, 50–51. *See also* Coverture
Stearns, Jonathan, 97
Steinem, Gloria, 260
Stennis, John, 291
Stern, Edith, 238
Stevens, Doris, 214–18, 226
Stewart, Maria, 95, 309
Stewart, Justice Potter, 276, 291
Stiles, Ezra, 39
Stockton, Richard, 55
Stone, Lucy, 83, 85, 94, 100–101, 110–11, 123, 149–50, 155–56, 169
Stone, William, 101
Storer, Horatio Robinson, 166
Story, Justice Joseph, 65, 69, 126–27, 252
Stowe, Harriet Beecher, 83, 88
Strong, Simeon, 54
Substantive due process. *See* Due process
Suffrage communities: defined, xi; in modern era, 168–71, 175–209, 268, 304, 309
Suffrage: and speech, xi, 168–73, 310–12; and heads of household, xiii, 65; in early America, 20, 39, 48; and revolution, 47–48, 55; in the early nation, 115, 123–34, 139, 146–55, 160–61; partial, 123–24, 147, 181–83, 193; and military service, 141; and black women, 143, 153, 155; and Civil War amendments, 148–50; and unlawful voting, 153–55; and professionalization, 168–70; in the modern era, 175–209; and ancillary rights, 185–88, 201–9, 259–62; and temperance, 187; parades, 196–98; and labor unions, 197; and states' rights sentiment, 200; and exclusionary devices, 206–7; and marital residence, 207; limits of, 208–9; linked to economic protection, 212; and self-defense, 244; and social purity, 244; and turnout, 259–62
Sullivan, Mark, 246
Sullivan, James, 53
Sumner, Helen, and *Women and Child Wage-Earners in the United States*, 221
Supreme Court: in constitutional history, xvi. *See also specific rulings*
Sutherland, Justice George, 228–29, 231–32
Sylvester, May, 187
Symbolic speech. *See* Deportment; speech

Taft, Chief Justice William Howard, 228–29, 253
Tailhook Association Convention, 296
Take Back the Night marches, 300

Takings, 69–70, 84, 107, 119, 228
Talbye, Dorothy, 32–33
Taney, Chief Justice Roger, 139, 172, 188
Tarbell, Ida, 226
Taussig, Frederick, 249
Taylor, Harriet, 118
Taylor, Susie King, 142
Taylor, John, 12
Teague, Kathleen, 261
Temperance reform, 60, 86–87, 96–97, 133, 187
Tenant in [by] curtesy, 75, 119, 184–85
Tennessee: and antisuffragism, 197; and suffrage, 200; and amendment ratification, 201
Terrel, Anne, 89
Terrell, Mary Church, 176, 219
Texas A & M University, and Texas Women's University, 283–84
Texas: and married women's property, 129–32, 184; and antisuffragism, 197
Textiles, 40–41, 135
Therapeutic exception, and abortion, 79
Thirteenth Amendment, 139, 146, 153, 156, 226
Thomas, Dr. L. Carey, 210
Thomas, Justice Clarence, 257, 279, 296
Thompson, William, 137
Thurston, Samuel, 131
Tiedeman, Christopher, 137
Tillmon, Johnie, 281
Title: in rights, 98; in self, 109; to land, 131–32; of suffrage statutes, 186–87, 202. See also Property rights
Title VII. See Civil Rights Act, of 1964
Title IX. See Education Amendments Act
Train, George Francis, 118, 155
Transportation, sex integration of, 145
Trask, David, 203
Treason: in revolution, 55; and petit kings, 32, 107–8, 111; and suffrage picketers, 197
Trespass, and rape or seduction, 77, 245
Triangle Shirtwaist fire, 220
Troy Female Academy, 90
Trumbull, John, 46
Trusts, 10–11, 24, 126–27, 132. See also Equity; marriage settlements
Truth, Sojourner [Isabella Baumfree; Isabella Van Wagoner], 83–85, 143
Tubman, Harriet, 142
Turner, Justice George, 186–87, 202, 255
Twenty-fourth Amendment, 259
Typewriting, 135

Union College of Law, 140
Unions, 208, 229, 238; and equal pay, 265; and harassment, 296. See also Economic rights; wage labor

Unitarianism, 87
United Automobile, Aircraft, and Agricultural Implement Workers of America, 264
United Auto Workers, 235, 268
University of Virginia, 284
Unmarried women, rights of, 10, 103–4, 123. See also Feme sole.
Utah: and suffrage, 164, 183; and hours legislation, 222; and spousal rape, 297

Vagrancy, 166
Van Valkenberg, Ellen, 154
Van Voorhis, John, 159
Vane, Governor Harry, 5–6
Vassar College, 176
Vaughan, Mary, 122
Veblen, Thorstein, 135, 168, 182
Vermont: and suffrage, 47–48; and married women's property, 129; and amendments, 201; and privacy, 252–53
Vest, George, 198
Virginia: and chancery, 11; and divorce, 14; and economic freedom, 22; and taxation of white laborers, 22; and speech, 31–32; and interracial sex crimes, 38; and late colonial era, 45, 48; and married women's property, 132; and racism within suffragism, 199
Virginia Military Institute (VMI), and Mary Baldwin College, 284–85
Virginia State Woman Suffrage Association, 147
Voluntary motherhood: societies, 247–48; as public policy, 255
Voting Rights Act, 209

Wadsworth-Taft Bill, 264
Wage discrimination, 256–83, 282–83. See also Economic rights
Wage and hour legislation, 211–12, 214–18, 221–22, 225, 228, 233–36, 268, 273–74, 277; in England, 218. See also Economic rights; protectionism
Wage labor: in early America, 23, 27, 41, 45; in nineteenth century, 114, 118, 128, 134–36, 140, 142, 145; and domesticity, 138; among blacks, 143, 236–38; and delinquency, 166; and clothing, 168; in modern era, 194, 201, 214–29, 230–34, 243, 246, 256–59, 263, 269, 272–73, 280–312; and suffrage, 208; and government jobs, 235; and birth control, 248; and ERA, 300–301. See also Capitalism
Waite, Chief Justice Morrison, 161
Wakerman, Sarah Rosetta [a.k.a. Lyons Wakerman], 141
Wald, Lillian, 211
Walker, Dr. Mary, 119, 141

Wallace, George, 301
Walsh-Healy Public Contracts Act, 233
Ward, Dr. Kay, 260
Warren, Chief Justice Earl, 204, 272
Warren, Mercy Otis, 46–47, 90
Washington University, 140
Washington, D.C.: and suffrage, 149, 157, 161; and bar admission, 162–63; and maternity, 292
Washington State: and political rights, 183, 200–202; and wage and hour legislation, 223; and abortion, 287
Washington Territory: and community property, 71, 129, 184–86; and suffragism, 183–87; and ancillary rights, 185–88; and custody, 185–86
Watkins, Dink, 145
Wayne, James, 68
Weed, Helen Hill, 264
Weld, Theodore, 82
Welfare state, 232–35, 281; and suffragism, 192; and Progressivism, 213–14; and birth control, 249–52
Wellesley College, 176
Wells, Alice Stebbins, 230
Wells, Elizabeth, and infanticide, 29
Wells, Ida Barnett, 145
Wesley, John, 18
Western settlement: and deportment, 89; and married women's property, 128–31; and labor, 130–31, 141; and racial unrest, 163; and suffragism, 178, 182–83. See also specific states or territories
West Virginia, and ratification of amendments, 201
Wheatley, Phillis, 57
Wheelwright, John, 5–9
White slavery, 214, 242–43
White supremacy, 199. See also Racism; xenophobia
White, Justice Byron, 278
White, William Allen, 195
Widows and widowers: in early America, 1, 12–13, 22–23, 42; and rights, 24; and suffrage, 54–55; in nineteenth century, 119, 126, 133, 141–42, 278. See also Dower
Wilkinson, Eliza, 89
Willard, Frances, and Evanston College for Ladies, and WCTU, 194, 243–44
Willard, Samuel, 17
Williams, George, 148–49
Willliams, Roger, 20
Wilson, Elizabeth, 31
Wilson, John, 5–9
Wilson, Robert, 297
Wilson, President Woodrow, 178–79, 196, 200–201

Window, Bridgett, 13
Winslow, Hubbard, 97
Winstanley, Gerrard, 25
Winthrop, Governor John, 5–9, 15, 18, 32–33, 50, 314
Wisconsin: and homestead exemptions, 127; and necessaries doctrine, 130; and bar admission, 163; and political rights, 188, 262; and rape law, 245; and abortion policy, 290
Witchcraft, 9, 21, 33–35, 95
Wittenmyer, Annie, 141
Wixon, Susan, 191
Wollstonecraft, Mary, 91
Woman suffrage. See Suffrage
Women's Bar Association of Baltimore, 235
Women's Bureau, U.S. Department of Labor, 221, 236, 265, 267
Women's Charter [1943], 263
Woman's Christian Temperance Union, 61, 104, 154, 177, 183, 227, 243
Women's Club of Denver, Reform Department, 215–16
Woman's Medical College of the New York Infirmary, 106
Women's Progressive Franchise Association, 155
Women's rights conventions, 60, 92–115, 150, 170, 269
Woman's State Temperance Society of New York, 96, 100
Women's Trade Union League, 208, 227
Wood, Justice Harlington, Jr., 258
Wood, Henry, 194
Woodhull, Victoria, 152–53, 170
Work, working women. See Labor; wage labor.
Working Girls' Home Association, 176
Working Women's National Association, 140
Working Women's Protective Union, 140
Working Women's Society of New York, 243
Wright, Frances [Fanny], 95, 97
Writing: in early America, 19, 45–46; in nineteenth century, 90, 92, 125–26; in Europe, 92
Wyoming: and married women's property, 130; and jury service, 182; and suffrage, 182, 187

Xenophobia: in suffragism, 163, 198–99, 208–9; in social reform, 242–43; and birth control, 248–49

Yale Medical School, 254
Young Women's Christian Association, 227, 236
Young Ladies Academy of Philadelphia, 36, 90
Younger, Maud, 197

6461